小小汉英词典

THE LITTLE POCKET
CHINESE-ENGLISH DICTIONARY

严英 编

外语教学与研究出版社

目 录

编 辑 说 明

　　这本小小汉英词典是为大、中学校学生、英语自学者和旅游者编写的。全书共收单字条目三千八百余，多字条目一万九千余。限于篇幅，只收普通词语。汉语条目、义项，主要依据中国社会科学院语言研究所词典编辑室编《现代汉语词典》（商务印书馆出版）。条目的英语释义和例证的译文主要依据北京外国语学院英语系《汉英词典》编写组编《汉英词典》（商务印书馆出版）。取舍损益不当之处以及其它缺点和错误，概由本书编者负责。

用 法 说 明

一、本词典所收条目分单字条目和多字条目。前者用大字排印，后者用小字排印，加鱼尾号（【】）。

二、单字条目按汉语拼音字母次序排列。同音异调的汉字按声调次序排列。同音同调的汉字，按笔画多少排列。单字条目用汉语拼音字母注音。书前附《汉语拼音音节索引》，供按音查字之用。另有《部首检字表》，供按汉字部首查字之用。

三、多字条目按第一个字排列在单字条目之后。同一单字条目后的多字条目不止一条时，按第二个字的汉语拼音字母次序排列。多字条目不注音。

四、条目一般用对应的英语释义。单字条目有两个或两个以上的英语释义时，分立义项，用①②③等数码标出顺序；多字条目的不同义项则用斜线号（/）隔开。同一义项有两个以上英语释义时，用分号（；）隔开。如：

　　改... ①change; transform ... ②alter; revise ③correct; rectify; put right ... 【改编】adapt; rearrange; revise / reorganize; redesignate ...

五、条目释义后，根据需要，收入词、词组或句子作为例证。例证与本单字条目或多字条目相同的部分，用代字号（～）表示。如：

　　动... ①move; stir ～了～嘴唇 stir one's lips

　　带... ②do sth. incidentally ... 请把门～上 please shut the door after you

　　【爱国】be patriotic ～心 patriotic feeling ～者 patriot ～主义 patriotism

六、条目释义、例证或其译文中，如有限定性（或补充性）说明、可省略部分或可替换部分，用圆括号（（ ））括出。如：

【改道】change one's route/(of a river) change its course

【电池】(electric) cell; battery

茶 ... tea ... 浓(淡)～ strong (weak) tea

汉语拚音音节索引

蔡碴 chǎ 叉 chà 权岔
诧刹差
chāi 拆差 chái 柴豺
chān 搀 chán 馋缠蝉潺
chǎn 产谄铲阐 chàn 忏
颤
chāng 昌猖娼 cháng 长场
肠尝常偿 chǎng 厂场敞
chàng 怅畅倡唱
chāo 抄吵钞绰超剿 cháo
巢朝潮嘲 chǎo 吵炒
chē 车 chě 扯 chè 彻澈撤
chēn 抻嗔 chén 尘臣沉陈
晨 chèn 衬称趁
chēng 称撑 chéng 成呈诚
承城乘盛程惩澄 chěng
逞 chèng 秤
chī 吃痴嗤 chí 池驰迟持
匙踟 chǐ 尺齿侈耻 chì
叱斥赤炽翅
chōng 冲充忡舂憧 chóng 虫
重崇宠 chòng 冲
chōu 抽 chóu 仇惆绸愁稠
酬筹踌 chǒu 丑 chòu 臭
chū 出初 chú 除厨锄雏橱
chǔ 处杵储楚 chù 处畜
触矗
chuāi 揣 chuǎi 揣 chuài
踹
chuān 川穿 chuán 传船
chuǎn 喘 chuàn 串

chuāng 创疮窗 chuáng 床
chuǎng 闯 chuàng 创
chuī 吹炊 chuí 垂捶锤
chūn 春 chún 纯唇 chǔn
蠢
chuō 戳 chuò 绰
cī 疵 cí 词祠瓷慈磁雌
cǐ 此 cì 次伺刺赐
cōng 从匆葱聪 cóng 从丛
còu 凑
cū 粗 cù 促醋簇
cuān 氽 cuán 攒 cuàn 窜
篡
cuī 催摧 cuǐ 脆淬啐粹
翠
cūn 村 cún 存 cǔn 忖
cùn 寸
cuō 搓磋撮蹉 cuò 挫措锉
错
　　D (91—132页)
dā 搭答 dá 打达沓答 dǎ
打 dà 大
dāi 呆待歹 dài 大代
带待贷袋逮戴
dān 丹单担耽 dǎn 胆掸
dàn 旦但担诞淡蛋弹氮
dāng 当 dǎng 挡党 dàng
当荡档
dāo 刀叨 dǎo 导岛倒捣祷
dào 到倒悼盗道稻
dé 得德

dēng 灯登 děng 等 dèng
凳澄瞪

dī 低堤提滴 dí 的敌涤笛
嘀嫡 dǐ 诋邸底抵 dì
地弟的帝递第缔

diān 掂颠巅 diǎn 典点碘
踮 diàn 电佃店玷垫 淀
惦奠殿

diāo 刁叼凋貂碉雕 diào
吊钓调掉

diē 爹跌 dié 迭谍喋牒叠
碟蝶

dīng 丁叮盯钉 dǐng 顶
鼎订钉定

diū 丢

dōng 东冬 dǒng 董懂
动冻洞恫栋

dōu 都兜 dǒu 生抖陡 dòu
斗豆逗痘

dū 都督嘟 dú 毒独读渎钍
牍黩 dǔ 肚堵赌睹 dù
杜肚妒度渡镀蠹

duān 端 duǎn 短 duàn
段断缎锻

duī 堆 duì 队对兑

dūn 吨敦墩蹲 dǔn 盹 dùn
囤盾钝顿遁

duō 多咄哆 duó 夺踱 duǒ
朵垛躲 duò 剁垛舵堕惰
踱

ē 阿 é 讹俄鹅蛾额 ě 恶
è 厄扼恶饿愕遏腭颚鳄鳄

ēn 恩 èn 摁

èr 儿而 ěr 尔耳 èr 二

fā 发 fá 乏伐罚阀筏 fǎ
法砝 fà 发珐

fān 帆番藩翻 fán 凡烦蕃
繁 fǎn 反返 fàn 犯泛
饭范贩

fāng 方芳妨 fáng 防坊
房 fǎng 访仿纺舫 fàng
放

fēi 飞妃非绯扉蜚 féi 肥
fěi 诽匪菲翡 fèi 沸废肺
费痱

fēn 分芬吩纷 fén 坟焚
fěn 粉 fèn 分份奋粪愤

fēng 丰风枫疯封峰烽锋蜂
féng 逢缝 fěng 讽 fèng
凤奉俸缝

fó 佛

fǒu 否

fū 夫肤孵敷 fú 伏凫扶拂
服俘浮符幅福辐 fǔ 抚
府斧俯辅腐 fù 父讣付
负妇附服赴复副富赋傅腹
缚覆馥

gā 咖嘎 gá 轧

gāi 该 gǎi 改 gài 钙盖概

gān 干甘杆肝泔柑竿尴 gǎn
　杆秆赶敢感擀橄　gàn 干

gāng 扛刚纲肛缸钢 gǎng
　岗港　gàng 杠钢

gāo 高羔膏糕篙 gǎo 搞稿
　镐 gào 告

gē 戈疙哥胳鸽割搁歌 gé
　革阁格搁隔嗝 gè 个各硌

gěi 给

gēn 根跟

gēng 更耕羹 gěng 埂耿哽
　梗 gèng 更

gōng 工弓公功攻供宫恭躬
　gǒng 巩拱 gòng 共贡供

gōu 勾沟钩篝 gǒu 苟狗
　gòu 构购垢够媾

gū 估沽咕孤姑辜箍 gú 骨
　gǔ 古谷股骨贾蛊鼓 gù
　固故顾雇痼

guā 瓜呱刮 guǎ 寡 guà
　卦挂褂

guǎi 乖掴 guǎi 拐 guài
　怪

guān 关观官冠棺鳏 guǎn
　馆管 guàn 贯冠惯盟灌
　罐

guāng 光 guǎng 广 guàng
　逛

guī 归龟规闺瑰 guǐ 轨诡
　鬼 guì 刿柜贵桂跪

gǔn 滚 gùn 棍

guō 锅 guó 国 guǒ 果裹
　guò 过

H（202—237页）

hā 哈

hāi 咳 hái 还孩 hǎi 海
　hài 骇害

hān 酣憨鼾 hán 含函涵寒
　hǎn 罕喊 hàn 汉汗旱悍
　捍焊憾

hāng 夯 háng 行吭航

hāo 蒿 háo 号毫豪壕嚎
　hǎo 好 hào 号户耗浩皓

hē 呵喝 hé 禾合何河和荷
　核盒 hè 吓和贺荷喝褐
　赫鹤壑

hēi 黑

hén 痕 hěn 很狠 hèn 恨

hēng 亨哼 héng 恒横衡
　hèng 横

hōng 轰哄烘 hóng 弘红宏
　洪虹鸿 hǒng 哄 hòng 哄

hóu 侯喉猴 hǒu 吼 hòu
　厚候

hū 呼忽糊 hú 囫狐弧胡壶
　核湖葫糊蝴 hǔ 虎唬琥
　hù 户互护糊

huā 花划 huá 划华哗滑 huà
　化划话画

huái 怀踝 huài 坏

huān 欢 huán 还环 huǎn
　缓 huàn 幻宦涣换唤焕

患

huāng 荒慌　huáng 皇黄惶
蝗　huǎng 恍晃谎幌　huàng
晃

huī 灰诙恢挥晖辉徽　huí
回茴蛔　huǐ 悔毁　huì
汇卉会讳海烩贿秽惠
慧

hūn 昏荤婚　hún 浑魂　hùn
混

huō 豁　huó 和活　huǒ 火
伙　huó 或和货获祸惑豁

J (237—299页)

jī 几讥击叽饥机肌鸡奇迹积
基缉缉畸稽激羁　jí 及汲
吉级极即急疾脊棘集嫉籍
jǐ 几己挤给脊　jì 计记
纪伎技忌际妓季剂济既
继寄寂祭

jiā 加夹佳枷家痂嘉　jiá 夹
荚颊　jiǎ 甲假　jià 价驾
架假嫁稼

jiān 尖奸间歼坚肩艰兼监缄
煎　jiǎn 拣茧柬俭捡检剪
减简碱　jiàn 见件俦建剑
荐贱涧舰健渐溅践腱毽
鉴箭

jiāng 江将姜浆僵疆　jiǎng
讲奖桨　jiàng 匠降将强
酱犟糨

jiāo 交郊浇娇骄胶教焦椒礁

jiáo 嚼　jiǎo 角侥狡绞
饺皎脚矫搅剿缴　jiào
叫觉校较轿教窖醮

jiē 阶皆结接秸揭街　jié 孑
节劫杰洁拮结捷睫竭截
jiě 姐解　jiè 介芥戒届诫
界借

jīn 巾今斤金津矜筋禁襟
jǐn 仅尽紧锦谨　jìn 尽进
近劲浸晋禁噤

jīng 京茎经荆惊晶睛兢鲸
jǐng 井阱景警　jìng
劲净径胫竟敬境静镜

jiǒng 迥炯窘

jiū 纠究阄揪　jiǔ 九久灸韭
酒　jiù 旧臼疚咎柩救厩
就舅

jū 拘狙居驹掬鞠　jú 局菊
橘　jǔ 沮咀举　jù 巨句
拒具炬俱剧惧据踞锯聚

juān 捐娟圈　juǎn 卷　juàn
卷倦绢眷圈

juē 撅　jué 决诀抉角觉绝倔
掘崛厥爵蹶攫　juě 倔

jūn 军均君龟菌　jùn 俊郡
浚骏菌竣

K (299—319页)

kā 咖　kǎ 卡咯

kāi 开揩　kǎi 凯慨楷

kān 刊看勘堪　kǎn 坎砍
砍　kàn 看

kāng 康慷糠 káng 扛 kàng
  亢抗炕
kǎo 考拷烤 kào 铐犒靠
kē 苛科棵窠磕嗑蚵 ké
  壳咳 kě 可渴 kè 克刻
  客恪课
kěn 肯垦恳啃
kēng 坑吭铿
kōng 空 kǒng 孔恐 kòng
  空控
kōu 抠 kǒu 口 kòu 扣寇
kū 枯哭窟骷 kǔ 苦 kù 库
  裤酷
kuǎ 垮 kuǎ 垮 kuà 挎胯跨
kuài 会快块脍筷
kuān 宽 kuǎn 款
kuāng 匡诓框筐 kuáng 狂
  kuàng 况旷矿框眶
kuī 亏盔窥 kuí 葵魁睽
  kuǐ 傀 kuì 溃愧
kūn 坤昆 kǔn 捆 kùn 困
kuò 扩括阔
  L (320—362页)
lā 拉垃 ló 拉 lǎ 喇 là
  落腊辣蜡瘌
lái 来赖癞
lán 兰拦栏阑蓝谰澜褴篮
  lǎn 览揽缆懒 làn 烂滥
láng 郎狼廊 lǎng 朗 làng 浪
lāo 捞 láo 牢劳痨 lǎo
  老 lào 涝烙落酪

le 乐勒
lēi 勒 léi 累雷 lěi 垒累
  磊 lèi 肋泪类擂
léng 棱 lěng 冷 lèng 愣
lí 离梨犁黎篱 lǐ 礼李里俚
  理鲤 lì 力历立厉吏沥丽
  励利例隶荔俪栗笠痢
liǎ 俩
lián 连帘伶涟莲联廉镰 liǎn
  敛脸 liàn 练炼恋链
liáng 良凉梁量梁粮 liǎng
  两 liàng 亮凉谅晾量踉
liāo 撩 liáo 辽疗聊寥僚寮
  撩缭嘹 liǎo 了潦 liào
  了料撂镣
liě 咧 liè 列劣烈猎裂
lín 邻林临淋琳磷鳞 lǐn 凛
  lìn 吝赁淋
líng 伶灵玲凌铃聆菱翎零
  龄 lǐng 岭领 lìng 另令
liū 溜熘 liú 浏流留硫瘤
  liǔ 柳绺 liù 六溜遛
lóng 龙聋隆 lǒng 垄拢
  笼 lòng 弄
lōu 搂 lóu 喽楼 lǒu 搂篓
  lòu 陋漏露
lú 卢庐芦炉颅 lǔ 卤房捋
  鲁橹 lù 陆录鹿禄碌路戮
  麓露
lǘ 驴 lǚ 侣旅捋铝偻屡
  缕膂履 lǜ 律虑率绿滤

luán 孪 luǎn 卵 luàn 乱
luě 掠
lūn 抡 lún 伦沦纶轮 lùn 论
luō 罗捋 luó 罗萝逻锣箩骡
　螺 luǒ 裸 luò 荦络骆
　落摞
M (362—393页)
mā 妈抹麻 mǎ 马吗玛码
　蚂 mà 骂
mái 埋 mǎi 买 mài 迈麦
　卖脉
mán 埋蛮馒瞒 mǎn 满
　màn 曼谩漫蔓慢幔
máng 忙芒杧盲茫 mǎng
　莽蟒
māo 猫 máo 毛矛茅锚
　mǎo 铆 mào 茂冒贸帽
　貌
méi 没玫眉梅媒煤霉 měi
　每美镁 mèi 妹昧谜媚魅
mēn 闷 mén 门扪 mèn
　闷焖 men 们
mēng 蒙 méng 萌蒙盟朦
　朦瞢 měng 猛蒙锰懵
　mèng 孟梦
mī 咪眯 mí 弥迷谜糜靡
　mǐ 米眯靡 mì 泌觅秘密
　蜜
mián 眠绵棉 miǎn 免勉
　miàn 面
miáo 苗描瞄 miǎo 秒渺藐

miào 妙庙
miè 灭蔑篾
mín 民 mǐn 泯悯闽敏
míng 名明鸣茗冥铭瞑 mìng
　命
miù 谬
mō 摸 mó 摹模膜摩磨蘑
　魔 mǒ 抹 mò 末没沫
茉抹陌脉莫漠寞蓦墨默磨
móu 牟谋眸 mǒu 某
mú 模 mǔ 母亩牡姆 mù
木目沐牧亩墓幕睦慕暮穆
N (394—410页)
ná 拿 nǎ 哪 nà 那呐纳捺
nǎi 乃奶 nài 奈耐
nān 囡 nán 男南难喃 nàn
　难
náng 囊
náo 挠 nǎo 恼脑 nào 闹
něi 哪馁 nèi 内
nèn 嫩
néng 能
ní 尼泥呢霓 nǐ 拟你 nì
　泥逆昵匿溺腻
niān 拈蔫 nián 年黏 niǎn
　捻碾撵 niàn 念
niáng 娘酿
niǎo 鸟 niào 尿
niē 捏 niè 啮镊镍蹑孽
níng 宁拧狞柠凝 nǐng 拧
　nìng 宁佞

niǔ 妞 niú 牛 niǔ 忸扭纽
niù 拗

nóng 农浓脓 nòng 弄

nú 奴 nǔ 努 nù 怒 nǚ 女

nuǎn 暖

nüè 疟虐

nuó 挪 nuò 诺懦糯

O （410—411页）

ōu 讴欧殴鸥 ǒu 呕偶藕
òu 沤怄

P （411—435页）

pā 趴 pá 扒爬耙 pà 怕

pāi 拍 pái 排徘牌 pǎi 迫
pài 派

pān 攀 pán 盘磐蹒 pàn
判叛盼畔襻

pāng 滂膀 páng 彷庞旁膀
磅螃 pǎng 耪 pàng 胖

pāo 抛泡 páo 刨咆袍 pǎo
跑 pào 泡炮疱

pēi 呸胚 péi 陪培赔 pèi
沛佩配

pēn 喷 pén 盆 pèn 喷

pēng 抨烹澎 péng 朋棚蓬
硼鹏篷膨 pěng 捧 pèng
碰

pī 批纰坯披砒劈霹 pí 皮
枇毗疲啤脾 pǐ 匹仳否痞
劈癖 pì 屁媲僻譬

piān 片偏翩篇 pián 便
piàn 片骗

piāo 剽漂缥飘 piǎo 嫖瓢
piáo 漂瞟 piào 票漂

piē 撇瞥 piě 撇

pīn 拼姘 pín 贫频 pǐn
品 pìn 牝聘

pīng 乒 píng 平评坪苹凭
屏瓶萍

pō 泊坡泼颇 pó 婆 pǒ 叵
笸 pò 迫破魄

pōu 剖 póu 抔 pǒu 掊

pū 仆扑铺 pú 仆匍菩脯葡
蒲 pǔ 朴圃普谱蹼 pù
铺堡曝

Q （436—471页）

qī 七沏妻凄栖戚期欺漆蹊
qí 齐祈其奇歧脐畦崎骑棋
旗 qǐ 乞岂企启绮 qì
气讫迄汽弃泣契砌器

qiā 掐 qiǎ 卡 qià 洽恰

qiān 千扦迁钎牵悭铅谦签
qián 前荨钳虔钱掮乾潜黔
qiǎn 浅遣谴缱 qiàn 欠
纤倩堑嵌歉

qiāng 枪戗戕腔锖锵 qiáng
强墙蔷樯 qiǎng 抢强襁
qiàng 呛

qiāo 悄跷敲锹橇 qiáo 乔
侨荞桥翘憔瞧 qiǎo 巧悄
qiào 壳俏诮窍峭撬鞘

qiē 切 qié 茄 qiě 且 qiè
切妾怯窃挈惬锲

qīn 亲侵钦　qín 芹琴禽勤
　擒噙　qǐn 寝　qìn 沁
qīng 青轻氢倾清蜻　qíng
　情晴擎　qǐng 顷请　qìng
　庆亲磬
qióng 穷穹琼
qiū 丘秋龟　qiú 囚求泅酋球
qū 区曲驱屈祛蛆趋　qú
　渠　qǔ 曲取娶龋　qù 去
　趣觑
quān 圈　quán 权全泉拳痊
　蜷　quǎn 犬　quàn 劝券
quē 缺　qué 瘸　què 却雀
　确鹊
qún 裙群

　　R (471—484页)

rán 然燃　rǎn 染
rāng 嚷　ráng 瓤　rǎng 壤
　攘嚷　ràng 让
ráo 饶　rǎo 扰　rào 绕
rě 惹　rè 热
rén 人仁　rěn 忍　rèn 刃
　认任妊纫韧
rēng 扔　réng 仍
rì 日
róng 荣茸绒容熔融　rǒng
　冗
róu 柔揉糅　ròu 肉
rú 如儒蠕孺　rǔ 乳辱　rù
　入褥
ruǎn 软

ruǐ 蕊　ruì 锐瑞
rùn 闰润
ruò 若弱

　　S (484—551页)

sā 撒　sǎ 洒撒　sà 飒
sāi 塞腮　sài 塞赛
sān 三　sǎn 伞散　sàn 散
sāng 丧桑　sǎng 嗓　sàng
　丧
sāo 搔骚缫臊　sǎo 扫嫂
　sào 扫臊
sè 色涩塞
sēn 森
sēng 僧
shā 杀沙纱刹砂煞　shǎ 傻
　shà 厦煞霎
shāi 筛　shài 晒
shān 山删衫姗珊舢扇膻
　shǎn 闪　shàn 讪扇善缮
　擅膳鳝
shāng 伤商墒　shǎng 晌赏
　shàng 上尚
shāo 烧捎梢稍　sháo 勺芍
　韶　shǎo 少　shào 少捎
　哨潲
shē 奢赊　shé 舌折蛇　shě
　舍　shè 设社舍涉射赦摄
　慑麝
shēn 申伸身呻绅参深　shén
　什神　shěn 审婶　shèn 肾
　甚渗慎

shēng 升生 声牲甥　shéng
　绳　shěng 省　shèng 圣
　胜盛剩

shī 尸失使师虱诗狮施湿嘘
　shí 十什石识时实拾食蚀
　shǐ 史矢使始驶屎　shì 士
　氏市示世仕式试势事侍视
　饰室恃拭柿是适逝释嗜誓
　噬螫

shōu 收　shǒu 手守首　shòu
　寿兽授售瘦

shū 书抒枢叔殊倏淑梳舒疏
　输蔬　shú 赎塾熟　shǔ 属
　暑署数鼠薯曙　shù 术戌
　束述树竖恕蔗数漱

shuā 刷　shuǎ 耍　shuà 刷

shuāi 衰摔　shuǎi 甩　shuài
　帅率

shuān 闩拴栓　shuàn 涮

shuāng 双霜缩　shuǎng 爽

shuí 谁　shuǐ 水　shuì 税
　睡

shùn 顺瞬

shuō 说　shuò 烁朔硕数

sī 司丝私思斯嘶嘶　sǐ 死
　sì 四寺拟伺饲肆

sōng 松嵩凇　sǒng 怂耸　sòng
　讼送诵颂

sōu 搜馊

sū 苏酥　sú 俗　sù 夙诉肃
　素速宿溯塑簌

suān 酸　suàn 蒜算

suī 尿虽　suí 绥随　suǐ 髓
　suì 岁祟遂碎隧燧穗

sūn 孙　sǔn 笋损

suō 唆梭缩　suǒ 所索琐锁

T (551—594页)

tā 它他她地塌　tǎ 塔　tà 榻
　踏

tāi 胎　tái 台抬苔　tài 太
　汰态泰

tān 坍贪滩瘫瘫　tán 坛昙
　谈弹痰潭檀　tǎn 忐坦祖
　毯　tàn 叹炭探碳

tāng 汤膛　táng 堂塘搪膛
　糖　tǎng 倘淌躺　tàng 烫

tāo 叨涛掏滔韬　táo 逃桃
　陶淘　tǎo 讨　tào 套

tè 特

téng 疼誊腾藤

tī 体剔梯踢　tí 啼缇题蹄
　tǐ 体　tì 屉剃涕惕替嚏

tiān 天添　tián 田恬甜填

tiāo 挑　tiáo 条迢调笤　tiǎo
　挑　tiào 眺跳

tiē 贴　tiě 铁　tiè 帖

tīng 厅听　tíng 延亭庭停
　tǐng 挺铤艇

tōng 通　tóng 同桐铜童瞳
　tǒng 统捅桶筒　tòng 痛

tōu 偷　tóu 头投　tòu 透

tū 凸秃突　tú 图涂途徒屠

tǔ 土吐 tù 吐兔

tuān 湍 tuán 团

tuī 推 tuí 颓 tuǐ 腿 tuì
退蜕褪

tūn 吞 tún 屯囤豚臀 tǔn
氽 tùn 褪

tuō 托拖脱 tuó 驮陀驼鸵
tuǒ 妥椭 tuò 拓唾

W (594—625页)

wā 洼挖蛙 wá 娃 wǎ 瓦
wà 瓦袜

wāi 歪 wài 外

wān 弯剜湾蜿豌 wán 丸纨
完玩顽 wǎn 宛挽惋晚碗
莞绾婉 wàn 万腕蔓

wāng 汪 wáng 亡王 wǎng
网枉往惘 wàng 妄忘旺
往望

wēi 危威逶偎煨微巍 wéi
为违围桅惟唯
伟苇纬尾委娓萎唯猥 wèi
卫为未位味畏胃谓尉喂蔚
慰

wēn 温瘟 wén 文纹闻蚊
wěn 刎吻紊稳 wèn 问

wēng 翁嗡 wěng

wō 涡窝蜗 wǒ 我 wò
沃卧握斡龌

wū 乌污巫呜诬屋钨 wú 无
芜梧蜈 wǔ 五午妩忤
武侮捂舞 wù 勿务坞物

误悟恶晤雾

X (625—681)

xī 夕汐西吸希昔析牺息惜
悉稀犀溪锡熄蜥膝嬉熹
蟋 xí 习席袭媳檄 xǐ
洗玺徙铣喜 xì 戏系细
隙

xiā 虾瞎 xiá 匣狎侠峡狭
遐瑕暇辖霞 xià 下吓夏

xiān 仙先纤掀锨鲜 xián 闲
贤弦咸衔舷嫌 xiǎn 险
显 xiàn 县现限线宪陷
馅羡献腺

xiāng 乡相香厢箱襄镶
xiáng 详降祥翔 xiǎng 享
响饷想 xiàng 向巷项相
象像橡

xiāo 削哮消宵逍萧硝销潇
箫霄嚣 xiáo 淆 xiǎo
小晓 xiào 孝肖效校笑
啸

xiē 些歇蝎 xié 协邪胁挟
谐偕斜携鞋 xiě 写血
xiè 泻泄卸屑械谢亵榭懈
邂蟹

xīn 心辛欣锌新薪馨 xín
寻 xìn 芯信衅

xīng 兴星惺猩腥 xíng 刑
行形型 xǐng 省醒擤
xìng 兴杏性幸姓悻

xiōng 凶凶汹胸 xióng 雄熊

xiū 休修羞　xiǔ 朽　xiù
秀袖绣臭锈嗅
xū 吁须虚需嘘　xú 徐　xǔ
许栩　xù 旭序恤叙畜酗
绪续絮婿蓄
xuān 轩宣喧　xuán 玄旋悬
漩檀
xuǎn 选　xuàn 炫绚眩旋
渲楦
xuē 削靴　xué 穴学　xuě
雪　xuè 血谑
xūn 勋熏　xún 旬驯寻巡询
循　xùn 讯训迅逊殉

Y (681—748)

yā 丫压呀押鸦鸭　yá 牙芽
涯崖　xǎ哑雅　yà 轧亚
yān 咽烟胭淹阉腌嫣　yán
延言严岩炎岩盐阎筵颜
檐　yǎn 奄掩眼演　yàn 厌
沿砚咽宴晏艳谚焰雁
燕赝
yāng 央殃秧　yáng 羊阳扬
杨佯洋　yǎng 仰养氧痒
yàng 怏恙样漾
yāo 夭吆幺妖要腰邀　yáo
肴窑谣遥摇徭　yǎo 杳咬
窈舀　yào 药要钥鹞耀
yē 耶掖椰噎　yé 爷揶
也治野　yè 业叶页曳夜
液掖谒腋
yī 一衣伊医依揖　yí 仪夷
宜怡饴贻姨胰移遗颐疑

yǐ 乙已以蚁倚椅　yì 义
亿忆艺刈议亦屹异译抑呓
邑役诣易疫益谊逸翌溢意
裔肄毅臆翼
yīn 因阴音茵洇姻荫殷　yín
吟淫银　yǐn 引饮隐瘾
yìn 印饮荫
yīng 应英莺婴嘤缨樱鹦鹰
yíng 迎盈荧莹萤营萦蝇
赢　yǐng 颖影　yìng 应
映硬
yōng 佣拥庸雍臃鳙　yǒng
永甬泳咏俑勇涌踊　yòng
用佣
yōu 优忧幽悠　yóu 尤由邮
犹油铀游　yǒu 友有莠　yòu
又右幼佑诱
yū 迂淤　yú 于余鱼谀隅
渔渝愉逾愚瑜舆璵　yǔ 与
予宇屿羽雨语　yù 玉驭
芋育郁狱浴预欲域谕寓裕
遇喻御誉愈
yuān 冤鸳渊　yuán 元园员
原圆援源猿辕缘　yuán
远　yuàn 怨院愿
yuē 曰约　yuè 月乐岳钥悦
阅跃越
yūn 晕　yún 云匀耘　yǔn
允陨殒　yùn 孕运晕酝
愠韵熨蕴

Z (748—830)

zā 扎杂砸

zāi 灾栽 zǎi 宰载 zài 再在载

zān 簪 zán 咱 zǎn 攒 zàn 暂赞

zāng 赃脏 zàng 脏葬藏

zāo 遭糟 záo 凿 zǎo 早枣蚤澡藻 zào 灶皂造噪燥躁

zé 则责泽择啧

zéi 贼

zěn 怎

zēng 曾憎增 zèng 赠

zhā 扎渣揸 zhá 扎札轧闸炸铡 zhǎ 眨 zhà 乍诈炸栅蚱榨

zhāi 斋摘 zhái 宅择 zhǎi 窄 zhài 债寨

zhān 占沾毡粘谵瞻 zhǎn 斩展崭辗握碾 zhàn 占战栈站绽湛颤蘸

zhāng 张章彰樟 zhǎng 长涨掌 zhàng 丈仗杖帐胀涨障瘴

zhāo 招昭朝 zháo 着 zhǎo 找沼 zhào 召兆照罩肇

zhē 折揸遮 zhé 折哲辙者褶 zhè 这蔗

zhēn 贞针侦珍真砧斟甄箴 zhěn 诊枕疹缜 zhèn 阵振赈震镇

zhēng 正争征徵挣峥狰症睁蒸 zhěng 拯整 zhèng 正证诤郑政挣症

zhī 之支枝只芝枝知肢织指脂掷蜘 zhí 执直侄指值职植殖 zhǐ 止只旨址纸指趾 zhì 至志治质制峙桎致秩挚掷窒痔滞痣智置稚

zhōng 中忠终盅钟衷 zhǒng 肿种 zhòng 中众仲种重

zhōu 州舟诌周洲粥 zhóu 妯轴 zhǒu 肘 zhòu 咒宙昼皱骤

zhū 朱诛侏珠株诸猪蛛潴 zhú 竹烛逐 zhǔ 主拄属煮嘱瞩 zhù 助住注贮驻妊祝柱著蛀筑铸

zhuā 抓 zhuǎ 爪

zhuài 拽

zhuān 专砖 zhuǎn 转 zhuàn 传转赚撰

zhuāng 妆庄桩装 zhuàng 壮状撞

zhuī 追椎锥 zhuì 坠缀惴赘

zhūn 谆 zhǔn 准

zhuō 拙卓捉桌 zhuó 灼茁浊酌着啄琢擢镯

zī 孜咨姿资滋辎 zǐ 子仔姊紫 zì 字自恣渍

zōng 宗综棕踪鬃　zǒng 总
　zòng 纵棕

zǒu 走　zòu 奏揍

zū 租　zú 足卒族　zǔ 阻诅
　组祖、

zuān 钻　zuàn 钻攥

zuǐ 嘴　zuì 最罪醉

zūn 尊遵　zǔn 撙

zuō 作　zuó 作昨琢　zuǒ
　左　zuò 坐作座做凿

部 首 检 字 表

（一）部首目录

部首左边的号码表示部首的次序

一画							
		17	刂	35	又	52	大
1	、	18	冖	36	廴	53	尢
2	一	19	冂	37	厶	54	寸
3	丨	20	亻	38	凵	55	扌
4	丿	21	亻	39	匕	56	弋
5	一	22	厂	三画		57	巾
6	乛	23	人（入）	40	氵	58	口
7	乙（乛乚）	24	八（丷）	41	忄	59	囗
二画		25	乂	42	爿（丬）	60	山
8	冫	26	勹	43	亠	61	屮
9	亠	27	刀（刂）	44	广	62	彳
10	冫	28	力	45	宀	63	彡
11	二	29	儿	46	门	64	夕
12	十	30	几（几）	47	辶	65	夂
13	厂	31	亠	48	工	66	丸
14	厂	32	卩	49	土（士）	67	尸
15	匚	33	阝（在左）	50	艹	68	忄
16	卜（卜）	34	阝（在右）	51	廾	69	犭

70	ㅋ(彑彑)	93	廿(卄)	117	尺	140	业
71	弓	94	木	118	月	141	目
72	己(巳)	95	不	119	殳	142	田
73	女	96	犬	120	欠	143	山
74	子(孑)	97	歹	121	风	144	申
75	马	98	瓦	122	氏	145	罒
76	幺	99	牙	123	比	146	皿
77	纟(糸)	100	车	124	屮	147	钅
78	巛	101	戈	125	水	148	矢
79	小(⺌)	102	止	**五　画**		149	禾
四　画		103	日	126	立	150	白
80	灬	104	曰	127	疒	151	瓜
81	心	105	中	128	穴	152	鸟
82	斗	106	贝	129	衤	153	皮
83	火	107	见	130	夫	154	癶
84	文	108	父	131	玉	155	矛
85	方	109	气	132	示	156	疋
86	户	110	牛(牜)	133	去	**六　画**	
87	礻	111	手	134	甘	157	羊(⺶⺷)
88	王	112	毛	135	甘	158	关
89	主	113	攵	136	石	159	米
90	天(夭)	114	片	137	龙	160	齐
91	韦	115	斤	138	戊	161	衣
92	少	116	爪(爫)	139	卌	162	亦(亦)

163	耳	181	血	198	谷	214	鬼
164	臣	182	舟	199	身	215	食
165	戈	183	羽	200	角	**十 画**	
166	覀(西)	184	艮(日)	**八 画**		216	高
167	束	**七 画**		201	青	217	髟
168	亚	185	言	202	卓	**十一画**	
169	而	186	辛	203	雨	218	麻
170	页	187	辰	204	非	219	鹿
171	至	188	麦	205	齿	**十二画**	
172	光	189	走	206	隹	220	黑
173	卢	190	赤	207	金	**十三画**	
174	虫	191	豆	208	鱼	221	鼓
175	缶	192	束	**九 画**		222	鼠
176	耒	193	酉	209	音	**十四画**	
177	舌	194	里	210	革	223	鼻
178	竹(⺮)	195	足	211	是		
179	臼	196	采	212	骨	224	余类
180	自	197	豸	213	香		

(二) 检字表

字右边的号码指词典正文的页码

三画	仰 692	侠 632	修 670	偿 56	盾 129
仕 516	似 543	佳 249	侯 216	假 250	(23)
付 159	伊 704	侍 518	侵 456	假 251	人(人)部
代 97	五画	供 182	俊 299	偎 410	人 474
仗 765	伴 13	供 183	俑 724	偷 582	入 482
们 374	位 611	使 514	八画	傀 318	一画
他 551	住 802	例 334	倦 295	偕 655	个 175
仙 635	佞 405	侄 785	倍 22	十画	二画
仪 705	估 705	侥 265	俯 158	傍 14	今 275
仔 814	何 211	侩 772	倩 449	储 77	介 273
四画	体 564	侣 335	债 759	傲 6	从 85
伙 236	体 566	侧 49	值 785	傅 162	从 85
仿 145	佑 733	侏 798	倚 708	十一画	仓 47
伪 608	但 100	侨 452	倒 104	催 88	以 707
伟 78	伸 500	侈 68	倒 105	傻 489	三画
传 807	作 826	佩 418	倘 558	十二画	令 348
伎 246	作 826	七画	倏 528	僧 488	四画
休 669	作 827	信 662	候 218	僚 341	伞 485
伏 156	伶 345	便 30	俱 293	十三画	全 467
优 725	佣 723	便 424	倜 57	僵 260	会 232
伐 118	佣 725	俩 335	倔 297	僻 423	会 315
伥 423	伯 36	俐 334	倔 297	十四画	企 439
仲 795	低 108	俏 453	倾 458	儒 481	众 795
份 151	你 401	俚 331	健 258	(22)	余 591
价 251	伺 84	保 16	九画	厂部	杂 87
伦 358	佛 543	促 87	偻 356	反 141	五画
伧 47	六画	俘 157	停 575	后 217	余 733
任 477	佯 691	俟 132	偏 424	质 789	六画
件 257	依 704	侮 623	做 829		合 498
伤 493		俭 254			
		俗 545			

舍	499	七画		匈	85	象	647	(29)
命	386	养	692	包	14	十三画		几部
十画		前	446	四画		劈	422	几 134
禽	456	菁	464	旬	680	劈	423	兆 768
舒	528	首	524	匐	434			先 635
(24)		八画		(27)		(28)		兜 121
八(")部		兼	253	刀(⺈)部		力部		(30)
八	6	九画		刀	103	力	332	几(几)部
一画		兽	526	一画		二画		几 237
丫	681	十二画		刃	476	办	12	几 243
二画		與	735	二画		三画		凤 140
分	149	(25)		切	453	加	248	凤 155
分	151	乂部		切	454	四画		朵 131
公	179	乂	709	三画		动	120	凤 545
三画		刈	709	召	768	五画		急 156
兰	322	杀	488	四画		励	333	咒 797
四画		希	626	危	604	助	802	凯 302
兴	663	肴	694	负	159	劲	279	凭 430
兴	667	(26)		争	776	劳	284	(31)
关	191	勹部		色	487	努	408	マ部
并	34	一画		五画		六画		予 736
五画		勺	497	龟	196	势	517	甬 724
兑	129	二画		龟	299	七画		勇 724
兵	34	匀	746	免	379	勃	37	疏 528
弟	111	勿	624	六画		勋	679	九画
六画		勾	183	兔	587	勉	379	勘 302
单	99	勾	184	八画		九画		十一画
其	438	三画		艳	689	勘	302	(32)
具	292	句	292	九画		十一画		卩部
典	112			剪	255	勤	456	卫 610

印	718
卸	656
(33)	
阝(左)部	
二画	
队	127
四画	
防	144
阱	283
阵	774
阳	690
阶	268
阴	714
五画	
陀	593
陆	354
际	246
阿	1
阿	132
陈	61
阻	823
附	160
六画	
陋	352
陌	389
降	644
降	644
限	639
七画	
院	744

陡	122	邻	343	**四画**		参	501	汐	625	泔	166
陨	747	邸	109	戏	630	能	400	汲	241	泄	656
陉	637	**六画**		观	192	**(38)**		汤	557	沽	185
除	75	郑	781	欢	225	**凵部**		**四画**		河	211
陲	26	郊	263	**五画**		凶	668	沁	457	沾	760
八画		郎	324	鸡	239	击	237	汪	602	泪	328
陪	418	耶	697	**六画**		凼	224	沛	418	沮	291
陵	346	郁	738	叔	527	函	204	沐	393	油	728
陶	560	**七画**		艰	253	**(39)**		汰	553	泗	463
陷	640	郡	299	**七画**		**匕部**		沍	436	泻	656
九画		**八画**		叙	674	匕	24	沤	411	泥	401
随	548	部	43	**八画**		北	20	沥	333	泥	401
隅	735	都	121	难	396	旨	786	沉	61	波	35
隆	351	**十一画**		难	397	顷	461	沧	142	泡	416
隐	717	鄙	26	**十一画**		肆	713	沧	47	泡	417
十画		**(35)**		叠	117	疑	707	沦	359	沿	686
隘	2	**又部**		**(36)**		**(40)**		汽	442	沿	689
隔	175	又	732	**夊部**		**氵部**		沃	618	泊	36
隙	631	**一画**		廷	575			沩	669	泊	431
十一画		叉	50	延	684	**二画**		沟	183	治	768
障	766	叉	52	建	257	汁	783	没	370	治	788
十二画		**二画**		**(37)**		汇	231	没	389	泼	431
隧	549	双	533	**厶部**		汉	205	沙	488	泯	383
(34)		劝	469	允	747	**三画**		**五画**		沸	148
阝(右)部		**三画**		台	552	汗	205	泌	377	泽	755
四画		圣	507	牟	390	污	618	泣	443	**六画**	
邪	654	对	127	县	638	江	259	注	802	洋	691
邦	13	发	135	参	46	池	67	泳	724	济	247
那	394	发	139	参	50	汛	681	沫	389	浏	348
五画								法	138	洲	797
								浅	448	洼	594

洁	271	海	202	添	569	滚	198	潜	447	忤	623
洪	216	涂	585	淆	650	滂	415	澎	420	怅	57
洒	484	涤	109	涮	533	溶	480	潭	555	快	315
浇	263	渔	227	淘	560	满	366	潮	59	忸	406
洞	121	浚	299	渔	735	漠	389	潦	342	**五画**	
润	715	涌	724	渗	504	源	743	潲	498	怯	454
测	49	浸	504	涵	204	滥	324	潺	54	怦	776
浊	812	涨	764	**九画**		滥	357	澄	66	怖	43
浑	234	涨	766	滋	814	滔	559	澄	108	怏	692
浓	407	涩	488	湾	597	溪	627	**十三画**		性	667
洗	629	**八画**		渲	677	滗	27	濒	33	怕	411
活	234	淡	100	渡	125	溜	348	激	753	怜	336
洽	444	淬	700	游	729	溏	351	激	240	怡	705
派	413	淤	733	港	170	滩	554	**十五画**		怪	191
津	275	淀	115	滞	790	溺	402	瀑	435	**六画**	
七画		清	459	湛	763	**十一画**		**十七画**		恼	398
涕	567	渍	818	湖	220	漾	693	灌	194	恃	519
流	348	鸿	216	湮	684	滴	108	**(41)**		恒	214
润	483	淋	344	渣	216	漪	757	**忄部**		恢	230
涧	258	淋	345	湉	381	漪	688	**一画**		恍	229
浪	324	渎	124	温	613	漂	425	忆	709	恫	121
涛	559	淹	684	湿	510	漂	426	**三画**		恬	570
涝	326	涯	682	渴	307	漂	426	忙	368	恤	674
酒	287	渐	558	溃	318	潇	649	忖	89	恰	444
涟	528	淘	558	渐	222	漱	531	忏	55	恨	214
消	648	淑	528	溅	258	漆	437	**四画**		**七画**	
涉	499	混	234	湍	587	漫	367	怀	224	悦	745
涡	617	深	501	渝	735	漏	352	忧	726	悟	625
浮	157	淫	716	**十画**		潘	799	怄	411	悄	451
浴	738	渊	741	溢	712	**十二画**		忡	69	悄	453
浩	209			溯	546	澜	323				
						激	60				

忄部		忄部		丬(爿)部 / 亡部 / 广部	
悯	383	惶	229	将	261
悭	445	愧	318	**(43)**	
悍	205	慨	302	**亡部**	
悔	231	**十画**		亡	602
八画		慎	504	妄	603
惊	281	慑	500	忘	603
惝	115	**十一画**		盲	368
惋	600	慷	304	赢	721
惆	460	慢	367	**(44)**	
悼	668	**十二画**		**广部**	
惜	627	憎	756	广	195
惵	455	懂	120	**三画**	
断	47	憔	452	庄	807
惕	105	懊	6	庆	462
惘	603	**十三画**		**四画**	
惧	293	懒	323	应	719
惕	567	憨	205	庐	353
惆	71	懈	657	床	80
惟	607	**十四画**		库	314
惨	47	懦	410	庇	26
九画		**十五画**		序	673
愤	151	懵	375	**五画**	
慌	228	**(42)**		庞	415
惰	132	**忄(爿)部**		店	114
愠	748	壮	808	庙	381
惺	664	妆	807	府	158
愕	133	状	809	底	109
愣	329	戕	450	庶	148
㥃	810	将	259		
愉	735				

广部 / 宀部		宀部		宀部 / 门部	
六画		宏	216	寇	313
度	125	牢	324	寄	247
庭	575	**五画**		寂	248
七画		实	512	宿	546
席	628	宝	16	**九画**	
座	829	宗	818	寒	204
八画		定	118	富	162
廊	324	宠	70	寓	739
庶	531	宜	705	**十画**	
庸	723	审	503	寝	457
康	303	官	192	塞	485
十画		**六画**		寒	488
廉	337	宣	675	寞	390
十一画		宦	227	**十一画**	
廒	159	室	519	蜜	378
(45)		宫	182	寨	759
宀部		宛	640	寐	189
二画		客	308	察	52
宁	405	**七画**		寥	341
宁	405	宰	749	**十二画**	
它	551	害	203	寮	341
三画		宽	315	**(46)**	
宇	736	家	249	**门部**	
守	524	宵	649	门	373
宅	759	宴	689	**一画**	
安	2	容	479	闩	533
字	814	宾	33	**二画**	
四画		案	4	闪	491
灾	749	**八画**			
完	598	密	378		

三画	二画	迊 571	逮 98	巧 452	坐 827
闭 26	边 28	六画	九画	巩 182	均 298
问 616	辽 341	迸 24	道 105	贡 183	声 506
闯 80	三画	送 544	遂 549	巫 619	坎 303
四画	迂 733	迷 376	遍 30	攻 181	坞 624
闵 373	过 200	逑 401	遇 24	项 646	圾 315
闶 374	达 92	迹 239	遐 632	(49)	五画
闱 483	迈 365	逃 559	遇 740	土(士)部	幸 668
闲 636	迁 444	选 676	遏 133	土 586	垃 320
间 252	迄 442	适 519	遗 706	士 515	坪 430
闷 257	迅 681	追 809	道 130	三画	坯 421
五画	巡 680	退 589	逾 735	寺 543	坦 555
闹 398	四画	逊 681	十画	吉 241	坤 318
闸 757	这 771	七画	遨 5	地 110	坡 431
六画	远 743	逍 111	遣 448	场 56	六画
闺 197	进 278	逗 123	遥 694	场 57	型 666
闻 615	运 747	速 546	遛 351	四画	垮 314
阀 138	违 606	逎 649	十一画	坟 150	垧 114
阁 174	还 202	逐 799	遮 770	坑 309	城 65
七画	环 226	逝 520	遭 752	坊 144	垢 185
阅 746	连 335	逞 66	十二画	志 788	垛 131
阃 287	近 279	造 754	遵 826	坛 554	垛 131
八画	返 142	透 583	遴 657	坚 253	垒 327
阐 54	迟 67	途 196	避 27	址 786	七画
阆 684	五画	通 576	十三画	坝 7	埂 177
阎 687	述 530	八画	邀 694	壳 307	埋 364
九画	迥 286	逻 360	(48)	壳 453	埋 366
阔 319	迷 117	逶 605	工部	坠 810	壶 220
阑 322	迫 413	逸 712	工 178	坍 553	八画
(47)	迫 432		功 181		培 418
辶部					堵 124

孼 27	七画	打 92	报 18	抹 362	拂 156
(52)	奎 561	扑 434	折 498	拔 7	六画
大部	八画	扒 6	折 770	拓 594	排 427
大 94	奢 498	扒 411	折 770	挑 351	挤 244
大 97	爽 534	扔 478	扳 10	拣 254	挖 594
一画	九画	三画	抓 804	拈 402	按 4
太 553	奥 6	扩 319	抇 13	担 99	挟 655
夫 156	(53)	扛 169	抢 451	担 100	拭 519
二画	尢部	扛 304	抢 358	抽 71	挂 190
头 582	尢 727	扪 374	投 583	拐 191	持 67
夯 206	尴 167	扣 312	抛 416	拍 411	拮 271
央 690	(54)	扦 444	抑 711	拖 592	拱 182
三画	寸部	托 591	抔 401	拆 43	挎 305
夹 249	寸 89	执 784	批 421	拆 53	挥 230
夹 250	寿 525	扫 487	抒 527	披 421	挎 314
夸 314	封 153	扫 487	把 7	抵 110	挠 398
夷 705	尉 612	扬 691	把 7	担 766	挡 102
五画	尊 826	四画	抉 296	拥 723	拽 804
奈 395	(55)	抖 122	抯 406	拘 290	挑 570
奇 239	扌部	抗 304	抄 58	抱 19	挑 572
奇 438	一画	护 221	五画	抬 552	挺 576
奔 22	扎 748	扶 156	拦 322	拨 35	括 319
奔 23	扎 757	抚 158	拌 13	拉 811	拴 533
奋 151	扎 757	技 246	拉 320	择 755	拾 514
奄 687	二画	拒 246	拉 320	择 759	挣 777
六画	打 91	抠 311	拄 801	抿 383	挣 781
契 443		抔 433	拧 405	拗 5	挪 409
牵 445		扰 473	拧 405	拗 406	拯 778
奖 261		扼 133	抨 419	拇 391	指 783
		找 768	抹 388		指 785
		扯 60	抹 389		指 787

叫	266	吻	616	咳	307	八画		嗜	520	十七画	
三画		吹	81	哄	215	哗	88	嗔	61	嚷	472
吁	672	呜	619	哄	216	哢	755	嗝	175	嚷	472
吓	212	君	299	哄	216	哚	812	喋	67	嚼	264
吓	634	邑	711	哑	683	唷	309	嗡	617	嚼	297
吐	586	叽	217	咧	342	啧	404	嗅	672		
吐	586	吵	548	品	428	唱	57	十一画		(59)	
吏	333	吵	59	咽	683	唾	594	嘀	109	口部	
吊	115	五画		咽	689	唯	607	嘈	48	二画	
吃	66	咏	724	咱	751	唯	610	嘎	163	囚	463
吸	626	味	611	响	645	啤	423	嘘	510	四	542
吆	693	哎	1	哈	202	啦	653	嘛	673	三画	
吗	364	咕	185	哈	202	九画		十二画		团	713
四画		呵	209	咯	300	喽	352	嘻	697	团	587
吭	206	呸	417	哆	131	啼	566	嘶	541	回	230
吭	310	咀	291	哪	394	喧	675	嘲	59	图	396
呈	64	呻	501	哪	399	喷	419	嘹	341	四画	
吱	813	呼	218	七画		喷	419	嘴	457	围	607
吒	711	呱	189	唁	689	喇	320	嗯	801	囤	741
呆	1	呢	401	哼	214	喃	397	十三画		困	319
呆	96	咖	163	哮	648	喊	205	噗	280	囵	129
吨	129	咖	299	唏	38	喋	117	嘴	824	囫	591
呕	410	岔	288	哽	178	喝	209	器	443	囹	219
呀	682	咆	416	哲	771	喂	612	十四画		五画	
员	741	鸣	386	哲	771	喘	80	嚎	207	囷	199
呐	394	咄	131	唢	498	十画		嚓	44	固	188
告	172	六画		唤	227	喉	217	十五画		图	584
吟	716	咨	813	唆	550	喻	740	嚷	568	七画	
含	204	咪	376	唉	1	十一画		十五画		圃	435
吩	150	咬	695	啊	1			嚣	650	圆	743
呛	451	咳	202	啊	123					八画	

9

(80)		心	657	慈	84	灼	812	烙	326	斋	759
灬部		三画		想	645	灸	287	七画		紊	616
		志	555	感	167	四画		焖	374	(85)	
五画		忍	476	愚	735	炎	686	焊	205	方部	
点	112	四画		愁	71	炕	304	烯	154	方	143
六画		态	553	愈	740	炉	353	焕	227	四画	
烈	343	念	403	十画		炬	292	八画		放	145
热	473	忿	544	愿	744	炖	129	焚	150	五画	
七画		忽	219	十一画		炊	81	焰	690	施	510
烹	419	五画		慧	233	炒	59	九画		六画	
八画		总	819	憨	204	五画		煤	371	旁	415
煮	801	怎	756	憋	32	烂	323	煳	605	旅	355
然	471	急	744	懂	612	炷	803	十画		七画	
九画		急	241	(82)		炫	677	熔	480	族	823
煎	254	怨	98	斗部		炼	338	熄	627	旋	676
照	768	怒	408			炽	68	熘	348	旋	677
煞	489	六画		斗	122	炯	286	十一画		十画	
煞	489	恋	818	斗	122	炸	758	熨	748	旗	439
十画		持	311	斟	774	炸	758	十二画		(86)	
熬	5	恩	134	斜	655	炮	15	燎	341	户部	
熬	5	恕	531	(83)		炮	417	燃	471	户	220
熙	627	七画		火部		烁	539	十三画		三画	
熏	679	悬	676			六画		爆	754	启	439
熊	669	患	227	火	235	烫	558	十五画		四画	
十一画		您	726	一画		烤	305	爆	20	房	144
熟	529	八画		灭	382	烘	215	(84)		肩	253
十二画		惹	473	二画		烦	140	文部		五画	
熹	628	惠	233	灯	107	烧	496			扁	29
(81)		惑	237	三画		烛	799	文	613	六画	
心部		惩	66	灶	754	烟	683	齐	345		
		九画		灿	47	烩	233				

扇	491	**(88)**	八画	**(91)**	二画	枕 774
扇	491	**王部**	琼 462	**韦部**	污 671	松 543
八画		王 602	斑 11	韧 478	朴 435	杵 77
扇	147	一画	琴 456	韬 559	机 238	析 626
雇	189	主 799	琳 344		杂 748	板 11
(87)		三画	琢 813	**(92)**	权 467	枪 449
ネ部		弄 352	琢 827	**耂部**	三画	枫 153
一画		弄 407	琥 220	老 326	忙 368	构 184
礼	330	玛 364	九画	考 304	来 321	枇 422
三画		四画	瑕 632	孝 652	杆 166	五画
社	499	玩 593	瑞 483	者 771	杆 167	染 472
四画		环 197	瑰 197		杜 125	栏 322
视	518	现 638	瑜 735	**(93)**	杠 170	柿 804
祈	437	玫 371	十二画	**廿(卄)部**	杖 765	柿 519
五画		五画	噩 134	共 182	村 89	柠 405
祛	465	垆 139		昔 626	材 44	标 30
祖	823	玷 10	**(89)**	巷 646	杏 667	栈 763
神	502	珊 491	**主部**	恭 182	极 241	柄 34
祝	803	玲 345	责 755	黄 228	枉 52	桥 166
祠	83	珍 772	表 31	李 330	杜 313	
六画		玻 36	毒 123	杨 691	枢 288	
祥	645	六画	素 546	四画	栋 121	
七画		班 10		杰 270	相 641	
祷	104	珠 798	**(90)**	柱 603	相 647	
祸	237	七画	**天(夭)部**	林 343	查 51	
八画		望 604	天 568	枝 783	柏 9	
禄	354	琉 350	夭 693	杯 20	柳 350	
九画		球 464	乔 452	枢 527	枷 249	
福	158	琐 550	吞 590	柜 198	架 251	
		理 331	蚕 46	查 695	栅 758	
			札 757	果 200	树 531	

癌 1	窗 80	**九画**	**（132）**	紫 721	**六画**
十三画	窘 286	褐 212	**示**	**八画**	硕 539
癞 322	**八画**	褪 590	示 516	蒙 374	砝 176
癣 423	窥 318	褴 591	祟 549	蒙 374	**七画**
（128）	窠 306	**十画**	祭 248	蒙 375	硫 350
穴部	窟 313	裤 482	禁 276		硬 722
穴 677	**（129）**	褶 323	禁 280	**（135）**	硝 649
二画	**衤部**	**十一画**	**（133）**	**甘部**	确 470
穷 462	**二画**	褶 771	**去部**	甘 166	**八画**
究 287	补 38	**十二画**	去 466	某 391	碰 420
三画	初 75	襁 451	圣 119	**（136）**	碎 549
空 310	**三画**	**十三画**	却 470	**石部**	碗 601
空 311	衬 62	襟 276	劫 270	石 511	碍 2
帘 336	衫 490	**十九画**	**（134）**	**三画**	碘 113
穹 462	**四画**	襕 415	**共部**	矿 317	碑 470
四画	袄 5	**（130）**	**二画**	码 364	碉 115
突 584	**五画**	**夬部**	劳 325	**四画**	硼 420
窈 454	袜 595	奉 155	**四画**	研 686	碌 354
穿 78	袒 556	奏 822	荧 720	砌 443	**九画**
五画	袖 671	春 82	荣 479	砚 689	磋 90
窍 453	被 22	泰 553	荤 233	砍 303	磁 84
窄 759	袍 416	舂 69	莘 361	砒 421	碧 27
窈 695	**七画**	蠢 82	**五画**	砥 489	碱 256
六画	裤 314	**（131）**	莹 720	泵 24	碴 52
室 790	裕 740	**玉部**	莺 719	**五画**	碟 117
窝 694	裙 471	玉 737	**六画**	砧 139	碳 557
七画	**八画**	玺 629	莹 721	硒 749	**十画**
窜 88	褂 190		营 720	砧 774	磅 14
窝 617	裸 361			破 432	磅 416
窨 268	裨 27				磕 306
					磊 328

硪	403
磐	414
十二画	
磷	344
礁	264

(137)

龙部

龙	351
垄	351
袭	628
龚	351

(138)

戊部

戊	530
成	63
咸	637
威	605
戚	436

(139)

⺌部

尝	56
党	102
堂	557
常	56
赏	494
掌	764

(140)

业部

业	699
澉	753
凿	830

(141)

目部

目	392
二画	
盯	117
四画	
盹	129
眨	758
看	302
看	303
盼	415
眉	371
五画	
眩	677
眠	378
六画	
眯	376
眵	377
眺	317
眺	572
静	778
眸	391
眼	687
八画	

睛	282
睦	393
睹	125
睫	272
瞄	381
督	123
睬	45
睡	537
睥	27
九画	
睽	318
十画	
瞒	632
瞌	307
購	366
瞑	386
十一画	
瞭	426
瞥	426
十二画	
瞳	580
瞬	538
瞧	452
瞩	801
瞪	108
十三画	
朦	375
瞻	760

(142)

田部

田	569
二画	
男	396
四画	
思	541
畏	612
胃	612
界	274
毗	422
五画	
畔	415
畜	77
畜	674
畛	349
六画	
畦	438
略	358
累	327
累	327
量	328
七画	
甥	506
八画	
畸	240

(143)

由部

由	727
胄	797
邮	727

(144)

申部

申	500
畅	57

(145)

罒部

三画	
罗	360
罗	360
四画	
罚	138
五画	
罡	7
八画	
署	530
置	791
罪	825
罩	770
十二画	
羁	240

(146)

皿部

四画	
盆	419
盈	720
五画	
益	711
盏	761

盐	687
监	254
盘	5
六画	
盗	105
盔	318
盛	65
盛	507
盒	212
八画	
盟	375
十一画	
盥	194

(147)

钅部

二画	
针	772
钉	118
钉	118
三画	
钎	444
钓	116
四画	
钙	165
钝	129
钟	794
钢	169
钢	170
钠	697
钥	745
钦	456

鹤 213	羊 690	眷 295	糕 172	李 357	（165）
鹳 697	三画	誊 563	糖 558	四画	戈部
十一画	差 50	（159）	糙 48	恋 338	栽 749
鹦 720	差 53	米部	十一画	六画	载 750
十三画	差 53	米 377	糠 304	蛮 366	载 751
鹰 720	美 372	三画	槽 752	（163）	裁 44
（153）	姜 259	类 328	十二画	耳部	截 272
皮部	四画	四画	糜 262	耳 135	戴 98
皮 422	羔 171	料 342	十四画	二画	（166）
皱 798	恙 693	粉 151	糯 410	取 465	襾（西）部
颇 431	羞 671	五画	（160）	四画	西 625
（154）	五画	粒 334	齐部	耿 178	要 693
癶部	着 767	粘 760	齐 437	耽 68	要 696
登 107	着 767	粗 86	剂 246	耻 99	栗 334
凳 108	着 812	六画	（161）	聋 544	贾 187
（155）	盖 165	粪 151	衣部	五画	票 426
矛部	六画	七画	衣 703	职 785	覆 163
矛 369	羹 641	粱 339	袋 98	聆 346	（167）
柔 480	善 492	粮 339	装 808	聊 341	束部
矜 275	翔 645	粲 47	裂 343	联 336	束 753
（156）	七画	八画	裔 713	七画	棘 242
疋部	群 471	粹 88	（162）	聘 428	（168）
蛋 100	十二画	粽 821	亦（亦）部	八画	亚部
楚 77	羲 157	精 282	亦 710	聚 294	亚 683
（157）	（158）	九画	二画	（164）	严 685
羊⺷芉部	⺷部	糊 219	变 29	臣部	恶 133
	券 469	糊 220	三画	臣 61	恶 133
	卷 294	糊 221	弯 597	卧 618	
	卷 295	糇 480			
	拳 469	十画			

恶	625	颇	427	虐	409	蝈	622	十八画		（178）	
晋	280	颓	589	虔	356	蜗	617	蠹	126	**竹(竹)部**	
（169）		颖	721	虑	447	蛾	132	（175）		竹	799
而部		八画		虚	672	蜂	154	**缶部**		三画	
而	134	颗	306	（174）		八画		缸	169	竿	166
耐	395	九画		**虫部**		蜻	469	缺	469	四画	
耍	532	颜	687	虫	70	蝉	54	罂	719	笔	25
（170）		颏	132	三画		蜿	598	罄	462	笑	653
页部		颚	134	虾	631	蜡	460	（176）		笋	549
页	699	十画		虹	216	蜥	627	**耒部**		五画	
二画		颠	112	蚁	708	蝇	721	四画		笠	335
顶	118	十三画		蛋	753	蜘	784	耕	177	笨	23
三画		颤	55	蚂	364	九画		耘	747	笛	351
顺	537	颧	763	四画		蝴	220	耗	209	笼	351
四画		（171）		蚊	615	蝶	117	耙	7	筐	432
顽	599	**至部**		蚌	14	蝎	654	耜	411	笛	109
顾	189	至	788	五画		蝌	307	十画		符	158
顿	130	到	104	蛙	804	蝗	229	耪	416	笞	572
颂	544	致	790	蛇	498	十画		（177）		第	111
颁	11	（172）		蛆	465	螃	416	**舌部**		六画	
预	738	**光部**		蛊	187	螟	368	舌	498	等	107
五画		光	194	蚱	758	融	480	乱	357	筑	804
颅	353	辉	230	蚯	463	十一画		刮	189	策	49
领	347	耀	697	六画		螫	520	舐	109	筐	316
颈	284	（173）		蛙	594	螺	361	甜	570	筛	489
六画		**虍部**		蛔	231	蟋	628	辞	83	筒	357
颊	250	虎	220	蛛	798	十三画				筏	138
七画		虏	353	七画		蟹	657			筵	687
颐	707			蜕	590	十四画				答	91
				蜇	770	蠕	482			答	92

醉	268	跷	451	蹩	32	（199）	
酷	314	跳	572	**十二画**		**身部**	
酸	547	踩	132	蹲	50	身	501
八画		跪	198	蹭	297	射	499
醇	825	路	354	蹼	435	躬	182
醋	87	跟	177	**十三画**		躯	465
九画		**七画**		蹿	754	躲	131
醒	667	踉	340			躺	558
		踌	72	（196）			
（194）		踊	724	**采部**		（200）	
里部		**八画**		采	45	**角部**	
		踮	113	采	45	角	265
里	331	踪	819	悉	627	解	272
野	698	踝	225	释	520	触	77
		踢	564	番	139		
（195）		踩	45			（201）	
足部		踟	67	（197）		**青部**	
足	822	踏	552	**豸部**		青	457
二画		**九画**		豹	19	静	286
趴	411	蹉	90	貂	115		
四画		蹀	566	貌	370	（202）	
距	293	蹂	131			**革部**	
趾	788	踹	78	（198）		乾	447
跃	746	蹂	480	**谷部**		朝	59
五画		**十画**		谷	186	朝	767
践	258	蹑	404	欲	739	幹	618
跋	7	蹒	414	豁	234		
跌	131	蹊	437	豁	237	（203）	
跛	37	**十一画**				**雨部**	
跑	416	蹬	557				
六画		蹦	24				
跨	314						

雨	736	辈	22
三画		翡	148
雪	679	蜚	147
五画		靠	305
雷	327		
零	346	（205）	
雾	625	**齿部**	
雹	16	齿	68
六画		龄	347
需	673	龋	466
七画		龌	618
震	775		
霄	649	（206）	
霉	371	**隹部**	
八画		售	526
霎	489	焦	264
霓	401	集	242
九画		雄	669
霜	534	雏	76
霞	633	雌	84
十三画		雕	115
霸	8		
霖	422	（207）	
露	353	**金部**	
露	355	金	275
		鉴	259
（204）			
非部		（208）	
非	147	**鱼部**	
韭	287	鱼	734
悲	147	**四画**	

鲁	353

六画

鲜	636

七画

鲤	331

八画

鲸	283

九画

鳄	134

十画

鳏	193

十二画

鳝	492
鳞	344

(209)　音部

音	715
章	764
竞	285
意	712
韵	748
韶	497

(210)　革部

革	174

二画

勒	327

三画

勒	327

四画

靴	677
靶	7

六画

鞍	3
鞋	655

七画

鞴	453

八画

鞠	290

九画

鞭	28

(211)　是部

是	519
题	566

(212)　骨部

骨	186
骨	187

五画

骷	313

十二画

髓	548

(213)　香部

香	643
馥	163
馨	662

(214)　鬼部

鬼	197
魂	234
魁	318
魅	373

(215)　食部

食	514
餐	46

(216)　高部

高	170
敲	452
膏	172

(217)　影部

鬓	819

(218)　麻部

麻	362
摩	388
磨	390
糜	377
靡	377
魔	388

(219)　鹿部

鹿	354
麓	355
麝	500

(220)　黑部

黑	213

三画

墨	390

四画

默	390
黔	448

八画

黥	124

九画

黯	5

(221)　鼓部

鼓	187

(222)　鼠部

鼠	530

(223)　鼻部

鼻	24
鼾	204

(224)　余类

三画

乡	641

四画

屯	591
巴	6

五画

东	119
民	382
凸	584
凹	5

七画

卵	357

九画

举	291
叛	415

A

A

阿 ā 【阿飞】teddy boy 【阿姨】one's mother's sister; auntie/nurse (in a family)

啊 ā á ǎ à eh; oh; o; ah; hey

AI

哎 āi hey; ah 【哎哟】ouch; ow

哀 āi ①grief; sorrow ～哭 wail ②mourning ③pity 【哀悼】grieve over sb.'s death 【哀歌】a mournful song; dirge; elegy 【哀号】cry; wail 【哀怜】feel compassion for 【哀求】entreat; implore 【哀伤】grieved; distressed 【哀思】sad memories (of the deceased) 【哀叹】bewail

挨 āi ①get close to; be next to ②in sequence; by turns 【挨次】in turn; one by one ～入场 file in

唉 āi right; yes 【唉声叹气】heave deep sighs; sigh in despair

呆 ái 【呆板】stiff; rigid; inflexible

挨 ái ①suffer; endure ～饿 suffer from hunger ～打 take a beating ～骂 get a scolding ～批评 be criticized ②drag out ～日子 suffer day after day ③delay; stall

癌 ái cancer; carcinoma 肝～ cancer of the liver

矮 ǎi ①short (of stature) ②low ～墙 a low wall ～凳 low stool 【矮墩墩】pudgy; stumpy 【矮胖】roly-poly 【矮小】short and small 【矮子】dwarf; a short person

蔼 ǎi friendly; amiable

爱 ài ①love; affection ～祖国 love one's country ②like; be keen on ～游泳 be fond of swimming ③be apt to; be in the habit of ～发脾气 be short-tempered 【爱称】term of endearment; pet name; diminutive 【爱戴】love and esteem 【爱抚】show tender care for 【爱国】be patriotic ～心 patriotic feeling ～者 patriot ～主义 patriotism 【爱好】love; like; be fond of; be keen on/interest; hobby ～者 amateur; enthusiast; fan; lover 【爱护】cherish; treasure ～公物 take good care of public property 【爱恋】be in love with; feel attached to 【爱面子】be concerned about face-saving 【爱慕】adore; admire ～虚荣 be vain 【爱情】love 【爱人】husband or wife/sweetheart 【爱惜】treasure; use sparingly

隘 ài ①narrow ②pass 【隘路】defile; narrow passage

碍 ài hinder; obstruct; be in the way of 【碍事】be a hindrance/be of consequence; matter

暖 ài 【暧昧】equivocal/shady 态度～ assume an ambiguous attitude ～关系 dubious relationship

AN

安 ān ①peaceful; quiet; tranquil; calm ～睡 sleep peacefully ②set (sb.'s mind) at ease ③rest content; be satisfied ～于现状 be content with things as they are ④safe; secure; in good health 欠～ be unwell ⑤place in a suitable position; find a place for ⑥install; fix; fit ～电灯

install electric lights ⑦bring (a charge against sb.); give (sb. a nickname) ⑧harbour (an intention) 【安插】place in a certain position; assign to a job; plant ～亲信 put one's trusted followers in key positions 【安定】stable; quiet; settled/stabilize; maintain ～团结 stability and unity ～人心 reassure the public 【安顿】find a place for; help settle down; arrange for/undisturbed; peaceful 【安放】lay; place 【安分】be law-abiding/know one's place 【安好】safe and sound; well 【安家】settle down; set up a home 【安静】quiet; peaceful 【安康】good health 【安乐】peace and happiness ～窝 cosy nest ～椅 easy chair 【安眠】sleep peacefully ～药 sleeping pill 【安宁】peaceful; tranquil/calm; composed; free from worry 【安排】arrange; plan; fix up ～参观游览 arrange visits and sightseeing trips 【安全】safe; secure ～行车 safe driving ～感 sense of security 【安然】safely/peacefully; at rest 【安如磐石】as solid as a rock 【安身】make one's home; take shelter 【安神】calm the nerves 【安适】quiet and comfortable 【安慰】comfort; console 【安稳】smooth and steady 【安息】rest; go to sleep 【安闲】carefree; leisurely 【安详】serene; composed 【安心】feel at ease; be relieved / keep one's mind on sth. ～工作 work contentedly 【安逸】comfortable; easy 贪图～ love comfort 【安营】pitch a camp 【安葬】bury (the dead) 【安置】help settle down; arrange for 【安装】install; fix; mount

氨 ān ammonia 【氨基】amino 【氨水】aqua ammoniae

鞍 ān saddle 【鞍马】pommelled horse; side horse

岸 àn bank; shore; coast 【岸标】shore beacon 【岸然】in a solemn manner

按 àn ①press; push down ～电钮 press a button ②leave aside; shelve ～下此事 leave this aside for the moment ③restrain; control (one's anger) ④keep one's hand on; keep a tight grip on ⑤according to; in accordance with; in the light of; on the basis of ～质定价 fix the price according to the quality ⑥note【按部就班】follow the prescribed order【按劳分配】distribution according to work【按理】according to reason; normally【按脉】feel the pulse【按摩】massage【按捺】restrain; control【按钮】push button【按期】on schedule; on time【按说】in the ordinary course of events; ordinarily【按需分配】distribution according to need【按语】note; comment【按照】according to; on the basis of ～实际情况 in the light of actual conditions ～群众的意见 in accordance with the opinions of the masses

案 àn ①table; desk ②(law) case 办～ handle a case ③record; file 有～可查 be on record ④proposal【案板】kneading or chopping board【案件】(law) case【案卷】records; files; archives【案情】details of a case; case【案头】on one's desk ～日历 desk calendar【案由】brief; summary【案子】long table; counter/(law) case

暗 àn ①dark; dim; dull ～绿 dark green ②hidden; secret ③unclear; hazy【暗暗】secretly; inwardly; to oneself【暗堡】bunker【暗藏】hide; conceal【暗淡】dim; faint; dismal; gloomy【暗害】kill secretly/stab in the back【暗含】imply【暗号】secret signal; cipher【暗合】(happen to) coincide【暗记】secret mark【暗箭】an arrow shot from hiding【暗礁】submerged rock【暗杀】assassinate【暗伤】internal injury/invisible damage【暗示】hint; suggest【暗室】darkroom【暗算】plot 遭人～ fall a prey to a plot【暗探】secret agent; detective【暗笑】snigger;

snicker【暗语】code word【暗中】in the dark/in secret

黯 àn dim; gloomy【黯然】dim; faint/dejected; low-spirited; downcast; depressed ～失色 be eclipsed

ANG

肮 āng 【肮脏】dirty; filthy ～的阴沟 a filthy sewer ～的勾当 dirty work; a foul deed

昂 áng ①hold (one's head) high ②high; soaring【昂昂】brave-looking【昂贵】expensive; costly【昂然】upright and unafraid【昂扬】high-spirited 斗志～ have high morale; be full of fight; be militant

盎 àng 【盎然】abundant; full; overflowing; exuberant【盎司】ounce

AO

凹 āo concave; hollow; sunken; dented【凹面镜】concave mirror【凹陷】hollow; sunken; depressed

熬 āo cook in water; boil ～白菜 stewed cabbage

遨 áo stroll; saunter【遨游】roam; travel ～太空 travel through space

熬 áo ①boil; stew; decoct ～粥 cook gruel ～药 decoct medicinal herbs ②endure; hold out【熬夜】stay up late or all night

翱 áo take wing【翱翔】hover; soar

袄 ǎo a short Chinese-style coat or jacket 皮～ a fur coat 棉～ a cotton-padded jacket

拗 ào 【拗口】hard to pronounce ～令 tongue twister

傲 ào ① proud; haughty ②refuse to yield to; brave; defy 【傲慢】 arrogant 【傲气】 haughtiness 【傲然】 loftily; unyieldingly

奥 ào profound; abstruse 【奥秘】 profound mystery 【奥妙】 subtle; secret

懊 ào ①regretful; remorseful ②annoyed 【懊悔】 feel remorse; repent; regret 【懊恼】 vexed; upset 【懊丧】 dejected; despondent; depressed

B

BA

八 bā eight 【八宝饭】 eight-treasure rice pudding 【八成】 eighty per cent/most likely 【八级工】 eighth-grade worker 【八角】 anise; star anise/octagonal 【八月】 August/ the eighth moon ～节 the Mid-Autumn Festival

巴 bā ①hope earnestly; wait anxiously ②cling to; stick to ③be close to; be next to 【巴不得】 be only too anxious (to do sth.); earnestly wish 【巴豆】 (purging) croton 【巴结】 fawn on; curry favour with; make up to 【巴望】 look forward to 【巴掌】 palm; hand

扒 bā ①hold on to; cling to ～着窗台 hold on to the window sill ②dig up; rake; pull down ～土 rake earth ③push aside ～开芦苇 push aside the reeds ④strip off; take off ～兔皮 skin a rabbit 【扒拉】 push lightly

芭 bā 【芭蕉】 *bajiao* banana ～扇 palm-leaf fan 【芭蕾舞】 ballet

疤 bā scar

拔 bá pull out; pull up ～草 pull up weeds ～牙 pull out a tooth 【拔除】pull out; remove 【拔河】tug-of-war 【拔尖儿】tiptop; top-notch/push oneself to the front

跋 bá ①cross mountains ②postscript 【跋扈】domineering; bossy 【跋涉】trudge; trek 长途～ make a long and difficult journey

把 bǎ ①hold; grasp ～着手教 take sb. by the hand and teach him how to do ②guard; watch ～门 guard a gate ③handle (of a pushcart, etc.) ④bundle; bunch 草～ a bundle of straw ⑤about; or so 个～月 about a month; a month or so 【把柄】handle 【把持】control; dominate; monopolize 【把风】keep watch; be on the lookout 【把关】guard a pass/check on 把好质量关 guarantee the quality (of products) 【把守】guard 【把头】labour contractor; gangmaster 【把握】hold; grasp/assurance ～时机 seize the opportunity 没有成功的～ have no certainty of success 【把戏】acrobatics/cheap trick

靶 bǎ target 打～ shooting practice 【靶场】range 【靶船】target ship 【靶机】target drone 【靶心】bull's-eye

把 bà ①grip; handle (of a teapot, etc.) ②stem (of a leaf, flower or fruit) 【把子】handle (of a knife, etc.)

坝 bà ①dam ②dyke; embankment

爸 bà pa; dad; father

耙 bà ①harrow ②draw a harrow over (a field)

罢 bà ①stop; cease 欲～不能 try to stop but cannot ②dismiss 【罢工】strike; go on strike 【罢官】dismiss from office 【罢教】teachers' strike 【罢课】students' strike 【罢免】recall ～权 right of recall 【罢市】shopkeepers'

strike 【罢手】give up 【罢休】let the matter drop

霸 bà ①chief of feudal princes; overlord ②tyrant; despot; bully ③hegemonism ④dominate; lord it over; tyrannize over 【霸道】overbearing; high-handed 【霸权】hegemony; supremacy ～主义 hegemonism 【霸占】forcibly occupy; seize

掰 bāi break off with the fingers and thumb ～玉米 break off corncobs ～腕子 hand wrestling

白 bái ①white ～发 white hairs ②clear 真相大～ everything is clear now ③pure; plain; blank ～纸 a blank sheet of paper ④in vain; for nothing ～忙 go to a lot of trouble for nothing ～跑一趟 make a fruitless trip ⑤free of charge; gratis ～送 give away free (of charge) ⑥White ～军 the White army ⑦wrongly written or mispronounced ⑧spoken part in opera, etc. 独～ monologue ⑨state; explain 自～ confessions 【白白】to no purpose 【白报纸】newsprint 【白布】plain white cloth; calico 【白菜】Chinese cabbage 【白痴】idiocy/idiot 【白饭】plain cooked rice 【白费】waste (one's energy, etc.) ～心思 bother one's head for nothing 【白果】ginkgo 【白喉】diphtheria 【白花花】shining white 【白话】vernacular ～文 writings in the vernacular 【白桦】white birch 【白金】platinum 【白净】fair and clear 【白酒】white spirit 【白卷】blank examination paper 交～ hand in an examination paper unanswered 【白开水】plain boiled water 【白兰地】brandy 【白茫茫】a vast expanse of whiteness 【白米】(polished) rice 【白面】wheat flour; flour 【白热】white heat; incandescence ～化 turn white-hot 【白人】white man or woman 【白刃】naked sword ～战

bayonet charge 【白色】 white (colour) ～恐怖 White terror ～政权 White regime 【白薯】 sweet potato 【白糖】 (refined) white sugar 【白天】 daytime; day 【白熊】 polar bear 【白血球】 white blood cell; leucocyte 【白眼】 supercilious look 【白杨】 white poplar 【白蚁】 white ant 【白银】 silver 【白纸黑字】 (written) in black and white 【白种】 the white race 【白昼】 daytime 【白字】 wrongly written or mispronounced character

百 bǎi ①hundred ②numerous; all kinds of ～花盛开 a hundred flowers in bloom 【百般】 in every possible way; by every means 【百倍】 a hundredfold; a hundred times 【百发百中】 a hundred shots, a hundred bull's-eyes; be a crack shot 【百分比】 percentage 【百分之百】 a hundred per cent; out and out; absolutely 【百分制】 hundred-mark system 【百合】 lily 【百花齐放，百家争鸣】 let a hundred flowers blossom and a hundred schools of thought contend 【百货】 general merchandise ～商店 department store; general store 【百科全书】 encyclopaedia 【百灵】 lark 【百年】 a hundred years; a century/lifetime 【百万】 million ～富翁 millionaire 【百姓】 common people 【百叶窗】 shutter; blind; jalousie

柏 bǎi cypress 【柏油】 pitch; tar; asphalt ～路 asphalt road

摆 bǎi ①put; place; arrange ～碗筷 set the table ②lay bare; state clearly ～矛盾 lay bare the contradictions ③put on; assume ～威风 put on airs ～老资格 flaunt one's seniority ④sway; wave ⑤pendulum 【摆布】 order about; manipulate 【摆动】 swing; sway 【摆渡】 ferry 【摆架子】 assume great airs 【摆阔】 parade one's wealth 【摆轮】 balance (of a watch) 【摆弄】 move back and forth; fiddle with 【摆设】 furnish and decorate 【摆摊子】 set up a stall / maintain a large staff or organization 【摆脱】 cast off; shake off; break away from; free oneself from ～困境 extricate oneself from a predicament

败 bài ①be defeated; lose (a battle, etc.) ②defeat; beat ③fail ④spoil ⑤counteract (a toxin) ⑥decay; wither 【败坏】 ruin; corrupt; undermine ～名誉 discredit; defame 道德～ morally degenerate 【败家子】 spendthrift; wastrel; prodigal 【败局】 lost game; losing battle 【败类】 scum of a community; degenerate 【败露】 fall through and stand exposed; be brought to light 【败落】 decline (in wealth and position) 【败诉】 lose a lawsuit 【败退】 retreat in defeat 【败兴】 disappointed 【败仗】 lost battle 打～ suffer a defeat

拜 bài ①do obeisance ～佛 worship Buddha ②make a courtesy call ③acknowledge sb. as one's master, godfather, etc. 【拜倒】 prostrate oneself; fall on one's knees; grovel 【拜访】 pay a visit; call on 【拜年】 pay a New Year call; wish sb. a Happy New Year

BAN

扳 bān pull; turn ～枪栓 pull back the bolt of a rifle ～道岔 pull railway switches ～成平局 equalize the score 【扳道员】 switchman 【扳机】 trigger 【扳手】 spanner; wrench / lever (on a machine)

班 bān ①class; team 作业～ work team ②shift; duty 上夜～ be on night shift ③squad 【班车】 regular bus (service) 【班次】 order of classes or grades at school / number of runs or flights ～比我高 be in a higher class than me 【班底】 ordinary members (of a theatrical troupe, etc.) 【班房】 jail 【班机】 airliner; regular air service 【班级】 classes and grades in school 【班轮】 regular steamship service 【班务会】a routine meeting of a squad, team or class 【班长】class monitor / squad leader / (work) team leader 【班主任】a teacher in charge of a class 【班子】theatrical troupe / organized group

般 bān sort; kind; way 暴风雨～的掌声 stormy applause 兄弟～的情谊 fraternal feelings

颁 bān promulgate; issue 【颁布】issue (a decree); publish 【颁行】issue for enforcement

斑 bān ①spot; speck; speckle; stripe ②spotted; striped 【斑白】grizzled; greying 【斑斑】full of stains or spots 【斑驳】mottled; motley 【斑点】stain 【斑鸠】turtledove 【斑斓】gorgeous; bright-coloured 【斑马】zebra

搬 bān ①take away; move; remove 把桌子～走 take the table away ②apply indiscriminately; copy mechanically 【搬家】move (house) 【搬弄】move sth. about; fiddle with/show off; display ～学问 show off one's erudition ～是非 sow discord; tell tales 【搬运】carry; transport ～工人 porter; docker

板 bǎn ①board; plank; plate 钢～ steel plate ②shutter ③bat; battledore ④clappers ⑤stiff; unnatural ⑥stop smiling; look serious ～着脸 keep a straight face 【板壁】wooden partition 【板擦】blackboard eraser 【板凳】wooden bench or stool 【板结】harden 【板栗】Chinese chestnut 【板书】writing on the blackboard 【板刷】scrubbing brush 【板鸭】pressed salted duck 【板烟】plug (of tobacco) 【板羽球】battledore and shuttlecock / shuttlecock

版 bǎn ①printing plate ②edition ③page (of a newspaper) 【版本】edition 【版画】print 【版刻】carving; engraving 【版面】space of a whole page / layout of a printed sheet 【版权】copyright ～所有 all rights reserved ～页 copyright page; colophon 【版税】royalty (on books)

【版图】domain; territory

办 bàn ①do; handle; manage; tackle; attend to 怎么～ what's to be done ②set up; run ～学习班 organize a study class ③buy a fair amount of; get sth. ready ～酒席 prepare a feast ④punish (by law); bring to justice 【办案】handle a case 【办报】run a newspaper 【办到】get sth. done; accomplish 【办法】way; means; measure 【办公】handle official business; work ～时间 office hours ～室 office ～桌 desk; bureau 【办理】handle; conduct; transact ～手续 go through the formalities 【办事】handle affairs; work ～处 office; agency ～机构 administrative body; working body ～员 office worker

半 bàn ①half; semi- ～小时 half an hour ～年 six months ②in the middle; halfway ～山腰 halfway up a hill ③very little; the least bit ④partly; about half 房门～开着 the door was left half open 【半百】fifty (years of age) 【半边】half of sth.; one side of sth. 【半场】half of a game or contest/half-court 【半成品】semi-finished articles 【半导体】semiconductor ～收音机 transistor radio 【半岛】peninsula 【半点】the least bit 【半封建】semifeudal 【半工半读】part work, part study; work-study programme 【半公开】semi-overt 【半官方】semi-official 【半价】(at) half price 【半截】half (a section) 【半径】radius 【半空中】in mid air; in the air 【半路】halfway; midway; on the way 【半票】half-price ticket; half fare 【半旗】half-mast 下～fly a flag at half-mast 【半日制学校】half-day school 【半身不遂】hemiplegia 【半身像】half-length photo / bust 【半生】half a lifetime 【半数】half the number; half 【半天】half of the day / (for) a long time; quite a while 【半途而废】give up halfway 【半夜】midnight ～三更 in the depth of night; late at

night【半元音】semivowel【半圆】semicircle【半月刊】
semimonthly; fortnightly【半殖民地】semi-colony

扮 bàn ①be dressed up as; disguise oneself as ② put
on (an expression)【扮相】the appearance of an
actor or actress in costume and makeup【扮演】play the
part of; act【扮装】makeup

伴 bàn ①companion; partner 作～ keep sb. company
②accompany【伴唱】vocal accompaniment/accompany
(a singer)【伴侣】companion; mate; partner【伴随】ac-
company; follow【伴奏】accompany (with musical instruments)～者 accompanist

拌 bàn mix【拌和】mix and stir; blend【拌面】noodles
served with soy sauce, sesame butter, etc.【拌种】
seed dressing【拌嘴】bicker; squabble; quarrel

绊 bàn (cause to) stumble; trip【绊脚石】stumbling
block; obstacle

瓣 bàn ①petal ②segment or section (of a tangerine,
etc.); clove (of garlic) ③valve; lamella ④fragment;
piece【瓣膜】valve

BANG

邦 bāng nation; state; country 邻～ a neighbouring
country【邦交】diplomatic relations

帮 bāng ①help; assist ～他搬行李 help him with his
luggage ②side (of a boat, truck, etc.); upper (of a
shoe) ③outer leaf (of cabbage, etc.) ④gang; band; clique
【帮厨】help in the mess kitchen【帮工】help with farm
work/helper【帮会】secret society【帮忙】help; give a
hand; do a favour; do a good turn【帮派】faction【帮
腔】speak in support of sb.; echo sb.; chime in with sb.
【帮手】helper; assistant【帮凶】accomplice; accessary

绑 bǎng ①bind; tie ②bind sb.'s hands behind him; truss up 【绑匪】kidnapper 【绑架】kidnap/staking 【绑票】kidnap (for ransom) 【绑腿】leg wrappings; puttee

榜 bǎng ①a list of names posted up ②announcement; notice 【榜样】example; model

膀 bǎng ①upper arm; arm ②shoulder ③wing (of a bird) 【膀臂】arm/reliable helper

蚌 bàng freshwater mussel; clam

谤 bàng slander; defame; vilify

傍 bàng draw near; be close to 【傍晚】toward evening; at nightfall; at dusk

棒 bàng ①stick; club; cudgel 垒球～ softball bat ② good; fine; excellent; strong 字写得～ write a good hand 【棒槌】wooden club 【棒球】baseball ～场 baseball field 【棒糖】sucker; lollipop

磅 bàng ①pound ②scales ③weigh ～体重 weigh oneself or sb. on the scales ④point (type) 【磅秤】platform scale; platform balance

镑 bàng pound (a currency)

BAO

包 bāo ①wrap ～书 wrap up a book in a piece of paper ②bundle; package; pack; packet; parcel 邮～ postal parcel ③bag; sack 书～ school bag ④bale; sack ⑤swelling; lump 起了个～ have a swelling ⑥surround; encircle; envelop ⑦include; contain 无所不～ all-inclusive ⑧undertake the whole thing 这事我～了 just leave it all to me ⑨assure; guarantee ⑩hire; charter ～机 a chartered plane 【包办】 take care of everything concerning a job/ run the whole show; monopolize everything ~婚姻 arranged marriage 【包庇】 shield; harbour; cover up 【包藏】 contain; harbour; conceal ~祸心 harbour evil intentions 【包产】 make a production contract; take full responsibility for output quotas ~到户 fixing of farm output quotas for each household 【包场】 make a block booking 【包抄】 outflank; envelop 【包饭】 board 【包袱】 cloth-wrapper/a bundle wrapped in cloth/load; weight; burden 【包干】 be responsible for a task until it is completed 【包管】 assure; guarantee 【包裹】 wrap up; bind up/bundle; package; parcel ~单 parcel form 【包含】 contain; embody; include 海水~盐分 sea water contains salt 【包涵】 excuse; forgive 【包金】 gild 【包括】 include; consist of; comprise; incorporate 运费~在帐内 the freight is included in the account 【包揽】 undertake the whole thing; take on everything 【包罗】 include; cover; embrace ~万象 all-embracing; all-inclusive 【包赔】 guarantee to pay compensations 【包皮】 wrapping; wrapper/ prepuce; foreskin 【包容】 pardon; forgive/contain; hold 【包围】 surround; encircle ~圈 ring of encirclement 【包厢】 box (in a theatre) 【包销】 have exclusive selling rights 【包扎】 wrap up; bind up; pack ~伤口 dress a wound 【包装】 pack; package ~箱 packing box ~纸 wrapping paper 【包子】 steamed stuffed bun

炮 bāo ①quick-fry; sauté ~羊肉 quick-fried mutton ②dry by heat

胞 bāo ①afterbirth ②born of the same parents ~兄弟 full brothers

剥 bāo shell; peel; skin ~花生 shell peanuts ~香蕉 peel a banana ~兔皮 skin a rabbit

褒 bāo praise; honour; commend 【褒贬】pass judgment on; appraise 【褒义】commendatory (term)

雹 báo hail 【雹灾】disaster caused by hail

薄 báo ①thin; flimsy ～纸 thin paper ②weak; light ～酒 light wine ③poor (land, etc.) 【薄板】sheet 【薄饼】thin pancake 【薄脆】crisp fritter 【薄页纸】tissue paper

宝 bǎo ①treasure ②precious; treasured 【宝宝】darling; baby 【宝贝】treasure/darling; baby 【宝贵】valuable; precious/value; treasure ～意见(经验) valuable suggestion (experience) 【宝剑】a double-edged sword 【宝库】treasure-house 【宝石】precious stone; gem 【宝塔】pagoda 【宝藏】precious deposits 【宝座】throne

饱 bǎo ①have eaten one's fill; be full ②full; plump ③fully; to the full ④satisfy 【饱和】saturation 【饱经风霜】weather-beaten; having experienced the hardships of life 【饱满】full; plump 精神～ full of vigour; energetic 颗粒～ plump-eared 【饱学】learned; erudite

保 bǎo ①protect; defend ②keep; maintain; preserve ～水～肥 preserve moisture and fertility (in the soil) ③guarantee; ensure ～质～量 guarantee both quality and quantity ④stand guarantor for sb. ⑤guarantor 作～ stand surety for sb. 【保安】ensure public security/ensure safety (for workers engaged in production) ～措施(人员) security measures (personnel) 【保镖】bodyguard 【保不住】most likely; may well 【保藏】keep in store; preserve 【保持】keep; maintain; preserve ～安静 keep quiet ～警惕 maintain vigilance; be on the alert ～车距 keep a safe distance between cars 【保存】preserve; conserve; keep ～实力 preserve one's strength 【保单】guarantee slip 【保管】

take care of / certainly; surely ～农具 take care of farm tools ～费 storage fee ～室 storeroom ～员 storeman; storekeeper 【保护】protect; safeguard ～环境 protect the environment ～现场 keep intact the scene of a crime or accident ～国 protectorate ～色 protective coloration 【保健】health protection; health care ～操 setting-up exercises ～费 health subsidies 【保洁箱】litter-bin 【保留】continue to have; retain/hold back; reserve 持～意见 have reservations ～剧目 repertory 【保密】maintain secrecy; keep sth. secret 【保姆】(children's) nurse / housekeeper 【保全】save from damage; preserve / maintain; keep in good repair 【保释】release on bail; bail 【保守】guard; keep / conservative ～思想 conservative ideas ～疗法 conservative treatment 【保送】recommend sb. for admission to school, etc. 【保卫】defend; safeguard ～祖国 defend one's country ～工作 security work ～科 security section 【保温】heat preservation 【保险】insurance / be sure; be bound to ～公司 insurance company ～柜 safe ～丝 fuse; fuse-wire 【保修】guarantee to keep sth. in good repair 【保养】take good care of one's health / maintain; keep in good repair 【保佑】bless and protect 【保育】child care; child welfare ～员 child-care worker; nurse ～院 nursery school 【保障】ensure; guarantee; safeguard ～生产队的自主权 ensure the production teams' power of decision 【保证】pledge; guarantee; assure; ensure 我可以向你～这消息可靠 I can assure you of the reliability of the information ～成功（安全，供应）ensure success (safety, supplies) ～书 guarantee ～金 earnest money; cash deposit ～人 guarantor; bail

葆 bǎo ①luxuriant growth ②preserve; nurture 永～青春 keep alive the fervour of youth

堡

bǎo fort; fortress 【堡垒】 stronghold; blockhouse ～战 blockhouse warfare

报

bào ①report; announce; declare ～户口 apply for a residence permit ～火警 report a fire ②reply; respond ～以热烈的掌声 respond with warm applause ③recompense; requite 无以为～ be unable to repay a kindness ④newspaper; ⑤periodical; journal 学～ college journal ⑥bulletin report 战～ war bulletin ⑦telegram; cable 发～ send a telegram 【报案】 report a case to the security authorities 【报表】 report forms 【报偿】 repay; recompense 【报仇】 revenge; avenge 【报酬】 reward; remuneration; pay 【报答】 repay; requite 【报到】 report for duty; check in; register 新生已开始～ the new students have started registering 【报道】 report (news); cover/news report; story 【报恩】 pay a debt of gratitude 【报废】 report sth. as worthless/discard as useless; reject; scrap 【报复】 make reprisals; retaliate 【报告】 report; make known/speech; talk; lecture 作～ give a talk or lecture 动员～ mobilization speech ～会 public lecture ～人 speaker; lecturer ～文学 reportage 【报捷】 report a success; announce a victory 【报界】 the press; journalistic circles 【报警】 report (an incident) to the police/give an alarm 鸣钟～ sound the alarm bell 【报刊】 newspapers and periodicals; the press 【报考】 enter oneself for an examination 【报名】 enter one's name; sign up 【报幕】 announce the items on a programme ～员 announcer 【报社】 newspaper office 【报失】 report the loss of sth. to the authorities concerned 【报时】 give the correct time 【报数】 number off; count off 【报摊】 news-stand; news stall 【报头】 masthead; nameplate 【报务员】 telegraph or radio operator 【报喜】 announce good news; report success 【报销】 submit an expense account/hand in a list of expended articles/write off; wipe out 【报信】notify; inform 【报应】retribution; judgment 【报帐】render an account / apply for reimbursement 【报纸】newspaper / newsprint

刨 bào ①plane sth. down; plane ～木板 plane a board ②plane; planing machine 【刨冰】water ice 【刨床】 planer 【刨花】wood shavings ～板 shaving board

抱 bào ①hold or carry in the arms; embrace; hug ～小 孩 take a child in one's arms ②hang together ～成 团 gang up ③cherish; harbour ～很大希望 entertain high hopes 不～幻想 cherish no illusions ④an armful (of hay, firewood, etc.) 【抱病】be ill; be in bad health ～工作 go on working in spite of ill health 【抱不平】be outraged by an injustice (done to another person) 打～ defend sb. against an injustice 【抱负】aspiration; ambition 很有～ have high aspirations 【抱恨】have a gnawing regret 【抱 愧】feel ashamed 【抱歉】be sorry; feel apologetic; regret 很～, 我不能来 I regret (to say) that I cannot come 【抱养】adopt (a child) 〖抱怨〗complain; grumble

豹 bào leopard; panther

暴 bào ①sudden and violent ～饮～食 eat and drink too much at one meal ②cruel; savage; fierce ③short-tempered; hot-tempered 脾气～ have a hot temper ④stick out; stand out; bulge 【暴病】sudden attack of a serious illness 【暴跌】steep fall (in price); slump 【暴动】insur-rection; rebellion 【暴发】break out/suddenly become rich ～户 upstart 【暴风】storm wind 【暴风雪】snowstorm 【暴风雨】rainstorm; storm; tempest 【暴风骤雨】violent storm; hurricane 【暴光】exposure 【暴君】tyrant; despot 【暴力】violence; force ～革命 violent revolution ～机关 organ of violence 【暴利】sudden huge profits 牟取～ reap staggering profits 【暴露】 expose; reveal; lay bare ～思想 lay bare one's thoughts ～目标 give away one's position 【暴乱】 riot; rebellion; revolt 平定～ quell a rebellion 【暴怒】 rage; fury 【暴虐】 brutal; tyrannical 【暴徒】 ruffian; thug 【暴行】 savage act: outrage 【暴雨】 torrential rain; rainstorm 【暴躁】 irascible; irritable 【暴涨】 (of floods, prices, etc.) rise suddenly and sharply 【暴政】 tyranny

爆 bào ①explode; burst ②quick-fry 【爆发】 erupt; burst out; break out 战争～ war broke out 【爆裂】 burst; crack 【爆破】 blow up; demolish; dynamite; blast ～手 dynamiter ～筒 bangalore (torpedo) ～音 plosive 【爆炸】 explode; blow up; detonate ～力 explosive force ～物 explosive 【爆竹】 firecracker 放～ let off firecrackers

BEI

杯 bēi ①cup; glass 茶～ teacup 一～茶 a cup of tea ②(prize) cup; trophy 银～ silver cup

卑 bēi ①low ②inferior ③modest; humble 【卑鄙】 base; mean; contemptible; despicable 【卑贱】 lowly / mean

背 bēi ①carry on the back ～着孩子 carry a baby on one's back ②bear; shoulder 【背包】 knapsack; rucksack; field pack/blanket roll 【背带】 braces; suspenders

悲 bēi ①sad; melancholy ②compassion 【悲哀】 grieved; sorrowful 【悲惨】 miserable; tragic 【悲悼】 mourn; grieve over sb.'s death 【悲愤】 grief and indignation 【悲歌】 sad melody / elegy; dirge / sing with solemn fervour 【悲观】 pessimistic ～主义 pessimism 【悲剧】 tragedy

碑 bēi stone tablet; stele 【碑林】 a rubbing from a stone inscription 【碑文】 an inscription on a tablet

北 běi north ～风 a north wind 【北斗星】 the Big Dipper; the Plough 【北方】 north / the northern part of the country ～话 northern dialect ～人 Northerner 【北极】the North Pole; the Arctic Pole/the north magnetic pole ～圈 the Arctic Circle ～星 Polaris

贝 bèi ①shellfish ②cowrie 【贝雕】shell carving 【贝壳】shell 【贝类】molluscs

备 bèi ①be equipped with; have ②prepare; get ready ③provide against; take precautions against 以～万一 prepare against all eventualities ④equipment 军～ military equipment 【备案】·put on record; enter (a case) in the records 【备查】for future reference 【备而不用】have sth. ready just in case; keep sth. for possible future use 【备荒】prepare against natural disasters 【备件】spare parts 【备考】for reference 【备课】(of a teacher) prepare lessons 【备料】get the materials ready 【备取】be on the waiting list (for admission to a school) 【备忘录】memorandum; aide-mémoire/memorandum book 【备用】reserve; spare; alternate ～机器 standby machine ～轮胎 spare tyre 【备战】prepare for war/be prepared against war 【备注】remarks ～栏 remarks column

背 bèi ①the back of the body ～痛 backache ②the back of an object 椅(手)～ the back of a chair (the hand) ③with the back towards ～山面海 with hills behind and the sea in front ④turn away 把脸～过去 turn one's face away ⑤hide sth. from; do sth. behind sb.'s back ～着人说话 talk behind sb.'s back ⑥recite from memory; learn by heart ～台词 speak one's lines ⑦violate; break ～约 violate an agreement 【背道而驰】run counter to 【背后】behind; at the back/behind sb.'s back 【背景】background 【背离】deviate from; depart from 【背面】the back; the reverse side; the wrong side 【背叛】betray; forsake 【背诵】recite; repeat from memory 【背心】a sleeveless garment 【背信弃义】 break faith with sb.; be perfidious

被 bèi quilt 棉~ cotton-wadded quilt 【被袋】 bedding bag 【被单】 (bed) sheet 【被动】 passive ~式 passive form ~语态 passive voice 【被服】 bedding and clothing ~厂 clothing factory 【被俘】 be captured; be taken prisoner 【被告】 defendant; the accused ~席 dock 【被害人】 the victim 【被里】 the underneath side of a quilt 【被面】 the facing of a quilt 【被迫】 be compelled; be forced; be constrained 【被褥】 bedding; bedclothes

倍 bèi ①times; -fold 四~ four times; fourfold 增长两 ~ increase by 200% ②double 【倍数】 multiple

辈 bèi ①people of a certain kind; the like 无能之~ people without ability ②generation ③lifetime; all one's life 【辈分】 seniority in the family or clan

BEN

奔 bēn ①run quickly ~马 a galloping horse ②hurry; hasten; rush ~赴前线 hurry to the front 【奔波】 rush about; be busy running about 【奔驰】 speed 【奔放】 bold and unrestrained; untrammelled 【奔流】 flow at great speed; pour/racing current ~入海 flow into the sea

本 běn ①the root or stem of a plant ②foundation; basis; origin ③capital; principal ④original ⑤one's own; native ~厂 this factory ⑥this; current; present ~周 this week ⑦based on ~着政策办事 act according to policy ⑧book 【本分】 one's duty 尽~ do one's duty 【本国】 one's own country ~资源 national resources 【本行】 one's line; one's own profession 【本届】 current; this year's ~毕业生 this year's graduates 【本金】 capital; principal 【本科】 undergraduate course; regular college course ~学生 undergraduate 【本来】 original/originally;

at first ～面目 true colours; true features 【本领】 skill; ability; capability 【本末】 the whole course of an event from beginning to end; ins and outs/the fundamental and the incidental 【本能】 instinct 【本钱】 capital 【本人】 I (me, myself)/oneself; in person 【本色】 true qualities; distinctive character 【本身】 itself; in itself 【本事】 source material; original story 【本土】 one's native country; metropolitan territory 【本位】 standard/one's own department or unit ～工作 one's own work ～主义 selfish departmentalism 【本性】 natural character; nature ～难移 it is difficult to alter one's character 【本义】 original meaning; literal sense 【本意】 original idea; real intention 【本源】 origin; source 【本职】 one's job 【本质】 essence; nature ～差别 an essential distinction 【本子】 book; notebook 改～ correct papers; go over students' written exercises 【本族语】 native language; mother tongue

奔 bèn ①go straight towards; head for 直～教室 head straight for the classroom ②approach; be getting on for 【奔头儿】 sth. to strive for; prospect

笨 bèn ①stupid; dull; foolish 脑子～ slow-witted ② clumsy; awkward ③cumbersome 【笨蛋】 fool; idiot

BENG

崩 bēng ①collapse ②burst ③be hit by sth. bursting 【崩溃】 crumble; fall apart 【崩裂】 break apart; crack 【崩陷】 fall in; cave in

绷 bēng ①stretch tight ～上块绳子 stretch a piece of silk on sth. ②spring; bounce ③baste; tack; pin 【绷带】 bandage 【绷子】 embroidery frame; hoop; tambour

甭 béng don't; needn't ～说了 don't say any more

绷 běng strain oneself ～住劲 strain one's muscles ～着脸 look displeased

迸 bèng spout; spurt; burst forth 【迸发】 burst (out) 【迸裂】 split; burst (open)

泵 bèng pump 【泵房】 pump house

绷 bèng ①split open; crack ②very ～脆 very crisp

蹦 bèng leap; jump; spring

BI

逼 bī ①force; compel; drive; coerce ～死 hound sb. to death ②extort ～租 press for payment of rent 【逼供】 extort a confession 【逼近】 press on towards; close in on; approach; draw near 【逼人】 pressing; threatening 形势～ the situation spurs us on 【逼真】 lifelike

荸 bí 【荸荠】 water chestnut

鼻 bí nose 【鼻孔】 nostril 【鼻梁】 bridge of the nose 【鼻腔】 nasal cavity 【鼻涕】 nasal mucus; snivel 流～ have a running nose 【鼻息】 breath 【鼻炎】 rhinitis 【鼻音】 nasal sound 【鼻祖】 the earliest ancestor; originator

匕 bǐ 【匕首】 dagger

比 bǐ ①compare; contrast ～得上 can compare with ②emulate; compete; match ～革命干劲 emulate each other in revolutionary drive ③draw an analogy; liken to; compare to ④copy; model after ⑤ratio; proportion 【比方】 analogy; instance 打～ draw an analogy 【比分】 score 【比画】 gesture; gesticulate 【比价】 price relations;

parity; rate of exchange 【比较】compare; contrast/fairly; comparatively; relatively; quite; rather ～级 comparative degree 【比例】proportion/scale ～尺 scale′ 【比率】ratio; rate 【比目鱼】flatfish 【比拟】draw a parallel; match/analogy; metaphor; comparison 【比如】for example; for instance; such as 【比赛】match; competition ～项目 event 【比试】have a competition/make a gesture of measuring 【比翼】fly wing to wing ～鸟 a pair of lovebirds — a devoted couple 【比喻】metaphor; analogy; figure of speech 【比照】according to; in the light of/contrast 【比值】specific value;′ratio 【比重】proportion/specific gravity

彼 bǐ ①that; those; the other; another ～时 at that time ②the other party 知己知～ know both your opponent and yourself 【彼此】each other; one another

笔 bǐ ①pen 毛～ writing brush ②technique of writing, calligraphy or drawing 文～ style of writing ③write 代～ write sth. for sb. ④stroke; touch 添几～ add a few touches 【笔画】strokes of a Chinese character 【笔迹】a person's handwriting; hand 对～ identify sb.'s handwriting 【笔记】take down (in writing)/notes 记～ take notes ～本 notebook 【笔架】pen rack; penholder 【笔尖】nib; pen point/the tip of a writing brush or pencil 【笔帽】the cap of a pen 【笔名】pen name; pseudonym 【笔墨】pen and ink; words; writing 【笔试】written examination 【笔算】do a sum in writing/written calculation 【笔筒】pen container; brush pot 【笔头】nib/ability to write/written; in written form ～练习 written exercises ～快 be good at writing 【笔误】a slip of the pen 【笔心】pencil lead/refill (for a ball-point pen) 【笔译】written translation 【笔者】the author; the writer 【笔直】perfectly straight

鄙 bǐ ①low; mean; vulgar; philistine; despicable ②my ③despise; scorn 【鄙陋】 superficial; shallow 【鄙人】 your humble servant; I 【鄙视】 disdain; look down upon

币 bì money; currency 外～ foreign currency 银～ silver coin 【币值】 currency value

必 bì ①certainly; surely; necessarily ②must; have to ～读书目 a list of required reading 【必定】 be bound to; be sure to 【必然】 certain ～结果 inevitable outcome ～规律 inexorable law ～性 necessity; inevitability; certainty 【必修课】 a required course 【必须】 must; have to 【必需】 essential; indispensable ～品 necessities; necessaries 【必要】 necessary; indispensable ～条件 essential condition

闭 bì ①shut; close ～眼 close one's eyes ～嘴 shut up ②stop up; obstruct ～住气 hold one's breath 【闭会】 end a meeting 【闭幕】 the curtain falls; lower the curtain/ close; conclude ～词 closing address ～式 closing ceremony 【闭塞】 stop up; close up/hard to get to; out-of-the-way

毕 bì ①finish; accomplish; conclude ②fully; completely 【毕竟】 after all; all in all; in the final analysis 【毕生】 all one's life; lifetime 【毕业】 graduate; finish school ～班 graduating class ～典礼 graduation (ceremony); commencement ～分配 job assignment on graduation ～论文 graduation thesis ～设计 graduation project ～生 graduate ～实习 graduation field work ～证书 diploma; graduation certificate

庇 bì shelter; protect; shield 【庇护】 put under one's protection; take under one's wing

陛 bì a flight of steps leading to a palace hall 【陛下】 Your (His, Her) Majesty

毙 bì die; get killed 倒～ drop dead ②shoot 枪～ execute by shooting 【毙命】 meet violent death; get killed

敝 bì ①shabby; worn-out; ragged ～衣 ragged clothing ②my; our; this ～校 my school

婢 bì slave girl; servant-girl

裨 bì benefit; advantage 【裨益】profit 大有～ be of great benefit

蓖 bì 【蓖麻】castor-oil plant ～蚕 castor silkworm ～油 castor oil ～子 castor bean

睥 bì 【睥睨】look at sb. disdainfully out of the corner of one's eye ～一切 be overweening

滗 bì decant; strain; drain 别把壶里的茶水～干 don't drain the teapot dry

碧 bì ①green jade ②bluish green; blue ～空 an azure sky ～玉 jasper

蔽 bì cover; shelter; hide ～风雨 shelter from the wind and rain 衣不～体 be dressed in rags

弊 bì ①fraud; abuse; malpractice ②disadvantage; harm 【弊病】malady; evil; corrupt practice/drawback

篦 bì comb with a double-edged fine-toothed comb ～头 comb one's hair with such a comb

避 bì ①avoid; evade; shun ～而不谈 evade the question ～雨 seek shelter from the rain ②prevent; keep away; repel 【避风】take shelter from the wind/lie low ～港 haven; harbour 【避雷器】lightning arrester 【避雷针】lightning rod 【避免】avoid; refrain from; avert ～错误 avoid mistakes 【避难】take refuge; seek asylum ～所 refuge; sanctuary 【避暑】be away for the summer holidays; spend a holiday at a summer resort/prevent sunstroke

壁 bì ①wall ②cliff ③rampart; breastwork 【壁报】wall newspaper 【壁橱】a built-in wardrobe or cupboard; closet 【壁灯】wall lamp; bracket light 【壁画】mural (painting); fresco 【壁龛】 niche 【壁垒】 rampart; barrier 【壁炉】 fireplace 【壁毯】 tapestry (used as a wall hanging)

臂 bì ①arm ②upper arm 【臂膀】 arm 【臂纱】 (black) armband 【臂章】 armband; armlet/shoulder emblem

BIAN

边 biān ①side 街道两~ both sides of the street ②margin; edge; brim; rim 碗~ the rim of a bowl ③border; frontier; boundary ~城 border town ④limit; bound 无~ boundless ⑤by the side of; close by 手~ at hand 耳~ in one's ears 【边地】 border district; borderland 【边防】 frontier defence ~部队 frontier guards ~战士 frontier guard 【边际】 limit; bound; boundary 漫无~ rambling; discursive 不着~ wide of the mark; not to the point 【边界】 boundary; border ~线 boundary line ~争端 boundary dispute 【边境】 frontier 【边框】 frame; rim 【边门】 side door 【边沿】 edge; fringe 【边缘】 edge; fringe; verge; brink

编 biān ①weave; plait ~筐子 weave baskets ②organize; group; arrange ~班 group into classes ③edit; compile ~教材 compile teaching material ④write; compose ~剧本 write a play ⑤fabricate; invent; make up ⑥part of a book; book; volume 【编导】 write and direct (a play, film, etc.)/playwright-director; scenarist-director 【编队】 form into columns; organize into teams/formation 【编号】number/serial number 【编辑】 edit; compile/editor; compiler ~部 editorial department ~委员会 editorial board 【编剧】 write a play, scenario, etc./playwright

鞭 biān ①whip ②a string of small firecrackers 【鞭策】 spur on; urge on 【鞭打】 whip; lash; flog; thrash 【鞭挞】 castigate

贬 biǎn ①demote; relegate ②reduce; devalue ③censure; depreciate 【贬词】 derogatory term; expression of censure 【贬低】 belittle; play down; disparage 【贬义】 derogatory sense ~词 derogatory term 【贬值】 devalue

扁 biǎn flat 【扁担】 carrying pole; shoulder pole 【扁豆】 hyacinth bean 【扁桃】 almond 【扁桃腺】 tonsil

匾 biǎn ① a horizontal inscribed board ② a silk banner embroidered with words of praise ③ a big round shallow basket

变 biàn ①change; become different 情况~了 the situation has changed ②change into; become 从缺粮~为有余粮 be changed from being short of grain to having surplus grain 从冷~热 change from cold to hot ③transform; alter ~废为宝 change waste material into things of value ④an unexpected turn of events 事~ incident 【变本加厉】 become aggravated; be further intensified 【变成】 change into; turn into 把理想~现实 translate an ideal into reality 【变电站】 (transformer) substation 【变动】 change; alteration 【变革】 transform ~现实 change reality 【变更】 alter; modify ~作息时间 alter the daily timetable 【变故】 event; accident; misfortune 【变卦】 go back on one's word; break an agreement 【变化】 change; vary 【变幻】 change irregularly; fluctuate 【变换】 vary; alternate ~手法 vary one's tactics ~位置 shift one's position 【变节】 make a political recantation; turn one's coat 【变脸】 suddenly turn hostile 【变乱】 turmoil; social upheaval 【变卖】 sell off (one's property) 【变迁】 changes; vicissitudes 【变色】 change colour; discolour / change countenance; become angry 【变态】 abnormal ~心理 abnormal psychology 【变通】 be flexible; adapt sth. to circumstances ~办法 accommodation; adaptation 【变戏法】 conjure; juggle

便 biàn ①convenient; handy ②informal; plain ～装 ordinary clothes ③relieve oneself 小～ piss ④piss or shit; urine or excrement 【便当】convenient; handy; easy 【便道】pavement; sidewalk/makeshift road 【便饭】a simple meal 来吃～ come along and take potluck 【便服】everyday clothes; informal dress/civilian clothes 【便壶】chamber pot 【便笺】notepaper; memo (pad) 【便览】brief guide 【便利】convenient; easy/facilitate 【便帽】cap 【便门】side door 【便桥】temporary bridge 【便条】(informal) note 【便鞋】cloth shoes; slippers 【便宴】informal dinner

遍 biàn all over; everywhere 【遍布】be found everywhere; spread all over 【遍及】extend all over

辨 biàn distinguish 【辨别】differentiate; discriminate ～是非 draw a clear distinction between right and wrong ～方向 take one's bearings 【辨认】identify; recognize 【辨析】differentiate and analyse

辩 biàn argue; dispute; debate 【辩白】offer an explanation; try to defend oneself 【辩驳】refute 【辩才】eloquence 【辩护】speak in defence of; argue in favour of/plead (for the accused); defend (a case) ～权 right to defence ～人 defender; counsel ～士 apologist 【辩解】provide an explanation 【辩论】argue; debate 【辩证】dialectical ～法 dialectics

辫 biàn plait; braid; pigtail 蒜～ a braid of garlic 【辫子】plait/handle 揪～ seize on sb.'s mistake

BIAO

标 biāo ①mark; sign 音～ phonetic symbol ②put a mark, tag or label on; label ～界 demarcate a boundary ③prize; award 夺～ win the championship ④outward sign; symptom 治～ seek temporary relief ⑤tender; bid 【标榜】

flaunt; advertise; parade/boost; excessively praise 【标本】specimen; sample 【标兵】parade guards/model; pace-setter 树～ set a good example 【标尺】surveyor's rod; staff/staff gauge/rear sight 【标灯】beacon 【标点】punctuation/punctuate ～符号 punctuation mark 【标记】sign; mark; symbol 【标价】mark a price/marked price 【标明】mark; indicate 【标签】label; tag 贴～ stick on a label 【标枪】javelin 掷～ javelin throw 【标题】title; heading; headline 【标语】poster 贴～ put up slogans ～牌 placard 【标志】sign; mark; symbol/indicate; mark; symbolize 【标致】beautiful; handsome 【标准】standard; criterion 合乎～ up to standard ～音 standard pronunciation ～语 standard speech

彪

biāo young tiger 【彪炳】shining; splendid 【彪形大汉】burly chap

膘

biāo fat (of an animal) 长～ get fat; put on flesh 牲口～肥体壮 the animals are plump and sturdy

表

biāo ①surface; outside; external ②show; express ～决心 declare one's determination ③table; form; list 时间～ timetable ④meter; gauge 温度～ thermometer ⑤watch 手～ wrist watch 【表白】vindicate 【表报】statistical tables and reports 【表册】statistical forms; book of tables or forms 【表层】surface layer 【表尺】rear sight 【表达】express; convey; voice 【表带】watchband; watch strap 【表格】form; table 【表决】decide by vote; vote 付～ put to the vote; take a vote ～权 right to vote; vote 【表露】show; reveal 【表蒙子】watch glass; crystal 【表面】surface; face; outside; appearance ～现象 superficial phenomenon ～化 come to the surface; become apparent 【表明】make clear; state clearly; indicate ～立场 make known one's position; declare one's stand 【表盘】dial 【表亲】cousin/cousinship 【表情】express one's feelings/

(facial) expression 【表示】show; express; indicate ～关切 show concern ～热烈欢迎 extend a warm welcome 【表率】example; model 【表态】make known one's position; declare where one stands 【表现】expression; manifestation/show; display; manifest 他在工作中～好 he is doing well in his work ～积极 be active; show initiative 好～ like to show off ～手法 technique of expression ～形式 manifestation 【表演】perform; act; play/performance; exhibition/demonstrate 杂技～ acrobatic performance 体育～ sports exhibition ～赛 exhibition match ～节目 put on a show 【表扬】praise; commend ～信 commendatory letter 【表语】predicative 【表彰】cite

BIE

憋 biē ①suppress; hold back ～住气 hold one's breath ～足了劲儿 be bursting with energy ②suffocate; feel oppressed 【憋闷】be depressed; be dejected

别 bié ①leave; part ～故乡 leave one's native place ②other; another ～处 another place; elsewhere ③difference; distinction 性～ sex distinction ④differentiate; distinguish ⑤fasten with a pin or clip 把文件～在一起 clip papers together ⑥stick in ⑦don't ～忘了 don't forget 【别出心裁】adopt an original approach 【别管】no matter (who, what, etc.) 【别具一格】having a unique style 【别离】take leave of; leave 【别名】another name 【别人】other people; others; people 【别墅】villa 【别有用心】have ulterior motives 【别针】safety pin/brooch 【别致】unique

蹩 bié sprain (one's ankle or wrist) 【蹩脚】inferior; shoddy ～货 inferior goods; poor stuff

瘪 biě shrivelled; shrunken ～花生 blighted peanuts 车胎～了 the tyre is flat

别 .biè 【别扭】 awkward; uncomfortable; difficult; un-natural/cannot see eye to eye 闹～ be at odds

BIN

宾 bīn guest 【宾词】 predicate 【宾馆】 guesthouse 【宾客】 guests; visitors 【宾语】 object 直接～ direct object

彬 bīn 【彬彬有礼】 refined and courteous; urbane

滨 bīn ①bank; brink; shore 海～ seashore ②be close to (the sea, a river, etc.); border on

缤 bīn 【缤纷】 in riotous profusion 五彩～ a riot of colour 落英～ petals falling in riotous profusion

濒 bīn ① be close to (the sea, a river, etc.); border on② be on the point of 【濒危】 be in imminent dan-ger/be critically ill 【濒于】 be on the brink of ～崩溃 verge on collapse ～绝境 face an impasse ～灭亡 near extinction

摈 bìn discard; get rid of 【摈斥】 reject; dismiss 【摈除】 dispense with 【摈弃】 abandon; cast away

殡 bìn ①lay a coffin in a memorial hall ②carry a cof-fin to the burial place 【殡仪馆】 the undertaker's

BING

冰 bīng ①ice ②put on the ice; ice ③feel cold 【冰雹】 hail; hailstone 【冰场】 skating rink; ice stadium 【冰川】 glacier 【冰蛋】 frozen eggs 【冰刀】 (ice) skates 【冰点】 freezing point 【冰冻】 freeze ～食物 frozen food 【冰棍儿】 ice-lolly; popsicle; ice-sucker 【冰河】 glacier 【冰窖】 icehouse 【冰凉】 ice-cold 【冰期】 glacial epoch 【冰淇淋】 ice cream 【冰橇】 sled; sledge; sleigh 【冰球】 ice hockey/puck 【冰山】 iceberg 【冰上运动】 ice-sports 【冰糖】 rock candy ～葫芦 candied haws on a stick 【冰箱】

icebox 【冰鞋】skates 【冰镇】iced 【冰砖】ice-cream brick

兵

bīng ①weapons; arms ②soldier ③rank-and-file soldier; private ④army; troops ⑤military 【兵变】mutiny 【兵船】man-of-war; naval vessel 【兵法】art of war; military strategy and tactics 【兵工厂】munitions factory; arsenal 【兵舰】warship 【兵力】military strength; armed forces; troops 【兵马】troops and horses; military forces 【兵团】large unit; formation; corps 【兵蚁】soldier ant; dinergate 【兵役】military service 服～ serve in the army; perform military service 【兵营】military camp; barracks

丙 bǐng third ～等 the third grade; grade C

秉 bǐng grasp; hold/control; preside over ～政 hold political power 【秉承】take (orders) 【秉公】justly

柄 bǐng ①handle (of a knife); shaft (of an axe) ②stem (of a flower, leaf or fruit) ③power; authority

饼 bǐng a round flat cake 【饼铛】baking pan 【饼肥】cake (fertilizer) 【饼干】biscuit; cracker

屏 bǐng ①hold (one's breath) ②reject; get rid of; abandon 【屏除】dismiss; brush aside 【屏弃】discard

禀 bǐng ①report (to one's superior); petition ②receive; be endowed with 【禀赋】natural endowment; gift 【禀告】report (to one's superior) 【禀性】natural disposition

并 bìng ①combine; merge; incorporate ②equally; side by side ③and 【并发】be complicated by; erupt simultaneously ～症 complication 【并肩】shoulder to shoulder; abreast ～作战 fight side by side 【并举】develop simultaneously 【并列】stand side by side; be juxtaposed ～分句 coordinate clauses ～句 compound sentence 【并排】side by side; abreast 【并且】and; besides; moreover; furthermore 【并入】 merge into; incorporate in 【并吞】 swallow up; annex; merge 【并行不悖】 not be mutually exclusive; run parallel 【并重】 lay equal stress on

病 bìng ①ill; sick 生～ fall ill ②disease ③fault; defect 语～ ill-chosen expression 【病变】 pathological changes 【病虫害】 plant diseases and insect pests 【病床】 hospital bed/sickbed 【病倒】 be laid up 【病毒】 virus 【病房】 ward; sickroom 【病根】 an incompletely cured illness; an old complaint/the root cause of trouble 【病故】 die of an illness 【病号】 sick personnel ～饭 patient's diet 【病假】 sick leave 请～ ask for sick leave ～条 certificate for sick leave 【病菌】 pathogenic bacteria; germs 【病况】 state of an illness; patient's condition 【病理】 pathology 【病历】 medical record; case history 【病例】 case (of illness) 【病人】 patient; invalid 【病容】 sickly look 【病势】 patient's condition ～心理 morbid psychology 【病痛】 slight illness; ailment 【病危】 be critically ill; be terminally ill 【病象】 symptom (of a disease) 【病因】 cause of disease; pathogeny 【病愈】 recover (from an illness) 【病院】 a specialized hospital

BO

波 bō wave ～长 wavelength 【波荡】 heave; surge 【波动】 undulate; fluctuate / wave motion 【波段】 wave band 【波及】 spread to; involve; affect 【波澜】 great waves; billows ～起伏 (of a piece of writing) with one climax following another ～壮阔 surging forward with great momentum; unfolding on a magnificent scale 【波纹】 ripple/corrugation 【波折】 twists and-turns

拨 bō ①move with hand, foot, stick, etc.; turn; stir; poke ～火 poke a fire ～电话号码 dial a telephone number ②set aside; assign (rooms, workers, etc.); allocate (funds, etc.) 【拨付】appropriate (a sum of money) 【拨号盘】(telephone) dial 【拨火棍】poker 【拨款】allocate funds / appropriation 【拨乱反正】bring order out of chaos; set to right things which have been thrown into disorder; set things right 【拨弄】move to and fro; fiddle with/stir up ~是非 stir things up

玻 bō 【玻璃】glass ~杯 glass; tumbler ~厂 glassworks ~丝 glass silk ~纸 cellophane; glassine

剥 bō 【剥夺】deprive; expropriate; strip ~权力 divest sb. of his power 【剥离】(of tissue, skin, covering, topsoil, etc.) come off; peel off; be stripped 【剥削】exploit ~阶级 exploiting class ~者 exploiter

菠 bō 【菠菜】spinach 【菠萝】pineapple

播 bō ①sow; seed ②broadcast 【播弄】order sb. about/ stir up ~是非 stir up trouble; sow dissension 【播送】transmit; beam ~新闻 broadcast news 【播音】broadcast ~室 broadcasting studio ~员 announcer

伯 bó ①father's elder brother; uncle ②the eldest of brothers 【伯母】wife of father's elder brother; aunt

驳 bó ①refute; contradict; gainsay ②barge ③transport by lighter 【驳斥】denounce ~一种论点 refute an argument 【驳船】barge; lighter 【驳倒】demolish sb.'s argument; outargue ~对方 refute an opponent 【驳回】reject; turn down; overrule 【驳壳枪】Mauser pistol 【驳杂】heterogeneous

泊 bó be at anchor; moor; berth ~岸 anchor alongside the shore ~位 berth

帛 bó silks

勃 bó suddenly 【勃勃】thriving; vigorous; exuberant 【勃发】thrive; prosper/break out 【勃然】agitatedly/vigorously 【勃兴】rise suddenly; grow vigorously

脖 bó neck 【脖颈】back of the neck; nape

博 bó ①rich; abundant; plentiful ②win; gain 【博爱】universal brotherhood; universal love 【博得】win; gain ～同情 win sympathy ～好评 have a favourable reception 【博览】read extensively ～会 (international) fair 【博取】try to gain; court ～欢心 curry favour ～信任 try to win sb.'s confidence 【博士】doctor ～学位 doctor's degree; doctorate 【博物】natural science ～馆 museum 【博学】learned; erudite

搏 bó ①fight; combat 肉～ hand-to-hand fight ②pounce on ③beat; throb 【搏动】pulsate 【搏斗】struggle; wrestle with sb.

箔 bó ①screen (of sorghum stalks, etc.) 苇～ reed screen ②foil; tinsel 金～ gold foil

薄 bó ①slight; meagre; small ～酬 small reward ②despisc; belittle 【薄利】small profits ～多销 small profits but quick turnover 【薄膜】membrane/film 【薄暮】dusk; twilight 【薄片】thin slice; thin section 【薄情】inconstant in love; fickle 【薄弱】weak; frail

跛 bǒ lame 【跛子】lame person; cripple

簸 bò winnow (with a fan) ～谷 winnow away the chaff; fan the chaff 【簸荡】roll; rock

薄 bò 【薄荷】field mint; peppermint ～糖(油) peppermint drops (oil)

簸 bò 【簸箕】dustpan/winnowing fan

BU

卜 bǔ ①divination; fortune-telling ②foretell; predict ③select; choose ～居 choose a place for one's home

补 bǔ ①mend; patch; repair ～衣服 (鞋) mend clothes (shoes) ～袜子 patch or darn socks ②fill; supply; make up for (a loss) ～牙 fill a tooth ③nourish ～血 enrich the blood ④benefit; use; help【补白】filler (in a newspaper or magazine)【补偿】compensate; make up 损失 make compensation for sb.'s losses ～贸易 compensatory trade【补充】replenish; supplement; complement/ complementary ～读物 supplementary reading material ～规定 (说明) additional regulations (remarks)【补丁】patch 打～ sew a patch on; patch up【补发】supply again (sth. lost, etc.); reissue ～工资 pay wages retroactively【补给】supply ～品 supplies ～线 supply line【补救】remedy【补考】make-up examination【补课】make up a missed lesson 教师给学生～ the teacher helped his pupils make up the lessons they had missed【补品】tonic【补习】take lessons after school or work ～学校 continuation school【补遗】addendum【补益】benefit; help【补语】complement【补种】reseed; resow; replant【补助】subsidy

捕 bǔ catch; seize; arrest【捕获】capture 当场～ catch sb. red-handed【捕捞】fish for (aquatic animals and plants); catch【捕食】catch and feed on; prey on

哺 bǔ feed (a baby); nurse【哺乳】breast-feed; suckle; nurse ～室 nursing room【哺育】feed/nurture; foster

不 bù not【不安】intranquil; unpeaceful; unstable/ uneasy; disturbed; restless【不备】unprepared; off guard【不比】unlike【不必】need not; not have to ～来 need not have come; did not need to come【不便】

inconvenient; inappropriate; unsuitable/be short of cash
【不测】accident; mishap; contingency 【不成】won't do
【不出所料】as expected 【不辞而别】leave without saying
good-bye 【不辞辛苦】make nothing of hardships 【不错】
correct; right / not bad; pretty good 【不大】not very;
not too / not often 【不但】not only 【不当】unsuitable;
improper; inappropriate 处理~ not be handled properly
【不倒翁】tumbler; roly-poly 【不道德】immoral 【不得】
must not; may not 【不得不】have no choice but to 【不
得了】desperately serious; disastrous / extremely 【不得
已】act against one's will; have no alternative but to;
have to 【不等】vary; differ (in size, in amount) 【不定】
indefinite ~冠词 indefinite article ~式 infinitive 【不断】
unceasing; uninterrupted; continuous; constant 【不对】
incorrect; wrong / amiss; queer 【不法】lawless; illegal;
unlawful 【不凡】out of the ordinary 【不妨】there is
no harm in; might as well 【不服】refuse to obey; not
give in to ~罪 not admit one's guilt ~老 refuse to
give in to old age 【不符】not agree with; not conform
to 【不干涉】noninterference; nonintervention 【不甘】un-
reconciled to; not resigned to ~落后 unwilling to lag
behind 【不敢当】I really don't deserve this; you flatter me 【不公】unjust; unfair 【不够】not enough; insufficient 【不顾】in spite of; regardless of 【不管】no matter
(what, how, etc.) ~怎样 anyway 【不规则】irregular ~
动词 irregular verb 【不过】only; merely / but; however
【不含糊】unambiguous; unequivocal; explicit / not ordinary; really good 【不寒而栗】tremble with fear 【不好
意思】feel embarrassed; be ill at ease / find it embarrassing (to do sth.) 【不合】not conform to; be unsuited
to; be out of keeping with ~标准 not up to the stan-

dard ～时宜 be out of keeping with the times 【不和】 not get along well; be on bad terms/discord 【不怀好意】 harbour evil designs 【不欢而散】 part on bad terms 【不会】 be unlikely; will not (act, happen, etc.) / have not learned to; be unable to 我～抽烟 I don't smoke 【不及】 not as good as; inferior to / (find it) too late (for, to) 【不计其数】 countless; innumerable 【不简单】 not simple; rather complicated / remarkable; marvellous 【不见】 not see; not meet ～不散 not leave without seeing each other 好久～ haven't seen you for a long time 【不见得】 not necessarily; not likely ～对 not necessarily correct 【不见了】 be missing 【不禁】 can't refrain from; can't help (doing sth.) 【不仅】 not only 【不久】 not long; before long / not long after; soon after 【不拘】 not stick to / whatever 【不倦】 tireless; untiring 【不堪】 cannot bear; cannot stand / utterly; extremely ～设想 dreadful to contemplate ～一击 cannot withstand a single blow 疲惫～ extremely tired 【不可】 cannot; should not; must not 【不客气】 impolite; rude; blunt / not at all; don't mention it / please don't bother 【不快】 be unhappy; be in low spirits/be out of sorts 【不愧】 be worthy of; deserve to be called; prove oneself to be 【不理】 refuse to acknowledge; pay no attention to; take no notice of; ignore 【不力】 not do one's best 【不利】 unfavourable; disadvantageous / unsuccessful 【不良】 bad; harmful; unhealthy 【不料】 unexpectedly; to one's surprise 【不灵】 not work; be ineffective 【不论】 no matter (what, who, how, etc.); whether ... or ...; regardless of 【不满】 resentful; discontented; dissatisfied 【不免】 unavoidable 【不妙】 (of a turn of events) not too encouraging; far from good 【不明】 not clear; unknown / fail to under-

stand ~是非 confuse right and wrong ~真相 be unaware
of the truth 【不能】 cannot; must not; should not 【不能
不】 have to; cannot but 【不平】 injustice; unfairness/
indignant; resentful 【不平衡】 disequilibrium 【不巧】
unfortunately; as luck would have it 【不切实际】 unreal-
istic; unpractical; impracticable 【不屈】 unyielding; unbending; indomitable 【不然】 not so / or else; otherwise; if
not 【不忍】 cannot bear to 【不容】 not tolerate; not allow;
not brook 【不如】 not equal to; not as good as; inferior
to/it would be better to 【不时】 frequently; often/at any
time 【不适】 unwell; out of sorts 【不通】 be obstructed;
be blocked up; be impassable/not make sense; be illogical;
be ungrammatical 【不同】 not alike; different; distinct
【不妥】 not proper; inappropriate 【不问】 pay no attention to; disregard; ignore/let go unpunished; let off 【不
惜】 not stint; not spare/not hesitate (to do sth.); not
scruple (to do sth.) 【不下于】 as many as; no less than/
not inferior to; as good as; on a par with 【不相干】 be
irrelevant; have nothing to do with 【不相容】 incompatible 【不相上下】 equally matched; about the same 【不
象话】 unreasonable/shocking; outrageous 【不屑】 disdain
to do sth.; think sth. not worth doing 【不懈】 untiring;
unremitting 【不行】 won't do; be out of the question/
be no good; not work 【不省人事】 be unconscious; be in
a coma 【不幸】 misfortune; adversity / unfortunately 【不
朽】 immortal 【不锈钢】 stainless steel 【不许】 not allow;
must not 【不言而喻】 it goes without saying 【不厌】 not
mind doing sth.; not tire of 【不要】 don't 【不要紧】 unimportant; not serious/it doesn't matter; never mind 【不
宜】 not suitable; inadvisable 【不遗余力】 spare no pains
【不义之财】 ill-gotten wealth 【不意】 unexpectedly/un-

awareness; unpreparedness 【不在】not be in; be out 【不在乎】not mind; not care 【不折不扣】a hundred per cent; to the letter/out-and-out 【不正之风】unhealthy tendency 【不知不觉】unconsciously; unwittingly 【不知所措】be at a loss 【不值】not worth 【不止】incessantly; without end/more than; not limited to 【不只】not only; not merely 【不至于】cannot go so far; be unlikely 【不中用】unfit for anything; no good; useless 【不准】not allow; forbid; prohibit 【不足】not enough; insufficient; inadequate/not worth/ cannot; should not 【不做声】keep silent; not say a word

布 bù ①cloth 花～ cotton prints ②declare; announce; publish 公～ make public ③spread; disseminate ④dispose; arrange; deploy 【布店】cloth store 【布尔什维克】Bolshevik 【布防】organize a defence 【布告】notice; bulletin ～栏 notice board; bulletin board 【布谷鸟】cuckoo 【布景】composition (of a painting) /setting 【布局】layout; distribution / composition (of a picture, piece of writing, etc.) 工业～ distribution of industry 作物～crop patterns 【布雷】lay mines 【布面】cloth cover 【布匹】cloth; piece goods 【布票】cloth coupon 【布纹纸】wove paper 【布置】fix up; arrange; decorate / assign; make arrangements for ～会场 fix up a place for a meeting ～工作 assign work

步 bù ①step; pace 快～ quick pace 大～ big strides ②stage; step 下一～ next move ③condition; situation; state ④walk; go on foot 散～ take a walk 【步兵】infantry/foot soldier 【步步】step by step; at every step 【步伐】step; pace 【步法】footwork 【步枪】rifle 【步哨】sentry; sentinel 【步行】go on foot; walk 【步骤】step; move; measure

怖 bù fear; be afraid of 可～ horrible; frightful

部 bù ①part; section 分为三～ divide into three parts ②unit; ministry; department; board 解放军某～ a certain PLA unit ③headquarters 前沿指挥～ advance command post 【部队】army; armed forces/troops; force; unit 【部分】part; share 【部件】parts; components; assembly 【部类】category; division 【部落】tribe 【部门】department; branch 【部署】dispose; deploy ～兵力 dispose troops for battle 【部位】position; place 【部下】troops under one's command/subordinate 【部长】minister; head of a department

埠 bù ①wharf; pier ②port 本～ this port 外～ other ports 商～ a commercial port

簿 bù book 【簿籍】account books, registers, records, etc. 【簿记】bookkeeping 【簿子】notebook

C
CA

拆 cā 【拆烂污】do slovenly work; leave things in a mess; be irresponsible

擦 cā ①rub; graze; scratch ～火柴 strike a match ②wipe; scrub ～桌子 wipe the table ～地板 mop the floor ～汗 wipe the sweat away ～枪 clean a gun. ～皮鞋 polish shoes ③spread on; put on ～碘酒 apply iodine (to a wound) ～粉 powder (one's face) ④brush; shave ～肩而过 brush past sb. ⑤scrape (into shreds) 【擦边球】touch ball 【擦拭】clean; cleanse 【擦网球】net ball 【擦音】fricative 【擦澡】take a sponge bath

CAI

猜 cāi ①guess; conjecture; speculate ②suspect 我～他病了 I suspect that he is ill 【猜测】surmise 【猜忌】be suspicious and jealous of 【猜谜】guess a riddle 【猜想】suppose; suspect 【猜疑】harbour suspicions; have misgivings

才 cái ①ability; talent; gift ②capable person ③people of a certain type ④just; only 【才干】ability; competence 【才华】literary or artistic talent 【才识】ability and insight 【才学】talent and learning; scholarship 【才智】ability and wisdom 【才子】gifted scholar

材 cái ①timber ②material ③ability; talent; aptitude ④capable person 【材料】material/data/makings; stuff 搜集～ gather material; collect data ～力学 mechanics of materials

财 cái wealth; money 【财宝】money and valuables 【财产】property 公共～ public (state) property ～权 property right ～税 property tax 【财阀】financial magnate; plutocrat; tycoon 【财富】wealth; riches 【财力】financial resources 【财贸】finance and trade 【财迷】miser 【财务】financial affairs ～科 finance section 【财物】property; belongings 个人～ personal effects 【财源】financial resources; source of revenue 【财政】(public) finance ～部 the Ministry of Finance ～收入 revenue ～支出 expenditure 【财主】rich man; moneybags

裁 cái ①cut (paper, cloth, etc.) into parts ～衣服 cut out garments ②reduce; dismiss ～员 reduce the staff ③judge; decide ④check; sanction 经济制～ economic sanction 【裁撤】dissolve (an organization) 【裁缝】tailor; dressmaker 【裁减】reduce; cut down ～军备 reduction of armaments 【裁决】ruling; adjudication 【裁判】judgment/umpire; judge; referee

采 cǎi ①pick; pluck; gather ～茶 pick tea ～药 gather medicinal herbs ②mine; extract ～油 extract oil ③ adopt; select ④complexion; spirit 【采伐】fell; cut 【采访】 (of a reporter) gather material; cover ～新闻 gather news 【采购】purchase ～员 purchasing agent 【采集】gather; collect 【采掘】excavate 【采矿】mining 【采煤】coal cutting 【采纳】accept; adopt 【采取】adopt; take ～措施 take measures ～主动 take the initiative 【采用】use; employ

彩 cǎi ①colour ～云 rosy clouds ②coloured silk ③ applause; cheer ～声 acclamation ④variety; splendour ⑤prize ～win a prize (in a lottery) 【彩绸】coloured silk 【彩带】coloured ribbon 【彩绘】coloured drawing or pattern 【彩礼】betrothal gifts; bride-price 【彩排】dress rehearsal 【彩棚】decorated tent/marquee 【彩票】lottery ticket 【彩旗】coloured flag; bunting 【彩色】multicolour; colour ～电视 colour television ～胶片 colour film

睬 cǎi pay attention to; take notice of 不要～他 take no notice of him; ignore him

踩 cǎi step on; trample ～庄稼 tread on the crops 【踩水】tread water 【踩线】step on the line; footfault

采 cài 【采邑】fief; benefice

菜 cài ①vegetable; greens 种～ grow vegetables ②(non-staple) food 买～ go to the market to buy food ③dish; course 做～ prepare the dishes; do the cooking 【菜场】food market 【菜单】menu; bill of fare 【菜刀】 kitchen knife 【菜地】vegetable plot 【菜豆】kidney bean 【菜花】cauliflower/rape flower 【菜窖】clamp 【菜农】 vegetable grower 【菜色】famished look 【菜苔】bolt (of rape, mustard, etc.) 【菜摊】vegetable stall 【菜心】heart (of a cabbage, etc.) 【菜肴】 cooked food (usu. meat dishes) 【菜油】 rape oil 【菜园】 vegetable farm 【菜籽】 rapeseed

CAN

参 cān ①join; enter; take part in ～战 enter a war ②refer; consult ③call to pay one's respects to 【参观】 visit; look around ～游览 visit places of interest; go sightseeing 欢迎～ visitors are welcome 【参加】 join; attend; take part in/give (advice, suggestion, etc.) ～党 join the Party ～会议 attend a meeting ～建设 take part in construction ～劳动 participate in (productive) labour 【参军】 join the army 【参看】 see (also) /consult/read sth. for reference 【参考】 consult; refer to/reference 仅供～ for reference only ～书 reference book ～书目 bibliography ～资料 reference material 【参谋】 staff officer/give advice ～长 chief of staff 【参与】 participate in; have a hand in

餐 cān ①eat 进～ dine ②food; meal 【餐车】 restaurant; dining car; diner 【餐巾】 table napkin 【餐具】 tableware; dinner set 【餐厅】 dining room / restaurant

残 cán ①deficient ～稿 an incomplete manuscript ② remaining ～敌 remnants of the enemy forces ③ injure; damage ④savage; ferocious 【残存】 surviving 【残废】 maimed; disabled / a maimed person; cripple 【残骸】 wreckage 【残害】 cruelly injure or kill 【残货】 shopworn goods 【残迹】 vestiges 【残酷】 cruel; ruthless; brutal 【残品】 damaged article 【残破】 broken; dilapidated 【残缺】 incomplete; fragmentary 【残杀】 murder; massacre; slaughter 【残余】 remnants; remains; survivals

蚕 cán silkworm 养～ raise silkworms 【蚕豆】 broad bean 【蚕蛾】 silk moth 【蚕茧】 silkworm cocoon 【蚕食】 nibble 【蚕丝】 natural silk 【蚕子】 silkworm seed

惭 cán feel ashamed 【惭愧】 be ashamed

惨 cǎn ①miserable; pitiful; tragic ～遭不幸 die a tragic death ②cruel; savage ～无人道 inhuman ③to a serious degree; disastrously 【惨案】 massacre / murder case 【惨白】 pale 【惨败】 crushing defeat 【惨淡】 gloomy; dismal; bleak 【惨祸】 horrible disaster; frightful calamity 【惨境】 miserable condition 【惨剧】 tragedy; calamity 【惨然】 saddened; grieved 【惨痛】 painful; bitter 【惨重】 heavy; disastrous 损失～ suffer grievous losses 伤亡～ suffer heavy casualties 【惨状】 pitiful sight

灿 càn 【灿烂】 magnificent; splendid; resplendent; bright ～的阳光 brilliant sunshine

粲 càn 【粲然】 ①bright; beaming ②smiling broadly ～一笑 give a beaming smile; grin with delight

CANG

仓 cāng storehouse; warehouse 谷～ barn 【仓促】 hurriedly; hastily ～应战 accept battle in haste 【仓皇】 in a flurry; in panic ～逃窜 flee in confusion ～退却 retreat in haste 【仓库】 storehouse; depository 清理～ take stock; check warehouse stocks ～保管员 warehouseman

伧 cāng rude; rough 【伧俗】 vulgar

沧 cāng dark blue 【沧海】 the blue sea

苍 cāng ①dark green ～松 green pines ②blue ～天 the blue sky ③grey; ashy ～髯 a grey beard 【苍白】 pale; pallid; wan 【苍苍】 grey/vast and hazy 【苍翠】 dark green; verdant 【苍老】 old; aged 【苍茫】 vast; boundless/indistinct 【苍天】 the blue sky/Heaven 【苍蝇】 fly ～拍子 flyswatter

舱 cāng ①cabin ②module 【舱口】hatchway; hatch 【舱位】cabin seat or berth / shipping space

藏 cáng ①hide; conceal ②store; lay by 【藏身】hide oneself 【藏书】collect books/a collection of books

CAO

糙 cāo rough; coarse ～纸 rough paper ～米 unpolished rice; brown rice 活儿做得～ this is slipshod work

操 cāo ①grasp; hold ～刀 hold a sword (in one's hand) ②act; do; operate ～之过急 act with undue haste ③ speak (a language or dialect) ④drill; exercise ⑤conduct; behaviour 【操场】playground; sports ground 【操持】manage; handle 【操劳】work hard/take care 【操练】drill; practice 【操切】rash; hasty 【操守】personal integrity 【操心】worry about; take pains / rack one's brains 【操行】behaviour or conduct of a student 【操纵】operate; control/rig; manipulate ～机器 operate a machine ～市场 rig the market ～杆 operating lever ～台 control board 【操作】operate; manipulate ～程序 operation sequence ～方法 method of operation ～规程 operating rules

嘈 cáo noise; din 【嘈杂】noisy 人声～ a hubbub of voices

槽 cáo ①trough 马～ manger 水～ water trough ②groove; slot 【槽坊】brewery; distillery 【槽牙】molar

草 cǎo ①grass; straw ～绳 straw rope ②careless; hasty; rough ～draft (a document, etc.) 【草案】draft (of a plan, law, etc.) 【草本】herbaceous 【草草】carelessly; hastily ～收场 hastily wind up the matter ～了事 get through with sth. any old way 【草叉】pitch-fork 【草创】start (an enterprise, etc.) 【草丛】a thick growth of grass 【草地】grassland; meadow/lawn 【草垛】haystack

【草房】thatched cottage 【草稿】rough draft 【草料】forage; fodder 【草绿】grass green 【草帽】straw hat 【草莓】strawberry 【草拟】draw up; draft 【草棚】straw shed 【草皮】sod; turf 【草坪】lawn 【草率】careless; rash 【草图】sketch (map); draft 【草席】straw mat 【草鞋】straw sandals 【草药】medicinal herbs 【草鱼】grass carp 【草原】grasslands; prairie 【草约】draft treaty 【草泽】grassy marsh; swamp 【草纸】rough straw paper / toilet paper 【草子】grass seed

CE

册 cè ①volume; book 画～ an album of paintings ② copy 【册子】book; volume 小～ pamphlet; booklet

厕 cè lavatory; toilet; washroom; W.C. 公～ public lavatory 男～ men's (room, toilet) 女～ women's (room, toilet)

侧 cè ①side 左～ left side ②incline; lean ～睡 sleep on one's side 击～ flank attack 【侧记】sidelights 【侧门】side door 【侧面】side; aspect; flank ～像 profile 【侧目】sidelong glance ～而视 look askance at sb. 【侧身】on one's side; sideways 【侧翼】flank 【侧影】silhouette; profile 【侧泳】sidestroke 【侧重】lay particular emphasis on

测 cè ①survey; fathom; measure ～雨量 gauge rainfall ②conjecture; infer 【测定】determine 【测度】estimate; infer 【测绘】survey and drawing; mapping ～板 plotting board ～员 surveyor 【测验】test 算术～ arithmetic test

策 cè ①plan; scheme; strategy ②whip 【策动】instigate; engineer; stir up 【策反】incite defection 【策划】plot; scheme ～阴谋 hatch a plot 【策略】tactics / tactful 【策应】support by coordinated action 【策源地】source; place of origin 战争～ a source of war

CEN

参 cēn 【参差】 irregular; uneven ～不齐 not uniform

CENG

层 céng ①layer; tier; stratum 一～冰 a sheet of ice ② storey; floor 【层层】 layer upon layer; tier upon tier ～包围 surround ring upon ring ～设防 set up successive lines of defence ～把关 check at each level 【层出不穷】 emerge in an endless stream 【层次】 administrative levels / arrangement of ideas (in writing or speech)

蹭 cèng ①rub ～破了手 have the skin rubbed off one's hand ②be smeared with ③dillydally; loiter

CHA

叉 chā ①fork 草～ hayfork ②work with a fork ～鱼 spear fish ③cross 打个～ put a cross above sth. 【叉腰】 akimbo

差 chā ①difference; dissimilarity 时～ time difference ②mistake 偏～ deviation 【差别】 disparity 【差错】 mistake; error; slip / mishap; accident 【差额】 balance; margin 【差价】 price difference 【差距】 gap; disparity 【差异】 discrepancy; divergence

插 chā ①stick in; insert ～上插头 plug in ～上门 bolt the door ③interpose 【插班】 join a class in the middle of the course 【插队】 go to live and work in a production team ～落户 go and settle in the countryside 【插话】 interpose (a remark, etc.); chip in / digression; episode 【插曲】 interlude/songs in a film or play/episode 【插入】 insert ～几句话 insert a few words ～语 parenthesis 【插身】squeeze in / take part in; get involved in 【插手】take part; lend a hand / have a hand in; meddle in 【插图】illustration; plate 【插销】bolt (for a door) / plug 【插秧】transplant rice seedlings　～机 rice transplanter 【插页】inset; insert 【插足】put one's foot in / participate 【插嘴】interrupt; chip in 【插座】socket; outlet

茌 chá ①stubble 麦～ wheat stubble ②crop; batch 换～ change crops 【茌口】crops for rotation

茶 chá　tea ～ make tea / 浓(淡)～ strong (weak) tea 【茶杯】teacup 【茶场】tea plantation 【茶匙】teaspoon 【茶炊】tea-urn 【茶点】tea and pastries; refreshments 【茶碟】saucer 【茶缸】mug 【茶馆】teahouse 【茶壶】teapot 【茶花】camellia 【茶会】tea party 【茶几】tea table 【茶具】tea set; tea-things; tea service 【茶末】tea dust 【茶盘】tea tray; teaboard 【茶钱】payment for tea (in a teahouse) / tip 【茶水】tea or boiled water (supplied to walkers) ～站 tea-stall 【茶托】saucer 【茶叶】tea; tea-leaves ～罐 tea caddy 【茶油】tea oil 【茶园】tea plantation / tea garden 【茶砖】brick tea 【茶座】teahouse / seats in a teahouse

查 chá ①check; examine ～卫生 make a public health and sanitation check ～血 have a blood test ②look into; investigate ～原因 find out the cause of sth. ③look up; consult ～词典 consult a dictionary ～资料 read up the literature ～档案 look into the archives 【查办】investigate and deal with accordingly 【查点】make an inventory of ～人数 check the number of people present ～存货 take stock 【查对】check; verify 【查房】make the rounds of the wards 【查封】seal up; close down 【查户口】check residence cards 【查获】hunt down and seize ～逃犯 track down a fugitive criminal 【查禁】ban; prohibit 【查究】investigate and ascertain (cause, re-

sponsibility, etc.) 【查看】 look over; examine 【查考】
examine; do research on; try to ascertain 【查明】 prove
through investigation; ascertain ~真相 find out the truth
现已~ it has been established that 【查票】 examine tickets
【查讫】 checked 【查清】 make a thorough investigation of
~来历 check up on sb. 【查哨】 inspect the sentries 【查
问】 question; interrogate 【查无实据】 investigation reveals
no evidence 【查询】 inquire about 【查夜】 go the rounds
at night/night patrol 【查阅】 consult; look up 【查帐】 audit
accounts 【查证】 verify ~属实 be checked and found to
be true; be verified

搽 chá put (powder, vanishing cream, etc.) on the skin;
apply ～药 apply ointment, lotion, etc. ～粉 powder

察 chá examine; look into; scrutinize 【察觉】 be conscious of; become aware of; perceive 【察看】 watch;
observe ～地形 survey the terrain

碴 chá 【碴儿】 broken pieces; fragments (of glass, etc.) /
sharp edge of broken glass, china, etc./the cause of
a quarrel/sth. just said or mentioned 找~ pick a quarrel
答~ make a reply

叉 chā part so as to form a fork; fork ～着腿站着
stand with one's legs apart

杈 chà branch (of a tree)

岔 chà ①branch off; fork ②turn off 【岔开】 branch off;
diverge / diverge to (another topic); change (the
subject of conversation) / stagger 【岔路】 branch road;
byroad 【岔子】 accident; trouble 你放心吧，出不了~
don't worry, everything will be all right

诧 chà be surprised 【诧异】 be astonished

刹 chà Buddhist temple 【刹那】instant; split second

差 chà ①differ from; fall short of ②wrong ③wanting; short of ④not up to standard; poor 【差不多】almost; nearly/about the same; similar/just about right; not far off; not bad 【差点儿】not good enough/almost; nearly ～没赶上车 very nearly miss the bus ～(没)哭出来 be on the verge of tears 【差劲】no good; disappointing

CHAI

拆 chāi ①tear open; take apart ～信 open a letter ② pull down; dismantle ～桥 dismantle a bridge ～毛衣 unravel a sweater 【拆除】demolish; remove 【拆穿】expose; unmask 【拆毁】pull down 【拆伙】part company 【拆开】take apart; open; separate 把机器～ disassemble a machine 【拆散】break (a set) / break up (a marriage, family, etc.) 【拆台】pull away a prop 别拆我的台 don't let me down 【拆洗】wash (padded coats, quilts, etc.); unpick and wash / strip and clean 【拆卸】dismantle; dismount; disassemble

差 chāi ①send on an errand; dispatch ②errand; job 【差遣】dispatch; assign 【差使】send; assign; appoint

柴 chái firewood 【柴火】faggot 【柴油】diesel oil ～机 diesel engine ～机车 diesel locomotive

豺 chái jackal

CHAN

搀 chān ①help by the arm ②mix 【搀扶】support sb. with one's hand 【搀和】mix 【搀假】adulterate 【搀杂】mingle

谗 chán slander; backbite 【谗害】calumniate sb. in order to have him persecuted; frame sb. up 【谗言】slanderous talk; calumny

馋 chán greedy; gluttonous; fond of good food 【馋涎欲滴】mouth drooling with greed 【馋嘴】gluttonous

缠 chán ①twine; wind ②tangle; tie up; pester 【缠绵】lingering / touching; moving / sentimental

蝉 chán cicada 【蝉联】continue to hold a post or title 【蝉翼】cicada's wings

潺 chán 【潺潺】murmur; babble; purl

产 chǎn ①give birth ②produce; yield ～油 produce oil ③product; produce 土～ local product ④property; estate 家～ family possessions 【产地】place of production; producing area 【产儿】newborn baby 【产房】delivery room 【产妇】lying-in woman 【产假】maternity leave 【产科】obstetrical department/obstetrics ～医生 obstetrician ～医院 maternity hospital 【产量】output; yield 【产品】product; produce 【产权】property right 【产生】produce; engender/emerge; come into being 【产物】outcome; result; product 【产业】estate; property/industrial ～工人 industrial worker 【产值】output value

谄 chǎn flatter; fawn on 【谄媚】toady 【谄笑】ingratiating smile

铲 chǎn ①shovel 锅～ slice ②lift or move with a shovel ～煤 shovel coal 【铲除】root out; uproot; eradicate

阐 chǎn explain 【阐发】elucidate 【阐明】expound ～观点 clarify one's views 【阐释】interpret 【阐述】elaborate 各方～了自己的立场 each side set forth its position 进行系统的～ make a systematic exposition

忏 chàn repent 【忏悔】be penitent/confess (one's sins)

颤 chàn quiver; tremble; vibrate 说话声音发～ one's voice quivered 【颤动】quiver 声带～ vibration of the vocal chords 【颤抖】shake; shiver 【颤巍巍】tottering; faltering 【颤音】trill / shake 【颤悠】flicker

CHANG

昌 chāng prosperous; flourishing 【昌明】thriving; well-developed 科学～ science is flourishing

猖 chāng 【猖獗】be rampant; run wild 这个地区过去风沙～ the area used to be struck by raging sandstorms 【猖狂】savage; furious ～的挑衅 reckless provocation

娼 chāng prostitute 【娼妇】bitch; whore 【娼妓】street-walker

长 cháng ①long ～河 long river ②length 全～六米 the overall length is 6 metres ③lasting 与世～辞 pass away ④steadily; regularly ⑤strong point; forte ～于绘画 be good at painting 【长波】long wave 【长处】good qualities; good points 【长笛】flute 【长度】length 【长方形】rectangle 【长工】long-term hired hand 【长颈鹿】giraffe 【长久】for a long time; permanently 【长空】vast sky 【长裤】trousers; slacks; pants 【长眠】eternal sleep; death 【长年】all the year round 【长袍】long gown; robe 【长跑】long-distance race 【长篇小说】novel 【长期】long-term ～战争 a long-drawn-out war; a protracted war ～观点 a long-term view 作～打算 make long-term plans ～性 protracted nature 【长枪】spear/long-barrelled gun 【长驱】make a long drive; push deep ～直入 drive straight in 【长寿】long life; longevity 【长叹】deep sigh 【长统袜】stockings 【长途】long-distance ～电话 long-distance call

～汽车 long-distance bus; coach 【长线产品】goods in excess supply 【长远】long-term; long-range ～利益 long-term interests ～规划 long-range plan 【长征】long march

场 cháng ①a level open space 打～ threshing ②一～大雨 a downpour 大干一～ go all out 【场院】threshing ground

肠 cháng intestines 【肠胃】intestines and stomach; stomach; belly ～不好 suffer from indigestion 【肠炎】enteritis 【肠衣】casing (for sausages)

尝 cháng ①taste; try the flavour of ②ever; once 【尝试】attempt; try 【尝新】have a taste of what is just in season

常 cháng ①ordinary; common; normal 习以为～ be used to sth. ②constant; invariable ～绿树 evergreen (tree) ③frequently; often; usually ～来往 keep in constant touch; pay frequent calls 【常备不懈】always be on the alert 【常备军】standing army 【常常】frequently; often; usually; generally 【常规】convention; rule; common practice; routine 打破～ break with convention ～疗法 routine treatment ～武器 conventional weapons ～战争 conventional war 【常会】regular meeting 【常见】common ～病 common disease 【常例】common practice 【常情】reason; sense 【常人】ordinary person 【常任】standing ～代表 permanent delegate 【常设】permanent ～机构 standing body 【常识】general knowledge / common sense 【常数】constant 【常态】normality 【常委】member of the standing committee 【常务】day-to-day business; routine 【常用】in common use ～词语 everyday expressions 【常驻】resident

偿 cháng ①repay; compensate for ～债 pay a debt ②meet; fulfil 【偿付】pay back 【偿还】repay 【偿命】pay with one's life; a life for a life 【偿清】 clear off (one's debts)

厂 chǎng ①factory; mill; plant; works ②yard; depot 【厂房】 factory building/workshop 【厂矿】 factories and mines 【厂商】 firm 【厂长】 factory director 【厂址】 the site of a factory 【厂主】 factory owner; millowner

场 chǎng ①a place where people gather 战～ battlefield ②farm ③stage ④scene 【场地】 space; place; site 比赛～ ground; court 施工～ construction site 【场合】 occasion; situation 【场面】 scene (in drama, fiction, etc.); spectacle/occasion/appearance; front facade 【场所】 arena

敞 chǎng ①spacious ②open; uncovered ～着门 leave the door open 【敞车】 open wagon / flatcar 【敞开】 open wide 【敞亮】 light and spacious / clear (in one's thinking)

怅 chàng disappointed; sorry 【怅然】 upset ～而返 come away disappointed 【怅惘】 distracted; listless

畅 chàng ①smooth; unimpeded ②free; uninhibited ～饮 drink one's fill 【畅快】 free from inhibitions; carefree 心情～ have ease of mind 【畅所欲言】 speak out freely 【畅谈】 speak glowingly of 【畅通】 unimpeded; unblocked 【畅销】 sell well; have a ready market ～国外 sell well on foreign markets ～书 best seller 【畅叙】 chat cheerfully 【畅游】 have a good swim/enjoy a sightseeing tour

倡 chàng initiate; advocate 【倡议】 propose 提出～ put forward a proposal ～召开会议 propose the calling of a conference 在他的～下 at his suggestion ～书 (written) proposal ～者 initiator

唱 chàng ①sing ②call; cry 【唱词】 libretto; words of a ballad 【唱段】 aria 【唱对台戏】 put on a rival show 【唱反调】 sing a different tune 【唱高调】 use high-flown words 【唱歌】 sing (a song) 【唱机】 gramophone; phonograph 【唱片】 gramophone record; disc 【唱头】 pickup 【唱戏】 act in an opera 【唱针】 gramophone needle; stylus

CHAO

抄 chāo ①copy; transcribe ～稿子 make a fair copy of the manuscript ②go off with 把字典～走 go off with a dictionary ③grab; take up ～起一把铁锹就干 take up a spade and plunge into the job ④search; ferret ～身 search sb. 【抄本】 hand-copied book; transcript 【抄后路】 turn the (enemy's) rear 【抄家】 search sb.'s house and confiscate his property 【抄件】 duplicate; copy 【抄袭】 plagiarize; lift 【抄写】 copy ～员 copyist

吵 chāo 【吵吵】 make a row; kick up a racket

钞 chāo ①bank note 现～ cash ②collected writings 诗 ～ collected poems 【钞票】 bank note; paper money

绰 chāo grab; take up ～起棍子 grab a stick

超 chāo ①exceed; surpass; overtake ②ultra-; super-; extra- ～高温 superhigh temperature ③transcend; go beyond 【超产】 overfulfil a production target ～粮 grain output in excess of a production target 【超等】 of superior grade; extra fine 【超短波】 ultrashort wave 【超短裙】 miniskirt 【超额】 above quota ～利润 superprofit 【超过】 outstrip; surpass; exceed ～限度 go beyond the limit ～历史最高水平 top all previous records 【超级】 super ～大国 superpower 【超假】 overstay one's leave 【超龄】 overage ～团员 overage Youth League member 【超然】 aloof; detached 【超人】 be out of the common run/superman 【超声波】 ultrasonic (wave) 【超脱】 unconventional/

be detached; stand aloof 【超音速】 supersonic speed ～
喷气机 superjet 【超越】 overstep; surpass ～障碍 surmount an obstacle 【超支】 overspend 【超重】 overload/
overweight

剿 chāo plagiarize

巢 cháo nest 【巢穴】 lair; den; nest; hideout

朝 cháo ①court; government ②dynasty ③facing; towards ～西 facing west ～南走 go southward 【朝拜】
pay respects to (a sovereign); pay religious homage to;
worship 【朝臣】 courtier 【朝贡】 pay tribute (to an imperial court) 【朝见】 have an audience with (a king,
etc.) 【朝廷】 royal court / royal government

潮 cháo ①tide 涨～ flood tide ②(social) upsurge; current; tide 思～ trend of thought ③damp; moist 返
～ get damp 【潮呼呼】 dank; clammy 【潮流】 tidal
current / trend 【潮气】 moisture in the air; humidity 【潮
湿】 moist; damp 【潮水】 tidewater; tidal water 【潮汐】
morning and evening tides; tide

嘲 cháo ridicule; deride 【嘲讽】 sneer at; taunt 【嘲弄】
mock; poke fun at 【嘲笑】 laugh at; jeer at

吵 chǎo ①make a noise ～嚷 be quiet ②quarrel; squabble ～翻天 kick up a terrific row 【吵架】 quarrel;
have a row 【吵闹】 wrangle / din; hubbub 【吵嚷】 make
a racket; shout in confusion; clamour 【吵嘴】 bicker

炒 chǎo stir-fry; fry ～鸡蛋 scrambled eggs 【炒菜】
stir-fry / a fried dish / a dish cooked to order 【炒冷
饭】 heat leftover rice—say or do the same old thing;
rehash 【炒米】 parched rice ～花 puffed rice 【炒面】 fried
noodles / parched flour 【炒勺】 round-bottomed frying pan

CHE

车 chē ①vehicle 军用~ army vehicle ②wheeled machine or instrument 滑~ pulley ③machine 开~ start the machine ④lathe; turn ~光 smooth sth. on a lathe ⑤lift water (by waterwheel) 【车把】handlebar (of a bicycle, etc.); shaft (of a wheelbarrow, etc.) 【车床】lathe 【车次】train number 【车刀】lathe tool 【车队】motorcade 【车费】fare 【车工】lathe work / turner; lathe operator 【车祸】traffic accident 【车技】trick-cycling 【车架】frame (of a car) 【车间】workshop; shop 【车库】garage 【车辆】vehicle; car 【车轮】wheel 【车马费】travel allowance 【车皮】railway wagon or carriage 【车票】ticket 【车胎】tyre 【车厢】railroad car 【车闸】brake 【车站】station; depot; stop 【车照】licence 【车辙】rut 【车轴】axle

扯 chě ①pull ②tear ~下假面具 tear off the mask ③buy (cloth) ④chat; gossip 【扯淡】(talk) nonsense 【扯后腿】hold sb. back (from action); be a drag on sb. 【扯谎】tell a lie 【扯皮】dispute over trifles; wrangle

彻 chè thorough; penetrating 【彻底】thorough; thoroughgoing ~性 (degree of) thoroughness 【彻骨】to the bone 【彻头彻尾】out and out; through and through; downright 【彻夜】all through the night ~不眠 lie awake all night

澈 chè (of water) clear; limpid

撤 chè ①remove; take away ②withdraw; evacuate 【撤兵】withdraw troops 【撤除】remove; dismantle 【撤换】dismiss; recall; replace 【撤回】recall; withdraw / revoke; retract 【撤离】leave; evacuate 【撤退】withdraw; pull out 【撤销】cancel; rescind; revoke ~处分 annul a penalty ～命令 countermand an order ～法令 repeal a decree 【撤职】 dismiss sb. from his post

CHEN

抻　chēn pull out; stretch 【抻面】 make noodles by drawing out the dough by hand/hand-pulled noodles

嗔　chēn ①be angry; be displeased ②be annoyed 【嗔怪】 blame; rebuke 【嗔怒】 get angry

尘　chén ①dust; dirt ②this world 【尘垢】 dirt 【尘世】 this world; this mortal life 【尘土】 dust

臣　chén official (under a feudal ruler); subject

沉　chén ①sink ～船 a sunken boat ②keep down; lower ～下心来 settle down (to one's work, etc.) 把脸一～ pull a long face ③deep; profound 睡得～ be in a deep sleep ④heavy 【沉淀】 sediment; precipitate 【沉积】 deposit 【沉寂】 quiet; still 【沉浸】 immerse; steep 【沉静】 quiet; calm / serene; placid 【沉沦】 sink into (vice, degradation, depravity, etc.) 【沉闷】 oppressive; depressing / depressed; in low spirits / withdrawn 【沉迷】 indulge; wallow 【沉湎】 wallow in; be given to 【沉没】 sink 【沉默】 reticent; taciturn / silent 【沉睡】 be sunk in sleep; be fast asleep 【沉思】 ponder; meditate; be lost in thought 【沉痛】 deep feeling of grief or remorse / deeply felt; bitter 【沉吟】 mutter to oneself 【沉冤】 gross injustice; unrighted wrong 【沉渣】 sediment; dregs 【沉重】 heavy / serious; critical 【沉住气】 keep calm; be steady 【沉着】 cool-headed; composed; steady ～应战 meet the attack calmly 【沉醉】 get drunk; become intoxicated

陈　chén ①lay out; put on display ②state; explain ③ old; stale 【陈兵】 mass troops ～百万 deploy a million troops 【陈词滥调】 hackneyed and stereotyped expressions 【陈腐】 old and decayed; stale; outworn 【陈规】 outmoded conventions 【陈货】 old stock; shopworn goods 【陈酒】 mellow wine 【陈旧】 outmoded; old-fashioned; out-of-date 【陈列】 display; set out; exhibit ～馆 exhibition hall ～品 exhibit ～室 showroom 【陈设】 display; set out/furnishings 【陈述】 state; recite; explain ～句 declarative sentence

晨 chén morning 【晨光】 dawn 【晨曦】 first rays of the morning sun 【晨星】 stars at dawn

衬 chèn ①line; place sth. underneath ②lining; liner ③set off 【衬布】 lining cloth 【衬裤】 underpants; pants 【衬裙】 underskirt; petticoat 【衬衫】 shirt 【衬托】 set off; serve as a foil to 【衬衣】 underclothes; shirt

称 chèn fit; match; suit 相～ well matched 【称身】 fit 【称心】 find sth. satisfactory; be gratified 【称职】 fill a post with credit; be competent

趁 chèn ①avail oneself of ～势 take advantage of a favourable situation ②while ～热喝吧 drink it while it's still hot ～亮儿走吧 let's start while it is still light ③be possessed of; be rich in ～钱 have pots of money 【趁便】 when it is convenient; at one's convenience 【趁机】 take advantage of the occasion; seize the chance 【趁空】 use one's spare time 【趁热打铁】 strike while the iron is hot 【趁早】 as early as possible; before it is too late

CHENG

称 chēng ①call 自～ style oneself ②name 俗～ popular name ③weigh 【称霸】 seek hegemony; dominate 【称病】 plead illness 【称得起】 deserve to be called 【称号】 title; name; designation 【称呼】 call; address / form of address

【称颂】praise; extol; eulogize 【称谓】appellation; title 【称羡】envy 【称谢】thank 【称雄】hold sway over a region; rule the roost 【称赞】praise; acclaim; commend

撑 chēng ①prop up; support ～住屋顶 sustain the roof ②push or move with a pole ～船 pole a boat; punt ③maintain ～场面 keep up appearances ④open; unfurl ～伞 open an umbrella ⑤fill to the point of bursting 【撑持】prop up; sustain ～局面 shore up a shaky situation 【撑竿跳高】pole vault 【撑腰】support; back up ～打气 bolster and pep up

成 chéng ①accomplish; succeed ②become; turn into ③achievement; result ④fully developed; fully grown ～人 adult ⑤established; ready-made 既～事实 established fact ⑥in considerable numbers or amounts ～千上万的人 tens of thousands of people ⑦all right; O.K. 【成本】cost ～核算 cost accounting ～价格 cost price ～会计 cost accounting 【成材】grow into useful timber/become a useful person 【成堆】form a pile; be in heaps/be piled up; be heaped up 【成分】composition; component part; ingredient/one's class status 【成功】succeed; success 【成规】established practice; set rules; groove 【成果】achievement; fruit; gain; positive result 【成婚】get married 【成活】survive ～率 survival rate 【成绩】result; achievement; success ～单 school report; report card 【成家】get married 【成见】preconceived idea; prejudice 【成交】strike a bargain; clinch a deal 【成就】achievement; attainment; success/achieve; accomplish 【成立】found; establish; set up/be tenable; hold water 举行～大会 hold an inaugural meeting 不能～的论点 untenable argument 【成名】become famous ～成家 establish one's reputation as an authority 【成年】grow up; come of age/adult; grown-up 【成批】

group by group; in batches ～生产 serial production 【成品】finished product 【成亲】get married 【成全】help (sb. to achieve his aim) 【成群】in groups; in large numbers ～结队 in crowds; in throngs 【成人】grow up; become full-grown/adult; grown-up 【成熟】ripe; mature 时机～ the time is ripe 【成套】form a complete set/whole set ～设备 complete sets of equipment 【成为】become; turn into 【成文】existing writings/written ～法 written law 【成问题】be a problem 【成效】effect; result 【成心】intentionally; on purpose; with deliberate intent 【成形】take shape/forming 【成性】by nature 【成药】medicine already prepared by a pharmacy 【成衣】readymade clothes 【成因】cause of formation 【成语】set phrase; idiom 【成员】member ～国 member state 【成灾】cause disaster 【成长】grow up; grow to maturity

呈 chéng ①assume (form, colour, etc.) ②submit; present ③petition; memorial 【呈报】submit a report; report a matter 【呈递】present; submit ～国书 present credentials 【呈文】memorial; petition 【呈现】present; appear; emerge

诚 chéng sincere; honest 【诚恳】sincere 【诚然】true; indeed; to be sure 【诚实】honest 【诚心】sincere desire; wholeheartedness 【诚意】good faith; sincerity 【诚挚】cordial

承 chéng ①bear; hold; carry ②undertake; contract (to do a job) ③be indebted ④continue; carry on 【承办】undertake 【承包】contract ～商 contractor 【承担】bear; undertake; assume ～费用 bear the costs ～责任 bear responsibility for; be held responsible for 【承继】adopted as heir to one's uncle / adopt one's brother's son (as one's heir) 【承蒙】be indebted (to sb. for a kindness); be granted a favour 【承认】admit; acknowledge; recognize/give diplomatic recognition ～错误 admit one's mistake; acknowledge one's fault 【承受】bear; support; endure / inherit (a legacy, etc.)

城 chéng ①city wall; wall ～外 outside the city ②city 内～ inner city ③town 【城堡】castle 【城池】city wall and moat; city 【城堞】battlements 【城防】the defence of a city 【城关】the area just outside a city gate 【城壕】moat 【城郊】outskirts of a town 【城里】inside the city; in town ～人 city dwellers; townspeople 【城楼】gate tower 【城门】city gate 【城墙】city wall 【城区】the city proper 【城市】town; city ～规划 city planning ～建设 urban construction ～居民 city dwellers

乘 chéng ①ride ～公共汽车 go by bus ～火车旅行 travel by train ②take advantage of; avail oneself of ～敌不备 take the enemy unawares ③multiply 【乘便】when it is convenient; at one's convenience 【乘法】multiplication ～表 multiplication table 【乘机】seize the opportunity 【乘客】passenger 【乘凉】enjoy the cool 【乘人之危】take advantage of sb.'s precarious position 【乘胜】exploit a victory ～追击 follow up a victory with hot pursuit 【乘务员】attendant on a train 【乘隙】take advantage of a loophole 【乘兴】while one is in high spirits

盛 chéng ①fill; ladle ～饭 fill a bowl with rice ～菜 dish out food ～汤 ladle out soup ②hold; contain ～一百斤粮食 hold 100 *jin* of grain

程 chéng ①rule; regulation ②order; procedure 议～ agenda ③journey 启～ set out on a journey ④distance 行～ distance of travel 【程度】level; degree/extent 【程式】form; pattern; formula ～化 stylization 【程序】order; procedure; course; sequence ～问题 point of order

惩 chéng penalize 【惩罚】 punish; penalize 【惩戒】 punish sb. to teach him a lesson; discipline sb. as a warning 【惩前毖后】 learn from past mistakes to avoid future ones 【惩治】 mete out punishment to

澄 chéng clear; transparent 【澄清】 clear; transparent/ clear up ～事实 clarify some facts 要求～ demand clarification

逞 chéng ①show off (one's strength, power, etc.); flaunt ②carry out (an evil design); succeed (in a scheme) ③indulge; give free rein to 【逞能】 show off one's skill; parade one's ability 【逞强】 flaunt one's superiority

秤 chèng balance; steelyard 【秤锤】 the sliding weight of a steelyard 【秤杆】 the arm of a steelyard

CHI

吃 chī ①eat; take ～药 take medicine ②have one's meals ～馆子 dine out ～食堂 have one's meals in the mess ③live on ～利钱 live on interest ④suffer; incur ～败仗 suffer a defeat 【吃不开】 be unpopular / won't work 【吃不下】 not feel like eating / be unable to eat any more 【吃醋】 be jealous 【吃大锅饭】 mess together / everybody sharing food from the same big pot 【吃饭】 eat; have a meal / keep alive; make a living 【吃紧】 be critical; be hard pressed 【吃惊】 be startled; be shocked; be amazed 【吃苦】 bear hardships 【吃亏】 suffer losses; come to grief / at a disadvantage 【吃老本】 live off one's past gains 【吃力】 entail strenuous effort; be a strain 【吃零嘴】 nibble between meals 【吃奶】 suck the breast ～的孩子 sucking child; suckling 【吃素】 be a vegetarian 【吃透】 have a thorough grasp ～精神 grasp the spirit of sth. 【吃香】 be very popular; be well-liked 【吃斋】 practise abstinence from meat 【吃重】arduous; strenuous

痴 chī ①silly; idiotic 白～idiot ②crazy about ～情 infatuation ③insane; mad ～子 madman 【痴呆】stupid 【痴想】wishful thinking; illusion; fond dream

嗤 chī sneer 【嗤笑】laugh at 【嗤之以鼻】give a snort of contempt; despise

池 chí ①pool; pond 游泳～swimming pool ②stalls (in a theatre)

驰 chí ①speed ～骋 gallop ②spread ～驰名 well-known; famous ～中外 renowned at home and abroad

迟 chí ①slow; tardy ②late 【迟到】be late; arrive late 【迟钝】slow (in thought or action); obtuse 【迟缓】 tardy; sluggish 行动～act slowly 【迟误】delay; procrastinate 【迟延】retard 【迟疑】hesitate ～不决 hesitate to make a decision; be irresolute 毫不～without hesitation 【迟早】sooner or later 【迟滞】slow-moving; sluggish

持 chí ①hold; grasp ～相反意见 hold a contrary opinion ～保留态度 have reservations ～不同政见者 dissident ②support; maintain ③manage; run 主～take charge of ④oppose 【持家】run one's home; keep house 【持久】lasting; enduring; protracted ～力 staying power; endurance ～战 protracted war ～和平 lasting peace 【持枪】 hold a gun/port arms 【持球】holding 【持续】continued; sustained 【持有】hold ～护照 hold a passport ～不同意 见 hold differing views 【持重】prudent; cautious

匙 chí spoon 汤～soup spoon 茶～teaspoon

踟 chí 【踟蹰】hesitate; waver ～不前 hesitate to move forward

尺 chí ①*chi*, a unit of length (=1/3 metre) ②rule; ruler 【尺寸】measurement; dimensions; size 量～

take sb.'s measurements 你穿什么～的鞋 what size shoes do you wear 【尺牍】a model of epistolary art /correspondence (of an eminent writer) 【尺度】yardstick; measure; scale

齿 chǐ tooth 锯～ the teeth of a saw 【齿轮】gear wheel; gear 【齿龈】gums

侈 chǐ ①wasteful; extravagant ②exaggerate 【侈谈】talk glibly about; prate about; prattle about

耻 chǐ shame; disgrace; humiliation 引以为～ regard as a disgrace 【耻笑】hold sb. to ridicule; sneer at; mock

叱 chǐ loudly rebuke; shout at; bawl at 【叱喝】scold roundly; curse; abuse 【叱责】upbraid

斥 chǐ ①upbraid; scold; reprimand 痛～ vehemently denounce ②repel; exclude; oust 【斥骂】reproach 【斥责】rebuke; excoriate

赤 chǐ ①red ②loyal; sincere ～心 loyalty; sincerity ③bare 【赤膊】barebacked 打～ be stripped to the waist 【赤诚】absolute sincerity 【赤道】the equator 【赤豆】red bean 【赤脚】barefoot ～医生 barefoot doctor 【赤金】pure gold 【赤裸裸】stark-naked / undisguised; out-and-out 【赤贫】utterly destitute 【赤手空拳】bare-handed; unarmed 【赤子】a newborn baby 【赤字】deficit 财政（贸易）～ financial (trade) deficit

炽 chǐ flaming; ablaze 【炽烈】burning fiercely; blazing ～的气氛 a fervent atmosphere 【炽热】red-hot; blazing / passionate

翅 chǐ ①wing ②shark's fin

CHONG

冲 chōng ①pour boiling water on ～茶 make tea ②rinse; flush 便后～水 flush the toilet after use ③ charge; rush; dash 向敌人～去 charge the enemy ④develop ～胶卷 develop a roll of film 【冲刺】 spurt; sprint 【冲淡】 dilute/water down; weaken 【冲动】 impulse/get excited; be impetuous 【冲锋】 charge; assault ～号 bugle call to charge ～枪 tommy gun 【冲击】 lash; pound/ charge; assault ～波 shock wave 【冲积】 alluviation 【冲垮】 shatter; burst 【冲力】 impulsive force 【冲破】 break through; breach 【冲散】 break up; scatter; disperse (a crowd) 【冲杀】 charge; rush ahead 【冲刷】 erode; scour; wash out 【冲突】 conflict; clash 【冲洗】 rinse; wash / develop 【冲撞】 collide; bump; ram / give offence; offend

充 chōng ①sufficient; full ②fill; charge ～电 charge (a battery) ③serve as; act as ～向导 serve as a guide ④pose as; pass sth. off as ～内行 pretend to be an expert ～好汉 pose as a hero 【充斥】 flood; congest; be full of 【充当】 serve as; act as 【充耳不闻】 turn a deaf ear to 【充分】 full; ample; abundant ～利用 fully utilize; make full use of 有～理由 have every reason 【充公】 confiscate 【充饥】 allay one's hunger 【充军】 banish 【充满】 full of; brimming with; permeated with; imbued with 【充沛】 plentiful; abundant; full of 【充其量】 at most; at best 【充塞】 fill (up); cram 【充实】 substantial; rich / substantiate; enrich; replenish 【充数】 make up the number 【充裕】 abundant; ample 时间很～ there is plenty of time 【充足】 adequate; sufficient

忡 chōng 【忡忡】 laden with anxiety; careworn 忧心～ heavyhearted; deeply worried

舂 chōng pound; pestle ～米 husk rice with mortar and pestle ～药 pound medicinal herbs in a mortar

憧 chōng 【憧憧】 flickering; moving 人影～ shadows of people moving about 【憧憬】 look forward to

虫 chóng insect; worm 【虫害】insect pest 【虫胶】shellac 【虫情】insect pest situation 【虫牙】carious tooth; decayed tooth 【虫灾】plague of insects

重 chóng ①repeat 这两个例子～了 these two examples duplicate each other ②again; once more ～起炉灶 begin all over again ③layer 双～领导 dual leadership 【重重】layer upon layer 被～包围 be encircled by ring 顾虑～ full of misgivings 【重迭】one on top of another; overlapping 【重返】return ～前线 go back to the front ～家园 return to one's homeland 【重犯】repeat (an error or offence) 【重逢】meet again 【重复】repeat; duplicate 【重婚】bigamy 【重建】rebuild; reconstruct; reestablish ～家园 rehabilitate one's homeland 【重申】reiterate; restate ～党的纪律 affirm anew the discipline of the Party 【重孙】great-grandson 【重孙女】great-granddaughter 【重提】bring up again 【重温】review ～旧梦 revive an old dream 【重现】reappear 【重新】again; anew; afresh ～做人 begin one's life anew ～考虑 reconsider ～部署 rearrange; redeploy 【重演】put on an old play/recur; reenact; repeat

崇 chóng ①high; lofty; sublime ②esteem; worship 【崇拜】adore ～偶像 worship of idols; idolatry 【崇奉】believe in (a religion) 【崇高】lofty; sublime; high 【崇敬】respect; revere 【崇尚】uphold; advocate

宠 chǒng dote on; bestow favour on 得～ find favour with sb. 失～ fall out of favour 【宠爱】make a pet of sb. 【宠儿】pet; favourite 【宠信】be specially fond of and trust unduly (a subordinate)

冲 chòng ①with plenty of dash; vigorously 干活儿～ do one's work with vim and vigour 说话～ speak bluntly ②(of smell) strong ③facing; towards 【冲床】punch

【冲压】punching

CHOU

抽　chōu ①take out (from in between) ②take (a part from a whole) ～出一部分劳力 release part of the labour force from other work ～时间 find time ③(of certain plants) put forth ～枝 branch out; sprout ～芽 bud ④obtain by drawing, etc. ～血 draw blood ⑤shrink ⑥lash ～陀螺 whip a top 【抽查】spot check 【抽打】lash; whip; thrash 【抽调】transfer (personnel or material) 【抽动】twitch; spasm 【抽筋】pull out a tendon/cramp (in the leg, etc.) 【抽空】manage to find time ～学习 study at odd moments 【抽泣】sob 【抽签】cast lots 【抽球】drive 【抽身】leave (one's work); get away 【抽水】draw water ～机 water pump ～马桶 water closet ～站 pumping station 【抽税】levy a tax 【抽缩】shrink; contract 【抽屉】drawer 【抽象】abstract 科学的～ scientific abstraction 【抽烟】smoke (a cigarette or a pipe)

仇　chóu ①enemy; foe ②hatred; enmity 记～ nurse a grievance 【仇恨】hostility 满腔～ seething with hatred 【仇人】personal enemy 【仇杀】kill in revenge 【仇视】look upon with hatred; be hostile to

惆　chóu 【惆怅】disconsolate; melancholy

绸　chóu silk fabric; silk ～伞 silk parasol 【绸缎】silks and satins 【绸缪】sentimentally attached

愁　chóu worry; be anxious 【愁苦】anxiety; distress 【愁眉】knitted brows; worried look ～不展 with a worried frown ～苦脸 pull a long face 【愁闷】feel gloomy; be depressed 【愁容】anxious expression ～满面 look extremely worried

稠 chóu ①thick ～粥 thick porridge ②dense 【稠密】 dense 人烟～ densely populated

酬 chóu reward; payment 【酬报】 requite; repay 【酬金】 monetary reward; remuneration 【酬劳】 recompense 【酬谢】 thank sb. with a gift

筹 chóu ①chip; counter ②prepare; plan ～款 raise money 【筹办】 make preparations; make arrangements 【筹备】 prepare; arrange ～工作 preparatory work ～会议 preliminary meeting 【筹划】 plan and prepare 【筹集】 raise (money) 【筹建】 prepare to construct or establish sth. 【筹码】 chip; counter 【筹募】 collect (funds) 【筹商】 discuss; consult

踌 chóu 【踌躇】 hesitate; shilly-shally ～不前 hesitate to move forward ～满志 enormously proud of one's success; smug; complacent

丑 chǒu ①ugly; unsightly; hideous 长得不～ not bad-looking ②disgraceful; shameful; scandalous 出～ make a fool of oneself 【丑恶】 ugly; repulsive 【丑化】 smear; uglify; defame; vilify 【丑剧】 farce 【丑角】 clown; buffoon 【丑事】 scandal 【丑态】 ludicrous performance; buffoonery

臭 chòu ①smelly; foul; stinking ～鸡蛋 a rotten egg ②disgusting; disgraceful ～架子 nauseating airs 【臭虫】 bedbug 【臭骂】 curse roundly 【臭名远扬】 notorious; of ill repute 【臭气】 bad smell; stink; offensive odour

CHU

出 chū ①go or come out ～城 go out of town ② exceed; go beyond ～月 after this month; next month ③issue; put up ～证明 issue a certificate ～考题 set the paper; set the examination questions ～主意

offer advice ～布告 post an announcement; put up a notice ④produce; turn out ～煤 produce coal ⑤arise; happen ～问题 go wrong; go amiss ～事故 have an accident ⑥rise well (with cooking) ⑦put forth; vent ～芽 put forth buds; sprout ～气 vent one's spleen ⑧pay out; expend 入不敷～ one's income falling short of one's expenditure ⑨a dramatic piece 一～戏 an opera; a play ⑩out 走～大厅 come out of the hall 【出版】 come off the press; publish; come out ～社 publishing house ～物 publication 【出榜】 publish a list of successful candidates or examinees 【出殡】 hold a funeral procession 【出兵】 dispatch troops 【出操】 (go out to) drill or do exercises 【出差】 be away on official business ～费 allowances for a business trip 【出产】 produce; manufacture 【出厂】 leave the factory ～价格 producer price ～日期 date of production 【出场】 come on the stage; appear on the scene 【出超】 favourable balance of trade 【出车】 dispatch a vehicle/be out driving a vehicle; be out with the car 【出丑】 make a fool of oneself 【出处】 source 注明～ give references 【出错】 make mistakes 【出点子】 offer advice; make suggestions 【出动】 set out; start off/send out; dispatch 【出发】 set out; start off/start from; proceed from 【出风头】 seek or be in the limelight 【出格】 exceed what is proper; go too far 【出工】 go to work 【出轨】 be derailed; go off the rails / overstep the bounds 【出国】 go abroad 【出海】 go to sea 【出汗】 perspire; sweat 【出航】 set out on a voyage; set sail/set out on a flight; take off 【出乎意料】 exceeding one's expectations; unexpectedly 【出活】 yield results in work; be efficient 【出击】 launch an attack; hit out; make a sally 【出嫁】 (of a woman) get married; marry 【出境】 leave the country 驱逐～

deport 办理～手续 go through exit formalities ～签证 exit visa ～许可证 exit permit 【出口】speak; utter/exit/ export ～货 exports; exportation ～贸易 export trade ～ 商品 export commodities 【出来】come out; emerge 【出类 拔萃】stand out from one's fellows ～的人物 an outstanding figure 【出力】put forth one's strength; exert oneself 【出笼】come out of the steamer/come forth; appear 【出路】way out; outlet 【出马】go into action; take the field 【出卖】offer for sale; sell/sell out; betray 【出毛病】 be or go out of order; go wrong 【出门】be away from home; go on a journey; go out 【出面】appear personally ～调停 act as a mediator 【出名】famous; well-known 【出没】appear and disappear; haunt 【出谋划策】give counsel; mastermind a scheme 【出纳】receive and pay out money or bills/cashier; teller 【出品】produce; manufacture; make/product 【出其不意】take sb. by surprise; catch sb. unawares 【出奇】unusually; extraordinarily 【出气】give vent to one's anger; vent one's spleen 【出勤】 turn out for work/be out on duty ～率 rate of attendance; attendance 【出去】go out; get out 【出让】sell (one's own things) 【出入】come in and go out/discrepancy; divergence ～证 pass 【出色】outstanding; remarkable; splendid ～当行 class origin; family background/one's previous experience or occupation 【出神】be spellbound; be in a trance 他坐在那里～ he sat there, lost in thought 【出生】be born ～登记 registration of birth ～地 birthplace ～率 birthrate ～证 birth certificate 【出师】finish one's apprenticeship/dispatch troops to fight; send out an army 【出使】serve as an envoy abroad; be sent on a diplomatic mission 【出示】show; produce (one's papers, etc.) 【出世】come into the world; be born/renounce the world 【出事】 meet with a mishap; have an accident 【出售】 offer for sale; sell 【出庭】 appear in court 【出头】 lift one's head/appear in public; come forward ～露面 be in the limelight 【出席】 attend (a meeting); be present (at a banquet) 【出现】 appear; arise; emerge 【出于】 start from; proceed from; stem from ～自愿 of one's own accord; on a voluntary basis ～无奈 as it cannot be helped; there being no alternative 【出院】 leave hospital ～证明 hospital discharge certificate 【出诊】 pay a home visit 【出征】 go on an expedition; go out to battle 【出众】 be out of the ordinary; be outstanding 【出走】 leave; run away; flee 【出租】 hire ～汽车 taxicab; taxi; cab

初 chū ①at the beginning of; in the early part of ～夏 early summer ②first (in order) ～战 first battle ③for the first time ④elementary; rudimentary ⑤original ～愿 one's original intention 【初版】 first edition 【初步】 initial; preliminary; tentative 【初次】 the first time 【初等】 elementary; primary ～教育 primary education ～数学 elementary mathematics 【初犯】 first offender; first offence 【初稿】 first draft 【初级】 elementary; primary ～读本 primer ～班 elementary course 【初交】 new acquaintance 【初恋】 first love 【初露锋芒】 display one's talent for the first time 【初期】 initial stage; early days 【初审】 first trial 【初试】 first try / preliminary examination 【初小】 lower primary school 【初选】 primary election 【初学】 begin to learn 【初叶】 early years (of a century) 【初诊】 first visit (to a doctor or hospital) 【初中】 junior middle school

除 chú ①get rid of; eliminate; remove 为民～害 rid the people of a scourge ②except ③besides ④divide 【除草】 weeding ～机 weeder ～剂 weed killer; herbicide

【除尘器】 dust remover 【除法】 division 【除非】 only if; only when/unless 【除根】 dig up the roots; cure once and for all; root out 【除名】 remove sb.'s name from the rolls 【除外】 except; not counting; not including 【除夕】 New Year's Eve

厨 chú kitchen 【厨房】 kitchen ～用具 cooking utensils 【厨师】 cook; *chef*

锄 chú ①hoe ②work with a hoe; hoe ～草 hoe up weeds ③uproot; eliminate; wipe out 【锄奸】 eliminate traitors; ferret out spies

雏 chú ①young (bird) ～鸡 chicken ②nestling; fledgling 【雏形】 embryonic form; embryo

橱 chú cabinet; closet 【橱窗】 display window; showcase; shopwindow/glass-fronted billboard 【橱柜】 cupboard/sideboard

处 -chǔ ①get along (with sb.) 相～得好 get on well with each other ②be situated in; be in a certain condition ③manage; handle; deal with ～事 handle affairs; manage matters ④punish; sentence ⑤dwell; live 【处罚】 penalize 【处方】 write out a prescription; prescribe/prescription; recipe 【处分】 take disciplinary action against; punish 【处境】 unfavourable situation; plight ～困难 be in a difficult situation ～危险 be in peril 【处决】 put to death; execute 【处理】 handle; deal with; dispose of/treat by a special process/sell at reduced prices ～heat treatment ～价格 reduced price ～品 goods sold at reduced prices; shopworn or substandard goods 【处女】 virgin; maiden ～地 virgin land; virgin soil ～膜 hymen 【处世】 conduct oneself in society 【处死】 put to death; execute 【处心积虑】 deliberately plan (to achieve evil ends) 【处刑】 condemn; sentence 【处之泰然】 take things calmly 【处置】 handle; deal with; manage/punish

杵 chǔ ①pestle ②a stick used to pound clothes in washing ③poke ~个窟窿 poke a hole

储 chǔ store up 【储备】 store for future use; lay in; lay up/reserve 外汇~ foreign exchange reserve ~粮 grain reserves 【储藏】 save and preserve; store; keep/deposit ~量 reserves ~室 storeroom 【储存】 lay in; lay up; store; stockpile 【储户】 depositor 【储蓄】 save; deposit ~存款 savings deposit ~额 total savings deposits ~所 savings bank

楚 chǔ ①clear; neat ②pang; suffering 【楚楚】 clear; tidy; neat 衣冠~ immaculately dressed

处 chǔ ①place 别~ another place; elsewhere ②point; part 长~ strong point ③department; office 总务~ general affairs department 【处处】 everywhere; in all respects 【处所】 place; location 【处长】 section chief

畜 chù domestic animal; livestock 【畜肥】 animal manure 【畜力】 animal power ~车 animal-drawn cart 【畜生】 domestic animal/beast; dirty swine

触 chù ①touch; contact ②strike; hit ~雷 strike a mine ③move sb.; stir up sb.'s feelings 【触电】 get an electric shock 【触动】 touch sth., moving it slightly/ move sb.; stir up sb.'s feelings 【触发】 detonate by contact; touch off; spark; trigger 【触犯】 offend; violate; go against ~法律 break the law 【触及】 touch ~灵魂 touch people to their very souls 【触礁】 strike a reef 【触角】 antenna; feeler 【触觉】 tactile sensation; sense of touch 【触媒】 catalyst; catalytic agent 【触目】 meet the eye ~惊心 startling; shocking; grim 【触怒】 make angry 【触手】 tentacle 【触痛】 touch a tender spot; touch sb. to the quick

矗 chù 【矗立】 stand tall and upright; tower over sth.

CHUAI

揣 chuāi hide or carry in one's clothes ～在怀里 hide in the bosom; tuck into the bosom ～着手儿 tuck each hand in the opposite sleeve

揣 chuǎi estimate; surmise 【揣测】 guess; conjecture 【揣摩】 try to fathom; try to figure out

踹 chuài ①kick ～开门 kick the door open ②tread; stamp ～在水坑里 step in a puddle

CHUAN

川 chuān ①river ②plain 【川流不息】 flowing past in an endless stream; never-ending 【川资】 travelling expenses

穿 chuān ①pierce through; penetrate 看～ see through ②pass through; cross ～马路 cross a street ③wear; be dressed in ～衣 put on one's clothes 【穿插】 alternate; do in turn/weave in; insert/subplot; interlude; episode 【穿戴】 apparel; dress 【穿孔】 bore a hole; perforate 【穿梭】 shuttle back and forth ～轰炸 shuttle bombing 【穿堂】 hallway ～风 draught 【穿越】 pass through; cut across 【穿针】 thread a needle ～引线 act as a go-between 【穿凿】 give a farfetched interpretation ～附会 give strained interpretations and draw farfetched analogies

传 chuán ①pass (on) ～球 pass a ball ～话 pass on a message ②hand down ～世 be handed down from ancient times ③pass on (knowledge, skill, etc.); impart; teach ④spread 消息很快～开了 the news spread quickly ⑤conduct ～热 transmit heat ⑥convey; express ⑦

summon ~证人 summon a witness ⑧ infect 【传播】 disseminate; propagate; spread 【传抄】 make private copies
【传达】 pass on (information, etc.); transmit (an order);
relay; communicate / janitor ~室 reception office; janitor's room 【传单】 leaflet; handbill 【传导】 conduction
【传递】 transmit (messages); deliver (mail); transfer 【传
动】 transmission; drive ~带 transmission belt 【传呼】
notify sb. of a phone call ~电话 neighbourhood telephone service 【传教】 do missionary work ~士 missionary 【传令】 transmit orders ~嘉奖 cite sb. in a dispatch 【传票】 (court) summons; subpoena/voucher 【传
奇】 legend; romance 【传染】 infect; be contagious ~病
infectious disease ~病院 hospital for infectious diseases
【传神】 vivid; lifelike 【传声筒】 megaphone; loud hailer
【传授】 pass on (knowledge, skill, etc.); instruct; impart;
teach 【传说】 it is said; they say/legend; tradition 【传
诵】 be on everybody's lips; be widely read 【传送】 convey; deliver ~带 conveyer belt 【传统】 tradition ~观
念 traditional ideas ~剧目 traditional theatrical pieces
【传闻】 it is said; they say/hearsay; rumour; talk 【传
讯】 summon for interrogation or trial; subpoena; cite
【传扬】 spread (from mouth to mouth) 【传阅】 pass
round for perusal 在党委成员中~ be circulated among
the members of the Party committee 【传真】 portraiture /
facsimile ~电报 phototelegraph ~照片 radiophoto

船 chuán boat; ship 上~ go on board; embark 下~
disembark 乘~ go by boat; embark for 【船舱】 ship's
hold/cabin 【船队】 fleet 【船票】 steamer ticket 【船期】 sailing
date 【船首】 stem; bow; prow 【船体】 the body of a ship;
hull 【船尾】 stern 【船坞】 dock; shipyard 【船舷】 side
【船员】 crew 【船长】 captain; skipper【船只】shipping; vessels

喘 chuǎn breathe heavily 【喘气】breathe (deeply); gasp (for breath) /take a breather 【喘息】pant/breather; breathing spell; respite 【喘吁吁】puff and blow

串 chuàn ①string together ～珠子 string beads ②conspire ～骗 gang up and swindle sb. ③get things mixed up ～线 get the (telephone) lines crossed ④run about; rove ～亲戚 go visiting one's relatives ⑤play a part (in a play); act 客～ be a guest performer ⑥string; bunch; cluster 一一钥匙 a bunch of keys 【串联】establish ties; contact 【串门儿】call at sb.'s home; drop in 【串通】gang up; collaborate; collude

CHUANG

创 chuāng wound 【创痕】scar 【创口】cut 【创伤】trauma 精神～ a mental scar 战争～ the wounds of war

疮 chuāng ①sore; skin ulcer 褥～ bedsore ②wound 【疮疤】scar 【疮口】the open part of a sore

窗 chuāng window ～玻璃 windowpane 【窗洞】an opening in a wall 【窗格子】window lattice 【窗花】paper-cut for window decoration 【窗口】wicket; window 【窗框】window frame 【窗帘】curtain 【窗纱】window screening 【窗扇】casement 【窗台】windowsill

床 chuáng bed 【床单】sheet 【床垫】mattress 【床架】bedstead 【床头】the head of a bed; bedside ～灯 bedside lamp ～柜 bedside cupboard 【床位】berth; bunk; bed 【床罩】bedspread; counterpane

闯 chuǎng ①rush; dash; charge ～进来 break in; force one's way in ②temper oneself (by battling through difficulties and dangers) ～出新路 break a new path 【闯祸】get into trouble; bring disaster 【闯江湖】make a living wandering from place to place 【闯劲】the spirit of a pathbreaker; pioneering spirit

创 chuàng start (doing sth.); achieve (sth. for the first time) ～记录 set a record 【创办】 establish; set up; found 【创见】 original idea 【创举】 pioneering work 【创刊】 start publication ～号 first issue 【创立】 originate ～学派 found an academic school 【创始】 initiate ～人 founder; originator 【创新】 bring forth new ideas; blaze new trails 【创业】 start an undertaking; do pioneering work 【创造】 create; produce; bring about ～力 creative power ～性 creativeness; creativity 【创制】 formulate; institute 【创作】 create; produce; write/creative work

CHUI

吹 chuī ①blow; puff ～火 blow a fire ～灯 blow out the lamp ～气 give a puff ～起床号 sound the reveille ②play (wind instruments) ～笛 play the flute ③boast; brag ④break off; break up; fall through 【吹风】 be in a draught; catch a chill/let sb. in on sth. in advance/dry (hair, etc.) with a blower ～机 blower; drier 【吹拂】 sway; stir 【吹鼓手】 trumpeter; bugler 【吹冷风】 blow a cold wind over; throw cold water on 【吹毛求疵】 find fault; pick holes; nitpick 【吹牛】 boast; brag; talk big 【吹捧】 flatter; laud to the skies 【吹嘘】 lavish praise on oneself or others 【吹奏】 play (wind instruments) ～乐 band music; wind music

炊 chuī cook a meal 【炊具】 cooking utensils 【炊事】 cooking; kitchen work ～班 cookhouse squad ～员 a cook/the kitchen staff 【炊烟】 smoke from kitchen chimneys 【炊帚】 pot-scouring brush

垂 chuí hang down; droop; let fall ～泪 shed tears; weep 【垂死】 moribund; dying ～挣扎 put up a last-ditch struggle 【垂头丧气】 crestfallen; dejected 【垂危】 critically ill 【垂涎】 drool; slaver; covet 【垂直】 perpendicular; vertical ～线 vertical line

捶 chuí beat; thump ～背 pound sb.'s back ～胸顿足 beat one's breast and stamp one's feet (in deep sorrow)

锤 chuí ①hammer ②hammer into shape 【锤炼】 hammer into shape/temper/polish (a piece of writing)

CHUN

春 chūn ①spring ～色 spring scenery ②love; lust ～情 stirrings of love ③life; vitality 【春饼】 spring pancake 【春播】 spring sowing 【春风】 spring breeze ～满面 beaming with satisfaction (smiles, happiness) 【春耕】 spring ploughing 【春光】 sights and sounds of spring; spring scenery 【春假】 spring vacation; spring holidays 【春节】 the Spring Festival 【春卷】 spring roll 【春雷】 spring thunder 【春笋】 bamboo shoots in spring 【春天】 springtime 【春意】 spring in the air; the beginning of spring/thoughts of love 【春游】 spring outing 【春装】 spring clothing

纯 chún ①pure; unmixed ～毛（金） pure wool (gold) ②simple ～属捏造 sheer fabrication 【纯粹】 pure; unadulterated 【纯度】 purity 【纯洁】 pure; clean and honest 【纯利】 net profit 【纯朴】 honest; simple; unsophisticated 【纯熟】 skilful; practised; well versed 【纯真】 sincere 【纯正】 pure; unadulterated 【纯种】 purebred ～牛 pedigree cattle

唇 chún lip 【唇膏】 lipstick 【唇枪舌剑】 cross verbal swords 【唇舌】 words; argument 【唇音】 labial (sound)

蠢 chǔn stupid; foolish; dull; clumsy 【蠢材】 idiot; fool 【蠢动】 wriggle/creat disturbances

CHUO

戳 chuō jab; poke; stab ～了眼睛 jab sb.'s eye ～一个洞 poke a hole 【戳穿】puncture; lay bare; expose

绰 chuò ample; spacious 【绰绰有余】more than sufficient; enough and to spare 【绰号】nickname

CI

疵 cī flaw; defect; blemish 【疵点】flaw; fault 【疵毛】defective wool

词 cí ①word; term ②speech; statement 【词典】dictionary 【词法】morphology 【词干】stem 【词根】root 【词汇】vocabulary; words and phrases ～表 word list; vocabulary; glossary ～学 lexicology 【词句】words and phrases; expressions 【词类】parts of speech 【词素】morpheme 【词头】prefix 【词尾】suffix 【词形】morphology ～变化 morphological changes; inflections 【词序】word order 【词义】the meaning of a word 【词语】words and expressions; terms 【词源】the origin of a word; etymology 【词缀】affix 【词组】word group; phrase

祠 cí ancestral temple 【祠堂】ancestral hall; memorial temple

瓷 cí porcelain; china 【瓷雕】porcelain carving 【瓷漆】enamel paint; enamel 【瓷器】chinaware 【瓷实】solid; firm; substantial 【瓷砖】ceramic tile; glazed tile

辞 cí ①diction; phraseology ②take leave ③decline ～让 politely decline ④dismiss 【辞别】bid farewell; take one's leave 【辞呈】resignation 【辞典】dictionary 【辞令】language appropriate to the occasion 外交～ diplomatic language 【辞书】lexicographical work 【辞退】dismiss; discharge 【辞谢】decline with thanks 【辞行】say good-bye before setting out on a journey 【辞藻】flowery language; rhetoric 【辞章】poetry and prose/art of writing; rhetoric 【辞职】resign

慈 cí kind; loving 【慈爱】love; affection; kindness 【慈悲】mercy; benevolence; pity 发～ have pity; be merciful 【慈和】kindly and amiable 【慈善】charitable; benevolent ～机关 charitable institution ～家 philanthropist ～事业 charities; good works

磁 cí ①magnetism ②porcelain; china 【磁场】magnetic field 【磁带】(magnetic) tape ～录音机 tape recorder 【磁铁】magnet 【磁针】magnetic needle

雌 cí female 【雌花】female flower 【雌雄】male and female/victory and defeat 决一～ see who's master

此 cǐ this ～地 this place; here 【此后】after this; hereafter; henceforth 【此起彼伏】rise one after another 【此时】this moment; right now 【此外】besides; in addition; moreover 【此致敬礼】with greetings

次 cì ①order; sequence 依～in due order; in succession ②second; next ～子 second son ～日 next day ③second-rate; inferior ～棉 poor quality cotton ④time 首～ first time 【次等】second-class; inferior 【次第】order; sequence/one after another 【次货】inferior goods; sub-standard goods 【次品】defective goods 【次数】number of times; frequency 【次序】order; sequence 【次要】secondary; subordinate; minor 【次之】take second place

伺 cì 【伺候】wait upon; serve 难～ hard to please

刺 cì ①thorn; splinter ②stab; prick ～伤 stab and wound ③assassinate ④irritate; stimulate ～鼻 irritate the nose ⑤criticize 【刺刀】bayonet 拼～ bayonet-fighting 【刺耳】grating on the ear ～的叫声 piercing cry ～的话

harsh words 【刺骨】piercing (to the bones); biting 【刺激】
stimulate/provoke; irritate; upset ～物 stimulus; stimulant
物质～material incentive 【刺客】assassin 【刺杀】assas-
sinate/bayonet charge 【刺探】pry; spy 【刺猬】hedgehog
【刺绣】embroider/embroidery 【刺眼】dazzling; offending
to the eye

赐 cì grant; favour; gift 【赐教】condescend to teach;
grant instruction 【赐予】grant; bestow

CONG

从 cōng 【从容】calm; unhurried; leisurely/plentiful
时间很～there's still plenty of time

匆 cōng hastily; hurriedly 【匆促】in a hurry 时间～
be pressed for time 【匆忙】hastily ～作出决定 make
a hasty decision

葱 cōng onion; scallion 【葱翠】fresh green 【葱花】
chopped green onion ～饼 green onion pancake 【葱
茏】verdant; luxuriantly green 【葱绿】pale yellowish
green; light green 【葱头】onion

聪 cōng ①faculty of hearing ②acute hearing 【聪明】
intelligent; bright; clever

从 cóng ①from; through ～现在起 from now on ②
ever ～不计较 never give any consideration to ③
follow; comply with; obey ～命 obey an order ～征 go
on a military expedition ④join; be engaged in ～军 join
the army; enlist ⑤follower; attendant 随～ retainer;
retinue ⑥secondary ～犯 accessary criminal 【从此】from
this time on; from now on; henceforth; thereupon 【从
而】thus; thereby 【从句】subordinate clause 【从来】al-
ways; at all times; all along 【从略】be omitted 【从前】
before; formerly; in the past 【从事】go in for; be engaged

in; work on/deal with 【从属】subordinate 【从速】as soon as possible; without delay 【从头】from the beginning/ anew; once again ～来 start afresh 【从小】from childhood; as a child 【从中】out of; from among; therefrom ～渔利 profit from; cash in on ～调解 mediate between two sides ～吸取教训 draw a lesson from it

丛 cóng ①clump; thicket; grove 草～ a patch of grass 灌木～ a clump of bushes ②crowd; collection 人～ a crowd of people 论～ a collection of essays 【丛林】 jungle; forest ～战 jungle warfare 【丛生】(of plants) grow thickly/(of disease, evils, etc.) break out 百病～ all kinds of diseases and ailments breaking out 【丛书】 a series of books; collection

COU

凑 còu ①gather together; pool; collect ～钱 pool money ～份子 club together (to present a gift to sb.) ～情 况 pool information ②happen by chance; take advantage of ～空儿 try to find time ③move close to; press near 【凑合】collect; assemble/make do / passable; not too bad 【凑集】gather together 【凑巧】luckily; fortunately 【凑趣】 join in (a game, etc.) just to please others/make a joke about; poke fun at 【凑热闹】join in the fun/add trouble to 【凑手】at hand; within easy reach 【凑数】make up the number or amount; serve as a stopgap

CU

粗 cū ①wide (in diameter); thick ～绳 a thick rope ②crude; rough ～盐 crude salt ～布 coarse cloth ③gruff; husky ～嗓子 a husky voice ④careless; negligent ⑤rude; unrefined; vulgar 说话很～ speak rudely ⑥ roughly; slightly 【粗暴】rude; rough; crude; brutal 【粗笨】clumsy; unwieldy 【粗糙】coarse; rough; crude 【粗大】thick; bulky/loud (voice).【粗豪】forthright 【粗话】vulgar language 【粗活】unskilled work 【粗粮】coarse food grain (e.g. maize, sorghum, etc.) 【粗劣】of poor quality; cheap; shoddy 【粗鲁】rude; boorish 【粗略】rough; sketchy 【粗浅】superficial; shallow; simple 【粗人】boor; unrefined person 【粗疏】careless; inattentive 【粗率】rough and careless; ill-considered 【粗俗】vulgar; coarse 【粗心】careless; thoughtless; negligent 【粗野】boorish; uncouth 【粗枝大叶】sloppy; slapdash 【粗制滥造】manufacture in a rough and slipshod way 【粗重】(of voice, etc.) loud and jarring/big and heavy; bulky/thick and heavy/strenuous 【粗壮】sturdy; thickset; brawny (arms) / thick and strong/ deep and resonant (voice)

促 cù ①(of time) short; hurried; urgent ②urge; promote ③close to; near 【促成】help to bring about; facilitate 【促进】promote; advance; accelerate 互相～ help each other forward ～派 promoter of progress 【促使】impel; urge; spur ～我们钻研技术 impel us to study technique ～我们刻苦学习 spur us on to study diligently

醋 cù ①vinegar ②jealousy (as in love affair) 吃～ feel jealous 【醋精】vinegar concentrate 【醋栗】gooseberry 【醋酸】acetic acid

簇 cù ①form a cluster; pile up ②cluster; bunch 一～花 a bunch of flowers 【簇新】brand new 【簇拥】cluster round

CUAN

爨 cuān quick-boil ～丸子 quick-boiled meat balls with soup

攒 cuán collect together; assemble

窜 cuàn ①flee; scurry 东逃西～ flee in all directions ②change (the wording in a text, manuscript, etc.); alter 【窜犯】raid; make an inroad into ～边境 invade the border area 【窜改】alter (the original text); tamper with; falsify 【窜扰】harass 【窜逃】flee in disorder; scurry off

篡 cuàn usurp; seize ～权 usurp power 【篡改】distort; misrepresent ～历史 distort history 【篡位】usurp the throne

CUI

催 cuī hasten; urge; hurry; press (sb. to do sth.) ～他一下 hurry him up 【催泪弹】tear bomb; tear-gas grenade 【催眠】lull (to sleep); hypnotize ～曲 lullaby; cradlesong ～术 hypnotism

摧 cuī break; destroy 【摧残】wreck; devastate ～身体 ruin one's health 【摧毁】destroy; smash; wreck

脆 cuì ①fragile; brittle ～金属 brittle metal ②crisp 又甜又～ be sweet and crisp ③(of voice) clear 【脆弱】fragile; frail; weak

淬 cuì temper by dipping in water, oil, etc.; quench 【淬火】quench

唾 cuì spit; expectorate

粹 cuì ①pure ②essence; the best 精～ quintessence

翠 cuì ①emerald green; green ～竹 green bamboos ② kingfisher ③ jadeite 【翠绿】emerald green; jade green 【翠鸟】kingfisher

CUN

村 cūn ①village; hamlet ②rustic; boorish 【村史】village history 【村长】village head

存 cún ①exist; live; survive ②store; keep ~粮 store up grain ③accumulate; collect ④deposit (money) ⑤leave with; check (one's luggage, etc.) ⑥reserve; retain ⑦remain on balance; be in stock ⑧cherish; harbour 不~幻想 harbour no illusions 【存案】register with the proper authorities 【存查】file for reference 【存车处】parking lot (for bicycles); bicycle park or shed 【存单】deposit receipt 【存档】keep in the archives; place on file 【存底】keep the original draft; keep a file copy 【存放】leave with; leave in sb.'s care/deposit (money) 【存根】counterfoil; stub 【存户】depositor 【存货】goods in stock; existing stock 【存款】deposit; bank savings 【存栏】amount of livestock on hand 【存身】take shelter; make one's home 【存亡】live or die; survive or perish 与阵地共~ defend one's position to the death 【存项】(credit) balance 【存心】cherish certain intentions/intentionally; deliberately; on purpose 【存疑】leave a question open; leave a matter for future consideration 【存在】exist; be 【存折】deposit book; bankbook

忖 cǔn turn over in one's mind; ponder; speculate 【忖度】conjecture; surmise 【忖量】think over

寸 cùn ①cun, a unit of length (= 1/3 decimetre) ②very little; very short; small ~进 a little progress ~土必争 fight for every inch of land 【寸步】a tiny step; a single step ~不离 follow sb. closely; keep close to ~不让 refuse to yield an inch ~难行 can't move a single step

CUO

搓
球

cuō rub with the hands ～手 rub one's hands together ～毛巾 scrub a towel【搓板】washboard【搓球】chop【搓澡】give sb. a rubdown with a damp towel

磋

cuō consult【磋商】exchange views 进行～ hold consultations with

撮
盐
糖

cuō ①gather; bring together ②scoop up (with a dustpan or shovel) ③take up with the fingers ～点盐 take a pinch of salt ④extract; summarize ⑤pinch 一～糖 a pinch of sugar【撮合】make a match; act as go-between【撮弄】make fun of; play a trick on; tease/abet; instigate; incite【撮要】make an abstract; outline essential points/abstract; synopsis; extracts

蹉

cuō【蹉跎】waste time ～岁月 let time slip by without accomplishing anything; idle away one's time

挫

cuò ①defeat; frustrate; foil ②subdue; lower【挫伤】dampen; blunt; discourage ～群众的积极性 dampen the enthusiasm of the masses【挫折】setback; reverse 遭受～ suffer setbacks

措

cuò ①arrange; manage; handle ②make plans【措辞】wording; diction ～不当 inappropriate wording ～强硬 a strongly worded【措施】measure; step 采取～ adopt a measure【措手不及】be caught unprepared

锉

cuò ①file ②make smooth with a file【锉刀】file【锉屑】filing

错

cuò ①intricate; complex 交～ interlock ② grind (one's teeth, etc.); rub ③alternate ～开 stagger ④wrong; mistaken ⑤fault; demerit ⑥bad; poor【错案】misjudged case【错别字】wrongly written or mispronounced characters【错处】fault; demerit【错怪】blame sb. wrongly

【错过】miss; let slip ～机会 miss an opportunity 【错觉】illusion; misconception 造成～ give sb. a false impression 【错乱】in disorder; in confusion　精神～ mentally deranged; insane 【错误】wrong; mistaken; erroneous / mistake; blunder 犯～ commit an error 【错杂】mixed; heterogeneous; jumbled 【错字】wrongly written character / misprint 【错综复杂】intricate; complex

D

DA

搭 dā ①put up; build ～桥 build a bridge ～帐篷 pitch a tent ②hang over; put over ～在绳上 hang sth. on a line ③come into contact; join ～上关系 establish contact with ④throw in more (people, money, etc.); add ⑤lift sth. together 把这包米～上去 lift the bag of rice onto sth. ⑥take (a ship, plane, etc.); travel by ～船 go by boat ～飞机 go by plane ～长途汽车 travel by coach 【搭档】cooperate; work together / partner 【搭伙】join as partner / eat regularly in (a mess) 【搭架子】build a framework 【搭救】rescue; go to the rescue of 【搭配】arrange in pairs or groups / collocation 这两个词不～ these two words don't go together 【搭腔】answer; respond / talk to each other 【搭讪】strike up a conversation with sb.; say something to smooth over an embarrassing situation

答 dā 【答应】answer; reply; respond / agree; promise; comply with 他～来 he agreed to come

打 dá dozen 一～铅笔 a dozen pencils

达 dá ①extend 四通八～ extending in all directions 直～列车 through train ②reach; amount to ③express; communicate 词不～意 the words fail to convey the idea ④eminent; distinguished ～官 ranking official 【达成】 reach ～协议 reach agreement ～交易 strike a bargain 【达到】 achieve; attain; reach ～目的 achieve the goal

杳 dá pile (of paper, etc.); pad 一～钞票 a wad of bank notes

答 dá ①answer; reply; respond ②return (a visit, salute, etc.); reciprocate 【答案】 answer; solution; key 练习的～ key to an exercise 【答辩】 reply (to a charge, query or an argument) 【答词】 thank-you speech; answering speech; reply 【答复】 answer; reply 请尽早～ please reply at your earliest convenience 【答谢】 express appreciation (for sb.'s kindness or hospitality); acknowledge ～宴会 a return banquet

打 dǎ ①strike; hit; knock ～门 knock at the door ～鼓 beat a drum ②break; smash ③fight; attack ④construct; build ～埂 ridging ⑤make (in a smithy) ～铁 forge iron ⑥mix; stir; beat ～鸡蛋 beat eggs ⑦tie up; pack ～行李 pack one's luggage; pack up ⑧knit; weave ～毛衣 knit a sweater ⑨draw; paint ～格儿 draw squares ～问号 put a question mark ⑩spray; spread ～农药 spray insecticide ⑪open; dig ～井 dig a well ⑫raise; hoist ～伞 hold up an umbrella ⑬send; dispatch; project ～电话 make a phone call ⑭issue or receive (a certificate, etc.) ⑮remove; get rid of ～蛔虫 take worm medicine ⑯ladle; draw ～粥 ladle gruel ⑰gather in; collect; reap ～柴 gather firewood ⑱buy ～酱油 buy soy sauce ⑲catch; hunt ～鱼 catch fish ⑳estimate; calculate; reckon ～work out ～草稿 work out a draft ㉑do; engage in ～短工 be a temporary worker ②play ～篮球 play basketball 【打靶】 target practice 【打败】 defeat; beat; worst / suffer a defeat; be defeated 【打扮】 dress up; make up; deck out 【打岔】 interrupt; cut in 【打场】 thresh grain 【打成一片】 become one with 【打倒】 overthrow 【打掉】 destroy; knock out; wipe out 【打动】 move; touch 【打赌】 bet; wager 【打断】 break / interrupt; cut short ～思路 interrupt sb.'s train of thought 【打盹】 doze off; take a nap; nod 【打耳光】 box sb.'s ears 【打发】 send; dispatch / dismiss; send away / while away (one's time) 【打嗝】 hiccup / belch; burp 【打官腔】 stall with official jargon 【打官司】 go to court; engage in a lawsuit / squabble 【打滚】 roll about 孩子们在草地上～ the kids rolled about on the lawn 疼得直～ writhe with pain 【打哈欠】 yawn 【打鼾】 snore 【打火】 strike a light ～机 lighter 【打击】 hit; strike; attack ～歪风 take strong measures against unhealthy tendencies ～报复 retaliate 【打架】 fight; scuffle 【打交道】 come into contact with; have dealings with 【打搅】 disturb; trouble 别～他 don't disturb him ～您一下 may I trouble you a minute 【打劫】 rob; plunder; loot 【打结】 tie a knot 【打开】 open; unfold / turn on; switch on ～盖子 take off the lid ～包袱 untie a bundle ～缺口 make a breach ～眼界 widen one's horizon ～收音机 turn on the radio 【打量】 measure with the eye; look sb. up and down; size up / think; suppose; reckon 【打猎】 go hunting 【打乱】 throw into confusion; upset (a scheme, etc.) 【打破】 break; smash 【打气】 inflate; pump up (a tyre) / encourage; cheer up ～筒 inflater; tyre pump 【打拳】 shadowboxing 【打扫】 sweep; clean 【打手】 hired roughneck; hatchet man 【打算】 plan; intend 【打胎】 have an abortion 【打听】 ask about; inquire about 【打消】give up (an idea, etc.); dispel (a doubt, etc.) ～顾虑 dispel misgivings 【打游击】fight as a guerrilla 【打杂】do odds and ends 【打战】shiver 【打仗】fight; go to war 【打针】give or have an injection 【打中】hit the mark ～要害 hit on the vital spot 【打字】typewrite; type ～带 typewriter ribbon ～稿 typescript ～机 typewriter ～员 typist ～纸 typing-paper

大 dà ①big; large; great ～城市 a big city ②heavy (rain, etc.); strong (wind, etc.) ③loud 说～声点 speak louder ④general; main ～路 main road ～问题 major issue ⑤greatly; fully ～吃一惊 be greatly surprised ⑥eldest ～哥 eldest brother ⑦your ～作 (札) your writing (letter) 【大半】more than half; greater part; most/very likely; most probably 【大便】defecate; shit/stool; human excrement; shit; faeces 【大部】greater part 【大车】cart 【大臣】minister 【大吹大擂】make a big noise 【大葱】green Chinese onion 【大大】greatly; enormously 【大胆】bold; daring; audacious 【大地】earth 【大典】grand ceremony / canon 【大殿】audience hall / main hall of a Buddhist temple 【大豆】soybean; soya bean 【大队】group/production brigade/a large body of ～人马 a large contingent of troops 【大多数】great majority 【大方】generous; liberal / natural and poised; easy; unaffected/in good taste; tasteful 【大方向】general orientation 【大风】gale; strong wind 【大副】mate; chief officer 【大概】general idea; broad outline/general; rough; approximate/probably; most likely; presumably 【大干】go all out; make an all-out effort 【大纲】outline 【大规模】large-scale; massive 【大汉】big fellow 【大号】large size 【大合唱】cantata; chorus 【大轰大嗡】raise a hue and cry 【大红】bright red; scarlet 【大后年】three years from now 【大后天】

three days from now 【大话】 big talk; boast; bragging 【大会】 plenary session; general membership meeting/mass meeting; mass rally 【大伙儿】 we all; you all; everybody 【大家】 great master; authority/all; everybody 【大家庭】 big family; community 【大将】 senior general/high-ranking officer 【大街】 main street 【大节】 political integrity 【大惊小怪】 be surprised at sth. perfectly normal; make a fuss 没什么可～的 there is nothing to get alarmed about 【大局】 general situation ～已定 the outcome is a foregone conclusion 【大举】 carry out (a military operation) on a large scale ～进攻 mount a large-scale offensive 【大军】 main forces; army/large contingent 【大考】 end-of-term examination; final exam 【大课】 a lecture given to a large number of students; enlarged class 【大快人心】 affording general satisfaction 【大理石】 marble 【大力】 energetically; vigorously 【大力士】 a man of unusual strength 【大量】 a large number; a great quantity/generous; magnanimous ～财富 enormous wealth ～事实 a host of facts 【大楼】 multi-storied building 【大陆】 continent; mainland ～架 continental shelf 【大略】 general idea; broad outline/generally; roughly 【大麻】 hemp/marijuana 【大麦】 barley 【大拇指】 thumb 【大脑】 cerebrum ～皮层 cerebral cortex 【大炮】 artillery; big gun; cannon 【大批】 large quantities of 【大气】 atmosphere; air 【大权】 power over major issues; authority 【大人】 adult; grown-up 【大人物】 important person; great personage; VIP 【大赦】 amnesty; general pardon 【大师】 master 【大师傅】 cook; chef 【大使】 ambassador ～馆 embassy 【大事】 great event; important matter; major issue / overall situation/in a big way 【大势】 general trend of events ～所趋 the trend of the times; the general trend ～已去

the game is as good as lost 【大是大非】 major issues of principle 【大手大脚】 wasteful; extravagant 【大蒜】 garlic 【大体】 cardinal principle; general interest/roughly; more or less; on the whole 【大厅】 hall 【大庭广众】 (before) a big crowd; (on) a public occasion 【大同小异】 alike except for slight differences; very much the same 【大头针】 pin 【大团圆】 happy reunion / happy ending 【大腿】 thigh 【大王】 king; magnate 【大无畏】 dauntless; utterly fearless; indomitable 【大喜】 great rejoicing ～过望 be overjoyed 【大小】 big or small/size 【大写】 capitalization ～字母 capital letter 【大型】 large-scale; large 【大选】 general election 【大学】 university; college ～生 university or college student 【大洋】 ocean/silver dollar 【大衣】 overcoat; topcoat 【大意】 general idea; gist/careless; negligent 【大雨】 heavy rain 【大元帅】 generalissimo 【大院】 courtyard; compound 【大约】 approximately; about/probably 【大灶】 ordinary mess 【大张旗鼓】 on a grand scale; in a big way 【大志】 high aim; exalted ambition; high aspirations 【大治】 great order 【大致】 roughly; approximately 【大众】 the masses; the people; the public ～歌曲 popular songs ～文艺 popular literature ～化 popular; in a popular style 【大专院校】 universities and colleges; institutions of higher education 【大宗】 a large amount/staple

DAI

呆 dāi ①slow-witted; dull ②blank; wooden ③stay ～在家里 stay at home 【呆若木鸡】 dumb as a wooden chicken; dumbstruck; transfixed

待 dāi stay ～了三天 stay for three days

歹 dǎi　bad; evil; vicious 为非作～ do evil 【歹徒】
scoundrel; ruffian; evildoer

大 dài　【大夫】doctor; physician

代 dài　①take the place of ～人受过 suffer for the
faults of another ②acting ～部长 acting minister③
historical period 古～ ancient times ④generation 一～
新人 a generation of people of a new type 【代办】do
sth. for sb.; act on sb.'s behalf/chargé d'affaires 【代办所】
agency 【代笔】write on sb.'s behalf 【代表】deputy;
delegate; representative / represent; stand for / on behalf of;
in the name of ～大会 congress; representative assembly
～人物 representative figure ～团 delegation; deputation
【代词】pronoun 【代购】buy on sb.'s behalf 【代号】code
name 【代价】price; cost 【代课】take over a class for an
absent teacher 【代理】act on behalf of someone in a
responsible position/act as agent ～人 agent; deputy/
attorney 【代乳粉】milk powder substitute 【代售】be commissioned to sell sth. (usu. as a sideline) 【代数】algebra
【代替】replace; substitute for; take the place of 【代销】
sell goods on a commission basis ～店 commission agent
【代谢】supersession/metabolize ～作用 metabolism 【代言
人】spokesman 【代用】substitute 【代字号】swung dash

带 dài　①belt; girdle; ribbon; band; tape 皮～ leather
belt ②tyre 自行车～ bicycle tyre ③zone; area; belt
热～ the torrid zone ④take; bring; carry ～雨衣 take
one's raincoat along 你～着笔吗 have you a pen about
you ～个话儿 take a message to sb. ⑤do sth. incidentally
～点茶叶来 get me some tea 请把门～上 please shut the
door after you ⑥bear; have 面～笑容 wear a smile ⑦
having sth. attached; simultaneous ～叶的橘子 tangerines

with their leaves on ⑧lead; head ～队 lead a group of people ～兵 lead troops ⑨look after; bring up; raise ～孩子 look after children ～徒弟 train an apprentice 【带病】 in spite of illness 【带动】 drive; spur on; bring along ～全局 promote the work as a whole ～生产 give an impetus to production 【带劲】 energetic; forceful/interesting: exciting; wonderful 【带领】 lead; guide 【带路】 show the way; act as a guide ～人 guide 【带头】 take the lead; be the first; set an example 起～作用 play a leading role 【带孝】 be in mourning 【带鱼】 hairtail

待 dài ①treat; deal with ～人诚恳 treat people sincerely ～人接物 the way one gets along with people ② entertain ～客 entertain a guest ③wait for; await ～机 await an opportunity 【待价而沽】 wait for the right price to sell 【待考】 need checking 【待命】 await orders 【待续】 to be continued 【待遇】 treatment / remuneration; pay

贷 dài ①loan ②borrow or lend ③shift (responsibility); shirk ④pardon; forgive 【贷方】 credit side; credit 【贷款】 provide a loan; extend credit to/loan; credit

怠 dài idle; remiss; lazy; indolent 【怠工】 slow down; go slow 【怠慢】 cold-shoulder; slight

袋 dài bag; sack; pocket; pouch 一～水泥 a sack of cement 【袋鼠】 kangaroo 【袋装】 in bags

逮 dài reach 【逮捕】 arrest; take into custody ～法办 bring to justice ～证 arrest warrant

戴 dài put on; wear ～手套 put on one's gloves ～眼镜 wear glasses 【戴孝】 be in mourning

DAN

丹 dān ①red ②pellet or powder 【丹方】 folk prescription 【丹田】 the pubic region 【丹心】 a loyal heart; loyalty

单 dān ①one; single ～扇门 single-leaf door ②odd ～号 odd numbers ～日 odd-numbered days ③singly; alone; only 不～ not only ④unlined (clothing) ⑤sheet ⑥bill; list 【单薄】(of clothing) thin/thin and weak; frail/insubstantial; flimsy 【单纯】simple; pure / alone; purely; merely 【单词】individual word; word / single-morpheme word 【单调】monotonous; dull; drab 【单独】alone; by oneself; on one's own 【单方面】one-sided; unilateral 【单干】work on one's own; go it alone 【单杠】horizontal bar/horizontal bar gymnastics 【单个】individually; alone/ an odd one 【单价】unit price 【单间】separate room (in a hotel, restaurant, etc.) 【单句】simple sentence 【单据】documents (e. g. receipts, bills, vouchers, invoices, etc.) 【单枪匹马】single-handed; all by oneself; alone 【单人床】single bed 【单身】unmarried; single/live alone ～汉 bachelor ～宿舍 bachelor quarters 【单数】odd number/singular number 【单位】unit 【单项】individual event 【单行本】separate edition / offprint 【单一】single; unitary 【单衣】unlined garment 【单音词】monosyllabic word; monosyllable 【单元】unit 【单子】list; bill; form 【单字】individual character; separate word

担 dān ①carry on a shoulder pole ～水 carry water ②take on; undertake 【担保】assure; guarantee; vouch for 【担当】take on; undertake; assume 【担负】bear; shoulder; take on; be charged with ～责任 shoulder responsibility ～费用 bear an expense 【担架】stretcher; litter 【担惊受怕】feel alarmed; be in a state of anxiety 【担任】assume the office of; hold the post of 【担心】worry

耽 dān ①delay ②indulge in (pleasure, etc.) 【耽搁】stop over; stay/delay 一分钟也不能～ not a single minute is to be lost 【耽误】delay; hold up ～功夫 waste time

胆 dǎn ①gallbladder ②courage; guts; bravery 【胆大】bold; audacious 【胆敢】dare 【胆寒】be terrified 【胆量】courage; pluck; spunk 【胆略】courage and resourcefulness 【胆识】courage and insight 【胆小】timid; cowardly ~鬼 coward 【胆战心惊】tremble with fear

掸 dǎn brush lightly; whisk ～衣服 brush the dust off one's clothes ～灰 whisk away the dust 【掸子】duster

旦 dàn ①dawn; daybreak ②day 元～ New Year's Day

但 dàn ①but ②only; merely 【但凡】in every case; without exception 【但是】but; yet; still; nevertheless 【但书】proviso 【但愿】if only; I wish ～如此 let's hope so

担 dàn a carrying pole and the loads on it; load; burden 一～水 two buckets of water (carried on a shoulder pole)

诞 dàn ①birth ②birthday ③absurd; fantastic 【诞辰】birthday 【诞生】be born; come into being; emerge

淡 dàn ①thin; light ～酒 light wine ②tasteless; weak ～茶 weak tea ③light; pale ～黄 light yellow ④indifferent ～然处之 treat with indifference ⑤slack; dull 生意清～ business is slack 【淡薄】thin; light/become indifferent; flag/faint; dim; hazy 兴趣渐渐～ one's interest has begun to flag 印象～了 these impressions became dim 【淡化】desalination (of sea water) 【淡季】slack season 【淡漠】indifferent; apathetic; nonchalant/faint; dim; hazy 【淡水】fresh water ～鱼 freshwater fish 【淡忘】fade from one's memory 【淡雅】simple and elegant; quietly elegant

蛋 dàn egg 【蛋白】egg white; albumen/protein 【蛋白质】protein 【蛋粉】egg powder 【蛋糕】cake 【蛋黄】yolk 【蛋壳】eggshell 【蛋品】egg products

弹 dàn ①ball; pellet ②bullet; bomb 【弹弓】catapult 【弹壳】shell case 【弹坑】(shell) crater 【弹片】shell fragment 【弹头】bullet; warhead 【弹丸】pellet; shot ～之地 a tiny area 【弹药】ammunition ～库 ammunition depot ～手 ammunition man ～箱 cartridge box 【弹子】a pellet shot from a slingshot/marble 打～ play marbles

氮 dàn nitrogen 【氮肥】nitrogenous fertilizer

DANG

当 dāng ①equal ②ought; should; must ③in sb.'s presence ～面 to sb.'s face ④just at (a time or place) ～场 on the spot ⑤work as; serve as; be ～兵 be a soldier 【当初】originally; in the first place 【当代】the present age 【当地】at the place in question; local 【当机立断】make a prompt decision 【当即】at once; right away 【当家】manage (household) affairs ～作主 be master in one's own house 【当局】the authorities 【当令】in season 【当年】in those years/the prime of life 【当前】before one; facing one / present; current 大敌～ a formidable enemy stands before us ～的任务 the task at present ～利益 immediate interests ～的经济形势 the present economic situation 【当权】be in power; hold power ～派 people in authority 【当然】as it should be; only natural/certainly; of course; to be sure / natural 【当时】then; at that time 【当事人】party (to a lawsuit); litigant / person concerned; interested parties 【当务之急】a task of top priority 【当下】instantly; at once 【当先】in the van; at the head 【当心】be careful; look out ～不要弄错 take care there's no mistake 【当选】be elected 【当政】be in office 【当中】in the middle; in the centre/among 【当众】

in public; in the presence of all

挡 dǎng ①keep off; ward off; block 〜雨 keep off the rain 〜风 shelter sth. from the wind ②block; get in the way of 〜路 be in the way 〜光 get in the light ③fender; blind 窗〜 window blind ④gear 【挡驾】 decline to receive a guest 【挡箭牌】 shield/excuse; pretext

党 dǎng ①political party; party ②the Party (the Communist Party of China) ③clique; faction; gang 死〜 sworn follower 【党报】 party newspaper/the Party organ 【党代表】 Party representative 【党费】 party membership dues 【党纲】 party programme 【党籍】 party membership 【党纪】 party discipline 【党课】 Party class; Party lecture 【党魁】 party chieftain 【党龄】 party standing 【党内】 within the party; inner-party 【党派】 political parties and groups; party groupings 【党旗】 party flag 【党徒】 member of a clique/henchman 【党外】 outside the party 〜人士 non-Party personages 【党委】 Party committee 【党务】 party affairs 【党小组】 Party group 【党校】 Party school 【党性】 Party spirit 【党员】 party member 【党章】 party constitution 【党证】 party card 【党支部】 Party branch 〜书记 Party branch secretary 【党中央】 the Party Central Committee 【党总支】 general Party branch 【党组】 leading Party group

当 dàng ①proper; right 用词不〜 inappropriate choice of words ②match; equal to ③treat as; regard as; take for ④think ⑤that very (day, month, etc.) ⑥pawn ①sth. pawned; pawn; pledge 【当年】 the same year; that very year 【当票】 pawn ticket 【当铺】 pawnshop 【当日】 the same day; that very day 【当时】 right away; at once; immediately 【当真】 take seriously / really true; really 【当做】 treat as; regard as; look upon as

荡 dàng swing; sway; wave ～秋千 play on a swing 【荡船】swingboat 【荡涤】cleanse; clean up; wash away 【荡漾】ripple; undulate

档 dàng ①shelves (for files); pigeonholes ②files; archives 查～ consult the files ③crosspiece (of a table, etc.) ④grade 高～商品 high-grade goods 【档案】files; archives; record; dossier ～馆 archives ～管理员 archivist ～柜 filing cabinet

DAO

刀 dāo ①knife; sword ②one hundred sheets (of paper) 【刀把子】(sword) hilt / military power; power 【刀背】the back of a knife blade 【刀兵】weapons; arms/ fighting; war 【刀叉】knife and fork 【刀豆】sword bean 【刀锋】the point or edge of a knife 【刀具】cutting tool 【刀口】the edge of a knife / the crucial point; the right spot / cut; incision 【刀片】razor blade 【刀枪】sword and spear; weapons 【刀鞘】sheath; scabbard

叨 dāo 【叨唠】talk on and on; chatter away

导 dǎo ①lead; guide ②transmit; conduct ～电 conduct electricity ③instruct; teach; give guidance to 教～ teach 【导弹】guided missile 【导航】navigation ～台 guidance station 【导火线】(blasting) fuse/a small incident that touches off a big one; an incident (that touches off a war) 【导师】tutor; teacher/guide of a great cause 【导线】lead; wire 【导言】introduction (to a piece of writing); introductory remarks 【导演】direct (a film, play, etc.) / director 【导游】conduct a sightseeing tour/guidebook ～图 tourist map ～者 guide 【导致】lead to; bring about; result in; cause

岛 dǎo island 【岛国】 island country 【岛屿】 islands and islets; islands

倒 dǎo ①fall; topple 摔～ fall over ②collapse; fail 内阁～了 the cabinet collapsed ③close down; go bankrupt; go out of business ④(of voice) become hoarse 嗓子～了 lose one's voice ⑤change; exchange ～车 change trains or buses ～肩 shift a burden from one shoulder to the other ～座位 change seats ⑥move around 【倒把】 speculate 【倒班】 change shifts; work in shifts 【倒闭】 close down; go bankrupt 【倒戈】 change sides in a war 【倒卖】 resell at a profit 【倒霉】 have bad luck; meet with reverses 【倒手】 change hands 【倒塌】 collapse; topple down 【倒台】 downfall 【倒胃口】 spoil one's appetite

捣 dǎo ①pound; smash ～碎 pound to pieces ～药 pound medicine in a mortar ②harass; disturb 【捣蛋】 make trouble 【捣鬼】 play tricks; do mischief 【捣毁】 smash up; demolish; destroy 【捣乱】 create a disturbance ～分子 trouble-maker

祷 dǎo pray 【祷告】 say one's prayers

到 dǎo ①arrive; reach 公共汽车～站 the bus has arrived at the stop ②go to; leave for ～群众中去 go among the masses ③up until; up to 活～老，学～老 a man should study till his dying day 【到场】 be present; show up 【到处】 at all places; everywhere 【到达】 arrive; get to; reach 【到底】 to the end; to the finish/at last, in the end; finally / on earth /after all 【到会】 attend a meeting 【到家】 reach a very high level; be perfect; be excellent 【到来】 arrival; advent 【到期】 become due; mature; expire 【到手】 in one's hands; in one's possession 【到头】 to the end; at an end

倒 dào ①inverted; inverse ～立 stand upside down ② move backward; turn upside down ～车 back a car ③pour; tip ～垃圾 tip rubbish 【倒彩】 booing; hooting; catcall 【倒流】 flow backwards 【倒数】 count backwards ～第三行 the third line from the bottom 【倒退】 go backwards; fall back 【倒行逆施】 go against the historical trend; try to put the clock back / perverse acts 【倒叙】 flashback 【倒因为果】 reverse cause and effect; take cause for effect 【倒影】 inverted image 【倒置】 place upside down; invert 【倒转】 turn the other way round; reverse 【倒装词序】 inverted word order

悼 dào mourn; grieve 【悼词】 memorial speech

盗 dào ①steal; rob ②thief; robber 【盗匪】 bandits; robbers 【盗卖】 steal and sell (public property) 【盗窃】 steal ～犯 thief ～罪 larceny 【盗取】 embezzle 【盗用】 usurp (a name, etc.); embezzle (public funds, etc.)

道 dào ①road; way 小～ path ②channel; course 河流改～ change of course of a river ③way; method 养生之～ the way to keep fit ④doctrine; principle 孔孟之～ the doctrines of Confucius and Mencius ⑤line 斜～ a slanting line 【道白】 spoken parts in an opera 【道德】 morals; morality; ethics 【道贺】 congratulate 【道具】 stage property; prop 【道理】 principle; truth/reason; argument; sense 【道路】 road; way; path 【道歉】 apologize; make an apology 【道听途说】 hearsay; rumour; gossip 【道谢】 express one's thanks; thank 【道义】 morality and justice ～上的支持 moral support

稻 dào rice; paddy 【稻草】 rice straw ～人 scarecrow 【稻糠】 rice chaff 【稻壳】 rice husk 【稻田】 rice field 【稻秧】 rice seedlings; rice shoots

DE

得 dé ①get; obtain; gain 他怎么~病的 what brought about his illness ②(of a calculation) result in ③fit; proper ~用 fit for use; handy ④satisfied; complacent 自~ pleased with oneself ⑤be finished; be ready 饭~了 dinner is ready 【得便】when it's convenient 【得不偿失】 the loss outweighs the gain 【得逞】have one's way; prevail; succeed 【得出】reach (a conclusion); obtain (a result) 【得当】apt; appropriate; proper; suitable 措词~ aptly worded 【得到】get; obtain; gain; receive 【得法】 do sth. in the proper way 【得分】score 【得计】succeed in one's scheme 【得奖】win a prize ~人 prizewinner 【得空】have leisure; be free 【得力】benefit from; get help from/capable; competent ~助手 capable assistant ~干部 competent cadre 【得胜】win a victory; triumph 【得失】 gain and loss; success and failure/advantages and disadvantages; merits and demerits 【得势】be in power/get the upper hand 【得手】go smoothly; come off; do fine; succeed 【得闲】have leisure; be at leisure 【得心应手】 with facility; with high proficiency/serviceable; handy 【得以】so that... can... 【得益】benefit; profit 【得意】 proud of oneself; pleased with oneself; complacent ~扬 扬 look triumphant ~忘形 get dizzy with success; have one's head turned by success 【得志】achieve one's ambition; have a successful career 少年~ enjoy success when young 【得罪】offend; displease

德 dé ①virtue; morals; moral character ②heart; mind ③kindness; favour 【德才兼备】have both ability and political integrity 【德高望重】be of noble character and high prestige 【德行】moral integrity; moral conduct 【德

语】German (language) 【德育】moral education 【德政】
benevolent rule 【德治】rule of virtue

DENG

灯 dēng ①lamp; lantern; light 电～ electric light ②
valve; tube ③burner 【灯光】the light of a lamp;
lamplight/(stage) lighting 【灯火】lights ～辉煌 ablaze
with lights ～管制 blackout 【灯笼】lantern 【灯笼裤】
knickerbockers 【灯谜】lantern riddles 【灯泡】(electric)
bulb; light bulb 【灯塔】lighthouse; beacon 【灯头】lamp
holder; electric light socket 【灯心绒】corduroy 【灯油】
lamp-oil 【灯罩】lampshade

登 dēng ①ascend; mount; scale (a height) ～岸 go
ashore ②publish; record; enter ～广告 advertise (in
a newspaper) ③pedal; treadle ～三轮车 pedal a pedicab
④step on; tread 【登报】publish in the newspaper 【登峰
造极】reach the peak of perfection; reach the limit 【登
高】ascend a height 【登记】register; check in; enter one's
name 结婚～ marriage registration ～簿 register; registry
～处 registration office 【登陆】land; disembark ～部队
landing force ～舰(艇) landing ship (boat) 【登门】call
at sb.'s house 【登山】mountain-climbing ～队 mountaineering party ～运动 mountaineering 【登台】mount a
platform; go up on the stage 【登载】publish

等 dēng ①class; grade; rank 分三～ classify into three
grades ②equal ③wait; await ～车 wait for a train,
bus, etc. 我～你的答复 I await your answer ④when;
till ⑤and so on; and so forth; etc. 【等待】wait; await ～时
机 wait for a chance 【等到】by the time; when 【等号】
equal-sign 【等候】wait; await; expect 【等级】grade;
rank/order and degree; social estate ～制度 hierarchy;

social estate system 【等价】of equal value; equal in value
～交换 exchange of equal values; exchange at equal
value ～物 equivalent 【等式】equality 【等同】equate; be
equal ～语 equivalent 【等外】substandard ～品 substandard produc.【等于】equal to / amount to 设想不～现实
presumption is not reality

凳 dèng stool; bench 方～ square stool / 长～ bench

澄 dèng (of a liquid) settle 【澄清】(of a liquid) settle;
become clear 【澄沙】sweetened bean paste

瞪 dèng open one's eyes wide; stare 【瞪眼】stare; glare/
glower and glare at sb.; get angry with sb. 干～
look on helplessly

DI

低 dī ①low ～年级学生 students of the junior years
②let droop; hang down ～头 hang one's head 【低
产】low yield 【低潮】low tide 【低沉】overcast lowering/
(of voice) low and deep / low-spirited; downcast 【低估】
underestimate 【低级】elementary; lower / vulgar; low ～
趣味 vulgar interests; bad taste 【低廉】cheap; low 物价
～ prices are low 【低劣】inferior; low-grade 【低烧】low
fever; slight fever 【低声】in a low voice 【低注】low-
lying 【低微】low; humble 【低温】low temperature / mi-
crotherm 【低息】low interest 【低压】low pressure

堤 dī dyke; embankment; dam

提 dī 【提防】take precautions against; be on guard
against; beware of

滴 dī ①drip ～眼药 put drops in one's eyes ②drop
一～水 a drop of water 【滴答】tick; ticktack

的 dí 【的确】 indeed; really 【的确良】 dacron; terylene

敌 dí ①enemy; foe ～机 an enemy plane ②oppose; fight; resist 与人民为～ oppose the people ③match; equal 【敌对】 hostile; antagonistic 【敌国】 enemy state 【敌后】 enemy's rear area 【敌军】 enemy troops 【敌情】 the enemy's situation 【敌视】 be antagonistic to; adopt a hostile attitude towards 【敌手】 match; opponent; adversary/enemy hands 【敌探】 enemy spy 【敌我矛盾】 contradictions between ourselves and the enemy 【敌意】 hostility

涤 dí wash; cleanse 【涤除】 wash away; do away with; eliminate 【涤荡】 clean up 【涤纶】 polyester fibre

笛 dí ①bamboo flute ②whistle 汽～ steam whistle

嘀 dí 【嘀咕】 whisper; talk in whispers/have misgivings about sth.; have sth. on one's mind

嫡 dí ①of or by the wife ～长子 the wife's eldest son ②of lineal descent; closely related 【嫡传】 handed down in a direct line from the master 【嫡派】 disciples taught by the master himself 【嫡亲】 blood relations ～弟兄 blood brothers 【嫡系】 direct line of descent/one's own clique ～部队 troops under one's direct control

诋 dǐ slander; defame 【诋毁】 slander; vilify; calumniate; defame

邸 dǐ the residence of a high official 官～ official residence

底 dǐ ①bottom; base 缸～ the bottom of a vat ～价 base price ②the heart of a matter; ins and outs 露～儿了 the whole thing came out 心里没～ feel unsure of sth. 心里有～ know how the matter stands ③rough draft ④a copy kept as a record 留～ keep a copy on file; duplicate and file (a letter, etc.) ⑤end 年～ the end of a year ⑥ground; background; foundation 白～ white background 【底层】ground floor; first floor/bottom; the lowest rung 社会的～ the bottom of society 【底稿】draft; manuscript 【底牌】cards in one's hand; hand 亮～ show one's hand 【底片】negative; photographic plate 【底细】ins and outs; exact details 【底下】under; below; beneath/next; later; afterwards

抵 dǐ ①support; sustain; prop 把门～住 prop sth. against the door ②resist; withstand ～住压力 withstand the pressure ③compensate for; make good ～命 pay with one's life ④mortgage 用房屋做～ mortgage a house ⑤balance; set off 收支相～ income balances expenditure ⑥be equal to 【抵触】conflict; contradict 【情绪 resentment; resistance 【抵达】arrive; reach 【抵挡】keep out; ward off; check 【抵抗】resist; stand up to ～力 resistance (to disease) 【抵赖】deny; disavow 【抵消】offset; cancel out; counteract 【抵押】mortgage ～品 security 【抵御】resist; withstand ～侵略 resist aggression 【抵制】boycott

地 dì ①the earth ②land; soil ③fields 麦～ wheat field ④ground; floor ⑤place; locality ⑥position; situation ⑦background; ground 【地板】floor board / floor 【地堡】bunker 【地步】condition; plight/extent 留～ leave room for manoeuvre 【地层】stratum; layer 【地产】landed estate; real estate 【地带】district; region; zone; belt 【地道】tunnel 【地点】place; site; locale 【地段】a sector of an area 【地方】locality/local ～戏 local opera ～武装 local armed forces 【地方】place; space; room/part; respect 【地基】ground/foundation 【地窖】cellar 【地界】the boundary of a piece of land 【地雷】(land) mine ～战 (land) mine warfare 【地理】geographical features of a place /

geography 【地利】 favourable geographical position/land productivity 【地面】 the earth's surface/ground; floor/region; area 【地名】 place name 【地皮】 land for building/ground 【地痞】 local ruffian 【地平线】 horizon 【地铺】 shakedown 【地壳】 the earth's crust 【地球】 the earth; the globe ～仪 (terrestrial) globe 【地区】 area; district; region/prefecture 【地势】 relief; terrain; topography 【地毯】 carpet; rug 【地图】 map 【地位】 position; place; status 【地下】 underground / secret (activity) ～室 basement; cellar ～铁道 underground (railway); tube; subway 【地形】 topography; terrain ～图 topographic map 【地狱】 hell; inferno 【地域】 region; district 【地震】 earthquake; seism 【地址】 address 【地质】 geology 【地主】 landlord/host ～阶级 the landlord class 【地租】 land rent

弟 dì　younger brother 【弟妇】 younger brother's wife; sister-in-law 【弟兄】 brothers 【弟子】 disciple; pupil

的 dì　target; bull's-eye

帝 dì　①emperor ②imperialism 【帝国】 empire ～主义 imperialis〔m〕 【帝王】 monarch 【帝制】 monarchy

递 dì　①hand over; pass; give 请把铲子～给我 please pass me the spade 请把报纸～给我 please reach me the newspaper ～眼色 wink at sb. ②successively; in the proper order ～升 promote to the next rank 【递加】 progressively increase 【递减】 decrease progressively 【递交】 hand over; present; submit 【递送】 send; deliver

第 dì 【第二性】 secondary 【第三者】 a third party (to a dispute, etc.) 【第五纵队】 fifth column 【第一】 first; primary; foremost ～书记 the first secretary 得名 win first place ～把手 first in command ～手 firsthand ～线 forefront; first line 【第一性】 primary

缔 dì form (a friendship); conclude (a treaty) 【缔交】establish diplomatic relations/contract a friendship 【缔造】found; create ～者 founder

DIAN

掂 diān weigh (in the hand) 【掂量】weigh in the hand / think over; weigh up

颠 diān ①crown (of the head) ②top; summit 山～ mountain top ③jolt; bump 卡车～得厉害 the truck jolted badly ④fall; turn over; topple down 【颠簸】jolt; bump; toss 船～起来 the boat was tossed about (by the waves) 【颠倒】turn upside down; reverse; invert/confused; disordered 别放～了 don't put it upside down 把这两个字～过来 transpose these two words 神魂～ infatuated ～黑白 (confuse right and wrong) ～是非 confuse truth and falsehood 【颠覆】overturn; subvert 【颠沛流离】drift from place to place 【颠三倒四】incoherent; disorderly; confused

巅 diān mountain peak; summit 泰山之～ the summit of Taishan Mountain

典 diān ①standard; law; canon ②standard work of scholarship ③allusion; literary quotation 用～ use allusions 【典当】pawn 【典范】model; example 【典故】allusion 【典礼】celebration 【典型】typical case; model; type/typical; representative 抓～ grasp typical cases ～性 typicalness; representativeness ～事例(人物) a typical instance (character) 【典雅】refined; elegant 【典章】institutions

点 diǎn ①drop (of liquid) 雨～ raindrops ②spot 圆～ dot 墨～ ink spots ③point 基准～ datum point ④ a bit 给我～纸 give me some paper ⑤aspect; feature 特～ characteristic feature ⑥touch; skim ～了这件事 touch on the matter ⑦drip ～眼药 put drops in the eyes ⑧check one by one ～货 check over goods ⑨select; choose ～菜 order dishes (in a restaurant) ⑩hint ～明 put one's finger on; point out ⑪light; burn; kindle ～灯 light a lamp ⑫o'clock 九～ nine o'clock 几～了 what time is it ⑬appointed time 误～ behind time 【点火】light a fire/ignition 【点名】call the roll/mention or criticize sb. by name ～册 roll book; roll 【点破】lay bare; point out bluntly 【点燃】light; kindle; ignite 【点收】check and accept 【点数】check the number; count 【点题】bring out the theme 【点头】nod one's head; nod 【点心】light refreshments; pastry 【点缀】embellish; ornament; adorn/use sth. merely for show 【点子】drop (of liquid)/spot; dot; speck/key point; essentials; right spot / idea; pointer

碘 diǎn iodine 【碘酊】tincture of iodine 【碘仿】iodoform 【碘酒】tincture of iodine

踮 diǎn stand on tiptoe ～着脚走 tiptoe; tip

电 diàn ①electricity ②give or get an electric shock ～了我一下 I got a shock ③telegram; cable ～复 reply by telegram ～贺 cable a message of congratulations 【电报】telegram; cable ～机 telegraph 【电表】meter (for measuring electricity) /electric meter 【电冰箱】electric refrigerator; fridge 【电唱机】electric gramophone; record player 【电车】tram/trolley 【电池】(electric) cell; battery 【电灯】electric lamp ～泡 electric bulb 【电动】electric 【电工】electrical engineering /electrician 【电光】lightning 【电焊】electric welding 【电化教育】education with electrical audio-visual aids 【电话】telephone; phone/phone call ～簿 telephone book ～机 telephone ～局 telephone office 别把～挂上 hold the line 打～ phone sb.; ring sb. up; give sb. a ring 您的～ there's a phone call for you; you're wanted on the phone ～断了 the line is dead 【电机】 electrical machinery ～厂 electrical machinery plant 【电缆】 cable 【电熨铁】 electric iron 【电力】 (electric) power 【电料】 electrical materials and appliances 【电铃】 electric bell 【电流】 electric current 【电炉】 electric stove 【电码】 code ～本 code book 【电门】 switch 【电钮】 (push) button 【电气】 electric ～化 electrification 【电器】 electrical equipment 【电扇】 electric fan 【电视】 television; TV 看～ watch television ～大学 television university ～台 television station ～影片 telefilm 【电台】 transceiver/broadcasting station 【电烫】 permanent hair styling; perm 【电梯】 elevator; lift ～司机 lift operator 【电筒】 (electric) torch; flashlight 【电文】 text (of a telegram) 【电线】 (electric) wire ～杆子 (wire) pole 【电信】 telecommunications ～局 telecommunication bureau 【电讯】 dispatch/telecommunications 【电影】 film; movie ～放映机 (film) projector ～剧本 scenario ～演员 film actor or actress ～院 cinema; movie (house) 【电源】 power supply 【电灶】 electric cooking stove 【电子】 electron ～管 valve ～计算机 electronic computer

佃 diàn rent land；【佃户】 tenant (farmer) 【佃农】 tenant-peasant; tenant farmer

店 diàn ①shop; store 书～ bookshop ②inn 住～ stop at an inn 【店员】 shop assistant; salesclerk; clerk

玷 diàn ①a flaw in a piece of jade ②blemish; disgrace 【玷辱】 bring disgrace on 【玷污】 stain; sully

垫 diàn ①fill up; pad ～平 level up ～路 repair a road by filling the holes ②pad; cushion; mat 椅～ chair cushion 【垫肩】 shoulder pad 【垫款】 money advanced for sb. to be paid back later 【垫上运动】 mat tumbling

DIE

爹 dié　father; dad; daddy; pa

跌 dié　①fall; tumble ～伤 fall down and injure oneself ②drop 物价下～ prices have dropped 【跌价】 go down in price【跌交】 trip and fall/make a mistake; meet with a setback

迭 dié　①alternate; change ②repeatedly 【迭次】 repeatedly; again and again 【迭起】 occur repeatedly

谍 dié　①espionage ②intelligence agent; spy 【谍报】 intelligence report

喋 dié　【喋喋不休】 chatter away; rattle on; talk endlessly 【喋血】 bloodshed; bloodbath

牒 dié　an official document or note; certificate 最后通～ ultimatum

叠 dié　①pile up; repeat ②fold ～被子 fold up a quilt ～信 fold the letter 【叠罗汉】 pyramid

碟 dié　small plate; small dish 一～炒卷心菜 a dish of fried cabbage

蝶 dié　butterfly 【蝶泳】 butterfly stroke

DING

丁 dīng　①man 成～ reach manhood 添～ have a baby born into the family ②fourth ～等 the fourth grade; grade D 【丁香】 lilac/clove

叮 dīng　①sting; bite 叫蚊子～了一下 get a mosquito bite ②say or ask again to make sure 【叮嘱】 warn; exhort

盯 dīng　fix one's eyes on; gaze at; stare at 【盯梢】 shadow sb.; tail sb.

钉 dīng ①nail; tack ②follow closely; tail ③urge; press 【钉锤】nail hammer 【钉耙】rake 【钉梢】shadow sb.; tail sb. 【钉鞋】spiked shoes; spikes 【钉子】nail/snag

顶 dǐng ①the crown of the head ②top 山～ hilltop 屋～ roof ③carry on the head ～着一罐水 carry a pitcher of water on one's head ④retort; turn down ～了他几句 say a few words to him in retort ⑤take the place of ～别人的名字 assume sb. else's name ⑥very; most; extremely 【顶端】top; peak 【顶风】against the wind/head wind 【顶峰】summit; pinnacle 【顶棚】ceiling 【顶事】be useful 【顶替】take sb.'s place; replace 【顶用】be of use; serve the purpose 不～ can't be of help 【顶针】thimble 【顶住】stand up to ～压力 withstand pressure ～风浪 weather a storm 【顶撞】contradict (one's elder or superior) 【顶嘴】reply defiantly; answer back

订 dìng ①conclude; draw up; agree on ～条约 conclude a treaty ～合同 enter into a contract ～计划 work out a plan ～日期 fix a date ～指标 set a target ②subscribe to (a newspaper, etc.); book (seats, tickets, etc.); order (merchandise, etc.) ③make corrections; revise ④staple together 【订单】order for goods 【订费】subscription (rate) 【订购】order (goods); place an order for sth. 欢迎～ orders are welcome 【订婚】be engaged (to be married); be betrothed 【订货】order goods 【订书机】stapler; stapling-machine

钉 dìng ①nail ～钉子 drive in a nail ②sew on ～扣子 sew a button on

定 dìng ①calm; stable; quiet 心神不～ feel restless ②decide; fix; set ～方针 decide on a policy ③fixed; settled; established ～评 accepted opinion 【定案】decide on a verdict/verdict; final decision 【定本】definitive edition 【定额】 quota; norm 【定稿】 finalize a manuscript, text, etc./final version or text 【定冠词】 definite article 【定计】 work out a scheme 【定价】 fix a price/fixed price 【定见】 set view 【定居】 settle down 【定局】 inevitable outcome 【定理】 theorem 【定量】 fixed quantity; ration/ determine the amounts of the components of a substance ～供应 rationing 【定律】 law 【定论】 final conclusion 【定期】 fix a date/regular ～刊物 periodical (publication) ～存款 fixed deposit; time deposit 【定钱】 deposit; earnest (money) 【定神】 collect oneself; compose oneself; pull oneself together/concentrate one's attention 【定时炸弹】 time bomb 【定向】 directional 【定型】 finalize the design; fall into a pattern 【定义】 definition 【定影】 fixing 【定语】 attribute ～从句 attributive clause 【定罪】 declare sb. guilty; convict sb. (of a crime) 【定做】 have sth. made to order

● DIU

丢 diū ①lose; mislay ～了本书 mislay a book ②throw; cast; toss 把火柴～给我 throw me the matches ③put aside ～在脑后 clean forget; completely ignore 【丢掉】 lose/throw away; cast away; discard 【丢脸】 lose face; be disgraced 【丢弃】 abandon; discard; give up 【丢三落四】 forgetful; scatterbrained 【丢手】 wash one's hands of; give up 【丢眼色】 wink at sb.; tip sb. the wink

DONG

东 dōng ①east 城～ east of the city ～风 east wind ～郊 eastern suburbs ②master; owner 房～ landlord ③host 做～ stand treat; stand host 【东奔西跑】 bustle about; rush about 【东道】 host 做～ play the host; stand treat 【东拉西扯】talk at random; ramble 【东鳞西爪】odds and ends; fragments 【东拼西凑】scrape together 【东西】thing 【东张西望】gaze around

冬 dōng 【冬耕】winter ploughing 【冬菇】dried mushrooms (picked in winter) 【冬瓜】wax gourd; white gourd 【冬眠】winter sleep 【冬笋】winter bamboo shoots 【冬衣】winter clothes

董 dǒng direct; superintend; supervise 【董事】director; trustee ～会 board of trustees or directors ～长 chairman of the board

懂 dǒng understand; know ～英语 know English 【懂得】know; grasp 【懂行】know the business; know the ropes 【懂事】sensible; intelligent

动 dòng ①move; stir ～了嘴唇 stir one's lips ②act 群众普遍地～起来了 the masses all got moving ③change; alter ～一两个字 change one or two words ④use ～脑筋 use one's head ⑤touch (one's heart); arouse ～感情 be carried away by emotion 【动笔】take up the pen; start writing 【动不动】easily; frequently 【动产】movables; personal property 【动词】verb ～不定式 infinitive 【动荡】turbulence; upheaval; unrest 【动工】start building 【动画片】animated drawing; cartoon 【动机】motive; intention ～不纯 have impure motives 【动静】the sound of sth. astir / movement; activity 【动力】motive power; power/motive force; impetus 【动乱】upheaval; turmoil; disturbance 【动脉】artery 【动名词】gerund 【动怒】lose one's temper; flare up 【动气】take offence; get angry 【动情】become excited / become enamoured; have one's (sexual) passions aroused 【动人】moving; touching 【动身】set out on a journey; leave (for a distant place) 【动手】start work; get to work / touch; ·handle / raise a hand to strike; hit out 【动手术】perform or have an operation 【动态】trends; developments 【动听】interesting or pleasant to listen to 【动武】use force; start a fight 【动物】animal ～园 zoo 【动向】trend; tendency 【动心】one's mind is perturbed; one's desire, enthusiasm or interest is aroused 【动刑】torture 【动摇】shake; vacillate; waver ～分子 wavering element 【动用】put to use; employ; draw on 【动议】motion 【动员】mobilize; arouse ～报告 mobilization speech ～大会 mobilization meeting 【动作】movement; motion; action/act; start moving

冻 dòng ①freeze ～肉 frozen meat ～坏 be damaged by frost ②jelly 肉～ jellied meat ③feel very cold; freeze 别～着了 don't catch cold 【冻冰】freeze 【冻疮】chilblain 【冻豆腐】frozen bean curd 【冻僵】frozen stiff; numb with cold 【冻结】freeze; congeal/(of wages, prices, etc.) freeze 【冻伤】frostbite 【冻死】freeze to death; die of frost 【冻土】frozen soil

洞 dòng ①hole; cavity 山～ mountain cave ②penetratingly; thoroughly ～悉 know clearly; understand thoroughly 【洞察】see clearly; have an insight into ～力 insight; discernment; acumen 【洞房】bridal chamber

恫 dòng fear 【恫吓】threaten; intimidate 虚声～ bluff; bluster

栋 dòng ridgepole 【栋梁】ridgepole and beam—pillar of the state

DOU

都 dōu ①all ②even ③already

兜 dōu ①pocket; bag ②wrap up in a piece of cloth, etc. ③move round 【兜风】catch the wind / go for a drive, ride or sail; go for a spin 【兜揽】 canvass; solicit (custom) /take upon oneself (sb. else's work, etc.) 【兜圈子】 go around in circles; circle/beat about the bush 【兜售】 peddle; hawk

斗蓬 dǒu ①dou, a unit of dry measure for grain (= 1 decalitre) ②a dou measure 【斗笠】 bamboo hat 【斗蓬】 cape; cloak

抖 dǒu ①tremble; shiver; quiver ②shake; jerk ~~~绳 give the reins a jerk ③stir up 【抖动】 shake; vibrate 【抖擞】 enliven; rouse ~精神 brace up; pull oneself together 精神~ full of energy 【抖威风】 throw one's weight about

陡 dǒu ①steep; precipitous ②suddenly; abruptly 【陡度】 gradient 【陡立】 rise steeply 【陡峭】 precipitous 【陡然】 suddenly

斗 dǒu ①fight; tussle ②denounce ~地主 struggle against the landlords ③contest with; contend with ④make animals fight (as a game) ⑤fit together ~榫 fit the tenon into the mortise; dovetail 【斗争】 struggle; fight; combat / accuse and denounce at a meeting / strive for; fight for ~会 public accusation meeting ~性 fighting spirit; militancy 【斗志】 will to fight; fighting will ~昂扬 have high morale 【斗智】 battle of wits

豆 dòu legumes; pulses; beans; peas 【豆包】 steamed bun stuffed with sweetened bean paste 【豆饼】 bean cake 【豆腐】 bean curd ~房 bean-curd plant ~干 dried bean curd ~皮 skin of soya-bean milk/ thin sheets of bean curd ~乳 fermented bean curd 【豆浆】 soya-bean milk 【豆角】 fresh kidney beans 【豆蓉】 fine bean mash 【豆沙】 sweetened bean paste 【豆芽】 bean sprouts 【豆油】 soya-bean oil 【豆制品】 bean products

逗 dòu ①tease; play with ～孩子玩 play with a child ②provoke (laughter, etc.); amuse ③funny 这话真～ what a funny remark 【逗号】comma 【逗留】stay; stop 【逗弄】tease; kid; make fun of

痘 dòu ①smallpox ②smallpox pustule 【痘苗】(bovine) vaccine

DU

都 dū ①capital ②big city; metropolis 【都】capital 【都市】city; metropolis

督 dū superintend and direct ～战 supervise operations 【督察】superintend; supervise 【督促】supervise and urge

嘟 dū ①toot; honk ②pout 【嘟噜】bunch; cluster / trill 【嘟囔】mutter to oneself; mumble

毒 dú ①poison; toxin 服～ take poison ②narcotics 贩～ traffic in drugs ③noxious ～汁 venom ～箭 a poisoned arrow ④poison ～死 kill with poison ⑤malicious; cruel; fierce 太阳正～ the sun was at its fiercest ～打 beat up 【毒害】poison (sb.'s mind) 【毒化】poison; spoil 【毒计】venomous scheme; deadly trap 【毒剂】toxic; toxicant 【毒辣】sinister; diabolic 【毒瘤】malignant tumour; cancer 【毒品】narcotic drugs; narcotics 【毒气】poisonous gas; poison gas ～弹 gas shell 【毒蛇】poisonous snake; viper 【毒手】murderous scheme 下～ resort to violent treachery 【毒刑】horrible torture 【毒性】toxicity 【毒药】poison; toxicant

独 dú ①only; single ～子 only son ②alone; by oneself; in solitude ～居 live a solitary existence ～坐 sit alone 【独霸】monopolize ～一方 be a local despot 【独白】monologue 【独裁】dictatorship; autocratic rule ～者 autocrat; dictator 【独唱】 (vocal) solo ～会 recital (of a vocalist) 【独出心裁】 show originality 【独创】 original creation 【独断】 arbitrary; dictatorial ～独行 act arbitrarily 【独力】 by one's own efforts 【独立】 stand alone/independence/independent; on one's own ～成分 independent element ～国 independent state ～王国 independent kingdom ～性 independence ～自主 maintain independence and keep the initiative in one's own hands 【独特】 unique; distinctive 【独舞】 solo dance 【独一无二】 unique; unparalleled; unmatched 【独占】 have sth. all to oneself; monopolize 【独自】 alone; by oneself 【独奏】 (instrumental) solo ～会 recital (of an instrumentalist)

读 dú read; read aloud 【读本】 reader; textbook 【读书】 read; study / attend school ～班 study class ～笔记 reading notes 【读物】 reading matter 【读音】 pronunciation 【读者】 reader

渎 dú ①show disrespect or contempt ②ditch; drain 【渎职】 malfeasance; dereliction of duty

犊 dú calf

牍 dú documents; archives; correspondence

黩 dú ①blacken; defile ②act wantonly 【黩武】 militaristic; warlike; bellicose ～主义 militarism

肚 dǔ tripe

堵 dǔ ①stop up; block up ～洞 stop up a hole 别～门 don't stand in the doorway ②stifled; suffocated; oppressed 【堵击】 intercept and attack 【堵塞】 stop up; block up 交通～ traffic jam ～漏洞 plug a hole 【堵嘴】 gag sb.; silence sb.

赌 dǔ ①gamble 禁~ ban gambling ②bet 打~ make a bet 【赌本】money to gamble with 【赌博】gambling 【赌场】gambling house 【赌棍】hardened gambler 【赌具】gambling device 【赌窟】gambling-den 【赌气】feel wronged and act rashly 他--就走了 he went off in a fit of pique 【赌徒】gambler 【赌咒】take an oath; swear 【赌注】stake

睹 dǔ see 目~ see with one's own eyes; be an eye-witness to

杜 dù ①birch-leaf pear ②shut out; stop; prevent 【杜鹃】cuckoo / azalea 【杜绝】stop (corrupt practices); put an end to (waste, etc.) 【杜撰】fabricate; make up

肚 dù belly; abdomen; stomach 【肚脐】navel; belly button 【肚子】belly ~痛 suffer from abdominal pain --~气 full of pent-up anger

妒 dù be jealous of; envy 【妒忌】be envious of

度 dù ① linear measure ②degree of intensity 硬~ hardness ③degree 九十~角 an angle of 90 degrees 摄氏一百~ 100 degrees centigrade ④time 再~ a second time 一年--~ once a year ⑤spend; pass ~假 spend one's holidays ~荒 tide over a lean year ⑥kilowatt-hour 【度量】tolerance; magnanimity 【度量衡】length, capacity and weight; weights and measures 【度日】subsist (in hardship); eke out an existence ~如年 days wear on like years 【度数】number of degrees; reading 那个表上的~是多少 what does that meter read

渡 dù ①cross (a river, the sea, etc.) ②tide over (a difficulty, etc.); pull through (people, goods, etc.) across 【渡场】crossing site 【渡船】ferryboat 【渡口】ferry

镀 dù plating 【镀金】gold-plating; gilding / get gilded 【镀锡】tin-plating 【镀银】silver-plating

蠹 dù ①moth ②moth-eaten; worm-eaten 【蠹虫】moth/a harmful person; vermin 【蠹鱼】silverfish; fish moth

DUAN

端 duān ①end; extremity 两~ both ends ②beginning ③point; item 举其一~ for instance ④reason; cause 无~ without reason ⑤upright; proper ~坐 sit up straight ⑥carry ~盘子 carry a tray 【端详】details/dignified and serene/look sb. up and down 【端正】upright; regular/ proper; correct/rectify 【端庄】dignified; sedate

短 duǎn ①short; brief ②lack; owe 理~ lack sound argument ~斤缺两 give short measure ③weak point; fault 【短波】shortwave 【短处】shortcoming; failing; weakness 【短促】very brief 【短见】shortsighted view/suicide 寻~ commit suicide 【短距离】short distance 【短裤】shorts 【短命】die young 【短跑】dash; sprint 【短篇小说】short story 【短片】short (film) 【短评】brief comment 【短期】short-term 【短浅】narrow and shallow 目光~ shortsighted 【短枪】short arm; handgun 【短缺】shortage 【短少】deficient; short; missing 【短统靴】ankle boots 【短途】short distance 【短线产品】goods in short supply 【短小】short 身材~ of small stature ~精悍 not of imposing stature but strong and capable/short and pithy; terse and forceful 【短训班】short-term training course 【短语】phrase 【短元音】short vowel 【短暂】of short duration; transient

段 duàn ①section; segment; part 一~衣料 a length of dress material ②passage/paragraph/phase; stage

断 duàn ①break; snap ~成两截 break in two ②break off; stop ~水 cut off the water supply ③give up; abstain from ~烟 quit smoking ④judge; decide 当机立~

make a prompt decision ⑥absolutely; decidedly ～不可信 absolutely incredible 【断定】conclude; judge; decide; determine 【断断续续】off and on; intermittently 【断根】be completely cured 【断交】break off a friendship/sever diplomatic relations 【断绝】break off; cut off; sever ～交通 stop traffic 【断奶】weaning 【断气】breathe one's last; die/cut off the gas 【断然】absolutely; flatly/resolute ～拒绝 flatly refuse ～否认 categorically deny 采取～措施 take drastic measures 【断送】forfeit (one's life, future, etc.); ruin 【断言】state with certainty; affirm 【断语】conclusion; judgment 【断章取义】quote out of context; garble a statement, etc.

缎 duàn　satin ～纹 satin weave

锻 duàn　forge 【锻工】forging / forger; blacksmith 【锻炼】take exercise; have physical training / temper (oneself); steel ～身体 build up a good physique

DUI

堆 duī　①pile up; heap up; stack ～满了书 be piled with books ②heap; pile; crowd 粪～ dung heap 一～人 a crowd of people 【堆砌】load one's writing with fancy phrases/pile up (hewn rocks, etc. to build sth.) 【堆栈】storehouse

队 duì　①a row of people; line ②team; group 篮球～ basketball team 【队部】the office or headquarters of a team 【队列】formation 【队旗】team pennant 【队伍】troops/ranks; contingent 【队形】formation 【队员】team member 【队长】captain/team leader

对 duì　①answer; reply 无言以～ have nothing to say in reply ②treat; cope with; counter ～事不～人 concern oneself with facts and not with individuals ③be trained on; be directed at ④mutual; face to face ～坐 sit facing each other ⑤ opposing ～岸 the opposite bank ⑥bring (two things) into contact; fit one into the other ～暗号 exchange code words ⑦suit; agree; get along ～胃口 suit one's taste ⑧compare check ～笔迹 identify the handwriting ～号码 check numbers ⑨set; adjust ～表 set one's watch ⑩right; correct　猜～了 guess right ⑪mix; add ～点儿水 add some water ⑫couplet　喜～ wedding couplet ⑬pair; couple　一～夫妇 a married couple 【对白】dialogue 【对比】contrast; balance 【对不起】sorry; excuse me; pardon me/let sb. down; be unworthy of; be unfair to 【对策】countermeasure; countermove 【对称】symmetry 【对待】treat; approach; handle/not let sb. down; treat sb. fairly; be worthy of 【对等】reciprocity; equity 【对方】the opposite side; the other party 【对付】deal with; cope with; counter; tackle/make do (with sth.) 【对号】check the number/fit; tally/tick ～入座 sit in the right seat 【对话】dialogue 【对劲儿】be to one's liking; suit one/normal; right 【对抗】antagonism; confrontation/resist; oppose ～赛 dual meet ～性 antagonism 【对立】oppose; set sth. against; be antagonistic to ～物 opposite; antithesis ～情绪 antagonism ～统一 unity of opposites 【对联】antithetical couplet (written on scrolls, etc.) 【对路】satisfy the need / be to one's liking; suit one 【对门】(of two houses) face each other / the building or room opposite 【对面】opposite / right in front / face to face 【对内】internal; domestic; at home ～政策 domestic policy 【对手】adversary / match; equal 【对台戏】rival show　唱～ put on a rival show 【对头】correct; right　你这样做不～ it doesn't befit you to do so 【对外】external; for-

eign ～政策 external policy ～贸易 foreign trade【对虾】
prawn【对象】target; object / boy or girl friend　找～
look for a partner in marriage【对应】corresponding【对
照】contrast; compare【对证】verify; check【对症下药】
suit the remedy to the case【对质】confrontation (in
court)【对峙】stand facing each other; confront each
other【对准】aim at

兑　duì ①exchange ②add (water, etc.)【兑换】exchange;
convert ～率 rate of exchange【兑现】cash (a cheque,
etc.) /honour (a commitment, etc.); fulfil 说话不～ not
live up to one's promise

DUN

吨　dūn　ton【吨位】tonnage

敦　dūn　honest; sincere ～请 cordially invite【敦促】
urge; press【敦睦】promote friendly relations

墩　dūn　①mound ② a block of stone or wood 树～ stump
桥～ pier (of a bridge)【墩布】mop; swab

蹲　dūn　①squat (on the heels) ②stay【蹲点】stay (at
a selected grass-roots unit)

盹　dǔn　doze 打～儿 doze off

囤　dùn　a grain bin

炖　dùn　①stew ～鸡 stewed chicken ②warm sth. by
putting the container in hot water ～酒 warm wine

盾　dùn　shield【盾牌】shield/pretext; excuse

钝　dùn　①blunt; dull ～刀 blunt knife ②stupid; dull-
witted【钝角】obtuse angle

顿 dùn ①pause ～了一下 after a short pause; come to a pause ②arrange; settle ③stamp (one's foot) ④ suddenly; immediately

遁 dùn escape; flee; fly 【遁词】subterfuge; quibble

DUO

多 duō ①many; much; more 相当～ a good many 害～益少 do more harm than good ②too many ～了个字 there is one word too many ③excessive; too much～疑 oversensitive; oversuspicious ④more; over; odd 两个～月 more than two months 六十～岁 over sixty years old ⑤much more; far more 病人今天好～了 the patient is much better today 【多半】the greater part; most / probably; most likely 【多变】changeable; varied 【多才多艺】versatile; gifted in many ways 【多次】many times; time and again 【多多益善】the more the better 【多方】in every way 【多方面】in many ways 【多亏】thanks to; luckily 【多么】how; what 【多面手】a versatile person 【多幕剧】a full-length drama 【多情】full of tenderness or affection (for a person of the opposite sex) 【多少】number; amount / somewhat; more or less; to some extent 【多少】how many; how much 这一班有～学生 how many pupils are there in this class 【多时】a long time 【多事】meddlesome/eventful ～之秋 an eventful period or year; troubled times 【多数】majority; most ～票 majority vote 【多谢】many thanks; thanks a lot 【多心】oversensitive; suspicious 【多样化】diversify; make varied 【多义词】polysemant 【多余】unnecessary; surplus; superfluous 【多种】varied; manifold ～经营 diversified undertakings 【多嘴】speak out of turn ～多舌 long-tongued

咄 duō　tut-tut 【咄咄逼人】overbearing; aggressive 【咄咄怪事】monstrous absurdity

哆 duō　【哆嗦】tremble; shiver 气得直～ tremble with rage 冷得打～ shiver with cold

夺 duó　①take by force; seize; wrest ～下刀子 wrest a knife ②force one's way ～门而出 force open the door and rush out ③contend for; compete for ～高产 strive for high yields ～得冠军 carry off the first prize ④deprive 【夺回】recapture; retake; seize back ～一局 win a game (after losing one or more) ～失去的时间 make up for lost time 【夺目】dazzle the eyes 【夺取】capture; seize; wrest / strive for ～主动权 seize the initiative ～政权 seize state power ～新胜利 strive for new victories 【夺权】seize power; take over power

踱 duó　pace; stroll ～来～去 pace to and fro ～方步 walk with measured tread

朵 duǒ　一～花 a flower 一～云 a cloud

垛 duǒ　①buttress ②battlements (on a city wall) 【垛口】crenel

躲 duǒ　①hide (oneself) ②avoid; dodge ～雨 take shelter from the rain 【躲避】hide (oneself) /elude; dodge 【躲藏】conceal oneself; go into hiding 【躲懒】shy away from work; shirk 【躲闪】dodge; evade 躲躲闪闪 be evasive; hedge; equivocate

剁 duò　chop; cut 把棍子～成两段 chop a stick into two pieces ～肉馅 chop up meat; mince meat

垛 duò　①pile up (logs, etc.) ②pile; stack 柴火～ a pile of faggots 麦～ a stack of wheat

舵 duò　rudder; helm 【舵轮】steering wheel 【舵手】steersman; helmsman

堕 duò fall; sink ～地 fall on the ground 【堕落】degenerate; sink low 【堕入】lapse into; land oneself in; fall into; sink into 【堕胎】induced abortion/have an (induced) abortion

惰 duò lazy; indolent 【惰性】inertia ～气体 inert gas ～元素 inert element

跺 duò stamp (one's foot) 气得直～脚 stamp one's foot with fury

E

E

阿 ē play up to; pander to 【阿谀】fawn on; flatter

讹 é ①erroneous; mistaken ②extort; blackmail ～人 bluff sb. 【讹传】false rumour 【讹误】error (in a text) 【讹诈】extort under false pretences; blackmail

俄 é very soon; presently; suddenly 【俄语】Russian (language)

鹅 é goose 【鹅黄】light yellow 【鹅卵石】cobble 【鹅毛】goose feather

蛾 é moth

额 é ①forehead ②a horizontal tablet ③a specified number or amount 贸易～ volume of trade 【额定】specified (number or amount); rated ～的人数 the maximum number of persons allowed 【额角】frontal eminence 【额外】extra; additional; added ～开支 extra expenses ～收入 additional income ～负担 added burden

恶 ě 【恶心】feel like vomiting; feel sick/nauseating; disgusting

厄 è ①strategic point ②adversity; disaster; hardship ③ be in distress; be stranded 【厄运】misfortune

扼 è ①clutch; grip ～住咽喉 clutch at sb.'s throat ② guard; control 【扼杀】strangle; smother; throttle 【扼守】hold (a strategic point); guard 【扼要】to the point 请～说明 please explain the main points briefly

恶 è ①evil; vice; wickedness ②fierce; ferocious ～战 a fierce battle ～狗 vicious dog; cur ③bad; wicked ～行 evil conduct ～势力 evil force 【恶霸】local tyrant; local despot 【恶报】retribution for evildoing; judgment 【恶臭】foul smell; stench 【恶毒】malicious; venomous ～攻击 viciously attack 【恶感】ill feeling; malice 并无 ～ bear no malice 【恶棍】ruffian; scoundrel 【恶果】evil consequence 【恶化】worsen; deteriorate 【恶劣】odious; abominable; disgusting 【恶魔】demon; devil; evil spirit 【恶人】evil person; villain 【恶习】bad habit 【恶性】pernicious ～通货膨胀 galloping inflation ～循环 vicious circle ～肿瘤 malignant tumour 【恶意】evil intentions; ill will; malice 【恶兆】ill omen 【恶浊】foul; filthy 【恶作剧】practical joke; mischief

饿 è ①hungry 挨～ go hungry ②starve 【饿殍】bodies of the starved

愕 è stunned 【愕然】astounded ～四顾 look around in astonishment 消息传来，大家为之～ everyone was stunned by the news

遏 è check; hold back 【遏制】keep within limits; contain ～愤怒 check one's anger

腭 è palate 硬～ hard palate 软～ soft palate

颚 è ①jaw 上～ upper jaw 下～ lower jaw ②palate

噩 è shocking; upsetting 【噩耗】 sad news of the death of one's beloved 【噩梦】 frightening dream; nightmare

鳄 è crocodile; alligator

EN

恩 ēn kindness; grace 【恩爱】 conjugal love ～夫妻 an affectionate couple 【恩赐】 bestow (favours, charity, etc.)/favour; charity 【恩惠】 favour; bounty 【恩情】 loving-kindness 【恩人】 benefactor 【恩怨】 feeling of gratitude or resentment/grievance; old scores

摁 èn press (with the hand or finger) ～电铃 ring an electric bell ～电钮 push a button 【摁钉】 drawing pin; thumbtack 【摁扣】 snap fastener

ER

儿 ér ①child ②youngster; youth ③son ④male 【儿歌】 children's song; nursery rhymes 【儿科】 (department of) paediatrics 【儿女】 sons and daughters; children/young man and woman (in love) ～情长 be immersed in love 【儿孙】 descendants; posterity 【儿童】 children ～读物 children's books ～节 (International) Children's Day (June 1) ～文学 children's literature ～医院 children's hospital 【儿媳妇】 daughter-in-law 【儿戏】 trifling matter

而 ér ①and 战～胜之 fight and defeat the enemy ② but 有其名～无其实 in name but not in reality ③ from 由南～北 from south to north 自远～近 approach from a distance 【而后】 after that; then 【而今】 now; at the present time 【而且】 and / but 【而已】 that is all; nothing more

尔 ěr ①you ②like that; so 果～ if so 【尔虞我诈】each trying to cheat or outwit the other

耳 ěr ①ear ②side ～房 side rooms ～门 side doors 【耳边风】unheeded advice 当作～ turn a deaf ear to sth. 【耳朵】ear ～尖 have sharp ears ～软 credulous; easily influenced 【耳光】a box on the ear 打～ slap sb.'s face 【耳环】earrings 【耳机】earphone 【耳闻】knowledge; information / one who spies for sb. else ～闭塞 ill-informed ～众多 eyes and ears everywhere ～一新 find everything fresh and new 【耳塞】earplug 【耳闻】hear of ～不如目见 seeing for oneself is better than hearing from others ～目睹 what one sees and hears 【耳语】whisper (in sb.'s ear) 【耳坠子】eardrop

二 èr ①two ～～得四 twice two is four ～路公共汽车 No. 2 bus ～嫂 wife of one's second elder brother; sister-in-law ②different ～心 disloyalty; half-heartedness 【二部制】two-shift system; two part-time shifts ～学校 two-shift school 【二重性】dual character; duality 【二副】second mate; second officer 【二流子】loafer; idler; bum 【二月】February/the second moon

F

FA

发 fā ①send out; issue; deliver; distribute ～货 deliver goods ～信号 give a signal ～工资 pay out wages ②utter; express ～牢骚 express one's grievances ③discharge; shoot; emit ～光 emit light ④develop; expand ～

育 growth; development ⑤(of foodstuffs) rise or expand when fermented or soaked ～豆芽 raise bean sprouts ⑥come or bring into existence ～电 generate electricity ⑦open up; discover 揭～ expose ⑧get into a certain state; become ～黄 turn yellow 脸色～白 lose colour; become pale ⑨show one's feeling ～怒 get angry ～笑 laugh ⑩feel; have a feeling 嘴里～苦 have a bitter taste in the mouth ～麻 tingle ～痒 itch ⑪start; set out; begin an undertaking 朝～夕至 set off in the morning and arrive in the evening 【发报】 transmit messages (by radio, telegraphy, etc.) ～机 transmitter 【发表】 publish; issue ～文章 publish an article ～声明 issue a statement ～意见 express an opinion ～演说 make a speech 【发病】 (of a disease) come on ～率 incidence of a disease 【发布】 issue; release ～命令 issue orders ～新闻 release news 【发财】 get rich 【发愁】 worry; be anxious 【发出】 issue; give out ～指示 issue a directive ～警告 send out a warning ～警报 sound the alarm 【发达】 developed; flourishing ～国家 developed country 【发呆】 stare blankly; be in a daze 【发动】 start (a machine); launch (a war)/call into action; mobilize; arouse (the masses) ～机 engine; motor 【发抖】 shiver; shake; tremble 【发放】 provide; extend ～贷款 grant credits 【发愤】 make a firm resolution ～图强 work with a will to make the country strong 【发疯】 go mad; go crazy 【发稿】 distribute news dispatches/send manuscripts to the press 【发光】 give out light; shine 【发号施令】 issue orders 【发还】 return sth. (usu. to one's subordinate); give back 把作业～给学生 return the homework to the pupils 【发慌】 feel nervous 【发挥】 bring into play / develop (an idea, a theme, etc.); elaborate

～专长 give full play to sb.'s professional knowledge or skill 【发昏】 feel giddy/lose one's head; become confused 【发火】 catch fire; ignite / detonate / go off/get angry 【发酵】 ferment 【发觉】 find; detect; discover 【发掘】 excavate; unearth; explore ～人才 seek gifted people 【发困】 feel sleepy 【发亮】 shine 【发霉】 go mouldy 【发面】 leaven dough/leavened dough 【发明】 invent/invention 【发胖】 get fat 【发脾气】 lose one's temper 【发票】 bill; receipt 开～ write a receipt 【发起】 initiate; sponsor/start; launch ～国 sponsor nation ～人 initiator; sponsor 【发球】 serve a ball 【发热】 give out heat / have a fever 【发散】 (of rays, etc.) diverge 【发烧】 run a fever; have a temperature 【发射】 launch; project; shoot; fire 【发生】 happen; occur; take place 【发誓】 vow; pledge; swear 【发酸】 turn sour/ache slightly 【发条】 clockwork spring 【发文】 outgoing message; dispatch 【发问】 ask a question 【发现】 find; discover ～线索 find a clue ～问题 discover problems 【发泄】 give vent to; let off ～不满 air one's grievances 【发信】 post a letter ～人 addresser 【发行】 issue; publish; distribute; put on sale ～纸币 issue paper money ～书刊 publish books and magazines 【发芽】 germinate; sprout 【发言】 speak; make a statement or speech 要求～ ask for the floor ～稿 the text of a speech ～权 right to speak; floor ～人 spokesman 【发炎】 inflammation 伤口～了 the wound has become inflamed 【发扬】 develop; carry on / make the most of ～正气 encourage healthy trends ～优良传统 carry forward the fine tradition ～火力 make full use of firepower 【发音】 pronunciation; enunciation ～部位 points of articulation ～器官 vocal organs 这个字怎么～ how do you pronounce this word 这个字母不～ this letter is not pronounced 【发育】 growth;

development ～健全 physically well developed 【发源】
rise; originate ～地 place of origin; source; birthplace
【发展】develop; expand; grow / recruit; admit ～经济
develop the economy ～新党员 recruit new Party members ～中国家 developing country 【发胀】swell 肚子
～ feel bloated 头脑～ have a swelled head 【发作】break
out; show effect/have a fit of anger

乏 fá ①lack 不～其人 there's no lack of such people
②tired; weary 走～了 be tired from a long walk ③
exhausted; worn-out 火～了 the fire's going out 【乏味】
dull; insipid; drab; tasteless

伐 fá ①fell; cut down ②send an expedition against;
strike; attack 【伐木】lumbering; felling; cutting ～
工 lumberman ～业 lumbering

罚 fá punish; penalize ～出场 foul out ～酒 be made
to drink as a forfeit 【罚金】fine; forfeit 【罚款】im-
pose a fine or forfeit/fine; forfeit; penalty 【罚球】penalty
shot; penalty kick

阀 fá ①a powerful person or family 军～ warlord
财～ financial magnate; plutocrat ②valve

筏 fá raft 橡皮～ rubber raft

法 fǎ ①law ②method; way; mode 教～ teaching method
③follow; model after ④standard; model 【法案】pro-
posed law; bill 【法办】deal with according to law; punish
by law 【法宝】a magic weapon 【法场】execution ground
【法典】code; statute book 【法定】legal; statutory ～年龄
lawful age ～期限 legal time limit ～人数 quorum 【法
官】judge; justice 【法规】laws and regulations 【法纪】
law and discipline 【法警】bailiff 【法兰绒】flannel 【法郎】
franc 【法力】supernatural power 【法令】decree 【法律】

law; statute ～根据 legal basis ～顾问 legal adviser ～手续 legal procedure 【法螺】conch 【法权】right 【法术】magic arts 【法庭】court; tribunal 【法网】the net of justice; the arm of the law 【法西斯】fascist 【法学】the science of law 【法医】legal medical expert 【法语】French (language) 【法院】court (of justice); law court 【法则】rule; law 【法治】rule by law 【法制】legal system; legality ～教育 education in legal matters 加强社会主义～ strengthen the socialist legal system 【法子】way; method

砝 fǎ 【砝码】weight (used on a balance)

发 fà hair 【发卡】hairpin 【发刷】hairbrush 【发网】hairnet 【发型】hair style; hairdo; coiffure

珐 fà 【珐琅】enamel

FAN

帆 fān sail 【帆布】canvas ～包 canvas bag; kit bag ～床 cot; campbed ～篷 canvas roof; awning ～鞋 plimsolls 【帆船】sailing boat; junk

番 fān time 三～五次 time and again 产量翻了一～ the output has doubled 【番号】designation (of a military unit) 【番茄】tomato ～酱 tomato ketchup ～汁 tomato juice 【番薯】sweet potato

藩 fān 【藩篱】hedge; fence 【藩属】vassal state

翻 fān ①turn over ～地 turn up the soil ～车 the cart turned over ～饼 turn a cake over 碰～ knock over ②cross; get over ～山 cross over a mountain ～墙 climb over a wall ③rummage; search ～抽屉 rummage the drawers ～参考书 look through reference works

④translate 把英文～成中文 translate the English into Chinese ⑤reverse ⑥multiply ⑦fall out; break up 闹～ quarrel and split up 【翻案】reverse a verdict 【翻版】 reprint; reproduction 【翻覆】overturn; turn upside down 【翻盖】renovate (a house) 【翻跟头】turn a somersault; loop the loop 【翻供】retract one's testimony 【翻滚】roll; toss; tumble 【翻悔】back out (of a commitment, promise, etc.) 【翻来复去】toss and turn/again and again; repeatedly 【翻脸】fall out; suddenly turn hostile 【翻领】turndown collar 【翻身】turn over/free oneself; stand up 【翻腾】seethe; rise; churn/turn sth. over and over; rummage 【翻天覆地】 earth-shaking; world-shaking 【翻新】renovate; recondition; make over ～车胎 retread a tyre 花样～ (the same old thing) in a new guise 【翻修】rebuild ～马路 repair the roads 【翻译】translate; interpret/translator; interpreter ～ 电码 decode; decipher ～本 translation ～片 dubbed film 【翻印】reprint; reproduce 【翻阅】look over; glance over ～报刊 look over newspapers and magazines ～目录 glance through a catalogue

凡 fán ①commonplace; ordinary 非～ extraordinary ②this mortal world 下～ come down to earth ③every; any; all 【凡例】notes on the use of a book 【凡人】ordinary person/mortal 【凡事】everything 【凡是】every; any; all

烦 fán ①be vexed; be irritated; be annoyed 心～ feel vexed ②be tired of 厌～ be fed up with ③superfluous and confusing ④trouble ～交 please forward (to) 【烦闷】 be unhappy; be worried 【烦恼】be vexed 【烦扰】bother/ feel disturbed 【烦琐】overelaborate; tedious; pedantic ～哲学 scholasticism/hairsplitting 【烦躁】be fidgety

蕃 fán ①luxuriant; growing in abundance ～茂 lush ②multiply; proliferate ～衍 increase gradually in number or quantity

繁 fán ①numerous; manifold ②propagate; multiply 【繁多】 various 【繁复】 heavy and complicated 【繁华】 bustling 【繁忙】 busy 工作～ be busily engaged 【繁茂】 lush; luxuriant 【繁密】 dense 【繁难】 hard to tackle; troublesome 【繁荣】 flourishing; prosperous; booming/make sth. prosper ～经济 promote economic prosperity ～昌盛 thriving and prosperous 市场～ the market is brisk 【繁杂】 miscellaneous 【繁殖】 breed; reproduce; propagate ～力 fecundity; fertility ～率 rate of reproduction; breeding rate 【繁重】 heavy; strenuous ～的任务 an onerous task

反 fán ①turn over ～败为胜 turn defeat into victory; turn the tide ②in an opposite direction; in reverse; inside out ～面 the reverse side ～其道而行之 do exactly the opposite ～科学 contrary to science ③on the contrary; instead ④return; counter ～问 ask in retort ～建议 counterproposal ⑤revolt; rebel ⑥oppose; combat ～封建 anti-feudal ～法西斯 anti-fascist ～霸 oppose hegemonism ～帝 anti-imperialist ～间谍 counterespionage 【反比】 inverse ratio 【反驳】 refute; retort 【反常】 unusual; abnormal; strange 【反衬】 set off by contrast 【反动】 reactionary / reaction ～分子 reactionary element; reactionary ～派 reactionaries 【反对】 oppose; be against; fight; combat ～贪污 fight against corruption ～官僚主义 combat bureaucracy ～党 opposition party; the Opposition ～派 opposition faction 【反而】 on the contrary; instead 【反复】 repeatedly; again and again/reversal; relapse ～思考 think a lot about sth. ～辩论 argue back and forth ～强调 repeatedly stress ～无常 changeable; fickle; capricious 【反感】 be disgusted with; be averse to; dislike 【反革命】 counterrevolutionary ～分子 a counterrevolutionary 【反

攻】counteroffensive; counterattack; strike back ～倒算 counterattack to settle old scores; retaliate 【反光】reflect light/reflection of light ～灯 reflector lamp ～镜 reflector 【反话】irony 【反悔】go back on one's word 【反击】strike back; beat back 【反抗】rebel; revolt; resist 【反面】reverse side; wrong side; back/opposite; negative side 【反派】villain (in drama, etc.); negative character 【反叛】revolt; rebel 【反扑】pounce on sb. again after being beaten off 【反射】reflex/reflection 【反响】repercussion; echo; reverberation 【反省】introspection; self-questioning; self-examination 【反宣传】counterpropaganda/slander campaign 【反义词】antonym 【反应】reaction/response; repercussion ～不一 reactions vary 作出～ make a response 【反映】reflect; mirror/report; make known ～论 theory of reflection 【反正】anyway; anyhow; in any case 【反之】on the contrary; otherwise 【反作用】counteraction

返 fǎn return ～校 return to school 一去不～ gone forever; gone never to return 【返潮】get damp 【返工】do poorly done work over again 【返航】return to base or port

犯 fàn ①violate; offend (against law, etc.) ～纪律 violate discipline ②attack; assail; work against ③criminal 战～ war criminal ④have a recurrence of (an old illness); revert to (a bad habit) ～脾气 get angry ⑤commit (a mistake, crime, etc.) 【犯不着】not worthwhile 【犯得着】is it worthwhile 【犯法】break the law 【犯规】break the rules/foul 【犯忌】violate a taboo 【犯禁】violate a ban 【犯人】prisoner; convict 【犯罪】commit a crime ～分子 offender; criminal ～行为 criminal offence

泛 fàn ①float ～舟 go boating ②be suffused with (blushes) ③ flood; inundate ④extensive; general; nonspecific 【泛泛】 general; not deepgoing 【泛滥】 be in flood; overflow; inundate/spread unchecked; run wild 【泛指】 make a general reference; be used in a general sense

饭 fàn ①cooked rice or other cereals ②meal 【饭菜】 meal; repast 【饭店】 hotel / restaurant 【饭锅】 rice cooker 【饭盒】 lunch-box; mess tin 【饭量】 appetite 【饭票】 meal ticket; mess card 【饭食】 food (esp. with regard to its quality) 【饭厅】 dining hall; mess hall 【饭桶】 rice bucket / big eater / fathead; good-for-nothing 【饭碗】 rice bowl/job 【饭桌】 dining table

范 fàn ①example; pattern ②model essay ②limits 就~ submit·【范文】model (for calligraphy or painting) 【范畴】 category 【范围】 scope; limits; range

贩 fàn ①buy to resell ②pedlar; vendor 【贩卖】 traffic; peddle; sell 【贩运】 transport goods for sale 【贩子】 dealer; monger

FANG

方 fāng ①square ～格 check ～桌 square table ②cubic metre (of lumber, earth, stone, etc.) ③direction ④side; party 我～ our side ⑤place; region; locality 远～ remote place ⑥method; way 多～ in various ways ⑦prescription 处~ make out a prescription ⑧just; at the time when 【方案】 scheme; plan 【方便】 convenient ～群众 make things convenient for the people 交通~ have a good transport service 【方才】 just now 【方法】 method; way; means 【方括号】 square brackets 【方面】 respect; aspect; side; field 【方式】 way; fashion; pattern 生活～ mode of life; life-style 斗争～ form of struggle 领导～ style of leadership 【方糖】 cube sugar 【方位】 position; bearing 【方向】 direction; orientation ～盘 steering wheel 【方兴

未艾】be just unfolding 【方言】dialect 【方针】policy; guiding principle 【方子】prescription

芳 fāng ①sweet-smelling; fragrant ～草 fragrant grass ②good (name or reputation); virtuous 【芳香】aromatic

妨 fāng 何～试试 what harm is there in trying 不～同他谈谈 we might as well have a talk with him

防 fáng ①guard against; provide ～病 prevent disease ～特 guard against enemy agents ②defend ～身 defend oneself 【防备】take precautions against 【防弹】shellproof ～玻璃 (背心) bulletproof glass (vest) 【防盗】guard against theft 【防毒】gas defence ～面具 gas mask 【防范】be on guard; keep a lookout 【防腐】antiseptic ～剂 preservative 【防护】protect; shelter ～堤 embankment ～林 shelter-forest 【防火】fire prevention; fireproof 【防空】air defence; antiaircraft ～洞 air-raid shelter 【防线】line of defence 【防疫】epidemic prevention ～针 (prophylactic) inoculation 【防雨布】waterproof cloth 【防御】defence ～部队 defending force ～工事 defences ～战 defensive warfare 【防止】forestall; avoid

坊 fáng workshop; mill 染～ dyer's workshop/ 油～ oil mill

妨 fáng hinder 【妨碍】impede; obstruct ～团结 hinder unity ～生产的发展 hamper the growth of production～工作 hinder one's work ～交通 block traffic 【妨害】impair; jeopardize ～健康 be harmful to one's health

房 fáng ①house ②room 【房产】house property 【房顶】roof 【房东】landlord or landlady 【房间】room 【房客】lodger 【房屋】houses; buildings 【房檐】eaves 【房主】house-owner 【房租】rent (for a house, flat, etc.)

访 fǎng ①visit ～友 call on a friend ②seek by inquiry or search; try to get 【访查】investigate 【访问】visit

仿 fǎng ①imitate; copy ～古 modelled after an antique ②resemble; be like 【仿佛】seem; as if/be more or less the same 【仿效】imitate; follow the example of 【仿制】modelled on ～品 imitation; replica; copy

纺 fǎng ①spin ～羊毛 spin wool ②a thin silk cloth 【纺车】spinning wheel 【纺绸】a soft plain-weave silk fabric 【纺纱】spinning ～工人 spinner ～机 spinning machine 【纺织】spinning and weaving ～厂 textile mill ～工人 textile worker ～品 textile; fabric

舫 fǎng boat 画～ a gaily-painted pleasure-boat

放 fàng ①let go; set free; release ～他走 let him go ～掉俘虏 release the captives 把水～了 let the water out (of sth.) ②let off; give out ～枪 fire a gun ～焰火 set off fireworks ～风筝 fly a kite ③put out to pasture ～牛 pasture cattle ④let oneself go; give way to ～声歌唱 sing heartily ⑤lend (money) for interest ～高利贷 practise usury ⑥let out; expand; make larger, longer, etc. ～裤腰 let the trousers out at the waist ⑦blossom; open 百花齐～ a hundred flowers in bloom ⑧put in; add 多点酱油 put a bit more soy sauce in ⑨put; place 把书～在桌上 put the book on the table ⑩leave alone; lay aside ⑪send away 流～ send into exile ⑫readjust (attitude, behaviour, etc.) to a certain extent ～明白点 be sensible ～慢点 slow down a little ⑬show ～电影 show a film ～电视 turn on the TV 【放出】give out; let out; emit 【放大】enlarge; magnify; amplify ～尺 pantograph ～机 enlarger ～镜 magnifying glass ～照片 enlarged photograph 【放荡】dissolute; dissipated/unconventional 【放过】let off; let slip 【放火】set fire to; set on fire 【放假】have a holiday or vacation; have a day off

你们什么时候放暑假 when is your summer vacation 【放宽】 relax 【放款】 make loans 【放炮】 fire a gun/blowout (of a tyre, etc.)/blasting 【放屁】 break wind; fart 【放弃】 abandon; give up; renounce ～原则 forsake one's principles 【放任】 not interfere; let alone; let things drift/noninterference 【放哨】 stand sentry; be on sentry go 【放射】 radiate ～线 radioactive rays ～性 radioactivity 【放手】 let go; let go one's hold/have a free hand; go all out 【放肆】 unbridled; wanton 【放松】 slacken; loosen 【放下】 lay down; put down 【放心】 set one's mind at rest; be at ease 对他不大～ not quite trust him～不下 feel anxious 这事你～好了 make yourself easy about the matter 【放学】 classes are over 【放映】 show (a film); project ～机 (film) projector 【放置】 lay up; lay aside; lie idle 【放逐】 exile; banish 【放纵】 let sb. have his own way; connive at; indulge/self-indulgent; undisciplined

FEI

飞 fēi ①fly; flit 直～北京 make a nonstop flight to Beijing ②swiftly ～奔 dash ～驰 speed along 【飞船】 airship 【飞弹】 missile / stray bullet 【飞机】 aircraft; aeroplane; plane ～场 airfield; airport 【飞快】 very fast; at lightning speed / extremely sharp 【飞速】 at full speed 【飞腾】 fly swiftly upward; soar 【飞舞】 dance in the air; flutter 【飞翔】 circle in the air; hover 【飞行】 flight; flying ～表演 demonstration flight ～服 flying suit ～帽 aviator's helmet ～员 pilot; aviator; flyer 【飞扬】 fly upward; rise 【飞扬跋扈】 arrogant and domineering 【飞跃】 leap 【飞涨】 (of prices, etc.) soar; shoot up; skyrocket

妃 fēi ①imperial concubine ②the wife of a prince 【妃色】 light pink

非 fēi ①wrong; evildoing 是～ right and wrong 为～作歹 do evil ②not conform to; run counter to ～分 assuming ③not; no 答～所问 give an irrelevant answer ～比寻常 unusual; out of the ordinary 【非常】 extraordinary; unusual; special / very; extremely; highly 【非但】 not only 【非法】 illegal; unlawful; illicit ～活动 illegal activities ～收入 illicit income 【非凡】 outstanding (achievements); extraordinary; uncommon 【非卖品】 (articles) not for sale 【非难】 blame; censure; reproach 【非刑】 brutal torture 【非议】 reproach; censure 【非正式】 unofficial; informal

绯 fēi red 【绯红】 bright red; crimson 脸羞得～ blush with shame ～的晚霞 rosy evening clouds

扉 fēi door leaf 【扉页】 title page

蜚 fēi 【蜚声】 make a name; become famous ～海外 enjoy a high reputation abroad 【蜚语】 rumours; gossip

肥 féi ①fat 一块～肉 a chunk of fat meat ～猪 a big porker ②fertile; rich ③fertilize ～田 fertilize the soil ④fertilizer ⑤loose-fitting; loose; large 【肥大】 loose; large / fat; plump; corpulent 【肥厚】 plump; fleshy 【肥料】 fertilizer; manure 【肥胖】 corpulent 【肥沃】 fertile; rich 【肥皂】 soap ～粉 soap powder ～泡 soap bubble ～片 soap flakes ～水 soapsuds

诽 fěi slander 【诽谤】 calumniate; libel

匪 fěi bandit; brigand; robber 【匪帮】 bandit gang 【匪集】 bandits' lair 【匪徒】 gangster

菲 fěi poor; humble; unworthy ～酌 a simple meal ～仪 my small gift 【菲薄】 humble / belittle; despise

翡 fěi 【翡翠】jadeite

沸 fèi boil ～水 boiling water 【沸点】boiling point 【沸腾】boiling / seethe with excitement; boil over

废 fèi ①give up; abandon 半途而～ give up halfway ②waste; useless; disused ～棉 cotton waste ～油 used oil ～井 a disused well ～矿 an abandoned mine ～水 waste water ～气 waste gas or steam 【废弛】(of a law, custom, etc.) cease to be binding/(of discipline, etc.) become lax 【废除】abolish; abrogate; annul; repeal 【废话】nonsense; rubbish 【废料】waste (material); scrap 【废票】invalidated ticket or ballot 【废品】waste product; reject/scrap; waste 【废弃】discard; cast aside 【废寝忘食】forget food and sleep 【废人】disabled person 【废物】waste material; trash/good-for-nothing ～利用 make use of waste material 【废墟】ruins 【废止】annul; put an end to 【废纸】waste paper

肺 fèi lungs 【肺癌】lung cancer 【肺病】pulmonary tuberculosis (TB) 【肺腑】the bottom of one's heart

费 fèi ①fee; dues; expenses; charge 学～ schooling fees ②spend; expend ～钱 cost a lot ～时 take time ③wasteful ～煤 consume too much coal 【费工】take a lot of work 【费工夫】be time-consuming 【费解】hard to understand; obscure 【费尽心机】rack one's brains in scheming 【费力】need or use great effort; be strenuous 【费神】may I trouble you (to do sth.); would you mind (doing sth.) 【费事】give or take a lot of trouble 【费心】give a lot of care 【费用】cost; expenses 生产～ production cost 生活～ living expenses

痱 fèi 【痱子】prickly heat ～粉 prickly-heat powder

FEN

分 fēn ①divide; separate; part ～阶段实行 carry out stage by stage ②assign; allot ～票子 distribute tickets ～田地 share out the land ③distinguish; differentiate ④branch (of an organization) ～店 branch (of a shop) ⑤fraction 二～之一 half ⑥one-tenth 有十～把握 be hundred-percent sure ⑦minute (= 1/60 of an hour or a degree) ⑧point; mark 连得二～ score two successive points 【分辨】distinguish; differentiate 【分辩】defend oneself; offer an explanation 【分别】part; leave each other/respectively; separately 【分布】be distributed (over an area); be dispersed 【分词】participle ～短语 participial phrase 【分寸】sense of propriety 说话有～ know what to say and what not to say 不知～ lack tact 【分担】share responsibility for ～费用 share the expenses ～家务劳动 share house-hold duties 【分等】grade; classify 【分队】element 【分发】distribute; issue ～学习材料 hand out study materials ～奖品 distribute prizes 【分割】cut apart; break up; carve up 【分工】divide the work ～合作 share out the work and cooperate with one another ～负责 division of labour with individual responsibility 【分管】be put in charge of 【分行】branch (of a bank) 【分号】semicolon/branch (of a firm, etc.) 【分化】split up; become divided; break up 【分机】extension (telephone) 【分级】grade; classify 【分家】break up the family and live apart 【分解】resolve; decompose / recount; disclose 【分居】 (of members of a family) live apart 【分句】clause 【分类】classify ～法 classification ～帐 ledger ～学 taxology 【分离】separate; sever 【分裂】split; divide; break up 【分泌】secrete 【分娩】childbirth 【分明】clearly demarcated; distinct / plainly; evidently 【分派】assign (to different persons) 【分配】distribute; allot; assign ～土地 distribute land ～住房 allot dwelling houses 【分批】in batches; in turn 【分期】by stages ～付款 payment by instalments; hire purchase 【分歧】difference; divergence 【分清】distinguish; draw a clear line of demarcation between 【分散】disperse; scatter ～注意力 divert one's attention 不要～精力 don't scatter your strength 【分手】part company 【分数】fraction / mark; grade 【分水岭】watershed; divide/line of demarcation; watershed 【分摊】share (the expenses, etc.) 【分析】analyse ～问题 analyse problems ～形势 size up a situation 【分享】share (joy, rights, etc.); partake of 【分心】distract one's attention 【分忧】share sb.'s cares and burdens 【分赃】share the booty 【分组】divide into groups ～讨论 discuss in groups

芬 fēn sweet smell 【芬芳】sweet-smelling; fragrant/ fragrance

吩 fēn 【吩咐】tell; instruct

纷 fēn ①confused; tangled; disorderly ②many and various; profuse 【纷繁】numerous and complicated 【纷纷】one after another; in succession/numerous and confused 对此议论～ this has become the subject of much discussion 【纷乱】numerous and disorderly 【纷扰】confusion; turmoil 【纷纭】diverse and confused 【纷争】dispute; wrangle 【纷至沓来】come thick and fast; keep pouring in

坟 fén grave; tomb 【坟地】graveyard; cemetery 【坟头】grave mound

焚 fén burn ～香 burn incense 【焚化】incinerate; cremate ～炉 incinerator; cremator 【焚毁】destroy by fire; burn down 【焚烧】set on fire

粉 fěn ①powder 磨成～ grind into powder ②pink ～色 pink colour 【粉笔】chalk ～槽 a ledge for chalk on a blackboard ～画 crayon 【粉红】pink 【粉剂】powder/ dust 【粉皮】sheet jelly made from bean starch 【粉扑】 powder puff 【粉饰】gloss over; whitewash 【粉刷】white-wash 【粉丝】vermicelli (made from bean starch) 【粉碎】smash; shatter; crush/broken to pieces 【粉条】noodles made from bean or sweet potato starch

分 fēn ①component 盐～ salt content ②what is within one's rights or duty 本～ one's duty 【分量】weight 给足～ give full measure 【分内】one's job 【分外】par-ticularly; especially / not one's job 【分子】member; ele-ment

份 fèn share; portion 股～ stock ～额 share 出一～力 do one's bit 复写三～ make three carbon copies 【份儿饭】table d'hôte; set meal

奋 fèn ①exert oneself; act vigorously ②raise; lift 【奋斗】struggle; fight; strive 【奋发】rouse oneself; exert oneself ～图强 go all out to make the country strong 【奋力】do all one can; spare no effort 【奋起】 rise (with force and spirit) 【奋勇】summon up all one's courage and energy ～前进 advance bravely; forge ahead/ courageously 【奋战】fight bravely

粪 fèn excrement; faeces; dung; droppings 【粪便】night soil 【粪车】dung-cart 【粪堆】dunghill 【粪肥】muck; dung 【粪坑】manure pit 【粪筐】manure basket 【粪桶】 manure bucket 【粪土】dung and dirt

愤 fèn indignation; anger; resentment 【愤愤不平】feel aggrieved 【愤恨】resent; detest 【愤慨】(righteous) indignation 【愤怒】anger; wrath 【愤世嫉俗】detest the world and its ways

FENG

丰 fēng ①abundant; plentiful ②great ③fine-looking; handsome 【丰碑】 monument/monumental work 【丰产】 bumper crop ～田 a high-yield plot 【丰富】 rich; abundant; plentiful/enrich 积累～的资料 accumulate a wealth of data ～自己的生活经验 enrich one's experience of life ～多彩 rich and colourful 【丰功伟绩】 great achievements; signal contributions 【丰厚】 rich and generous 【丰满】 plentiful/full and round; well-developed/chubby (cheeks, face); plump (figure) 【丰茂】 luxuriant; lush 【丰年】 good year 【丰饶】 rich and fertile 【丰润】 plump and smooth-skinned 【丰盛】 sumptuous 【丰收】 bumper harvest ～在望 a good harvest is in sight 【丰硕】 plentiful and substantial 取得～的成果 reap rich fruits 【丰裕】 well provided for; in plenty

风 fēng ①wind ②put out to dry or air ～干 air-dry ③winnow ④style; practice; custom 节约成～ thrift has become the prevailing practice 不正之～ unhealthy tendencies ⑤scene; view ⑥news; information 走～ leak news 【风暴】 windstorm; storm; tempest 【风波】 disturbance 【风采】 graceful bearing 【风潮】 agitation; unrest 【风尘】 travel fatigue/hardships or uncertainties in an unstable society ～仆仆 be travel-worn and weary 【风斗】 wind scoop 【风度】 demeanour; bearing 有～ have poise 大方 have an easy manner 【风格】 style 【风光】 scene; view; sight 【风寒】 chill; cold 【风华】 elegance and talent ～正茂 in one's prime 【风化】 morals and manners; decency 【风纪】 conduct and discipline ～扣 hook and eye 【风景】 scenery; landscape ～画 landscape painting ～区 scenic spot 【风镜】 goggles 【风浪】 stormy waves; storm 【风雷】

wind and thunder; tempest 【风力】 wind-force/wind power 【风凉】 cool ～话 irresponsible and sarcastic remarks 【风流】 distinguished and admirable/talented in letters and unconventional in life style/dissolute; loose 【风气】 general mood; atmosphere; common practice 【风琴】 organ 【风情】 amorous feelings; flirtatious expressions 【风趣】 humour; wit 说话有～ speak in a humorous vein 【风骚】 coquettish 【风色】 how the wind blows 看～ see which way the wind blows; see how things stand 【风扇】 (electric) fan 【风尚】 prevailing custom 【风俗】 custom 【风味】 special flavour; local colour ～菜 typical local dish 【风闻】 learn through hearsay; get wind of 【风险】 risk; hazard 冒～ take risks 【风箱】 bellows 【风行】 be in fashion; be popular 【风雅】 literary pursuits/elegant; refined 【风言风语】 groundless talk; slanderous gossip 【风雨】 wind and rain; trials and hardships ～无阻 regardless of the weather; rain or shine 【风云】 wind and cloud—a stormy or unstable situation ～变幻 a changeable situation ～人物 man of the hour 【风韵】 graceful bearing; charm 【风筝】 kite 放～ fly a kite

枫 fēng ①Chinese sweet gum ②maple

疯 fēng mad; insane; crazy 【疯狗】 mad dog 【疯狂】 insane/frenzied; unbridled 【疯人院】 madhouse 【疯瘫】 paralysis 【疯子】 madman

封 fēng ①seal ～存 seal up for safekeeping ～信 seal a letter ～门 seal up a door ②bank (a fire) ③confer (a title, territory, etc.) upon ～王 make sb. a prince ～闭 seal / seal off; close 【封官许愿】 offer official posts and make lavish promises 【封建】 the system of enfeoffment/feudalism ～残余思想 surviving feudal ideology ～

社会 feudal society ～主义 feudalism 【封口】 seal/heal 伤～了 the wound has healed 【封面】 the front and back cover of a book/front cover 【封锁】 blockade; block; seal off ～边境 close the border ～消息 block the passage of information ～线 blockade line 【封套】 big envelope 【封条】 paper strip seal

峰 fēng ①peak; summit 山～ mountain peak ～峦 ridges and peaks 科学高～ the heights of science ②hump 驼～ camel's hump

烽 fēng beacon 【烽火】 beacon-fire/flames of war ～台 beacon tower

锋 fēng ①the sharp point or cutting edge (of a sword, etc.) ②van 【锋利】 sharp; keen/incisive; sharp; poignant 【锋芒】 cutting edge; spearhead (of struggle, etc.)/ talent displayed; abilities 不露～ be able but modest ～毕露 make a showy display of one's abilities

蜂 fēng ①wasp ②bee; honeybee ③in swarms ～聚 gather in swarms ～起 rise in swarms ～拥 swarm; flock 【蜂巢】 honeycomb 【蜂刺】 the sting of a bee or wasp 【蜂毒】 bee venom 【蜂糕】 steamed sponge cake 【蜂蜡】 beeswax 【蜂蜜】 honey 【蜂鸣器】 buzzer 【蜂鸟】 hummingbird 【蜂群】 (bee) colony 【蜂乳】 royal jelly 【蜂王】 queen bee/queen wasp 【蜂窝】 honeycomb ～炉 honeycomb briquet stove ～煤 honeycomb briquet 【蜂箱】 beehive

逢 féng meet; come upon 重～ meet again 【逢场作戏】 join in the fun on occasion 【逢集】 market day 【逢凶化吉】 turn ill luck into good 【逢迎】 fawn on; curry favour with

缝 féng stitch; sew ～被子 stitch a quilt ～扣子 sew on a button 【缝补】 sew and mend 【缝合】 suture; sew up (a wound) 【缝纫】 sewing; tailoring ～机 sewing machine

讽 fěng satirize; mock 【讽刺】satirize ～画 satirical drawing; caricature; cartoon ～小品 satirical essay 【讽喻】parable; allegory

凤 fèng phoenix 【凤梨】pineapple 【凤毛麟角】rarity of rarities 【凤尾鱼】anchovy 【凤仙花】garden balsam

奉 fèng ①give or present with respect ②receive (orders, etc.) ③esteem; revere ④believe in ⑤wait upon; attend to 【奉承】flatter; fawn upon; toady ～话 flattery 【奉告】let sb. know; inform 无可～ no comment 【奉公守法】be law-abiding 【奉还】return sth. with thanks 【奉命】act under orders ～出发 receive orders to set off 【奉陪】keep sb. company 恕不～ sorry, I won't be able to keep you company 【奉劝】may I offer a piece of advice 【奉送】offer as a gift 【奉献】present with all respect 【奉行】pursue (a policy, etc.) 【奉养】support and wait upon sb.

俸 fèng pay; salary 【俸禄】an official's salary

缝 fèng ①seam 无～钢管 seamless steel tube ②crack; crevice; fissure; chink

FO

佛 fó ①Buddha ②Buddhism ③image of Buddha 【佛法】Buddhist doctrine/power of Buddha 【佛教】Buddhism ～徒 Buddhist 【佛经】Buddhist Scripture

FOU

否 fǒu ①negate; deny ～认 deny ②no 【否定】negate; deny/negative ～的答复 an answer in the negative 【否决】veto; overrule ～权 veto (power) 【否则】otherwise; if not; or else

FU

夫 fū ①husband ②man 【夫妻】 man and wife 【夫权】 authority of the husband 【夫人】 Lady; Madame; Mrs.

肤 fū skin 【肤皮潦草】 cursory; casual; perfunctory 【肤浅】 superficial; shallow 【肤色】 colour of skin

孵 fū hatch; brood; incubate ～小鸡 hatch chickens 【孵化】 hatching ～场 hatchery

敷 fū ①apply (powder, ointment, etc.) ②spread; lay out ③be sufficient for 【敷料】 dressing 【敷设】 lay (pipelines, a railway track, etc.) 【敷衍】 be perfunctory; go through the motions ～了事 muddle through one's work ～塞责 perform one's duty in a perfunctory manner

伏 fú ①bend over ～案 bend over one's desk ②lie prostrate ～地不动 lie on the ground with one's face downward ③subside; go down 此～彼起 down here, up there ④hide 昼～夜出 hide by day and come out at night ⑤hot season ⑥admit (defeat or guilt) 【伏笔】 foreshadowing 【伏兵】 (troops in) ambush 【伏法】 be executed 【伏击】 ambush 【伏贴】 fit perfectly

凫 fú ①wild duck ②swim

扶 fú ①support with the hand ②help sb. up; straighten sth. up ～苗 straighten up the seedlings ③help; relieve 【扶病】 in spite of illness 【扶持】 help sustain; give aid to; help sb. to stand or walk; support 【扶手】 handrail; rail; banisters / armrest 【扶梯】 staircase 【扶养】 provide for; foster; bring up 【扶植】 foster; prop up 【扶助】 help; assist; support

拂 fú ①stroke 春风～面 a spring breeze stroking the face ②whisk; flick ～去桌上的尘土 whisk the dust

off a desk ③go against (sb.'s wishes)【拂拭】whisk or
wipe off【拂晓】before dawn

服 fú ①clothes; dress 工作～ work clothes ②take (medicine) ③serve (in the army) ④be convinced; obey
我～了 I'm convinced 不～指导 refuse to obey directions
⑤be accustomed to (the climate)【服从】obey; submit
(oneself) to; be subordinated to ～命令 obey orders ～多
数 submit to the majority【服毒】take poison【服气】
be convinced【服饰】dress and personal adornment; dress
【服侍】wait upon; attend ～病人 attend the sick【服输】
admit defeat【服贴】docile; obedient; submissive/fitting;
well arranged【服务】give service to; serve ～行业 service
trades ～台 service desk ～员 attendant ～站 neighbourhood service centre【服刑】serve a sentence ～期满
complete a term of imprisonment【服役】enlist in the
army【服装】dress; clothing; costume ～厂 clothing factory
～商店 clothes shop ～设计 dress designing【服罪】admit
one' guilt

俘 fú ①capture; take prisoner ②captive【俘获】capture
【俘房】take prisoner/captured personnel; prisoner
of war

浮 fú ①float ～在水上 float on water ②swim ③on the
surface; superficial ～土 dust on the surface ④tem-
porary; provisional ～支 expenditure not in the regular
account ⑤flighty; unstable; superficial ⑥hollow; inflated
～名 bubble reputation【浮冰】floating ice; (ice) floe
【浮雕】relief (sculpture)【浮动】float; drift/be unsteady;
fluctuate【浮泛】reveal; display/superficial; too abstract
【浮华】showy; ostentatious; flashy【浮夸】be boastful;
exaggerate【浮力】buoyancy【浮面】surface【浮皮】outer
skin/surface【浮浅】superficial; shallow【浮桥】pontoon

bridge 【浮筒】 float; buoy 【浮现】 appear before one's eyes 【浮想】 thoughts or recollections flashing across one's mind 【浮云】 floating clouds 【浮躁】 impetuous 【浮肿】 dropsy

符 fú ①symbol ②tally with; accord with 【符号】 symbol; mark / insignia 【符合】 accord with; tally with; be in keeping with ～要求 accord with the demands ～实际情况 conform to reality 【符咒】 incantations

幅 fú ①width of cloth ②size 【幅度】 range; scope; extent 大～增长 increase by a big margin 【幅员】 the size of a country

福 fú good fortune; blessing; happiness 【福利】 material benefits; well-being; welfare ～费 welfare funds 【福气】 happy lot; good fortune

辐 fú spoke (of a wheel, etc.) 【辐射】 radiation 【辐照】 irradiation

抚 fú ①comfort; console ②nurture; foster 【抚爱】 caress; fondle 【抚摩】 stroke 【抚弄】 stroke; fondle 【抚慰】 comfort; console; soothe 【抚恤】 comfort and compensate a bereaved family 【抚养】 foster; raise; bring up 【抚育】 nurture; tend

府 fú ①seat of government; government office 首～ capital ②official residence; mansion 总统～ presidential palace 【府绸】 poplin 【府第】 mansion (house) 【府上】 your home; your family/your native place

斧 fǔ axe; hatchet 【斧正】 (please) make corrections

俯 fǔ bow (one's head) 【俯冲】 dive 【俯视】 look down at; overlook 【俯首】 bow one's head (in submission) ～就范 meekly submit ～听命 obey submissively

辅 fǔ assist; complement; supplement 【辅币】 fractional currency 【辅导】 give guidance in study or training;

coach ~报告 guidance lecture ~材料 guidance material ~员 assistant; instructor 【辅课】 subsidiary course 【辅音】 consonant 【辅助】 assist / supplementary; auxiliary ~机构 auxiliary body ~劳动 auxiliary labour ~人员 auxiliary staff members

腐 fǔ rotten; putrid; stale; corroded ~肉 rotten meat 【腐败】 rotten; decayed; putrid (food) /corrupt ~无能 corrupt and incompetent 【腐化】 degenerate; corrupt; dissolute /rot; decay ~分子 degenerate; a depraved person 【腐烂】 decomposed; putrid / corrupt; rotten 【腐乳】 fermented bean curd 【腐蚀】 corrode; etch / corrupt

父 fù father 【父老】 elders (of a country or district) 【父母】 father and mother; parents 【父系】 paternal line ~亲属 relatives on the paternal side

讣 fù obituary 【讣告】 announce sb.'s death / obituary (notice)

付 fù ①hand over to; commit to ~表决 put to the vote ~诸实施 put into effect ~之一笑 dismiss with a laugh ②pay ~税 pay taxes 【付出】 pay; expend ~代价 pay a price ~生命 give one's life 【付方】 credit side 【付款】 pay a sum of money ~办法 methods of payment ~人 payer; drawee 【付排】 send to the compositor 【付讫】 (of a bill) paid 【付清】 pay off; clear (a bill) 【付息】 payment of interest 【付现】 (pay in) cash 【付印】 send to the press/turn over to the printing shop (after proofreading) 【付邮】 take to the post; post 【付帐】 pay a bill 【付之一炬】 commit to the flames

负 fù ①shoulder; bear ~薪 carry firewood on one's back 如释重~ feel greatly relieved 身~重任 shoulder an important task ~主要责任 assume the main responsibility ②have at one's back; rely on ③suffer ~伤 get wounded ④enjoy ～盛名 enjoy a good reputation ⑤owe ～债 be in debt ⑥fail in one's duty, obligation, etc. 忘恩～义 be ungrateful; betray ⑦lose (a battle, game, etc.); be defeated ～于对方 lose the match 不分胜～ end in a draw; break even ⑧minus; negative 【负担 (a burden); shoulder/burden; load 家庭～ family burden 工作～ work load 思想～ mental burden 减轻学生～ lighten the student's load 【负号】 negative sign 【负片】 negative 【负气】 do sth. in a fit of pique 【负伤】 be wounded; be injured 【负数】 negative number 【负约】 break a promise 【负责】 be responsible for; be in charge of

妇 fù ①woman ②married woman ③wife 【妇科】 (department of) gynaecology ～医生 gynaecologist 【妇女】 woman ～病 women's disease ～节 International Working Women's Day (March 8)

附 fù ①add; attach; enclose ～笔 add a word or two (in a letter, etc.) ～表 attached list or chart ～寄 enclosed herewith sth. ②get close to; be near ③agree to 【附带】 in passing ～说一下 mention in passing; by the way 不～任何条件 have no strings attached 【附和】 echo; chime in with 【附加】 add; attach/attached; appended ～费 extra charges ～税 additional tax ～条款 additional article 【附件】 appendix; annex/enclosure/accessories; attachment 【附近】 nearby; neighbouring/close to; in the vicinity of 【附录】 appendix 【附上】 enclosed herewith 【附设】 have as an attached institution 这个学院～一所中学 there is a middle school attached to the institute 【附属】 subsidiary; auxiliary ～国 dependency ～机构 subsidiary body ～品 accessory; appendage 【附图】 attached map or drawing; figure 【附小】 attached primary school 【附言】 postscript 【附议】 second a motion 【附庸】 dependency;

vassal 【附中】 attached middle school 【附注】 annotations 【附着】 adhere to; stick to ～力 adhesive force; adhesion

服 fú dose 一～药 a dose of medicine

赴 fù go to; attend ～约 keep an appointment ～宴 attend a banquet ～任 go to one's post 【赴汤蹈火】 go through fire and water

复 fù ①duplicate ②compound; complex ～姓 compound surname ③turn round; turn over ④answer; reply 请 即电～ cable reply immediately ⑤recover; resume ～职 resume one's post ⑥revenge 报～ retaliate; take revenge ⑦again 【复本】 duplicate 【复辟】 restoration of a dethroned monarch/restoration of the old order 【复查】 check; re-examine 【复仇】 revenge; avenge 【复电】 telegram in reply (to one received) 【复发】 have a relapse; recur; have an attack (of an old illness) 【复方】 compound 【复工】 return to work (after a strike) 【复合】 compound; complex; composite ～词 compound (word) ～句 compound or complex sentence ～元音 compound vowel 【复核】 check ～数字 check the figures 【复会】 resume a session 【复活】 bring back to life; revive 【复句】 a sentence of two or more clauses 【复刊】 resume publication 【复课】 resume classes 【复赛】 intermediary heat 【复审】 reexamine/review a case 【复述】 repeat (an order); retell (a story) 【复数】 plural (number)/complex number 【复苏】 resuscitate/recovery 【复习】 review; revise ～功课 review lessons 【复写】 make carbon copies; duplicate ～纸 carbon paper 【复信】 write a letter in reply/letter in reply; reply 【复兴】 revive; resurge; rejuvenate 【复学】 go back to school; resume one's interrupted studies 【复印】 duplicate ～机 duplicator ～纸 duplicating paper 【复员】 demobilize ～

费 demobilization pay ～军人 demobilized soldier 【复原】 recover from an illness; be restored to health/restore; rehabilitate 【复杂】 complicated; complex ～的心情 mixed feelings 使问题～化 complicate matters; perplex problems 【复职】 resume one's post 【复制】 duplicate; make a copy of; reproduce ～品 replica

副 fù ①deputy; assistant; vice ～部长 vice-minister ～书记 deputy secretary ～教授 associate professor ②auxiliary; subsidiary; secondary ③correspond to; fit 【副本】 transcript; copy 【副产品】 by-product 【副词】 adverb 【副官】 adjutant 【副刊】 supplement 【副品】 substandard goods 【副食】 non-staple food ～商店 grocer's; grocery 【副手】 assistant 【副业】 sideline; side occupation ～生产 sideline production 家庭～ household sideline production 【副作用】 side effect; by-effect

富 fù rich; wealthy; abundant ～于养分 be rich in nutrition ～于创造性 be highly creative 【富贵】 riches and honour; wealth and rank 【富豪】 rich and powerful people 【富矿】 rich ore 【富丽堂皇】 sumptuous; gorgeous; splendid 【富农】 rich peasant 【富强】 prosperous and strong 【富饶】 fertile; abundant ～的国家 richly endowed country ～的土地 fertile land 【富翁】 man of wealth 【富有】 rich; wealthy/rich in; full of ～经验 rich in experience ～战斗性 very militant ～代表性 typical 【富裕】 prosperous; well-off ～中农 well-to-do middle peasant 【富余】 have enough and to spare 【富源】 natural resources 【富足】 plentiful

赋 fù ①bestow on; endow with; vest with 秉～ natural endowments ②tax ③compose (a poem) 【赋税】 taxes

傅 fù ①teach; instruct ②teacher; instructor ③lay on; apply ～粉 put powder on; powder (the face, etc.)

腹 fù belly; abdomen; stomach 【腹背受敌】be attacked front and rear 【腹地】hinterland 【腹稿】mental notes 【腹腔】abdominal cavity 【腹痛】abdominal pain 【腹泻】diarrhoea

缚 fù tie up; bind fast

覆 fù ①cover ②overturn; upset ～舟 capsized boat 【覆盖】cover/plant cover; vegetation 【覆灭】destruction; complete collapse 【覆没】capsize and sink/be overwhelmed; be annihilated 全军～ the whole army was destroyed 【覆亡】fall (of an empire, nation, etc.) 【覆辙】the track of an overturned cart

馥 fù fragrance

G

GA

咖 gā 【咖喱】curry ～牛肉 beef curry ～粉 curry powder

嘎 gā 【嘎巴】crack; snap 【嘎嘎】quack 【嘎吱】creak

轧 gá ①press hard against each other ②make friends ③check ～帐 check the accounts

GAI

该 gāi ①ought to; should 早就～办 ought to have done it long ago 本～如此 that's just as it should be 你～理发了 you could do with a haircut ②be sb.'s turn to do sth. 这回～我了 it's my turn now ③deserve ～受到表扬 deserve to be commended ④most likely; probably 水库～完工了 the reservoir will have been completed ⑤owe 我不～他钱 I don't owe him any money ⑥this; that ～厂 this factory ～校 the above-mentioned school 【该当】 deserve/should 【该死】 damn

改 gǎi ①change; transform 这儿～样了 the place has changed ②alter; revise ③correct; rectify; put right ～作业 correct students' homework or papers ④switch over to (doing sth. else) ～种水稻 switch over to growing rice 【改版】 correcting 【改编】 adapt; rearrange; revise/reorganize; redesignate 【改变】 change; alter; transform ～主意 change one's mind 【改道】 change one's route/(of a river) change its course 【改掉】 give up; drop ～坏习惯 give up bad habits 【改订】 reformulate; rewrite 【改动】 change; alter; modify 【改革】 reform 【改观】 change the appearance of 大为～ have changed greatly 【改过】 mend one's ways; correct one's mistakes ～自新 turn over a new leaf 【改行】 change one's profession 【改换】 change over to; change ～名称 rename 【改悔】 repent 毫无～之意 absolutely unrepentant 【改嫁】 (of a woman) remarry 【改进】 improve; make better ～工作作风 improve one's work style 【改口】 correct oneself 【改良】 improve; ameliorate/reform ～派 reformists ～主义 reformism change the date 【改日】 another day; some other day 【改善】 improve; ameliorate ～供应 supplying more and better commodities 【改头换面】 change the appearance 【改邪归正】 give up evil and return to good 【改写】 rewrite; adapt 【改选】 reelect 班委会每年～一次 a new class committee is elected every year 【改造】 transform; reform ～思想 remould one's ideology ～自然 remake nature

～主观世界 remould one's subjective world 【改正】correct; amend; put right ～错误 correct one's mistakes 【改锥】screwdriver 【改组】reorganize; reshuffle ～内阁 reshuffle the cabinet

钙 gài calcium 【钙化】calcification 【钙镁磷肥】calcium magnesium phosphate

盖 gài ①lid; cover 茶壶～ teapot lid ②cover ～住秧苗 cover the seedlings ③affix (a seal) ④build ～房 build houses 【盖世】unparalleled; matchless ～英雄 peerless hero 【盖章】seal; stamp 【盖子】lid; cover; cap; top

概 gài ①general ②approximate ③without exception; categorically ～不追究 no action will be taken (against sb. for his past offences) 【概况】general situation; survey 【概括】summarize; generalize / briefly; in broad outline ～性 generality 【概略】outline; summary 【概论】outline; introduction 【概念】concept; conception; notion; idea ～化 deal in generalities; write or speak in abstract terms 【概要】essentials; outline

GAN

干 gān ①be concerned with 与你何～ what has this to do with you ②dry 衣服～得慢 the washing dries slowly ③dried food 萝卜～ dried radish ④empty; hollow; dry ～号 cry aloud (but shed no tears) ⑤taken into nominal kinship ～儿子 (nominally) adopted son ⑥(do sth.) for nothing; futilely 【干巴】dried up; wizened 【干巴巴】dull and dry; insipid; dryasdust 【干杯】drink a toast 【干瘪】shrivelled 【干菜】dried vegetable 【干草】hay 【干脆】clear-cut; straightforward/simply; just; altogether 【干电池】dry cell 【干饭】cooked rice 【干果】dry fruit (e.g. nuts) / dried fruit 【干旱】arid; dry 【干净】clean;

neat and tidy/completely; totally 忘得～ have completely forgotten; clean forgot【干净利落】neat and tidy; neat; efficient 他办事～ he's very efficient【干枯】dried-up; shrivelled ～的树木 withered trees ～的皮肤 wizened skin【干酪】cheese【干粮】solid food; field rations; rations for a journey ～袋 haversack; ration bag【干扰】disturb; interfere; obstruct / interference; jam 排除～ overcome obstruction ～台 jamming station【干涉】interfere; intervene; meddle / interference【干洗】dry-clean【干系】implication 脱不了～ cannot shirk the responsibility【干燥】dry; arid / dull; uninteresting

甘 gān ①sweet; pleasant ～泉 sweet spring water ② willingly; of one's own accord 不～落后 unwilling to lag behind【甘拜下风】candidly admit defeat (in friendly competition, etc.)【甘苦】sweetness and bitterness; weal and woe; joys and sorrows / hardships and difficulties experienced in work【甘美】sweet and refreshing【甘薯】sweet potato【甘心】willingly; readily / resign oneself to; be content with【甘于】be willing to; be ready to【甘蔗】sugarcane

杆 gān pole; staff 旗～ flagstaff; flagpole 电线～ pole (for telephone or electric power lines, etc.)

肝 gān liver【肝癌】cancer of the liver【肝火】irascibility 动～ fly into a rage; be worked up ～旺 hot-tempered【肝炎】hepatitis

泔 gān【泔水】swill; slops; hogwash

柑 gān mandarin orange【柑橘】oranges and tangerines/ citrus ～酱 marmalade

竿 gān pole; rod 竹～ bamboo pole 钓鱼～ fishing rod

尴 gān 【尴尬】awkward; embarrassed 处境～ in an awkward position 样子～ look embarrassed

杆 gǎn the shaft or arm of sth. 枪～ the barrel of a rifle 【杆秤】steelyard 【杆菌】bacillus

秆 gǎn stalk 高粱～ sorghum stalk 麻～ hemp stalk

赶 gǎn ①catch up with; overtake ～先进 catch up with the advanced ②try to catch; make a dash for; rush for ～头班车 catch the first bus ③hurry through ～任务 rush through one's job ④drive ～大车 drive a cart ⑤drive away; expel ～苍蝇 whisk the flies off ⑥happen to; find oneself in (a situation); avail oneself of (an opportunity) 【赶集】go to market; go to a fair 【赶紧】lose no time; hasten 【赶快】at once; quickly 【赶路】hurry on with one's journey 【赶忙】hurry; make haste 【赶巧】happen to; it so happened that 【赶上】overtake; catch up with; keep pace with / run into (a situation); be in time for 没～车 miss the bus or the train 【赶时髦】follow the fashion

敢 gǎn ①bold; courageous; daring ②dare to ～想 ～干 dare to think and dare to act ③have the confidence to; be certain 【敢情】why; so; I say/of course; indeed; really 【敢干】be bold in; have the courage to ～斗争, ～胜利 dare to struggle and dare to win

感 gǎn ①feel; sense 略～不适 not feel very well ② move; touch; affect ～人 touching; moving ③be grateful; be obliged ④sense; feeling 责任～ sense of responsibility 读后～ reaction to a book or an article 【感触】thoughts and feelings; feeling 深有～地说 say with deep feeling 【感动】move; touch ～得流下眼泪 be moved to tears 【感恩】feel grateful; be thankful 【感官】sense organ; sensory organ 【感光】 sensitization ～纸 sensitive paper 【感化】 help sb. to change by persuasion, setting an example, etc. 【感激】 feel grateful; be thankful 【感觉】 sense perception; sensation; feeling / feel; perceive; become aware of 你～怎么样 how do you feel now 【感慨】 sigh with emotion 【感冒】 common cold 患～ catch cold 【感情】 emotion; feeling; sentiment / affection; attachment; love 动～ be carried away by one's emotions; get worked up 伤～ hurt sb.'s feelings 怀有深厚的～ cherish a deep affection for ～用事 be swayed by one's emotions; act impetuously 【感染】 infect/influence; affect 【感伤】 sorrowful; sentimental 【感受】 be affected by/experience; feel 【感叹】 sigh with feeling ～词 interjection ～号 exclamation mark; exclamation point ～句 exclamatory sentence 【感想】 reflections; thoughts 请你谈谈～ please tell us your impressions 【感谢】 thank; be grateful ～信 letter of thanks 【感性】 perceptual 【感应】 response; reaction 【感召】 move and inspire; impel

擀 gǎn roll (dough, ect.) ～面条 make noodles 【擀面杖】 rolling pin

橄 gǎn 【橄榄】 Chinese olive/olive ～球 Rugby (football) ～油 olive oil ～枝 olive branch

干 gàn ①trunk; main part 树～ tree-trunk ②cadre 高～ senior cadre ③do; work 咱们～吧 let's get started ～社会主义 work for socialism ④fight; strike ～到底 fight to the bitter end ⑤capable; able 【干部】 cadre ～政策 cadre policy 【干才】 ability; capability / capable person 【干掉】 kill; get rid of 【干活】 work; work on a job 【干将】 capable person; go-getter 【干劲】 drive; vigour; enthusiasm 鼓～ rouse one's enthusiasm ～十足 be full of vigour 【干练】 capable and experienced 【干吗】 why on earth; whatever for/what to do 下午～ what are we going to do this afternoon 你想～ what are you up to 【干事】 clerical worker in charge of sth. 【干线】 main line; trunk line 【干校】 cadre school

GANG

扛 gāng ①lift with both hands ②carry together

刚 gāng ①firm; strong; indomitable ②just; exactly 大小～合适 just the right size ③barely; only just ④ only a short while ago; just 她～走 she has just gone 【刚才】 just now; a moment ago 【刚好】 just; exactly/ happen to; it so happened that 【刚健】 energetic; robust ～的舞姿 vigorous movements of a dancer 【刚劲】 bold; vigorous; sturdy 【刚强】 firm; staunch 【刚毅】 resolute and steadfast 【刚正】 upright; honourable; principled

纲 gāng ①the headrope of a fishing net ②key link; guiding principle ③outline; programme 总～ the general programme 【纲领】 programme; guiding principle ～性文件 programmatic document 【纲要】 outline; sketch/ essentials; compendium

肛 gāng 【肛门】 anus

缸 gāng vat; jar; crock 水～ water vat 金鱼～ goldfish bowl 【缸子】 mug; bowl 茶～ (tea) mug

钢 gāng steel 【钢板】 steel plate/stencil steel board 【钢笔】 pen; fountain pen 【钢材】 steel products; steels 【钢锭】 steel ingot 【钢骨水泥】 reinforced concrete 【钢管】 steel tube 【钢轨】 rail 【钢筋】 reinforcing bar 【钢精】 aluminium (as used for utensils) 【钢盔】 (steel) helmet 【钢琴】 piano ～家 pianist 【钢丝】 (steel) wire 走～ high-wire walking 【钢铁】 iron and steel; steel ～意志 iron will ～战士 a dauntless fighter ～厂 steelworks 【钢印】 steel seal/embossed stamp 【钢珠】 steel ball

岗 gǎng ①hillock; mound ②ridge; welt; wale ③sentry; post 站～ stand sentry 【岗楼】 watchtower 【岗哨】 lookout post/sentry; sentinel 【岗亭】 sentry box 【岗位】 post; station 坚守～ stand fast at one's post 走上新的 ～ take up a new post

港 gǎng port; harbour 天然～ natural harbour 【港口】 port; harbour 沿海～ coastal port

杠 gàng ①thick stick; stout carrying pole ②bar ③thick line ④cross out; delete 【杠杆】 lever 【杠铃】 barbell

钢 gàng sharpen; whet; strop ～剃刀 strop a razor 【钢刀布】 (razor) strop

GAO

高 gāo ①tall; high 它有六英尺 it's six feet high ② of a high level or degree ～年级 higher grades ～质量 high quality ～风格 fine style ③loud ～喊 shout loudly ④dear; expensive 要价太～ ask too high a price ⑤your ～见 your opinion ～差不多 be about the same height 【高昂】 hold high (one's head, etc.)/ high; elated; exalted/dear; expensive 【高傲】 arrogant; haughty 【高不可攀】 too high to reach 【高才生】 outstanding student 【高产】 high yield; high production ～品种 high-yield variety 【高超】 superb; excellent 【高潮】 high tide/upsurge; climax 【高大】 tall and big; tall/lofty 【高档】 top grade; superior quality ～商品 high-grade goods 【高等】 higher ～教育 higher education ～院校 institutions of higher learning; colleges and universities 【高低】 height/ relative superiority or inferiority 争个～ vie with each other to see who is better 难分～ hard to tell which is better 不知～ have no sense of propriety ～杠 uneven (parallel) bars 【高调】 lofty tone 唱～ mouth high-sounding words 【高度】 altitude; height/a high degree of ～赞扬 speak highly of ～政治觉悟 a high level of political consciousness ～的精神文明 a high ethical and cultural level 给予～重视 attach great importance to 【高尔夫球】 golf/golf ball ～场 golf course; golf links 【高峰】 peak; summit; height 【高跟鞋】 high-heeled shoes 【高贵】 noble; high/highly privileged; elitist 【高级】 senior; high-level; high / high-grade ～干部 senior cadre ～将领 high-ranking general officers ～读本 advanced reader ～小学 higher primary school ～中学 senior middle school 【高价】 high price 【高空】 high altitude; upper air ～飞行 high-altitude flight ～作业 work high above the ground 【高利贷】 usury 【高粱】 Chinese sorghum 【高龄】 advanced age 【高帽子】 tall paper hat (worn as a sign of humiliation) /flattery 【高妙】 ingenious; masterly 【高明】 brilliant; wise 另请～ find someone better qualified (than myself) 【高强】 excel in; be master of 【高跷】 stilts 【高尚】 noble; lofty ～的思想情操 noble thoughts and feelings 【高烧】 high fever 【高射炮】 antiaircraft gun 【高深】 advanced; profound; recondite 【高手】 past master 【高耸】 stand tall and erect; tower 【高速】 high speed ～前进 advance at high speed ～发展 develop by leaps and bounds 【高温】 high temperature 【高兴】 glad; happy; cheerful 【高血压】 high blood pressure 【高压】 high pressure/high-handed 【高音喇叭】 tweeter 【高原】 plateau 【高瞻远瞩】 stand high and see far 【高涨】 rise; upsurge 【高姿态】 lofty stance

 gāo lamb; kid; fawn 【羔皮】 lambskin; kidskin

膏 gāo ①fat; grease; oil ②paste; cream; ointment 牙~ toothpaste 【膏剂】 medicinal extract; electuary

糕 gāo cake; pudding 【糕点】 cake; pastry 【糕干】 sweetened rice flour

篙 gāo punt-pole

搞 gāo ①do; carry on; be engaged in ～生产 engage in production ②make; produce; work out ～计划 draw up a plan ③set up; start ～个商店 set up a shop ④get; get hold of; secure ～点吃的 get something to eat ⑤cause to become 把事～糟 make a mess of things 把问题～清 get a clear understanding of the question ～坏机器 break the machine 把思想～通 straighten out one's ideas ～好团结 strengthen unity ～好关系 build good relations

稿 gāo ①draft; sketch 初～ first draft ②manuscript; original text 定～ finalize a text 【稿费】 contribution fee; author's remuneration 【稿件】 contribution; manuscript 【稿约】 notice to contributors 【稿纸】 squared or lined paper (for making drafts or copying manuscripts)

镐 gāo pick; pickaxe

告 gāo ①tell; inform; notify 盼～ please inform me ②accuse; go to law against; bring an action against ③ask for; request; solicit ～假 ask for leave ④declare; announce 不一而别 go away without taking leave 【告别】 leave; part from/bid farewell to; say good-bye to 【告词】 farewell speech ～会 farewell banquet ～仪式 farewell ceremony 【告吹】 fizzle out; fail 【告辞】 take leave (of one's host) 【告发】 report (an offender); inform against 【告急】 be in an emergency/report an emergency 【告捷】 win victory/report a victory 【告诫】 warn 【告

密】inform against sb. ～者 informer 【告示】official notice; bulletin; placard 【告诉】tell; let know 【告知】inform; notify 【告终】come to an end; end up 以失败～ end in failure 【告状】go to law against sb. / lodge a complaint against sb. with his superior

GE

戈 gē dagger-axe 【戈壁】gobi/the Gobi Desert

疙 gē 【疙瘩】pimple; lump/knot/a knot in one's heart 解开我心上的～ get rid of my hang-up

哥 gē (elder) brother 【哥儿】brothers; boys 【哥儿们】brothers/buddies; pals

胳 gē 【胳膊】arm ～腕子 wrist ～肘儿 elbow

鸽 gē pigeon; dove 家～ pigeon 野～ wild pigeon; dove 通信～ carrier pigeon

割 gē cut ～草 cut grass 【割爱】give up what one treasures; part with some cherished possession 【割草机】mower 【割除】cut off; excise 【割地】cede territory 【割断】sever; cut off ～联系 sever relations ～电线 cut wires ～历史 apart from historical context 【割据】set up a separatist regime 封建～ feudal separatist rule 军阀～ separatist warlord regimes 【割裂】cut apart; separate; isolate 【割让】cede 【割舍】give up 难以～ find it hard to part with

搁 gē ①put 汤里～点盐 put some salt in the soup ～在这儿 leave it here ②put aside; leave over; shelve 【搁浅】run aground; reach a deadlock 船～了 the ship got stranded 【搁置】shelve; lay aside ～动议 shelve a motion

歌 gē ①song ②sing 【歌本】songbook 【歌唱】sing ～家 vocalist 【歌词】words of a song 【歌功颂德】sing the praises of sb. 【歌剧】opera ～剧本 libretto ～团 opera troupe ～院 opera house 【歌片儿】song sheet 【歌谱】music of a song 【歌曲】song 【歌手】singer 【歌颂】sing the praises of; extol 【歌舞】song and dance ～剧 song and dance drama ～团 song and dance ensemble 【歌谣】ballad; folk song 【歌咏】singing ～比赛 singing contest ～队 singing group; chorus

革 gé ①leather; hide ～制品 leather goods ～履 leather shoes ②change; transform ③remove from office; expel 【革除】abolish; get rid of/expel 【革命】revolution ～干部 revolutionary cadre ～家 revolutionist ～军人 revolutionary armyman ～烈士 revolutionary martyr ～化 revolutionize ～性 revolutionary character 【革新】innovation 技术～ technological innovation

阁 gé ①pavilion ②cabinet 组～ form a cabinet 【阁楼】attic; loft; garret

格 gé ①squares formed by crossed lines; check 在纸上打方～儿 square off the paper ②division (horizontal or otherwise) 横～纸 ruled paper ③standard; pattern; style 合～ up to standard ④case 主～ the nominative case 宾～ the objective case 【格调】style 【格斗】grapple; wrestle; fistfight 【格格不入】incompatible with; out of tune with 【格局】pattern; setup; structure 【格式】form; pattern 公文～ the form of an official document 【格外】especially; all the more ～小心 be especially careful 显得～壮丽 looks especially magnificent 【格言】maxim 【格子】check; chequer

搁 gé bear; stand; endure ～不住压 cannot stand crushing

隔 gé ①separate; partition; stand or lie between 把屋子~成两间 partition a room into two ②at a distance from; after or at an interval of 相~千里 be a thousand li away from each other ~两天再来吧 come back in two days' time ~行写 write on every other line 【隔壁】 next door 住在~ live next door 【隔断】 cut off; separate; obstruct 【隔阂】 estrangement; misunderstanding/barrier 【隔绝】 completely cut off; isolated 和外界~ be cut off from the outside world 【隔离】 keep apart; isolate; segregate ~病房 isolation ward 【隔膜】 lack of mutual understanding / unfamiliar with 【隔夜】 of the previous night 【隔音】 sound insulation / syllable-dividing

嗝 gé ①belch ②hiccup

个 gè individual 【个把】 one or two 【个别】 individual; specific/very few; one or two ~辅导 individual coaching ~照顾 special consideration for individual cases ~谈话 private talk ~情况 isolated cases 【个个】 each and every one; all 【个儿】 size; height; stature 【个人】 individual (person) ~利益 personal interests ~负责 individual responsibility 以~名义 in one's own name ~迷信 personality cult ~主义 individualism 【个体】 individual ~经济 individual economy ~劳动者 self-employed labourer 【个性】 individuality; personality

各 gè each; every; various; different 全国~地 in all parts of the country ~不相让 neither being ready to give way ~不相同 have nothing in common with each other ~就位 on your marks 【各别】 distinct; different ~对待 treat differently 【各持己见】 each sticks to his own view 【各个】 each; every; various / one by one; separately ~击破 destroy one by one 【各级】 all or

different levels 【各界】 all walks of life; all circles ～人
士 personalities of various circles 【各尽所能】 from
each according to his ability 【各取所需】 each takes
what he needs 【各人】 each one; everyone 【各色】 of all
kinds; assorted 【各抒己见】 each airs his own views 【各
位】 everybody/every ～代表 fellow deputies 【各行其是】
each goes his own way 【各有所好】 each follows his
own bent 【各自】 each; respective ～为政 each does things
in his own way

硌 gè (of sth. hard or bulging) press or rub against
鞋里有砂子, ～脚 there's some grit in the shoe, and
it hurts my foot

GEI

给 gěi ①give; grant ～他一个星期的假 grant him a
week's leave ②for; for the benefit of ～旅客送水
bring drinking water for the passengers ③let; allow
～我看看 let me have a look 【给以】 give; grant ～重
视 pay attention to ～照顾 show consideration for

GEN

根 gēn ①root; foot; base 树～ the root of a tree 城
墙～ the foot of a city wall ②cause; origin; source
祸～ the root of trouble or disaster ③thoroughly;
completely ～除 completely do away with; eradicate 【根本】
basic; fundamental; essential; cardinal / at all; simply/
radically; thoroughly 【根底】 foundation / cause; root 【根
基】 foundation; basis 【根究】 get to the bottom of;
probe into 【根据】 on the basis of; according to; in the
light of / basis; grounds; foundation ～地 base area; base
【根绝】 stamp out; exterminate 【根深蒂固】 deep-rooted;

ingrained; inveterate 【根源】 source; origin; root 战争的 ~ the source of war 思想~ the ideological roots 【根治】 effect a radical cure

跟 gēn ①heel 鞋后 ~ the heel of a shoe ②follow ~我来 come along with me ~党走 follow the Party ~我念 read after me ③with; about; as ~他一起劳动 work with him ~我们说说 tell us about it ~往常一样 be the same as before ④and 你~我 you and I 【跟前】 in front of; close to; near 【跟上】 keep pace with; catch up with 【跟头】 (have a) fall / (turn a) somersault 【跟着】 follow in the wake of 【跟踪】 follow the tracks of ~追击 go in hot pursuit of ~敌舰 shadow the enemy warships

GENG

更 gēng ①change; replace ②watch 打~ beat the watches 【更动】 change; alter 人事~ personnel changes 【更改】 change; alter ~设计 alter the design 【更换】 replace ~位置 change places 【更生】 regenerate; revive / renew 【更新】 renew 设备~ renewal of equipment 【更衣】 change one's clothes ~室 changeroom; locker room 【更正】 make corrections (of errors in statements or newspaper articles)

耕 gēng plough; till 深~ deep ploughing 【耕畜】 farm animal 【耕地】 plough; till / cultivated land 【耕牛】 farm cattle 【耕耘】 ploughing and weeding; cultivation 【耕作】 tillage; farming

羹 gēng a thick soup 鸡蛋~ egg custard 【羹匙】 soup spoon; tablespoon

埂 gěng ①a low bank of earth between fields ②a long, narrow mound ③an earth dyke

耿 gěng ①dedicated ②honest and just; upright 【耿耿】 devoted; dédicated / have sth. on one's mind ～于怀 brood on (an injury); take sth. to heart

哽 gěng choke (with emotion); feel a lump in one's throat 【哽咽】 choke with sobs

梗 gěng ①stalk; stem 菠菜～ spinach stalk ②a slender piece (of wood or metal) 火柴～ matchstick ③obstruct; block 从中作～ place obstacles in the way 【梗概】 broad outline; main idea 故事～ the gist of a story; synopsis 【梗塞】 block; obstruct; clog 交通～ traffic jam 心肌～ myocardial infarction 【梗直】 honest and frank; upright

更 gèng ①more; still more ②further; furthermore ～进一步 go a step further ～上一层楼 climb one storey higher; scale new heights

GONG

工 gōng ①worker; the working class 女～ woman worker ②work; labour 上～ go to work 省～ save labour (construction) project 动～ begin a project ④industry 化～ chemical industry ⑤man-day 工程需要五千个～ the project will take 5,000 man-days to complete ⑥skill; craftsmanship 唱～ (art of) singing ⑦ be good at ～诗 be well versed in poetry 【工本】 cost (of production) 【工厂】 factory; mill; plant; works 【工场】 workshop 【工潮】 strike movement 【工程】 engineering; project ～兵 engineer ～队 construction brigade ～师 engineer 【工地】 buildsng site 【工分】 workpoint ～值 cash value of a workpoint 【工蜂】 worker (bee) 【工夫】 time/work; labour; effort 有～再来 come again if you have time 花了好大～ put in a lot of work 【工会】 trade union; labour union 【工间操】 work-break exercises 【工件】 workpiece 【工具】

tool; means; instrument ～袋 kit bag ～房 toolhouse ～书 reference book ～箱 toolbox; workbox 【工科】 engineering course ～大学 college of engineering 【工龄】 length of service; standing; seniority 【工农】 workers and peasants ～干部 worker and peasant cadres ～联盟 worker-peasant alliance 【工棚】 builders' temporary shed/work shed 【工钱】 charge for a service/wages; pay 【工区】 work area 【工人】 worker ～运动 labour movement ～阶级 working class 【工伤】 industrial injury 【工时】 man-hour 【工事】 defence works 【工头】 overseer 【工效】 work efficiency 【工休日】 day off; holiday 【工序】 process 【工业】 industry ～国 industrial country ～化 industrialization ～品 manufactured goods 【工艺】 technology; craft ～美术 industrial art ～品 handiwork; handicraft ～水平 technological level 【工贼】 scab; blackleg 【工长】 section chief; foreman 【工装裤】 overalls 【工资】 wages; pay 【工作】 work; job ～单位 place of work ～队 work team ～服 work clothes ～量 work load ～面 face ～人员 working personnel ～日 workday ～证 employee's card; I.D. card ～者 worker

弓 gōng ①bow ～箭 bow and arrow ②bend; arch; bow ～背 arch one's back 【弓弦】 bowstring

公 gōng ①public; state-owned; collective ～与私 public and private (interests) 交～ turn over to the authorities ②common; general ③metric ～里 kilometre ④make public ～之于世 make known to the world ⑤fair; just 秉～办理 handle affairs equitably or impartially; be evenhanded ⑥public affairs; official business ～余 after work 因～外出 be away on official business ⑦husband's father; father-in-law ⑧male (animal) ～鸡 cock 【公安】 public security ～部 the Ministry of Public Security ～机关 public security organs ～局 public security bureau ～人员 public security officer 【公报】bulletin; *communiqué* 【公布】announce; publish; make public ～法令 promulgate a decree ～名单 publish a name list 【公尺】metre 【公出】be away on official business 【公道】justice/fair; just 主持～ uphold justice 办事～ be impartial 价钱～ the price is reasonable 【公德】social morality 【公敌】public enemy 【公断】arbitration 【公法】public law 【公费】at public expense ～医疗 free medical service 【公分】centimetre/gram 【公愤】public indignation 【公告】announcement 【公共】public; common～财产 public property ～场所 public places ～汽车 bus ～食堂 canteen ～卫生 public health ～秩序 public order 【公害】social effects of pollution 【公函】official letter 【公积金】accumulation fund 【公斤】kilogram; kilo 【公开】open; overt; public/make public; make known to the public ～化 come out into the open ～信 open letter 【公款】public money 【公里】kilometre 【公理】generally acknowledged truth 【公路】highway; road ～交通 highway communication ～运输 road transportation 【公论】public opinion 是非自有～ public opinion is the best judge 【公民】citizen ～权 citizenship 【公亩】are 【公墓】cemetery 【公平】fair; just; impartial ～交易 fair deal 【公仆】public servant 【公顷】hectare 【公然】openly; brazenly 【公社】(primitive) commune/people's commune 【公审】public trial 【公使】envoy; minister ～馆 legation 【公式】formula ～化 formulism/formulistic; stereotyped 【公事】public affairs ～包 portfolio 【公司】company; corporation 【公诉】public prosecution 提起～ institute proceedings against sb. ～人 the prosecution 【公文】official document ～袋 document envelope 【公务】official business

～人员 government functionary ～员 orderly 【公物】 public property 【公休】 general holiday 【公演】 perform in public 【公议】 public or mass discussion 【公益】 public good ～金 public welfare fund 【公意】 public will 【公用】 for public use; public; communal ～电话 public telephone ～事业 public utilities 【公有】 publicly-owned; public ～制 public ownership 【公寓】 flats; apartment house 【公元】 the Christian era ～一九八二年 A. D. 1982 ～前五〇〇年 500 B. C. 【公园】 park 【公约】 convention; pact/joint pledge 【公允】 just and sound 【公债】 (government) bonds 【公章】 official seal 【公正】 just; fair; impartial 【公证】 notarization ～人 notary 【公职】 public employment 担任～ hold public office 开除～ discharge from public employment 【公众】 the public 【公主】 princess

功 gōng ①meritorious service; merit; exploit 立大～ render outstanding service ②achievement; result 劳而无～ work hard but to no avail ③skill 练～ practise one's skill 【功臣】 a person who has rendered outstanding service; meritorious workers 【功德】 merits and virtues 【功绩】 contribution 【功课】 schoolwork; homework 做～ do homework 【功劳】 meritorious service; credit ～簿 record of merits 【功利】 utility; material gain 【功能】 function 【功效】 efficacy; effect 【功用】 function; use

攻 gōng ①attack; take the offensive 主～方向 the main direction of the offensive ②accuse; charge 群起而～之 everyone points an accusing finger at him ③study ～读 diligently study/specialize in 【攻打】 attack; assault 【攻关】 storm a strategic pass/tackle key problems 【攻击】 assault; launch an offensive/accuse; charge; vilify 【攻坚】 storm fortifications ～战 storming of heavily fortified positions 【攻克】 capture; take ～技术难关 surmount a technical difficulty 【攻破】make a breakthrough; breach 【攻势】offensive 【攻占】attack and occupy

供 gōng ①supply; feed ～不上 be in short supply ②for (the use or convenience of) 仅～参考 for your reference only 【供不应求】supply falls short of demand 【供给】supply; provide; furnish ～制 the supply system 【供养】provide for (one's parents or elders) 【供应】supply 市场～ market supplies ～点 supply centre ～线 supply line

宫 gōng palace 【宫灯】palace lantern 【宫女】maid of honour 【宫廷】palace/court ～政变 palace coup

恭 gōng respectful; reverent 【恭贺】congratulate ～新禧 Happy New Year 【恭候】await respectfully ～光临 we request the pleasure of your company 【恭顺】respectful and submissive 【恭维】flatter; compliment ～话 flattery 【恭喜】congratulations

躬 gōng ①personally ～逢其盛 be present in person on the grand occasion ② bend forward; bow ～身 bend at the waist

巩 gōng consolidate 【巩固】strengthen; solidify/strong; solid ～阵地 consolidate a position ～的根据地 stable base areas ～的国防 strong national defence

拱 gǒng ①hump up; arch 猫～腰 the cat arched its back ②arch ～顶 vault ～门 arched door ～桥 arch bridge ～道 archway ③push without using one's hands 用肩～门 push the door with one's shoulder

共 gòng ①common; general ～性 general character ②share ～命运 share a common fate ③doing the same thing; together ～聚一堂 gather in the same hall ～饮一江水 drink from the same river ④altogether; in all; all told 【共产党】the Communist Party ～员 Communist; Party member 【共产主义】communism 【共存】

coexist 【共和】 republicanism; republic ～国 republic 【共计】 amount to; add up to; total 【共鸣】 resonance/sympathetic response 【共青团】 the Communist Youth League ～员 League member 【共事】 work together; be fellow workers 【共同】 common/together; jointly ～点 common ground ～纲领 common programme ～战斗 fight side by side ～努力 make joint efforts ～对敌 join forces to oppose the enemy ～行动 act in concert 【共享】 enjoy together; share

贡 gòng tribute 进～ pay tribute 【贡献】 contribute; dedicate; devote 为革命～一份力量 do one's bit for the revolution

供 gòng ①lay (offerings) ②offerings ③confess; own up 4confession; deposition 口～ oral confession 【供词】 confession 【供品】 offerings 【供认】 confess 【供养】 make offerings to; consecrate 【供状】 written confession; deposition 【供桌】 altar

GOU

勾 gōu ①cancel; cross out; strike out; tick off ～掉名字 cross out one's name ～重要项目 tick off the important items ②delineate; draw ～出轮廓 draw an outline ③induce; evoke; call to mind ～起回忆 evoke memories of sth. ④collude with 【勾搭】 gang up with/seduce 【勾画】 draw the outline of; delineate 【勾结】 collaborate with 【勾销】 liquidate; strike out ～一笔 write off at one stroke 【勾引】 tempt; entice; seduce

沟 gōu ①ditch; channel; trench 交通～ communication trench ②groove; rut; furrow 开～ make furrows ③gully; ravine 乱石～ boulder-strewn gully 【沟渠】 irrigation canals and ditches 【沟通】 link up

钩 gōu ①hook 挂衣 ~ clothes-hook ②check mark; tick ③secure with a hook; hook 把掉到井里的水桶~上来 fish up the bucket which had dropped into the well ④sew (with large stitches) ～贴边 sew on an edging ⑤crochet ～花边 crochet lace 【钩心斗角】intrigue against each other; jockey for position 【钩针】crochet hook

篝 gōu cage 【篝火】bonfire; campfire

苟 gǒu ①careless; negligent ②if 【苟安】seek momentary ease 【苟合】illicit sexual relations 【苟活】live cn in degradation 【苟且】drift along; be resigned to circumstances / perfunctorily; carelessly / illicit (sexual relations); improper ～偷生 drag out an ignoble existence 【苟全】preserve (one's own life) at all costs 【苟延残喘】be on one's last legs

狗 gǒu dog 【狗急跳墙】a cornered beast will do something desperate 【狗腿子】lackey; henchman 【狗窝】kennel; doghouse 【狗熊】black bear / coward

勾 gòu 【勾当】business; deal 罪恶～ criminal activities 肮脏～ a dirty deal

构 gòu ①construct; form; compose ～词 form a word ②make up 虚～ fabrication ③literary composition 佳～ a good piece of writing 【构成】constitute; form ～威胁 pose a threat 【构词法】word-building 【构思】work out the plot (of a literary work) 【构图】composition (of a picture) 【构陷】make a false charge against sb.; frame sb. up 【构造】structure 人体～ the structure of the human body ～简单 be simple in construction

购 gòu buy ～粮 purchase grain 【购货单】order (form) 【购买】purchase; buy ～力 purchasing power ～农具 purchase farm implements

垢 gòu ①dirty; filthy ②dirt; filth 油～ grease stain

够 gòu ①enough; sufficient; adequate 一句话就～了 one word will suffice 这几个图钉～不～ will these drawing pins be enough ②reach; be up to (a certain standard, etc.) 你～得着吗 can you reach it ③quite; rather 【够本】 break even 【够格】 be qualified; be up to standard

媾 gòu ①wed 婚～ marriage ②reach agreement ～和 make peace ③coition 交～ copulate

GU

估 gū appraise ～产 estimate the yield / assess 【估计】 estimate; appraise ～错误 miscalculate ～形势 make an appraisal of the situation ～他会来 reckon he will come 【估价】 evaluate/appraised price

沽 gū ①buy ～酒 buy wine ②sell 待价而～ wait to sell at a good price 【沽名钓誉】 fish for fame and compliments

咕 gū (of hens, etc.) cluck; (of turtledoves, etc.) coo 【咕咚】 thud; splash; plump 【咕嘟】 bubble; gurgle 【咕噜】 rumble; roll/murmur 【咕哝】 mutter; grumble

孤 gū ①fatherless; orphaned ②solitary; alone ～岛 an isolated island 【孤单】 alone/lonely; friendless 【孤独】 lonely; solitary 【孤儿】 orphan 【孤军】 an isolated force ～作战 fight in isolation 【孤苦伶仃】 orphaned and helpless 【孤立】 isolated/isolate ～无援 isolated and cut off from help ～敌人 isolate the enemy ～主义 isolationism 【孤僻】 unsociable and eccentric

姑 gū ①father's sister; aunt ②husband's sister; sister-in-law 【姑夫】 the husband of one's father's sister; uncle 【姑母】 father's sister; aunt 【姑娘】 girl/daughter

【姑且】tentatively; for the moment ～不谈 leave sth. aside for the moment 【姑息】appease; indulge; tolerate ～养奸 to tolerate evil is to abet it

辜 gū guilt; crime 无～ guiltless; innocent 【辜负】fail to live up to; be unworthy of; disappoint 不～党的期望 live up to the expectations of the Party ～群众的信任 let the masses down

箍 gū ①hoop; band 铁～ hoop iron ②bind round; hoop ～桶 bind a bucket 【箍桶匠】cooper; hooper

骨 gú bone 【骨头】bone/character; a person of a certain character 懒～ lazybones ～架子 skeleton

古 gǔ ancient; age-old; palaeo- ～时 in ancient times; in olden days ～画 ancient painting ～瓷 old china 【古奥】archaic and abstruse 【古板】old-fashioned and inflexible 【古代】ancient times; antiquity ～史 ancient history 【古典】classical allusion/classical ～文学 classical literature ～音乐 classical music ～作品 classic 【古董】antique; curio / old fogey 【古怪】eccentric; odd; strange 【古迹】historic site 【古旧】antiquated; archaic ～词语 archaisms 【古老】ancient; age-old 【古人】ancient; our forefathers 【古诗】ancient poetry 【古书】ancient books 【古铜色】bronze 【古玩】antique; curio 【古为今用】make the past serve the present 【古文】prose written in the classical literary style; ancient Chinese prose 【古物】ancient objects; antiquities 【古装】ancient costume

谷 gǔ ①valley; gorge 深～ a deep valley ②cereal; grain ③millet 【谷仓】granary; barn 【谷草】millet straw 【谷壳】husk (of rice)

股 gǔ ①thigh ②section (of an office, enterprise, etc.) ③strand; ply 三～的线 three-ply thread ④one of several equal parts; share in a company 分～ divide into equal parts ⑤ ~~线 a skein of thread 一~泉水 a stream of spring water 一~香味 a whiff of fragrance 一~热气 a puff of hot air 一~劲 a burst of energy 一~敌军 a horde of enemy soldiers 【股本】 capital stock 【股东】 shareholder 【股份】 share; stock ~公司 stock company ~有限公司 limited company 【股票】 share certificate; share; stock ~行市 current prices of stocks ~交易 buying and selling of stocks ~交易所 stock exchange ~市场 stock market 【股息】 dividend 【股长】 section chief

骨 gǔ ①bone ②skeleton; framework ③character; spirit 傲~ lofty and unyielding character 【骨粉】 bone meal; bone dust 【骨干】 backbone 起~作用 be a mainstay ~工程 key projects ~分子 core member 【骨骼】 skeleton 【骨灰】 bone ash/ashes of the dead ~盒 cinerary casket 【骨架】 skeleton; framework (of a house, novel, etc.) 【骨节】 joint 【骨科】 (department of) orthopaedics ~医生 orthopaedist 【骨牌】 dominoes 【骨气】 strength of character; moral integrity; backbone 【骨肉】 flesh and blood; kindred ~兄弟 blood brothers ~之亲 blood relations ~团聚 a family reunion 【骨髓】 marrow 【骨折】 fracture 【骨子】 frame; ribs 伞~ umbrella frame 扇~ the ribs of a fan 【骨子里】 in one's heart of hearts

贾 gǔ ①merchant ②engage in trade ③sell; afford

蛊 gǔ a legendary venomous insect 【蛊惑】 poison and bewitch ~人心 confuse and poison people's minds

鼓 gǔ ①drum 打~ beat a drum ~声 drumbeats ②beat; strike; sound ~掌 clap one's hands; applaud ③blow with bellows, etc. ④rouse; agitate; pluck up ~起勇气 muster one's courage ⑤bulge; swell ~着嘴 pout 【鼓吹】 advocate / preach; advertise 【鼓动】 agitate; arouse / instigate 【鼓励】 encourage; urge 精神~和物质~ moral encouragement and material reward 【鼓舞】 inspire; hearten ~斗志 enhance the morale of sb. 【鼓噪】 make an uproar; clamour 【鼓足干劲】 go all out

固 gù ①solid; firm 加~ make sth. more solid ②firmly; resolutely ~辞 resolutely refuse ③solidify; consolidate ~堤 strengthen the dyke 【固定】 fixed; regular ~价格 fixed price ~职业 permanent occupation ~资本 fixed capital 【固然】 no doubt; it is true/of course; admittedly 【固守】 be firmly entrenched in ~阵地 tenaciously defend one's position 【固体】 solid (body) ~酱油 solidified soy sauce ~燃料 solid fuel 【固有】 intrinsic; inherent; innate 【固执】 obstinate/persist in; cling to ~己见 stubbornly adhere to one's opinions

故 gù ①incident; happening 变~ unforeseen event ②reason; cause 无~缺勤 be absent without reason ③on purpose; intentionally ~作镇静 pretend to be calm ④hence; therefore; for this reason ⑤former; old ~道 old course (of a river) ⑥friend; acquaintance 非亲非~ neither relative nor friend; a perfect stranger ⑦die; pass away ~died of illness 【故步自封】 be complacent and conservative 【故都】 onetime capital 【故宫】 the Imperial Palace 【故伎】 old tactics 【故居】 former residence 【故弄玄虚】 be deliberately mystifying 【故人】 old friend 【故世】 die; pass away 【故事】 story; tale ~会 story-telling session ~片 feature film ~员 story-teller 【故土】 native land 【故乡】 native place; hometown; birthplace 【故意】 intentionally; wilfully; deliberately ~刁难 place obstacles in sb.'s way 我不是~的 I didn't do it on purpose 【故障】 hitch; stoppage; trouble 排除~ fix a breakdown 出了~ be out of order

顾 gù ①turn round and look at; look at 相一一笑 smile at each other knowingly ②attend to; take into consideration 兼～ give consideration to both 【顾及】take into account; give consideration to 【顾忌】scruple; misgiving 【顾客】customer; shopper; client 【顾虑】apprehension; worry 打消～ dispel one's misgivings 【顾全】show consideration for and take care to preserve ～大局 take the interests of the whole into account ～面子 save sb.'s face 【顾问】adviser; consultant

雇 gù hire; employ ～船 hire a boat 【雇工】hire labour/hired hand 【雇农】farmhand 【雇佣】employ; hire ～军 mercenary army ～观点 hired hand mentality ～劳动 wage labour 【雇员】employee 【雇主】employer

痼 gù chronic; inveterate 【痼疾】obstinate illness 【痼习】confirmed habit

GUA

瓜 guā melon, gourd, etc. 【瓜分】carve up; divide up; partition 【瓜葛】connection; implication; association 【瓜子】melon seeds

呱 guā clip-clop; clack ～板儿 bamboo clappers 【呱呱叫】tiptop; top-notch

刮 guā ①scrape ～胡子 shave the beard ②smear with (paste, etc.) ③plunder; fleece ～钱 extort money from sb. ④blow ～大风 it's blowing hard 【刮刀】scraper 【刮脸】shave (the face) ～刀 razor 【刮目相看】look at sb. with new eyes

寡 guǎ ①few; scant 以～敌众 pit a few against many ～不敌众 be hopelessly outnumbered ②tasteless ③widowed 【寡妇】widow 【寡头】oligarch ～垄断 oligopoly ～政治 oligarchy

卦 guà divinatory symbols 占～ divination

挂 guà ①hang; put up 把它～在墙上 hang it up on the wall ②hitch; get caught ～拖车 hitch up the trailer ③ ring off ～断电话 hang up (the receiver) 先别～(电话) hold the line ④call up; put sb. through to 请给我～拖拉机站 please put me through to the tractor station ⑤ be concerned about ⑥ register (at a hospital, etc.) ～外科 register for surgery 【挂彩】be wounded in action 【挂车】trailer 【挂钩】couple (two railway coaches) /link up with; establish contact with; get in touch with 【挂号】register (at a hospital, etc.) /send by registered mail ～处 registration office ～费 registration fee ～信 registered letter 【挂虑】be anxious about; worry about 【挂面】fine dried noodles; vermicelli 【挂名】titular; nominal; only in name 【挂念】miss 【挂失】report the loss of (identity papers, cheques, etc.) 【挂帅】be in command; take command 【挂锁】padlock 【挂毯】tapestry 【挂图】wall map/hanging chart 【挂衣钩】clothes-hook 【挂钟】wall clock

褂 guà gown; unlined garment 短～ short gown 大～儿 long gown

GUAI

乖 guāi ①well-behaved (child); good; obedient ②clever; shrewd; alert 学～了 become a little wiser 【乖觉】alert; quick 【乖戾】perverse (behaviour); disagreeable (character) 【乖谬】absurd; abnormal 【乖僻】eccentric; odd 【乖巧】clever/cute; lovely

掴 guāi slap; smack ～耳光 box sb.'s ears; slap sb. on the face

拐 guǎi ①turn 往左～ turn to the left ②limp ③crutch 架着～走 walk with crutches ④abduct; kidnap ⑤ swindle; make off with 【拐棍】 walking stick 【拐角】 corner; turning 【拐骗】 abduct/swindle (money out of sb.) 【拐弯】 turn (a corner) /turn round; pursue a new course 【拐弯抹角】 talk in a roundabout way; beat about the bush 【拐杖】 walking stick 【拐子】 cripple / abductor

怪 guài ①strange; odd; queer; bewildering ～现象 something quite unusual ～题 odd questions ②monster; demon; evil being ③blame 不能～他们 it's not their fault 只能～自己 have only oneself to blame 【怪不得】 no wonder; so that's why/not to blame 【怪诞】 weird; strange 【怪话】 cynical remark; grumble; complaint 【怪模怪样】 queer-looking; grotesque 【怪僻】 eccentric; peculiar 【怪物】 monster; monstrosity; freak / an eccentric person 【怪异】 monstrous; unusual

GUAN

关 guān ①shut; close ～上门 close the door ②turn off ～灯 turn off the light ③lock up (in prison); shut in ④close down ～了几家店铺 a few shops closed down ⑤pass 把～ guard the pass; check ⑥customhouse ⑦ barrier; critical juncture 技术难～ technical barriers ⑧ concern; involve 这不～他的事 that doesn't concern him 【关闭】 close; shut/close down; shut down 【关怀】 show loving care for; show solicitude for ～儿童的健康成长 pay attention to the healthy growth of children 【关键】 hinge; key; crux 问题的～ the key to the question ～时刻 a critical moment 【关节】 joint/links ～炎 arthritis 【关口】 pass / juncture 【关联】 be related; be connected 【关门】 close / slam the door on sth. / behind closed doors 【关切】 be deeply concerned; show one's concern over 【关税】 customs duty; tariff 【关头】 juncture; moment 【关系】 relation; relationship / bearing; impact; significance / concern; have to do with 外交～ diplomatic relations 群众～ relations with the masses ～重大 have an important bearing on sth. 【关心】 be concerned with; show solicitude for; be interested in; care for ～国家大事 concern oneself with affairs of state 【关押】 lock up; put in prison 【关于】 about; on; with regard to; concerning 【关照】 look after; keep an eye on/notify by word of mouth ～我一声 let me know 【关注】 follow with interest; pay close attention to

观 guān ①look at; watch; observe ～日出 see the sunrise ②sight; view 外～ outward appearance ③outlook; view; concept 【观察】 observe; watch; survey ～动静 watch what is going on ～家 observer ～所 observation post ～员 observer 【观点】 point of view; viewpoint; standpoint 【观感】 impressions 【观光】 go sightseeing; visit; tour ～团 visiting group ～者 sightseer 【观看】 watch; view 【观礼】 attend a celebration or ceremony ～台 reviewing stand 【观摩】 view and emulate 【观念】 sense; idea; concept ～形态 ideology 【观赏】 view and admire; enjoy the sight of 【观望】 wait and see; look on 【观众】 spectator; viewer; audience

官 guān ①government official; officer ～兵一致 unity between officers and men ②organ 感～ sense organ 【官场】 official circles 【官邸】 official residence 【官方】 of or by the government; official ～人士 official quarters ～消息 official sources 【官复原职】 be reinstated 【官架子】 bureaucratic airs 【官阶】 official rank 【官僚】 bureaucrat ～机构 bureaucratic apparatus ～主义 bureaucracy 【官能】 (organic) function; sense 【官腔】 (speak in a) bureaucratic tone; (still with) official jargon 【官司】 lawsuit 【官衔】 official title 【官样文章】 officialese 【官员】 official 【官职】 government post; official position

冠 guān ①hat ②corona; crown (of a tree) 花～ corolla ③crest; (cock's) comb 【冠冕】 royal crown; official hat ～堂皇 highfalutin; high-sounding

棺 guān coffin

鳏 guān wifeless; widowered 【鳏夫】 bachelor; widower

馆 guān ①accommodation for guests 旅～ hotel ②embassy, legation or consulate ③shop 饭～ restaurant ④a place for cultural activities 文化～ cultural centre

管 guǎn ①tube; pipe 钢～steel tube ②wind instrument 铜～乐器 brass wind ③valve; tube 电子～ electron tube ④manage; run; be in charge of ～家务 keep house ～机器 tend a machine ⑤subject sb. to discipline 孩子要～children need discipline ⑥bother about; mind 别～我 don't bother about me 不要你～ mind your own business ⑦provide; guarantee ～住 provide accommodation 【管保】 guarantee; assure/certainly; surely 【管道】 pipeline; piping; conduit; tubing 【管风琴】 organ 【管家】 manager; house-keeper 【管教】 subject sb. to discipline 【管理】 manage; run; administer; supervise ～生产 manage production 企业～ administration of enterprises ～处 management office ～费 costs of administration 【管事】 run affairs; be in charge/efficacious; effective; of use 【管束】 restrain; check; control 【管辖】 have jurisdiction over; administer ～权 jurisdiction 【管弦乐】 orchestral music ～队 orchestra 【管乐队】 wind band 【管乐器】

wind instrument 【管制】control/put under surveillance

贯 guàn ①pass through; pierce ②be linked together 鱼～而入 file in ③birthplace; native place 籍～ the place of one's birth or origin 【贯彻】carry out; implement; put into effect 【贯穿】run through; penetrate 【贯串】run through; permeate 【贯通】have a thorough knowledge of; be well versed in/joined up 【贯注】concentrate on; be absorbed in

冠 guàn precede; crown with/first place; the best 全国之～ rank first in the whole country 【冠词】article 【冠军】champion

惯 guàn ①be used to; be in the habit of ②indulge; spoil (a child) 【惯犯】habitual offender; repeater 【惯匪】hardened bandit 【惯技】old trick 【惯例】convention; usual practice 【惯窃】hardened thief 【惯用】habitually practise; consistently use

盥 guàn wash 【盥洗】wash one's hands and face ～室 washroom ～台 washstand ～用具 toilet articles

灌 guàn ①irrigate ②fill; pour ～田 irrigate the fields ～药 pour medicine down the throat ～醉 get sb. drunk 【灌肠】sausage 【灌唱片】cut a disc 【灌溉】irrigate ～面积 irrigated area ～渠 irrigation canal ～网 irrigation network 【灌木】bush; shrub 【灌输】instil into; inculcate; imbue with 【灌音】have one's voice recorded

罐 guàn jar; pot; tin 茶叶～ tea caddy 【罐头】tin; can ～食品 tinned food 【罐子】pitcher; jug; pot

GUANG

光 guāng ①light; ray 日～ sunlight ②brightness; lustre 金属的～ the lustre of metals ③honour; glory 为国争～ win honour for one's country ④scenery 春～

spring scene ⑤smooth; glossy; polished 两面～ be smooth on both sides 磨～ polish ⑥used up; nothing left ⑦bare; naked ～着头 be bareheaded ⑧solely; only; merely; alone 【光波】light wave 【光彩】lustre; splendour; radiance/honourable; glorious 【光复】recover 【光棍儿】unmarried man; bachelor 【光棍】ruffian 【光华】brilliance; splendour 【光滑】smooth; glossy; sleek 【光辉】radiance; brilliance; glory/brilliant; magnificent; glorious ～著作 magnificent works ～榜样 a shining example ～的一生 a glorious life 【光景】scene / circumstances; conditions 【光亮】bright; luminous; shiny 【光临】presence (of a guest, etc.) 敬请～ your presence is cordially requested 欢迎～指导 we welcome you and would appreciate your advice 【光芒】rays of light; brilliant rays; radiance ～万丈 shining with boundless radiance; gloriously radiant 【光明】light / bright; promising/openhearted; guileless ～磊落 open and aboveboard 【光荣】honour; glory; credit ～榜 honour roll ～花 rosette 【光天化日】broad daylight 【光头】bareheaded/shaven head; shaven-headed 【光线】light; ray 别在～不好的地方看书 don't read in a poor light 【光阴】time ～似箭 time flies like an arrow; how time flies 【光泽】lustre; gloss

广 guǎng ①wide; vast; extensive ②numerous ③expand; spread 【广播】broadcast; be on the air ～电台 radio station ～稿 broadcast script ～节目 broadcast programme ～剧 radio play ～体操 setting-up exercises to radio music ～员 announcer; broadcaster ～站 broadcasting station 【广博】wide; extensive (knowledge) 【广场】(public) square 【广大】vast; wide; extensive/large-scale; widespread/numerous ～青年学生 the mass of student youth ～读者 the reading public 【广度】scope; range 【广泛】extensive;

wide-ranging; widespread ～的兴趣 wide interests ～征求意见 solicit opinions from all sides 【广告】 advertisement 做～ advertise ～画 poster ～栏 advertisement column ～牌 billboard ～色 poster colour 【广阔】 vast; wide; broad ～的前景 broad prospects 交游～ have a wide acquaintance 【广漠】 vast and bare 【广义】 broad sense

逛 guàng stroll; ramble; roam ～大街 stroll around the streets 【逛荡】 loiter; loaf about

GUI

归 guī ①go back to; return ～期 date of return 无家可～ be homeless ②give back to; return sth. to (its rightful owner, etc.) ③converge; come together; sum up ④turn over to; put in sb.'s charge ～集体所有 be turned over to the collective 【归案】 bring (a criminal) to justice 【归并】 incorporate into; merge into/lump together; add up 【归档】 place on file; file 【归队】 rejoin one's unit/return to the profession one was trained for 【归根结底】 in the final analysis 【归功于】 give the credit to; attribute the success to 【归国】 return to one's country ～观光 return to one's homeland on a sightseeing tour ～华侨 returned overseas Chinese 【归还】 return; revert 【归结】 sum up; put in a nutshell 【归类】 sort out; classify 【归纳】 induce; conclude; sum up ～法 inductive method; induction 【归入】 classify; include 【归属】 belong to; come under the jurisdiction of 【归宿】 a home to return to 【归心似箭】 impatient to get back; anxious to return 【归于】 belong to; be attributed to / result in; end in 【归罪】 put the blame on; impute to

龟 guī tortoise; turtle 【龟甲】 tortoise-shell 【龟缩】 withdraw into passive defence; hole up

规 guī ①compasses; dividers ②regulation; rule 校～ school regulations ③advise ④map out ～划 plan ⑤ gauge 线～ wire gauge 【规避】evade; dodge; avoid 【规程】rules; regulations 【规定】stipulate; provide/fix; set ～的指标 a set quota ～动作 compulsory exercise 【规范】standard; norm 合乎～ conform to the standard ～化 standardization 【规格】specifications; standards; norms 统一的～ unified standards 不合～ not be up to standard 【规划】programme; plan 【规矩】rule; established practice; custom/well-behaved; well-disciplined 守～ abide by the rules; behave oneself 没～ have no manners 【规律】law; regular pattern ～性 regularity 【规模】scale; scope; dimensions 【规劝】admonish; advise 【规则】rule; regulation/regular

闺 guī boudoir 【闺女】girl; maiden/daughter

瑰 guī rare; marvellous 【瑰宝】rarity; treasure; gem 【瑰丽】surpassingly beautiful; magnificent

轨 guī ①rail; track 单～ single track 出～ be derailed ②course; path 常～ normal practice 正～ right path 【轨道】track/orbit; trajectory/course; path 【轨范】standard; criterion

诡 guī deceitful; tricky; cunning 【诡辩】sophistry; sophism; quibbling ～术 sophistry 【诡计】crafty plot; trick; ruse 【诡秘】surreptitious (in one's movements); secretive 【诡诈】crafty; treacherous

鬼 guī ①ghost; spirit; apparition ②stealthy; surreptitious ③sinister plot; dirty trick 心里有～ have a guilty conscience 这里边有～ I smell a rat ④terrible; damnable; horrible ⑤clever; smart; quick 【鬼怪】ghosts and monsters 【鬼鬼祟祟】sneaking; furtive; stealthy 【鬼话】lie 【鬼混】

lead an aimless or irregular existence; fool around 【鬼脸】 funny face; wry face; grimace 【鬼迷心窍】 be possessed; be obsessed 【鬼神】 ghosts and gods; spirits 【鬼主意】 evil plan; wicked idea 【鬼子】 devil

刽 guì cut off; chop off 【刽子手】 executioner; headsman/slaughterer; butcher

柜 guì cupboard; cabinet 书～ bookcase 衣～ wardrobe 【柜台】 counter; bar 站～ serve behind the counter

贵 guì ①expensive; costly; dear 价钱太～ it is too dear ②highly valued; worth; valuable; precious 春雨如油 rain in spring is as precious as oil ③noble ④your ～国 your country ～姓 may I ask your name 【贵宾】 honoured guest; distinguished guest 【贵金属】 precious metal 【贵族】 noble; aristocrat

桂 guì ①cassiabarktree ②laurel; bay tree ③sweet-scented osmanthus 【桂冠】 laurel 【桂花】 sweet-scented osmanthus 【桂皮】 cassia bark 【桂圆】 longan ～肉 dried longan pulp

跪 guì kneel; go down on one's knees 【跪拜】 worship on bended knees; kowtow 【跪倒】 throw oneself on one's knees; prostrate oneself; grovel

GUN

滚 gǔn ①roll; trundle ～铁环 trundle a hoop ②get away; beat it ③bind; trim ～上花边 trim sth. with lace 【滚蛋】 beat it; scram 【滚动】 roll; trundle 【滚滚】 roll; billow; surge ～浓烟 billowing smoke ～向前 surge forward; roll on 【滚珠】 ball ～轴承 ball bearing

棍 gùn ①rod; stick ②scoundrel; rascal 恶～ ruffian 赌～ gambler 【棍棒】 club; cudgel; bludgeon/a stick or staff used in gymnastics

GUO

锅 guō ①pot, pan, boiler, cauldron, etc. 沙～ clay pot 炒菜～ frying pan ②bowl (of a pipe, etc.) 【锅巴】 rice crust 【锅炉】 boiler ～房 boiler room 【锅台】 the top of a kitchen range 【锅贴儿】 lightly fried dumpling 【锅子】 bowl (of a pipe, etc.)/chafing dish

国 guó ①country; state; nation ②of the state; national ～营 state-run ③of our country; Chinese 【国宝】 national treasure 【国宾】 state guest 【国策】 national policy 【国产】 made in our country; made in China 【国耻】 national humiliation 【国都】 (national) capital 【国法】 (national) law 【国防】 national defence ～部 the Ministry of National Defence ～建设 the building up of national defence ～力量 defence capability ～生产 defence production ～线 national defence line ～支出 expenditure on national defence 【国歌】 national anthem 【国画】 traditional Chinese painting 【国徽】 national emblem 【国会】 parliament; Congress 【国货】 Chinese goods 【国籍】 nationality 【国计民生】 the national economy and the people's livelihood 【国际】 international ～地位 international status ～形势 world situation ～影响 impact abroad ～歌 *The Internationale* ～主义 internationalism 【国家】 country; state; nation 【国界】 national boundaries 【国境】 territory ～线 boundary line 【国库】 national treasury; exchequer 【国力】 national power 【国民】 national ～经济 national economy ～生产总值 gross national product 【国难】 national calamity 【国内】 internal; domestic; home 【国旗】 national flag 【国情】 the condition of a country; national conditions 【国庆】 National Day ～节 National Day (October 1) 【国事】 state affairs ～

访问 state visit 【国手】 national champion; grand master 【国土】 territory; land 【国外】 external; overseas; abroad 【国王】 king 【国务会议】 state conference 【国务院】 the State Council 【国宴】 state banquet

果 guǒ ①fruit 结~ bear fruit ②result; consequence 恶~ dire consequences ③determined 行必~ be resolute in action ④really; sure enough ~不出所料 just as one expected ⑤if indeed; if really ~能如此 if that is so 【果断】 resolute; decisive 【果脯】 preserved fruit; candied fruit 【果敢】 courageous and resolute 【果酱】 jam 【果木】 fruit tree 【果皮】 peel; rind 【果品】 fruit 【果然】 really; as expected; sure enough 【果仁儿】 kernel 【果肉】 the flesh of fruit; pulp 【果实】 fruit/gains; fruits 【果树】 fruit tree 【果园】 orchard 【果汁】 fruit juice 【果子】 fruit ~酒 fruit wine ~露 fruit syrup

裹 guǒ bind; wrap ~伤 bind up the wound 【裹腿】 puttee 【裹胁】 force to take part; coerce 【裹足不前】 hesitate to move forward

过 guò ①cross; pass ~草地 plod through grasslands ②across; past; through; over 穿~激流 cut across swift currents ③spend (time); pass (time) 假期~得怎样 how did you spend your holiday ④after; past ~了几个月 after several months ⑤undergo a process; go through 把稿子再~一遍 go over the draft once again ⑥exceed; go beyond 小心别~了站 be sure you don't go past your station ⑦excessively; unduly ~早 too early ~长 too long ⑧fault; mistake 改~ correct one's mistakes 【过不去】 cannot get through; be impassable/be hard on; make it difficult for 【过场】 interlude/cross the stage 走~ do sth. as a mere formality 【过程】 course; process 【过错】 fault; mistake 【过道】 passageway; corridor 【过得去】 be able to pass; can get through/passable; so-so; not too bad 【过度】 excessive; undue; over- 饮酒~ excessive drinking ~兴奋 be overexcited ~疲劳 be overtired 【过渡】 transition; interim 【过分】 excessive; undue ~强调 put undue stress on 做得太~ go too far; overdo sth. 【过关】 pass a barrier/pass a test; reach a standard 【过后】 afterwards; later 【过户】 transfer ownership 【过活】 make a living; live 【过火】 go too far; go to extremes; overdo ~行动 excesses 【过激】 too drastic; extremist 【过节】 celebrate a festival 【过境】 be in transit 【过客】 passing traveller 【过来】 come over; come up 【过路】 pass by on one's way ~人 passerby 【过虑】 be overanxious 【过滤】 filter ~嘴 filter tip (of a cigarette) 【过敏】 allergy 【过目】 look over (papers, lists, etc.) so as to check or approve 【过年】 celebrate the New Year 【过期】 exceed the time limit; be overdue ~作废 in valid after the specified date ~胶卷 expired film ~杂志 back number of a magazine 【过谦】 too modest 【过去】 in or of the past; formerly; previously / go over; pass by 【过人】 surpass; excel 精力~ surpass many others in energy 勇气~ excel in courage 【过剩】 excess; surplus 生产~ overproduction 【过失】 fault; slip; error/offence ~杀人 manslaughter 【过时】 out-of-date; outmoded 【过手】 take in and give out (money, etc.); receive and distribute; handle 【过头】 go beyond the limit; overdo 【过问】 concern oneself with 亲自~ take a personal interest in a matter 无人~ not be attended to by anybody 你不必~ you needn't bother about this 【过细】 meticulous; careful 【过夜】 pass the night; stay overnight 【过意不去】 feel sorry 【过瘾】 enjoy oneself to the full 【过硬】 have a perfect mastery of sth.; be really up to the mark 【过于】 too; unduly

H

HA

哈 hā ①breathe out (with the mouth open) ②aha ～，我猜着了 aha, I've guessed it ～～大笑 laugh heartily; roar with laughter 【哈欠】yawn 打～ give a yawn 【哈腰】bend one's back; stoop/bow

HAI

咳 hāi oh; what; dammit

还 hái ①still; yet ②even more; sitll more 你～要什么呢 what more do you want ③also; too; as well; in addition ④passably; fairly ⑤even 【还好】not bad; passable/fortunately 【还是】still; nevertheless; all the same

孩 hái child 【孩子】child / son or daughter; children 【孩子气】childishness

海 hǎi ①sea or big lake 出～ put out to sea ②a great number of people or things coming together 人～ a sea of people ③extra large; of great capacity ～碗 a very big bowl 【海岸】seacoast; seashore ～线 coastline,【海拔】elevation 【海报】playbill 【海豹】seal 【海滨】seaside 【海产】marine products 【海船】seagoing vessel 【海带】kelp 【海岛】island (in the sea) 【海盗】pirate; sea rover ～行为 piracy 【海堤】sea wall 【海底】seabed; sea floor ～电报 cablegram 【海防】coast defence ～部队 coastal defence force 【海风】sea breeze; sea wind 【海港】seaport; harbour 【海关】customs ～检查 customs inspection 【海角】

cape 【海景】 seascape 【海军】 navy ～航空兵 naval air force ～基地 naval base ～陆战队 marine corps; marines ～武官 naval *attaché* ～学校 naval academy 【海里】 sea mile 【海路】 sea route; sea-lane; seaway 走～ travel by sea 【海米】 dried shrimps 【海绵】 sponge/foam rubber or plastic ～垫 foam-rubber cushion ～球拍 sponge table-tennis bat 【海鸥】 sea gull 【海上】 at sea; on the sea ～作业 operation on the sea ～保险 marine insurance 【海参】 sea cucumber 【海市蜃楼】 mirage 【海誓山盟】 (make) a solemn pledge of love 【海水】 seawater; brine; the sea ～浴 seawater bath; sea bathing 【海滩】 seabeach; beach 【海图】 marine chart 【海外】 overseas; abroad ～华侨 overseas Chinese 【海湾】 bay; gulf 【海王星】 Neptune 【海味】 choice seafood 【海峡】 strait; channel 【海员】 seaman; sailor; mariner 【海运】 ocean shipping 【海战】 sea warfare 【海蜇】 jellyfish

骇 hài be astonished; be shocked 【骇然】 gasping with astonishment; struck dumb with amazement 【骇人听闻】 shocking; appalling

害 hài ①evil; harm; calamity 为民除～ rid the people of a scourge ～多利少 more harm than good ②harmful; destructive; injurious ③do harm to; impair ～人不浅 do people great harm ④kill; murder 遇～ be murdered ⑤contract (an illness); suffer from ～大病 have a serious attack of illness ⑥feel (ashamed, afraid, etc.) 【害虫】 injurious insect 【害处】 harm 吸烟对身体有～ smoking is harmful to one's health 【害鸟】 harmful bird 【害怕】 be afraid; be scared 【害群之马】 an evil member of the herd; black sheep 【害臊】 feel ashamed; be bashful 【害兽】 destructive animal 【害羞】 be bashful; be shy 【害眼】 have eye trouble

HAN

酣 hān (drink, etc.) to one's heart's content ～睡 be fast asleep ～饮 drink to the full; carouse ～战 hard-fought battle ～歌 sing to one's heart's content 【酣畅】merry and lively (with drinking)/fully

憨 hān ①foolish; silly ②naive; ingenuous 【憨厚】simple and honest; straightforward and good-natured

鼾 hān snore 【鼾声】sound of snoring 【鼾睡】sound, snoring sleep

含 hán ① keep in the mouth ～着糖 with a drop in one's mouth ②contain ～泪 with tears in one's eyes ～沙量 silt content ③nurse; cherish; harbour ～恨 nurse one's hatred 【含苞】be in bud 【含糊】ambiguous; vague/careless; perfunctory ～其词 talk ambiguously 【含混】indistinct 【含怒】in anger 【含沙射影】attack by innuendo 【含笑】have a smile on one's face 【含羞】with a shy look; bashfully 【含蓄】contain; embody/implicit; veiled/reserved 【含义】meaning; implication

函 hán ①case; envelope ②letter ～复 reply by letter ～告 inform by letter ～购 purchase by mail 【函授】teach by correspondence ～学校 correspondence school

涵 hán ①contain ②culvert 【涵洞】culvert 【涵养】ability to control oneself; self-restraint/conserve 有～ know how to exercise self-control

寒 hán ①cold ～风 cold wind 受～ get a cold ②tremble (with fear) 胆～ be terrified ③poor; needy 贫～ in indigent circumstances ④humble ～舍 my humble home 【寒伧】ugly; unsightly/shabby; disgraceful 【寒带】frigid zone 【寒假】winter vacation 【寒噤】shiver (with cold or fear) 【寒冷】frigid 【寒流】cold current 【寒气】cold air;

cold draught 【寒暑表】thermometer 【寒酸】miserable and shabby 【寒心】be bitterly disappointed 【寒暄】exchange of conventional greetings

罕 hǎn rarely; seldom ～闻 seldom heard of ～见 seldom seen; rare

喊 hǎn ①shout; cry out; yell ～口号 shout slogans ②call (a person) 【喊话】propaganda directed to the enemy at the front line/communicate by tele-equipment 【喊冤叫屈】cry out about one's grievances

汉 hàn ①the Han nationality ②Chinese (language) ③man 老～ an old man 【汉奸】traitor (to China) 【汉语】Chinese (language) ～拼音字母 the Chinese phonetic alphabet 【汉字】Chinese character 【汉子】fellow

汗 hàn sweat; perspiration 出～ sweat; perspire 【汗背心】sleeveless undershirt; vest; singlet 【汗流浃背】streaming with sweat 【汗马功劳】distinctions won in battle; war exploits/one's contributions in work 【汗毛】fine hair on the human body 【汗衫】undershirt

旱 hàn ①dry spell; drought 抗～ combat drought ②dryland 一稻 dry rice ③on land 【旱季】dry season 【旱路】overland route 走～ travel by land 【旱田】dry farmland 【旱象】signs of drought 【旱烟】tobacco (smoked in a long-stemmed Chinese pipe)

悍 hàn ①brave; bold ②fierce; ferocious 【悍然】outrageously; brazenly; flagrantly

捍 hàn defend; guard 【捍卫】guard; protect ～国家主权 uphold state sovereignty

焊 hàn weld; solder 【焊工】welder 【焊接】welding 【焊枪】welding torch 【焊条】welding rod

憾 hàn regret 引以为～ deem it regrettable 死而无～ die without regret 【憾事】a matter for regret

HANG

夯 háng ①rammer; tamper ②ram; tamp; pound 把土~实 ram the earth

行 háng ①line; row 排成两~ fall into two lines ② seniority among brothers and sisters ③trade; profession; line of business 改~ change one's profession 他干哪~ what's his line ④business firm 【行当】 trade; profession; line of business/type of role (in traditional Chinese operas) 【行话】 jargon; cant 【行家】 expert; connoisseur 【行列】 ranks 【行情】 quotations (on the market); prices ~表 quotations list

吭 háng throat 引~高歌 sing lustily

航 háng ①boat; ship ②navigate (by water or air) 夜~ night navigation 民~ civil aviation 【航标】 navigation mark 【航程】 voyage; passage; range 【航道】 channel; lane; course 【航海】 navigation 【航空】 aviation ~版 airmail edition ~兵 air arm ~港 air harbour ~公司 airline company; airways ~母舰 aircraft carrier ~线 airline; airway ~信 airmail (letter); air letter ~学院 aeronautical engineering institute 【航天】 spaceflight ~飞机 space shuttle 【航图】 chart 【航线】 air or shipping line; route; course 【航向】 course (of a ship or plane) 【航行】 navigate by water; sail / navigate by air; fly 内河(空中)~ inland (aerial) navigation 【航运】 shipping ~公司 shipping company

HAO

 薅 hāo pull up (weeds, etc.) 【薅草】 weeding

号 háo ①howl; yell 北风怒～ a north wind is howling ②wail 哀～ cry piteously; wail 【号啕】 cry loudly ～大哭 cry one's eyes out

毫 háo ①fine long hair ②writing brush 挥～ wield one's writing brush ③in the least; at all 一不动摇 not waver in the least ～无道理 utterly unjustifiable 【毫厘】 the least bit; an iota 【毫毛】 soft hair on the body

豪 háo ①bold and unconstrained; forthright ～饮 unrestrained drinking ～雨 torrential rain ②despotic; bullying 【豪富】 powerful and wealthy / the rich and powerful 【豪华】 luxurious; sumptuous 【豪杰】 person of exceptional ability; hero 【豪迈】 bold and generous; heroic 【豪门】 rich and powerful family; wealthy and influential clan 【豪气】 heroism; heroic spirit 【豪爽】 despotic; tyrannical / despot; bully 【豪情】 lofty sentiments ～满怀 full of pride and enthusiasm ～壮志 lofty sentiments and aspirations 【豪爽】 straightforward; forthright 【豪兴】 exuberant spirits 【豪言壮语】 brave words

壕 háo ①moat ②trench 掘～ dig trenches 【壕沟】 trench / ditch 【壕堑战】 trench warfare

嚎 háo howl; wail 狼～ the howl of a wolf 【嚎啕】 cry loudly; cry one's eyes out

好 hǎo ①good; fine; nice ～看 good-looking; pleasant to the eye; beautiful ②friendly; kind ～朋友 good friend ③be in good health; get well 我病～了 I'm well now ④O.K.; all right; well ⑤be easy (to do); be convenient 这个问题～回答 this question is easy to answer ⑥so as to; so that 早点睡，明儿～赶火车 let's turn in early, so as to get up early tomorrow to catch the train 【好比】 can be compared to; may be likened to 【好吃】 good to eat; tasty; delicious 【好处】 good; benefit; advantage / gain;

profit 对革命有～ be good for the revolution 计划生育～多 family planning has many advantages 得不到～ can gain nothing【好歹】good and bad; what's good and what's bad/mishap; disaster/in any case; anyhow【好感】good opinion; favourable impression【好过】have an easy time / feel well【好汉】brave man; true man; hero【好话】a good word / fine words【好评】favourable comment; high opinion【好人】good person/a healthy person【好日子】wedding day/good days; happy life【好容易】with great difficulty; have a hard time (doing sth.)【好事】good deed; good turn【好手】good hand; past master【好受】feel better【好玩】amusing; interesting【好戏】good play/great fun【好象】seem; be like ～要下雨 it looks like rain【好笑】laughable; funny; ridiculous【好些】quite a lot; a good deal of【好心】good intention; kindness 谢谢您的～ thank you for your kindness【好在】fortunately; luckily【好转】take a turn for the better; improve 形势～ the situation took a favourable turn 病情～ the patient is on the mend

号 hào ①name 绰～ nickname ②assumed name; alternative name ③business house 分～ branch (of a firm, etc.) ④mark; signal 加～ plus sign ⑤number 编～ serial number ⑥size 大～ large size ⑦date ⑧order ⑨any brass-wind instrument 小～ trumpet ⑩anything used as a horn 螺～ conch ⑪bugle call 起床～ reveille【号称】be known as / claim to be【号角】bugle; horn / bugle call【号令】verbal command; order【号码】number ～机 numbering machine【号手】trumpeter; bugler【号外】extra (of a newspaper)【号召】call; appeal

好 hào ①like; love; be fond of ～学 eager to learn ～表现 like to show off ②be liable to ～伤风 be subject to colds 【好吃懒做】 be gluttonous and lazy 【好高务远】 aim too high 【好客】 be hospitable 【好奇】 be curious ～心 curiosity 【好强】 eager to do well in everything 【好胜】 seek to do others down 【好事】 meddlesome; officious 【好恶】 likes and dislikes; taste 【好逸恶劳】 love ease and hate work 【好战】 bellicose; warlike

耗 hào ①consume; cost ―电量 power consumption ② waste time; dawdle 别～着了 stop dawdling ③bad news 【耗费】 expend (time, money, etc.) 【耗尽】 exhaust; use up 【耗损】 consume; waste; lose 【耗子】 mouse; rat

浩 hào great; vast; grand 【浩大】 very great; huge 【浩荡】 vast and mighty 东风～ the east wind blows with mighty power 【浩繁】 vast and numerous 【浩劫】 great calamity; catastrophe 【浩气】 noble spirit

皓 hào ①white ～齿 white teeth ～首 hoary head ② bright; luminous ～月 bright moon

HE

呵 hē breathe out (with the mouth open) ～一口气 give a puff 【呵斥】 berate; excoriate 【呵欠】 yawn

喝 hē ①drink ～茶 drink tea ②drink alcoholic liquor ～醉 be drunk

禾 hé standing grain (esp. rice) 【禾本科】 the grass family ～植物 grass 【禾苗】 seedlings of cereal crops

合 hé ①close; shut ～眼 close one's eyes ②join; combine ～力 joint effort ③whole (family) ④suit; agree (with) ～胃口 suit one's taste ―得来 get along well ⑤be equal to; add up to 一公顷～十五市亩 a hectare is equal to 15 *mu* 【合并】 merge; amalgamate 【合唱】 chorus ～团 chorus 【合成】 compose; compound / synthetize ～词 compound word ～纤维 synthetic fibre 【合订本】 one-volume edition; bound volume 【合法】 legal; lawful; legitimate; rightful ～地位 legal status ～斗争 legal struggle ～化 legalize ～权利 legitimate right ～途径 legal means ～政府 legal government 【合格】 qualified; up to standard 产品～ the product is up to standard ～证 certificate of inspection; certificate of quality 【合乎】 conform with; correspond to; accord with; tally with ～实际 conform to the actual situation ～规律 be in conformity with the law of sth. ～事实 tally with the facts ～需要 meet the needs of sth. ～规格 up to the specifications ～逻辑 logical ～情理 reasonable; sensible 【合伙】 form a partnership 【合击】 make a joint attack on 【合计】 amount to; add up to; total 【合计】 think over; figure out/consult 【合剂】 mixture 【合金】 alloy ～钢 alloy steel 【合刊】 combined issue (of a periodical) 【合理】 rational; reasonable; equitable ～分工 rational division of labour ～的价格 a reasonable price ～施肥 apply fertilizer rationally ～化 rationalize 【合力】 join forces; pool efforts 【合流】 flowing together; confluence/collaborate 【合谋】 conspire; plot together 【合拍】 in time; in step; in harmony 【合情合理】 fair and reasonable 【合群】 get on well with others/be gregarious 【合身】 fit 【合适】 suitable; appropriate; becoming 【合算】 paying; worthwhile/reckon up 【合同】 contract 签订～ sign a contract 撕毁～ tear up a contract ～工 contract worker ～医院 assigned hospital 【合页】 hinge 【合意】 suit; be to one's liking 【合影】 group photo ～留念 have a group photo taken to mark the occasion 【合著】 write in collaboration with; coauthor 【合奏】 instrumental ensemble 【合作】 cooperate; collaborate; work together ～经济 cooperative economy ～社 cooperative; co-op ～医疗 cooperative medical service

何 hé ～人 who ～时 when ～处 where ～往 whither 【何必】 there is no need; why 【何不】 why not 【何妨】 why not; might as well ～一试 why not have a try 【何苦】 why bother; is it worth the trouble 【何况】 much less; let alone 【何以】 how; why ～自解 how are you to explain yourself ～见得 what makes you think so 【何在】 where 困难～ wherein lies the difficulty 原因～ what is the reason for it 【何止】 far more than

河 hé river 【河岸】 river bank 【河床】 riverbed 【河沟】 brook; stream 【河谷】 river valley

和 hé ①gentle; mild; kind ～风 gentle breeze ②harmonious; on good terms 不～ on bad terms ③peace 讲～ make peace ④draw; tie 那盘棋～了 that game of chess ended in a draw ⑤together with ～衣而卧 sleep in one's clothes ⑥with; as ～这件事没有关系 have nothing to do with the matter ～我一样高 be the same height as I ⑦and 工人～农民 workers and peasants 【和蔼】 kindly; affable; amiable; genial 【和好】 become reconciled ～如初 be on good terms again 【和缓】 gentle; mild/ease up; relax 【和会】 peace conference 【和解】 become reconciled ～的态度 conciliatory attitude 【和局】 drawn game; draw; tie 【和睦】 harmony; concord; amity ～相处 live in harmony 家庭～ family harmony 【和平】 peace ～攻势 peace offensive ～共处 peaceful coexistence ～主义 pacifism 【和气】 gentle; kind; polite; amiable 说话～ speak politely; be soft-spoken 伤了～ hurt sb.'s feelings 【和善】 kind and gentle; genial 【和尚】 Buddhist monk 【和谈】 peace talks 【和谐】 harmonious 音调～ in perfect harmony; melodious; tuneful 【和煦】 pleasantly warm; genial (sunshine) 【和颜悦色】 with a kind and pleasant countenance 【和约】 peace treaty

荷 hé lotus 【荷包】small bag; pouch/pocket (in a garment ～蛋 fried eggs 【荷花】lotus 【荷叶】lotus leaf

核 hé ①pit; stone 桃～ peach-pit ②nucleus 细胞～ cell nucleus ③examine; check ～准 check and approve; ratify 【核定】check and ratify 【核对】check ～数字 check figures ～事实 check the facts 【核计】assess; calculate 【核仁】kernel (of a fruit-stone) 【核实】verify; check 【核试验】nuclear test 【核酸】nucleic acid 【核算】business accounting ～单位 accounting unit 【核桃】walnut 【核武器】nuclear weapon 【核心】nucleus; core; kernel ～力量 force at the core ～人物 key person 【核战争】nuclear war 【核装置】nuclear device

盒 hé box; case 一～火柴 a box of matches 铅笔～ pencil case 【盒子枪】Mauser pistol

吓 hé threaten; intimidate

和 hé ①join in the singing ②compose a poem in reply

贺 hé congratulate 【贺词】congratulations; greetings 【贺电】message of congratulation 【贺礼】gift 【贺年】extend New Year greetings or pay a New Year call ～片 New Year card 【贺喜】congratulate sb. on a happy occasion 【贺信】congratulatory letter

荷 hè carry sth. on one's shoulder or back ～枪 carry a rifle ②burden 肩负重～ shoulder heavy responsibilities 【荷载】load

喝 hè shout loudly ～问 shout a question to ～令 shout an order 大～一声 give a loud shout 【喝彩】acclaim; cheer 【喝倒彩】make catcalls; hoot; boo

褐 hè brown 【褐煤】brown coal 【褐色土】drab soil

赫 hè conspicuous; grand 【赫赫】illustrious; very impressive ～战功 illustrious military exploits

鹤 hè crane 【鹤嘴锄】pick; pickaxe; mattock

壑 hè gully; big pool

黑 hēi ①black ～发 black hair ②dark 天～了 it's dark ③secret; shady ～交易 shady deal ④wicked; sinister ～后台 sinister backstage boss 【黑暗】dark ～统治 dark rule ～面 a dark aspect ～势力 forces of darkness 【黑白】black and white; right and wrong ～电视 black-and-white television ～片 black-and-white film 【黑板】blackboard ～报 blackboard newspaper ～擦子 eraser 【黑帮】reactionary gang; sinister gang 【黑豆】black soya bean 【黑话】(bandits') argot; (thieves') cant/double-talk; malicious words 【黑货】smuggled goods; contraband/sinister stuff; trash 【黑面包】black bread 【黑名单】blacklist 【黑幕】inside story of a plot, shady deal, etc. 【黑人】Black people; Black; Negro 【黑色】black ～火药 black powder ～金属 ferrous metal 【黑市】black market 【黑体】boldface (type) 【黑眼镜】sunglasses 【黑油油】jet-black

痕 hén mark; trace 刀～ a mark or scar left by a knife-cut 泪～ tear stains 【痕迹】mark; trace; vestige

很 hěn very; quite; awfully ～满意 feel very satisfied; feel quite pleased ～有道理 contain much truth

狠 hěn ①ruthless; relentless ②suppress (one's feelings); harden (the heart) ③firm; resolute ～～打击歪风邪

气 take vigorous measures to counter evil trends 【狠毒】 vicious; venomous 【狠心】 cruel-hearted; heartless

恨 hèn ①hate 怀～ nurse hatred in one's heart ②regret 遗～ eternal regret 【恨不得】 how one wishes one could; itch to 【恨事】 a matter for regret

HENG

亨 hēng go smoothly 【亨通】 go smoothly; be prosperous 万事～ everything is going smoothly

哼 hēng ①groan; snort ～了一声 give a snort ②hum; croon ～曲子 hum a tune 【哼赤】 puff hard

恒 héng ①permanent; lasting 永～ eternal; everlasting ②perseverance 持之以～ persevere in (doing sth.) ③usual; common; constant 【恒心】 constancy of purpose 【恒星】 (fixed) star

横 héng ①horizontal; transverse ～断面 transverse section ②across; sideways ～写 write words sideways ③move cross-wise; traverse 这条铁路～贯五省 the railway traverses five provinces ④unrestrainedly; turbulently 江河～溢 turbulent waters overflowing their banks ⑤violently; fiercely; flagrantly ～加阻挠 wilfully obstruct ～加干涉 flagrantly interfere 【横冲直撞】 push one's way by shoving or bumping; barge about 【横队】 rank; row 【横幅】 horizontal scroll of painting or calligraphy／banner; streamer 【横格纸】 lined paper 【横跨】 stretch over or across 【横眉】 frown; scowl ～怒目 dart fierce looks of hate 【横批】 a horizontal scroll (bearing an inscription) 【横扫】 sweep away 【横竖】 in any case; anyway 【横心】 steel one's heart; become desperate 【横行】 run amuck; be on a rampage ～一时 run wild for a time ～霸道 play the tyrant 【横征暴敛】 levy exorbitant taxes

衡 héng ①the graduated arm of a steelyard ②weighing apparatus 【衡器】measure; judge ～得失 weigh up the gains and losses 请你～一下该怎么办 will you please consider what to do about it

横 héng ①harsh and unreasonable; perverse 发～ act in an brutal way ②unexpected 【横暴】perverse and violent 【横财】ill-gotten wealth 发～ get rich by foul means 【横祸】unexpected calamity; sudden misfortune 【横死】meet with a sudden death

HONG

轰 hōng ①bang; boom ～的一声炸了 be blown up with a bang ②rumble; bombard; explode 万炮齐～ ten thousand cannons booming ③shoo away; drive off ～他出去 throw him out 【轰动】make a stir ～全国 cause a sensation throughout the country ～一时 create a furore 全场～ make a stir in the hall 【轰轰烈烈】on a grand and spectacular scale; vigorous; dynamic 【轰击】shell; bombard 【轰隆】rumble; roll 【轰鸣】thunder; roar 【轰然】with a loud crash 【轰炸】bomb ～机 bomber

哄 hōng ①roars of laughter ②hubbub 【哄传】(of rumours) circulate widely 【哄动】cause a sensation; make a stir 【哄然】boisterous ～大笑 burst into uproarious laughter 【哄抬】drive up (prices) 【哄堂大笑】the whole room rocking with laughter

烘 hōng ①dry or warm by the fire ～面包 bake bread ②set off 【烘焙】cure (tea or tobacco leaves) 【烘烤】toast; bake 【烘托】add shading around an object to make it stand out/set off by contrast 【烘箱】oven

弘 hóng ①great; grand; magnificent ②enlarge; expand 【弘大】grand

红 hóng ①red ～墙 a red ochre wall ②revolutionary; red 又～又专 both red and expert 【红榜】honour board 【红宝石】ruby 【红茶】black tea 【红豆】ormosia/ love pea 【红果】haw 【红军】the Red Army/Red Army man 【红利】bonus; extra dividend 【红脸】blush / flush with anger; get angry 【红领巾】red scarf/Young Pioneer 【红领章】red collar tab 【红绿灯】traffic light 【红木】padauk 【红旗】red flag or banner 【红润】ruddy; rosy 【红烧】braise in soy sauce 【红薯】sweet potato 【红糖】brown sugar 【红通通】bright red; glowing 【红星】red star 【红血球】red blood cell 【红药水】mercurochrome 【红晕】blush; flush 脸上泛出～ one's face blushing scarlet

宏 hóng great; grand; magnificent 【宏大】grand; grand 规模～ on a grand scale 【宏图】great plan

洪 hóng ①big; vast ～涛 big waves ②flood 防～ control or prevent flood 【洪大】loud 【洪峰】flood peak 【洪亮】loud and clear; sonorous 【洪流】mighty torrent; powerful current 【洪水】flood; floodwater

虹 hóng rainbow 【虹吸管】siphon 【虹吸现象】siphonage

鸿 hóng ①swan goose ②letter ③great; grand ～图 great plans 【鸿沟】wide gap; chasm 不可逾越的～ an impassable chasm 【鸿雁】swan goose

哄 hōng ①fool; humbug 你～我 you're kidding me ②coax; humour ～孩子 coax a child 【哄骗】cheat

哄 hòng uproar; horseplay 一～而散 break up in an uproar

HOU

侯 hóu ①marquis ②a nobleman or a high official 【侯爵】marquis ～夫人 marquise

喉 hóu larynx; throat 【喉结】Adam's apple 【喉咙】throat ～痛 have a sore throat 【喉舌】mouthpiece

猴 hóu ①monkey ②clever boy 【猴皮筋】rubber band 【猴戏】monkey show

吼 hóu roar; howl 狮～ the roar of a lion 远方传来大炮的～声 guns rumbled in the distance

后 hóu ①behind; back; rear 屋～ behind a house ②after; afterwards; later 课～ after class 不久以～ before long ③offspring 无～ without issue ④empress; queen 【后半】latter half; second half ～生 the latter half of one's life ～夜 the small hours 【后备】reserve ～部队 reserve units ～军 reserves / reserve force ～力量 reserve forces 【后辈】younger generation / posterity 【后代】later periods/later generations; descendants; posterity 为～着想 for the sake of future generations 【后爹】stepfather 【后盾】backing 【后方】rear ～工作 rear-area work ～医院 base hospital ～基地 rear base 【后顾】turn back (to take care of sth.)/look back (on the past) ～之忧 fear of disturbance in the rear 【后果】consequence; aftermath 【后患】future trouble ～无穷 no end of trouble for the future 【后悔】regret; repent ～不已 be overcome with regret ～莫及 too late to repent 【后记】postscript 【后继】succeed; carry on ～有人 there is no lack of successors 【后进】lagging behind; less advanced; backward 【后劲】delayed effect; aftereffect/reserve strength 【后来】afterwards; later ～人 successors ～居上 the latecomers surpass the old-timers 【后路】route of retreat/a way of escape 抄～ attack (the enemy) from the rear 切断～ cut off the (enemy's) route of retreat 留～ leave oneself a way out 【后门】back door / backdoor influence 走～ get in by the "back door"; get sth. done through pull 【后

面】at the back; in the rear; behind/later 【后年】the year after next 【后娘】stepmother 【后排】back row 【后期】later stage; later period 【后起】(of people of talent) of new arrivals; of the younger generation ～之秀 an up-and-coming youngster 【后勤】rear service; logistics ～部 rear-service department ～机关 rear-service establishments 【后世】later ages/later generations 【后事】funeral affairs 料理～ make arrangements for a funeral 【后台】backstage/backstage supporter ～老板 backstage boss 【后天】day after tomorrow/postnatal; acquired 【后退】draw back; retreat 【后裔】descendant; offspring 【后援】backing 【后院】backyard 【后者】the latter 【后缀】suffix

厚 hòu ①thick ～棉衣 a heavy padded coat ②deep; profound 深情～谊 profound friendship ③kind; magnanimous 忠～ honest and kind ④large; generous ～礼 generous gifts ⑤rich or strong in flavour ～味 rich food ⑥favour; stress 【厚道】honest and kind 【厚度】thickness 【厚望】great expectations 不负～ live up to sb.'s expectations 【厚颜无耻】impudent; brazen; shameless 【厚意】kind thought; kindness

候 hòu ①wait; await 请稍～ please wait a moment ～领 to be kept until claimed ②inquire after 致～ send one's regards 【候补】be a candidate (for a vacancy); be an alternate 【候车室】waiting room 【候机室】airport lounge or waiting room 【候鸟】migratory bird; migrant 【候选人】candidate 提出～ nominate candidates 【候诊】wait to see the doctor ～室 waiting room

HU

呼 hū ①breathe out; exhale ～出二氧化碳 exhale carbon dioxide ②shout; cry out ～口号 shout slogans

③call 真～其名 address sb. disrespectfully (by name) 【呼号】call sign; call letters/catchword (of an organiza-tion) 【呼唤】call; shout to 【呼救】call for help 【呼哨】whistle 【呼声】cry; voice 【呼吸】breathe; respire ～新鲜空气 have a breath of fresh air ～急促 be short of breath ～困难 breathe with difficulty; lose one's breath ～道 respiratory tract ～系统 respiratory system 【呼啸】whistle; scream; whizz 【呼应】echo; work in concert with 【呼吁】appeal; call on ～书 (letter of) appeal

忽 hū ①neglect; overlook; ignore ②suddenly 【忽略】neglect; overlook; lose sight of 【忽然】suddenly; all of a sudden 【忽视】ignore; neglect 不可～的力量 a force not to be ignored ～困难 overlook the difficulties

糊 hū plaster ～一层泥 spread a layer of mud

囫 hū 【囫囵】whole ～吞 swallow sth. whole 【囫囵吞枣】swallow dates whole--read without understanding

狐 hú fox 【狐臭】body odour 【狐媚】bewitch by ca-jolery; entice by flattery 【狐裘】fox-fur robe 【狐群狗党】a gang of scoundrels 【狐疑】doubt; suspicion

弧 hú arc 【弧度】radian 【弧光】arc light ～灯 arc lamp; arc light 【弧圈球】loop drive 【弧形】arc; curve

胡 hú ①introduced from the northern and western nationalities or from abroad ～桃 walnut ② reckless-ly; wantonly; outrageously ～吹 talk big ～编 recklessly concoct ③moustache, beard or whiskers 【胡扯】(talk) nonsense 【胡蜂】wasp; hornet 【胡搞】mess things up; carry on an affair with sb.; be promiscuous 【胡话】rav-ings; wild talk 樣得直说～ be delirious from fever 【胡椒】pepper 【胡搅】pester sb.; be mischievous/argue te-diously and vexatiously; wrangle ～蛮缠 pester sb. endless-

ly; harass 【胡来】 fool with sth./run wild; make trouble
【胡乱】 carelessly; casually; at random ～猜测 make wild
guesses 【胡萝卜】 carrot ～素 carotene 【胡闹】 run wild
【胡思乱想】 go off into wild flights of fancy 【胡同】
lane; alley 【胡须】 beard, moustache or whiskers

壶 hú ①kettle; pot 茶～ teapot 油～ oil can ②bottle;
flask 行军～ water bottle; canteen

核 hú 【核儿】 stone; pit; core 杏～ apricot stone 梨～
pear core 煤～ cinders

湖 hú lake 【湖滨】 lakeside 【湖泊】 lakes 【湖色】 light
green

葫 hú 【葫芦】 bottle gourd; calabash

糊 hú ①paste ②stick with paste ③(of food) burnt 【糊
精】 dextrin 【糊墙纸】 wall paper 【糊涂】 muddled;
confused ～观念 a muddled idea 别装～ don't play the
fool ～虫 blunderer ～帐 chaotic accounts; a mess

蝴 hú 【蝴蝶】 butterfly ～结 bow

虎 hǔ ①tiger ②brave; vigorous ～将 brave general 【虎口】
tiger's mouth—jaws of death ～余生 survive a disaster; have a narrow escape 【虎头蛇尾】 in like a lion, out
like a lamb; fine start and poor finish 【虎穴】 tiger's den

唬 hǔ bluff 你别～人 quit bluffing 她没被～住 she
wasn't intimidated

琥 hǔ 【琥珀】 amber ～油 amber oil

户 hù ①door 足不出～ never step out of doors ②
household; family 家家～～ each and every family
③(bank) account 存～ (bank) depositor 【户籍】 household register/registered permanent residence ～警 police-

man in charge of household registration 【户口】 number of households and total population / registered permanent residence ～簿 residence booklet 【户头】 (bank) account 开～ open an account 【户主】 head of a household

互 hù mutual; each other ～通情报 exchange information; keep each other informed 【互访】 exchange visits 【互惠】 mutually beneficial; reciprocal 【互利】 mutually beneficial; of mutual benefit 【互相】 mutual; each other ～排斥 be mutually exclusive ～配合 work in coordination ～利用 each using the other for his own ends ～勾结 work in collusion 【互助】 help each other ～组 mutual aid group/mutual aid team

护 hù ①protect; guard; shield ～林 protect a forest ～厂 guard a factory ②be partial to; shield from censure ～孩子 be partial to one's own child 【护航】 escort; convoy ～舰 convoy ship 【护理】 tend and protect; nurse (the sick or the wounded) ～人员 nursing staff 【护身符】 protective talisman 【护士】 (hospital) nurse ～学校 nurses' school ～长 head nurse 【护送】 escort 【护照】 passport

糊 hù paste 玉米～ (cornmeal) mush 【糊弄】 fool; deceive/be slipshod in work; go through the motions

HUA

花 huā ①flower; blossom; bloom 桃～ peach blossom ②pattern; design ③coloured; variegated ～衣服 bright-coloured clothes ④blurred; dim 把眼睛都弄～了 blur one's eyes ⑤spend; expend ～钱 spend money 【花瓣】 petal 【花边】 decorative border / lace 【花布】 cotton print; print 【花茶】 scented tea 【花丛】 flowering shrubs 【花房】 greenhouse 【花费】 expend; cost ～时间 spend time ～心血 take pains 【花岗岩】 granite 【花环】 garland; floral hoop 【花

椒】 Chinese prickly ash 【花卷】 steamed twisted roll 【花篮】 a basket of flowers/gaily decorated basket 【花露水】 toilet water 【花名册】 register (of names); membership roster; muster roll 【花呢】 fancy suiting 【花炮】 fireworks and firecrackers 【花盆】 flowerpot 【花瓶】 flower vase 【花圃】 flower nursery 【花圈】 (floral) wreath 【花色】 design and colour/variety of designs, sizes, colours, etc. 【花生】 peanut; groundnut ~酱 peanut butter ~壳 peanut shell ~米 shelled peanut ~糖 peanut brittle ~油 peanut oil 【花饰】 ornamental design 【花束】 bouquet 【花坛】 flower bed 【花纹】 decorative pattern; figure 【花言巧语】 sweet words 【花样】 pattern; variety/trick ~翻新 the same old thing in a new guise 玩~ play tricks ~滑冰 figure skating 【花椰菜】 cauliflower 【花园】 (flower) garden 【花招】 flourish/trick; game

划 huá ①paddle; row (a boat) ②be to one's profit; pay ~不来 it doesn't pay ③scratch; cut the surface of ~玻璃 cut a piece of glass ~火柴 strike a match 【划拳】 finger-guessing game 【划算】 calculate; weigh / be to one's profit; pay 【划子】 small rowboat

华 huá ①magnificent; splendid ~屋 magnificent house ②prosperous; flourishing 繁~ bustling ③best part 精~ the cream ④flashy; extravagant; luxurious 【华贵】 luxurious; sumptuous; costly 【华丽】 resplendent; gorgeous ~的词藻 flowery language 【华侨】 overseas Chinese 【华裔】 foreign citizen of Chinese origin

哗 huá noise; clamour 【哗变】 mutiny 【哗然】 in an uproar; in commotion 【哗笑】 uproarious laughter 【哗众取宠】 try to please the public with claptrap

滑 huá ①slippery; smooth 路~ the road is slippery ②slip; slide ~一跤 slip and fall ③cunning; crafty;

slipery 【滑冰】 ice-skating; skating 【滑动】 slide 【滑稽】 funny; amusing; comical ~戏 farce 【滑润】 smooth 【滑梯】 (children's) slide 【滑头】 slippery; sly 【滑翔】 glide ~机 glider; sailplane 【滑行】 slide; coast 【滑雪】 skiing ~板 skis ~鞋 ski boots ~杖 ski pole

化 huà ①change; turn; transform ~公为私 appropriate public property ②convert; influence ③melt; dissolve; (of snow, ice) thaw 用水~开 dissolve in water ④digest ~食 help digestion ⑤burn up 焚~ burn up; incinerate ⑥chemistry ⑦-ize; -ify 工业~ industrialize 现代~ modernize 简~ simplify 【化肥】 chemical fertilizer 【化工】 chemical industry ~厂 chemical plant 【化脓】 fester; suppurate 伤口~ the wound is festering 【化身】 incarnation; embodiment 【化石】 fossil 【化为乌有】 melt into thin air; vanish; come to naught 【化学】 chemistry ~成分 chemical composition ~反应 chemical reaction ~武器 chemical weapons ~纤维 chemical fibre ~药品 chemicals ~元素 chemical element ~战争 chemical warfare ~作用 chemical action 【化验】 chemical examination; laboratory test ~单 laboratory test report ~室 laboratory ~员 laboratory technician 【化妆】 put on makeup; make up ~品 cosmetics 【化装】 (of actors) make up / disguise oneself ~师 makeup man ~室 dressing room

划 huà ①delimit; differentiate ~界 delimit a boundary ②transfer; assign ~款 transfer money ③draw; mark; delineate ~线 draw a line 【划定】 delimit; designate 【划分】 divide / differentiate ~势力范围 carve out spheres of influence 【划清】 draw a clear line of demarcation ~是非界限 make a clear distinction between right and wrong 跟他~界线 make a clean break with him 【划时代】 epoch-making ~的意义 epoch-making significance 【划—】 standardized; uniform

话 huà ①word; talk 说几句～ say a few words 留～ leave word ②talk about; speak about. ～家常 exchange small talk 【话别】 say good-bye 【话柄】 subject for ridicule; handle 【话剧】 modern drama; stage play ～团 modern drama troupe 【话题】 topic of conversation 转～ change the subject 【话筒】 microphone / telephone transmitter/megaphone 【话头】 thread of discourse 打断～ interrupt sb. 【话务员】 (telephone) operator

画 huà ①draw; paint ～画 draw a picture ～圈 describe a circle ～草图 make a sketch ②drawing; painting 油～ oil painting 这公园美景如～ the park is a picture itself ③be decorated with paintings or pictures ～栋雕梁 painted pillars and carved beams 【画板】 drawing board 【画报】 pictorial 【画笔】 (painting) brush 【画布】 canvas (for painting) 【画册】 picture album 【画家】 painter; artist 【画架】 easel 【画匠】 artisan-painter 【画境】 picturesque scene 【画具】 painter's paraphernalia 【画廊】 painted corridor / gallery 【画面】 tableau / frame 【画片】 a miniature reproduction of a painting 【画室】 studio 【画图】 draw designs, maps, etc. / picture 【画像】 draw a portrait / portrayal 【画展】 art exhibition

HUAI

怀 huái ①bosom ②mind ③keep in mind ～着真诚的愿望 cherish sincere hopes ～着深厚的感情 with deep feelings ④think of; yearn for ～乡 yearn for one's native place; be homesick.⑤conceive (a child) 【怀抱】 bosom 回到祖国的～ return to the embrace of one's homeland 【怀表】 pocket watch 【怀恨】 nurse hatred 【怀念】 cherish the memory of 【怀疑】 doubt; suspect 引起～

raise doubts 消除～ clear up suspicion 受～ come under suspicion 持～态度 take a sceptical attitude 【怀孕】 be pregnant ～期 period of pregnancy

踝 huái ankle

坏 huài
①bad ～书 a harmful book ～天气 foul weather ②go bad; spoil; ruin 鱼～了 the fish has gone bad ③badly; awfully; very 吓～了 be badly scared 气～了 be beside oneself with rage 累～了 be dead tired ④evil idea; dirty trick 使～ play a dirty trick 【坏处】 harm; disadvantage 【坏蛋】 bad egg; scoundrel 【坏东西】 bastard; rogue 【坏分子】 bad element; evildoer 【坏话】 malicious remarks; vicious talk/unpleasant words 【坏人】 bad person; evildoer 【坏事】 bad thing; evil deed/ruin sth.

HUAN

欢 huān
①joyous; merry; jubilant ～唱 sing merrily ②vigorously; with great drive; in full swing 雨越下越～ it's raining harder and harder 【欢畅】 thoroughly delighted; elated 【欢度】 spend (an occasion) joyfully ～佳节 celebrate a festival with jubilation 【欢呼】 hail; cheer; acclaim 长时间的～ prolonged cheers 【欢聚】 happy reunion ～一堂 happily gather under the same roof 【欢快】 cheerful and light-hearted; lively 【欢乐】 happy; joyous; gay 【欢庆】 celebrate joyously 【欢送】 see off; send off ～会 send-off meeting ～仪式 seeing-off ceremony 【欢腾】 great rejoicing; jubilation 【欢喜】 joyful; happy/like; be fond of; delight in 【欢笑】 laugh heartily 【欢心】 favour; liking; love 【欢欣鼓舞】 be filled with exultation; be elated 【欢迎】 welcome; greet ～词 welcoming speech ～会 a party to welcome sb. ～批评 criticisms

are welcome 这本书很受～ the book had a favourable reception

还 huán ①go back ～家 return home ～乡 return to one's native place ②give back; return; repay ～书 return the books ～本 repay capital ～钱 pay sb. back ③ give or do sth. in return 【还击】 fight back; return fire 【还价】 counter-offer 【还礼】 return a salute / present a gift in return 【还清】 pay off (one's debts, etc.) 【还手】 strike back 【还原】 restore 【还债】 repay a debt

环 huán ①ring; hoop 耳～ earring ②link 薄弱的一～ weak link ③surround; encircle; hem in 四面～山 be surrounded by mountains 【环抱】 surround; encircle 【环顾】 look about ～四周 look all round 【环节】 link 【环境】 environment; surroundings 换换～ have a change of environment ～保护 environmental protection ～卫生 general sanitation 【环球】 round the world / the earth; the whole world 【环绕】 encircle; revolve around 【环行】 going in a ring ～一周 make a circuit ～公路 ring road

缓 huán ①slow; unhurried ～步而行 walk unhurriedly ②delay; postpone; put off ～办 postpone doing sth. ～口气 have a respite ③not tense; relaxed ④recuperate; revive; come to ～过劲儿 feel refreshed after a breathing spell 【缓冲】 buffer; cushion ～作用 cushioning effect ～地带 buffer zone ～国 buffer state 【缓和】 relax; ease (up); mitigate; alleviate/*détente* ～紧张局势 relax the tension ～矛盾 mitigate a contradiction 【缓慢】 slow 【缓期】 postpone a deadline; suspend ～付款 delay payment 【缓刑】 reprieve; probation

幻 huàn ①unreal; imaginary; illusory 虚～ unreal; visionary ②magical; changeable 变～ change irregularly; fluctuate 【幻灯】 slide show / slide projector ～片 slide

放～ show slides 【幻境】dreamland; fairyland 【幻梦】illusion; dream 【幻灭】vanish into thin air 【幻术】magic 【幻想】fancy ～曲 fantasia 抱～ cherish illusions 丢掉 ～ cast away illusions 沉湎于～ indulge in fantasy 【幻象】mirage 【幻影】unreal image

宦 huàn ①official ～海 official circles ～途 official career ②eunuch

涣 huàn melt; vanish 【涣然】melt away; disappear 疑虑 ～冰释 one's misgivings have all vanished 【涣散】lax; slack 纪律～ be lax in discipline ～斗志 sap sb.'s morale

换 huàn ①exchange; barter; trade ～货 exchange goods ②change ～衣服 change one's clothes ～句话说 in other words 【换班】change shifts/relieve a person on duty/changing of the guard 【换车】change trains or buses 【换气】take a breath (in swimming) 【换钱】change money/sell 【换取】exchange sth. for; get in return 【换人】substitution (of players) 【换算】conversion ～表 conversion table 【换文】exchange of notes

唤 huàn call out 【唤起】arouse/call; recall 【唤醒】wake up; awaken

焕 huàn shining; glowing 【焕发】shine; glow; irradiate ～精神 call forth all one's vigour ～革命青春 radiate the revolutionary vigour of one's youth 【焕然一新】take on an entirely new look; look brand-new

患 huàn ①trouble; peril; disaster 防～于未然 provide against possible trouble ②anxiety; worry ③contract ～病 suffer from an illness ～处 affected part (of a patient's body) 【患得患失】worry about personal gains and losses 【患难】trials and tribulations; adversity; trouble ～之交 tested friend ～与共 go through thick and thin together 【患者】sufferer; patient

HUANG

荒 huāng ①waste 地～了 the land lies waste ②uncultivated land 垦～ open up wasteland ③desolate; barren ～村 deserted village ～岛 desert island ～山 barren hill ④famine; crop failure 储粮备～ store up grain against natural disasters ⑤neglect; be out of practice 别把功课～了 don't neglect your lessons ⑥shortage; scarcity 房～ housing shortage 【荒诞】 fantastic; absurd; incredible 【荒地】 wasteland; uncultivated land 【荒废】 leave uncultivated; lie waste/fall into disuse/neglect 【荒唐】 absurd; fantastic; preposterous/dissipated; loose; intemperate 【荒芜】 lie waste; go out of cultivation 【荒野】 wilderness; the wilds 【荒淫】 dissolute; licentious

慌 huāng flurried; flustered 别～ don't panic ～了手脚 be alarmed and confused ～了神儿 be scared out of one's wits 【慌忙】 in a great rush; hurriedly

皇 huáng emperor; sovereign 【皇帝】 emperor 【皇宫】 (imperial) palace 【皇冠】 imperial crown 【皇后】 empress 【皇权】 imperial power 【皇上】 the emperor; the throne; the reigning sovereign/Your or His Majesty 【皇室】 imperial family 【皇太后】 empress dowager 【皇太子】 crown prince 【皇族】 imperial kinsmen

黄 huáng yellow; sallow 【黄澄澄】 glistening yellow; golden 【黄豆】 soya bean; soybean 【黄蜂】 wasp 【黄瓜】 cucumber 【黄昏】 dusk 【黄金】 gold ～储备 gold reserve ～价格 price of gold ～时代 golden age 【黄牛】 cattle 【黄泉】 netherworld 【黄雀】 siskin 【黄色】 yellow/decadent; obscene ～电影 sex film ～书刊 pornographic books and periodicals ～音乐 decadent music 【黄铜】 brass 【黄土】 loess ～高原 loess plateau 【黄莺】 oriole 【黄油】

butter 【黄鱼】 yellow croaker 【黄种】 the yellow race

惶 huáng fear; trepidation 【惶惶】 in a state of anxiety; on tenterhooks; alarmed 【惶惑】 perplexed and alarmed; apprehensive 【惶恐】 terrified

蝗 huáng locust ～灾 plague of locusts

恍 huǎng ①all of a sudden; suddenly ②seem; as if ～如梦境 as if in a dream 【恍惚】 in a trance; absent-minded/dimly; faintly 【恍然大悟】 suddenly see the light

晃 huǎng ①dazzle ～眼的阳光 dazzling sunshine ②flash past 半个月一～就过去了 a fortnight passed in a flash

谎 huǎng lie; falsehood 说～ tell a lie ～报 lie about sth.; give false information; make a false report

幌 huǎng 【幌子】 shop sign; signboard/pretence; cover; front

晃 huàng shake; sway ～～手 shake one's hand 【晃动】 rock; sway 【晃悠】 wobble; stagger; shake from side to side

HUI

灰 huī ①ash 飞～ fly ash ②dust 一层～ a layer of dust ③lime; mortar 和～ mix mortar ④grey ～马 a grey horse ⑤discouraged 心～意懒 feel disheartened 【灰暗】 murky grey; gloomy 【灰白】 greyish white; ashen; pale 脸色～ look pale 【灰尘】 dust; dirt 【灰烬】 ashes 化为～ be reduced to ashes 【灰溜溜】 gloomy; dejected; crest-fallen 【灰蒙蒙】 dusky; overcast ～的夜色 a dusky night scene 【灰色】 grey; ashy/pessimistic; gloomy/obscure; ambiguous 【灰心】 lose heart; be discouraged; be disheartened

诙 huī 【诙谐】 humorous; jocular ～曲 humoresque

恢 huī extensive; vast 【恢复】renew; resume (diplomatic relations, etc.) /recover (one's health, consciousness, etc.) /restore; reinstate ～名誉 rehabilitation (of a person's reputation) 他精神～了 he retrieved his spirits

挥 huī ①wave; wield ～刀 wield a sword ～镰 wield a scythe ～笔 put pen to paper ②wipe off ～泪 wipe away tears ～汗 drip with sweat ③command (an army) ～师南下 command an army to march south ④scatter 【挥动】brandish; wave; wield ～拳头 shake one's fist 【挥发】volatilize ～性 volatility ～油 volatile oil 【挥霍】spend freely; squander 【挥手】wave (one's hand) ～致意 wave greetings to ～告别 wave farewell

晖 huī sunshine; sunlight

辉 huī ①brightness; splendour ②shine 【辉煌】brilliant; glorious ～的战果 a brilliant military victory

徽 huī emblem; badge 校～ school badge 帽～ cap insignia 【徽号】title of honour 【徽章】badge; insignia

回 huī ①circle; wind 迂～ winding; roundabout ②return; go back ～到生产第一线 go back to one's post on the production front ③turn ～身 turn round ④answer; reply ～信 send a letter in reply; write back 【回避】evade; dodge; avoid (meeting sb.) ～要害问题 evade the crucial question ～困难 dodge difficulties 【回答】answer; reply; response 【回访】pay a return visit 【回顾】look back; review 【回合】round; bout 【河击】fight back; return fire; counterattack 【回教】Islam 【回绝】decline; refuse 【回来】return; come back; be back 【回声】echo 【回收】retrieve; recover 【回头】turn one's head; turn round/repent/later ～见 see you later ～路 the road back (to one's former position) 【回味】aftertaste/call sth. to mind and ponder over it 【回乡】 return to one's home village 【回想】 think back; recollect; recall 【回心转意】 change one's views 【回信】 write in reply; write back/a letter in reply/a verbal message in reply; reply 我给你个～ I'll let you know 望早日～ I'm looking forward to hearing from you soon 【回形针】 (paper) clip 【回忆】 call to mind; recollect; recall ～录 recollections 【回音】 echo / reply 【回执】 receipt 【回转】 turn round

茴 huí 【茴香】 fennel / aniseed ～豆 beans flavoured with aniseed ～油 fennel oil

蛔 huí 【蛔虫】 roundworm; ascarid ～病 roundworm disease; ascariasis

悔 huǐ regret; repent 【悔改】 repent and mend one's ways 毫无～之意 show no sign of repentance 【悔过】 repent one's error; be repentant ～书 a written statement of repentance 【悔恨】 regret deeply 【悔悟】 realize one's error and show repentance 【悔罪】 show repentance

毁 huǐ ①destroy; ruin; damage ～于一旦 be destroyed in a moment ②burn up 焚～ destroy by fire; burn down ③defame 【毁谤】 slander; malign; calumniate 【毁灭】 exterminate ～性打击 crushing blow 【毁约】 break one's promise/scrap a contract or treaty

汇 huì ①converge ～成巨流 converge into a mighty torrent ②gather together ③things collected; assemblage; collection 词～ vocabulary ④remit (money) 电～ telegraphic transfer 【汇报】 report; give an account of ～工作 report to sb. on one's work ～会 report-back meeting ～演出 report-back performance 【汇编】 compilation; collection 【汇兑】 remittance 【汇费】 remittance fee 【汇合】 converge; join 【汇集】 collect; compile/come together; converge; assemble 【汇款】 remit money; make a remittance/remittance ～单 money order ～人 remitter 【汇率】 exchange rate 【汇票】 draft; bill of exchange

卉 huì (various kinds of) grass 奇花异～ rare flowers and grasses

会 huì ①get together; assemble 在门口～齐 assemble at the gate ②see ～见 meet with sb. ③meeting; gathering; party 全组～ a meeting of the whole group ④ association; society; union 工～ trade union ⑤can; be able to ～英文 know English ⑥be skilful in ～做工作 be good at doing work ⑦be likely to ～犯错误 be sure to make mistakes ⑧pay a bill 【会餐】 have a dinner party 【会场】 meeting-place 【会费】 membership dues 【会合】 join; meet; converge; assemble 【会话】 conversation 【会聚】 assemble; flock together 【会客】 receive a visitor ～时间 visiting hours 不～ no visitors ～室 reception room 【会商】 hold a conference or consultation 【会审】 joint hearing/make a joint checkup 【会师】 join forces; effect a junction 【会谈】 talks ～纪要 notes on talks 【会堂】 (assembly) hall 【会心】 understanding; knowing ～的微笑 an understanding smile 【会演】 joint performance 文艺～ theatrical festival 【会议】 meeting; conference ～地点 meeting-place ～室 meeting room 【会员】 member ～国 member state ～证 membership card 【会长】 the president of an association or society 【会帐】 pay a bill 【会诊】 consultation of doctors

讳 huì ①avoid as taboo 直言不～ speak bluntly ②forbidden word; taboo 【讳言】 dare not or would not speak up 毫不～ confess freely 无可～ there's no denying the fact

诲 huì teach; instruct 【诲人不倦】 be tireless in teaching 【诲淫诲盗】 propagate sex and violence

绘 huì　paint; draw 【绘画】 drawing; painting 【绘声绘色】 vivid; lively ～的描述 a vivid description

烩 huì　①braise ～虾仁 braised shrimp meat ②cook (rice or shredded pancakes) with meat, vegetables, etc.

贿 huì　bribe 受～ take bribes 行～ practise bribery 【贿赂】 bribe/bribery 【贿买】 buy over; suborn

晦 huì　dark; obscure 【晦暗】 dark and gloomy 【晦气】 unlucky 自认～ be resigned to one's bad luck 【晦涩】 hard to understand ～的语言 obscure language

秽 huì　①dirty 污～ filthy ～土 rubbish; refuse ② ugly; immoral ～行 abominable behaviour

惠 huì　favour; kindness; benefit 受～receive kindness; be favoured 互～ mutual benefit 【惠存】 please keep (this photograph, book, etc. as a souvenir)

慧 huì　intelligent; bright 【慧黠】 clever and artful; shrewd 【慧心】 wisdom 【慧眼】 insight; acumen

HUN

昏 hūn　①dusk 晨～ at dawn and dusk ②dark; dim ③ confused; muddled ④lose consciousness; faint ～倒 go off into a faint 【昏暗】 dim; dusky 【昏沉】 murky/ dazed; befuddled 【昏花】 dim-sighted (from old age) 【昏厥】 faint; swoon 【昏乱】 dazed and confused; befuddled 【昏迷】 stupor; coma ～不醒 remain unconscious 【昏睡】 lethargic sleep; lethargy 【昏头昏脑】 muddleheaded / forgetful 【昏眩】 dizzy; giddy 【昏庸】 fatuous; stupid

荤 hūn　meat or fish ～菜 meat dishes ～油 lard 他不吃～ he's a vegetarian

婚 hūn　①wed; marry ②marriage; wedding 【婚礼】 wedding (ceremony) 【婚期】 wedding day 【婚姻】 marriage; matrimony ～法 marriage law 【婚约】 engagement

浑 hún ①muddy; turbid ～水 muddy water ②foolish; stupid ③simple and natural ④whole; all over 【浑厚】 simple and honest/simple and vigorous 【浑身】 from head to foot; all over ～疼 aching all over ～是劲 brimming with energy 【浑水摸鱼】 fish in troubled waters

魂 hún ①soul ②mood; spirit 【魂不附体】 as if the soul had left the body

混 hùn ①mix; confuse ～在一起 mix things up ②pass for; pass off as ～在革命队伍中 lurk in the revolutionary ranks ③muddle along ～日子 drift along aimlessly ④get along with sb. ～得很熟 be quite familiar with sb. ⑤thoughtlessly; recklessly ～出主意 put forward irresponsible suggestions 【混充】 pass oneself off as 【混纺】 blending ～织物 blend fabric 【混合】 mix; blend; mingle ～物 mixture 【混进】 infiltrate; sneak into 【混乱】 confusion; chaos 【混凝土】 concrete 【混同】 confuse; mix up 【混为一谈】 lump together; confuse sth. with sth. else 【混淆】 obscure; blur ～黑白 mix up black and white ～是非 confuse right and wrong ～视听 mislead the public 【混血儿】 half-breed 【混杂】 mix; mingle

HUO

豁 huō ①slit; break; crack ②give up; sacrifice 【豁出去】 go ahead regardless; be ready to risk everything 【豁口】 break; breach 城墙～ an opening in the city wall 【豁嘴】 harelip/a harelipped person

和 huó mix (powder) with water, etc. 【和面】 knead dough

活 huó ①live ～到八十岁 live to be eighty ②alive; living ～捉 capture alive ③save (the life of a person) ④vivid; lively 脑子很～ have a quick mind ⑤mov-

able; moving ～水 flowing water ⑥exactly; simply ～
象 look exactly like ⑦work 重～ heavy work ⑧pro-
duct【活茬】farm work【活动】move about; exercise/
shaky; unsteady/movable; flexible/activity;manoeuvre 站
起来～ stand up and move about 这颗牙齿～了 this
tooth's loose 政治～ political activities ～余地 room for
manoeuvre 替他～～ use one's influence on his behalf ～
家 activist; public figure【活该】serve sb. right【活活】
while still alive ～烧死 be burnt alive【活计】handicraft
work; manual labour/handiwork; work【活结】slipknot【活
力】vigour; vitality; energy【活路】means of subsistence;
way out / workable method【活命】earn a bare living;
eke out an existence / save sb.'s life ～哲学 the philosophy of survival【活泼】lively; vivacious; vivid【活期】
current ～储蓄 current deposit ～存款帐户 current ac-
count【活页】loose-leaf (binder, selections, etc.)【活跃】
brisk; active; dynamic/enliven; animate

火 huǒ ①fire 生～ make a fire 有～吗 have you got
a light ②firearms; ammunition 交～ exchange shots
③fiery; flaming ④anger; temper 心头～起 flare up in an-
ger【火柴】match ～盒 matchbox【火车】train ～票 railway
ticket ～时刻表 railway timetable ～司机 engine driver;
(locomotive) engineer ～头 (railway) engine; locomotive ～站 railway station【火攻】fire attack【火光】flame;
blaze【火锅】chafing dish【火红】red as fire; fiery;
flaming【火花】spark【火碱】caustic soda【火箭】rocket
～部队 rocket troops ～弹 rocket shell ～发射场 rocket
launching site ～炮 rocket gun ～筒 rocket projector【火
警】fire alarm【火炬】torch【火坑】fiery pit【火辣辣】
burning【火力】firepower; fire ～点 firing point ～发电
厂 thermal power plant【火炉】(heating) stove【火苗】a

tongue of flame; flame 【火炮】cannon; gun 【火热】burning hot; fiery/intimate ～的心 a fervent heart 打得～ carry on intimately with 【火山】volcano ～口 crater 【火伤】burn (caused by fire) 【火上加油】pour oil on the fire 【火舌】tongues of fire 【火石】flint 【火腿】ham 【火险】fire insurance 【火线】front line 【火星】spark/Mars 【火焰】flame 【火药】gunpowder; powder ～库 powder magazine ～桶 powder keg ～味 the smell of gunpowder 【火灾】fire (as a disaster); conflagration 【火葬】cremation

伙 huǒ ①mess; board; meals 在学校入～ board at school ②partner; mate ②partnership; company 合～ enter into partnership 拆～ part company (halfway) ④ group; crowd; band 一～强盗 a band of robbers ⑤combine; join ～买 club together to buy sth. ～着用 share in the use of sth. 【伙伴】partner; companion 【伙房】kitchen 【伙计】partner/fellow; mate 【伙食】mess; food; meals

或 huò ①perhaps; maybe; probably ②or; either ... or ... 【或然】probable ～率 probability

和 huò ①mix; blend 油和水～不到一块儿 oil and water do not mix 【和稀泥】try to smooth things over

货 huò ①goods; commodity ②money 【货币】money; currency 【货车】goods train/goods van; freight car/truck 【货船】freighter; cargo ship 【货机】air freighter 【货价】price of goods 【货架子】goods shelves 【货款】payment for goods 【货品】kinds or types of goods 【货色】goods / stuff; trash; rubbish 【货摊】stall; stand 【货物】goods; commodity; merchandise 【货箱】packing box 【货样】sample (goods) 【货源】source of goods 【货运】freight transport 【货栈】warehouse

获 huò ①capture; catch ②obtain; win ～胜 win victory ～奖 win the prize ～利 reap profits 【获得】gain;

obtain; win ～解放 win liberation ～独立 gain independence ～成绩 achieve success ～知识 acquire knowledge

祸 huò ①misfortune; disaster; calamity; mishap 车～ traffic accident ②bring disaster upon; ruin 【祸根】 the cause of ruin 【祸国殃民】 bring calamity to the country and the people 【祸害】 curse; scourge/damage 【祸心】 evil intent 包藏～ harbour malicious intentions

惑 huò ①be puzzled; be bewildered ②delude; mislead

豁 huò ①clear; open ～达大度 open-minded and magnanimouse ②exempt; remit 【豁亮】 roomy and bright 【豁免】 exempt; remit 【豁然开朗】 suddenly see the light

J

JI

几 jī a small table 茶～ teapoy 【几乎】 nearly; almost ～一夜没睡 lay awake almost the whole night

讥 jī ridicule; mock 【讥讽】 satirize 【讥笑】 jeer; sneer at; deride

击 jī ①beat; hit; strike ～鼓 beat a drum ～掌 clap one's hands ②attack; assault 声东～西 feint in the east and attack in the west ③come in contact with; bump into 撞～ collide with; ram 【击败】 defeat; vanquish ～对手 beat one's opponent 【击毙】 shoot dead 【击沉】 send (a ship) to the bottom 【击毁】 smash; wreck; destroy 【击中】 hit ～目标 hit the target ～要害 hit sb.'s vital point

叽 jī 【叽咕】 whisper; mutter 【叽叽喳喳】 chirp; twitter; jabber

饥 jī ①be hungry; starve; famish ②famine 【饥饿】 hunger; starvation 【饥寒交迫】 suffer hunger and cold 【饥民】 famine victim

机 jī ①machine; engine 蒸汽～ steam engine ②aircraft; aeroplane 客～ passenger plane ③crucial point; pivot; key link 转～ a turning point ④chance; occasion 趁～ seize the chance 见～行事 do as one sees fit 不可失 don't let slip an opportunity 【机场】 airport; airfield 【机车】 locomotive; engine 【机床】 machine tool 【机动】 power-driven; motorized / flexible; mobile / in reserve ～车 motor vehicle ～力量 reserve force ～时间 time kept in reserve ～粮 grain reserve for emergency use ～性 mobility 【机构】 mechanism/organization; setup/organizational structure 【机关】 mechanism; gear/machine-operated/office; organ; body ～报 official newspaper; organ ～炮 machine cannon ～枪 machine gun 【机会】 chance; opportunity 错过(抓住)～ lose (seize) a chance ～主义 opportunism 【机警】 alert; sharp-witted; vigilant 【机灵】 clever; smart; sharp; intelligent 【机密】 secret; classified; confidential 【机敏】 alert and resourceful 【机能】 function 【机器】 machine; machinery; apparatus ～人 robot ～油 lubricating oil ～制造 machine building 【机枪】 machine gun ～手 machine gunner 【机群】 a group of planes 【机务人员】 maintenance personnel/ground crew 【机械】 machinery; machine; mechanism / mechanical; inflexible; rigid ～师 machinist ～工业 engineering industry ～化 mechanize 【机要】 confidential (work, etc.) 【机翼】 wing 【机油】 engine oil 【机缘】 good luck 【机长】 aircraft commander 【机智】 quick-witted; resourceful

肌 jī muscle; flesh 【肌肤】 (human) skin 【肌肉】 muscle ～发达 muscular 【肌体】 organism

鸡 jī chicken 公～ cock 母～ hen【鸡蛋】(hen's) egg ～糕 (sponge) cake【鸡尾酒】cocktail ～会 cocktail party【鸡窝】henhouse; roost

奇 jī ①odd (number) ～数 odd number

迹 jī ①mark; trace 足～ footmark 血～ bloodstain ②remains; ruins; vestige【迹象】sign; indication

积 jī ①amass; store up; accumulate ～谷 store up grain ②long-standing; long-pending; age-old ～案 a long-pending case【积弊】age-old malpractice【积存】store up; lay up; stockpile【积肥】collect manure【积极】positive/active; energetic; vigorous ～工作 work hard 调动～因素 mobilize positive factors 采取～措施 adopt vigorous measures ～分子 activist; enthusiast ～性 zeal; initiative.【积累】accumulate ～资金 (经验) accumulate funds (experience)【积木】toy bricks【积少成多】many a little makes a mickle【积蓄】put aside; save/savings【积压】keep long in stock

基 jī ①base; foundation 路～ roadbed; bed 房～ foundations (of a building) ②basic; key; primary; cardinal ③radical; base; group 氨～ amino【基本】basic; fundamental; elementary/main; essential/basically; in the main; on the whole ～词汇 basic vocabulary ～功 basic skill; essential technique ～建设 capital construction【基层】basic level; grass-roots unit ～单位 basic unit ～干部 cadre at the basic level【基础】foundation; base; basis 打～ lay a foundation ～工业 basic industries ～教育 elementary education ～课 basic courses (of a college curriculum) ～知识 rudimentary knowledge【基地】base【基点】basic point; starting point【基调】main key/keynote【基督】Christ ～教 Christianity; the Christian religion ～徒 Christian 【基金】 fund 【基于】 because of; in view of ～以上理由 for the above-mentioned reasons

绩 jī ①twist hempen thread ②achievement; accomplishment; merit 战～ military exploit

缉 jī seize; arrest 【缉拿】 arrest ～凶手 apprehend the murderer 【缉私】 suppress smuggling

畸 jī ①lopsided; unbalanced ②irregular; abnormal 【畸形】 deformity/unbalanced ～发展 lopsided development ～现象 abnormal phenomenon

稽 jī ①check; examine; investigate 有案可～ be on record ②delay; procrastinate ～延 be considerably delayed 【稽考】 ascertain; verify 无可～ be unverifiable

激 jī ①swash; surge; dash ②stimulate; excite ～起热情 arouse one's enthusiasm ～于义愤 be stirred by righteous indignation ③sharp; fierce; violent ～战 fierce fighting 【激昂】 excited and indignant; roused 【激荡】 agitate; surge; rage 【激动】 excite; stir; agitate ～得流下眼泪 be moved to tears 【激愤】 wrathful; indignant 【激光】 laser ～束 laser beam 【激化】 sharpen; intensify 【激进】 radical ～派 radicals 【激励】 encourage; impel; urge ～斗志 inspire one's fighting will 【激烈】 intense; sharp; fierce ～的争论 heated argument 【激流】 torrent; rapids 【激怒】 enrage; infuriate 【激起】 arouse; evoke; stir up ～公愤 arouse public indignation ～反抗 evoke opposition 【激情】 fervour; passion 【激增】 increase sharply; soar

羁 jī ①bridle; headstall ②control; restrain ③stay; delay; detain 事务～身 be detained by one's duties 【羁绊】 trammels; fetters; yoke 【羁留】 stay; stop over

及 jí ①reach; come up to 目力所～ as far as the eye can reach 力所能～ within one's power ②in time for ③and 【及格】 pass (a test, examination, etc.) 【及时】

timely; in time; seasonable/promptly; without delay ～雨 timely rain 【及物动词】 transitive verb 【及早】 as soon as possible; before it is too late 【及至】 up to; until

汲 jí　draw (water) 【汲取】 draw; derive (from) ～营养 derive nourishment ～力量 draw strength

吉 jí　lucky 【吉普车】 jeep 【吉庆】 auspicious; propitious; happy 【吉他】 guitar 【吉兆】 good omen

级 jí　①level; rank; grade 甲～产品 grade A products 三～工 grade-3 worker ②grade; class; form 同～不同班 be in different classes of the same grade ③step 石 ～ stone steps ④degree 比较～ the comparative degree

极 jí　①the utmost point; extreme ～而言之 talk in extreme terms ②pole ～圈 polar circle ～地 polar region ③extremely; exceedingly ～重要 of the utmost importance ～少数 a tiny minority 【极点】 the limit; the extreme 【极端】 extreme; exceeding 【极力】 do one's utmost; spare no effort 【极盛】 heyday; zenith; acme

即 jí　①approach; reach; be near 可望而不可～ within sight but beyond reach ②assume; undertake ～位 ascend the throne ③at present; in the immediate future 成功在～ success is in sight ④prompted by the occasion ～兴 impromptu ⑤be; mean; namely 非此～彼 it must be either this or that 【即将】 be on the point of 比赛～ 开始 the match is about to begin 【即刻】 at once; immediately; instantly 【即使】 even; even if; even though

急 jí　①impatient; anxious ～着想知道 be impatient to know ～worry 把人～死 be worried to death ②irritated; annoyed; nettled 我没想到他真～了 I didn't expect him to get angry ④fast; rapid; violent 水流很～ the current is swift ⑤urgent; pressing 事情很～ the matter is pressing ⑥urgency 应～ meet an emergency ⑦be eager to help (those in need) 【急促】 hurried; rapid/short; pressing 时间很～ time is running short 【急电】 urgent telegram 【急风暴雨】 violent storm; tempest 【急件】 urgent document or dispatch 【急进】 radical 【急救】 first aid ～包 first-aid dressing ～药品 first-aid medicine ～站 first-aid station 【急剧】 rapid; sharp; sudden 【急流】 torrent; rapids/jet stream ～勇进 forge ahead against a swift current ～勇退 resolutely retire at the height of one's official career 【急忙】 in a hurry; in haste 【急迫】 urgent; imperative 【急切】 eager; impatient / in a hurry; in haste 【急速】 very fast; at high speed 【急行军】 rapid march 【急需】 be in need of/urgent need 以应～ meet a crying need 【急用】 urgent need 以备～ against a rainy day 【急于】 eager; anxious; impatient ～求成 overanxious for quick results 【急躁】 irritable; irascible/impetuous; rash; impatient ～情绪 impetuosity 【急诊】 emergency call or treatment ～病人(室) emergency case (ward) 【急智】 quick-wittedness

疾　jí ①disease; sickness; illness 眼～ eye trouble ② suffering; pain; difficulty ～苦 sufferings; hardships ③hate; abhor ～恶如仇 hate evil like an enemy ④fast; quick ～驰而过 speed past ～风 strong wind; gale

脊　jí 【脊梁】 back (of the human body) ～骨 backbone; spine

棘　jí ①sour jujube ②thorn bushes; brambles ③spine; spina 【棘手】 thorny; troublesome; knotty; sticky

集　jí ①gather; collect ～各家之长 incorporate the strong points of different schools ②country fair; market 赶～ go to market ③collection; anthology 诗～ a collection of poems ④volume; part 分三～出版 be published in three volumes 这部影片分上、下两～ this film is in two parts 【集成电路】integrated circuit 【集合】gather; assemble; muster; call together ～地点 assembly place ～号 bugle call for fall-in; assembly ～名词 collective noun 【集会】assembly; rally; gathering; meeting 【集结】concentrate; build up ～军队 mass troops; concentrate forces ～力量 build up strength 【集权】centralization of state power 【集市】country fair; market ～贸易 country fair trade 【集思广益】pool the wisdom of the masses 【集体】collective ～的智慧 collective wisdom ～观念 collective spirit ～经济 collective economy ～领导 collective leadership ～宿舍 dormitory ～所有制 collective ownership ～舞 group dancing 【集团】group; clique; circle; bloc ～军 group army 【集训】assemble for training ～队 team of athletes in training 【集邮】stamp collecting; philately ～簿 stamp-album 【集镇】(market) town 【集中】centralize; focus ～精力 concentrate one's energy ～目标 concentrate on the same target ～财富 amass fortunes ～注意力 focus one's attention on ～管理 centralized management ～营 concentration camp

嫉 jí ①be envious ②hate 【嫉妒】be jealous of; envy 【嫉恨】hate out of jealousy

籍 jí ①book; record 古～ ancient books ②registry; roll 户～ household register ③native place; birthplace 回～ return to one's native place ④membership 党～ party membership 国～ nationality

几 jǐ ①how many ～天可以完工 how many days will it take to finish the work ～点钟了 what's the time ②a few; several; some 说～句 say a few words 过～天 in a couple of days 相差无～ not much difference 【几分】a bit; somewhat; rather 有～醉意 a bit tipsy 让他 ～ humour him a little 【几何】geometry ～级数 ge ometric series ~图形 geometric figure 【几时】what time

己 jĭ oneself; one's own; personal 引为~任 regard as one's duty 【己方】one's own side

挤 jĭ ①squeeze; press ~水 squeeze the water out ~奶 milk (a cow, etc.) ~时间 find time ②jostle; push against ~进去 force one's way in; squeeze in ~上去 push to the front ③crowd; pack; cram ~做一团 pressed close together ~不下那么多人 it's impossible to pack so many people 【挤眉弄眼】make eyes; wink

给 jĭ ①supply; provide 粮食自~ produce all one's own food grain ②ample; well provided for 【给养】provisions; victuals 【给予】give; render ~支持 give support to ~协助 render assistance to ~同情 show sympathy for ~纪律处分 take disciplinary measures against sb.

脊 jĭ ①spine; backbone ②ridge 山~ the ridge of a hill or mountain 屋~ the ridge of a roof 【脊背】back (of a human being) 【脊髓】spinal cord 【脊柱】spinal column 【脊椎】vertebra ~骨 vertebra; spine

计 jĭ ①count; compute; calculate; number 数以万~ numbering tens of thousands 不~报酬 not be concerned about pay ②meter; gauge 雨量~ rain gauge ③idea; ruse; stratagem; plan 作归~ plan to go home 为长远~ from a long-term point of view 【计策】stratagem; plan 【计划】plan; project; programme / map out; plan ~供应 planned supply ~经济 planned economy ~生产 planned production ~生育 family planning; birth control 【计件】reckon by the piece ~工资 piece rate wage ~工作 piecework 【计较】haggle over; fuss about / argue; dispute / think over ~小事 be too particular about trifles 不~个人得失 give no thought to personal gains or losses 【计时】reckon by time ~工资 time wage ~工作 timework 【计数】 count 【计算】 count; compute; calculate/ consideration; planning ～尺 slide rule ～机 computer

记 jì ①remember; bear in mind ～错 remember wrong-ly ～不清 cannot recall exactly ～仇 bear grudges ②write down; record ～下电话号码 jot down the tele-phone number ③notes; record 游～ travel notes ④mark; sign 暗～ secret mark 【记分】 record the points (in a game)/register a student's marks ～册 (teacher's) mark-book ～牌 scoreboard ～员 scorer; marker 【记功】 record a merit 【记过】 record a demerit 【记号】 mark; sign【记录】 take notes/ record/minutes; notes/notetaker; recorder 创～ set a record ～本 minute book ～片 documentary (film) 【记名】 put down one's name; sign 【记事】 keep a record of events/account; chronicles 【记述】 record and narrate 【记诵】 learn by heart 【记性】 memory 【记叙】 narrate ～ 文 narration; narrative 【记忆】 remember; recall/memory ～力 (the faculty of) memory 【记载】 put down in writing/ record; account 【记帐】 keep accounts / charge to an ac-count 【记者】 reporter; correspondent ～协会 journalists' association ～招待会 press conference ～证 press card

纪 jì ①discipline 军～ military discipline ②put down in writing; record ～事 chronicle ③age; epoch 世～ century 【纪律】 discipline 遵守～ keep discipline ～严明 highly disciplined ～检查委员会 commission for inspecting discipline 【纪念】 commemorate; mark / souvenir / an-niversary ～碑 monument ～册 autograph album ～馆 memorial hall; museum ～品 souvenir ～日 commemora-tion day ～塔 memorial tower ～邮票 commemorative stamp ～章 souvenir badge 【纪实】 on-the-spot report 【纪要】 summary (of minutes) 会谈～ summary of talks 【纪元】 the beginning of an era/epoch; era

伎 jì skill; ability; trick 故～ old tricks 【伎俩】intrigue; manoeuvre

技 jì skill; ability; trick 使无所施其～ make it impossible to play any tricks 【技工】skilled worker / mechanic; technician 【技能】technical ability 【技巧】skill; technique; craftsmanship ～运动 acrobatic gymnastics 【技师】technician 【技术】technology; skill; technique ～服务 technical service ～革新 technological innovation ～工人 skilled worker ～力量 technical force ～名词 technical term ～人员 technical personnel 【技艺】artistry

系 jì tie; fasten; do up; button up ～领巾 wear a scarf ～鞋带 tie shoe laces

忌 jì ①be jealous of; envy ～才 be jealous of other people's talent ②fear; dread; scruple 横行无～ ride roughshod ③avoid; shun; abstain from ～生冷 avoid cold and uncooked food ～口 be on a diet ④quit; give up ～酒 abstain from wine ～烟 quit smoking 【忌惮】dread; fear; scruple 肆无～ stopping at nothing; unscrupulous

际 jì ①border; boundary; edge 水～ waterside 天～ horizon ②between; among; inter 校～比赛 interschool matches ③inside 脑～ in one's head ④occasion; time 临别之～ at the time of parting ⑤one's lot; circumstances

妓 jì prostitute 【妓女】prostitute 【妓院】brothel

季 jì season 四～ the four seasons (of the year) 【季度】quarter (of a year) 【季风】monsoon 【季节】season 农忙～ a busy farming season 收获～ harvest time ～性 seasonal ～工 seasonal worker 【季刊】quarterly

剂 jì a pharmaceutical or other chemical preparation 针～ injection 麻醉～ narcotic 一～中药 a dose of Chinese herbal medicine 【剂量】dosage; dose

济 jì ①cross a river 同舟共～ people in the same boat help each other ②aid; relieve; help ～人之急 relieve sb. in need ③be of help 无～于事 not help matters

既 jì ①already ～得权利 vested right ②since; as; now that ～...both ...and; as well as ～学外科又学内科 study medicine as well as surgery【既成事实】accomplished fact 造成～ make sth. an accomplished fact 承认～ accept a *fait accompli*【既得利益】vested interest ～集团 vested interests【既定】set; fixed; established ～目标 set objective; fixed goal ～方案 existing plan【既然】since; as; now that ～如此 since it is so; such being the case【既往不咎】forgive sb.'s past misdeeds

继 jì continue; succeed; follow ～位 succeed to the throne【继承】inherit; carry on ～财产 inherit property ～优良传统 carry forward the good traditions ～革命事业 carry on the revolutionary cause ～权 right of succession ～人 heir; successor; inheritor【继父】stepfather【继母】stepmother ～任 succeed sb. in a post【继续】continue; go on ～工作 continue working ～有效 remain in force ～执政 continue in office

寄 jì ①send; post; mail ～信 post a letter ～包裹 send a parcel by post ～钱 remit money ②entrust; deposit; place ～希望于人民 place hopes on the people ③depend on; attach oneself to ～食 live with a relative, etc.【寄存】deposit; leave with; check【寄放】leave with; leave in the care of【寄卖】consign for sale on commission ～商店 commission shop; secondhand shop【寄生】parasitism/parasitic ～生活 parasitic life ～虫 parasite【寄宿】lodge/(of students) board ～生 resident student; boarder ～学校 boarding school【寄托】entrust to the care of sb. / place (hope, etc.) on; find sustenance in

寂 jì ①quiet; still; silent ②lonesome; solitary 【寂静】quiet; still 【寂寞】lonely

祭 jì ①hold a memorial ceremony for ②offer a sacrifice to ~天 offer a sacrifice to Heaven ③wield (a magic wand, etc.) 【祭奠】hold a memorial ceremony for 【祭礼】sacrificial rites / memorial ceremony 【祭品】sacrificial offerings 【祭坛】sacrificial altar

JIA

加 jiā ①add; plus 二~三等于五 two plus three makes five ②increase; augment ~工资 raise sb.'s wages ③put in; add; append ~点盐 put some salt in ~注 append notes to 【加班】work overtime ~费 overtime pay 【加倍】double; redouble ~努力 redouble one's efforts ~注意 be doubly careful 【加工】process/machining; working ~厂 processing factory 文章需要~ the article needs polishing 【加固】reinforce; consolidate 【加害】injure; do harm to 【加紧】step up; intensify ~生产 step up production ~准备 speed up preparation 【加剧】aggravate; intensify 病势~ the patient's condition has taken a turn for the worse 【加快】quicken; speed up ~步子 quicken one's step 火车~了速度 the train picked up speed 【加宽】broaden; widen 【加码】raise the price of commodities/raise the quota 【加强】strengthen; enhance; augment; reinforce ~党的领导 strengthen Party leadership ~社会主义法制 strengthen socialist legal system ~纪律性 strengthen discipline ~控制 tighten one's control 【加入】add; mix; put in / join; accede to (a treaty) 【加深】deepen ~理解 get a deeper understanding 【加速】quicken; speed up; accelerate ~发展工业 speed up the development of industry 【加重】make or become heavier; increase the weight of ～任务 add to one's tasks ～语气 say sth. with emphasis ～危机 aggravate the crisis

夹 jiā ①press from both sides; place in between ～菜 pick up food (with chopsticks) ～着皮包 carry a briefcase under one's arm ②mix; mingle; intersperse ～在人群里 mingle with the crowd ③clip, clamp, folder, etc. 纸～ paper clip【夹板】boards for pressing sth. or holding things together / splint【夹道】a narrow lane; passageway / line both sides of the street【夹缝】crack; crevice【夹攻】attack from both sides【夹生】half-cooked ～饭 half-cooked rice【夹馅】stuffed (pastry, etc.)【夹心】with filling～饼干 sandwich biscuits

佳 jiā good; fine; beautiful ～宾 a welcome guest ～肴 delicacies【佳话】a story on everybody's lips; a much-told tale【佳期】wedding day

枷 jiā cangue【枷锁】yoke; chains; fetters 精神～ spiritual shackles

家 jiā ①family; household ～事 family matters; domestic affairs ②home 回～ go home 不在～ not be in; be out 上我～去吧 come to my place ③ a person or family engaged in a certain trade 船～ boatman ④a specialist in a certain field 科学～ scientist 文学～ writer ⑤school 法～ the Legalist School ⑥my 父 my father ⑦domestic; tame ～兔 rabbit【家产】family property【家常】the daily life of a family ～话 small talk; chitchat ～便饭 homely food / common occurrence【家丑】family scandal【家畜】domestic animal; livestock【家当】family belongings; property【家访】a visit to the parents of schoolchildren or young workers【家鸽】pigeon【家伙】tool; utensil; weapon/fellow; guy【家教】family education; upbringing ～严 be strict with one's children【家

境】family financial situation; family circumstances 【家具】furniture 【家眷】wife and children; one's family 【家妻】wife 【家禽】domestic fowl; poultry 【家属】family members; dependents 【家庭】family; household ～背景 family background ～成员 family members ～出身 family origin ～负担 family responsibilities ～妇女 housewife ～副业 household sideline production ～教师 private teacher ～教育 family education ～生活 home life ～作业 homework 【家务】household duties ～劳动 housework 【家乡】hometown; native place 【家信】a letter to or from one's family 【家业】family property; property 【家用】family expenses 【家喻户晓】widely known; known to all 做到～ make known to every household 【家园】home; homeland 【家长】the head of a family; patriarch / the parent or guardian of a child ～会 a parents' meeting ～制 patriarchal system 【家族】clan; family

痂 jiā　scab; crust

嘉 jiā　①good; fine ～宾 welcome guest ②praise 【嘉奖】commend; cite ～令 citation 【嘉许】approve

夹 jiā　double-layered; lined ～袄 lined jacket

荚 jiá　pod 结～ bear pods 【荚果】pod; legume

颊 jiá　cheek 两～红润 with rosy cheeks 【颊骨】cheekbone

甲 jiǎ　①first ～级 first rate; Class A ②shell; carapace 龟～ tortoise shell ③nail ④armour 【甲虫】beetle 【甲板】deck 【甲壳】crust 【甲鱼】soft-shelled turtle

假 jiǎ　①false; fake; phoney ～肢 artificial limb ～腿 artificial leg ～民主 sham dmocracy ～检讨 insincere self-criticism ②borrow; avail oneself of ③if; suppose 【假扮】 disguise oneself as; dress up as 【假充】 pretend to be 【假定】 suppose; assume; grant; presume/hypothesis 【假发】 wig 【假公济私】 use public office for private gain 【假花】 artificial flower 【假话】 lie; falsehood 【假借】 make use of ～名义 in the name of; under false pretences 【假冒】 pass oneself off as 【假面具】 mask; false front 【假如】 if; supposing; in case 【假手】 do sth. through sb. else 【假托】 on the pretext of (illness, etc.)/under sb. else's name 【假想】 imagination; supposition/hypothetical; fictitious 【假象】 false appearance 【假牙】 false tooth 【假意】 unction; insincerity; hypocrisy / pretend; put on 【假造】 forge; counterfeit 【假装】 pretend; feign; simulate

价 jià ①price 要～ ask a price ②value 估～ estimate the value of 【价款】 cost 【价目】 marked price; price ～表 price list 【价钱】 price 讲～ bargain ～公道 a fair price 【价值】 value/worth ～规律 law of value

驾 jià ①harness; draw (a cart, etc.) ②drive (a vehicle); pilot (a plane); sail (a boat) 【驾驶】 drive (a vehicle); pilot (a ship or plane) ～盘 steering wheel ～室 driver's cab ～台 bridge ～员 driver; pilot ～执照 driving license 【驾驭】 drive (a cart, horse, etc.)/control

架 jià ①frame; rack; shelf; stand 衣～ clothes hanger 书～ bookshelf ②put up; erect ～桥 build a bridge ～电话线 set up telephone lines ③support; prop; help ～着拐走 walk on crutches ④kidnap 强行～走 carry sb. away by force ⑤fight; quarrel 劝～ step in and patch up a quarrel 【架设】 erect 【架势】 posture; manner 【架子】 frame; stand/framework; outline/airs

假 jià ①holiday 暑～ summer vacation ②leave of absence 病～ sick leave 请～ ask for leave 【假期】 vacation/period of leave 【假条】 application for leave/leave permit 病～ doctor's certificate (for sick leave)

嫁 jià ①marry ～人 get married ～女儿 marry off a daughter ②shift; transfer 【嫁祸于人】 put the blame on sb. else 【嫁娶】 marriage 【嫁妆】 dowry; trousseau

稼 jià ①sow (grain) ②cereals; crops 庄～ standing grain

JIAN

尖 jiān ①point; tip; top 针～ the point of a needle 指～ fingertip ②pointed; tapering 把铅笔削～ sharpen a pencil ③shrill; piercing ～叫 scream ④sharp; acute 耳朵～ have sharp ears 眼～ be sharp-eyed 【尖兵】 point/pathbreaker; pioneer 【尖刀】 sharp knife; dagger 【尖端】 pointed end; acme; peak/most advanced ～产品 highly sophisticated products ～科学 most advanced branches of science; frontiers of science 【尖刻】 caustic; biting 【尖利】 sharp; keen; cutting/shrill; piercing 【尖锐】 sharp-pointed/penetrating; incisive; sharp; keen/shrill; piercing/intense; acute ～化 sharpen; intensify 【尖酸】 acrid; acrimonious; tart 【尖子】 the best of its kind; the pick of the bunch

奸 jiān ①wicked; evil; treacherous ～计 an evil plot ②traitor 内～ hidden traitor 锄～ eliminate traitors ③illicit sexual relations 【奸猾】 treacherous; crafty; deceitful 【奸商】 unscrupulous merchant; profiteer 【奸污】 rape or seduce 【奸细】 spy; enemy agent 【奸险】 wicked and crafty; malicious 【奸诈】 fraudulent

间 jiān ①between; among 同志之～ among comrades ②within a definite time or space 田～ (in) the fields 晚～ (in the) evening; (at) night ③room

歼 jiān annihilate; wipe out; destroy 【歼击机】 fighter (plane) 【歼灭战】 war or battle of annihilation

坚 jiān ①hard; solid ～冰 solid ice ②fortification; stronghold 攻～ storm strongholds ③firmly; steadfastly ～信 firmly believe ～拒 flatly refuse 【坚持】 persist in; persevere in; uphold; insist on; stick to ～原则 adhere to principle ～真理 hold firmly to the tru'h ～己见 hold on to one's own views ～错误 persist in one's errors ～不懈 unremitting ～不渝 persistent 【坚定】 firm; staunch; steadfast ～不移 unswerving; unflinching ～的步伐 firm strides 【坚固】 sturdy; strong 【坚决】 firm; resolute; determined ～支持 firmly support ～反对 resolutely oppose 采取～措施 take resolute measures 【坚强】 strong; firm; staunch/strengthen 【坚韧】 tough and tensile/firm and tenacious ～不拔 persistent and dauntless 【坚如磐石】 solid as a rock 【坚实】 solid; substantial ～的基础 a solid foundation 【坚守】 stick to; stand fast ～岗位 stand fast at one's post ～阵地 hold fast to one's position 【坚硬】 hard; solid 【坚贞】 faithful; constant

肩 jiān ①shoulder ②take on; bear 【肩负】 shoulder; bear ～光荣的任务 undertake a glorious task 【肩章】 shoulder loop/epaulet

艰 jiān difficult; hard 【艰巨】 arduous; formidable 【艰苦】 arduous; difficult; tough ～的生活 hard life ～的斗争 arduous struggle ～朴素 hard work and plain living ～的环境 difficult circumstances 【艰难】 difficult; hard 行动～ walk with difficulty 生活～ live in straitened circumstances 【艰深】 difficult to understand

兼 jiān ①double; twice ～程 travel at double speed ②simultaneously; concurrently ～管 be concurrently in charge of ～而有之 have both at the same time 【兼

并】annex (territory, property, etc.) 【兼顾】give consideration to two or more things 【兼课】do some teaching in addition to one's main occupation/hold two or more teaching jobs concurrently 【兼任】hold a concurrent post/part-time 【兼职】part-time teacher 【兼职】hold two or more posts concurrently/concurrent post

监 jiān ①supervise; inspect; watch ②prison; jail 【监察】supervise; control ~委员会 control commission ~员 controller ~制度 supervisory system 【监督】supervise; superintend; control 【监工】supervise work; oversee/overseer; supervisor 【监禁】take into custody; imprison 【监考】invigilate ~人 invigilator 【监视】keep watch on ~哨 lookout 【监听】monitor 【监狱】prison; jail

缄 jiān seal; close 【缄口】keep one's mouth shut; hold one's tongue 【缄默】keep silent; be reticent

煎 jiān ①fry in shallow oil ~鸡蛋 fried eggs ②simmer in water; decoct ~药 decoct medicinal herbs

拣 jiān choose; select; pick out 拣子~重的挑 choose the heavy loads to carry

茧 jiān ①cocoon 蚕~ silkworm cocoon ~绸 pongee ②callus 老~ thick callus

柬 jiān card; note; letter 请~ invitation card

俭 jiǎn thrifty; frugal 【俭朴】thrifty and simple; economical 生活 ~ lead a thrifty and simple life

捡 jiǎn pick up; collect; gather ~麦穗 pick up ears of wheat ~粪 collect manure

检 jiǎn ①check up; inspect; examine ~定 examine and determine ②restrain oneself 行为不~ depart from correct conduct 【检查】check up; inspect / self-criticism ~工作 check up on work ~质量 check on the quality of sth. ～护照 inspect sb.'s passport ～行李 examine sb.'s luggage ～身体 have a health check 作～ criticize oneself 写～ write a self-criticism 把练习～一遍再交 look over your exercises before handing them in 【检察】 procuratorial work ～官 public procurator ～机关 procuratorial organ ～院 procuratorate ～长 chief procurator 【检点】 examine; check / be cautious (about what one says or does) 行为有失～ be careless about one's acts 生活不～ commit an indiscretion 【检举】 report (an offence) to the authorities; inform against (an offender) ～箱 a box for accusation letters ～信 letter of accusation; written accusation 【检讨】 self-criticism 【检修】 overhaul 【检验】 test; examine; inspect 【检疫】 quarantine 【检阅】 review; inspect ～台 reviewing stand

剪 jiǎn ①scissors; shears; clippers ②cut (with scissors); clip ～指甲 trim one's nails ～羊毛 shear a sheep ～票 punch a ticket 【剪报】 newspaper cutting 【剪裁】 cut out (a garment); tailor / cut out unwanted material (from a piece of writing) 【剪除】 wipe out; annihilate 【剪刀】 scissors; shears 【剪辑】 montage/editing and rearrangement 【剪贴】 clip and paste (sth. out of a newspaper, etc.) in a scrapbook or on cards/cutting out (as schoolchildren's activity) ～簿 scrapbook 【剪纸】 paper-cut

减 jiǎn ①subtract 十～五 subtract five from ten 四～二等于二 four minus two is two ②reduce; decrease ～半 reduce by half 【减产】 reduction of output 【减低】 reduce; lower; cut ～速度 slow down 【减价】 reduce the price 【减轻】 lighten; ease; alleviate ～负担 lighten the burden ～病人的痛苦 ease a patient's suffering ～处分 mitigate a punishment 【减弱】 weaken; abate 【减色】 lose lustre; impair the excellence of 【减少】 reduce; lessen; cut down ～开支 reduce expenditure ～层次 eliminate duplication【减退】drop; go down 记忆力～ one's memory is failing【减刑】reduce a penalty【减员】depletion of numbers

简 jiǎn simple; simplified 从～ conform to the principle of simplicity ～而言之 in brief; in short【简报】bulletin【简编】short course【简便】simple and convenient; handy 操作～ easy to operate【简称】abbreviation/be called sth. for short【简单】simple; uncomplicated 头脑～ simple-minded ～化 oversimplify【简化】simplify【简洁】succinct; terse; pithy【简介】synopsis【简历】biographical notes【简练】terse; succinct; pithy【简略】simple (in content); brief; sketchy【简慢】negligent (in attending to one's guest)【简明】concise ～扼要 brief and to the point ～新闻 news in brief【简谱】numbered musical notation【简图】sketch; diagram【简写】simplify a book for beginners ～本 simplified edition【简讯】news in brief【简易】simple and easy/simply constructed ～读物 easy reader【简章】general regulations

碱 jiǎn ①alkali ②soda 洗涤～ washing soda【碱地】alkaline land【碱化】alkalization【碱性】basicity

见 jiàn ①see; catch sight of 所～所闻 what one sees and hears ②meet with; be exposed to ③show evidence of; appear to be ～之于行动 be translated into action ④refer to; see ～上 see above ～下 see below ⑤meet; call on; see 你～到他没有 did you meet him ⑥view; opinion; 依我之～ in my opinion【见地】insight; judgment【见多识广】experienced and knowledgeable【见怪】mind; take offence【见机】as the opportunity arises: according to circumstances ～行事 do as one sees fit【见解】view; opinion; understanding【见面】meet; see【见世面】see the world; enrich one's experience【见识】widen one's knowledge; enrich one's experience / experience; knowledge; sensibleness 长～ widen one's knowledge 【见闻】 knowledge; information 【见习】 learn on the job ～技术员 technician on probation ～生 probationer ～医生 intern 【见效】 become effective; produce the desired result 【见证】 witness; testimony ～人 eyewitness; witness

件 jiàn ①piece 一～工作 a piece of work; a job 三～行李 three pieces of luggage ②letter; correspondence 密～ confidential documents; secret papers

间 jiàn ①space in between; opening 乘～ seize an opportunity ②separate 黑白相～ chequered with black and white ③sow discord ④thin out (seedlings) 【间谍】 spy ～活动 espionage ～网 espionage network 【间断】 be disconnected; be interrupted 从不～ without interruption 【间隔】 interval; intermission /space 【间接】 indirect; secondhand ～宾语 indirect object ～经验 indirect experience 【间隙】 gap; space 【间歇】 intermission

建 jiàn ①build; erect ～新厂房 construct a new factory building ②establish; set up; found ～新功 make new contributions ③propose; advocate 【建党】 found a party / Party building 【建都】 found a capital 【建国】 establish a state / build up a country 【建交】 establish diplomatic relations 【建军】 found an army / army building ～节 Army Day (August 1) 【建立】 establish; found ～信心 build up one's confidence ～功勋 perform meritorious deeds 【建设】 build; construct ～性 constructive 社会主义～ socialist construction 【建树】 contribute 【建议】 propose; suggest / proposal; suggestion 【建制】 organizational system (of the army, etc.) 【建筑】 build; erect / building; structure; edifice / architecture ～材料 building materials ～工人 builder ～师 architect ～物 building; structure

剑 jiàn sword; sabre ～柄 the handle of a sword; hilt ～鞘 scabbard 【剑拔弩张】 at daggers drawn

荐 jiàn ①recommend ②grass; straw 【荐举】 propose sb. for an office; recommend

贱 jiàn ①low-priced; inexpensive ～卖 sell cheap ② lowly; humble 贫～ poor and lowly ③base

涧 jiàn ravine; gully

舰 jiàn warship; naval vessel; man-of-war 【舰队】 fleet; naval force 【舰艇】 naval vessels 【舰长】 captain

健 jiàn ①healthy; strong ②strengthen; toughen ～胃 be good for the stomach ③be strong in ～谈 be a good talker 【健儿】 valiant fighter / good athlete 【健将】 master sportsman; top-notch player 【健康】 health; physique / healthy; sound 身体～ be in good health 祝你～ I wish you good health 【健美】 strong and handsome; vigorous and graceful 【健全】 sound; perfect / strengthen; amplify ～社会主义民主 strengthen socialist democracy 【健身房】 gym 【健忘】 forgetful 【健壮】 robust

谏 jiàn remonstrate with; expostulate with; admonish (against sth.) ～止 plead with sb. not to do sth.

渐 jiàn gradually; by degrees 天气～冷 the weather is getting cold 雨～小 the rain is beginning to let up 【渐变】 gradual change 【渐渐】 gradually; little by little 【渐进】 advance gradually; progress step by step

溅 jiàn splash; spatter ～一身泥 be spattered with mud 【溅落】 splash down ～点 splash point

践 jiàn ①trample; tread ②act on; carry out 【践踏】 tread on; trample underfoot 【践约】 keep a promise

腱 jiàn tendon 【腱鞘】 tendon sheath ～炎 tenosynovitis

毽 jiàn shuttlecock 【毽子】 shuttlecock 踢～ kick the shuttlecock (as a game)

鉴 jiàn ①reflect; mirror ②warning; object lesson 引以为～ take warning from it ③inspect; examine 请～核 please examine 【鉴别】 distinguish; differentiate ～文物 make an appraisal of a cultural relic 【鉴定】 appraisal (of a person's strong and weak points) /appraise; identify 毕业～ graduation appraisal ～产品质量 appraise the quality of a product 【鉴赏】 appreciate ～力 ability to appreciate (music, etc.); connoisseurship

箭 jiàn arrow 【箭靶】 target for archery 【箭杆】 arrow shaft 【箭筒】 quiver 【箭头】 arrowhead/arrow

JIANG

江 jiāng river 【江湖】 rivers and lakes/all corners of the country ～医生 quack ～艺人 itinerant entertainer 【江米】 polished glutinous rice ～酒 fermented glutinous rice 【江山】 rivers and mountains; land; landscape/country 打～ fight to win state power

将 jiāng ①support; take; bring ②take care of (one's health) ～息 rest; recuperate ③do sth.; handle (a matter) ④put sb. on the spot ⑤with; by means of; by ～功折罪 expiate one's crime by good deeds ⑥be going to; be about to; will; shall 船～启碇 the ship is about to weigh anchor 【将计就计】 turn sb.'s trick against him 【将近】 close to; nearly; almost 【将就】 make do with; make the best of; put up with 【将军】 general 【将来】 future 在不远的～ in the not too distant future; before long 【将要】 be going to; will; shall

姜 jiàng ginger

浆 jiāng ①thick liquid 糖～ syrup ②starch ～衣服 starch clothes ～洗 wash and starch 【浆果】 berry

僵 jiāng ①stiff; numb 冻～ be numb with cold ②deadlocked 他把事搞～ he's brought things to a deadlock 【僵持】 (of both parties) refuse to budge 【僵化】 become rigid; ossify 【僵局】 deadlock; impasse; stalemate 打破～ break a deadlock 陷入～ have reached an impasse 【僵尸】 corpse 【僵死】 ossified 【僵硬】 stiff / rigid; inflexible

疆 jiāng boundary; border 【疆场】 battlefield 【疆域】 territory; domain

讲 jiǎng ①speak; say; tell ～故事 tell stories ～几句话 say a few words ②explain; make clear; interpret ～清道理 state the reasons clearly ③discuss; negotiate ～条件 negotiate the terms ④stress; pay attention to ～卫生 pay attention to hygiene ～质量 stress quality 【讲稿】 lecture notes 【讲和】 make peace; settle a dispute 【讲话】 speak; talk; address / speech / guide; introduction 【讲价】 bargain 【讲解】 explain ～员 guide 【讲究】 be particular about; pay attention to; stress; strive for/exquisite; tasteful / careful study 【讲课】 teach; lecture ～时数 teaching hours 【讲理】 reason with sb.; argue / listen to reason; be reasonable; be sensible 【讲明】 state explicitly; explain; make clear ～立场 state one's stand 【讲评】 comment on and appraise ～学生的作业 comment on the students' work 【讲情】 intercede; plead for sb. 【讲求】 be particular about; stress ～效率 strive for efficiency 【讲师】 lecturer 【讲授】 lecture; instruct; teach ～提纲 an outline for a lecture 【讲述】 tell about; narrate; relate 【讲台】 platform; dais 【讲堂】 lecture room; classroom 【讲习】 lecture and study ～班 study group 【讲学】 give lectures; discourse on an academic subject 【讲演】 lecture;

speech 【讲义】teaching materials 【讲座】a course of lectures 英语广播~ English lessons over the radio

奖 jiǎng ①encourage; praise; reward 有功者~ those who have gained merit will be rewarded ②award; prize 发~ give awards 得~ win a prize 【奖杯】cup (as a prize) 【奖金】money award; bonus; premium 【奖励】award; reward 物质~ material reward ~发明创造 encourage innovations by giving awards 【奖品】prize; award; trophy 【奖券】lottery ticket 【奖学金】scholarship; exhibition 【奖章】medal 【奖状】certificate of merit

桨 jiǎng oar

匠 jiàng craftsman; artisan 巧~ skilled craftsmen 石~ stonemason 【匠心】ingenuity; craftsmanship

降 jiàng fall; drop; lower ~雨 a fall of rain; rainfall ~价 lower prices 【降低】reduce; drop; lower ~成本 reduce costs ~消耗 cut down the consumption 【降格】lower one's standard or status ~以求 accept a second best 【降级】reduce to a lower rank; demote/send (a student) to a lower grade 【降临】befall; arrive; come 【降落】descend; land ~场 landing field ~伞 parachute 【降水】precipitation 人工~ artificial precipitation

将 jiàng general 【将领】high-ranking military officer 【将士】officers and men

强 jiàng stubborn; unyielding 倔~ unbending 【强嘴】reply defiantly; answer back; talk back

酱 jiàng ①a thick sauce made from soya beans, flour, etc. ②cooked or pickled in soy sauce ~肉 braised pork seasoned with soy sauce ③sauce; paste; jam 苹果~ apple jam 【酱菜】vegetables pickled in soy sauce; pickles 【酱油】soy (sauce) 【酱园】sauce and pickle shop

犟 jiàng obstinate; stubborn; self-willed; pigheaded; bullheaded

糨 jiàng thick 粥太~ the porridge is too thick 【糨糊】 paste

JIAO

交 jiāo ①hand over; give up; deliver ~活 turn over a finished item ~团费 pay League membership dues ②meet; join 春夏之~ when spring is changing into summer ③reach (a certain hour or season) ~好运 have good luck ④cross; intersect 两条铁路在此相~ the two railways cross here ⑤associate with ~友 make friends ⑥friend; friendship; relationship 一面之~ a passing acquaintance 知~ bosom friend ⑦have sexual intercourse ⑧mate; breed 杂~ crossbreed ⑨mutual; reciprocal; each other ~换 exchange ⑩together; simultaneous 内外~困 be beset with difficulties at home and abroad ⑪deal; bargain 成~ strike a bargain 【交班】 hand over to the next shift 【交叉】 intersect; cross; crisscross / alternate; stagger ~进行 do alternately ~点 intersect ~火力 cross fire 【交出】 surrender; hand over 【交错】 interlock; crisscross 【交代】 hand over (work to one's successor) /make clear; brief; tell; explain (policy, etc.) /account for; justify oneself/confess (a crime, etc.) 【交底】 tell sb. what one's real intentions are 【交锋】 cross swords; engage in a battle or contest 思想~ confrontation of ideas 【交付】 pay/ hand over; deliver; consign ~使用 be made available to the users ~表决 put to the vote 【交工】 hand over a completed project 【交公】 hand over to the collective or the state 【交换】 exchange; swop ~意见 exchange views ~场地 change of courts, goals or ends 商品~ exchange of commodities ～机 switchboard; exchange ～价值 exchange value 【交货】delivery ～期 date of delivery 【交集】be mixed; occur simultaneously 【交际】social intercourse; communication ～舞 ballroom dancing; social dancing 【交接】join; connect/hand over and take over, associate with ～班 relief of a shift ～手续 handing over procedure 【交卷】hand in an examination paper/ fulfil one's task 【交流】exchange; interflow; interchange ～经验 exchange experience 【交纳】pay; hand in ～会费 pay membership dues 【交情】friendship; friendly relations 讲～ do things for the sake of friendship 【交涉】 negotiate; make representations 办～ carry on negotiations with 【交售】sell (to the state) 【交谈】talk with each other; converse; chat 【交替】supersede; replace/alternately; in turn 新旧～ the new replaces the old 【交通】traffic; communications ～便利 have transport facilities 妨碍～ interfere with the traffic ～安全 traffic safety ～部 the Ministry of Communications ～规则 traffic regulations ～警 traffic police ～事故 traffic accident ～要道 vital communication line 【交作】association; contact 【交响乐】 symphony ～队 symphony orchestra 【交易】business; deal; trade; transaction 做成～ make a deal 政治～ a political deal ～额 volume of trade ～所 exchange 【交战】be at war; fight; wage war ～状态 state of war ～国 belligerent countries 【交帐】hand over the accounts / account for 【交织】interweave; intertwine; mingle

郊 jiāo suburbs 西～ the western suburbs 【郊区】suburban district 【郊外】outskirts 【郊游】outing; excursion

浇 jiāo ①pour liquid on; sprinkle water on (被雨)～ 得浑身湿透 be drenched through (with rain) ②irrigate; water ～花 water flowers ～地 irrigate the fields

娇 jiāo ①tender; lovely ②fragile; frail; delicate 【娇惯】 coddle; spoil; pamper (a child) 【娇媚】 coquettish / sweet and charming 【娇气】 squeamish; finicky 【娇小玲珑】 delicate and exquisite 【娇艳】 tender and beautiful

骄 jiāo proud 【骄傲】 arrogant; conceited / be proud; take pride in (the achievements of) / pride (of the nation, etc.) 【骄气】 overbearing airs; arrogance

胶 jiāo ①glue; gum ②stick with glue; glue ③gluey; sticky; gummy ④rubber 【胶布】 rubberized fabric / adhesive plaster 【胶合】 glue together; veneer 一板 plywood; veneer board 【胶卷】 roll film 【胶水】 mucilage; glue 【胶鞋】 rubber overshoes; galoshes/rubber-soled shoes; tennis shoes; sneakers 【胶印】 offset 【胶着】 deadlocked; stalemated

教 jiāo teach; instruct 【教书】 teach 在小学~ teach in a primary school

焦 jiāo ①burnt; scorched; charred 饼烤~了 the pancake is burnt ②coke 炼~ coking ~比 coke ratio ③worried; anxious 【焦点】 focal point / central issue 争论的~ the point at issue 【焦黄】 sallow; brown 【焦急】 anxious; worried 正在~地等着 be waiting anxiously 【焦煤】 coking coal 【焦炭】 coke 【焦头烂额】 badly battered; in a terrible fix 【焦躁】 restless with anxiety; impatient

椒 jiāo any of several hot spice plants 辣~ chili; red pepper 胡~ pepper ~盐 spiced salt

礁 jiāo reef 触~ strike a reef; run up on a rock 【礁石】 reef; rock

矫 jiāo 【矫情】 argumentative; contentious; unreasonable

嚼 jiāo masticate; chew; munch 【嚼舌头】 chatter; gossip / argue meaninglessly; squabble 【嚼子】 bit

角 jiǎo ①horn 牛～ ox horn 鹿～ antler ②horn 号～ bugle ③corner 眼～ corner of the eye ④angle 直～ right angle ⑤cape; promontory; headland 【角度】angle/point of view 【角落】corner; nook 找遍每一个～ search every nook and cranny 【角膜】cornea

侥 jiǎo 【侥幸】lucky; by luck ～取胜 win by a fluke ～心理 the idea of leaving things to chance

狡 jiǎo crafty; foxy; cunning ～计 crafty trick; ruse 【狡辩】quibble; indulge in sophistry 【狡猾】sly; tricky 【狡赖】deny (by resorting to sophistry)

绞 jiǎo ①twist; wring; entangle ～干衣服 wring out wet clothes ～脑汁 rack one's brains ②wind (a windlass, etc.) ③hang by the neck 【绞车】winch 【绞架】gallows 【绞盘】capstan 【绞肉机】meat mincer 【绞杀】strangle 【绞索】noose 【绞刑】death by hanging

饺 jiǎo dumpling 【饺子】dumpling (with meat and vegetable stuffing) ～皮 dumpling wrapper

皎 jiǎo clear and bright; glistening white ～月当空 a bright moon hung in the sky

铰 jiǎo ①cut with scissors ～成两半 cut in two ②bore with a reamer; ream ～孔 ream a hole 【铰链】hinge

脚 jiǎo ①foot 赤～ barefoot ②base; foot 墙～ the foot of a wall ③leg 【脚背】instep 【脚本】script; scenario 【脚步】step; pace ～声 footstep 【脚蹬子】pedal; treadle 【脚跟】heel 站稳～ stand firm 【脚尖】tiptoe 【脚镣】fetters 【脚面】instep 【脚踏实地】earnest and down-to-earth 【脚腕子】ankle 【脚印】footprint; footmark; track 【脚掌】sole 【脚指头】toe 【脚注】footnote

矫 jiǎo ①rectify; straighten out; correct ②strong; brave ③pretend; feign; dissemble ～命 issue false orders 【矫健】strong and vigorous 【矫揉造作】affected; artificial

【娇饰】feign in order to conceal sth.; dissemble; affect 【矫枉过正】exceed the proper limits in righting a wrong; overcorrect 【矫正】correct; put right; rectify ～发音 correct sb.'s pronunciation mistakes ～视力 correct defects of vision

攪 jiǎo ①stir; mix ～粥 stir the porridge ②disturb; annoy 【搅拌】stir; agitate ～机 mixer ～器 stirrer; agitator 【搅和】mix; blend; mingle/mess up; spoil 【搅乱】confuse; throw into disorder 【搅扰】disturb; annoy

劋 jiǎo send armed forces to suppress; put down ～匪 suppress bandits 【剿灭】exterminate; wipe out

缴 jiǎo ①pay; hand over; hand in ～税 pay taxes ②capture ～枪不杀 lay down your arms and we'll spare your lives 【缴获】capture; seize 【缴械】disarm / lay dawn one's arms

叫 jiào ①cry; shout 大～一声 give a loud cry ②call; greet 有人～你 somebody is calling you ③hire; order ～汽车 call a taxi ～菜 order dishes ④name; call 他～什么名字 what's his name ⑤ask; order ～他进来吗 shall I ask him in 【叫喊】shout; yell; howl 【叫好】applaud 【叫唤】cry out; call out 【叫苦】complain of hardship or suffering; moan and groan 暗暗～ groan inwardly ～不迭 pour out endless grievances 【叫骂】shout curses 【叫卖】cry one's wares; peddle; hawk 【叫门】call at the door to be let in 【叫醒】wake up 【叫做】be called; be known as

觉 jiào sleep 睡一～ have a sleep 午～ midday nap

校 jiào check; proofread; collate ～条样 read galley proofs 【校订】check against the authoritative text 【校对】proofread; proof/proofreader 【校样】proof sheet; proof 【校正】proofread and correct; rectify

较 jiào ①compare ②comparatively; quite; rather ～好 fairly good; quite good ～差 relatively poor 【较量】 have a contest; have a test of strength/argue; dispute

轿 jiào sedan (chair) 【轿车】 (horse-drawn) carriage ②bus or car 大～ bus; coach 小～ car; limousine

教 jiào ①teach; instruct 言传身～ teach by precept and example 请～ consult ②religion 信～ believe in a religion 【教案】 teaching plan; lesson plan 【教材】 teaching material 【教程】 course of study/(published) lectures 【教导】 instruct; teach / teaching; guidance ～员 (battalion) political instructor 【教皇】 pope 【教会】 (the Christian) church ～学校 missionary school 【教具】 teaching aid 【教科书】 textbook 【教练】 train; drill / coach 【教师】 teacher; schoolteacher 【教士】 priest; clergyman 【教室】 classroom; schoolroom 【教授】 professor/instruct; teach 副～ associate professor 【教唆】 instigate; abet ～犯 abettor 【教堂】 church; cathedral 【教条】 dogma; doctrine; creed; tenet ～主义 dogmatism 【教徒】 believer of a religion 【教务】 educational administration ～处 Dean's Office ～长 Dean of Studies 【教学】 teaching; education/teaching and studying/teacher and student ～大纲 teaching programme; syllabus ～方法 teaching method ～方针 principles of teaching ～改革 reform in education ～内容 content of courses 【教训】 lesson; moral/chide; teach sb. a lesson 【教研室】 teaching and research section 【教养】 bring up; train; educate/ breeding; upbringing; education; culture 【教义】 religious doctrine; creed 【教益】 benefit gained from sb.'s wisdom; enlightenment 【教育】 education/teach; educate; inculcate ～程度 level of education ～方针 policy for education ～家 educationist; educator ～界 educational circles ～学 pedagogy; education ～制度 system of education 【教

员】teacher; instructor ～休息室 staff room

窖 jiào ①cellar or pit for storing things 菜～ vegetable cellar ②store sth. in a cellar or pit

酵 jiào ferment; leaven【酵母】yeast ～菌 saccharomycete【酵素】ferment; enzyme

JIE

阶 jiē ①steps; stairs 台～ a flight of steps ②rank 军～ military rank【阶层】(social) stratum【阶段】stage; phase 过渡～ transitional stage 历史～ historical period【阶级】(social) class ～成分 class status ～斗争 class struggle ～观点 class viewpoint ～觉悟 class consciousness ～立场 class stand【阶梯】a flight of stairs; ladder

皆 jiē all; each and every 人人～知 it is known to all【皆大欢喜】everybody is happy

结 jiē bear (fruit); form (seed)【结巴】stammer/stammerer【结实】solid; durable / strong; sturdy

接 jiē ①come into contact with; come close to 短兵相～ fighting at close quarters ② connect; join ～线 connect wires ～线头 tie broken threads ③catch; take hold of ～球 catch a ball ④receive ～信 receive a letter ～电话 answer the phone ⑤meet; welcome 到车站～人 go to the station to meet sb. ⑥take over ～工作 take over a job【接班】take one's turn on duty; carry on; take over from ～人 successor【接触】come into contact with; get in touch with/engage (the enemy)/contact ～不良 loose contact【接待】receive; admit ～单位 host organization ～人员 reception personnel ～室 reception room ～站 reception centre【接管】take over (control)【接济】give material assistance to【接见】receive sb. ～外宾 receive foreign guests【接近】be close to; near; approach【接力】

relay ～棒 relay baton ～赛跑 relay (race) 【接连】 on end; in a row; in succession ～几天 for days on end ～三小时 for three hours at a stretch 【接洽】 arrange (business, etc.) with; consult with 来～工作 be here to talk business ～车辆 arrange transport 【接生】 deliver a child ～员 midwife 【接收】 receive (radio signals, etc.) / take over (property, etc.); expropriate / admit; recruit (new members, etc.) 【接手】 take over (duties, etc.) 【接受】 accept ～邀请 accept an invitation ～任务 accept an assignment ～意见 take sb.'s advice ～教训 draw a lesson ～考验 face up to a test 【接替】 take over; replace 【接通】 put through 电话～了吗 have you got through (电话)给你～了 you are in connexion 【接头】 connect; join; joint / contact; get in touch with; meet / have knowledge of; know about 【接吻】 kiss 【接续】 continue; follow 【接应】 come to sb.'s aid; coordinate with

秸 jiē stalks; straw 秫～ sorghum stalks 麦～ wheat straw

揭 jiē ①tear off; take off 把画儿～下来 take that picture off ②uncover; lift (the lid, etc.) ～盖子 take the lid off sth. ～不开锅 have nothing in the pot; go hungry ③expose; show up; bring to light ～矛盾 expose contradictions 【揭穿】 expose; lay bare; show up ～谎言 expose a lie ～假面具 unmask sb. ～阴谋 lay bare an evil plot 【揭发】 expose; unmask; bring to light 【揭开】 uncover; open ～奥秘 reveal the secrets ～序幕 raise the curtain on sth. 【揭露】 expose; unmask; ferret out ～阴谋 expose the plot ～真面目 expose sb.'s true colours 【揭示】 announce; promulgate/reveal ～客观规律 bring to light the objective laws 【揭晓】 announce; make known; publish

街 jié street 【街道】street / residential district; neighbourhood ～办事处 subdistrict office ～工厂 neighbourhood factory ～委员会 neighbourhood committee 【街谈巷议】street gossip 【街头】street (corner) 十字～ (at the) crossroads 流落～ tramp the streets 涌上～ pour into the streets

孑 jié lonely; all alone 【孑孓】wiggler; wriggler 【孑然】solitary ～一身 all alone in the world

节 jié joint; node; knot 骨～ joint (of bones) ②division; part 音～ syllable ③section; length ④festival; holiday 过～ celebrate a festival ⑤abridge ～译 abridged translation ⑥economize; save ～煤 save coal ⑦item 细～ details ⑧chastity 气～ moral integrity 【节本】abridged edition 【节俭】thrifty; frugal 【节节】successively; steadily ～胜利 win many victories in succession ～败退 keep on retreating 【节流】reduce expenditure 【节录】extract 【节目】item (on a programme); number ～单 programme 【节日】festival; red-letter day 【节省】economize; save; cut down on ～时间 save time ～篇幅 save space ～人力 use manpower sparingly 【节余】surplus (as a result of economizing) 【节育】birth control 【节约】practise thrift; save ～粮食 save on food ～用电 economize on electricity ～开支 cut down expenses 【节制】control; check/temperance ～饮食 be moderate in eating and drinking 【节奏】rhythm

劫 jié ①rob; plunder; raid 打～ loot ②coerce; compel ③calamity; disaster; misfortune 【劫持】kidnap; hijack ～飞机 hijack an aeroplane ～者 hijacker 【劫夺】seize by force 【劫掠】plunder; loot

杰 jié ①prominent ②outstanding person; hero 【杰出】outstanding; remarkable ～贡献 a brilliant contribution 【杰作】 masterpiece

诘 jié closely question; interrogate; cross-examine 【诘责】 censure; rebuke; denounce

洁 jié clean 【洁白】 spotlessly white; pure white 【洁身自好】 preserve one's purity/mind one's own business in order to keep out of trouble

拮 jié 【拮据】 in straitened circumstances; short of money; hard up

结 jié ①tie; knit; knot; weave ～网 weave a net ② knot 打～ tie a knot ③congeal; form; forge; cement ～痂 form a scab ④settle; conclude ～帐 settle accounts 【结案】 wind up a case 【结伴】 go with ～而行 go or travel in a group 【结冰】 freeze; ice up 【结肠】 colon 【结成】 form 【结仇】 start a feud 【结存】 cash on hand; balance/goods on hand; inventory 【结党营私】 form a clique to pursue selfish interests 【结构】 structure, composition, construction 【结果】 result, outcome 【结合】 combine; unite; integrate; link/be united in wedlock 【结核】 tuberculosis 【结婚】 marry ～登记 marriage registration ～证书 marriage certificate 【结集】 mass; concentrate (troops) 【结交】 make friends with, associate with 【结晶】 crystallize/crystal/crystallization 【结局】 final result, outcome; ending (of a novel, etc.) 【结论】 conclusion; verdict 得出～ draw a conclusion 还不能下～ be still an open question 【结盟】 form an alliance; ally; align 【结清】 settle; square (accounts with sb.) 【结社】 form an association 【结识】 get acquainted with sb. 【结束】 end; finish; conclude; wind up～语 concluding remarks 【结算】 settle accounts; close an account 【结尾】 ending; winding-up stage 【结业】 complete a course 【结余】 (cash) surplus; balance 【结怨】 incur hatred 【结扎】 ligature; tie up

捷 jié ①victory; triumph 报～ announce a victory ② prompt; nimble; quick 【捷报】news of victory; report of a success 【捷径】shortcut 【捷足先登】the swift-footed arrive first; the race is to the swiftest

睫 jié 【睫毛】eyelash; lash

竭 jié use up 【竭诚】wholeheartedly 【竭尽】use up; exhaust ～全力 spare no effort 【竭力】do one's utmost ～支持 give all-out support ～反对 actively oppose

截 jié ①cut; sever ～成两段 cut in two ②section; chunk; length 一～儿木头 a log ③stop; check; stem ～球 intercept a pass 【截断】cut off; block/cut short; interrupt ～河流 dam a river 【截获】intercept and capture 【截击】intercept ～机 interceptor 【截然】sharply ～不同 completely different 【截止】end; close 登记已经～ registration has closed 【截至】by (a specified time); up to ～本月底 by the end of this month ～目前为止 up to now

姐 jiě ①elder sister 【姐夫】elder sister's husband; brother-in-law 【姐妹】sisters

解 jiě ①separate; divide 瓦～ disintegrate ②untie; undo ～扣儿 unbutton ③allay; dispel; dismiss ～惑 remove doubts ④explain; interpret; solve ～题 solve a (mathematical, etc.) problem ⑤understand; comprehend 费～ hard to understand; obscure ⑥solution 求～ find the solution 【解除】remove; relieve; get rid of ～合同 terminate a contract ～武装 disarm ～禁令 lift a ban ～警报 sound the all clear ～婚约 renounce an engagement ～顾虑 free one's mind of apprehensions 【解答】answer 【解放】liberate; emancipate / liberation ～军 liberation army / the PLA / PLA man ～区 liberated area ～战争 war of liberation 【解雇】discharge; dismiss; fire 【解救】save;

rescue; deliver 【解决】solve; resolve; settle ～争端 settle
a dispute ～困难 overcome a difficulty ～问题 solve a
problem 把敌人完全～了 finish off all the enemy troops
【解开】untie; undo ～头巾 untie a kerchief ～这个谜
find a clue to the mystery ～疙瘩 get rid of a hang-up
【解渴】quench one's thirst 【解闷】divert oneself (from
boredom) 【解剖】dissect ～刀 scalpel ～学 anatomy 【解
散】dismiss/dissolve; disband (an organization, etc.) 【解
释】explain; expound; interpret ～生词 explain a new
word ～法律 interpret laws 【解说】explain orally; comment ～词 commentary; caption ～员 announcer; narrator
【解体】disintegrate 【解脱】extricate oneself 【解围】force
an enemy to raise a siege/save sb. from embarrassment
【解约】terminate an agreement; cancel a contract

介 jiè ①be situated between; interpose ②take seriously;
take to heart; mind 【介词】preposition 【介壳】shell
(of oysters, snails, etc.) 【介入】intervene; get involved in
【介绍】introduce; present / let know; brief / recommend;
suggest 自我～ introduce oneself ～对象 find sb. a boy
or girl friend ～一本书 recommend a book ～情况 brief
sb. on the situation ～经验 pass on experience ～信
letter of introduction ～人 sponsor / matchmaker 【介意】
take offence; mind 对此不必过分～ don't regard this
very seriously

芥 jiè mustard 【芥菜】leaf mustard 【芥蒂】unpleas-
antness; grudge 心存～ bear a grudge 【芥末】mustard

戒 jiè ①guard against ～浮夸 avoid boasting and ex-
aggeration ②exhort; admonish 引以为～ warn sb.
as an object lesson ③give up; drop; stop ～烟 give up
smoking ～酒 stop drinking ④(finger) ring 钻～ diamond ring 【戒备】guard; take precautions ～森严 be heavi-

ly guarded 处于～状态 be on the alert【戒骄戒躁】guard
against arrogance and rashness【戒心】religious discipline
【戒律】vigilance; wariness 怀有～ keep a wary eye on
sb.【戒严】enforce martial law; impose a curfew

届 jiè fall due ～期 on the appointed date 本～毕业
生 this year's graduates【届满】at the expiration of
one's term of office【届时】on the occasion

诚 jiè ①warn; admonish 告～ give warning; admonish
②commandment

界 jiè ①boundary 国～ national boundary ～河 boundary river ②scope; extent 眼～ field of vision ③
circles 新闻～ press circles ④primary division; kingdom
动物～ the animal kingdom【界限】demarcation line

借 jiè ①borrow (sth. from sb.) ②lend 把书～给我 lend
me your book ③ make use of 我愿～此机会向大家
表示感谢 I wish to take this opportunity to thank you
all ④use as a pretext【借贷】borrow or lend money/debit
and credit sides【借调】temporarily transfer; loan【借读】
study at a school on a temporary basis【借故】find an
excuse (to refuse, etc.) ～不去开会 absent oneself from a
meeting on some pretext【借火】ask for a light 请借个
火儿 would you mind giving me a light【借鉴】use for
reference; draw lessons from【借据】receipt for a loan
【借口】use as an excuse / excuse; pretext【借款】borrow
or lend money / loan【借书处】loan desk (of a library)
【借书证】library card【借宿】stay overnight at sb. else's
place; put up for the night【借以】so as to; for the purpose
of; by way of【借用】borrow; have the loan of/use sth.
for another purpose【借债】borrow money; raise a loan
【借支】ask for an advance on one's pay【借重】rely on
for support; enlist sb.'s help【借助】have the aid of

JIN

巾 jīn ① a piece of cloth (as used for a towel, scarf, kerchief, napkin, etc.) 【巾帼】ancient woman's headdress/ woman ～英雄 heroine

今 jīn ①modern; present-day ～人 moderns; contemporaries ②today ～晚 tonight; this evening ③this (year) ～冬 this winter ④now; the present 至～ until now ～胜于昔 the present is superior to the past 【今后】 from now on; henceforth; hereafter; in future 【今年】this year 【今生】this life 【今天】today/the present; now

斤 jīn *jin* a unit of weight (= 1/2 kilogram) 【斤斤 计较】haggle over every ounce; be calculating

金 jīn ①metals 合～ alloy ②money 现～ ready money ③gold 镀～ gild ～golden ～字 golden characters 【金 笔】(quality) fountain pen 【金币】gold coin 【金箔】 goldleaf; gold foil 【金额】sum of money 【金刚石】diamond 【金光】golden ray ～闪闪 glittering; glistening 【金黄】 golden (yellow) 【金库】state treasury; exchequer 【金块】 gold bullion 【金钱】money 【金融】finance; banking ～机 关 financial institution ～市场 money market ～资本 financial capital 【金色】golden 【金属】metal ～加工 metal processing ～结构 metal structure 【金条】gold bar 【金 星】Venus 【金鱼】goldfish 【金元】gold dollar 【金字塔】 pyramid

津 jīn ①ferry crossing; ford ②saliva 【津津乐道】take delight in talking about 【津津有味】with relish; with gusto 【津贴】subsidy; allowance

矜 jīn ①pity; sympathize with ②self-important; conceited 【矜持】restrained; reserved 举止～ have a reserved manner

筋 jīn ①muscle ②tendon; sinew 【筋斗】 somersault/fall; tumble 【筋骨】 bones and muscles—physique 【筋疲力尽】 exhausted; worn out; tired out 【筋肉】 muscles

禁 jīn ①bear; stand; endure 这鞋～穿 these shoes are durable ②contain oneself 不～流下眼泪 cannot hold back one's tears 【禁不起】 be unable to stand (tests, trials, etc.) 【禁不住】 be unable to bear or endure/can't help (doing sth.) 【禁得起】 be able to stand (tests, trials, etc.) 【禁得住】 be able to bear or endure

襟 jīn ①front of a garment ②brothers-in-law whose wives are sisters 【襟怀】 bosom; (breadth of) mind

仅 jīn only; merely; barely ～次于 second only to 这～供你参考 this is for your reference only 这～～是开始 this is only the beginning 这～～是时间问题 it is merely a matter of time

尽 jīn ①to the greatest extent ～早 as early as possible ②within the limits of ～着三天把事情办好 get the job done in three days at the outside ③give priority to ～着年纪大的坐 let the older people sit down first 【尽管】 feel free to; not hesitate to / though; even though; in spite of; despite 【尽可能】 as far as possible 【尽快】 as quickly as possible 请～答复 please reply at your earliest convenience 【尽量】 to the best of one's ability

紧 jīn ①tight; taut; close 拉～绳子 pull the rope taut 拧～螺丝 tighten the screw 我的鞋子太～ the shoe pinches me 日程安排得很～ the programme is packed ②tighten ～～背包带 tighten the knapsack straps ③urgent; pressing; tense 任务～ the task is urgent ④strict; stringent 管得～ be strict with ⑤hard up 手头～ be short of money 银根～ money is tight 【紧凑】 compact; terse; well-knit 布局～ be compactly laid out 情节～ have a well-knit plot 【紧跟】follow closely ～时代的步伐 keep in step with the times ～形势 keep abreast of the situation 【紧急】urgent; pressing; critical ～措施 emergency measures ～会议 emergency meeting ～集合 emergency muster ～任务 urgent task ～状态 state of emergency 情况～ the situation is critical ～行动起来 act promptly 【紧紧】closely; firmly; tightly ～相连 closely linked ～盯着 stare fixedly ～依靠群众 rely firmly on the masses 【紧密】close together; inseparable / rapid and intense 【紧迫】urgent; imminent 时间～ be pressed for time 【紧身】close-fitting undergarment 【紧缩】reduce; retrench; tighten ～开支 cut down expenses 【紧要】critical; crucial; vital ～关头 critical moment 无关～ of no consequence 【紧张】nervous / tense / tight 神情～ look nervous 别～ don't be nervous ～局势 a tense situation ～气氛 a tense atmosphere ～的战斗 intense fighting 关系～ relations are strained 供应～ be in short supply

锦 jǐn ①brocade ②bright and beautiful ～【锦标】prize; trophy; title ～赛 championships 【锦缎】brocade 【锦纶】polyamide fibre 【锦囊妙计】wise counsel 【锦旗】silk banner 【锦绣】beautiful; splendid ～山河 a land of charm and beauty

谨 jǐn ①careful; cautious ～记在心 bear in mind ② solemnly; sincerely ～致谢意 please accept my sincere thanks 【谨防】guard against; beware of ～扒手 beware of pickpockets 【谨上】sincerely yours 【谨慎】prudent; cautious 说话～ be guarded in one's speech 从事 act with caution 【谨小慎微】overcautious 【谨严】careful and precise 治学～ careful and exact scholarship

尽 jǐn ①exhausted; finished 取之不～ inexhaustible ② to the utmost; to the limit 用～气力 exert oneself to the utmost ③use up; exhaust 一饮而～ empty a glass at one gulp ④try one's best; put to the best use ～do one's duty 【尽最大努力】 exert one's utmost effort ⑤all; exhaustive 不可～信 not to be believed word for word 【尽力】 do all one can; do one's best 【尽量】 (drink or eat) to the full 【尽情】 to one's heart's content; as much as one likes 【尽人皆知】 be known to all 【尽善尽美】 perfect 【尽头】 end 【尽心】 with all one's heart 【尽兴】 enjoy oneself to the full 【尽义务】 fulfil one's obligation/ work for no reward 【尽职】 fulfil one's duty

进 jìn ①advance; move ahead 不～则退 move forward, or you'll fall behind ②enter; come or go into; get into ～屋 enter a house or room ～大学 enter college ～医院 be sent to hospital ③receive ～款 income ④eat; drink; take 共～晚餐 have supper together ⑤submit; present ～～言 give a word of advice ⑥into; in 走～车间 walk into the workshop 【进逼】 close in on; advance on 【进步】 advance; progress; improve / progressive 你的发音很有～ your pronunciation has greatly improved 思想～ have progressive ideas 【进程】 course; process; progress 【进出口】 imports and exports / exits and entrances; exit 【进度】 rate of progress / planned speed; schedule ～表 progress chart 【进犯】 intrude into; invade 【进攻】 attack; assault; offensive 【进化】 evolution ～论 the theory of evolution; evolutionism 【进军】 march; advance 向现代化～ march towards the modernization 【进口】 enter port / import / entrance ～货 imports ～商 importer ～税 import duty 【进款】 income; receipts 【进来】 come in; enter 请他～ ask him in 【进取】 be eager to make progress; be enterprising ～心 enterprising spirit; initiative 【进去】 go in; get in; enter 【进入】 enter; get into ～阵地 get into position ～决赛阶段 enter the finals ～角色 live one's part ～高潮 reach a high tide 【进退】 advance and retreat ～自如 free to advance or retreat ～两难 in a dilemma 【进项】 income; receipts 【进行】 be in progress; go on / carry on; conduct / march; advance ～社会主义革命 carry out socialist revolution ～争论 carry on a debate ～调查 make investigations ～科学实验 engage in scientific experiment ～表决 put a question to the vote ～斗争 wage a struggle ～抵抗 put up a resistance ～曲 march 【进修】 engage in advanced studies; take a refresher course 在职～ in-service training 教师的业务～ teachers' vocational studies ～班 class for advanced studies ～生 graduate student 【进一步】 go a step further; further 【进展】 make progress

近 jìn ①near; close ～邻 near neighbour 靠～些 come closer 由～及远 form the close to the distant 切勿～火 keep away from fire ～几年来 in recent years ② approximately; close to 年～六十 approaching sixty 【近代】 modern times ～史 modern history 【近郊】 outskirts; suburbs; environs 【近况】 recent developments; how things stand ～如何 how are things with you 【近来】 recently; of late; lately 【近路】 shortcut 走～ take a shortcut 【近期】 in the near future 【近亲】 close relative 【近日】 recently; in the past few days / within the next few days 【近视】 nearsightedness 【近似】 approximate; similar ～值 approximate value 【近因】 immediate cause

劲 jìn ①strength; energy 用～ put forth strength 有使不完的～ have inexhaustible energy ②vigour; spirit; drive; zeal 工作有～ be full of drive in one's work

浸 jìn soak; steep; immerse 把衣服～在水里 soak the clothes in water 【浸膏】 extract 【浸剂】 infusion 【浸

软】macerate 【浸润】infiltrate 【浸透】saturate; infuse

晋 jìn ①enter; advance ②promote 【晋级】rise in rank; be promoted 【晋见】have an audience with; call on (sb. holding high office)

禁 jìn ①prohibit; forbid; ban ～赌 suppress gambling 解～ remove a ban ② detain 监～ imprison ③taboo 【禁闭】confinement (as a punishment) 【禁忌】taboo/ avoid; abstain from 【禁令】prohibition; ban 【禁区】restricted zone or area 【禁书】banned book 【禁运】embargo 【禁止】prohibit; ban; forbid 砍树 felling trees is forbidden ～入内 no admittance ～停车 no parking ～通行 closed to traffic ～倒垃圾 no garbage here ～招贴 post no bills

噤 jìn ①keep silent ②shiver (with cold) 【噤若寒蝉】as silent as a cicada in cold weather — keep quiet out of fear

JING

京 jīng ①capital (of a country) 进～ go to the capital ②short for Beijing 【京剧】Beijing opera

茎 jīng stem (of a plant); stalk

经 jīng ①manage; deal in ～商 engage in trade ②constant; regular ～常 frequent ③scripture; canon; classics 圣～ the Holy Bible ④menses ⑤pass through; undergo 途～上海 pass through Shanghai ⑥as a result of; after; through ～某人建议 upon sb.'s proposal ⑦stand; bear; endure ～得起考验 can stand the test 【经常】day-to-day; everyday; daily / frequently; constantly; regularly; often ～工作 day-to-day work ～开支 running expenses ～发生 frequently crop up ～化 become a regular practice 【经典】classics / scriptures / classical 【经费】funds; outlay 【经管】be in charge of 【经过】pass; go through; undergo / as a result of; after; through / process; course ～充分讨论 after thorough discussion 事件的～ the course of the incident 【经纪】manage (a business) ～人 broker; agent 【经济】economy/economic/financial condition/economical; thrifty ～部门 economic departments ～成分 economic sector ～地位 economic status ～核算 business accounting ～基础 economic base ～危机 economic crisis ～学 economics ～学家 economist ～责任制 system of economic responsibility (in industry) ～作物 industrial crop 【经久】prolonged/durable 【经理】manage/manager; director 【经历】go through; undergo/experience 【经商】engage in trade; be in business 【经手】handle; deal with 【经受】undergo; withstand ～各种考验 experience all sorts of trials ～锻炼 be tempered 【经售】sell (on commission); deal in 【经心】careful; mindful; conscientious 【经验】experience 交流～ exchange experience 介绍～ pass on one's experience ～丰富 be very experienced ～不足 not be sufficiently experienced ～主义 empiricism 【经营】manage; run; engage in 改善～ improve management 苦心～ take great pains to build up (an enterprise, etc.) 【经由】via; by way of

荆 jīng chaste tree; vitex 【荆棘】thistles and thorns; brambles 【荆条】twigs of the chaste tree

惊 jīng ①start; be frightened ～呆了 be stupefied ②surprise; shock; alarm ③shy; stampede 马～了 the horse shied 【惊动】alarm; alert; disturb ～敌人 alert the enemy 别～他 don't trouble him 【惊呼】cry out in alarm 【惊慌】alarmed; scared 【惊叫】cry in fear; scream 【惊恐】terrified; panic-stricken; seized with terror 【惊奇】wonder;

be surprised; be amazed 【惊扰】 alarm; agitate 【惊人】 astonishing; alarming ～成就 astonishing achievements ～毅力 amazing willpower 【惊叹】 wonder at; marvel at; exclaim ～号 exclamation mark 【惊涛骇浪】 terrifying waves/a situation or life full of perils 【惊天动地】 earth-shaking; world-shaking 【惊喜】 pleasantly surprised 【惊险】 breathtaking; thrilling ～小说 thriller 【惊心动魄】 soul-stirring; profoundly affecting 【惊醒】 wake up with a start/awaken 【惊讶】 surprised; amazed; astonished

晶 jīng ①brilliant; glittering ②quartz; (rock) crystal 【晶石】 spar 【晶体】 crystal ～学 crystallography ～管 transistor 【晶莹】 sparkling and crystal-clear

睛 jīng eyeball 定～一看 give sth. or sb. a good look 目不转～地看着 gaze fixedly

精 jīng ①refined; picked; choice ～盐 refined salt ② essence; extract ～讲多练 teach only the essential and ensure plenty of practice ③perfect; excellent ～良 superior; of the best quality ④meticulous; fine; precise ～收细打 careful reaping and threshing ⑤smart; sharp; clever ⑥skilled; proficient ～于绘画 skilled in painting ⑦energy; spirit 聚～会神 concentrate one's attention ⑧ sperm; semen; seed 受～ fertilization ⑨goblin; spirit; demon 害人～ ogre 【精兵】 picked troops 【精彩】 brilliant; splendid; wonderful 【精萃】 cream; pick 【精粹】 succinct; pithy; terse 【精打细算】 careful calculation and strict budgeting 【精当】 precise and appropriate 【精到】 precise and penetrating 【精雕细刻】 work at sth. with the care and precision of a sculptor 【精读】 read carefully and thoroughly/intensive reading 【精干】 small in number but highly trained; crack/keen-witted and capable 【精悍】 capable and vigorous/pithy and poignant 【精华】 cream;

essence; quintessence 取其～ select the essence 【精簡】
retrench; simplify; cut; reduce ～会议 cut meetings to a
minimum ～机构 simplify the administrative structure ～
报表 reduce the number of forms 【精力】 energy; vigour;
vim ～充沛 very energetic 集中～ concentrate one's effort
【精练】 concise; succinct; terse 【精良】 excellent; superior
【精灵】 spirit; demon 【精美】 exquisite; elegant 【精密】
precise; accurate ～仪器 precision instrument 【精明】 astute; shrewd 【精疲力竭】 exhausted; worn out 【精辟】 penetrating; incisive 【精巧】 ingenious 【精确】 accurate; exact
【精锐】 crack; picked ～部队 crack troops 【精深】 profound
【精神】 spirit; mind/essence; gist ～负担 a load on one's
mind ～鼓励 moral encouragement ～枷锁 spiritual shackles ～面貌 mental attitude ～生活 cultural life ～世界
mental world ～文明 ethical and cultural level; cultural
development 【精神】 vigour; vitality; drive/lively; spirited;
vigorous 【精神病】 mental disease; psychosis ～人 mental
patient ～医生 psychiatrist ～院 psychiatric hospital 【精
髓】 marrow; pith; quintessence 【精通】 master ～业务 be
proficient in professional work ～英语 have a good command of English 【精细】 meticulous; fine; careful 【精心】
meticulously; painstakingly; elaborately ～护理 nurse with
the best of care 【精盐】 refined salt 【精液】 semen 【精益
求精】 constantly improve sth. 【精制】 refine 【精致】 fine;
exquisite; delicate 【精装】 (of books) clothbound; hard-
cover ～本 de luxe edition 【精壮】 able-bodied; strong
【精子】 sperm

兢

jīng 【兢兢业业】 cautious and conscientious ～地工
作 work conscientiously

鲸

jīng whale 【鲸吞】 swallow like a whale; annex
【鲸油】 whale oil

井 jǐng well 打～ sink a well 矿～ pit 【井井有条】in perfect order 【井然】orderly; neat and tidy

陉 jǐng trap; pitfall; pit

颈 jǐng neck 【颈椎】cervical vertebra

景 jǐng ①view; scenery; scene 外～ exterior view 雪～ a snow scene ②situation; condition 好～不长 good times do not last long ③scenery (of a play or film) ④ scene (of a play) ⑤admire; revere; respect ～慕 esteem 【景况】situation; circumstances 【景片】a piece of (stage) scenery; flat 【景气】prosperity; boom 不～ depression; slump 【景色】scenery; view; scene; landscape 【景象】scene; sight; picture 丰收～ panorama of bumper crops

警 jǐng ①alert; vigilant ～醒 be a light sleeper ②warn; alarm ③alarm 火～ fire alarm ④police 【警报】alarm; alert 台风～ a typhoon warning 战斗～ combat alert 【警备】guard; garrison 【警察】police; policeman 【警笛】police whistle / siren 【警告】warn; caution; admonish / warning (as a disciplinary measure) 【警戒】warn; admonish/be on the alert against; guard against ～部队 outpost troops 【警句】aphorism 【警觉】vigilance; alertness 【警犬】police dog 【警惕】be on guard against; watch out for ～性 vigilance 【警卫】(security) guard ～室 guard-room ～团 guards regiment ～员 bodyguard 【警钟】tocsin

劲 jìng strong; powerful; sturdy ～松 sturdy pines 【劲敌】formidable adversary 【劲旅】strong contingent

净 jìng ①clean ～水 clean water 擦～ wipe sth. clean ②completely 用～ use up ③only; merely; nothing but ～说不干 all talk, no action ④net ～收入 net income 【净化】purify 水的～ purification of water 【净利】net profit 【净余】remainder; surplus 【净值】net worth; net value 【净重】net weight

径 jìng ①footpath; path; track 曲～ a winding path ②way; means 捷～ an easy way ③directly ～行办理 deal with the matter straightaway 【径赛】track

胫 jìng shin 【胫骨】shin bone; tibia

痉 jìng 【痉挛】convulsion; spasm

竞 jìng compete; contest; vie 【竞技】sports; athletics ～场 arena ～状态 form (of an atehlete) 【竞赛】competition; emulation; race 【竞选】campaign for (office); run for 【竞争】compete 【竞走】heel-and-toe walking race

竟 jìng ①finish; complete 未～之业 unaccomplished cause; unfinished task ②throughout; whole ～夜 the whole night ③in the end; eventually 有志者事～成 where there's a will there's a way 【竟敢】dare; have the audacity 【竟然】unexpectedly; to one's surprise; actually / go to the length of; have the impudence to ～不顾事实 go so far as to disregard the facts

敬 jìng ①respect; esteem 致～ pay one's respects ②offer politely ～酒 propose a toast; toast ～茶 serve tea 【敬爱】respect and love 【敬辞】term of respect 【敬老院】old folks' home 【敬礼】salute / extend one's greetings 此致～ with high respect 【敬佩】esteem; admire 【敬仰】revere; venerate 【敬意】respect; tribute 【敬重】honour

境 jìng ①border; boundary 越～ cross the border ②place; area 敌～ enemy territory ③situation 困～ difficult position 【境界】boundary / state; realm 思想～ realm of thought 理想～ ideal state 【境况】condition; circumstances 【境遇】one's lot

静 jìng still; quiet; calm 请～～ please be quiet 【静脉】 vein ～注射 intravenous injection 【静默】 become silent / mourn in silence 【静穆】 solemn and quiet 【静物】 still life 【静养】 rest quietly to recuperate; convalesce 【静止】 static; motionless; at a standstill 【静坐】 sit quietly / sit still as a form of therapy ～罢丁 sit-down (strike)

镜 jìng ①looking glass; mirror 平如～ as smooth as a mirror ②lens; glass 【镜框】 picture frame / spectacles frame 【镜片】 lens 【镜头】 camera lens / shot; scene

JIONG

迥 jiǒng ①far away ②widely different 【迥然】 far apart ～不同 utterly different; not in the least alike

炯 jiǒng bright; shining 【炯炯】 (of eyes) bright; shining 一双眼睛～有神 a pair of bright piercing eyes

窘 jiǒng ①in straitened circumstances 一度生活很～ be hard up for a time ②awkward; ill at ease 露出～态 show signs of embarrassment ③embarrass; disconcert 【窘境】 predicament; plight 【窘迫】 poverty-stricken; very poor /hard pressed 生活～ live in poverty

JIU

纠 jiū ①entangle ②gather together ③correct; rectify 有错必～ mistakes must be corrected whenever discovered 【纠察】 maintain order at a public gathering/picket ～队 pickets ～线 picket line 【纠缠】 get entangled; be in a tangle / nag; worry; pester 【纠纷】 dispute; issue 【纠葛】 entanglement 【纠集】 get together; muster 【纠偏】 rectify a deviation; correct an error 【纠正】 correct; put right ～错误 correct a mistake; redress an error ～姿势 correct sb's posture ～不正之风 check unhealthy tendencies

究 jiū　study carefully; go into　～办 investigate and deal with　～其根源 trace sth. to its source【究竟】outcome; what actually happened/actually; exactly/after all; in the end

阄 jiū　lot 抓～ draw lots 拈～决定 decide by lot

揪 jiū　①hold tight; seize　～住一个小偷 grab a thief ②pull; tug; drag　～一下绳子 give a pull at the rope【揪辫子】seize sb.'s queue / seize upon sb.'s mistakes or shortcomings【揪出】uncover; ferret out【揪心】anxious, worried

九 jiǔ　nine【九九表】multiplication table【九泉】grave, the nether world【九死一生】a narrow escape from death【九霄云外】beyond the highest heavens 抛到～ cast sth. to the winds【九月】September/the ninth moon

久 jiǔ　for a long time; long　～别重逢 meet after a long separation 两个月之～ for as long as two months 你来了有多～ how long have you been here【久而久之】in the course of time; as time passes【久久】for a long time【久违】I haven't seen you for ages【久仰】I'm very pleased to meet you【久远】far back, ages ago; remote 年代～ of the remote past; age-old

灸 jiǔ　moxibustion

韭 jiǔ　fragrant-flowered garlic; (Chinese) chives 青～ young chives; chive seedlings【韭黄】hotbed chives

酒 jiǔ　alcoholic drink; wine; liquor; spirits【酒吧间】bar; barroom【酒菜】food and drink【酒厂】winery; distillery【酒店】wineshop; public house【酒鬼】drunkard/wine bibber【酒壶】wine pot【酒会】cocktail party【酒窖】wine cellar【酒精】alcohol　～灯 alcohol burner

【酒量】capacity for liquor 【酒酿】fermented glutinous rice 【酒窝】dimple 【酒席】feast 【酒意】a tipsy feeling 已有几分～ be mellow 【酒盅】a small handleless wine cup

旧 jiù ①past; bygone; old ～思想 old way of thinking ～事重提 bring up a matter of the past ②used; worn; old ～衣服 used clothes 【旧案】a court case of long standing/old regulations; former practice 【旧恶】old grievance; old wrong 【旧货】junk ～店 secondhand shop; junk shop ～市场 flea market 【旧交】old acquaintance 【旧诗】classical poetry 【旧时】old times; old days 【旧式】old type 【旧书】used book / books by ancient writers

臼 jiù ①mortar 石～ stone mortar ②joint (of bones) 脱～ dislocation (of joints) 【臼齿】molar

疚 jiù remorse 感到内～ have a guilty conscience

咎 jiù ①fault; blame 归～于人 lay the blame on sb. else ～由自取 have only oneself to blame ② censure

柩 jiù a coffin with a corpse in it 【柩车】hearse

救 jiù ①rescue; save; salvage ～国 save the nation ～孩子 rescue a child 呼～ call out for help ②help; relieve; succour ～荒 send relief to a famine area 【救兵】relief troops; reinforcements 【救护】relieve a sick or injured person; give first aid (to the wounded, etc.) 【救车】ambulance 【救活】bring sb. back to life 【救火】fire fighting ～车 fire engine ～队 fire brigade ～队员 fireman; fire fighter 【救急】help meet an urgent need 【救济】relieve; succour ～费 relief fund ～粮 relief grain 【救命】save sb.'s life ～稻草 a straw to clutch at ～恩人 saviour 【救生】lifesaving ～带 life belt ～圈 life buoy ～艇 lifeboat ～衣 life jacket ～员 lifeguard; lifesaver 【救死扶伤】

heal the wounded and rescue the dying 【救援】rescue; come to sb.'s help 【救灾】provide disaster relief; send relief to a disaster area 【救治】treat and cure 【救助】help sb. in danger or difficulty; succour

厩 jiù stable; cattle-shed; pen 【厩肥】barnyard manure

就 jiù ①come near; move towards ～着路灯 by the light of a street lamp ②undertake; engage in; enter upon ～学 go to school ～座 take one's seat ③accomplish; make 功成业～ (of a person's career) be crowned with success ④accomodate oneself to; suit; fit ～你的时间吧 make it anytime that suits you ⑤go with 咸菜～饭 have some pickles to go with the rice ⑥with regard to; concerning; on ～我所知 so far as I know ⑦at once 我这～去 I'll be going right away ⑧as early as; already 他一九七八年～参军了 he joined the army as early as 1978 ⑨as soon as; right after 说干～干 act without delay ⑩only; just ～等你一个了 you're the only one we're waiting for 【就此】at this point; here and now; thus 讨论～结束 the discussion was thus brought to a close 【就地】on the spot ～取材 use local materials 【就范】submit; give in 【就近】nearby; without having to go far ～找个住处 find accommodation in the neighbourhood 【就事论事】consider sth. as it stands 【就算】even if 【就绪】be in order 一切都已～ everything is ready 【就要】be about to; be going to 【就业】obtain employment; get a job 充分～ full employment 【就医】seek medical advice; go to a doctor 【就义】die a martyr 英勇～ face execution bravely 【就职】assume office

舅 jiù ①mother's brother; uncle ②wife's brother; brother-in-law 【舅母】wife of mother's brother; aunt

JU

拘 jū ①detain ②limit; constrain 长短不～ with no limit on the length 【拘捕】 arrest 【拘谨】 overcautious; reserved 【拘禁】 take into custody 【拘礼】 be punctilious; stand on ceremony 【拘留】 detain, intern ～所 house of detention; lockup 【拘泥】 be a stickler for (form, etc.); rigidly adhere to (form, formalities, etc.) ～于形式 be formalistic ～于细节 be very punctilious 【拘禁】 warrant 【拘束】 restrain; restrict / constrained; awkward

狙 jū 【狙击】 snipe ～手 sniper ～战 sniping action

居 jū ①reside; dwell; live 侨～国外 reside abroad ② residence; house 迁～ move house ③be (in a certain position); occupy (a place) ～中 be in the middle ～首位 occupy first place ④claim; assert 以专家自～ be a self-styled expert 【居多】 be in the majority 【居功】 claim credit for oneself 【居间】 (mediate) between two parties ～人 mediator 【居留】 reside ～权 right of residence ～证 residence permit 【居民】 resident; inhabitant ～点 residential area ～委员会 residents' committee 【居然】 unexpectedly; to one's surprise / go so far as to; have the impudence to. 【居心】 harbour (evil) intentions 【居住】 live; dwell ～面积 living space ～条件 housing conditions

驹 jū ①colt ②foal 怀～ be in foal

掬 jū hold with both hands 以手～水 scoop up some water with one's hands 笑容可～ radiant with smiles

鞠 jū rear; bring up 【鞠躬】 bow ～致谢 bow one's thanks 【鞠躬尽瘁】 bend oneself to a task and exert oneself to the utmost

局 jú ①chessboard ②game; set; innings 第一～ the first game ③situation; state of affairs 战～ the war situation ④limit ⑤office; bureau; shop 书～ publishing house 邮～ post office 【局部】 part ～地区 parts of an area ～利益 partial and local interests ～麻醉 local anaesthesia ～战争 partial war 【局促】 (of place) narrow; cramped/(of time) short/feel or show constraint 【局面】 aspect; phase; situation 打开～ open up a new prospect 【局势】 situation 【局外人】 outsider 【局限】 limit; confine

菊 jú chrysanthemum 【菊科】 the composite family

橘 jú tangerine 【橘红】 tangerine (colour); reddish orange 【橘黄】 orange (colour) 【橘汁】 orange juice

沮 jǔ ①stop; prevent ②turn gloomy 【沮丧】 dejected; depressed; dispirited; disheartened

咀 jǔ chew 【咀嚼】 masticate / ruminate; chew the cud

举 jǔ ①lift; raise; hold up ～杯 raise one's glass ② act; deed; move 壮～ a heroic undertaking ③start ～义 rise in revolt ④elect; choose ～他当代表 choose him as representative ⑤cite; enumerate ～出几件事 cite a few instances ～不胜～ too numerous to mention ⑥ whole; entire 【举办】 conduct; hold; run; put on ～训练班 conduct a training course ～学习班 run a study class ～展览会 hold an exhibition ～音乐会 give a concert 【举动】 move; act; activity ～缓慢 be slow in movement 轻率的～ a rash act 【举国】 the whole nation / throughout the nation ～欢腾 the whole nation is jubilant 【举荐】 recommend (a person) 【举例】 give an example ～说明 illustrate with examples 【举棋不定】 be unable to make up one's mind 【举世】 throughout the world; universally

～皆知 known to all ～闻名 of world renown; world-famous ～无双 unrivalled; matchless 【举手】put up one's hand or hands ～表决 vote by a show of hands 【举行】hold (a meeting, ceremony, etc.) ～会谈 hold talks ～宴会 give a banquet ～罢工 stage a strike 【举止】bearing; manner; mien ～庄重 carry oneself with dignity ～大方 have poise 【举重】weight lifting ～运动员 weight lifter 【举足轻重】hold the balance; prove decisive ～的力量(地位) a decisive force (position)

巨 jù huge; gigantic ～款 a huge sum of money 【巨大】tremendous; enormous; gigantic; immense 【巨额】a huge sum ～投资 huge investments ～利润 enormous profits ～赤字 huge financial deficits 【巨人】giant 【巨头】magnate; tycoon 【巨著】monumental work

句 jù sentence 【句法】sentence structure / syntax 【句号】full stop; full point; period 【句型】sentence pattern 【句子】sentence ～成份 sentence element; member of a sentence

拒 jù ①resist; repel ～敌 resist the enemy ②refuse; reject ～不接受 refuse to accept 【拒捕】resist arrest 【拒付】refuse payment 【拒绝】refuse / reject; decline ～参加 refuse to participate ～发表意见 refuse to comment ～无理要求 turn down unreasonable demands ～别人的批评 reject other people's criticism

具 jù ①utensil; tool; implement 农～ farm tool ②possess; have 初～规模 have begun to take shape 【具名】affix one's signature 【具体】concrete; specific; particular 【具有】possess; have; be provided with ～深远的历史意义 have profound historical significance

炬 jù ①torch ②fire 付之一～ be burnt down; be committed to the flames

俱 jù all; complete 【俱乐部】club 【俱全】complete in all varieties

剧 jù ①theatrical work; drama; play; opera ②acute; severe; intense ～痛 a severe pain '～变 a violent change 【剧本】drama; play; script ～创作 play writing 【剧场】theatre 【剧烈】violent; acute; severe; fierce ～运动 strenuous exercise 【剧目】a list of plays or operas 【剧评】a review of a play or opera; dramatic criticism 【剧情】the story of a play or opera ～简介 synopsis 【剧团】theatrical company; (opera) troupe 【剧务】stage management/stage manager 【剧照】stage photo; still 【剧中人】characters in a play or opera 【剧种】type of drama 【剧作家】playwright; dramatist

惧 jù fear; dread 毫无所～ not cowed in the least 【惧色】a look of fear 面无～ look undaunted

据 jù ①occupy; seize ～为己有 take forcible possession of; appropriate ②rely on; depend on ③according to ～道报 it is reported that ～我看 in my opinion ～我所知 as far as I know ～理力争 argue strongly on just grounds ②evidence; certificate 查无实～ investigation reveals no evidence 【据传】rumour has it that 【据此】on these grounds; accordingly 【据点】strongpoint 【据守】guard; be entrenched in 【据说】it is said; they say

距 jù ①distance 行～ the distance between rows of plants ②be apart from; be at a distance from 相～十里 be 10 *li* apart ～今十年 that was ten years ago 【距离】distance/be away from 保持～ keep at a distance

飓 jù 【飓风】hurricane

锯 jù ①saw 手～ handsaw ②cut with a saw ～木头 saw wood 【锯齿】sawtooth 【锯床】sawing machine

【锯末】sawdust 【锯木厂】lumber-mill 【锯条】saw-blade

聚 jù assemble; gather; get together ～在一起商量 get together and talk it over 【聚餐】dine together; have a dinner party 【聚光灯】spotlight 【聚会】get together; meet / get-together 【聚积】accumulate; collect; build up 【聚集】gether; assemble; collect 【聚精会神】concentrate one's attention ～地工作 be intent on one's work ～地听 listen with rapt attention 【聚居】inhabit a region 【聚敛】amass wealth by heavy taxation

JUAN

捐 juān ①relinquish; abandon ②contribute (money); donate; subscribe 募～ solicit contributions ③tax 上～ pay a tax 【捐款】contribute money/donation; subscription 【捐躯】sacrifice one's life; lay down one's life for 【捐税】taxes and levies 【捐赠】contribute (as a gift) 【捐助】offer (financial or material assistance)

娟 juān beautiful; graceful 【娟秀】graceful 字迹～ beautiful handwriting; a graceful hand

圈 juān ①shut in a pen; pen in 把羊～起来 herd the sheep into the pens ②lock up; put in jail

卷 juǎn ①roll up ～袖子 roll up one's sleeves ②sweep off; carry along 把小船～走 sweep the boat away ③roll 花～ twisted steamed roll 铺盖～ bedding roll ④roll; spool; reel 一～手纸 a roll of toilet paper 一～软片 a roll of film 【卷笔刀】pencil sharpener 【卷尺】band tape 【卷发】curly hair 【卷】be drawn into (a whirlpool, etc.) ～纠纷 be involved in a dispute 【卷逃】abscond with valuables 【卷土重来】stage a comeback 【卷心菜】cabbage 【卷烟】cigarette / cigar ～工业 cigarette industry ～机 cigarette machine ～纸 cigarette paper

卷 juàn ①book 手不释～ always have a book in one's hand ②volume 藏书十万～ have 100,000 volumes ③ examination paper 交～ hand in an examination paper ④file; dossier 【卷子】 examination paper 看～ mark examination papers 【卷宗】 folder / file; dossier

倦 juàn weary; tired 面有～容 look tired 毫无～意 not feel in the least tired

绢 juàn thin, tough silk 【绢本】 silk scroll 【绢纺】 silk spinning 【绢花】 silk flower 【绢丝】 spun silk

眷 juàn ①family dependant 女～ female members of a family ②have tender feeling for 【眷恋】 be sentimentally attached to 【眷念】 think fondly of 【眷属】 family dependants

圈 juàn pen; fold; sty 猪～ pigsty 【圈肥】 barnyard manure

JUE

撅 jue ①stick up (the tail, etc.) ～嘴 pout (one's lips) ②break; snap 把棍子一～断 break the stick in two

决 jue ①decide; determine 犹豫不～ hesitate ～一胜负 fight it out ②definitely; certainly ～非恶意 bear no ill will whatsoever ～不退让 will under no circumstances give in ③execute a person 枪～ execute by shooting 【决策】 make policy/policy decision ～机构 policy-making body ～人 policymaker 【决定】 decide; resolve; make up one's mind/decision; resolution/determine 我们～不去 we conclude not to go ～性胜利 a decisive victory ～因素 decisive factor; determinant ～权 power to make decisions 【决斗】 duel / decisive struggle 【决断】 make a decision / resolve; resolution 【决计】 have decided; have made up one's mind / definitely; certainly 【决口】 (of a dyke, etc.) be breached; burst 【决裂】break with; rupture 【决赛】finals 【决胜】determine the victory 【决死】life-and-death (struggle, fight, etc.) 【决算】final accounts 【决心】determination; resolution 表～ pledge one's determination 下～ make up one's mind ～书 written pledge 【决议】resolution ～案 draft resolution 【决意】have one's mind made up; be determined 【决战】decisive battle

诀 jué ①rhymed formula ②knack ③bid farewell; part 永～ part for ever 【诀别】bid farewell; part 【诀窍】secret of success; tricks of the trade; knack

抉 jué pick out; single out 【抉择】choose 作出～ make one's choice

角 jué ①role; part 主～ main character ②actor or actress ③contend ～斗 wrestle 口～ quarrel 【角逐】contend; tussle; enter into rivalry

觉 jué ①sense; feel ～着不舒服 not feel well ②wake (up); awake 如梦初～ as if waking from a dream 【觉察】detect; become aware of; perceive ～到其中有问题 sense there was something wrong 【觉得】feel / think 不～累 not feel tired 你～怎么样 what do you think of it 【觉悟】consciousness; awareness; understanding/come to understand; become aware of 【觉醒】awaken

绝 jué ①cut off; sever 掌声不～ prolonged applause ②exhausted; used up; finished 弹尽粮～ have run out of ammunition and provisions ③desperate; hopeless ～境 hopeless situation; impasse ④unique; superb; matchless ⑤extremely; most ～大多数 the overwhelming majority ～早 extremely early ⑥absolutely ～无此意 have absolutely no such intentions ～非偶然 by no means fortuitous 【绝版】out of print 【绝壁】precipice 【绝对】absolute/absolutely; perfectly; definitely 【绝后】without offspring/never to be seen again 【绝迹】 disappear; vanish; be stamped out 【绝技】 unique skill 【绝交】 break off relations 【绝路】 road to ruin 【绝密】 top-secret; most confidential 【绝妙】 extremely clever; ingenious; excellent; perfect 【绝命书】 suicide note/note written on the eve of one's execution 【绝望】 give up all hope; despair ～情绪 feeling of despair ～的挣扎 desperate struggle 【绝无仅有】 the only one of its kind 【绝症】 incurable disease

倔 jué 【倔强】 stubborn; unbending

掘 jué dig ～井 dig a well 自～坟墓 dig one's own grave 【掘墓人】 gravedigger 【掘土机】 excavator

崛 jué 【崛起】 rise abruptly; suddenly appear on the horizon / rise (as a political force)

厥 jué faint; lose consciousness; fall into a coma 昏～ fall to the ground in a faint

爵 jué peerage 封～ confer a title upon 【爵士】 knight/Sir 【爵士音乐】 jazz 【爵位】 the rank of nobility

蹶 jué ①fall ②suffer a setback 一～不振 collapse after one setback / never recover from a setback

嚼 jué masticate; chew

攫 jué 【攫取】 seize; grab ～别国的资源 grab the resources of other countries ～暴利 rake in exorbitant profits

倔 juè gruff; blunt 脾气～ be rather surly 【倔头倔脑】 blunt of manner and gruff of speech

JUN

军 jūn ①armed forces 正规～ regular troops ②army 第四～ the Fourth Army 【军备】 armament; arms ～

竞赛 arms race 【军部】 army headquarters 【军车】 military vehicle 【军阀】 warlord 【军法】 military criminal code 【军费】 military expenditure 【军服】 (mili'ary) uniform ～呢 army coating 【军港】 naval port 【军功】 military exploit 【军官】 officer 【军管】 military control ～会 military control commission 【军国主义】 militarism 【军号】 bugle 【军火】 munitions ～工业 armament industry ～库 arsenal ～商 arms dealer 【军机】 military plan/military secret 贻误～ delay or frustrate the fulfilment of a military plan 泄漏～ leak a military secret 【军籍】 military status 【军纪】 military discipline 【军舰】 warship; naval vessel 【军阶】 rank; grade 【军界】 the military 【军龄】 length of military service 【军令】 military orders 【军旗】 army flag 【军情】 military situation 【军区】 military region 【军人】 soldier; armyman 【军师】 army adviser 【军事】 military affairs ～部署 military deployment ～工业 war industry ～体育 military sports ～学院 military academy 【军衔】 military rank 【军校】 military school 【军械】 armament 【军心】 army's morale 【军需】 military supplies 【军训】 military training 【军医】 medical officer 【军营】 military camp; barracks 【军用】 military ～飞机 warplane ～列车 military train ～物资 military supplies 【军援】 military aid 【军乐】 martial music ～队 military band 【军长】 army commander 【军职】 military appointment 【军种】 (armed) services

均 jūn ①equal; even ～摊 share equally 劳逸不～ uneven allocation of work ②without exception; all 各项工作～已就绪 all the work has been completed 【均等】 impartial; fair 【均分】 divide equally 【均衡】 balanced; proportionate; harmonious 【均势】 balance of power; equilibrium 【均匀】 even; well-distributed

君 jūn ①monarch; supreme ruler ②gentleman; Mr. 【君权】 monarchical power 【君主】 monarch; sovereign ～国 monarchy 【君子】 gentleman; a man of noble character; a man of moral integrity

龟 jūn 【龟裂】 (of parched earth) be full of cracks / (of skin) chap

菌 jūn ①fungus ②bacterium 【菌肥】 bacterial manure 【菌苗】 vaccine

俊 jùn ①handsome; pretty ②a person of outstanding talent 【俊杰】 hero 【俊俏】 pretty and charming

郡 jùn prefecture

浚 jùn dredge 【浚泥船】 dredger

峻 jùn ①high 高山～岭 high mountains ②harsh; severe; stern 严刑～法 harsh law and severe punishment 【峻峭】 high and steep

骏 jùn 【骏马】 fine horse; steed

菌 jùn mushroom

竣 jùn complete; finish 告～ have been completed 【竣工】 (of a project) be completed

K

KA

咖 kā 【咖啡】 coffee ～馆 café ～色 coffee (colour) 【咖啡因】 caffeine

卡 kǎ block; check ～住这条路 block this road 【卡宾枪】 carbine 【卡车】 lorry; truck 【卡片】 card ～柜 card cabinet ～目录 card catalogue ～索引 card index

咯 kǎ cough up 【咯痰】 cough up phlegm 【咯血】 spit blood

KAI

开 kāi ①open ～锁 open a lock ②make an opening; open up; reclaim ～个窗口 make a window ～稻田 open up paddy fields ③open out; come loose 花～了 the flowers are open ④thaw; become navigable 河～了 the river is open ⑤lift (a restriction, etc.) ～禁 lift a ban ⑥start; operate ～机器 operate a machine ～灯 turn on a light ～飞机 fly an airplane ～船 set sail ⑦(of troops, etc.) set out; move ⑧set up; run ～工厂 set up a factory ⑨begin; start ～拍 start shooting (a flim) ⑩hold (a meeting, exhibition, etc.) ～运动会 hold an athletic meet ⑪write out ～个单子 make a list ～方子 write a prescription 我去～介绍信 I'm going to get a letter of introduction ⑫pay (wages, fares, etc.) ⑬boil 水～了 the water is boiling 【开采】 extract; exploit ～煤炭 mine coal ～石油 recover petroleum 【开场】 begin 戏已经～了 the play had already begun ～白 opening remarks 【开车】 drive or start a car, train, etc./set a machine going 【开除】 expel; discharge ～学籍 expel from school 【开创】 start; initiate 【开刀】 perform or have an operation 给病人～ operate on a patient 【开导】 enlighten 【开动】 start; set in motion ～脑筋 use one's brains 【开发】 open up; exploit ～山区 develop mountain areas 【开饭】 serve a meal 【开放】 lift a ban, restriction, etc./open to traffic or public use/be open (to the public) 【开工】 (of a factory, etc.) go into operation/(of work on a construction project, etc.) start 【开关】switch 【开航】become open for navigation/set sail 【开户】open an account 【开花】blossom; bloom 玫瑰在～ the roses are in flower 【开怀】to one's heart's content 【开会】hold or attend a meeting 【开火】open fire 【开卷】open a book; read ～有益 reading is always profitable ～考试 open-book examination 【开课】school begins/give a course; teach a subject 【开口】open one's mouth; start to talk 【开快车】step on the gas/(of a machine) speed up/make short work of a job 【开矿】open up a mine 【开阔】open; wide/tolerant/widen; broaden ～地 open terrain 【开朗】open and clear/sanguine; optimistic 【开列】draw up (a list) 【开路】open a way ～先锋 pioneer 【开绿灯】give the green light 【开门】open the door/open-door 【开明】enlightened ～人士 enlightened persons 【开幕】the curtain rises / open; inaugurate ～词 opening speech ～式 opening ceremony 【开炮】open fire with artillery; fire 【开辟】open up; start ～航线 open an air or sea route ～专栏 start a special column ～财源 tap new financial resources 【开枪】fire with a rifle, pistol, etc.; shoot ～射击 open fire ～还击 return fire 【开始】begin; start / initial stage; beginning; outset 今天从第五课～ today we'll begin with Lesson 5 【开庭】open a court session 【开玩笑】joke; make fun of 【开胃】whet the appetite 【开小差】(of a soldier) desert/be absent-minded 思想～ be woolgathering 【开销】pay expenses/expense 【开心】feel happy; rejoice / make fun of sb. 【开学】school opens; term begins 【开演】(of a play, movie, etc.) begin 【开业】(of a shop, etc.) start business/ (of a lawyer, doctor, etc.) open a private practice 【开夜车】work late into the night 【开展】develop; launch;

unfold / open-minded 【开战】 make war; open hostilities/ battle (against nature, conservative forces, etc.) 【开张】 open a business / the first transaction of a day's business 【开帐】 make out a bill / pay the bill (at a restaurant, hotel, etc.) 【开支】 pay (expenses) /expenses; expenditure

揩 kāi wipe ～桌子 wipe the table 【揩油】 get petty advantages at the expense of other people; scrounge

凯 kǎi ①triumphant strains ②victorious 【凯歌】 a song of triumph; paean 【凯旋】 triumphant return

慨 kǎi ①indignant ②deeply touched 感～ sigh with emotion ③generous ～允 consent readily; kindly promise 【慨然】 with deep feeling/generously

楷 kǎi ①model; pattern ②regular script 大(小)～ regular script in big (small) characters

KAN

刊 kān ①print; publish 停～ suspend or stop publication ②periodical; publication 周～ weekly (publication) ③delete or correct ～误 correct errors in printing 【刊登】 publish; carry ～广告 advertise 【刊物】 publication

看 kān ①look after; take care of; tend ～孩子 look after children ～瓜 keep watch in the melon fields ～牛 tend cattle ～机器 mind a machine ②keep under surveillance; keep an eye on sb. 【看管】 look after; attend to/watch; guard (prisoners, etc.) 【看护】 nurse (the sick) / hospital nurse 【看家】 mind the house 【看门】 guard the entrance/look after the house 【看守】 watch; guard (a storehouse, prisoners, etc.)/turnkey; warder

勘 kān ①collate ②investigate 【勘测】 survey 【勘察】 reconnaissance 【勘探】 exploration; prospecting 【勘误】 correct errors in printing ～表 errata; corrigenda

堪 kān ①may; can ～当重任 be capable of shouldering important tasks ②bear; endure 不～一击 cannot withstand a single blow

坎 kǎn ①bank; ridge ②pit; hole 【坎肩】sleeveless jacket 【坎坷】bumpy; rough (road)/full of frustrations

砍 kǎn ①cut; chop; hack ～树枝 cut off a branch ～柴 cut firewood ～去一半 cut down by half ②throw sth. at 【砍刀】chopper【砍伐】fell (trees)【砍头】behead

看 kàn ①see; look at; watch ～电影 see a film; go to the movies ～电视 watch TV ～球赛 watch a ball game ②read ～报 read a newspaper ～书 read (a book) ③think; consider ～清形势 make a correct appraisal of the situation ④look upon; regard ⑤treat (a patient or an illness) ⑥look after ～顾 take care of ⑦call on; visit; see 明天去～他 go and see him tomorrow ⑧depend on ～天气 depend on the weather 【看病】(of a doctor) see a patient/(of a patient) consult a doctor 【看不惯】cannot bear the sight of; frown upon 【看不起】scorn; despise 【看成】look upon as 【看出】make out; see 【看穿】see through 【看法】view 【看风使舵】trim one's sails 【看见】catch sight of; see 【看来】it seems; it appears; it looks as if 【看轻】underestimate; look down upon 【看上】take a fancy to (a girl, etc.); settle on 【看台】bleachers; stand 【看望】call on; visit; see 【看重】regard as important; value 【看做】look upon as; regard as

KANG

康 kāng well-being; health 【康复】restored to health 祝您早日～ I wish you a speedy recovery 【康健】healthy; in good health 【康乐】peace and happiness 【康庄大道】broad road; main road

慷 kāng 【慷慨】 vehement; fervent / generous; liberal ~陈词 present one's views vehemently ~解囊 help sb. generously with money ~激昂 impassioned ~就义 die a martyr's death

糠 kāng ①chaff; bran; husk ②(usu. of a radish) spongy

扛 káng carry on the shoulder ~着锄头 carry a hoe on one's shoulder ~枪 shoulder a gun

亢 kàng ①high; haughty 高~ resounding ②excessive; extreme 【亢奋】 stimulated; excited

抗 kàng ①resist; combat; fight ~灾 fight natural calamities ~暴斗争 struggle against violent repression ~旱 combat a drought ②refuse; defy 【抗衡】 contend with; match 【抗击】 beat back; resist (the aggressors, etc.) 【抗拒】 resist; defy 【抗议】 protest 提出~ lodge a protest 【抗战】 war of resistance against aggression

炕 kàng ①*kang*; a heatable brick bed ②bake or dry by the heat of a fire 【炕席】 *kang* mat

KAO

考 kǎo ①give or take an examination, test or quiz 我~~你 let me quiz you 应~ take an examination ~上大学 be admitted to a university ②check; inspect ③study; investigate; verify 待~ remain to be verified 【考查】 examine; check ~学生成绩 check students' work 【考察】 inspect; make an on-the-spot investigation / observe and study ~团 observation group ~组 study group 【考场】 examination hall or room 【考古】 engage in archaeological studies / archaeology 【考核】 examine; check; assess (sb.'s proficiency) ~干部 check on cadres 技术~ assess technical proficiency 【考究】 observe and

study; investigate / fastidious; particular / exquisite; fine
【考卷】 examination paper 【考虑】 think over; consider
【考勤】 check on work attendance ～簿 attendance record
【考取】 pass an entrance examination; be admitted to
school or college 【考生】 candidate for an entrance examination; examinee 【考试】 examination; test 【考题】 examination questions 出～ set an examination paper 【考
问】 examine orally; question 【考验】 test; trial 经受了
严峻的～ have stood a severe test 【考证】 textual research;
textual criticism

拷 kǎo torture 【拷贝】 copy 【拷打】 torture; flog; beat
【拷问】 interrogate with torture

烤 kǎo ①bake; roast; toast ～白薯 baked sweet potatoes ～馒头 toasted steamed bun ～面包 toast ②scorch-
ing 【烤火】 warm oneself by a fire 【烤炉】 oven 【烤肉】
roast meat; roast 【烤鸭】 roast duck 【烤烟】 flue-cured
tobacco

铐 kào ①handcuffs ②put handcuffs on 把犯人～起来
handcuff the criminal

犒 kào 【犒劳】 reward with food and drink 【犒赏】 reward a victorious army, etc. with bounties

靠 kào ①lean on ～着墙 lean against the wall ②keep
to; get near; come up to ～右走 keep to the right
③rely on ～他维持生活 depend on him for support ④
trust ～ reliable 【靠岸】 pull in to shore; draw alongside 【靠背】 back (of a chair) ～椅 chair 【靠边】 keep
to the side (of the road, etc.) ～儿站 stand aside; get
out of the way 【靠不住】 unreliable; untrustworthy 【靠
得住】 dependable; trustworthy 【靠垫】 cushion (for leaning on) 【靠近】 near; close to 【靠山】 backer; patron 【靠
手】 armrest

KE

苛 kē severe; exacting ～待 treat harshly; be hard upon 【苛捐杂税】 exorbitant taxes and levies 【苛刻】 harsh (terms, etc.) 【苛求】 be overcritical 【苛政】 tyranny

科 kē ①a branch of academic or vocational study 理～ the sciences ②section 财务～ finance section 卫生～ health section; clinic 猫～动物 animals of the cat family ④pass a sentence ～以罚金 impose a fine on sb.; fine 【科班】 old-type opera school / regular professional training ～出身 be a professional by training 【科技】 science and technology ～大学 university of science and technology 【科教片】 popular science film; science and educational film 【科举】 imperial examinations 【科目】 subject (in a curriculum); course / headings in an account book 【科室】 administrative or technical offices ～人员 office staff 【科学】 science; scientific knowledge ～工作者 scientific worker; scientist ～实验 scientific experiment ～仪器 scientific instruments ～院 academy of sciences 【科研】 scientific research 【科员】 section member 【科长】 section chief

棵 kē 一～树 a tree 一～大白菜 a (head of) Chinese cabbage

窠 kē nest; burrow 【窠臼】 set pattern (usu. of writing, etc.) 不落～ show originality; be unconventional

颗 kē 一～珠子 a pearl 一～黄豆 a soya bean 【颗粒】 pellet / grain ～归仓 every grain to the granary

磕 kē ①knock (against sth. hard) 脸上～破了皮 graze one's face ②knock sth. out of a vessel, container, etc. 【磕碰】 collide with; bump against / clash; squabble 【磕头】 kowtow

瞌 kē 【瞌睡】sleepy; drowsy 打～ doze off; nod; have a nap

蝌 kē 【蝌蚪】tadpole

壳 ké ①shell 鸡蛋～ egg shell 核桃～ walnut shell ② housing; casing; case 涡轮～ turbine casing

咳 ké cough 【咳嗽】cough ～糖浆 cough syrup

可 kě ①approve 不置～否 decline to comment ②can; may 由此～见 thus it can be seen that; this proves ③need (doing); be worth (doing) ④fit; suit ～了他的心 it suited him perfectly ⑤but; yet 【可爱】lovable; likable; lovely 【可悲】sad; lamentable 【可鄙】contemptible 【可耻】shameful; disgraceful 【可观】considerable; impressive 【可见】it is thus clear that 【可惊】surprising; startling 【可敬】worthy of respect; respected 【可靠】dependable; trustworthy ～消息 reliable information ～性 reliability 【可可】cocoa 【可口】good to eat; tasty 【可怜】pitiful; pitiable; poor/have pity on/miserable 【可能】possible; probable/probably; maybe ～性 possibility 【可是】but 【可恶】hateful; detestable 【可惜】it's a pity; it's too bad 【可喜】heartening ～的成就 gratifying achievements ～的进展 encouraging progress 【可笑】laughable; ridiculous; funny 【可行】feasible 【可疑】suspicious; dubious 【可以】can; may/passable; not bad

渴 kě ①thirsty ②yearningly 【渴望】thirst for; long for; yearn for

克 kè ①can; be able to 不～分身 can't get away ②restrain ③overcome; subdue; capture (a city, etc.) 攻无不～ carry all before one ④gram 【克敌制胜】vanquish the enemy 【克服】overcome; conquer/put up with (hardships, inconveniences, etc.) ～官僚主义 get rid of bureaucracy ～困难 surmount a difficulty【克制】restrain (one's passion, etc.) 表现很大的～ exercise great restraint

刻 kè ①carve; engrave; cut ～图章 engrave a seal ～蜡版 cut stencils ②a quarter (of an hour) 五点一～ a quarter past five ③moment 此～ at the moment ④cutting; penetrating 尖～ acrimonious; biting【刻板】cut blocks for printing / mechanical; stiff; inflexible【刻薄】unkind; harsh; mean 说话～ speak unkindly 待人～ treat people meanly【刻不容缓】brook no delay; be of great urgency【刻刀】burin; graver【刻毒】venomous; spiteful【刻骨】deeply ingrained; deep-rooted ～仇恨 inveterate hatred【刻画】depict; portray (characters, etc.)【刻苦】hardworking; painstaking ～钻研 study assiduously 生活～ lead a simple and frugal life

客 kè ①visitor; guest ～房 guest room ②traveller; passenger ～舱 passenger cabin ③customer 房～ boarder; lodger ④settle or live in a strange place 作～他乡 live in a strange land【客车】passenger train/bus【客船】passenger ship【客串】be a guest performer【客店】inn【客观】objective ～规律 objective law ～世界 objective world【客满】full house【客票】passenger ticket【客气】polite; courteous / modest 别～ please don't stand on ceremony; please don't bother 您太～了 you are being too modest【客人】visitor; guest / guest (at a hotel, etc.)【客套】polite formula【客厅】drawing room【客运】passenger transport

恪 kè scrupulously and respectfully【恪守】scrupulously abide by (a treaty, promise, etc.)

课 kè ①subject; course 必修～ required courses ②class 上～ go to class 讲～ give a lecture ③lesson 第一～ Lesson One ④tax ⑤levy (a tax on sb.)【课本】textbook

【课表】school timetable 【课程】course; curriculum ～表 school timetable 【课间操】setting-up exercises during the break 【课时】class hour; period 【课堂】classroom; schoolroom ～教学 classroom teaching ～讨论 classroom discussion ～作业 classwork 【课题】a question for study or discussion/problem; task 【课外】extracurricular; outside class; after school ～辅导 instruction after class ～活动 extracurricular activities ～阅读 outside reading ～作业 homework 【课文】text 【课业】lessons 【课余】after class

KEN

肯 kěn ①agree; consent 他不～ he did not agree 首～ nod assent ②be willing to; be ready to ～干 be willing to do hard work ～接受意见 be ready to listen to criticism ～学习 be eager to learn 【肯定】affirm; confirm; approve/positive; affirmative/definite; sure ～成绩 affirm the achievements ～的判断 a positive assessment ～的答复 a definite answer 我不能～ I'm not sure ～按时送到 guarantee delivery on time

垦 kěn cultivate (land); reclaim (wasteland) 【垦荒】bring wasteland under cultivation; open up virgin soil

恳 kěn ①sincerely ～谈 talk earnestly ②request 【恳切】earnest; sincere 言词～ speak in an earnest tone ～希望 earnestly hope 【恳请】earnestly request ～协助 your assistance is earnestly requested 【恳求】implore; entreat

啃 kěn gnaw; nibble ～骨头 gnaw a bone ～老玉米 nibble at an ear of corn ～书本 delve into books

KENG

坑 kēng ①hole; hollow 泥～ mud puddle 粪～ manure pit ②tunnel; pit 矿～ pit ③entrap; cheat ～人 cheat people 【坑道】 gallery/tunnel ～战 tunnel warfare 【坑害】 lead into a trap 【坑坑洼洼】 bumpy; rough 【坑木】 pit prop

吭
kēng utter a sound or a word 一声不～ without saying a word 【吭哧】 puff and blow / hum and haw

铿
kēng clang; clatter 【铿锵】 ring 【铿然】 loud and clear

KONG

空
kōng ①empty; hollow; void ～箱子 an empty box ～论 empty talk ②sky; air 晴～ a clear sky ③for nothing; in vain ～忙 make fruitless efforts 【空荡荡】 empty; deserted 【空洞】 cavity / empty; hollow 【空泛】 vague and general; not specific 【空话】 empty talk; idle talk 【空间】 space 外层～ outer space 【空降】 airborne ～兵 airborne force 【空军】 air force ～部队 air (force) unit ～基地 air base ～司令部 air command ～司令员 commander of the air force 【空气】 air / atmosphere 新鲜 ～ fresh air ～紧张 a tense atmosphere 【空前】 unprecedented 盛况～ an unprecedentedly grand occasion ～绝后 unprecedented and unrepeatable; unique 【空谈】 (indulge in) empty talk 【空头支票】 bad cheque / empty promise; lip service 【空投】 air-drop; paradrop 【空文】 ineffective law, rule, etc. 【空袭】 air raid; air attack ～警报 air raid alarm 【空想】 idle dream; fantasy ～家 dreamer 【空心】 hollow ～砖 hollow brick 【空虚】 hollow; void 生活～ lead a life devoid of meaning 思想～ lack mental or spiritual ballast 【空运】 air transport; airlift 【空战】 air battle 【空中】 in the sky; in the air; aerial; overhead ～楼阁 castles in the air 【空竹】 diabolo 【空转】 (of a motor, etc.) idling; racing / (of a wheel) turn without moving forward; spin

孔 kǒng hole; opening; aperture 钥匙～ keyhole 【孔道】 pass; narrow passage 【孔雀】 peacock

恐 kǒng ①fear; dread 惊～ be alarmed ②terrify; intimidate ～吓 threaten; intimidate 【恐怖】 terror 【恐吓信】 blackmailing letter 【恐慌】 panic; panic-stricken 【恐惧】 fear; dread 【恐怕】 I'm afraid/perhaps; I think

空 kòng ①leave empty or blank 请把座位～出来 please leave the seats vacant ～两格 leave two blank spaces ②unoccupied; vacant ～房 a vacant room ③empty space ④free time; spare time 今天没～ I'm busy today 【空白】 blank space 填补～ fill the gaps ～表格 blank form ～支票 blank cheque ～点 gap; blank 【空地】 open ground; open space 【空额】 vacancy 【空格】 blank space (on a form) 【空缺】 vacancy 【空隙】 space; gap; interval 【空闲】 idle; free/leisure 【空子】 gap; opening / chance; opportunity

控 kòng ①accuse ②control; dominate 遥～ remote control 【控告】 charge; accuse; complain 提出～ file charges; lodge complaints 【控诉】 denounce; condemn ～会 accusation meeting ～人 accuser 【控制】 control; dominate; command ～数字 control figure ～局面 have the situation under control ～不住自己的感情 lose control of one's feelings ～人口增长 control population growth

KOU

抠 kōu ①dig; dig out; scratch ～个洞 scratch a hole 把豆粒～出来 dig out the beans from sth. ②carve; cut ～点花 carve a design on sth. ③delve into ④stingy

口 kǒu ①mouth ②opening; entrance 入～ entrance 出～ exit 瓶～ the mouth of a bottle ③cut; hole 伤～ wound; cut ④edge (of a knife) ⑤一～井 a well 三～猪 three pigs 【口才】 eloquence 【口吃】 stutter 【口齿】 enuncia-

tion/ability to speak ～清楚 have clear enunciation ～
伶俐 be clever and fluent 【口袋】 pocket / bag; sack 【口
供】 a statement made by the accused under examination
【口号】 slogan 【口红】 lipstick 【口惠】 (pay) lip service
【口技】 vocal mimicry 【口径】 bore; calibre/specifications;
line of action ～不合 not meet the requirements 对～
arrange to give the same story 【口诀】 a pithy formula
(often in rhyme) 【口角】 quarrel; wrangle 【口渴】 thirsty
【口口声声】 keep on saying 【口粮】 grain ration 【口令】
word of command/password; watchword; countersign 【口
气】 tone; note/manner of speaking 改变～ change one's
tone ～不小 talk big 听他的～ judging by the way he
spoke 【口腔】 oral cavity ～卫生 oral hygiene ～医院 stom-
atological hospital 【口琴】 mouth organ; harmonica 【口
哨】 whistle 【口舌】 quarrel; dispute / talking round 【口
实】 handle 【口试】 oral test 【口是心非】 say one thing
and mean another 【口授】 oral instruction/dictate 【口述】
oral account 【口水】 saliva 流～ slobber 【口头】 oral ～
通知 notify orally ～表决 voice vote ～汇报 oral report
～声明 oral statement 【口味】 taste / the flavour or taste
of food 合～ suit one's taste 【口吻】 tone; note 【口香糖】
chewing gum 【口信】 (oral) message 【口译】 oral interpretation 【口音】 voice / accent 【口语】 spoken language 【口
罩】 gauze mask 【口子】 opening; hole; cut; tear

扣 kòu ①button up; buckle ～上皮带 buckle a belt
～上门 latch the door ～扣子 do up the buttons ②
place a cup, bowl, etc. upside down 用碗把菜～上 cover
the food with a bowl ③detain; arrest ④deduct (a part of
sb.'s pay, etc.) ⑤discount 打九～ give a 10 per cent discount ⑥knot; button; buckle 系个～ tie a knot ⑦smash
(the ball) 【扣除】 deduct ～房租 deduct rent (from wages,

etc.】已从工资中～ have been stopped out of one's wages 【扣留】detain; arrest; hold in custody ～走私犯 detain the smuggler ～行车执照 suspend a driving licence 【扣帽子】put a label on sb. 【扣压】withhold; pigeonhole

寇 kòu ①bandit; invader 海～ pirate 敌～ the (invading) enemy ②invade 入～ invade (a country)

枯 kū ①withered ～草 withered grass ～叶 dead leaves ②dried up ～井 a dry well ③dull ～坐 sit in boredom 【枯竭】dried up; exhausted 【枯燥】dull and dry

哭 kū cry; weep ～起来 burst into tears 【哭哭啼啼】endlessly weep and wail 【哭泣】sob 【哭穷】complain of being hard up 【哭丧着脸】put on a long face 【哭笑不得】not know whether to laugh or to cry

窟 kū ①hole; cave 石～ grotto ②den 匪～ a robbers' den 赌～ a gambling-den 【窟窿】hole; cavity

骷 kū 【骷髅】human skeleton / human skull; death's-head

苦 kū ①bitter ②hardship; suffering; pain 阶级～ bitterness of class oppression ③cause sb. suffering; give sb. a hard time ④be troubled by ～旱 suffer from drought ⑤painstakingly; doing one's utmost ～劝 earnestly advise ～求 entreat piteously 【苦干】work hard ～精神 hardworking spirit 【苦工】hard work 【苦功】painstaking effort 【苦海】sea of bitterness 脱离～ get out of the abyss of misery 【苦口】(admonish) in earnest ～相劝 earnestly advise/bitter to the taste 【苦闷】depressed; dejected; feeling low 【苦难】suffering; misery; distress ～的深渊 the abyss of misery 【苦恼】vexed; worried 【苦思】think hard; cudgel one's brains 【苦于】suffer from (a disadvantage)

~时间紧 hard pressed for time 【苦战】 struggle hard

库 kù warehouse; storehouse 【库存】 stock; reserve ~物资 goods kept in stock

裤 kù trousers; pants 短~ shorts 【裤衩】 underpants 【裤裆】 crotch 【裤脚】 bottom of a trouser leg 【裤腿】 trouser legs 【裤褶】 creases 【裤腰】 waist of trousers

酷 kù ①cruel ~吏 an oppressive official ②very; extremely ~似 be exactly like ~爱 ardently love 【酷暑】 the intense heat of summer 【酷刑】 cruel torture

KUA

夸 kuā ①exaggerate; overstate; boast ~口 brag; talk big ②praise 人人都~她 everyone praised her 【夸大】 overstate; magnify ~困难 exaggerate the difficulties ~敌情 overestimate the enemy 【夸奖】 praise; commend 【夸耀】 brag about; show off; flaunt 【夸赞】 speak highly of 【夸张】 exaggerate; overstate ~的语言 inflated language

垮 kuǎ collapse; fall; break down 墙要~了 the wall's going to collapse 冲~堤坝 burst the dyke 打~敌人 put the enemy to rout 【垮台】 collapse; fall from power

挎 kuà ①carry on the arm ~着个篮子 with a basket on one's arm ~着胳膊 arm in arm ②carry sth. over one's shoulder ~着照相机 have a camera slung over one's shoulder ~着手枪 carry a pistol at one's side

胯 kuà hip 【胯骨】 hipbone; innominate bone

跨 kuà ①step; stride ~进大门 step into a doorway ~过小沟 stride over a ditch ②bestride; straddle ~上战马 mount a war-horse ③cut across ~年度 go beyond the year 【跨越】 stride across; leap over; cut across ~障碍 surmount an obstacle

KUAI

会 kuài 【会计】 accounting / bookkeeper; accountant ~ 年度 financial year

快 kuài ①fast; quick; rapid 别说得那么~ don't speak so fast 进步很~ make rapid progress ②speed 这车能跑我~ how fast can this car go ③hurry up; make haste ~跟我走 quick, come with me ④soon; before long 他~ 回来了 he'll be back soon ⑤quick-witted; ingenious 他脑子~ he understands things quickly ⑥sharp ~刀 a sharp knife ⑦forthright; plainspoken ~人~语 straightforward talk from a straightforward person ⑧pleased; happy 不~ feel unhappy 【快报】bulletin 【快餐】quick meal; snack 【快车】express train or bus 【快递】express delivery ~邮件 express mail 【快干】quick-drying (paint, etc.) 【快感】pleasant sensation; delight 【快活】happy; merry; cheerful; joyful 【快手】quick worker; deft hand 【快艇】speedboat 【快信】express letter 【快意】satisfied; comfortable

块 kuài ①piece; lump; chunk 糖~ fruit drops; lumps of sugar ~煤 lump coal 把肉切成~ cut the meat into cubes ②piece; cake·两~肥皂 two cakes of soap

脍 kuài meat chopped into small pieces 【脍炙人口】win universal praise; enjoy great popularity

筷 kuài 【筷子】chopsticks 火~ fire-tongs; tongs

KUAN

宽 kuān ①wide; broad ~肩膀 broad-shouldered 眼界 ~ have a broad outlook ②breadth ③relax; relieve 把心放~一点 don't worry ④generous; lenient 处理从~ treat with leniency ~以待人 be lenient with others

【宽敞】spacious; roomy【宽大】spacious; roomy / lenient; magnanimous【宽待】be lenient in dealing with ～俘虏 treat prisoners of war leniently【宽厚】generous【宽阔】broad; wide【宽容】tolerant; lenient【宽恕】forgive【宽慰】comfort; console【宽心】feel relieved ～话 reassuring words【宽银幕】wide-screen (film)【宽裕】well-to-do; comfortably off; ample 经济～ in easy circumstances 时间～ there's plenty of time.

款 kuǎn ①receive with hospitality; entertain ②section of an article; paragraph ③fund 公～ public funds 汇～ remit money【款待】treat cordially; entertain ～客人 entertain guests【款式】pattern; style; design

KUANG

匡 kuāng ①rectify; correct (mistakes) ②assist; save

诓 kuāng deceive; hoax; dupe 我哪能～你 how could I deceive you

框 kuāng ①frame; circle ②draw a frame round 把标题～起来 frame the heading【框框】frame / restriction; set pattern 突破旧～ throw convention to the winds

筐 kuāng basket

狂 kuáng ①mad; crazy 发～ go mad ②violent ③wild; unrestrained ～奔的马 a bolting horse 欣喜若～ be wild with joy ④arrogant; overbearing【狂暴】violent; wild【狂飙】hurricane【狂风】fierce wind ～暴雨 a violent storm【狂欢】revelry; carnival【狂热】fanaticism ～的信徒 fanatic; zealot【狂人】madman【狂妄】wildly arrogant; presumptuous ～自大 arrogant and conceited ～的野心 a wild ambition【狂笑】laugh wildly【狂言】ravings

况 kuàng ①condition; situation 近～如何 how have you been recently ②compare 以古～今 draw parallels from history 【况且】moreover; besides; in addition

旷 ①vast; spacious ～野 wilderness ②free from worries and petty ideas 【旷废】neglect (one's studies) 【旷费】waste (one's time) 【旷工】stay away from work without leave or good reason 【旷课】cut school 旷一堂课 cut a class 【旷日持久】long-drawn-out; prolonged

矿 kuàng ①mineral deposit 报～ report where deposits are found ②ore 铁～ iron ore ③mine 煤～ coal mine; colliery 【矿藏】mineral resources 【矿产】mineral products; minerals 【矿床】deposit 【矿灯】miner's lamp 【矿工】miner 【矿井】mine; pit 【矿脉】mineral vein; lode 【矿苗】outcrop; crop 【矿区】mining area 【矿泉】mineral spring 【矿山】mine 【矿石】ore 【矿物】mineral ～学 mineralogy 【矿业】mining industry 【矿渣】slag

框 kuàng frame; case 门～ door frame 窗～ window case 镜～ picture frame 眼镜～ rims (of spectacles)

眶 kuàng the socket of the eye 热泪盈～ one's eyes filling with tears

KUI

亏 kuī ①lose (money, etc.); have a deficit 盈～ profit and loss ②deficient; short 理～ be in the wrong ③ treat unfairly ④fortunately; luckily; thanks to ～他提醒了我 luckily he reminded me 【亏本】lose money in business ～生意 a losing proposition 【亏待】treat unfairly 【亏空】be in debt / debt; deficit 拉～ get into debt 弥补～ meet a deficit; make up a loss 【亏损】loss; deficit/ general debility 【亏心】have a guilty conscience ～事 a deed that troubles one's conscience

盔 kuī helmet 【盔甲】a suit of armour

窥 kuī peep; spy 【窥测】spy out ~方向 see which way the wind blows ~时机 bide one's time 【窥见】catch a glimpse of; detect 【窥视】peep at; spy on 【窥伺】lie in wait for; be on watch for 【窥探】pry about

葵 kuí 【葵花】sunflower ~油 sunflower oil ~子 sunflower seeds 【葵扇】palm-leaf fan

魁 kuí ①chief; head 罪~ chief criminal ②of stalwart build 【魁梧】big and tall; stalwart

睽 kuí 【睽睽】stare; gaze 众目~之下 in the public eye

傀 kuǐ 【傀儡】puppet/stooge ~戏 puppet show ~政府 puppet government ~政权 puppet regime

溃 kuì ①(of a dyke or dam) burst ②break through (an encirclement) ③be routed ~不成军 be utterly routed ④fester; ulcerate 【溃败】be defeated 【溃烂】fester; ulcerate 【溃灭】crumble and fall 【溃散】be defeated and dispersed 【溃逃】escape in disorder 【溃疡】ulcer

馈 kuì make a present of ~送 present (a gift); make a present of sth.

愧 kuì ashamed; conscience-stricken 问心无~ have a clear conscience 于心有~ have a guilty conscience; feel ashamed 【愧色】a look of shame 毫无~ look unabashed

KUN

坤 kūn female; feminine ~表 woman's watch ~角儿 actress

昆 kūn elder brother 【昆虫】insect ~学 insectology ~学家 entomologist

捆 kǔn ①tie; bind; bundle up ～干草 truss hay ～行李 tie up one's baggage 把他～起来 tie him up ～住手脚 bound hand and foot ②bundle

困 kùn ①be stranded; be hard pressed ～于异乡 be stranded in a strange land ②surround; pin down ③tired ④sleepy 你～了就睡 go to bed if you feel sleepy 【困乏】tired; fatigued 【困惑】perplexed; puzzled 【困境】predicament 陷于～ fall into dire straits 摆脱～ extricate oneself from a difficult position 【困窘】in straitened circumstances; embarrassed 【困倦】sleepy 【困苦】(live) in privation 【困难】difficulty/financial difficulties 生活～ live in straitened circumstances ～户 families with material difficulties 【困守】stand a siege

KUO

扩 kuò expand; enlarge; extend 【扩充】strengthen; augment; expand (forces, etc.) ～设备 augment the equipment 【扩大】enlarge; expand; extend ～战果 exploit the victory ～眼界 widen one's outlook ～影响 extend influence ～企业自主权 enhance the power of decision of enterprises ～会议 enlarged meeting ～再生产 expanded reproduction ～化 broaden the scope; magnify 【扩建】extend (a factory, mine, etc.) 【扩散】spread; diffuse 【扩音器】megaphone/audio amplifier 【扩展】expand; spread; develop 【扩张】expand; enlarge 对外～ expansionism

括 kuò ①draw together (muscles, etc.); contract ②include 【括号】brackets 【括弧】parentheses

阔 kuò ①wide; broad; vast ②wealthy; rich 【阔步】take big strides ～前进 advance with giant strides 【阔绰】ostentatious; liberal with money 【阔老】rich man 【阔气】luxurious; lavish 摆～ display one's wealth

L

LA

拉 lā ①pull; draw; tug; drag ～车 pull a cart 把我～到一边 draw me aside ②transport by vehicle; haul 去～肥料 haul (back) the fertilizer ③move (troops to a place) ④play ～小提琴 play the violin 【拉出去】 pull out; drag out 【拉倒】 forget about it; drop it 你不同意，就～ since you don't agree let's forget about it 【拉关系】 try to establish underhand connections (for the sake of personal gain) 【拉后腿】 hold sb. back 【拉交情】 try to form ties with; cotton up to 【拉脚】 transport by cart at a charge 【拉开】 pull open; draw back/space out ～抽屉 open the drawer ～窗帘 draw back the curtain 【拉扯】 pull sb. about/exchange flattery and favours 【拉拉队】 cheering squad; rooters 【拉力】 pulling force ～器 chest-expander 【拉链】 zipper 【拉拢】 draw sb. over to one's side; rope in 【拉屎】 shit 【拉手】 handle (of a door, window, drawer, etc.) 【拉杂】 rambling; jumbled

垃 lā 【垃圾】 rubbish; garbage; refuse ～箱 dustbin; ash can ～堆 rubbish heap; garbage heap 清除～ remove refuse dump

拉 lá ①slash; slit; cut; make a gash in ～开皮子 slit the leather ②chat ～家常 have a chat

喇 lǎ 【喇叭】 a popular name for *suona*, a woodwind instrument / brass-wind instruments in general or any of these instruments / loudspeaker ～花 morning glory ～裤 flared trousers ～筒 megaphone 【喇嘛】 lama

落 là ①leave out; be missing ～两个字 two words are missing ②leave behind; forget to bring 我把票～在家里了 I left my ticket at home ③lag behind ～下很远 be left far behind ～了一个星期的课 miss a week's lessons

腊 là cured (fish, meat, etc.) sausage 【腊肠】sausage 【腊梅】wintersweet 【腊肉】bacon 【腊月】the twelfth moon

辣 là ①peppery; hot ②(of smell or taste) burn; bite; sting ～眼睛 make one's eyes sting ③vicious; ruthless 【辣酱】thick chilli sauce 【辣酱油】pungent sauce 【辣椒】hot pepper; chilli ～油 chilli oil

蜡 là ①wax ②candle 点～ light a candle 【蜡版】mimeograph stencil (already cut) 【蜡笔】wax crayon ～画 crayon drawing 【蜡黄】wax yellow; waxen; sallow 【蜡台】candlestick 【蜡纸】wax paper/stencil (paper)

痢 là 【痢痢】favus of the scalp 【痢痢头】a person affected with favus on the head

LAI

来 lái ①come; arrive 他什么时候～ when is he coming ②crop up; take place 问题一～就解决 solve a problem as soon as it crops up ③future; coming; next ～年 next year ④about; around 二十～个 around twenty 五十～岁 about fifty 【来宾】guest; visitor ～席 seats for guests 【来犯】come to attack us; invade our territory 【来访】come to visit; come to call 【来复枪】rifle 【来回】make a round trip; make a return journey / back and forth; to and fro ～走动 pace up and down ～摇摆 oscillate; vacillate ～票 return ticket 【来人】bearer; messenger 【来生】next life 【来势】oncoming force ～汹汹 bear down menacingly 【来头】connections; backing / the motive behind (sb.'s words, etc.); cause 【来往】come and go 街上～

的人 people coming and going on the streets ～信件 correspondence 【来往】 dealings; contact; intercourse 跟他们有～ have dealings with them 经常～ have frequent contacts with 【来文】 document received 【来信】 send a letter here / incoming letter ～收到 I have received your letter 人民～ letters from the people 【来意】 one's purpose in coming 说明～ make clear what one has come for 【来源】 source; origin / originate; stem from 经济～ source of income 知识～于实践 knowledge stems from practice

赖 lài ①rely; depend 有～于大家的努力 depend on everyone's efforts ②hold on to a place ～着不走 hang on and refuse to clear out ③deny one's error or responsibility; go back on one's word ～是～不掉的 you simply can't deny it ④blame sb. wrongly 自己错了还～别人 blame others for one's own mistake 【赖皮】 rascally; unreasonable 耍～ act shamelessly 【赖帐】 repudiate a debt

癞 lài ①leprosy ②favus of the scalp 【癞蛤蟆】 toad 【癞皮狗】 mangy dog / loathsome creature

LAN

兰 lán orchid 【兰草】 fragrant thoroughwort 【兰花】 cymbidium; orchid

拦 lán bar; block; hold back ～路 block the way ～网 block 【拦挡】 obstruct 【拦河坝】 a dam (across a river) 【拦截】 intercept 【拦腰】 by the waist

栏 lán ①fence; railing; balustrade; hurdle 凭～ lean on a railing ②pen; shed 牛～ cowshed ③column 布告～ notice board 【栏杆】 banisters

阑 lán ①late ②railing; balustrade 【阑干】 crisscross; athwart/banisters 【阑尾】 appendix ～炎 appendicitis

蓝 lán ①blue ②indigo plant 【蓝宝石】sapphire 【蓝本】chief source / original version (of a literary work) 【蓝靛】indigo 【蓝皮书】blue book 【蓝图】blueprint

谰 lán calumniate; slander 【谰言】calumny 无耻～a shameless slander

澜 lán billows

褴 lán 【褴褛】ragged; shabby 衣衫～shabbily dressed; out at elbows; in rags

篮 lán ①basket ②goal; basket 投～shoot (a basket) 【篮板】backboard; bank ～球 rebound 【篮球】basketball ～场 basketball court ～队 basketball team ～架 basketball stands 【篮圈】ring; hoop

览 lǎn ①look at; see; view 游～tour 一～无余 take in everything at a glance ②read 博～read extensively

揽 lǎn ①pull sb. into one's arms; take into one's arms 把孩子～在怀里 clasp the child to one's bosom ② fasten with a rope, etc. 用绳子～上 put a rope around sth. ③take on; canvass ～买卖 canvass business orders ④grasp; monopolize ～权 arrogate power to oneself

缆 lǎn ①hawser; mooring rope 解～cast off; set sail ②thick rope; cable 【缆车】cable car 【缆道】cableway

懒 lǎn ①lazy; indolent; slothful ②languid 发～feel sluggish 【懒得】not feel like (doing sth.); not be in the mood to 【懒汉】sluggard; idler; lazybones 【懒散】negligent; indolent 【懒洋洋】listless

烂 làn ①sodden; mashed; pappy 牛肉烧得～the beef is very tender ②rot; fester 伤口～了 the wound is festering ③worn-out 衣服穿～了 the clothes are worn-out ④messy 【烂糊】(of food) mashed; pulpy 【烂漫】bright-coloured; brilliant/unaffected 【烂泥】mud; slush

滥 làn ①overflow; flood ②excessive; indiscriminate ～施轰炸 wanton bombing ～发钞票 reckless issuing of banknotes【滥调】hackneyed tune; worn-out theme【滥用】abuse; misuse ～职权 abuse one's power

LANG

郎 láng 令～ your son 新～ bridegroom 货～ street vendor【郎舅】a man and his wife's brother

狼 láng wolf【狼狈】in a difficult position; in a tight corner; in a sorry plight ～逃窜 flee in panic 陷于～境地 find oneself in a fix ～为奸 act in collusion with each other【狼狗】wolfhound【狼吞虎咽】gobble up

廊 láng porch; corridor; veranda 回～ winding corridor 画～ picture gallery【廊檐】the eaves of a veranda

朗 lǎng ①light; bright ②loud and clear【朗读】read aloud【朗诵】recite; declaim

浪 làng ①wave; billow 白～ white breakers ②unrestrained 放～ dissolute【浪潮】tide; wave【浪荡】loaf about / dissipated【浪费】waste; squander; be extravagant 反对～ combat waste ～时间 waste time【浪花】spray; spindrift【浪漫】romantic ～主义 romanticism【浪头】wave/trend 赶～ follow the trend【浪子】prodigal; loafer

LAO

捞 lāo ①drag for; scoop up from the water 水草 dredge up water plants ～鱼 catch fish ②get by improper means【捞本】win back lost wagers【捞取】fish for; gain ～政治资本 seek political advantage【捞一把】reap some profit; profiteer【捞着】get the opportunity

牢 láo ①prison; jail 坐～ be in prison ②firm; fast; durable【牢不可破】unbreakable; indestructible【牢

固】firm; secure 【牢记】keep firmly in mind; remember well; bear in mind 【牢靠】firm; strong; sturdy/dependable 办事～ reliable in handling matters 【牢牢】firmly;safely 【牢笼】cage; bonds/trap; snare 陷入～ fall into a trap; be entrapped 【牢骚】discontent; grievance; complaint 满腹～ be querulous 发～ grumble

劳 láo ①work; labour 多～多得 more pay for more work ②put sb. to the trouble of ～你帮个忙 will you please do me a favour ③fatigue ④meritorious deed; service ⑤express one's appreciation (to the performer of a task); reward ～军 bring greetings and gifts to army units 【劳保】labour insurance 【劳动】work; labour/ manual labour ～创造世界 labour creates the world ～布 denim ～定额 work norm ～观点 attitude to labour ～教养 reeducation through labour ～节 International Labour Day ～竞赛 labour emulation ～人民 labouring people ～日 workday ～生产率 productivity ～者 labourer; worker 【劳动力】work force; labour/capacity for physical labour 丧失～ lose one's ability to work 【劳改】reform (of criminals) through labour ～农场 reform-through-labour farm 【劳绩】merits and accomplishments 【劳驾】excuse me; may I trouble you 【劳苦】toil; hard work ～大众 toiling masses 【劳累】tired; run-down; over-worked 【劳力】labour 【劳民伤财】waste money and manpower 【劳模】model worker 【劳心】work with one's mind or brains 【劳役】forced labour/corvée 【劳逸】work and rest ～结合 strike a proper balance between work and rest ～不均 uneven allocation of work 【劳资】labour and capital ～关系 labour-capital relations

痨 láo consumptive disease; tuberculosis; consumption 肺～ pulmonary tuberculosis

老 lǎo ①old; aged ②old people 扶～携幼 bringing along the old and the young ③of long standing; old ～朋友 an old friend ～干部 a veteran cadre ④outdated ～式 old-fashioned ⑤overgrown 菠菜要～了 the spinach will be overgrown ⑥(of colour) dark ⑦for a long time ～没见你啊 I haven't seen you for ages ⑧always (doing sth.) ⑨very ～早 very early ～远 far away 【老百姓】 common people; civilians 【老板】 boss 【老本】 principal; capital 【老兵】 veteran 【老粗】 uneducated person; rough and ready chap 【老搭档】 old partner 【老大娘】 aunty; granny 【老大爷】 uncle; grandpa 【老调】 hackneyed theme; platitude ～重弹 play the same old tune 【老底】 sb.'s past 揭～ dig up sb.'s unsavoury past 【老虎】 tiger 【老虎钳】 vice/pincer pliers 【老化】 ageing 【老话】 old saying 【老家】 native place; old home 【老将】 veteran; old-timer 【老练】 seasoned; experienced 【老毛病】 old trouble; old weakness 【老谋深算】 experienced and astute 【老年】 old age ～人 old people 【老牌】 old brand / old-line 【老婆】 wife 【老师】 teacher 【老师傅】 master craftsman; experienced worker 【老实】 honest; frank / well-behaved; good / naive 做～人 be an honest person ～说 to be frank 【老手】 old hand; veteran 【老鼠】 mouse; rat 【老兄】 brother; man; old chap 【老爷】 master; bureaucrat; lord 【老一辈】 older generation 【老一套】 the same old stuff 【老帐】 old debts

涝 lào waterlogging 【涝地】 waterlogged lowland 【涝灾】 damage or crop failure caused by waterlogging

烙 lào ①brand; iron ②bake in a pan ～张饼 bake a pancake 【烙饼】 a kind of pancake 【烙铁】 flatiron; iron/soldering iron 【烙印】 brand 阶级～ the brand of a class

落 lào 【落色】 discolour; fade 【落枕】 stiff neck

酪 lào ①junket ②thick fruit juice; fruit jelly 红果~ haw jelly ③sweet nut paste 核桃~ walnut cream

LE

乐 lè ①happy; cheerful; joyful 助人为~ find pleasure in helping others ②be glad to; find pleasure in; enjoy ~此不疲 always enjoy it ③laugh; be amused 你~什么 what are you laughing at【乐得】readily take the opportunity to; be only too glad to【乐观】optimistic; hopeful; sanguine ~主义 optimism【乐趣】delight; pleasure; joy【乐意】be willing to; be ready to / pleased; happy

勒 lè ①rein in (the horse) ②force; coerce ~交 force sb. to hand sth. over ~令 compel; order【勒索】blackmail ~钱财 extort money from sb.

LEI

勒 lēi tie or strap sth. tight ~紧裤带 tighten the belt

累 léi【累累】clusters of; heaps of 果实~ fruit hanging in clusters【累赘】burdensome/burden; nuisance

雷 léi ①thunder ②mine 布~ lay mines 扫~ sweep mines【雷达】radar ~荧光屏 radar screen ~兵 radarman【雷管】detonator【雷厉风行】vigorously and speedily; resolutely【雷声】thunderclap; thunder【雷霆】thunderbolt/thunder-like power or rage; wrath【雷同】duplicate; identical【雷阵雨】thunder shower

垒 lěi ①build (by piling up bricks, stones, earth, etc.) ~墙 build a wall ~猪圈 build a pigsty ②rampart ③base【垒球】softball ~棒 softball bat

累 lěi ①pile up; accumulate 成千~万 thousands upon thousands ②continuous; repeated; running ~戒不改

refuse to mend one's ways despite repeated warnings ③ involve 连～ implicate; get sb. into trouble 【累犯】 recidivism / recidivist 【累积】 accumulate 【累计】 add up/ accumulative total 【累进】 progression ～税 progressive tax 【累累】 again and again; many times / innumerable 罪行～ commit countless crimes

磊 lěi 【磊落】 open and upright 胸怀～ openhearted and upright 光明～ open and aboveboard

肋 lèi ①rib ②costal region 两～ both sides of the chest 【肋骨】 rib 【肋膜】 pleura ～炎 pleurisy 【肋条】 pork ribs

泪 lèi tear 【泪痕】 tear stains 【泪花】 tears in one's eyes 喜悦的～ tears of joy 【泪水】 tear; teardrop 【泪汪**汪**】 (eyes) brimming with tears 【泪眼】 tearful eyes

类 lèi ①kind; type; class; category 同～ be of a kind ②resemble; be similar to ～平神话 sound like a fairy tale 【类比】 analogy 【类别】 classification; category 【类似】 similar; analogous 【类推】 analogize 【类型】 type

累 lèi ①tired; fatigued; weary 不怕苦, 不怕～ fear neither hardship nor fatigue ②tire; strain; wear out ～活 tiring work ～眼睛 strain one's eyes ③work hard; toil

擂 lèi beat (a drum) 【擂台】 ring (for martial contests); arena 摆～ give an open challenge 打～ take up the challenge

LENG

棱 léng arris; edge 桌～儿 edges of a table ②corrugation; ridge 搓板的～儿 ridges of a washboard 【棱角】 edges and corners/edge; pointedness 【棱镜】 prism

冷 lěng ①cold 你～不～ do you feel cold ②cold in manner; frosty ③shot from hiding ～枪 a sniper's shot 【冷冰冰】 ice cold ～的脸色 frosty looks ～的态度 icy manners 【冷不防】 unawares; suddenly; by surprise 【冷餐】 buffet 【冷藏】 refrigeration; cold storage ～车 refrigerator car ～库 cold storage; freezer 【冷场】 awkward silence (on the stage or at a meeting) 【冷嘲热讽】 freezing irony and burning satire 【冷淡】 cheerless; desolate/cold/treat coldly 反映～ a cold response 表示～ show indifference towards sth. 【冷冻】 freezing ～厂 cold storage plant ～机 freezer 【冷汗】 cold sweat 出～ break out in a cold sweat 【冷荤】 cold meat; cold buffet 【冷静】 sober; calm 头脑～ sober-minded 保持～ keep calm 【冷酷】 unfeeling; callous ～无情 cold-blooded ～的现实 grim reality 【冷冷清清】 cold and cheerless; desolate 【冷落】 unfrequented; desolate / treat coldly; cold-shoulder; leave (a guest, etc.) out in the cold 【冷漠】 unconcerned; indifferent 【冷盘】 cold dish; *hors d'oeuvres* 【冷僻】 deserted/rare ～的字眼 rarely used words ～的典故 unfamiliar allusions 【冷气】 air conditioning ～机 air conditioner 【冷清】 desolate; lonely; deserted 【冷热病】 malaria/capricious changes in mood 【冷食】 cold drinks and snacks ～部 cold drink and snack counter 【冷霜】 cold cream 【冷水】 cold water / unboiled water ～浴 cold bath 【冷飕飕】 (of wind) chilling 【冷笑】 sneer; laugh grimly 【冷言冷语】 sarcastic comments; ironical remarks 【冷眼】 cool detachment/cold shoulder ～旁观 look on coldly/look on with a critical eye 【冷饮】 cold drink 【冷战】 cold war

愣 lèng ①distracted; stupefied; blank 发～ stare blankly ～住 be struck dumb ②rash; reckless; foolhardy

LI

离 lí ①leave; part from ～别 bid farewell ～京 leave Beijing ～家 be away from home ②off; away; from

③without; independent of 【离婚】divorce 【离间】 sow discord; set one party against another 【离境】leave a country or place ～签证 exit visa ～许可证 exit permit 【离开】leave; depart from 【离奇】odd; fantastic; bizarre 【离任】leave one's post 【离散】dispersed; scattered about 【离题】digress from the subject

梨 lí   pear 【梨膏】pear syrup (for the relief of coughs)

犁 lí   ①plough ②work with a plough 【犁铧】ploughshare; share

黎 lí   multitude; host 【黎民】the common people; the multitude 【黎明】dawn; daybreak

篱 lí   hedge; fence 竹～ bamboo fence 树～ hedgerow 【篱笆】bamboo or twig fence ～墙 wattled wall

礼 lǐ   ①ceremony; rite 丧～ funeral (ceremony) ②courtesy; manners 行～ (give a) salute ③gift; present 送～ send a gift 【礼拜】religious service / week/day of the week 下～ next week 今天～几 what day is it today 做～ go to church; be at church ～寺 mosque ～堂 church ～天 Sunday 【礼服】full dress; formal attire 【礼花】fireworks display 【礼节】courtesy; etiquette; protocol ～性拜访 a courtesy call 社交～ social etiquette 【礼貌】courtesy; politeness; manners 有～ courteous; polite 没～ have no manners; be impolite 【礼炮】salvo; (gun) salute 【礼品】gift; present ～部 gift and souvenir counter 【礼让】comity 国际～ the comity of nations 【礼尚往来】courtesy demands reciprocity/deal with a man as he deals with you 【礼堂】assembly hall; auditorium 【礼遇】courteous reception 受到～ be accorded courteous reception

李 lǐ   plum

里 lǐ ①lining; inside 衣服～儿 the lining of a garment ②inner ～间 inner room ③native place 返～ return to one's hometown ④li, a Chinese unit of length (=1/2 kilometre) ⑤in; inside 【里边】inside; in; within 【里程】mileage ～表 odometer ～碑 milestone 【里带】inner tube

俚 lǐ vulgar 【俚俗】unrefined; uncultured 【俚语】slang

理 lǐ ①texture; grain (in wood, skin, etc.) 肌～ skin texture ②reason; logic; truth 合～ reasonable ～当如此 that's just as it should be ③natural science, esp. physics ～工科 science and engineering ④manage; run ～家 keep house ⑤tidy up ～东西 put things in order ⑥pay attention to; acknowledge 置之不～ pay no attention to sth. 【理财】manage money matters 【理睬】show interest in 不予～ ignore; pay no heed to 无人～ nobody pays any attention to 【理发】haircut; hairdressing 去～ go to have a haircut (or one's hair done) ～馆 barbershop; barber's ～员 barber 【理解】understand; comprehend 加深～ deepen one's comprehension 不可～ beyond one's comprehension ～力 understanding 【理科】science department in a college/science (as a school subject) 【理亏】be in the wrong 自知～ know that one is in the wrong 【理论】theory ～家 theorist ～水平 theoretical level 【理事】member of a council; director ～会 council; board of directors 【理所当然】of course; naturally 【理想】ideal ～主义 idealism 【理性】reason ～认识 rational knowledge 【理应】ought to; should ～归公 ought to be handed over to the state or collective 【理由】reason; ground; argument 【理智】reason; intellect 丧失～ lose one's senses

鲤 lǐ carp

力 lì ①power; strength; ability 兵～ military strength 能～ capability 人～ manpower ②force 磁～ magnetic force ③physical strength ④do all one can; make every effort 办事不～ not do one's best in one's work 【力不从心】 ability not equal to one's ambition 【力不胜任】 be unequal to one's task 【力戒】 strictly avoid ～浪费 do everything possible to avoid waste ～骄傲 guard against arrogance 【力量】 power; force 群众的～ the strength of the masses 【力求】 make every effort to; do one's best to 【力挽狂澜】 make vigorous efforts to turn the tide 【力学】 mechanics 【力争】 work hard for; do all one can to/contend vigorously ～主动 do all one can to gain the initiative 据理～ argue strongly on just grounds

历 lì ①go through; undergo; experience ～尽艰辛 have gone through all kinds of hardships and difficulties ②all previous (occasions, sessions, etc.) ③covering all; one by one ④calendar 【历程】 course 战斗～ the course of the struggle 【历次】 all previous (occasions, etc.) ～指示 successive directives ～比赛 all past contests 【历代】 successive dynasties 【历届】 all previous (sessions, governments, etc.) ～毕业生 graduates of all previous years 【历来】 always; constantly; all through the ages ～如此 this has always been the case ～认为 have invariably insisted 【历历】 distinctly; clearly ～在目 come clearly into view 【历年】 over the years ～积蓄 savings over the years 【历史】 history; past records ～清白 have a clean record 隐瞒～ conceal one's past record ～观 conception of history ～剧 historical play ～人物 historical figure ～唯物主义 historical materialism ～唯心主义 historical idealism ～小说 historical novel ～学家 historian 【历书】 almanac

立 lì ①stand 起~ stand up ②erect; set up 把梯子~起来 set up the ladder ③upright; erect; vertical ④found; establish; set up ~国 found a state ~合同 sign a contract ⑤exist; live 自~ be on one's feet ⑥instantaneous ~见功效 feel the effect immediately ～候回音 awaiting your prompt reply 【立案】register; put on record 【立场】position; stand; standpoint 阐明~ make clear one's position on sth. 丧失~ depart from the correct stand ~坚定 take a firm stand 【立法】legislation ~机关 legislative body ～权 legislative power 【立方】cube/cubic metre; stere 【立功】do a deed of merit; win honour; make contributions 【立柜】clothes closet; wardrobe 【立刻】immediately; at once; right away 【立论】set forth one's views/argument; position 【立体】stereoscopic/solid ~几何 solid geometry ～声 stereophony; stereo 【立正】stand at attention 【立志】resolve ~改革 be determined to carry out reforms 【立足】have a foothold somewhere / base oneself upon ～点 foothold / stand

厉 lì ①strict; rigorous ～禁 strictly forbid ②stern; severe ～声 in a stern voice 【厉行】strictly enforce; make great efforts to carry out ～节约 practise strict economy

吏 lì official; mandarin

沥 lì ①drip; trickle 滴~ patter ②drop 余~ last drops 【沥青】pitch; asphalt; bitumen

丽 lì beautiful ～人 a beauty

励 lì encourage 【励精图治】rouse oneself for vigorous efforts to make the country prosperous

利 lì ①sharp ～刃 a sharp sword or blade ～爪 sharp claws ②favourable 形势不～ the situation is unfavourable ③advantage; benefit ④profit; interest 连本带～ profit as well as capital ⑤do good to; benefit ～己～人 benefit other people as well as oneself 【利弊】 pros and cons 权衡～ weigh the advantages and disadvantages 【利害】 gains and losses 不计～ regardless of gains or losses 【利己主义】 egoism 【利令智昏】 be blinded by lust for gain 【利率】 interest rate 【利落】 agile; nimble; dexterous/ neat; orderly 【利润】 profit ～率 profit rate 【利息】 interest 【利益】 interest; benefit; profit 【利用】 use; utilize/take advantage of ～国外资金 utilize foreign capital ～废料 make use of scrap material ～职权 exploit one's office 【利诱】 lure by promise of gain

例 lì ①example; instance 举～ give an example ②precedent 破～ break all precedents 援～ follow a precedent ③case (of illness,etc.); instance ④rule; regulation 不在此～ that is an exception ⑤regular; routine 【例会】 regular meeting 【例假】 official holiday/(menstrual) period 【例句】 illustrative sentence 【例如】 for instance; for example; such as 【例题】 example 【例外】 exception 【例语】 illustrative phrase 【例证】 illustration; example; case in point

隶 lì be subordinate to; be under 【隶属】 be under the jurisdiction or command of

荔 lì 【荔枝】 litchi

俪 lì ①pair; couple ②husband and wife; married couple

栗 lì ①chestnut ②tremble; shudder 不寒而～ tremble with fear 【栗色】 chestnut colour; maroon

粒 lì grain; granule; pellet 砂～ grains of sand 一～米 a grain of rice 【粒状】 granular 【粒子】 particle

笠 lì a large bamboo or straw hat with a conical crown and broad brim

痢 lì 【痢疾】dysentery

LIA

俩 liǎ ①two 咱～ we two; both of us ②some; several 给他～钱儿 give him some money

LIAN

连 lián ①link; join; connect 把零散的土地～成一片 join together scattered pieces of land 这两句～不上 the two sentences are disconnected ②in succession; one after another; repeatedly ～发三封电报 send three telegrams in succession ～战皆捷 win battle after battle ③including ～你一共十个人 there'll be ten people, including you ④company ⑤even 【连词】conjunction 【连队】company 【连贯】link up; piece together; hang together/coherent; consistent ～性 coherence; continuity 【连环】chain of rings ～画 picture-story book ～计 series of stratagems 【连接】join; link 【连襟】husbands of sisters 【连累】implicate; involve ～点头 nod again and again 【连忙】promptly; at once 【连绵】continuous; uninterrupted 【连年】in consecutive years; for years running ～干旱 successive years of drought ～丰收 reap rich harvests for many years running 【连篇】throughout a piece of writing/one article after another 空话～ pages and pages of empty verbiage ～累牍 lengthy and tedious; at great length 【连任】be reappointed or reelected consecutively 【连日】for days on end; day after day ～来 for the last few days ～刮大风 it blew hard for several days running 【连天】 reaching the sky/incessantly/sky-rending 叫苦～ incessantly complain to high heaven 炮火～ gunfire licked the heavens 【连续】 successive; in a row; running ～五天 five consecutive days ～作战 consecutive operations ～丰收 reap bumper harvests in succession ～性 continuity; continuance 【连夜】 the same night 【连衣裙】 a woman's dress 【连用】 use together 这两个词不能～ these two words do not go together 【连载】 publish in instalments; serialize 长篇～ serial (of a novel, etc.) 【连长】 company commander 【连字号】 hyphen

帘 lián flag as shop sign ②curtain; (hanging) screen 窗～ window curtain

怜 lián sympathize with; pity 【怜爱】 love tenderly; have tender affection for 【怜悯】 have compassion for

涟 lián ①ripples ②continual flow (of tears) 【涟漪】 ripples

莲 lián lotus 【莲花】 lotus (flower) 【莲蓬】 seedpod of the lotus 【莲蓬头】 shower nozzle 【莲子】 lotus seed

联 lián ①ally oneself with; unite; join ②couplet 【联邦】 federation; union; commonwealth ～共和国 federal republic ～制 federalism 【联播】 radio hookup; broadcast over a radio network ～节目时间 network time 【联产计酬责任制】 production responsibility introduced whereby remuneration is determined by farm output; output-related responsibility 【联队】 wing (of an air force) 【联防】 joint defence 军民～ army-civilian defence 【联合】 unite; ally/alliance; union; coalition/joint; combined ～举办 jointly organize or sponsor ～进攻 concerted attack ～公报 joint communiqué ～企业 integrated complex ～政府 coalition government 【联合国】 the United Nations (U.N.) 【联合会】 federation; union 妇女～ women's federation 学生～

students' union 【联欢】 have a get-together 节日～ gala celebrations ～会 get-together ～节 festival ～晚会 (evening) party 【联结】 bind; tie; join 【联军】 allied forces 【联系】 get in touch with; come into touch with/contact; liaison ～感情 make friendly contacts ～处 liaison office ～点 contact point ～官 liaison officer ～员 liaison man 【联盟】 alliance; coalition; league; union 【联名】 jointly (signed) ～发起 jointly initiate ～上书 submit a joint letter 【联赛】 league matches 【联席会议】 joint conference 【联系】 contact; touch; connection; relation / integrate; relate 取得～ get in touch with 保持～ keep in contact with 社会～ social connections 理论～实际 integrate theory with practice 密切～群众 maintain close links with the masses 【联想】 associate; connect in the mind

廉 lián ①honest and clean ②low-priced; inexpensive; cheap 【廉耻】 sense of honour 【廉价】 low-priced; cheap ～部 bargain counter ～品 cheap goods; bargain 【廉洁】 honest ～奉公 be honest in performing one's official duties

镰 lián sickle

敛 lián ①hold back; restrain ～足 hold back from going ②collect ～财 accumulate wealth by unfair means

脸 liǎn face; countenance 笑～ a smiling face 丢～ lose face 【脸蛋儿】 cheeks; face 【脸红】 blush with shame / flush with anger; get excited 【脸面】 face; self-respect; sb.'s feelings 【脸盆】 washbasin 架 washstand 【脸皮】 face; cheek ～厚 thick-skinned; shameless ～薄 shy; sensitive 【脸色】 complexion; look / facial expression

练 lián ①practise; train; drill ～跑 practise running ～字 practise calligraphy ～节目 rehearse ～球 practise a ball game ～本领 perfect one's skill ～身体 do exercises to build up one's health ②experienced; skilled; seasoned 【练兵】(troop) training ～场 drill ground 【练操】(of troops) drill 【练功】do exercises in gymnastics, acrobatics, etc.; practise one's skill 【练习】practise/exercise ～写文章 practise writing 做～ do exercises 算术～ arithmetic exercises ～簿 exercise-book ～题 exercises

炼 liàn ①smelt; refine ～钢 steel-smelting ～糖 refine sugar ②temper with fire 【炼乳】condensed milk 【炼油】oil refining/extract oil by heat/heat edible oil

恋 liàn ①love 初～ first love ②long for; feel attached to 【恋爱】love 谈～ be in love 【恋恋不舍】be reluctant to part with

链 liàn chain 铁～ iron chain 【链球】hammer 【链套】chain case 【链条】chain

LIANG

良 liáng ①good; fine ～策 good plan ～马 a fine horse ②good (people) 【良方】effective prescription/sound strategy 【良好】good; well ～的愿望 good intentions ～的气氛 favourable atmosphere ～的基础 sound foundation 情况～ be in a good state 【良机】golden opportunity 【良师益友】good teacher and helpful friend 【良田】fertile farmland 【良心】conscience 说句～话 to be fair 没～ conscienceless; ungrateful 【良种】improved variety (of rice, etc.)/fine breed ～马 a horse of fine breed

凉 liáng ①cold; cool ～风 cool breeze ②discouraged; disappointed 【凉菜】cold dish 【凉粉】bean jelly 【凉快】nice and cool / cool off 【凉棚】mat-awning 【凉爽】pleasantly cool 【凉水】cold water/unboiled water 【凉台】balcony 【凉席】summer sleeping mat 【凉鞋】sandals

梁 liáng ①roof beam ②bridge ③(mountain) ridge

量 liáng measure ～地 measure land ～米 mete out rice ～身材 take sb.'s measurements ～尺寸 take sb.'s measurements ～体温 take sb.'s temperature 【量规】 gauge 【量具】 measuring tool

梁 liáng ①a fine strain of millet ②fine grain; choice food

粮 liáng grain; food; provisions ～棉双丰收 a bumper harvest of grain and cotton 交公～ pay grain tax to the state 【粮仓】 granary; barn 【粮店】 grain shop 【粮库】 grain depot 【粮票】 grain coupon 【粮食】 grain; cereals; food ～产量 grain yield ～储备 grain reserves ～供应 staple food supply ～加工 grain processing

两 liǎng ①two ～匹马 two horses ②both (sides); either (side) ～利 benefit both ③ a few; some 我想讲～句 I'd like to say a few words ④liang, a unit of weight (= 50 grams) 【两败俱伤】 both sides suffer 【两半】 two halves; in half; in two 【两边】 both sides; both directions ～讨好 try to please both sides ～倒 lean now to one side, now to the other; waver 【两便】 be convenient to both; make things easy for both 【两重】 double; dual; twofold ～任务 a twofold task ～性 dual nature; duality 【两回事】 two entirely different things; two different matters 【两口子】 husband and wife; couple 【两面】 two sides; two aspects/dual; double ～性 dual character ～派 double-dealer ～手法 double game 【两难】 be in a dilemma 【两旁】 both sides; either side 【两栖】 amphibious ～部队 amphibious forces ～动物 amphibious animal 【两全】 have regard for both sides ～的办法 measures satisfactory to both sides ～其美 satisfy rival claims 【两手】 dual tactics 作～准备 prepare oneself for both eventualities 【两条心】 not of one mind 【两头】 both ends; either end/both parties ～尖 pointed at both ends ～为难 find it hard to please either party

亮 liàng ①bright; light 天～了 it's light already ② shine 屋里～着灯 lights were shining in the room ③loud and clear 嗓子～ have a resonant voice ④show ～思想 lay bare one's thoughts ～观点 air one's view 【亮度】 brightness; brilliance 【亮晶晶】 glittering; sparkling; glistening 【亮堂】 light; bright/clear; enlightened

凉 liàng make or become cool 把水～～再喝 let the water cool before you drink it

谅 liàng ①forgive; understand 尚希望～ I hope you will excuse me ②I think; I suppose 前信～已收到 I expect you have received my last letter 【谅解】 understand; make allowance for 互相～ mutual understanding 达成～ reach an understanding 得到～ gain the forgiveness

晾 liàng dry in the air or sun ～衣服 sun clothes 【晾干】 dry by airing 【晾衣绳】 clothesline

量 liàng ①capacity 酒～ capacity for liquor ②quantity; amount; volume 工业产～ the volume of industrial output ③estimate; measure 【量变】 quantitative change 【量词】 classifier; measure word 【量力】 estimate one's own strength or ability (and act accordingly) ～而行 act according to one's capability

踉 liàng 【踉跄】 stagger ～而行 stagger along

LIAO

撩 liāo ①hold up (a curtain, skirt, etc. from the bottom) ②sprinkle (with one's hand)

辽 liáo distant 【辽阔】 vast; extensive 【辽远】 distant; faraway

疗 liáo cure; treat (a patient) 诊～ make a diagnosis and give treatment 【疗程】 course of treatment 【疗法】 therapy 【疗效】 curative effect 【疗养】 recuperate; convalesce ～院 sanatorium

聊 liáo ①merely; just ～表谢意 just to show my appreciation ～以自慰 just to console oneself ②a little; slightly ～胜于无 it's better than nothing ③chat

寥 liáo ①few; scanty ～～可数 just a sprinkling ～～无几 very few ②silent; deserted 寂～ deserted and lonely 【寥廓】 boundless; vast 【寥落】 sparse; scattered

僚 liáo ①official 官～ bureaucrat ②an associate in office 同～ colleague 【僚机】 wing plane; wingman

寮 liáo small house; hut 茶～ teahouse 【寮棚】 shed

撩 liáo ①tease; tantalize ②provoke; stir up 【撩拨】 banter / incite

嘹 liáo 【嘹亮】 resonant; loud and clear ～的号角 a clarion call

缭 liáo ①entangled ②sew with slanting stitches ～贴边 stitch a hem 【缭乱】 confused; in a turmoil 心绪～ in a confused state of mind 【缭绕】 curl up; wind around

燎 liáo burn 【燎泡】 blister raised by a burn or scald 【燎原】 set the prairie ablaze

了 liǎo ①know clearly; understand ②end; finish; settle; dispose of 未～之事 unfinished task 【了不得】 terrific; extraordinary 【了不起】 amazing; terrific; extraordinary【了结】 finish; settle; wind up; bring to an end 【了解】 understand; comprehend/find out; acquaint oneself with 【了局】end / solution; settlement 【了如指掌】have sth. at one's fingertips 【了事】dispose of a matter; get sth. over

潦 liáo 【潦草】(of handwriting) hasty and careless; illegible/sloppy; slovenly 【潦倒】be frustrated

了 liào 【了望】watch from a height or a distance; keep a lookout ～台 observation tower

料 liào ①expect; anticipate 不出所～ as was expected ②material; stuff 燃～ fuel ③(grain) feed 【料到】foresee; expect 【料酒】cooking wine 【料理】arrange; manage; attend to ～家务 manage household affairs ～后事 make arrangements for a funeral 【料想】think; presume 【料子】material for making clothes/woollen fabric

撂 liào put down; leave behind ～下筷子就走 put down one's chopsticks and left at once 【撂挑子】throw up one's job

镣 liào fetters 【镣铐】fetters and handcuffs; shackles; irons; chains

LIE

咧 liě 【咧嘴】grin 疼得直～ grin with pain 他咧着嘴笑 his face broadened into a grin

列 liè ①arrange; line up ～队欢迎 line up to welcome sb. ～出理由 set out one's reasons ～表 arrange sth. in tables or columns; tabulate ②list; enter in a list ～入议程 be placed on the agenda ③row; file; rank 站在前～ stand in the front row ④kind; sort 不在讨论之～ not among the subjects to be discussed ⑤various; each and every ～国 various countries 【列兵】private 【列车】train ～时刻表 train schedule; timetable ～员 attendant (on a train) ～长 head of a train crew 【列岛】a chain of islands; archipelago 【列举】 enumerate; list ～大量事实 cite numerous facts —表上项目 enumerate the items on a list 【列宁主义】 Leninism 【列强】 big powers 【列席】 attend (a meeting) as a nonvoting delegate ～代表 nonvoting delegate 【列传】 biographies

劣 liè bad; inferior; of low quality 【劣等】 of inferior quality; low-grade; poor 【劣根性】 deep-rooted bad habits 【劣迹】 misdeed 【劣绅】 evil gentry 【劣势】 inferior strength or position 【劣质】 inferior (coal, etc.)

烈 liè ①strong; violent; intense ～风 strong gale ～酒 a strong drink ～焰 raging flames ②staunch; upright; stern 刚～ fiery and forthright 【烈火】 raging fire 【烈日】 burning sun; scorching sun 【烈士】 martyr ～纪念碑 a monument to revolutionary martyrs ～墓 the grave of a revolutionary martyr 【烈属】 members of a revolutionary martyr's family 【烈性】 spirited/strong

猎 liè hunt ～虎 tiger hunting 【猎场】 hunting field 【猎刀】 hunting knife 【猎狗】 hound 【猎获】 capture or kill in hunting; bag ～物 bag 【猎奇】 hunt for novelty; seek novelty 【猎枪】 shotgun; hunting rifle 【猎取】 hunt/pursue; seek; hunt for 【猎人】 hunter

裂 liè split; crack ～开 rend; split open ～成两半 be rent in two 杯子～了 the cup's cracked 【裂缝】 rift; crevice; crack; fissure 【裂口】 breach; gap 【裂纹】 crackle

LIN

邻 lín ①neighbour ②near; adjacent ～邦 a neighbouring country ～座 an adjacent seat 【邻近】 close to

林 lín ①forest; woods; grove 竹～ bamboo grove ②circles 艺～ art circles ③forestry 【林场】 forestry centre; tree farm 【林带】 forest belt 【林地】 forest land;

woodland 【林区】 forest (region) 【林业】 forestry ～工人 forest worker; forester 【林荫道】 boulevard; avenue

临 lín ①face; overlook 东～大海 border on the sea in the east ②arrive; be present 亲～指导 come personally to give guidance ③just before; be about to ～行 on the point of leaving ～睡 at bedtime ～刑 just before execution ④copy ～画 copy a painting ～帖 practise calligraphy after a model 【临别】 just before parting ～赠言 words of advice at parting ～纪念 parting souvenir 【临产】 about to give birth; parturient 【临床】 clinical ～经验 clinical experience 【临机】 as the occasion requires ～应变 adapt to changing circumstances 【临摹】 copy (a model of calligraphy or painting) 【临时】 at the time when sth. happens/temporary ～忙乱 be in a rush at the last moment ～凑合 make do for the moment ～办法 makeshift measures ～动议 extempore motion ～费用 incidental expenses ～工 casual labourer ～户口 temporary residence permit ～政府 provisional government 【临死】 on one's deathbed

淋 lín pour; drench 【淋巴】 lymph 【淋漓】 dripping (with sweat, blood, etc.) ～尽致 incisively and vividly; thoroughly 【淋浴】 shower

琳 lín 【琳琅】 beautiful jade; gem ～满目 a feast for the eyes

磷 lín phosphorus ～肥 phosphate fertilizer

鳞 lín scale (of fish, etc.)

凛 lín ①cold ②strict; stern; severe ③afraid; apprehensive 【凛冽】 piercingly cold 【凛凛】 cold/stern; awe-inspiring 威风～ majestic-looking 【凛然】 stern 正气～

awe-inspiring righteousness

吝 lìn stingy; mean; closefisted 【吝啬】 niggardly; miserly ～鬼 miser; niggard; skinflint 【吝惜】 grudge; stint

赁 lìn rent; hire 房屋出～ house to let ～费 rent; rental

淋 lìn strain; filter 用纱布把药～一下 strain the herbal medicine with a piece of gauze

LING

伶 líng actor or actress 【伶仃】 left alone without help; lonely 【伶俐】 clever; bright; quick-witted

灵 líng ①quick; clever; sharp 耳朵～ have sharp ears ②efficacious; effective ～药 an effective remedy ③spirit; intelligence 心～ heart; mind; soul ④fairy; sprite ～怪 elf; goblin ⑤(remains) of the deceased; bier 守～ keep vigil beside the bier 【灵便】 nimble; agile/easy to handle; handy 【灵车】 hearse 【灵丹妙药】 miraculous cure; panacea 【灵感】 inspiration 【灵魂】 soul; spirit ～深处 in the depth of one's soul 出卖～ sell one's soul 【灵活】 nimble; agile; quick/flexible; elastic ～性 flexibility; adaptability; mobility 【灵机】 sudden inspiration; brainwave 【灵柩】 a coffin containing a corpse; bier 【灵敏】 sensitive; keen; agile; acute ～度 sensitivity 【灵巧】 dexterous; skilful; ingenious 一双～的手 a pair of clever hands 动作～ one's movements are nimble 【灵堂】 mourning hall 【灵通】 have quick access to information; well-informed 消息～人士 well-informed sources 【灵性】 intelligence (of animals) 【灵验】 efficacious; effective/accurate; right

玲 líng 【玲珑】 ingeniously and delicately wrought; exquisite 小巧～ small and exquisite/clever and nimble 娇小～ petite and dainty

凌 líng ①insult ②approach ～晨 before dawn ③rise high ～霄 reach the clouds【凌驾】place oneself above; override【凌空】be high up in the air; soar or tower aloft【凌厉】swift and fierce (attack, etc.)【凌乱】in disorder; in a mess【凌辱】insult; humiliate

铃 líng ①bell ～铛 small bell ②boll; bud 棉～ cotton boll

陵 líng ①hill; mound ②imperial tomb【陵墓】mausoleum; tomb【陵园】tombs surrounded by a park

聆 líng listen; hear ～教 hear your words of wisdom ～听 listen (respectfully)

菱 líng ling; water chestnut; water caltrop【菱形】rhombus; lozenge

翎 líng plume; tail feather 孔雀～ peacock plumes; peacock feathers

零 líng ①zero sign; nought ②odd; with a little extra 五百挂～儿 five hundred odd ③zero 一减一等于～ one minus one leaves zero ④nil; love ～比～ no score; love 'all 二比～ two-nil【零度】zero ～以下 below zero【零工】odd job / odd-job man【零花】incidental expenses / pocket money【零活】odd jobs【零件】spare parts; spares【零落】withered and fallen / decayed / scattered; sporadic ～的枪声 sporadic shooting【零卖】retail; sell retail / sell by the piece or in small quantities【零七八碎】scattered and disorderly / miscellaneous and trifling things【零钱】small change / pocket money【零散】scattered【零时】zero hour【零食】between-meal nibbles; snacks 吃～ nibble between meals【零售】retail; sell retail ～店 retail shop ～额 turnover (from retail trade) ～价格 retail price【零碎】scrappy; fragmentary; piecemeal / odds and ends; oddments【零头】odd / remnant (of cloth)【零星】

odd; piecemeal/scattered ～材料 fragmentary material

龄 líng ①age; years 学～儿童 school-age children ②length of time; duration 工～ length of service

岭 líng ①mountain range ②mountain; ridge

领 líng ①neck ②collar; neckband 大衣～ coat collar ③outline 要～ main points; essentials ④lead; usher ～兵 lead troops ～我们参观学校 show us round the school ⑤receive; draw; get ～奖 receive a prize ～工资 draw one's pay 【领带】necktie; tie ～扣针 tiepin 【领导】lead; exercise leadership / leadership; leader ～班子 leading group ～方法 method of leadership ～干部 leading cadre ～核心 leading nucleus ～机关 leading body ～权 leadership; authority ～人 leader ～小组 leading group ～艺术 the art of leadership ～作风 the work style of the leadership 【领地】manor (of a feudal lord)/territory 【领队】lead a group/the leader of a group, sports team, etc. 【领海】territorial sea 【领航】navigate; pilot ～员 navigator; pilot 【领会】understand; comprehend; grasp ～文件的精神 grasp the essence of a document 【领结】bow tie 【领巾】scarf 【领空】territorial sky 【领口】collarband 【领扣】collar button 【领款】draw money ～人 payee 【领路】lead the way 【领略】realize; appreciate 【领情】feel grateful to sb.; appreciate the kindness 【领取】draw; receive 【领事】consul ～馆 consulate 【领头】take the lead 【领土】territory 【领先】lead 遥遥～ hold a safe lead ～五分 lead by five points 【领袖】leader 【领养】adopt (a child) 【领有】possess; own 【领域】territory/field; sphere; domain; realm 【领章】collar badge

另 lìng other; another; separate ～想办法 try to find some other way ～有打算 have other plans ～搞--

套 go one's own way ～行安排 make separate arrangements 【另外】in addition; moreover; besides

令 líng ①command; order 下～ issue an order ②make; cause ～人满意 satisfactory; satisfying ～人鼓舞 heartening; inspiring; encouraging ～人深思 make one ponder ③season 当～ in season ④your ～尊 your father

LIU

溜 liū ① slide; glide 顺山坡往下～ slide down a slope ② smooth 滑～ slippery ③sneak off; slip away 从后门～ 出去 slip out through the back door ～进房间 slide into a room 【溜冰】skating/roller-skating ～场 skating rink 【溜达】stroll; saunter; go for a walk

熘 liū sauté (with thick gravy); quick-fry ～肝尖 liver sauté ～鱼片 fish slices sauté

浏 liú ①(of water) clear; limpid ②(of wind) swift 【浏览】glance over; skim through ～报刊 browse among newspapers and magazines

流 liú ①flow 江水东～ the river flows east ～鼻涕 have a running nose ～汗 sweat; perspire ～泪 shed tears ②drifting; wandering ～民 refugees ③spread; circulate ④stream of water 中～ midstream ⑤current 气～ air current 电～ electric current ⑥class; rate; grade 第一～ 作品 a first-rate work 【流弊】corrupt practices; abuses 【流产】abortion; miscarriage/miscarry; fall through 【流畅】easy and smooth 【流程】technological process / circuit ～图 flow diagram 【流传】circulate; hand down 广泛～ spread far and wide 【流窜】flee (hither and thither) 【流弹】stray bullet 【流动】flow / going from place to place; on the move; mobile ～红旗 mobile red banner ～货车 shop-on-wheels ～基金 circulating fund ～人口 floating population ～图书馆 travelling library ～性 mobility; fluidity ～资本 circulating capital 【流毒】 exert a pernicious influence / baneful influence 【流芳百世】 leave a good name for a hundred generations 【流放】 banish; send into exile / float (logs) downstream 【流感】 flu 【流寇】 roving bandits / roving rebel bands 【流浪】 roam about; lead a vagrant life ～街头 roam the streets ～儿 waif ～汉 tramp 【流离失所】 be forced to leave home and wander about 【流利】 fluent; smooth 口才 a flow of eloquence 她说一口～的英语 she speaks fluent English 【流露】 reveal; betray; show unintentionally 真情的～ a revelation of one's true feelings 【流落】 wander about destitute ～他乡 wander destitute far from home 【流氓】 rogue; hoodlum; gangster/indecency 【流派】 sect; schools (of thought) 【流气】 rascally behaviour 【流沙】 drift sand; quicksand 【流失】 run off; be washed away 【流逝】 (of time) pass; elapse 随着时间的～ with the passage of time 光阴～ time flows away 【流水】 running water / turnover (in business) ～线 assembly line ～帐 current account ～作业 flow process 【流体】 fluid 【流通】 circulate 空气～ circulation of air ～费用 circulation costs ～手段 medium of circulation 【流亡】 go into exile ～政府 government-in-exile 【流线型】 streamline ～汽车 streamlined car 【流星】 meteor; shooting star 【流行】 prevalent; popular; fashionable; in vogue ～病 epidemic disease 【流血】 bleed; shed blood 【流言】 rumour; gossip 【流域】 valley; river basin

留 liú ①remain; stay ～在原地 stay where you are 会后请～一下 will you please remain after the meeting ②ask sb. to stay 我不～你了 I won't keep you any longer ③reserve; keep; save ～座 reserve a seat for sb. ～饭 save food for sb. ④grow; wear ～胡子 grow a beard

⑤accept; take ～下礼物 accept a present ⑥leave ～个条 leave a note for sb. ～话 leave word; leave a message 【留步】don't bother to see me out; don't bother to come any further 【留后路】leave a way out 【留后手】leave room for manoeuvre 【留级】repeat the year's work; stay down 【留空】leave a blank or a space 【留恋】can't bear to part (from sb. or with sth.) / yearn for (the past) 【留难】put obstacles in sb.'s way 【留念】accept or keep as a souvenir 【留情】show mercy 【留神】be careful; take care 【留声机】gramophone 【留守】stay behind to take care of things; stay behind for garrison or liaison duty ～处 rear office ～人员 rear personnel 【留宿】put up a guest for the night/stay overnight 【留心】be careful; take care ～别写错 mind you don't write it wrong ～听讲 listen attentively to a lecture 【留学】study abroad ～生 student studying abroad; returned student 【留意】look out; keep one's eyes open 【留影】have a picture taken as a souvenir 【留用】continue to employ; keep on 【留有余地】leave some leeway; allow for unforeseen circumstances

琉 liú 【琉璃】coloured glaze ～塔 glazed pagoda ～瓦 glazed tile

硫 liú sulphur 【硫磺】sulphur 【硫酸】sulphuric acid

瘤 liú tumour

柳 liú willow 【柳条】willow twig; osier; wicker ～筐 wicker basket ～箱 wicker suitcase 【柳絮】catkin

绺 liú tuft; lock; skein 一～丝线 a skein of silk thread 一～头发 a wisp of hair

六 liú six 【六月】June / the sixth moon

溜 liū ①swift current ②rainwater from the roof ③roof gutter ④row 一～平房 a row of one-storeyed houses

遛 liù saunter; stroll 出去～～ let's go for a stroll ～马 walk a horse

LONG

龙 lóng ①dragon ～船 dragon boat ～灯 dragon lantern ②imperial ～袍 imperial robe 【龙卷风】 tornado 【龙头】 tap; cock 开(关)～turn the cock on (off) 【龙王】 the Dragon King 【龙虾】 lobster 【龙眼】 longan

聋 lóng deaf; hard of hearing 聋哑 deaf-mute ～人 deaf-mute ～症 deaf-mutism 【聋子】 a deaf person

笼 lóng ①cage; coop 鸟～ birdcage ～鸟 cage bird 鸡～ chicken coop ②basket; container 【笼屉】 food steamer 【笼头】 headstall; halter

隆 lóng ①grand ②prosperous; thriving ③intense; deep 【隆冬】 midwinter 【隆隆】 rumble (of thunder, gunfire, etc.) 【隆重】 grand; solemn; ceremonious ～的典礼 a grand ceremony ～的接待 a grand reception ～开幕 be solemnly opened

垄 lǒng ①ridge (in a field) ②raised path between fields 【垄断】 monopolize ～市场 monopolize the market ～集团 monopoly group ～价格 monopoly price 【垄沟】 field ditch; furrow

拢 lǒng ①approach; reach ～岸 come alongside the shore ②add up ～帐 sum up the accounts ③hold together 把柴火～上 tie the firewood in a bundle ④comb (hair) 【拢共】 all told; in all 【拢子】 a fine-toothed comb

笼 lóng ①envelop; cover ②a large box or chest; trunk 【笼络】 win sb. over by any means; draw over; rope in ～人心 try to win people's support by hook or by crook 【笼统】general; sweeping 说得很~ speak in very general terms 【笼罩】envelop; shroud

弄 lòng lane; alley; alleyway 里~ lanes and alleys; neighbourhood

LOU

搂 lōu gather up; rake together ~柴火 rake up twigs, etc. ②hold up; tuck up ~起袖子 tuck up one's sleeves ③squeeze (money) ~钱 extort money

喽 lóu 【喽罗】the rank and file of a band of outlaws/ underling; lackey

楼 lóu ① a storied building 办公~ office building ② storey; floor 【楼板】floor 【楼道】passageway 【楼房】a building of two or more storeys 【楼上】upstairs 【楼梯】stairs; staircase 【楼下】downstairs

搂 lǒu hold in one's arms 【搂抱】hug; embrace; cuddle

篓 lǒu basket 字纸~ wastepaper basket; wastebasket

陋 lòu ①plain 丑~ ugly ②humble ~室 a humble room ~巷 a mean alley ③vulgar; undesirable ~习 corrupt customs; bad habits ④(of knowledge) scanty; limited 浅~ shallow; superficial 【陋规】objectionable practices

漏 lòu ①leak 船~了 the ship leaks ~水了 the water has leaked out ②divulge; leak 走~消息 leak information ③be missing; leave out ~了一行 a line is missing 【漏报】fail to report sth. 【漏洞】leak / flaw; hole ~百出 be full of holes 堵塞~ stop up all loopholes 【漏斗】funnel 【漏风】air leak / (of secrets) leak out 【漏光】light leak 【漏勺】strainer; colander 【漏税】evade taxation 【漏网】slip through the net; escape unpunished

露 lòu reveal; show 【露马脚】give oneself away 【露面】show one's face; make an appearance; appear or reappear on public occasions 【露头】show one's head / appear; emerge 【露馅儿】let the cat out of the bag; give the game away 【露一手】show off

LU

卢 lú 【卢比】rupee 【卢布】rouble

庐 lú hut; cottage 【庐舍】house; farmhouse

芦 lú reed 【芦根】reed rhizome 【芦花】reed catkins 【芦笋】asparagus 【芦苇】reed 【芦席】reed mat

炉 lú ①stove; furnace; oven ②heat 一～钢 a heat of steel 【炉膛】the chamber of a stove or furnace 【炉条】fire bars; grate 【炉灶】kitchen range 【炉渣】slag; cinder

颅 lú cranium; skull 【颅骨】skull 【颅腔】cranial cavity

卤 lǔ ①bittern ②halogen ～族 halogen family ③stew (chickens meat, etc.) in soy sauce ～鸡 pot-stewed chicken ④thick gravy used as a sauce for noodles, etc. 【卤味】pot-stewed fowl, meat, etc. served cold

虏 lǔ ①take prisoner ②captive; prisoner of war 【虏获】capture / men and arms captured

掳 lǔ carry off; capture 【掳掠】pillage; loot

鲁 lǔ ①stupid; dull ②rash; rough; rude 【鲁钝】dull-witted; obtuse 【鲁莽】crude and rash

橹 lǔ scull; sweep

陆 lù land 【陆地】 dry land 【陆军】 ground force; land force; army 【陆路】 land route 走～ travel by land ～交通 land communication 【陆续】 in succession 代表们～到达 the delegates arrived one after another 【陆运】 land transportation 【陆战队】 marines

录 lù ①record; write down; copy 抄～ copy down ②employ; hire 收～ take sb. on the staff ③tape-record 把讲话～下来 have a speech taped ④record; register; collection 回忆～ memoirs; reminiscences 【录取】 enroll; recruit; admit ～新学员 enroll students ～通知书 admission notice 【录像机】 videocorder 【录音】 sound recording 放～ play back the recording ～报告 tape-recorded speech ～带 (magnetic) tape ～机 (tape) recorder ～室 recording room 【录用】 employ

鹿 lù deer 公～ stag 母～ doe 小～ fawn 【鹿角】 deerhorn/abatis 【鹿皮】 deerskin 【鹿茸】 pilose antler

禄 lù official's salary in feudal China; emolument 高官厚～ high position and handsome salary

碌 lù ①commonplace ②busy 【碌碌】 mediocre; commonplace/busy with miscellaneous work ～无能 incompetent; devoid of ability 忙忙～～ busy going about one's work

路 lù ①road; path; way 大～ broad road 小～ path; trail ②journey; distance 走远～ walk a long distance ③means 生～ means of livelihood; a way out ④sequence; line; logic 思～ train of thought ⑤region; district 外～人 nonlocal people ⑥route 八～军 the Eighth Route Army ⑦sort; grade; class 一～货 the same sort 【路标】 road sign; route sign 【路程】 distance travelled; journey 【路道】 way; approach/behaviour 【路灯】 street lamp 【路费】 travelling expenses 【路轨】 rail/track 【路过】

pass by or through (a place) 【路基】roadbed 【路劫】
highway robbery 【路警】railway police 【路径】route;
way/method 【路口】crossing; intersection 十字~ crossroads 【路牌】street nameplate 【路人】passerby; stranger
视若~ treat sb. like a stranger 【路上】on the road / on
the way; en route 【路途】road; path / way; journey
~遥远 far away 【路线】route; itinerary / line 旅行的
~ the route of a journey ~斗争 two-line struggle

戮 lù ①kill; slay ②unite; join —力 join hands 【戮力
同心】make concerted efforts

麓 lù the foot of a mountain

露 lù ①dew 朝~ morning dew ②syrup 果子~ fruit
syrup ③show; reveal ~出原形 betray oneself 【露
骨】thinly veiled; barefaced 说得很~ speak undisguised-
ly ~地干涉 flagrantly interfere 【露酒】alcoholic drink
mixed with fruit juice 【露水】dew 【露宿】sleep in the
open 【露天】in the open (air); outdoors ~堆栈 open-
air depot ~剧场 open-air theatre ~开采 opencast mining
~矿 open-pit; strip mine ~煤矿 opencut coal mine

LÜ

驴 lǘ donkey; ass

侣 lǚ companion; associate 伴~ partner 情~ lovers

旅 lǚ ①travel ②brigade ③troops; force 劲~ a crack
force 【旅伴】travelling companion; fellow traveller
【旅程】route; itinerary 【旅店】inn 【旅费】travelling expenses 【旅馆】hotel 【旅居】reside abroad; sojourn 【旅
客】hotel guest; traveller; passenger ~登记簿 hotel re-

gister【旅途】journey; trip【旅行】travel; journey; tour ～包 travelling bag ～车 station wagon ～社 travel service ～团 touring party ～支票 traveller's cheque ～证 travel certificate ～指南 guidebook【旅游】tour; tourism ～事业 tourist trade; tourism【旅长】brigade commander

捋 lǚ smooth out with the fingers; stroke ～胡子 stroke one's beard

铝 lǚ aluminium【铝箔】aluminium foil【铝土矿】bauxite

偻 lǚ ①crooked (back) 伛～ hunchback(ed) ②instantly; directly; at once

屡 lǚ repeatedly; time and again ～战～胜 score one victory after another【屡次三番】over and over again; many times【屡见不鲜】common occurrence; nothing new 【屡教不改】refuse to mend one's ways despite repeated admonition【屡试不爽】time-tested

缕 lǚ ①thread ②wisp; strand; lock 一～烟 a wisp of smoke 一～麻 a strand of hemp ③detailed【缕述】state in detail【缕析】make a detailed analysis

膂 lǚ backbone【膂力】muscular strength; brawn ～过人 possessing extraordinary physical strength

履 lǚ ①shoe 革～ leather shoes ②tread on; walk on ③footstep ～carry out; fulfil ～约 keep an appointment【履带】caterpillar tread; track【履历】personal details; antecedents【履行】perform; fulfil; carry out ～职责 do one's duty ～诺言 perform what one has promised; carry out one's promise ～义务 fulfil obligations

律 lǚ ①law; statute; rule ②restrain 严以～己 be strict with oneself【律师】lawyer

虑 lǚ ①consider; ponder; think over 深思熟～ careful deliberation ②concern; anxiety; worry

率 lǜ rate; proportion; ratio 人口增长～ the rate of population increase 废品～ the rate of rejects

绿 lǜ green ～叶 green leaves 【绿宝石】 emerald 【绿茶】 green tea 【绿灯】 green light 开～ give the green light to 【绿豆】 green gram ～芽 mung bean sprouts 【绿肥】 green manure ～作物 green manure crop 【绿化】 afforest ～山区 afforest the mountain district ～城市 plant trees in and around the city 【绿洲】 oasis

滤 lǜ strain; filter 【滤过性病毒】 filterable virus 【滤色镜】 filter 【滤液】 filtrate 【滤纸】 filter paper

LUAN

李 luán 【李生】 twin ～姐妹 twin sisters

卵 luǎn ovum; egg; spawn 【卵白】 white of an egg; albumen 【卵巢】 ovary 【卵黄】 yolk 【卵石】 cobble; pebble; shingle 【卵翼】 shield

乱 luàn ①in disorder; in a mess; in confusion 屋里很～ the room is in a mess 稿子太～ the manuscript's too messy ～了阵脚 be in disarray ②disorder; chaos; riot; turmoil 内～ internal unrest 叛～ mutiny ③confuse; mix up; jumble 扰～ create confusion; disturb ④ confused (state of mind) 我心里很～ my mind is in a turmoil ⑤indiscriminate; random; arbitrary 给人～扣帽子 slap political labels on people right and left ～来 act recklessly ～花钱 spend money extravagantly ⑥promiscuity 【乱兵】 mutinous soldiers/totally undisciplined troops 【乱哄哄】 in noisy disorder; in a hubbub 【乱伦】 commit incest 【乱蓬蓬】 tangled; jumbled ～的头发 dishevelled hair 【乱七八糟】 in a mess; in a muddle 【乱世】 troubled times 【乱说】 speak carelessly; make irresponsible remarks; gossip 【乱弹琴】act or talk like a fool; talk nonsense 这简直是~ that's a lot of nonsense 【乱套】muddle things up; turn things upside down 那就~了 it will be in a muddle 【乱腾】confusion; disorder; unrest 【乱糟糟】chaotic/confused ~的屋子 a chaotic room 心里~的 feel very perturbed 【乱子】disturbance; disorder 闹~ cause trouble

LUE

掠 luè ①plunder; pillage; sack ②sweep past; brush past; graze ~过天空 sweep past the sky ~过水面 skim over the water 【掠夺】rob; pillage ~别国的资源 plunder the resources of other countries 【掠美】claim credit due to others 【掠取】seize; grab; plunder

略 luè ①brief; sketchy ~述大意 give a brief account ②slightly; a little; somewhat ~加修改 edit slightly ~有所闻 have heard a little about the matter ~有出入 vary slightly ③summary; brief account; outline 史~ brief history ④omit; delete; leave out ~去不提 make no mention of; leave out altogether ⑤strategy; plan; scheme 策~ tactics ⑥capture; seize 攻城~地 attack cities and seize territories 【略】slightly; briefly 【略见一斑】get a rough idea of 【略胜一筹】a notch better; slightly better 【略图】sketch 【略微】a little; somewhat 【略语】abbreviation; shortening

LUN

抡 lūn brandish; swing ~刀 brandish a sword ~起大铁锤 swing a sledgehammer

伦 lún ①human relations ②logic; order ③peer; match 绝~ peerless; matchless 【伦次】coherence; logical sequence 语无～ speak incoherently 【伦理】ethics

沦 lún ①sink 沉～ sink into depravity, etc. ②fall ～
于敌手 fall into enemy hands ～为乞丐 be reduced
to begging 【沦落】 fall low; come down in the world;
be reduced to poverty ～街头 be driven onto the streets
(to become a tramp, beggar or prostitute) 【沦亡】 be an-
nexed; be subjugated 【沦陷】 be occupied by the enemy

纶 lún ①black silk ribbon ②fishing line ③synthetic
fibre 锦～ polyamide fibre 涤～ polyester fibre

轮 lún ①wheel ⑦disc; ring 日～ the sun's disc 年～
annual ring ③steamboat 江～ river steamer ④take
turns ～值 on duty by turns 现在～到你了 it's your
turn now ⑤round 第一～比赛 the first round of the match
新的一～会谈 a new round of talks 【轮班】 in shifts; in
relays; in rotation 【轮唱】 round 【轮船】 steamer; steamship
【轮渡】 (steam) ferry 【轮番】 take turns ～轰炸 bomb
in waves 【轮换】 rotate; take turns 【轮机】 turbine/engine
～室 engine room ～员 engineer ～长 chief engineer
【轮空】 bye 【轮廓】 outline; contour; rough
sketch 画个～ draw an outline 厂房的～ the outline of
the factory buildings 【轮流】 take turns; do sth. in turn
【轮胎】 tyre 【轮休】 have holidays by turns; rotate days
off 【轮训】 training in rotation 【轮椅】 wheelchair

论 lùn ①discuss; discourse 就事～事 talk about a matter in isolation ②view 舆～ public opinion ③disser-
tation; essay ④theory 进化～ the theory of evolution
⑤ mention; regard; consider 又当别～ should be regarded
as a different matter ⑥decide on 按质～价 determine
the price according to the quality ⑦by; in terms of 鸡
蛋～斤卖 eggs are sold by the *jin* 【论处】 decide on sb.'s
punishment 以违反纪律～ be punished for a breach of

discipline 【论敌】one's opponent in a debate 【论点】thesis 【论调】view; argument 错误～ erroneous views 【论断】judgment 作出～ draw an inference 【论功行赏】award people according to their contributions 【论据】grounds of argument ～不足 insufficient grounds 有力的～ valid reasons 【论理】normally; as things should be/logic ～学 logic 【论述】discuss; expound 精辟的～ brilliant exposition 【论说】exposition and argumentation ～文 argumentation 【论坛】forum; tribune 【论文】thesis; dissertation; paper 学术～ an academic thesis 科学～ a scientific treatise 【论战】polemic; debate 【论证】demonstration; proof/expound and prove 【论著】treatise; work

LUO

罗 luó 【罗嗦】long-winded; wordy 我再～几句 bear with me a little longer

挣 luó rub one's palm along (sth. long) ～起袖子 push up one's sleeve

罗 luó ①a net for catching birds ②catch birds with a net ③collect; gather together ④display; spread out ⑤sieve; sift ～面 sift flour ⑥silk gauze ～扇 silk gauze fan 【罗锅儿】hunchbacked/hunchback 【罗口灯泡】screw socket bulb 【罗口灯头】screw socket 【罗列】spread out; set out / enumerate ～事实 enumerate the facts 【罗盘】compass 【罗圈腿】bowlegs/bowlegged 【罗网】net; trap 自投～ walk right into the trap 【罗织】frame up ～罪名 cook up charges 【罗致】enlist the services of

萝 luó trailing plants 藤～ Chinese wistaria 【萝卜】radish

逻 luó patrol 【逻辑】logic ～思维 logical thinking ～学 logic ～学家 logician ～主语 logical subject

锣 luó gong 【锣槌】(gong) hammer 【锣鼓】gong and drum/traditional percussion instruments

笊 luó a square-bottomed bamboo basket 【笊筐】a large bamboo or wicker basket

骡 luó mule

螺 luó spiral shell; snail 【螺号】conch; shell trumpet 【螺母】(screw) nut 【螺丝】screw ～刀 screwdriver 【螺旋】spiral; helix/screw 【螺旋桨】propeller; screw 飞机～ airscrew; aircraft propeller

裸 luǒ bare; exposed 【裸露】uncovered 【裸体】naked; nude

荦 luò prominent; outstanding 【荦荦】conspicuous; apparent; obvious ～大端 salient points

络 luò ①sth. resembling a net 橘～ tangerine pith ② twine; wind ～纱 winding yarn 【络腮胡子】whiskers 【络绎不绝】in an endless stream

骆 luò 【骆驼】camel 单峰～ one-humped camel ～队 caravan ～绒 camel hair cloth

落 luò ①fall; drop 秋天叶子～下 leaves fall in autumn ②go down; set 太阳～山了 the sun has set ③ lower ～下帘子 lower the blinds ④decline; sink 衰～ go downhill ～到这一步 come to such a pass ⑤lag behind ⑥leave behind 不～痕迹 leave no trace ⑦fall on; rest with 一切费用～在我身上 all the expenses fell on me 【落笔】put pen to paper 【落泊】be down and out 【落潮】ebb tide 【落成】completion (of a building, etc.) 【落得】get; end in 【落地】fall to the ground/(of babies) be born ～窗 French window ～灯 floor lamp ～式收音机 console set 【落后】fall behind/backward ～于现实 lag behind reality ～地区 backward areas ～分子 backward element 【落户】 settle 【落花流水】 like fallen flowers carried away by the flowing water; utterly routed 【落花生】 peanut; groundnut 【落价】 drop in price 【落脚】 stay (for a time); stop over; put up ～处 temporary lodging 【落空】 come to nothing; fail; fall through 两头～ fall between two stools 希望～ fail to attain one's hope 这事有～的危险 there is a danger that nothing will come of it 【落泪】 shed tears; weep 【落实】 practicable; workable/ fix in advance; ascertain; make sure / carry out; fulfil; put into effect ～政策 implement the policies 【落网】 be caught; be captured 【落伍】 fall behind the ranks; straggle; drop behind 【落选】 fail to be elected; lose an election 【落叶】 fallen leaves/deciduous leaf ～树 deciduous tree

摞 luò ①pile up; stack up 把砖一～起来 stack up the bricks ②pile; stack 一～书 a stack of books

M

MA

妈 mā ①ma; mother ②aunt 姑～ (paternal) aunt 姨～ (maternal) aunt

抹 mā ①wipe ～桌子 wipe a table ②rub sth. down 把帽子～下来 slip one's cap off 【抹布】 rag

麻 má ①a general term for hemp, flax, etc. ②sesame ～糖 sesame candy ③pocked; pitted; spotty 有～点 there are pits in sth. ④tingle 腿发～ have pins and needles in one's legs ⑤anaesthesia 药～ drug anaesthesia 【麻痹】 paralysis/benumb; lull; blunt/lower one's guard ～人们的斗志 lull people's fighting will ～大意 be off one's guard

【麻布】gunny; sackcloth/linen 【麻袋】gunny-bag; gunny-sack; sack 【麻刀】hemp; hair 【麻烦】troublesome; inconvenient/trouble sb.; bother 如果不～的话,请来一下 please come, if it is not inconvenient to you ～你给他打个电话 may I trouble you to call him up 别～他了 don't bother him 自找～ ask for trouble 【麻花】fried dough twist 【麻酱】sesame paste 【麻利】quick and neat; dexterous; deft 【麻木】numb/apathetic; insensitive 【麻雀】sparrow 【麻纱】yarn of ramie, flax, etc./cambric; hair-cords 【麻绳】rope (made of hemp, etc.) 【麻线】flaxen thread 【麻药】anaesthetic 【麻油】sesame oil 【麻子】pock-marks/a person with a pockmarked face 【麻醉】anaesthesia; narcosis/anaesthetize; poison ～剂 anaesthetic ～品 narcotic; drug ～师 anaesthetist

马 mǎ horse 母～ mare 种～ stallion; stud 小～ pony 【马鞍】saddle 【马鞭】horsewhip 【马不停蹄】without a stop 【马车】(horse-drawn) carriage/cart 【马达】motor 【马刀】sabre 【马灯】lantern 【马镫】stirrup 【马队】caravan/cavalry 【马粪纸】strawboard 【马蜂】hornet; wasp ～窝 hornet's nest 【马虎】careless; casual ～了事 get it done in a slapdash manner 【马厩】stable 【马克思列宁主义】Marxism-Leninism ～者 Marxist-Leninist 【马克思主义】Marxism ～哲学 Marxist philosophy ～者 Marxist ～政治经济学 Marxist political economy 【马口铁】tinplate 【马裤】riding breeches ～呢 whipcord 【马拉松】marathon 【马力】horsepower 开足～ at full speed 【马铃薯】potato 【马路】road; street; avenue 【马枪】carbine 【马球】polo 【马上】at once; immediately 你～就走吗 are you leaving right away 【马术】horsemanship 【马蹄】horse's hoof ～表 alarm clock ～声 hoofbeat ～形 U-shaped ～铁 horse-shoe/horseshoe magnet 【马桶】nightstool 【马戏】circus

~团 circus troupe【马靴】riding boots【马扎】campstool

吗
mǎ 【吗啡】morphine

玛
mǎ 【玛瑙】agate

码
mǎ ①a sign or thing indicating number 页~ page number 价~ marked price ②pile up; stack ~砖 stack bricks ③yard【码头】wharf; dock; quay; pier ~工人 docker; stevedore; longshoreman

蚂
mǎ 【蚂蟥】leech【蚂蚁】ant

骂
mà ①abuse; curse; swear ~人话 swearword; curse ②condemn; rebuke; reprove 把他~了一顿 give him a scolding【骂街】shout abuses in the street; call people names in public【骂名】bad name; infamy

MAI

埋
mái cover up (with earth); bury ~地雷 lay a mine 【埋藏】lie hidden in the earth; bury ~在心底 bury deep in one's heart【埋伏】ambush 设下~ lay an ambush 中~ fall into an ambush【埋没】bury; cover up/ neglect; stifle ~人材 stifle real talents【埋头】be engrossed in ~苦干 quietly immerse oneself in hard work ~读书 bury oneself in books ~业务 engross oneself in vocational work【埋葬】bury

买
mǎi buy; purchase ~东西 buy things; go shopping ~得起 can afford ~不起 cannot afford【买办】comprador【买方】the buying party; buyer【买价】buying price【买空卖空】speculate (in stocks, etc.)【买卖】buying and selling; business; deal 做成一笔~ make a deal ~怎么样 how was business ~婚姻 mercenary marriage

～人 businessman; trader; merchant 【买通】 bribe; buy over 【买主】 buyer; customer

迈 mài step; stride ～门槛 step over the threshold ～着矫健的步伐 walk with vigorous strides 【迈步】 take a step; step forward 迈出第一步 make the first step 【迈进】 stride forward; forge ahead

麦 mài ①a general term for wheat, barley, etc. ②wheat 【麦麸】 wheat bran 【麦秸】 wheat straw 【麦精】 malt extract 【麦克风】 microphone; mike 【麦片】 oatmeal ～粥 oatmeal porridge 【麦乳精】 extract of malt and milk 【麦收】 wheat harvest 【麦穗】 ear of wheat 【麦芽】 malt ～糖 malt sugar; maltose

卖 mài ①sell ～得快 sell well ～不出去 not sell well ②betray ～友 betray one's friend ③exert to the utmost; not spare ～力 spare no effort ④show off ～乖 show off one's cleverness 【卖方】 the selling party 【卖关子】 keep people guessing 【卖国】 betray one's country ～集团 traitorous clique ～条约 traitorous treaty ～行为 treasonable act ～贼 traitor (to one's country) ～主义 national betrayal 【卖价】 selling price 【卖力气】 do one's very best/make a living by manual labour 【卖命】 work oneself to the bone for sb. / die (unworthily) for 【卖弄】 show off; parade ～学问 parade one's knowledge ～小聪明 show off one's smartness 【卖俏】 (play the) coquette; flirt 【卖艺】 make a living as a performer 【卖淫】 prostitution 【卖主】 seller 【卖座】 (of a theatre, play, etc.) draw large audiences

脉 mài ①arteries and veins ②pulse 号～ feel sb.'s pulse ③vein 叶～ veins in a leaf 矿～ ore vein 【脉搏】 pulse 时代的～ the pulse of our times 【脉络】 arteries and veins/ vein (of a leaf, etc.) / thread of thought; sequence of ideas

埋 mán 【埋怨】 blame; complain; grumble

蛮 mán rough; fierce; reckless; unreasoning ～劲 sheer animal strength 【蛮干】 act rashly; be foolhardy 【蛮横】 rude and unreasonable; arbitrary; peremptory

馒 mán 【馒头】 steamed bun; steamed bread

瞒 mán hide the truth from 不～你说 to tell you the truth 【瞒哄】 deceive 【瞒上欺下】 deceive those above and bully those below

满 mǎn ①full; filled; packed 箱子～了 the box is full ②fill 给你～上一杯 let me fill your glass ③expire; reach the limit 年～十八岁 reach the age of 18 假期已～ the holidays are over ④entirely; completely ～不在乎 not worry at all ⑤satisfied 不～ dissatisfied ⑥complacent; conceited 【满城风雨】 (become) the talk of the town 闹得～ create a scandal 【满打满算】 at the very most 【满额】 fulfil the (enrolment, etc.) quota 【满分】 full marks 【满腹】 have one's mind filled with ～牢骚 full of grievances 【满怀】 have one's heart filled with; be imbued with ～豪情 full of pride and enthusiasm ～信心 with full confidence ～深情 imbued with ardent love 撞了个～ bump right into sb. 【满口】 profusely; glibly ～称赞 praise unreservedly ～答应 readily promise ～谎言 spout lies 【满面】 have one's face covered with 泪流～ tears streaming down one's cheeks ～笑容 be all smiles ～红光 glowing with health 【满腔】 have one's bosom filled with ～仇恨 burning with hatred ～怒火 filled with rage ～热忱 filled with ardour and sincerity 【满身】 be covered all over with ～是汗 sweat all over 【满师】 serve out one's apprenticeship 【满天】 all over the sky ～星斗 a star-studded sky 【满心】 have one's heart filled with ～欢喜 filled with joy 【满眼】 have one's eyes filled with/meet the eye on every side 【满意】 satisfied; pleased 表示～ express satisfaction 对工作很～ be pleased with one's work 【满员】 at full strength / all seats taken 【满月】 full moon / a baby's completion of its first month of life 【满载】 loaded to capacity; fully loaded ～而归 come back with fruitful results 【满足】 satisfied; content; contented / satisfy; meet ～现状 be content with things as they are ～需要 satisfy the needs of sb. ～要求 meet one's demands 【满座】 capacity audience; full house

曼　màn ①graceful ②prolonged; long-drawn-out 【曼妙】 lithe and graceful 【曼声】 (sing or recite in) lengthened sounds 【曼陀林】 mandolin

谩　màn disrespectful; rude 【谩骂】 hurl invectives; fling abuses; rail

漫　màn ①overflow; flood ～灌 flood irrigation ②all over the place; everywhere ③free; unrestrained; casual ～无目标 aimless; at random ～无止境 know no bounds 【漫不经心】 careless; negligent 【漫步】 stroll; ramble; roam 【漫长】 very long; endless 【漫画】 caricature; cartoon 【漫漫】 very long; boundless ～长夜 endless night 【漫谈】 (have an) informal discussion; talk 【漫无边际】 boundless/rambling; discursive 【漫游】 roam; wander

蔓　màn 【蔓生植物】 trailing plant 【蔓延】 spread; extend

慢　màn ①slow ～车 slow train 反应～ be slow to react ②postpone; defer ～点儿告诉她 don't tell her about it yet 【慢坡】 gentle slope 【慢腾腾】 at a leisurely pace; unhurriedly; sluggishly 【慢性】 chronic (disease, etc.)/slow (in taking effect)

幔 màn curtain; screen 布～ cotton curtain

MANG

忙 máng ①busy; fully occupied 你～不～ are you busy ②hurry; hasten 你～什么 what's the hurry 【忙碌】 be busy; bustle about 【忙乱】 be in a rush and a muddle

芒 máng awn; beard; arista

杧 máng 【杧果】 mango

盲 máng blind 【盲肠】 caecum 【盲从】 follow blindly 【盲动】 act blindly; act rashly ～主义 putschism 【盲目】 blind ～崇拜 worship blindly ～乐观 be unrealistically optimistic ～飞行 blind flight ～性 blindness (in action) 【盲人】 blind person 【盲文】 braille

茫 máng ①boundless and indistinct ②ignorant 【茫茫】 vast ～大海 a vast sea ～草原 the boundless grasslands 【茫然】 in the dark; at a loss ～无知 be utterly ignorant 显出～的神情 look blank

莽 mǎng ①rank grass ②rash 【莽汉】 a boor 【莽莽】 luxuriant; rank/(of fields, plains, etc.) vast; boundless 【莽撞】 crude and impetuous; rash

蟒 mǎng boa 【蟒蛇】 boa; python

MAO

猫 māo cat 雄～ tomcat 小～ kitten ～叫 mewing 【猫头鹰】 owl 【猫熊】 panda

毛 máo hair; feather 腋～ armpit hairs 绒～ down ②wool ～袜 woollen stockings ③mildew 长～ become mildewed ④semifinished ～坯 semifinished product ⑤gross ～利 gross profit ～重 gross weight ⑥little; small ～孩子 a mere child ⑦crude; rash ～手～脚 careless (in handling things) ⑧panicky; flurried 心里发～ feel scared 【毛笔】writing brush 【毛病】trouble; mishap/defect; fault; mistake/illness 发动机出了～ there's some trouble with the engine 工作风上的～ defects in one's work style 胃有～ have stomach trouble 【毛玻璃】frosted glass 【毛糙】crude; coarse 【毛虫】caterpillar 【毛豆】young soya bean 【毛纺】wool spinning ～厂 woollen mill 【毛巾】towel ～被 towelling coverlet ～布 towelling ～架 towel rail or rack 【毛孔】pore 【毛料】woollen cloth; woollens 【毛毛雨】drizzle 【毛皮】fur; pelt 【毛茸茸】hairy; downy 【毛瑟枪】Mauser 【毛毯】woollen blanket 【毛细管】capillary 【毛虾】shrimp 【毛线】knitting wool ～针 knitting needle 【毛衣】woollen sweater; sweater; woolly 【毛泽东思想】Mao Zedong Thought 【毛毡】felt 【毛织品】wool fabric; woollens/woollen knitwear

矛 máo lance; pike; spear 【矛盾】contradictory / contradiction 【矛头】spearhead ～所向 the target of attack

茅 máo 【茅草】cogongrass ～棚 thatched shed ～屋 thatched cottage 【茅房】latrine

锚 máo anchor 抛～ drop anchor 起～ weigh anchor

铆 máo riveting 【铆钉】rivet ～枪 riveting gun 【铆工】riveting/riveter 【铆机】riveter

茂 mào ①luxuriant; profuse ②rich and splendid 【茂密】dense; thick ～的森林 a dense forest 【茂盛】exuberant; flourishing 长得～ grow luxuriantly

冒 mào ①emit; send out ～泡 send up bubbles ～气 give off steam ②risk; brave ～雨 braving the rain ～风险 run risks ～着风浪出海 put to sea in spite of wind and wave ③boldly; rashly ～猜一下 make a bold guess ④falsely (claim, etc.); fraudulently 【冒充】pretend to be (sb. or sth. else); pass sb. or sth. off as ～内行 pose as an expert 【冒犯】offend; affront 【冒号】colon 【冒火】get angry; flare up 【冒进】rash advance 【冒领】falsely claim as one's own 【冒昧】make bold; venture; take the liberty 【冒名】go under sb. else's name ～顶替 take another's place by assuming his name 【冒牌】imitation ～货 fake 【冒失】rash; abrupt 说话～speak without due consideration 【冒头】begin to crop up 【冒险】take a risk; take chances/adventure 军事～military adventure ～家 adventurer ～政策 adventurist policy ～主义 adventurism

贸 mào trade 外～foreign trade 【贸然】rashly; hastily ～下结论 draw a hasty conclusion 【贸易】trade ～额 volume of trade ～协定 trade agreement

帽 mào headgear; hat; cap 草～straw hat 军～service cap 笔～the cap of a pen 【帽徽】insignia on a cap 【帽舌】peak (of a cap); visor 【帽檐】the brim of a hat 【帽子】headgear; hat; cap/label; tag; brand 扣～put a label on sb.

貌 mào looks; appearance 美～good looks 新～new look 【貌似】seemingly; in appearance ～强大 outwardly strong ～公正 seemingly impartial

MEI

没 méi 【没词儿】can find nothing to say/be at a loss for words 【没错儿】quite sure/can't go wrong 【没

法子】can do nothing about it; can't help it 【没关系】
it doesn't matter; it's nothing; that's all right; never
mind 【没精打采】 in low spirits; out of sorts 【没命】 lose
one's life; die/recklessly; desperately 【没趣】 feel put out
自讨～ ask for a snub 【没什么】 it doesn't matter; it's
nothing 【没事儿】 have nothing to do; be free/that's all
right; never mind 【没事找事】 ask for trouble/try hard
to find fault 【没有】 not have; there is not; be without

玫 méi 【玫瑰】 rugosa rose; rose

眉 méi ①eyebrow; brow ②the top margin of a page
【眉笔】 eyebrow pencil 【眉开眼笑】 beam with joy
【眉来眼去】 make eyes at each other 【眉目】 features;
looks/logic; sequence of ideas 【眉梢】 the tip of the brow

梅 méi plum 【梅毒】 syphilis 【梅花】 plum blossom 【梅
雨】 plum rains 【梅子】 plum

媒 méi ①go-between 做～ act as a matchmaker ②inter-
mediary 【媒介】 medium; vehicle

煤 méi coal 块～ lump coal 【煤仓】 coal bunker 【煤
层】 coal seam 【煤场】 coal yard 【煤尘】 coal dust
【煤斗】 scuttle 【煤灰】 coal ash 【煤焦油】 coal tar 【煤精】
jet; black amber 【煤矿】 coal mine; colliery ～工人 coal
miner 【煤气】 gas ～厂 gasworks ～灯 gas light ～管
gas pipe ～炉 gas stove ～设备 gas fittings ～灶 gas range
～中毒 gas poisoning 【煤球】 egg-shaped briquet 【煤炭】
coal 【煤田】 coalfield 【煤烟】 smoke from burning coal/
soot 【煤窑】 coalpit 【煤油】 kerosene; paraffin ～灯 kerosene lamp ～炉 kerosene stove 【煤渣】 coal cinder ～
路 cinder road ～跑道 cinder track 【煤砖】 briquet

霉 méi mould; mildew 【霉菌】 mould 【霉烂】 mildew
and rot

每 měi ①every; each; per ～星期五 every Friday ～时～刻 all the time; at all times ②often 【每当】whenever; every time 【每况愈下】steadily deteriorate; go from bad to worse

美 měi ①beautiful; pretty ②very satisfactory; good ～酒 good wine 【美德】virtue; moral excellence 【美感】aesthetic feeling; sense of beauty 【美工】art designing/art designer 【美观】pleasing to the eye; beautiful; artistic 【美国】the United States of America ～人 American 【美好】fine; happy; glorious 【美化】prettify; embellish ～环境 beautify the environment ～自己 prettify oneself 【美景】beautiful scenery 【美丽】beautiful 【美满】happy; perfectly satisfactory ～的生活 a happy life ～婚姻 a happy marriage; conjugal happiness 【美梦】fond dream 【美妙】beautiful; splendid; wonderful ～的青春 the wonderful days of one's youth 【美名】good name; good reputation 【美人】beautiful woman; beauty ～计 use of a woman to ensnare a man; sex-trap 【美容】improve (a woman's) looks/cosmetology ～院 beauty parlour; beauty shop 【美术】the fine arts; art / painting ～工作者 art worker ～馆 art gallery ～家 artist ～明信片 picture postcard ～片 cartoons, puppet films, etc. ～设计 artistic design ～字 artistic calligraphy; art lettering 【美味】delicious food; delicacy / delicious; dainty ～小吃 dainty snacks 【美学】aesthetics 【美言】put in a good word for sb. 【美育】art education 【美元】American dollar; U.S. dollar 【美洲】America

镁 měi magnesium 【镁光】magnesium light

妹 mèi younger sister; sister 【妹夫】younger sister's husband; brother-in-law

昧 mèi ①have hazy notions about; be ignorant of 素 ~平生 have never made sb.'s acquaintance ②hide; conceal 拾金不~ not pocket the money one has picked up ~着良心 (do evil) against one's conscience

谜 mèi 【谜儿】 riddle 猜~ guess a riddle

媚 mèi ①fawn on; curry favour with; flatter ~外 toady to foreign powers ②charming; fascinating

魅 mèi evil spirit; demon 【魅力】 glamour; enchantment 艺术~ artistic charm

MEN

闷 mēn ①stuffy; close ~热 sultry; muggy 这儿太~了 the air here is too close ②cover tightly ③(of a sound) muffled ④shut oneself or sb. indoors

门 mén ①entrance; door; gate 前~ front door 校~ school gate 炉~ stove door ②valve; switch 气~ air valve ③way to do sth.; knack 摸着~儿 know one's way around ④family 豪~ wealthy and influential family ⑤(religious) sect; school (of thought) ⑥class; category 分~别类 divide into different categories 【门把】 door knob; door handle 【门板】 door plank/shutter 【门洞儿】 gateway; doorway 【门房】 gate house; porter's lodge/doorman 【门岗】 gate sentry 【门户】 door/gateway/faction; sect ~之见 sectarianism 【门环】 knocker 【门禁】 entrance guard 【门径】 access; key; way 【门槛】 threshold 【门口】 entrance; doorway 在~等候 wait at the door 学校~ school entrance 把客人送到~ see the guest to the door 【门类】 class; kind; category 【门帘】 door curtain 【门路】 knack; way/social connections; pull 找~ solicit help from potential backers 摸到一些~ have learned the ropes 【门面】 the façade of a shop; shop front/appearance; façade 装点～ put up a façade; put on a front ～话 lip service 装点～ put up a façade; put on a front ～话 lip service 【门牌】 (house) number plate/house number 【门票】 entrance ticket; admission ticket 【门扇】 door leaf 【门市】 retail sales ～部 retail department; salesroom 【门闩】 (door) bolt; bar 【门厅】 entrance hall 【门徒】 disciple; follower 【门外汉】 layman; the uninitiated 【门牙】 front tooth; incisor 【门诊】 outpatient service ～病人 outpatient; clinic patient ～部 clinic

扪 mén touch; stroke 【扪心自问】 examine one's conscience

闷 mèn ①bored ②tightly closed; sealed 【闷闷不乐】 depressed; in low spirits 【闷气】 (be in the) sulks

焖 mèn boil in a covered pot over a slow fire; braise ～饭 cook rice over a slow fire ～牛肉 braised beef

们 men 他～ they 人～ people 同志～ comrades

MENG

蒙 mēng ①cheat; deceive; dupe 你～我 you're kidding me ②make a wild guess ～对了 make a lucky guess ③unconscious 给打～了 be knocked senseless 脑袋发～ feel one's head swimming 【蒙蒙亮】 first glimmer of dawn; daybreak 【蒙头转向】 lose one's bearings

萌 méng shoot forth 【萌芽】 sprout; germinate; shoot; bud/rudiment; seed; germ 处于～状态 in the bud

蒙 méng ①cover ～上一层灰 be covered with a layer of dust ～住眼睛 be blindfolded ②ignorant; illiterate 启～ enlighten 【蒙蔽】 hoodwink; deceive; pull the wool over sb.'s eyes ～群众 hoodwink the masses 被花言巧语所～ be fooled by honeyed words 【蒙哄】 swindle;

cheat; delude 【蒙混】 mislead (people) ～过关 get by under false pretences 【蒙昧】 uncivilized; uncultured/ignorant; benighted ～时代 age of barbarism ～无知 unenlightened; illiterate ～主义 obscurantism 【蒙蒙】 misty ～细雨 a fine drizzle 烟雾～ misty 【蒙受】 suffer; sustain ～损失 sustain a loss ～耻辱 be humiliated

盟 méng ①alliance 结～ form an alliance ②sworn (brothers) 【盟国】 allied country; ally 【盟军】 allied forces 【盟友】 ally 【盟员】 a member of an alliance 【盟约】 treaty of alliance 【盟主】 the chief of an alliance

曚 méng 【曚昽】 dim daylight

朦 méng 【朦胧】 dim moonlight/obscure; dim; hazy ～的景色 a hazy view

矇 méng 【矇眬】 half asleep; somnolent 睡眼～ eyes heavy with sleep; drowsy ～睡去 doze off

猛 měng ①fierce; violent; energetic; vigorous ～虎 a fierce tiger 用力过～ use too much strength ～击一掌 give sb. a powerful shove ②suddenly; abruptly ～地往前一跳 suddenly jump forward 【猛进】 push ahead vigorously 【猛力】 vigorously; with sudden force ～扣杀 smash with all one's strength 【猛烈】 fierce; violent ～的进攻 vigorous offensive ～的炮火 heavy shellfire 【猛禽】 bird of prey 【猛然】 suddenly; abruptly ～一拉 pull with a jerk 【猛士】 brave warrior 【猛兽】 beast of prey

蒙 měng 【蒙古】 Mongolia ～包 yurt ～人 Mongolian ～语 Mongol (language)

锰 měng manganese 【锰钢】 manganese steel 【锰铁】 ferromanganese

懵 měng muddled; ignorant

孟 mèng eldest (brother) 【孟浪】 rash; impetuous; impulsive 【孟什维克】 Menshevik

梦 mèng dream 【梦话】 words uttered in one's sleep; somniloquy/daydream; nonsense 【梦幻】 illusion; reverie 【梦见】 see in a dream; dream about 【梦境】 dreamland 【梦想】 vainly hope/fond dream 【梦魇】 nightmare

MI

咪 mī 【咪咪】①mew; miaow ②smilingly 笑～ be all smiles; be wreathed in smiles

眯 mī ①narrow (one's eyes) ～着眼笑 narrow one's eyes into a smile ～着眼瞧 squint at ② take a nap

弥 mí ①full; overflowing ②cover; fill ～缝 plug up holes; gloss over faults 【弥补】 make up; remedy; make good ～损失 make up for a loss ～赤字 make up a deficit ～缺陷 remedy a defect 【弥合】 close; bridge ～裂痕 close a rift 【弥留】 be dying ～之际 on one's deathbed 【弥漫】 fill the air; spread all over the place 烟雾～ heavy with smoke; be enveloped in mist

迷 mí ①be confused; be lost ②be fascinated by 对游泳着～ be crazy about swimming ③fan; enthusiast; fiend 棋～ a chess fiend ④confuse; perplex; fascinate ～人的景色 scenery of enchanting beauty 【迷航】 drift off course; lose one's course 【迷糊】 misted; blurred; dimmed/dazed; confused; muddled 睡～了 dazed with sleep 【迷惑】 puzzle; confuse; baffle 感到～ feel perplexed ～敌人 confuse the enemy 【迷恋】 be infatuated with; madly cling to 【迷路】 lose one's way; get lost 【迷梦】 pipe dream; fond illusion 【迷失】 lose (one's way, etc.) ～方向 lose one's bearings; get lost 【迷途】 lose one's way/wrong path 走入～ go astray ～知返 recover one's bearings and return to the fold; realize one's errors and mend one's ways 【迷惘】 be perplexed; be at a loss 【迷信】 superstition; superstitious belief; blind worship/have blind faith in

谜 mí ①riddle; conundrum 猜～ guess a riddle ②enigma; mystery; puzzle 不解之～ insoluble puzzle 【谜底】 answer to a riddle/truth

麋 mí ①gruel ②rotten ③wasteful; extravagant 【麋费】 waste (money, etc.) 【麋烂】 rotten to the core; dissipated; debauched/erosion 生活～ lead a fast life

靡 mí waste 奢～ wasteful; extravagant 【靡费】 spend extravagantly

米 mǐ ①rice ②shelled or husked seed 花生～ peanut seed ③metre 【米饭】 (cooked) rice 【米粉】 rice flour/rice-flour noodles 【米酒】 rice wine 【米粒】 grain of rice 【米色】 cream-coloured 【米制】 the metric system

眯 mí (of dust, etc.) get into one's eye 我～了眼了 something has got into my eyes

靡 mí blown away by the wind 【靡靡之音】 decadent music

泌 mí secrete 【泌尿科】 urological department 【泌尿器官】 urinary organs

觅 mí look for; hunt for; seek ～食 look for food

秘 mí ①secret ②keep sth. secret; hold sth. back ～而不宣 not let anyone into a secret 【秘本】 treasured private copy of a rare book 【秘方】 secret recipe 【秘诀】 secret (of success) 【秘密】 secret; confidential ～会议 secret meeting; closed-door session ～活动 clandestine activities ～文件 confidential document 【秘史】 secret history; inside story 【秘书】 secretary ～处 secretariat ～长 secretary-general

密 mì ①close; dense; thick ～林 dense forest ②intimate; close ～友 bosom friend ③fine; meticulous 周～ carefully considered ④secret 绝～ top secret 【密布】densely covered 【密电】cipher telegram / secretly telegraph sb. ～码 cipher code 【密度】density; thickness 人口～ population density 【密封】seal up / seal airtight ～舱 sealed cabin 【密集】concentrated; crowded together ～队形 close formation ～炮火 concentrated fire 【密件】a confidential paper; classified material 【密码】secret code ～电报 cipher telegram ～机 cipher machine ～员 cryptographer 【密谋】conspire; plot; scheme 【密切】close; intimate/carefully; intently ～配合 act in close coordination ～相关 be closely related ～联系 maintain close ties with ～注视 watch closely 【密商】hold private counsel 【密使】secret emissary 【密室】a room used for secret purposes 策划于～ plot behind closed doors 【密谈】private talk; talk behind closed doors 【密探】secret agent; spy 【密纹唱片】long-playing record; microgroove record 【密约】secret treaty 【密植】close planting

蜜 mì ①honey ②honeyed; sweet 【蜜蜂】honeybee; bee 【蜜柑】mandarin orange 【蜜饯】candied fruit; preserved fruit 【蜜橘】tangerine 【蜜源】nectar source 【蜜月】honeymoon 【蜜枣】candied date or jujube 【蜜渍】candied

MIAN

眠 mián ①sleep 不～之夜 a sleepless night; a white night ②dormancy 冬～ hibernate

绵 mián ①silk floss ②continuous ③soft 【绵亘】(of mountains, etc.) stretch in a long and unbroken chain 【绵绵】continuous; unbroken 【绵软】soft / weak 【绵延】be continuous 【绵羊】sheep 【绵纸】tissue paper

棉 mián ①cotton ②cotton-padded; quilted ~衣 cotton-padded clothes 【棉袄】 quilted jacket 【棉被】 a quilt with cotton wadding 【棉布】 cotton (cloth) 【棉纺】 cotton spinning ~厂 cotton mill 【棉猴儿】 hooded cotton-padded coat; parka; anorak 【棉花】 cotton 【棉裤】 cotton-padded trousers 【棉毛裤】 cotton (interlock) trousers 【棉毛衫】 cotton (interlock) jersey 【棉纱】 cotton yarn 【棉毯】 cotton blanket 【棉桃】 cotton boll 【棉田】 cotton field 【棉线】 cotton (thread) 【棉絮】 cotton fibre/a cotton wadding (for a quilt) 【棉织品】 cotton goods 【棉籽】 cottonseed

免 mián ①excuse sb. from sth.; exempt; dispense with ~试 be excused from an examination ②remove from office; dismiss; relieve 任~事项 appointments and removals ③avoid; avert ~于受灾 avert a disaster 【免不了】 be unavoidable; be bound to be 【免除】 prevent; avoid/remit; excuse; exempt ~债务 remit a debt ~一项任务 relieve sb. of a task 【免得】 so as not to ~引起误会 to avoid any misunderstanding 【免费】 free of charge ~医疗 free medical care ~入场 be admitted gratis 【免票】 free pass; free ticket / free of charge 【免税】 exempt from taxation/tax-free ~货物 duty-free goods 【免验】 exempt from customs examination ~放行 pass without examination 【免职】 relieve sb. of his post

勉 mián ①exert oneself; strive ~力为之 do one's best ②encourage; urge; exhort 自~ spur oneself on ③ strive (to do what is beyond one's power) 【勉励】 encourage; urge 【勉强】 manage with an effort/reluctantly; grudgingly/force sb. to do sth./inadequate; strained/barely enough ~同意 reluctantly agree ~笑笑 force a smile 别~他 don't force him 这个理由很~ the reason is rather unconvincing ~维持生活 eke out a bare living

面 miàn ①face ～无惧色 not look at all afraid ②face (a certain direction) ～向南 face south ③surface; top 桌～ tabletop 路～ road surface ④personally; directly ～告 tell sb. personally ⑤cover; outside 书～ the cover of a book 被～the top covering of a quilt ⑥side; aspect 四～包围 surround on all sides 问题的一～ one aspect of the question ⑦extent; range; scale; scope 知识～ range of knowledge ⑧flour 白～ wheat flour ⑨powder 胡椒～ ground pepper ⑩noodles 【面包】bread ～房 bakery ～干 rusk 【面不改色】not change colour 【面茶】seasoned millet mush 【面对】face; confront ～现实 face reality 【面对面】facing each other ～地坐着 sit face-to-face ～的斗争 a face-to-face struggle 【面粉】(wheat) flour ～厂 flour mill 【面红耳赤】be flushed 争得～ argue until everyone is red in the face 【面积】area 【面颊】cheek 【面筋】gluten 【面具】mask 【面孔】face 板起～ put on a stern expression 【面临】be faced with; be confronted with 【面貌】face; features / appearance (of things); look; aspect 精神～ mental outlook ～一新 take on a new look 【面目】face; features; visage / appearance (of things); look; aspect ～可憎 repulsive in appearance ～全非 be changed beyond recognition ～一新 take on an entirely new look; assume a new aspect 还其本来～ reveal sth. in its true colours 政治～不清 of dubious political background 【面前】in (the) face of; in front of; before 【面容】facial features; face 【面色】complexion / facial expression ～苍白 look pale ～红润 have rosy cheeks ～忧郁 look worried 【面纱】veil 【面生】look unfamiliar 【面食】cooked wheaten food 【面熟】look familiar 【面谈】take up a matter with sb. personally 【面条】noodles 【面团】dough 【面向】turn one's face to; face/be geared to

the needs of; cater to 【面罩】 face guard 【面值】 par value;
face value/denomination 【面子】 outer part; outside/repu-
tation; prestige, face 丢～ lose face 爱～ be concerned
about face-saving 有～ enjoy due respect 给～ show due
respect for sb.'s feelings

MIAO

苗 miáo ①young plant; seedling 麦～ wheat seedling
②the young of some animals 鱼～ fry 【苗床】 seed-
bed 【苗圃】 nursery (of young plants) 【苗条】 slender;
slim 【苗头】 symptom of a trend

描 miáo ①trace; copy (designs, etc.) ②touch up; re-
摹 touch 【描画】 draw; paint 【描绘】 depict; portray 【描
描】 delineate 【描述】 describe 【描图】 tracing ～员 tracer

瞄 miáo concentrate one's gaze on 【瞄准】 take aim;
train on; lay; sight ～心 aim at the bull's-eye

秒 miǎo second 【秒表】 stopwatch 【秒针】 second hand

渺 miǎo ①vast ②vague ～若烟云 as vague as mist
③tiny; insignificant 【渺茫】 distant and indistinct;
vague/uncertain 前途～ have an uncertain future 希
望～ have slim hopes 【渺小】 tiny; negligible; paltry

藐 miǎo ①small; petty ②slight 【藐视】 despise; look
down upon 【藐小】 tiny; insignificant

妙 miào ①wonderful; excellent; fine ～不可言 too
wonderful for words ②ingenious; clever; subtle 回
答得～ make a clever answer 【妙计】 brilliant scheme
【妙诀】 knack 【妙品】 fine quality goods / fine work of art
【妙用】 magical effect 【妙语】 witty remark; witticism

庙 miào ①temple; shrine ②temple fair 【庙会】 temple
fair 赶～ go to the fair

MIE

灭 miè ①go out 火～了 the fire has gone out 灯～了 the lights went out ②put off; turn off —火 extinguish a fire —灯 turn off the lights ③submerge ④destroy; exterminate; wipe out ～蝇 kill flies 【灭顶】be drowned; be swamped 【灭迹】destroy the evidence 【灭口】do away with a witness or accomplice 【灭亡】be destroyed; become extinct; die out 自取～ court destruction

蔑 miè ①slight; disdain ②smear 诬～ slander; vilify 【蔑视】despise; show contempt for; scorn

篾 miè thin bamboo strip 【篾席】a mat made of thin bamboo strips

MIN

民 mín ①the people ②a person of a certain occupation 农～ peasant ③folk ～歌 folk song ④civilian ～船 a boat for civilian use 【民办】run by the local people ～小学 a primary school run by the local people 【民变】mass uprising 【民兵】militia/militiaman 【民不聊生】the people have no means of livelihood 【民法】civil law 【民房】a house owned by a citizen 【民愤】popular indignation 【民工】a labourer working on a public project 【民国】the Republic of China (1912-1949) 【民航】civil aviation ～机 civil aircraft 【民间】among the people; popular; folk/nongovernmental ～传说 folk legend; folklore ～故事 folktale ～来往 people-to-people exchange ～文学 folk literature ～舞蹈 folk dance ～艺术 folk art ～音乐 folk music 【民警】people's police 【民力】financial resources of the people 【民气】popular morale 【民情】condition of the people/public feeling 【民权】

civil rights 【民生】 the people's livelihood 【民事】 civil ~案件 civil case ~审判庭 civil court ~诉讼 civil lawsuit 【民心】 popular feelings ~所向 (what conforms to) the common aspiration of the people 深得~ enjoy the ardent support of the people 【民谣】 folk rhyme 【民意】 popular will ~测验 (public opinion) poll 【民用】 civil 【民政】 civil administration ~机关 civil administration organ 【民众】 the masses of the people; the common people ~团体 people's organization 【民主】 democracy/democratic ~作风 democratic work-style ~集中制 democratic centralism 【民族】 nation; nationality/national

泯 mǐn vanish; die out; disappear 【泯没】 sink into oblivion; become lost

抿 mǐn ①smooth (hair, etc. with a wet brush) ②close lightly; furl ~着嘴笑 smile with closed lips ③sip

悯 mǐn ①commiserate; pity ②sorrow

敏 mǐn quick; agile 【敏感】 sensitive; susceptible 【敏捷】 nimble; agile 动作~ be quick in movement 【敏锐】 sharp; acute; keen 目光~ have sharp eyes

MING

名 míng ①name 地~ place name ②given name ③fame; reputation; renown ~闻中外 well known both at home and abroad ④famous; celebrated ~句 a well-known phrase ⑤express; describe 不可~~状 indescribable; nondescript 【名不副实】 be unworthy of the name or title 【名不虚传】 deserve the reputation one enjoys 【名册】 register; roll 学生~ students' register 工作人员~ personnel roll 【名产】 famous product 【名垂青史】 go down in history 【名词】 noun; substantive/term; phrase 【名次】 position in a name list; place in a competition 【名存实亡】 exist in name only 【名单】 name list 【名额】 quota of people 招生～ the number of students to be enrolled; planned enrolment figure 由于～有限 since the number of people allowed is limited 【名副其实】 be worthy of the name 【名贵】 famous and precious; rare ～药材 rare medicinal herbs 【名家】 famous expert; master 【名将】 famous general 足球～ a football hero 【名利】 fame and wealth ～思想 desire for personal fame and gain 【名流】 celebrities 【名目】 names of things; items ～繁多 names of every description 【名牌】 famous brand 【名片】 visiting card 留下～ leave one's card 【名气】 reputation; fame; name 【名人】 famous person 【名声】 reputation; repute; renown 有好～ enjoy a good reputation 【名胜】 scenic spot ～古迹 places of historic interest and scenic beauty 【名堂】 variety; item / result; achievement / what lies behind sth.; reason 【名望】 fame and prestige 【名言】 famous remark 【名义】 name/nominal; titular; in name 【名誉】 fame; reputation/honorary 【名著】 famous work

明 míng ①bright; brilliant; light ～月 a bright moon ②clear; distinct 情况不～ the situation is not clear 去向不～ whereabouts unknown ③open; overt; explicit 对你～说吧 be frank with you ④sharp-eyed; clear-sighted 眼～手快 quick of eye and deft of hand ⑤aboveboard; honest ⑥sight 复～ regain one's sight ⑦understand; know 不～真相 not know the facts ⑧immediately following in time ～年 next year ～晚 tomorrow evening 【明白】 clear; plain / frank; explicit / sensible; reasonable / realize 讲得很～ speak clearly 问题很～ the matter is quite clear ～人 a sensible person ～事理 know what's what; have good sense 你～我的意思吗 do you get me 不～你的

意思 I don't see what you mean 【明辨是非】make a clear distinction between right and wrong 【明澈】bright and limpid; transparent 【明处】in the open; in public 【明净】 bright and clean 【明镜】bright mirror 【明快】lucid and lively (style, etc.)/straightforward ～的节奏 sprightly rhythm 【明朗】bright and clear/obvious/bright and cheerful ～的天空 a clear sky ～的性格 an open and forthright character 局势逐渐～ the situation is becoming clear 态度～ adopt an unequivocal attitude 【明亮】light; bright; well-lit 灯光～ be brightly lit ～的眼睛 bright eyes 【明了】 understand; be clear about/clear; plain 简单～ simple and clear 【明令】explicit order; formal decree ～取缔 proscribe by formal decree ～嘉奖 mention in a citation 【明码】 plain code (telegram) / with the price clearly marked 【明确】clear; explicit / make clear ～的目标 a clear aim ～的立场 a clear-cut stand ～的答复 a definite answer ～的语言 unequivocal terms ～学习目的 be clear about the purpose of one's study 【明天】tomorrow / the near future 【明文】(of laws, regulations, etc.) proclaimed in writing ～规定 stipulate in explicit terms 【明晰】distinct; clear 【明虾】prawn 【明显】obvious; evident ～的优势 clear superiority ～的改进 distinct improvement ～的成效 tangible result 【明信片】postcard 【明星】 star 【明喻】simile 【明哲保身】be worldly wise and play safe 【明争暗斗】both open strife and veiled struggle 【明证】 clear proof 【明知】know perfectly well; be fully aware ～故犯 knowingly violate (discipline, etc.); deliberately break (a rule, etc.); do sth. one knows is wrong ～故问 ask while knowing the answer 【明智】sagacious; wise ～的态度 a sensible attitude 【明珠】bright pearl 【明子】 pine torch

鸣 míng ① the cry of birds, animals or insects 鸡～ the crow of a cock ② ring; sound ～笛 blow a whistle ～枪示警 fire a warning shot ③ express; voice; air ～不平 cry out against an injustice 【鸣禽】songbird; singing bird 【鸣冤叫屈】voice grievances

茗 míng ①tender tea leaves ②tea 品～ sip tea (to judge its quality); sample tea

冥 míng ①dark; obscure 幽～ dark hell ②deep; profound ～思 be deep in thought ③dull; stupid ～顽 thickheaded ④ underworld ～府 the nether world 【冥思苦想】cudgel one's brains 【冥王星】Pluto 【冥想】deep thought; meditation

铭 míng ①inscription 座右～ motto ②engrave (on one's mind) 【铭感】be deeply grateful 【铭记】bear firmly in mind; always remember 【铭文】epigraph

瞑 míng 【瞑目】close one's eyes in death—die content 死不～ die discontent

命 míng ①life 逃～ run for one's life ～在旦夕 be dying ②lot; fate; destiny ～苦 cruel fate ③order; command 待～ await orders ④assign (a name, title, etc.) 【命案】 homicide case 【命定】 determined by fate; predestined 【命根子】 one's very life; lifeblood 【命令】 order; command ～句 imperative sentence ～主义 commandism 【命脉】 lifeblood; lifeline 【命名】 name (sb. or sth.) ～大会 naming ceremony 【命题】 assign a topic; set a question/proposition 【命中】 hit the mark

MIU

谬 miù wrong; false; erroneous; mistaken ～传 a false report 【谬论】 fallacy; absurd theory; falsehood 【谬误】 error; mistake

4

MO

摸 mō ①feel; stroke; touch ～～刀口 feel the edge of a knife ～孩子的头 stroke the child's head ②feel for; grope for; fumble ～出一张五元的钞票 fish out a five-yuan note ③try to find out; feel out ～敌情 find out about the enemy's situation ～不着头脑 be unable to make head or tail of sth. 【摸底】 know the real situation / sound sb. out; feel sb. out 【摸索】 grope; feel about; fumble / try to find out (laws, secret, etc.)

摹 mó copy; trace 【摹本】 facsimile 【摹拟】 imitate; simulate 【摹写】 copy; imitate / describe; depict

模 mó ①pattern; standard 楷～ paragon ②imitate ③model 【模本】 calligraphy or painting model 【模范】 model; fine example 劳动～ model worker 起～作用 play an exemplary role ～事迹 exemplary deeds ～地执行 carry out sth. in an exemplary way 【模仿】 imitate; copy; model oneself on 【模糊】 blurred; indistinct; dim/obscure; confuse; mix up ～的景物 a hazy scene ～的印象 a vague idea of sth. ～的认识 confused ideas 泪水～了眼睛 tears blurred one's eyes 【模棱两可】 ambiguous (formulation, etc.); equivocal (attitude, etc.) 【模拟】 imitate; simulate ～人像 effigy 【模特儿】 model 【模型】 model / mould

膜 mó ①membrane 细胞～ cell membrane ②film; thin coating 【膜拜】 prostrate oneself; worship

摩 mó ①rub; scrape; touch ②mull over; study 【摩擦】 rub / friction / clash (between two parties) 制造～ create friction 发生～ have a brush with sb. ～力 frictional force ～音 fricative 【摩登】 modern; fashionable 【摩挲】 stroke; caress 【摩天】 skyscraping ～楼 skyscraper 【摩托】 motor ～车 motorcycle

磨 mó ①rub; wear ～出泡来 be blistered from the rubbing ②grind; polish ～剪子 sharpen scissors ～墨 rub an ink stick against an inkstone ③dawdle; waste time 别～时间 stop dawdling 【磨蹭】move slowly; dawdle 【磨床】grinder 【磨刀石】grindstone 【磨光】polish ～玻璃 polished glass ～机 polishing machine 【磨练】temper oneself; steel oneself 【磨灭】wear away; efface; obliterate 不可～的印象 an indelible impression 【磨难】hardship; suffering 【磨砂玻璃】ground glass

蘑 mó 【蘑菇】mushroom/worry; pester; keep on at ～云 mushroom cloud

魔 mó ①evil spirit; demon; devil; monster 着了～似的 like one possessed ②magic; mystic 【魔窟】den of monsters 【魔力】magic power; magic; charm 【魔术】magic; conjuring; sleight of hand ～演员 magician; conjurer 【魔王】Prince of the Devils / tyrant; despot 【魔掌】devil's clutches; evil hands 【魔爪】devil's talons; claws

抹 mǒ ①put on; apply; smear; plaster ～点果酱 spread some jam ～药膏 apply ointment ～浆糊 smear sth. with paste ②wipe ～眼泪 be weeping ～把脸 wipe one's face ③strike out; erase ～去这一行 cross out this line ～掉录音 erase the recording (from a tape) 【抹黑】blacken sb.'s name; throw mud at; bring shame on 【抹杀】blot out; obliterate 一笔～ write off at one stroke ～事实 deny the fact 【抹子】trowel

末 mò ①tip; end ②nonessentials; minor details 本～倒置 put the nonessentials before the essentials ③end; last stage 周～ weekend ～一天 the last day ④powder; dust 茶叶～ tea dust 锯～ sawdust 肉～ minced meat 煤～ coal dust 【末班车】last bus 【末代】the last reign of a dynasty 【末了】last; finally; in the end 【末路】dead end; impasse 【末期】 last phase; final phase

没 mò ①sink; submerge 潜艇～入水中 the submarine submerged ②rise beyond 洪水～过大坝 the flood overflowed the dam ③hide 出～ now appear, now disappear ④take possession of ⑤till the end (of one's life) 【没落】 decline; wane 【没收】 confiscate; expropriate

沫 mò foam; froth 啤酒～ froth on beer 肥皂～ soap-suds 口吐白～ foam at the mouth

茉 mò 【茉莉】 jasmine ～花茶 jasmine tea

抹 mò daub; plaster (a wall, etc.) 【抹不开】 feel embar-rassed 【抹灰】 plastering ～工 plasterer

陌 mò ①a path between fields ②road 【陌生】 strange; unfamiliar ～人 stranger

脉 mò 【脉脉】 affectionately; lovingly; amorously 温情～ full of tender affection; sentimental

莫 mò ①no one; nothing; none ②no; not ～知所措 not know what to do ③don't ～性急 don't be im-patient 【莫不】 there's no one who doesn't or isn't ～感动 there was no one who was unmoved 【莫测高深】 unfath-omable; enigmatic 【莫大】 greatest; utmost ～的幸福 the greatest happiness ～的侮辱 a gross insult 【莫非】 can it be that; is it possible that 【莫过于】 nothing is more ... than 【莫名其妙】 be unable to make head or tail of sth.; be baffled/without rhyme or reason; inexplicable 【莫如】 would be better; might as well 【莫须有】 unwarranted; groundless ～的罪名 a fabricated charge

漠 mò ①desert ②indifferent; unconcerned 【漠漠】 misty; foggy / vast and lonely 【漠然】 indifferently; apa-thetically ～置之 look on with unconcern 【漠视】 treat with indifference; ignore; overlook

寞 mò lonely; deserted

蓦 mò suddenly 【蓦地】unexpectedly; all of a sudden 我～想起一个主意 an idea rushed into my mind

墨 mò ①ink stick ②ink 油～ printing ink ③handwriting or painting 遗～ writing or painting left by the deceased ④black; pitch-dark 【墨斗鱼】inkfish; cuttlefish 【墨盒】ink box 【墨迹】ink marks/sb.'s writing or painting ～未干 before the ink is dry 【墨晶】smoky quartz 【墨镜】sunglasses 【墨绿】blackish green 【墨守成规】stick to conventions 【墨水】ink ～池 inkwell ～瓶 ink bottle ～台 inkstand 【墨汁】prepared Chinese ink

默 mò ①silent; tacit ～不作声 keep silent ②write from memory ～生字 write the new words from memory 【默哀】stand in silent tribute 【默祷】say a silent prayer 【默读】read silently 【默默】quietly; silently ～无言 without saying a word ～无闻 unknown to the public 【默契】tacit agreement 【默然】silent; speechless ～无语 fall silent 【默认】tacitly approve; acquiesce in

磨 mò ①mill 电～ electric mill ②grind ～麦子 grind wheat ～面 mill flour ③turn (the cart, etc.) round 【磨面机】flour-milling machine 【磨盘】millstones

MOU

牟 móu try to gain; seek (profit) 【牟取】try to gain; seek; obtain ～暴利 seek exorbitant profits

谋 móu ①stratagem; plan; scheme 有勇无～ brave but not astute ②seek; plot 为大多数人～利益 work for the interests of the vast majority ～刺 plot to assassinate ③consult 【谋财害命】murder sb. for his money 【谋反】conspire against the state; plot a rebellion 【谋害】plot to mur-

der / plot a frame-up against 【谋划】plan; scheme 【谋略】
astuteness and resourcefulness; strategy 【谋求】seek; strive
for; be in quest of ～解决办法 try to find a solution
【谋杀】murder 【谋生】seek a livelihood; make a living
【谋士】adviser 【谋事】plan matters / look for a job

眸 móu pupil (of the eye); eye 凝～ fix one's eyes on

某 mǒu certain; some ～日 at a certain date ～人 a
certain person ～部 a certain unit 在～种程度上 to
some extent 在～种意义上 in a sense 【某某】so-and-so

MU

模 mú mould; matrix; pattern; die 【模板】formwork
【模压】mould pressing ～机 moulding press 【模样】
appearance; look / about; around 半小时～ about half an
hour

母 mǔ ①mother ②one's female elders ③female (animal)
～鸡 hen ～狗 bitch ～马 mare 【母爱】mother love
【母畜】dam 【母老虎】tigress/shrew 【母系】maternal side/
matriarchal ～亲属 maternal relatives ～社会 matriarchal society 【母校】one's old school; Alma Mater 【母性】
maternal instinct 【母音】vowel

亩 mǔ *mu*, a unit of area (= 0.0667 hectares) ～产量
per *mu* yield

牡 mǔ male ～牛 bull 【牡丹】tree peony; peony 【牡
蛎】oyster

拇 mǔ 【拇指】thumb/big toe

木 mù ①tree 伐～ fell trees ②timber; wood ～片 wood
chip 松～ pinewood ③made of wood; wooden ～
箱 wooden box ④coffin 行将就～ have one foot in the

grave ⑤numb; wooden ～头～脑 wooden-headed; dull-witted 【木板】plank; board ～床 plank bed 【木版】block ～画 woodcut; wood engraving ～印刷 block printing 【木本植物】woody plant 【木材】wood; timber; lumber ～厂 timber mill 【木柴】firewood 【木耳】an edible fungus 【木筏】raft 【木工】woodwork 【木屐】clogs 【木匠】carpenter 【木结构】timber structure 【木刻】woodcut; wood engraving ～术 xylography 【木料】timber; lumber 【木马】vaulting horse; pommelled horse/rocking horse ～计 Trojan horse 【木棉】silk cotton; kapok 【木偶】wooden image; carved figure/puppet; marionette ～剧 puppet show; puppet play ～片 puppet film 【木排】raft 【木器】wooden furniture 【木琴】xylophone 【木然】stupefied 【木梳】wooden comb 【木炭】charcoal ～画 charcoal drawing 【木头】wood; log; timber ～人儿 woodenhead; blockhead 【木屋】log cabin 【木锨】wooden winnowing spade 【木星】Jupiter

【目】 mù ①eye ②look; regard ③item 细～ detailed items ④order 亚～ suborder ⑤list; catalogue 书～ book list 【目标】objective; target / goal; aim 命中～ hit the mark 军事～ military objective 共产主义的伟大～ the great goal of communism 【目不转睛】look with fixed eyes 【目次】contents 【目瞪口呆】gaping; stupefied 吓得～ be struck dumb with fear 【目的】aim; goal; end ～明确 have a definite purpose ～地 destination 【目光】sight; vision; view/gaze 【目击】see with one's own eyes; witness ～者 witness 【目力】eyesight; vision 【目录】catalogue; list / contents ～学 bibliography 【目前】at present; at the moment ～形势 the current situation 到～为止 up till now; so far 【目送】watch sb. go; gaze after 【目无法纪】disregard law and discipline 【目眩】dizzy 【目中无人】consider everyone beneath one's notice

沐 mù wash one's hair 【沐浴】 take a bath/bathe; immerse

牧 mù herd; tend ～马 herd horses ～羊 tend sheep 【牧草】 herbage; forage grass 【牧场】 grazing land; pasture 【牧歌】 pastoral (song) 【牧区】 herdsman pastoral area 【牧师】 pastor; minister; clergyman 【牧童】 shepherd boy 【牧畜】 livestock breeding 【牧业】 stock raising 【牧主】 herd owner

募 mù raise; collect; enlist; recruit ～款 raise money ～兵 recruit soldiers 【募集】 collect; raise (a fund) 【募捐】 solicit contributions; collect donations

墓 mù grave; tomb; mausoleum 【墓碑】 tombstone 【墓地】 cemetery 【墓穴】 coffin pit 【墓志铭】 epitaph

幕 mù ①curtain; screen ～启 the curtain rises ～落 the curtain falls 夜～ the veil of night ②act 第一～ the first act; Act 1 【幕布】 (theatre) curtain; (cinema) screen 【幕后】 behind the scenes; backstage 退居～ retire backstage ～操纵 pull strings behind the scenes ～活动 backstage manoeuvring ～交易 behind-the-scenes deal ～人物 wirepuller 【幕间休息】 interval 【幕僚】 aides and staff

睦 mù peaceful; harmonious 【睦邻】 good-neighbourliness ～政策 good-neighbour policy

慕 mù admire; yearn for 仰～ look up to with admiration ～名 out of admiration for a famous person

暮 mù ①dusk; evening; sunset ②towards the end; late ～春 late spring 【暮霭】 evening mist 【暮年】 declining years; old age 【暮气】 lethargy; apathy ～沉沉 lethargic; lifeless 【暮色】 dusk; twilight; gloaming

穆 mù solemn; reverent 【穆斯林】 Moslem; Muslim

N

NA

拿 ná ①hold; take ～去 take it away ～来 bring it here ～在手里 hold in one's hand ②seize; capture ～下碉堡 capture the blockhouse ③be able to do; be sure of ～不准 feel uncertain 你～得稳吗 are you sure of it 【拿不出手】 not be presentable 【拿获】 apprehend (a criminal) 【拿架子】 put on airs 【拿乔】 strike a pose to impress people 【拿手】 adept; expert; good at ～好戏 a game or trick one is good at 【拿主意】 make a decision; make up one's mind 我的主意拿定了 my mind is made up

哪 nǎ which; what 【哪个】 which/who 你们是一班的 which class are you in 【哪里】 where/wherever 你到～去 where are you going 【哪怕】 even; even if; even though 【哪些】 which; who; what ～是你的 which ones are yours ～人出席这次会议 who will attend the meeting 你们讨论了～问题 what problems did you discuss

那 nà ①that ～是谁 who is that ②then ～我们就不再等了 in that case, we won't wait any longer 【那个】 that ～孩子 that child 【那会儿】 at that time; then 【那里】 that place; there 【那么】 like that; in that way/then; in that case 【那时】 at that time; then; in those days 【那些】 those 【那样】 of that kind; like that; such

呐 nà 【呐喊】 shout loudly; cry out ～助威 shout encouragement; cheer

纳 nà ①receive; admit 闭门不～ refuse to admit ② accept ～降 accept the enemy's surrender ③enjoy ④ pay; offer ⑤sew close stitches (over a patch, etc.) ～鞋底子 stitch soles (of cloth shoes) 【纳贿】 take bribes/offer bribes 【纳凉】 enjoy the cool (in the open air) 【纳闷】 feel puzzled; wonder 【纳入】 bring into ～正轨 put sth. on the right course ～国家计划 bring sth. into line with the state plan 【纳税】 pay taxes ～人 taxpayer

捺 nà press down; restrain ～着性子 control one's temper 勉强～住心头的怒火 barely manage to restrain one's anger

NAI

乃 nǎi ①be ②so; therefore ③only then ④you; your 【乃至】 and even

奶 nǎi ①breasts ②milk ③suckle; breast-feed ～孩子 suckle a baby 【奶茶】 tea with milk 【奶粉】 milk powder 【奶酪】 cheese 【奶妈】 wet nurse 【奶名】 infant name 【奶奶】 grandma 【奶牛】 milk cow 【奶皮】 skin on boiled milk 【奶品】 milk products 【奶瓶】 nursing bottle 【奶糖】 toffee 【奶头】 nipple 【奶羊】 milch goat 【奶油】 cream 【奶罩】 bra 【奶嘴】 nipple (of a feeding bottle)

奈 nài 【奈何】 how; to no avail 徒唤～ utter bootless cries 无可～ be utterly helpless

耐 nài be able to bear or endure ～劳 stand hard work ～穿 be endurable 【耐寒】 cold-resistant; resistant to low temperature 【耐火】 fire-resistant; refractory ～材料 fireproof material ～砖 refractory brick; firebrick 【耐磨】 wear-resisting; wearproof 【耐热】 heat-resisting; heatproof 【耐人寻味】 afford food for thought 【耐心】 patient 【耐性】 patience; endurance 【耐用】 durable ～物品 durable goods; durables

NAN

囡 nān child 【囡囡】 little darling

男 nán ①man; male ～病房 men's ward ～护士 male nurse ～主人公 hero ～生 boy student; schoolboy ～用人 manservant ②son; boy 长～ one's eldest son 【男厕所】 men's lavatory 【男低音】 bass 【男方】 the bridegroom's or husband's side 【男高音】 tenor 【男孩】 boy 【男女】 men and women ～青年 young men and women ～平等 equality of the sexes 【男朋友】 boyfriend 【男人】 man / menfolk 【男声】 male voice ～合唱 male chorus 【男性】 the male sex/man 【男中音】 baritone 【男装】 men's clothing

南 nán south ～风 south wind 城～ south of the city ～屋 a room with a northern exposure 【南北】 north and south / from north to south 【南部】 southern part; south 【南方】 south/the southern part of the country 住在～ live in the South ～风味 southern style ～话 southern dialect ～人 a southerner 【南瓜】 pumpkin; cushaw 【南极】 the South Pole

难 nán ①difficult; hard; troublesome 这道题～解 this problem is hard to solve 路～走 the going is hard ②put sb. into a difficult position 把我～住了 put me on the spot ③hardly possible ～说 it's hard to say ～忘 unforgettable ④bad; unpleasant ～吃 taste bad ～听 unpleasant to the ear 【难保】 one cannot say for sure 【难产】 difficult labour / be difficult of fulfilment; be slow in coming 【难倒】 daunt; baffle 【难道】 can; can't; how can ～你忘了自己的诺言吗 can you have forgotten your promise 【难得】 hard to come by; rare / seldom; rarely ～的机会 a rare chance 这很～ it is hard to come by 【难

度】degree of difficulty ～很大 be extremely difficult【难怪】no wonder / understandable; pardonable【难关】difficulty; crisis 渡过～ tide over a crisis 攻克技术～ break down a technical barrier; resolve key technical problems【难过】have a hard time/feel sorry; be grieved【难解难分】be inextricably involved (in a dispute); be locked together (in a struggle)【难堪】unbearable / embarrassed 感到～ feel very much embarrassed 处于～的境地 be in an extremely awkward situation【难看】ugly; unsightly / shameful【难免】hard to avoid; can't help 犯错误是～的 mistakes are hard to avoid【难能可贵】difficult of attainment, hence worthy of esteem; estimable; commendable【难色】appear to be embarrassed 面有～ show signs of reluctance or embarrassment【难舍难分】loath to part from each other【难说】it's hard to say; no one can tell【难题】difficult problem; poser【难听】unpleasant to hear; not very pleasing to the ear/offensive; coarse【难忘】unforgettable; memorable【难为情】ashamed; shy / embarrassing; disconcerting【难为】embarrass; press / be a tough job to【难闻】smell unpleasant; smell bad【难以】difficult to ～捉摸 difficult to pin down; elusive ～想象 unimaginable ～形容 indescribable

喃 nán【喃喃】mutter; murmur ～自语 mutter to oneself

难 nàn ①calamity; disaster; adversity 逃～ flee from danger ②take to task 非～ blame; reproach【难民】refugee ～营 refugee camp【难友】fellow sufferer

NANG

囊 náng bag; pocket 胶～ capsule【囊空如洗】with empty pockets【囊括】include; embrace【囊肿】cyst

NAO

挠 náo ①scratch ~痒痒 scratch an itch ②hinder 阻~ obstruct ③yield; flinch 不屈不~ unyielding 【挠头】 scratch one's head/difficult to tackle

恼 nǎo ①angry; annoyed ②unhappy; worried 【恼恨】 resent; hate 【恼火】 irritated; vexed 感到~ be annoyed at 【恼怒】 angry; indignant; furious 【恼人】 irritating; annoying 【恼羞成怒】 be shamed into anger; fly into a rage from shame

脑 nǎo brain 用~过度 overtax one's brain 【脑充血】 encephalemia 【脑袋】 head 【脑海】 brain; mind 【脑筋】 brains; mind; head 动~ use one's brain 【脑壳】 skull 【脑力劳动】 mental work ~者 mental worker 【脑膜】 meninx 【脑神经】 cranial nerve 【脑髓】 brains 【脑溢血】 cerebral haemorrhage

闹 nào ①noisy 这屋里太~ this room is too noisy ② make a noise; stir up trouble 又哭又~ make a tearful scene ~名誉地位 be out for fame and position ③give vent (to one's anger, resentment, etc.) ~脾气 lose one's temper ④suffer from; be troubled by ~肚子 have diarrhoea ⑤go in for; do; make ~生产 go in for production 【闹别扭】 be difficult with sb. 【闹病】 fall ill 【闹翻】 fall out with sb. 【闹风潮】 carry on agitation; stage strikes, demonstrations, etc. 【闹革命】 make revolution 【闹鬼】 be haunted / play tricks 【闹哄哄】 clamorous; noisy 【闹剧】 farce 【闹乱子】 cause trouble 【闹情绪】 be in low spirits 【闹市】 busy streets; downtown area 【闹事】 make trouble 【闹意见】 be on bad terms 【闹意气】 feel resentful (because something is not to one's liking); sulk 【闹着玩】 joke 【闹钟】 alarm clock

NEI

哪 něi which; what

馁 něi ①hungry; famished ②disheartened; dispirited 气～ lose heart; be discouraged

内 nèi ①inner; within; inside 三天之～ within three days 党～ inner-Party ②one's wife or her relatives ～弟 wife's younger brother; brother-in-law 【内部】 inside; internal; interior ～联系 internal relations ～规律性 inherent laws ～消息 inside stuff ～传阅 For Inside Circulation Only ～刊物 restricted publication 【内地】 inland; interior; hinterland ～城市 inland city 【内分泌】 endocrine; internal secretion 【内服】 to be taken orally 【内阁】 cabinet ～大臣 cabinet minister 【内海】 inland sea/continental sea 【内行】 expert; adept 充～ pose as an expert 【内河】 inland river ～运输 inland water transport 【内讧】 internal strife 【内奸】 hidden traitor 【内景】 indoor scene 【内径】 inside diameter 【内疚】 compunction; guilty conscience 【内科】 (department of) internal medicine ～病房 medical ward ～医生 physician 【内涝】 waterlogging 【内陆】 inland; interior ～国 landlocked country ～河 continental river 【内乱】 civil strife; internal disorder 【内幕】 inside story 【内亲】 a relative on one's wife's side; in-law 【内勤】 office staff/internal or office work 【内情】 inside story 了解～ be an insider 【内燃机】 internal-combustion engine 【内燃机车】 diesel locomotive 【内容】 content; substance ～提要 synopsis; résumé 【内伤】 internal injury 【内胎】 the inner tube of a tyre 【内外】 inside and outside; domestic and foreign / about ～夹攻 attack from both within and without ～交困 beset with difficulties both at home and abroad 【内务】 internal affairs/ daily routine tasks to keep the barracks, etc. clean and tidy ～条令 interior service regulations 【内线】 planted agent/interior lines/inside (telephone) connections ～自动电话机 interphone 【内详】 name and address of sender enclosed 【内向】 introversion 【内销】 sold inside the country; for the domestic market 【内心】 heart; innermost being ～深处 in one's heart of hearts ～世界 inner world 【内因】 internal cause 【内忧外患】 domestic trouble and foreign invasion 【内在】 inherent; intrinsic ～规律 inherent law ～联系 inner link ～矛盾 inner contradictions ～因素 internal factor 【内脏】 internal organs 【内债】 internal debt 【内战】 civil war 【内政】 internal affairs

NEN

嫩 nèn ①tender; delicate ～叶 tender leaves 肉炒得～ the stir-fried meat is tender ②light ～色 light colour ～绿 light green; soft green ③inexperienced; unskilled

NENG

能 néng ①ability; capability; skill 无～ incompetent ②energy 原子～ atomic energy ③able; capable ～人 able person ④can; be able to 【能动】 active; dynamic ～性 dynamic role; activity 【能干】 competent 【能手】 dab; expert; a good hand 技术革新～ a crackajack at technical innovation 【能说会道】 have the gift of the gab 【能源】 energy (resources) ～危机 energy crisis

NI

尼 ní Buddhist nun 【尼庵】 Buddhist nunnery 【尼龙】 nylon ～丝 nylon yarn ～袜 nylon socks

泥 ní ①mud; mire ②mashed vegetable or fruit 枣~ jujube paste 土豆~ mashed potato 【泥垢】dirt; grime 【泥浆】slurry; mud 【泥坑】mud pit; morass 【泥煤】peat 【泥泞】muddy; miry 【泥鳅】loach 【泥人】clay figurine 【泥沙】silt 【泥石流】mud-rock flow 【泥水匠】bricklayer; tiler; plasterer 【泥塑】clay sculpture 【泥塘】mire; bog 【泥土】earth; soil/clay 【泥沼】swamp; slough

呢 ní wool; woollen cloth; wool coating; wool suiting 制服~ uniform coating 【呢绒】woollen goods

霓 ní secondary rainbow 【霓虹灯】neon light

拟 ní ①draw up; draft ~稿 make a draft ②intend; plan ③imitate 【拟订】draw up; work out ~计划 draft a plan ~有效办法 work out effective measures 【拟人】personification 【拟议】proposal; recommendation/draw up

你 ní you ~爸爸 your father ~方 your side ~校 your school 【你好】how do you do; how are you; hello 【你们】you 【你死我活】life-and-death ~的斗争 a life-and-death struggle 排个~ fight to the bitter end

泥 ní daub with plaster, putty, etc.; putty; plaster ~墙 cover the crevices in a wall with mud or plaster

逆 ní ①contrary; counter ~风 contrary wind ②go against; disobey; defy ~时代潮流而动 go against the trend of the times ③traitor ~产 traitor's property 【逆差】trade deficit 【逆耳】grate on the ear ~的话 words unpleasant to hear 【逆风】against the wind/head wind 【逆境】adversity 【逆料】anticipate; foresee 不难~ can be foreseen 尚难~ it's still hard to say 【逆流】adverse current; countercurrent 【逆水】against the current ~行舟 不进则退 a boat sailing against the current must forge ahead or it will be driven back 【逆转】reverse; become worse; deteriorate 【逆子】 unfilial son

昵 nì close; intimate 亲~ very intimate

匿 nì hide; conceal 【匿迹】 go into hiding 【匿名】 anonymous ~信 anonymous letter

溺 nì ①drown ~死 be drowned ~婴 infanticide ② be addicted to ~于酒色 given over to wine and woman 【溺爱】 spoil (a child) 【溺职】 neglect of duty

腻 nì ①greasy; oily 汤太~了 the soup is too oily ② be bored with 听~了 be tired of listening to sth. ③meticulous 【腻烦】 be bored; be fed up/loathe; hate

NIAN

拈 niān pick up 信手~来 pick up at rankom ~起一根针 pick up a needle 【拈阄儿】 draw lots

蔫 niān ①fade; wither; shrivel up 花儿~了 the flowers drooped ②listless; spiritless; droopy 孩子有点~ the child looks a bit listless

年 nián ①year ~复一~ year after year ②annual; yearly ~产量 annual output ③age 多大~纪 be of an age ④New Year ⑤a period in one's life 童~ childhood ⑥ a period in history 近~来 in recent years ⑦harvest 丰 ~ rich harvest 【年报】 annual (report) 【年表】 chronological table 【年成】 the year's harvest ~不好 a lean year 【年初】 the beginning of the year 【年代】 age; years; time/a decade of a century 战争~ during the war years 八十~ the eighties 【年底】 the end of the year 【年度】 year ~计划 annual plan 【年份】 a particular year/age; time 【年糕】 New Year cake 【年华】 time; years 虚度~ waste one's life 【年画】 Spring Festival pictures 【年会】 annual meeting 【年级】 grade; year 大学三~学生 third year university student 小学一～学生 first grade primary school pupil 【年纪】age 上～ advanced in years 【年鉴】yearbook; almanac 【年历】single-page calendar 【年利】annual interest ～率 annual interest rate 【年龄】age 【年轮】annual ring 【年迈】old; aged 【年青】~young 【年轻】young ～人 young people ～力壮 young and vigorous 【年限】fixed number of years 学习～ the number of years set for a course 【年终】the end of the year; year-end ～结帐 year-end settlement of accounts

黏 nián sticky; glutinous ～米 glutinous rice 【黏附】adhere ～力 adhesion 【黏结】cohere ～力 cohesion 【黏土】clay 【黏性】stickiness; viscosity 【黏液】mucus

捻 niǎn twist with the fingers ～线 twist thread 把煤气灯～小 turn the gaslight low 【捻子】spill/wick

碾 niǎn ①roller 石～ stone roller ②grind with a roller ～米 husk rice ③crush ～碎 be crushed to pieces 【碾坊】grain mill 【碾米机】rice mill

撵 niǎn ①drive out; oust ～走 drive sb. away ～下台 oust from a leading position ②catch up with sb.

念 niàn ①think of; miss 想老～着你 miss you very much ②thought; idea 杂～ distracting thoughts ③read aloud ④study; attend school ～书 read; study ～过中学 have been to middle school 【念头】thought; idea; intention 只有一个～ have only one thing in mind 放弃这个～ give up the idea 【念珠】beads

NIANG

娘 niáng ma; mother 【娘家】a married woman's parents' home 【娘胎】mother's womb 出了～ be born

酿 niàng ①make (wine, vinegar, etc.); brew (beer) ②make (honey) ③result in ～祸 lead to disaster ④wine

佳～ good wine【酿成】lead to; bring on; breed ～大错 lead to big mistake【酿酒】make wine; brew beer ～厂 winery ～业 wine-making industry

NIAO

鸟 niǎo bird【鸟粪】birds' droppings/guano【鸟瞰】get a bird's-eye view (of the city, etc.)/general survey of a subject【鸟类】birds ～学 ornithology【鸟笼】bird-cage【鸟枪】fowling piece/air gun【鸟兽】birds and beasts; fur and feather【鸟嘴】beak; bill

尿 niào ①urine ②make water; pass water【尿布】dia-per; napkin; nappy【尿床】wet the bed【尿盆】cham-ber pot【尿素】urea; carbamide

NIE

捏 niē ①hold between the fingers; pinch 把虫子～出来 pick the worms out ②knead; mould ～泥人 mould clay figurines ③fabricate; make up【捏合】mediate; act as go-between【捏一把汗】be breathless with anxiety or tension【捏造】fabricate; concoct; fake ～事实 invent a story ～罪名 trump up charges ～数字 conjure up figures

啮 niè gnaw【啮齿动物】rodent【啮合】clench the teeth/(of gears) mesh; engage

镊 niè ①tweezers ②pick up sth. with tweezers

镍 niè nickel ～币 nickel coin; nickel

蹑 niè ①lighten (one's step); walk on tiptoe ～手～脚 walk gingerly ～着脚走出病房 tiptoe out of the ward ②tread; step on; walk with ～足其间 join (a pro-fession); follow (a trade); associate with

孽 niè evil; sin 妖～ evildoer 【孽障】evil creature; vile spawn

NING

宁 níng peaceful; tranquil 【宁静】tranquil; quiet ～的夜晚 a tranquil night ～下来 calm down

拧 níng ①twist; wring ～毛巾 twist a wet towel 把衣服～干 wring out wet clothes ②pinch; tweak

狞 níng ferocious; hideous 【狞笑】grin hideously

柠 níng 【柠檬】lemon ～水 lemonade; lemon squash ～酸 citric acid ～糖 lemon drops ～汁 lemon juice

凝 níng ①congeal; curdle; coagulate 冷～ condensation ②with fixed attention ～思 be lost in thought 【凝点】condensation point 【凝固】solidify ～点 solidifying point 【凝结】coagulate; congeal; condense ～力 coagulability ～物 coagulum 【凝聚】(of vapour) condense 【凝练】concise; condensed; compact 【凝神】with fixed attention 【凝视】gaze fixedly; stare

拧 nǐng ①twist; screw ～开瓶盖 screw the cap off a bottle ～紧螺丝 tighten up a screw ②wrong ③disagree

宁 nìng rather; better 【宁可】would rather ～小心一点 better safe than sorry 【宁缺毋滥】rather go without than have something shoddy—put quality before quantity 【宁死不屈】rather die than submit

佞 nìng given to flattery ～人 sycophant; toady

NIU

妞 niū girl!

牛 niú ox 母～ cow 公～ bull 小～ calf 【牛车】ox cart 【牛痘】cowpox/smallpox pustule; vaccine pustule 种～ give or get smallpox vaccination 【牛鬼蛇神】monsters and demons—forces of evil; class enemies of all descriptions 【牛角】ox horn ～制品 hornware ～尖 the tip of a horn—an insignificant or insoluble problem 【牛栏】cattle pen 【牛毛】ox hair 多如～ countless 【牛虻】gadfly 【牛奶】milk ～场 dairy 【牛糖 toffee 【牛排】beefsteak 【牛棚】cowshed 【牛皮】cattlehide 吹～ talk big; brag ～糖 a sticky candy ～纸 kraft paper 【牛肉】beef 【牛尾】oxtail 【牛仔裤】close-fitting pants; jeans

忸 niǔ 【忸怩】blushing; bashful ～作态 behave coyly; be affectedly shy

扭 niǔ ①turn round ～头看 look over one's shoulder ②twist; wrench 把门～开 wrench the door open ③ sprain ～了筋 wrench a tendon ～了腰 sprain one's back ④roll; swing 走路一～一～的 walk with a rolling gait ⑤seize; grapple with ～送公安部门 seize sb. and hand him over to the public security authorities 【扭打】wrestle; grapple 【扭伤】wrench ～手腕 sprain one's wrist 【扭转】turn round/turn back; reverse ～局势 turn the tide

纽 niǔ handle; knob 秤～ the lifting cord of a steelyard 【纽带】link; tie; bond 【纽扣】button

拗 niù stubborn; obstinate; difficult ～不过 unable to dissuade; fail to talk sb. out of doing sth.

NONG

农 nóng ①agriculture; farming 务～ go in for agriculture ②peasant; farmer 菜～ vegetable grower 【农产品】agricultural products; farm produce 【农场】farm 【农村】rural area; countryside; village ～集市 village fair;

rural market 【农户】peasant household 【农活】farm work 【农家】peasant family ～肥 farm manure 【农具】farm tools 【农历】the lunar calendar 【农忙】busy season (in farming) 【农民】peasant ～阶级 the peasantry ～起义 peasant uprising ～协会 peasant association ～战争 peasant war 【农奴】serf ～制度 serf system ～主 serf owner 【农时】farming season 不违～ do farm work in the right season 【农田】farmland; cropland ～基本建设 farmland capital construction 【农闲】slack season (in farming) 【农学】agronomy; agriculture ～家 agronomist 【农谚】farmer's proverb 【农药】farm chemical; pesticide ～污染 pesticide pollution 【农业】agriculture; farming ～工人 farm labourer ～国 an agricultural country ～合作化 cooperative transformation of agriculture ～机械 farm machinery ～集体化 the collectivization of agriculture ～税 agricultural tax ～技术 agrotechnique 【农艺师】agronomist 【农艺学】agronomy 【农作物】crops

浓 nóng ①dense; thick; concentrated ～烟 dense smoke ～茶 strong tea ②great; strong 兴趣很～ take a great interest in sth. 香味很～ have a heavy fragrance; have a rich perfume 【浓度】consistency; density 【浓厚】dense; thick/strong; pronounced ～的地方色彩 pronounced local colour ～的农村生活气息 a strong flavour of rural life 【浓眉】heavy eyebrows 【浓缩】concentrate; enrich ～物 concentrate ～铀 enriched uranium

脓 nóng pus 【脓包】pustule / worthless fellow 【脓疮】running sore 【脓肿】abscess

弄 nòng ①play with; fool with ～沙土 play with sand 别～那只钟 don't meddle with the clock ②do; manage; handle ～饭 prepare a meal; cook 我替你～吧 let me do it for you 把我～糊涂了 make me feel puzzled

③get; fetch 去～点水来 go and get some water ④play ～手段 play tricks 【弄错】make a mistake; misunderstand 【弄好】do well / finish doing sth. 【弄坏】ruin; put out of order; make a mess of 【弄假成真】what was make-believe has become reality 【弄僵】(bring to a) deadlock 【弄巧成拙】try to be clever only to end up with a blunder; outsmart oneself 【弄清】make clear; clarify; understand fully ～情况 gain a clear idea of the situation ～事实 set the facts straight ～是非 thrash out the rights and wrongs 【弄死】put to death; kill 【弄通】get a good grasp of 【弄虚作假】practise fraud; employ trickery

NU

奴 nú ①bondservant; slave ②enslave 【奴才】flunkey; lackey ～相 servile behaviour; servility 【奴化】enslave ～政策 policy of enslavement 【奴隶】slave ～起义 slave uprising ～社会 slave society ～主 slave owner ～主义 slavishness 【奴仆】servant; lackey 【奴性】servility 【奴颜婢膝】servile 【奴役】enslave; keep in bondage

努 nǔ ①put forth (strength); exert (effort) ②protrude; bulge ～嘴 pout one's lips (as a signal) ～着眼睛 with bulging eyes 【努力】make great efforts; try hard ～工作 work hard ～发展生产 actively expand production ～奋斗 exert oneself in the struggle for

怒 nù anger; rage; fury ～骂 curse furiously 【怒不可遏】be beside oneself with anger; boil with rage 【怒潮】raging tide 【怒斥】angrily rebuke 【怒冲冲】in a rage; furiously 【怒放】in full bloom 心花～ be wild with joy 【怒号】howl; roar 狂风～ a violent wind is howling 【怒吼】roar; howl 大海～ the sea roared 【怒目】glaring eyes; fierce stare ～而视 stare angrily 【怒气】anger; rage;

fury ～冲天 be in a towering rage【怒容】an angry look

NÜ

女 nǚ ①woman; female ～教师 woman teacher ～民兵 militiawoman ～演员 actress ～英雄 heroine ～飞行员 aviatrix ～职工 women staff members and women workers ②daughter; girl【女厕所】women's lavatory【女车】lady's bicycle【女低音】alto【女儿】daughter; girl【女方】the bride's side; the wife's side【女服务员】air hostess; stewardess/waitress【女高音】soprano【女工】woman worker【女郎】young woman; maiden; girl【女朋友】girl friend【女色】woman's charms【女神】goddess【女生】woman student; girl student; schoolgirl【女声】female voice ～合唱 women's chorus【女士】lady; madam【女王】queen【女巫】witch【女性】the female sex/woman【女婿】son-in-law【女主角】leading lady

NUAN

暖 nuǎn ①warm; genial 天～了 it's getting warm ② warm up ～～手 warm one's hands【暖和】warm/warm up【暖气】central heating【暖水瓶】thermos flask

NÜE

疟 nüè malaria【疟疾】malaria; ague 恶性～ pernicious malaria【疟蚊】malarial mosquito

虐 nüè cruel; tyrannical【虐待】maltreat; ill-treat; tyrannize【虐政】tyrannical governmeht; tyranny

NUO

挪 nuó move; shift 往前～几步 move a few steps forward【挪借】get a short-term loan【挪用】divert (funds) / embezzle; misappropriate (public funds, etc.)

诺 nuò ①promise ②yes ～～连声 keep on saying "yes" 【诺言】promise 履行～ fulfil one's promise

懦 nuò cowardly; weak 【懦夫】coward; craven; weakling

糯 nuò glutinous (cereal) 【糯稻】glutinous rice 【糯米】polished glutinous rice

O

OU

讴 ōu ①sing ②folk songs; ballads 【讴歌】sing the praises of; eulogize

欧 ōu short for Europe 【欧化】Europeanize; westernize 【欧洲】Europe

殴 ōu hit ～伤 beat and injure 【殴打】beat up; hit 互相～ come to blows

鸥 ōu gull 海～ sea gull

呕 ǒu vomit 【呕吐】vomit; throw up; be sick ～不止 keep vomiting 【呕心】exert one's utmost effort ～沥血 shed one's heart's blood; work one's heart out

偶 ǒu ①image; idol 木～ wooden image; puppet ②even (number); in pairs ③mate 配～ spouse ④by chance; by accident; occasionally ～遇 meet by chance ～一为之 do sth. once in a while 【偶尔】once in a while; occasionally 【偶犯】casual offence/casual offender 【偶合】coincidence 【偶然】accidental; fortuitous; chance ～现象 accidental phenomena ～性 contingency; fortuity; chance

【偶数】even number 【偶像】image; idol ～崇拜 idolatry

藕 ǒu lotus root 【藕粉】lotus root starch 【藕荷】pale pinkish purple 【藕节】joints cf a lotus root

沤 òu soak; steep; macerate ～麻 ret flax or hemp ～肥 make compost/wet compost

怄 òu ①irritate; annoy ②be irritated 【怄气】be difficult and sulky 别～ don't sulk

P

PA

趴 pā ①lie on one's stomach; lie prone ～在地上 lie on the ground ②bend over; lean on ～在桌子上 bend over the desk

扒 pá ①gather up; rake up ②stew; braise ～鸡 braised chicken 【扒犁】sledge; sleigh 【扒手】pickpocket

爬 pá ①crawl; creep ②climb; clamber; scramble ～树 climb a tree 【爬虫】reptile 【爬泳】the crawl

耙 pá ①rake 木～ wooden rake ②make smooth with a rake; rake

怕 pà ①fear; dread; be afraid of 不～疲劳 not be afraid of fatigue 不～困难 brave difficulties ②I'm afraid; I suppose; perhaps 【怕生】(of a child) be shy with strangers 【怕事】be afraid of getting into trouble 【怕死】fear death ～鬼 coward 【怕羞】coy; shy; bashful

PAI

拍 pāi ①clap; pat; beat ～巴掌 clap one's hands ～桌子 strike the table ～球 bounce a ball ②bat; racket 乒乓球～ ping-pong bat; table-tennis bat ③beat; time —

节四~ four beats to a bar ④take (a picture); shoot ~电影 shoot a film ⑤send (a telegram, etc.) ⑥flatter; fawn on 【拍打】 pat; slap ~身上的雪 beat the snow off one's clothes 【拍发】 send (a telegram) 【拍马屁】 lick sb.'s boots; flatter; fawn on 【拍卖】 auction/selling off goods at reduced prices; sale 【拍摄】 take (a picture); shoot 把话剧~成电影 film a modern drama 在~外景 be on location 【拍手】 clap one's hands; applaud ~叫好 clap and shout "bravo!" ~ 称快 clap and cheer 【拍照】 take a picture; photograph 【拍纸簿】 (writing) pad

排

pái ①arrange; put in order ~座位 arrange seats ~课桌 put the desks in order ~节目单 arrange the programme ②row; line 前~ front row 一~椅子 a line of chairs ③rehearse ~戏 rehearse a play ④raft 木~ timber raft ⑤exclude; eject; discharge ~脓 discharge pus ~水 drain the water away ⑥push ~闼直入 push the door open and go straight in ⑦pie 苹果~ apple pie ⑧ platoon 【排场】 (go in for) ostentation and extravagance 【排斥】 repel; exclude; reject ~异己 exclude outsiders 【排除】 get rid of; remove; eliminate; get over ~障碍 remove an obstacle ~故障 fix a breakdown ~私心杂念 get rid of all selfish ideas 【排挡】 gear (of a car, tractor, etc.) 【排队】 form a line; line up; queue up ~买票 line up for tickets ~上车 queue up for a bus 【排骨】 spareribs 【排灌】 irrigation and drainage ~设备 irrigation and drainage equipment 【排挤】 push aside; push out; elbow out 互相~ each trying to squeeze the other out 【排解】 mediate; reconcile ~纠纷 reconcile a quarrel 【排涝】 drain flooded fields 【排练】 rehearse ~节目 have a rehearsal 【排列】 arrange (in a line, etc.); range; put in order 【排球】 volleyball 【排水】 drain off water ~工程 drainage works

~管 drain pipe 【排外】 exclusive; antiforeign 盲目~ blind opposition to everything foreign ~主义 exclusivism; antiforeignism 【排泄】 drain/excrete ~器官 excretory organ ~物 excreta 【排长】 platoon leader 【排字】 composing; typesetting

徘 pái 【徘徊】 pace up and down/hesitate; waver ~歧路 hesitate at the crossroads

牌 pái ①plate; tablet 门~ doorplate 车~ number plate 路~ signpost ②brand 名~货 goods of a well-known brand ③cards, dominoes, etc. 一副扑克~ a pack of playing cards 【牌价】 list price/market quotation 【牌照】 license plate; license tag 【牌子】 plate; sign/brand; trademark

迫 pǎi 【迫击炮】 mortar ~弹 mortar shell

派 pài ①group; school; faction; clique 学~ school of thought ②style; manner and air 气~ bearing ③send; dispatch; assign; appoint ~兵 dispatch troops ~工作 set sb. a task ~勤务 assign fatigue duties 【派出所】 police substation 【派款】 impose levies of money 【派遣】 send; dispatch ~代表团 send a delegation 【派生】 derive ~词 derivative 【派头】 style; manner 【派系】 factions 【派性】 factionalism

PAN

攀 pān ①climb; clamber ~着绳子往上爬 climb up a rope hand over hand ②seek connections in high places ③involve; implicate (sb. in a crime) 【攀登】 climb; scale ~峭壁 climb up a cliff ~科学技术新高峰 scale new heights in science and technology 【攀亲】 claim kinship/arrange a match 【攀谈】 engage in small talk; chitchat 【攀缘】 climb; clamber ~植物 climber 【攀折】

pull down and break off (twigs, etc.)

盘 pán ①tray; plate 茶~ tea tray 一~菜 a dish ②coil; wind; twist ~山小道 a winding mountain path ③ build ~灶 build a brick cooking range ④check; examine ~请 question ⑤game; set 下~棋 play a game of chess ⑥coil 一~香 a coil of incense 一~电线 a coil of wire 【盘剥】 practise usury; exploit 【盘查】 interrogate and examine 【盘缠】 travelling expenses 【盘存】 take inventory 【盘点】 check; make an inventory of 【盘踞】 illegally or forcibly occupy; be entrenched 【盘弄】 play with; fiddle with; fondle 【盘绕】 twine; coil; wreathe 【盘算】 calculate; figure; plan 【盘梯】 spiral staircase 【盘腿】 cross one's legs 【盘问】 cross-examine; interrogate 【盘香】 incense coil 【盘旋】 spiral; circle; wheel 在空中~ be wheeling in the air

磐 pán 【磐石】 huge rock 坚如~ as solid as a rock ~一般的团结 rocklike unity

蹒 pán 【蹒跚】 walk haltingly; limp; hobble

判 pàn ①distinguish; discriminate ②obviously different ~若两人 be quite a different person ③judge; decide ~案 decide a case ~卷子 mark examination papers ④ sentence; condemn ~徒刑 be sentenced to imprisonment 【判别】 differentiate ~真假 distinguish the true from the false 【判处】 condemn ~死刑 sentence sb. to death 【判词】 court verdict 【判断】 judge; decide; determine ~情况 assess the situation ~力 judgment 【判决】 court decision; judgment ~书 court verdict 【判例】 legal precedent 【判明】 ascertain ~是非 distinguish between right and wrong ~真相 ascertain the facts 【判罪】 declare guilty; convict

叛 pàn rebel against; betray (one's country, the Party, etc.) 【叛变】turn traitor; turn renegade 【叛军】rebel army; rebel forces 【叛离】desert 【叛乱】armed rebellion 【叛卖】betray; sell ～活动 acts of treason 【叛徒】traitor; renegade; turncoat

盼 pàn ①hope for; long for; expect ～复 I await your reply ～你下午来 you will be expected this afternoon ②look 【盼头】sth. hoped for and likely to happen; good prospects 这事有～了 things are looking up 【盼望】hope for; long for; look forward to

畔 pàn ①side; bank 河～ river bank; riverside 湖～ the shore of a lake ②the border of a field

襻 pàn ①loop 纽～ button loop 鞋～ shoe strap ②fasten with a string, etc.; tie 用绳子～上 fasten with a rope

PANG

滂 pāng 【滂湃】(of water) roaring and rushing 【滂沱】torrential 大雨～ it's raining in torrents

膀 pāng swell ～肿 swollen; bloated

彷 páng 【彷徨】walk back and forth, not knowing which way to go ～歧途 hesitate at the crossroads

庞 páng ①huge ②innumerable and disordered ③face 【庞大】huge; enormous; colossal; gigantic 机构～ an unwieldy organization 开支～ an enormous expenditure 【庞然大物】huge monster; giant

旁 páng ①side 马路两～ both sides of the street ②other; else 别说～的话 don't say anything else 【旁白】aside (in a play) 【旁边】side 坐在他～ sit by his side 【旁观】look on; be an onlooker ～者 spectator 【旁观者清】the spectator sees most clearly 【旁门】side door 【旁

敲侧击】attack by innuendo 【旁人】other people 【旁听】
be a visitor at a meeting, in a school class, etc. ～生 audi-
tor ～席 visitors' seats 【旁系亲属】collateral (relative)
【旁证】circumstantial evidence

膀 páng 【膀胱】(urinary) bladder ～炎 cystitis

磅 páng 【磅礴】boundless; majestic /'fill; permeate

螃 páng 【螃蟹】crab

耪 pǎng loosen soil with a hoe ～地 hoe the soil

胖 pàng fat; stout; plump 他一起来了 he's putting on
weight 【胖头鱼】bighead 【胖子】fat person; fatty

PAO

抛 pāo ①throw; cast; toss; fling ～球 toss a ball ②
leave behind; cast aside 【抛光】polishing 【抛锚】drop
anchor /(of vehicles) break down 【抛弃】abandon; forsake; cast aside 【抛售】sell (goods, etc.) in big quantities 【抛头露面】show one's face in public

泡 pāo ①sth. puffy and soft 豆腐～儿 beancurd puff
②spongy 【泡桐】paulownia

刨 páo dig; excavate ～个坑 dig a hole ～白薯 dig
(up) sweet potatoes 【刨根儿】get to the bottom of sth.

咆 páo 【咆哮】roar; thunder ～如雷 roar with rage

袍 páo robe; gown

跑 pǎo ①run ～得快 run fast ～百米 run the 100-
metre dash ②run away; escape; flee 敌军～了 the

enemy soldiers ran off 车带～气了 air is escaping from the tyre ③run about doing sth.; run errands ～材料 run about collecting material ④away; off 吓～ frighten away 刮～ blow off 【跑步】run; march at the double 【跑车】racing bike 【跑道】runway/track 【跑龙套】play a bit role; be a utility man 【跑腿儿】run errands; do legwork

泡 pào ①bubble 肥皂～ soap bubbles 冒～ rise in bubbles ②sth. shaped like a bubble 起～ get blisters 电灯～ electric light bulb ③steep; soak 放在水里～一下 steep sth. in water ④dawdle 别～了 stop dawdling 【泡菜】pickles 【泡茶】make tea 【泡饭】soak cooked rice in water/cooked rice reheated in boiling water 【泡蘑菇】play for time/importune; pester 【泡沫】foam; froth ～玻璃 cellular glass ～灭火器 foam extinguisher ～塑料 foamed plastics 【泡影】visionary hope, plan, scheme, etc.; bubble 化为～ melt into thin air; go up in smoke

炮 pào big gun; cannon; artillery piece 【炮兵】artillery; artillerymen ～部队 artillery (troops) ～连 battery ～阵地 artillery position 【炮弹】(artillery) shell 【炮轰】bombard 【炮灰】cannon fodder 【炮火】artillery fire; gunfire 【炮舰】gunboat ～政策 gunboat policy ～外交 gunboat diplomacy 【炮楼】blockhouse 【炮声】report of a gun ～隆隆 roar of guns 【炮手】gunner 【炮塔】turret 【炮台】fort; battery 【炮艇】gunboat 【炮筒】barrel (of a gun) 【炮战】artillery action 【炮仗】firecracker

疱 pào blister; bleb 【疱疹】bleb/herpes

PEI

呸 pēi pah; bah; pooh

胚 pēi 【胚胎】embryo ～学 embryology

陪 péi accompany; keep sb. company ～外宾参观工厂 show foreign visitors round a factory ～病人 look after a patient 【陪衬】serve as a contrast or foil; set off/ foil; setoff 【陪嫁】dowry 【陪审】act as an assessor (in a law case)/serve on a jury ～团 jury ～员 juror

培 péi ①bank up with earth; earth up (the roots, etc.) ②cultivate; foster 【培养】foster; train; develop/culture ～学生自学能力 foster the students' ability to study on their own ～和造就接班人 train and bring up successors ～细菌 culture of bacteria

赔 péi ①compensate; pay for ②stand a loss 【赔本】 sustain losses in business 【赔不是】apologize 【赔偿】 compensate; pay for ～损失 make good a loss 战争～ war reparations ～费 damages 【赔款】pay an indemnity; pay reparations / indemnity; reparations 【赔礼】offer an apology 【赔笑】smile obsequiously or apologetically

沛 pèi copious; abundant ～然降雨 a copious rain began to fall 精力充～ be full of energy

佩 pèi ①wear (at the waist, etc.) ～刀 wear a sword ②ad- mire 【佩带】wear ～徽章 wear a badge 【佩服】admire

配 pèi ①join in marriage 婚～ marry ②mate (animals) ～种 breeding ③compound; mix ～颜色 mix colours (on a palette) ～药 make up a prescription ④apportion ～售 ration ⑤find sth. to fit or replace sth. else ～钥匙 have a key made to fit a lock ～零件 replace parts ⑥ match 颜色不～ the colours don't match ⑦deserve; be worthy of; be qualified 【配备】allocate; provide; fit out/ dispose (troops, etc.); deploy / outfit; equipment ～助手 provide assistants ～火力 dispose firepower 现代化的～

modern equipment 【配搭】supplement; match; accompany 【配方】make up a prescription/directions for producing chemicals or metallurgical products 【配合】coordinate; cooperate; concert ～作战 coordination of military operations ～行动 take concerted action 【配给】ration 证 ration card 【配角】supporting role; minor role 【配偶】spouse 【配色】match colours; harmonize colours 【配套】form a complete set 【配戏】play a supporting role 【配音】dub (a film, etc.) 【配乐】dub in background music 【配制】compound; make up

PEN

喷 pēn ①spout; gush ～水 spurt water ②spray; sprinkle ～农药 spray an insecticide 【喷灌】spray irrigation ～器 sprinkler 【喷壶】sprinkling can 【喷火器】flamethrower 【喷漆】spray paint ～枪 paint gun 【喷气发动机】jet engine 【喷气式】jet-propelled ～飞机 jet (plane) ～客机 jet airliner 【喷枪】spray gun 【喷泉】fountain 【喷射】spray; spurt; jet ～火焰 spurt flames 【喷嚏】sneeze 【喷雾】spraying ～器 sprayer 【喷嘴】spray nozzle

盆 pén basin; tub; pot 脸～ washbasin 【盆地】basin 【盆花】potted flower 【盆景】potted landscape

喷 pèn ①in season ②crop 【喷香】fragrant; delicious

PENG

抨 pēng 【抨击】attack (in speech or writing); assail; lash out at

烹 pēng ①boil; cook ～茶 brew tea ②fry quickly in hot oil and stir in sauce ～对虾 quick-fried prawns in brown sauce 【烹饪】cooking 【烹调】cook (dishes)

澎 pēng splash; spatter 【澎湃】surge 波涛～ waves surge 心潮～ feel an upsurge of emotion

朋 péng friend 【朋比为奸】act in collusion with; conspire 【朋友】friend/boy friend or girl friend

棚 péng ①canopy of reed mats, etc. 凉～ awning ②shed; shack 牲口～ livestock shed 草～ straw mat shed

蓬 péng fluffy; dishevelled ～着头 with dishevelled hair 【蓬勃】vigorous; flourishing 【蓬松】puffy

硼 péng boron 【硼砂】borax 【硼酸】boric acid ～盐 borate

鹏 péng roc 【鹏程万里】(make) a roc's flight of 10,000 li—have a bright future

篷 péng ①covering or awning on a car, boat, etc. ②sail (of a boat) 【篷布】tarpaulin

膨 péng 【膨大】expand; inflate 【膨体纱】bulk yarn 【膨胀】expand; swell; dilate; inflate

捧 péng ①hold or carry in both hands ～着西瓜 hold a watermelon in both hands ～着孩子的脸 cup the child's face in one's hands ②exalt; extol 【捧场】be a member of a *claque*/boost; sing the praises of; flatter

碰 pèng ①touch; bump ～翻 knock sth. over 头～在门上 bump one's head against the door ②meet; run into ～到一个熟人 run into an acquaintance ～到困难 run up against difficulties ③take one's chance 【碰杯】clink glasses 【碰壁】run up against a stone wall; be rebuffed 【碰钉子】meet with a rebuff 【碰见】meet unexpectedly; run into 【碰巧】by chance; by coincidence 我～也在那儿 I happened to be there too 【碰头】meet and discuss; put (our, your, their) heads together ～会 brief meeting 【碰运气】try one's luck; take one's chance 【碰撞】collide; run into

PI

批 pī ①slap ～颊 slap sb.'s face ②criticize; refute ③ write comments on (a report, etc.) ～文件 write instructions on documents ④wholesale ～购 buy goods wholesale ⑤batch; lot; group 一一化肥 a lot of chemical fertilizer 分～下乡 go to the countryside in separate batches【批驳】veto an opinion or a request/refute; criticize; rebut【批发】wholesale / be authorized for dispatch ～部 wholesale department ～价格 wholesale price 【批改】correct ～作业 correct students' papers【批判】 criticize/critique ～地 critically ～会 criticism meeting ～文章 critical article ～现实主义 critical realism【批评】criticize/criticism【批示】written instructions or comments on a report, memorandum, etc.【批语】remarks on a piece of writing【批准】ratify; approve; sanction ～书 instrument of ratification 计划须经～ the plan is subject to approval

纰 pī (of cloth, thread, etc.) become unwoven or untwisted; be spoilt【纰漏】small accident; slip

坯 pī ①base; semifinished product; blank ②unburnt brick; earthen brick; adobe

披 pī ①drape over one's shoulders; wrap around ～上衣服 throw on some clothing ～着合法的外衣 under the cloak of legality ②open; unroll; spread out ～卷 open a book ③split open; crack 竹竿～了 the bamboo stick has split【披风】cloak【披肩】cape/shawl【披露】 publish; announce 在报上～ be published in the press 【披头散发】with hair dishevelled

砒 pī arsenic【砒霜】(white) arsenic

劈 pī ①split; chop; cleave ～木柴 chop wood ～山引水 cleave hills and lead in water ②right against (one's face, chest, etc.) 【劈头】 straight on the head; right in the face/at the very start

霹 pī 【霹雳】 thunderbolt; thunderclap 晴天～ a bolt from the blue

皮 pí ①skin 香蕉～ banana skin 土豆～ potato peel 西瓜～ watermelon rind ②leather; hide ～大衣 fur coat ③cover; wrapper 书～ book cover; jacket ④surface 水～儿 the surface of the water ⑤sheet 铁～ iron sheet ⑥become soft and soggy ⑦naughty ⑧case-hardened ⑨rubber ～筋儿 rubber band 【皮袄】 fur-lined jacket 【皮包】 leather handbag; briefcase; portfolio 【皮鞭】 leather-thonged whip 【皮尺】 tape (measure) 【皮带】 leather belt / belt 【皮蛋】 preserved egg 【皮筏】 skin raft 【皮肤】 skin ～病 skin disease ～科 dermatological department 【皮革】 leather; hide 【皮猴】 fur parka; fur anorak 【皮货】 fur; pelt ～商 furrier 【皮夹子】 wallet; pocketbook 【皮匠】 cobbler/tanner 【皮毛】 fur/smattering 【皮棉】 ginned cotton; lint (cotton) 【皮球】 (rubber) ball 【皮桶子】 fur lining 【皮线】 rubber-covered wire 【皮箱】 leather suitcase 【皮鞋】 leather shoes ～油 shoe polish 【皮衣】 fur clothing/leather clothing 【皮影戏】 shadow play 【皮张】 pelt 【皮掌】 outsole

枇 pí 【枇杷】 loquat

毗 pí 【毗连】 adjoin; be adjacent to; border on ～地区 contiguous zone

疲 pí tired; weary; exhausted 【疲惫】 tired; weary 作不～的斗争 wage tireless struggle 【疲劳】 tired; fatigued/fatigue 感到～ feel weary 【疲塌】 slack; negligent 工作～ be slack at one's work 【疲于奔命】 be kept constantly on the run; be weighed down with work

啤 pí 【啤酒】beer 生～ draught beer 黑～ porter; brown ale; stout ～厂 brewery ～花 hops

脾 pí spleen 【脾气】temperament; disposition/bad temper ～很好 have a good temper ～大 hot-tempered 发～ lose one's temper 【脾胃】taste

匹 pǐ ①be equal to; be a match for ～敌 be well matched ②三～马 three horses 一～布 a bolt of cloth 【匹夫】ordinary man/an ignorant person 【匹配】mate

仳 pǐ 【仳离】(of husband and wife) be separated/divorce one's spouse, esp. forsake one's wife

否 pǐ ①bad; wicked; evil ②censure 【否极泰来】out of the depth of misfortune comes bliss

痞 pǐ ①a lump in the abdomen ②ruffian; riffraff 地～ local ruffian

劈 pǐ ①divide; split ～成三股 split sth. into three strands ②break off; strip off ～白菜帮子 strip the outer leaves off cabbages 【劈叉】do the splits 【劈柴】firewood

癖 pǐ addiction; weakness for 嗜酒成～ be addicted to drinking 【癖好】favourite hobby; fondness for 【癖性】natural inclination; propensity

屁 pì wind (from bowels) 放～ break wind 【屁股】buttocks; bottom/rump; haunch 【屁话】nonsense

辟 pì ①open up (territory, land, etc.); break (ground) 开～果园 lay out an orchard 另～专栏 start a new column (in a newspaper, etc.) ②penetrating; incisive 精～ profound ③refute; repudiate ～谣 refute a rumour

媲 pì 【媲美】compare favourably with; rival

僻 pì ①out-of-the-way; secluded ～巷 side lane ②eccentric ③rare ～字 rare word 【僻静】secluded; lonely

譬 pì example; analogy 【譬如】 for example; for instance; such as 【譬喻】 metaphor; simile

PIAN

片 piān 【片盒】 film magazine 【片子】 a roll of film/ film; movie/gramophone record; disc

偏 piān ①inclined to one side; slanting; leaning 太阳~西 the sun is to the west 指标~低 the target is on the low side ②partial; prejudiced ~爱 have partiality for sth. 【偏差】 deviation; error 纠正~ correct deviations 【偏方】 folk prescription 【偏废】 do one thing and neglect another 【偏护】 be partial to and side with 【偏激】 extreme 意见~ hold extreme views 【偏见】 prejudice; bias 【偏离】 deviate; diverge ~航线 drift off the course 【偏僻】 remote; out-of-the-way 【偏巧】 it so happened that; as luck would have it 【偏题】 a catch question (in an examination) 【偏听偏信】 listen only to one side; be biased 【偏向】 erroneous tendency; deviation/ be partial to 【偏心】 partiality; bias 【偏重】 lay particular stress on

翩 piān 【翩翩】 lightly (dance, flutter, etc.) /elegant ~少年 an elegant young man 【翩跹】 lightly trippingly ~起舞 dance with quick, light steps

篇 piān ①a piece of writing 诗~ a poem ②sheet (of paper, etc.) 歌~ song sheet 【篇幅】 length (of a piece of writing) /space (on a printed page) ~有限 have limited space 【篇目】 (table of) contents; list of articles 【篇章】 sections and chapters; writings

便 piān 【便宜】 cheap/petty gains/let sb. off lightly 贪小~ out for small advantages ~货 goods sold at bargain prices

片 piàn ①a flat, thin piece; slice; flake 布～ small pieces of cloth 牛肉～ slices of beef 纸～ scraps of paper ②part of a place 切成～ cut into slices ～肉片 slice meat ～鱼片 flake a fish ④incomplete; fragmentary; partial; brief ⑤slice; stretch 一一～面包 a slice of bread 一一汪洋 a vast sheet of water 【片段】part; passage; extract; fragment 小说的～ certain passages of a novel 生活的～ a slice of life ～的消息 bits of information ～的回忆 fragments of sb.'s reminiscences 【片剂】tablet 【片刻】a short while; an instant; a moment 【片面】unilateral/one-sided ～之词 an account given by one party only ～观点 a lopsided view ～地看问题 take a one-sided approach to problems ～强调 put undue emphasis on

骗 piàn ①deceive; fool; hoodwink 受～ be deceived ②cheat; swindle ～钱 cheat sb. out of his money 【骗局】fraud; hoax; swindle 政治～ a political fraud 【骗取】gain sth. by cheating; trick sb. out of sth. ～财物 defraud sb. of his money and belongings ～信任 worm one's way into sb.'s confidence ～支持 fool sb. into giving his support ～选票 wangle votes 【骗子】swindler

剽 piāo ①rob ～掠 plunder; loot ②nimble; swift 【剽悍】agile and brave 【剽窃】plagiarize; lift

漂 piāo float; drift 在水上～着 be floating on the water 顺流～去 drift down the stream 【漂泊】lead a wandering life; drift

缥 piāo 『缥缈』dimly discernible; misty 虚无～ visionary; illusory

飘 piāo wave to and fro; float (in the air); flutter 红旗～～ red flags are fluttering ～来阵阵花香 the

scent of the flowers was wafted to us【飘带】streamer;
ribbon【飘荡】drift; wave; flutter 随波～ be drifting
with the tide【飘忽】(of clouds) move swiftly; fleet/
mobile; uncertain【飘零】faded and fallen/wandering;
adrift【飘飘然】smug; self-satisfied; complacent【飘摇】
sway; shake; totter 风雨～ precarious; tottering

嫖 piáo visit prostitutes; go whoring

瓢 piáo gourd ladle; wooden dipper【瓢虫】ladybug;
ladybird【瓢泼大雨】torrential rain; down pour

漂 piǎo ①bleach ②rinse【漂白】bleach ～棉布 bleach-
ed cotton cloth ～粉 bleaching powder

瞟 piǎo look askance at; glance sideways at ～了一眼
cast a sidelong glance at sb.

票 piào ①ticket 火车～ train ticket ②ballot 投～ cast
a ballot ③bank note; bill 零～ change【票额】deno-
mination; face value【票房】booking office; box office
～价值 box-office value【票根】counterfoil; stub【票价】
the price of a ticket; admission fee; entrance fee/fare
～一元 admission one yuan【票据】bill; note/voucher;
receipt ～交换所 clearinghouse【票箱】ballot box

漂 piào【漂亮】handsome; good-looking; pretty; beau-
tiful/remarkable; brilliant; splendid ～话 fine words

PIE

撇 piē ①cast aside; neglect 把别的事～在一边 neglect
everything else ②skim ～油 skim off the grease ～
沫 skim off the scum【撇开】leave aside ～这个问题
bypass this issue【撇弃】cast away; abandon; desert

瞥 piē shoot a glance at; dart a look at【瞥见】get a
glimpse of; catch sight of

撇 piē throw; fling; cast ～手榴弹 throw hand grenades 【撇嘴】 curl one's lip; twitch one's mouth

PIN

拼 pīn ①put together; piece together 把两张桌子～起来 put two tables together ②be ready to risk one's life (in fighting, work, etc.); go all out in work ～到底 fight to the bitter end 【拼版】 makeup 【拼刺】 bayonet drill / bayonet charge 【拼凑】 piece together; rig up ～小集团 knock together a clique 【拼命】 risk one's life; defy death/exerting the utmost strength; with all one's might ～奔跑 run for all one is worth ～工作 work with all one's might ～排扎 wage a desperate struggle 【拼盘】 assorted cold dishes; *hors d'oeuvres* 【拼写】 spell; transliterate ～法 spelling; orthography 【拼音】 combine sounds into syllables/spell; phoneticize ～文字 alphabetic writing ～字母 phonetic alphabet

姘 pīn have illicit relations with 【姘居】 live illicitly as husband and wife; cohabit 【姘头】 paramour

贫 pín poor; impoverished ②inadequate; deficient ～油国 oil-poor country ③loquacious 嘴～ be garrulous 【贫乏】 short; lacking 经验～ lack experience 语言～ flat, monotonous language 【贫雇农】 poor peasants and farm labourers 【贫寒】 poor; poverty-stricken ～人家 an impoverished family 【贫瘠】 barren 【贫困】 in straitened circumstances 生活～ live in poverty ～化 pauperization 【贫民】 poor people; pauper 城市～ the urban poor ～窟 slum ～区 slum area 【贫农】 poor peasant 【贫穷】 needy 【贫弱】 (of a country) poor and weak 【贫血】 anaemia

频 pín ①frequently; repeatedly 【频道】 frequency channel 【频繁】 frequently; often ～的交往 frequent contacts 【频率】 frequency 【频频】 repeatedly ～举杯 propose repeated toasts ～招手 wave one's hand again and again

品 pǐn article; product 农产～ farm produce ②grade; class; rank 上～ top grade ③character; quality 人～ moral quality ～学兼优 (of a student) of good character and scholarship ④taste; sample; savour ～茶 sample tea ～味 savour the flavour 【品德】 moral character 【品格】 one's character and morals 【品级】 official rank in feudal times / grade (of products, commodities, etc.) 【品类】 category; class 【品貌】 looks; appearance / character and looks 【品名】 the name of an article 【品行】 conduct; behaviour ～端正 well-behaved ～不端 ill-behaved 【品性】 moral character 【品质】 character; quality ～证书 certificate of quality 【品种】 breed; variety/assortment 羊的优良～ improved breeds of sheep 货物～齐全 have a rich assortment of goods 增加花色～ increase the variety of colours and designs

牝 pìn female (of some birds and animals) ～马 mare ～牛 cow ～鸡 hen

聘 pìn engage ～为顾问 engage sb. as a consultant 【聘礼】 betrothal gifts; bride-price 【聘请】 engage; invite 【聘书】 letter of appointment; contract

PING

乒 pīng 【乒乓球】 table tennis; ping-pong/table tennis ball ～拍 table tennis bat ～台 table tennis table

平 píng ①flat; level; even; smooth 桌面不～ the table is not level 把纸铺～ smooth out the paper ～地 level the ground ②be on the same level; be on a par; equal ～世界纪录 equal a world record ③make the same score; tie; draw 打成十五～ tie at 15-15 ④equal; fair

～分 divide equally ⑤suppress ～叛 put down a rebellion ⑥average; common ～日 on ordinary days 【平安】 safe and sound; without mishap ～无事 all is well 【平白】 for no reason 【平板】 dull and stereotyped; flat 【平板车】 flatbed (tricycle) 【平辈】 of the same generation 【平常】 ordinary; common/generally; usually; as a rule 【平淡】 flat; insipid; prosaic; pedestrian 【平等】 equality ～待遇 equal treatment ～待人 treat others as equals ～互利 equality and mutual benefit ～协商 consultation on the basis of equality 【平定】 calm down / suppress; put down 【平凡】 ordinary; common 在～的岗位上 at an ordinary post 【平反】 redress (a mishandled case) 宣布给某人～ announce sb.'s rehabilitation 复查和～了冤案 unjust cases were re-examined and their verdicts reversed 【平复】 calm down; subside; be pacified/be cured 事态～ the situation has quietened 伤口～ the wound is healed 【平和】 gentle; mild; moderate 【平衡】 balance; equilibrium 收支～ balance between income and expenditure 失去～ lose one's balance 保持～ keep one's balance ～力 equilibrant ～木 balance beam 【平滑】 level and smooth ～肌 smooth muscle 【平静】 calm; quiet; tranquil 【平局】 draw; tie 打成～ end in a draw 扳成～ equalize the score 【平均】 average; mean/equally ～速度 average speed ～亩产量 per mu yield ～分摊 share out equally ～利润 average profit ～寿命 average life span ～数 average; mean ～值 average value ～主义 equalitarianism 【平列】 place side by side 【平面】 plane ～几何 plane geometry ～镜 plane mirror ～图 plan/plane figure 【平民】 the common people; the populace 【平权】 equal rights 【平绒】 velveteen 【平时】 at ordinary times; in normal times/in peacetime 【平台】 terrace; platform 【平坦】 level;

even 地势～ smooth terrain 【平信】ordinary mail/surface
mail 【平行】of equal rank; on an equal footing/parallel
～作业 parallel operations ～的会谈 simultaneous talks ～
线 parallel lines 【平易】unassuming; amiable/easy; plain
～近人 amiable and easy of approach 【平庸】indifferent;
commonplace 【平原】plain; flatlands 【平装】paper-cover
～本 paperback (book); paperbound edition

评 píng ①criticize; review / judge; apprais:
博得好～
receive favourable comments 被～为劳动模范 be elected a model worker 【评比】appraise through comparison;
compare and assess ～产品质量 make a public appraisal
of the quality of different products 【评定】evaluate; assess 【评断】judge ～是非 arbitrate a dispute 【评分】give
a mark; mark (students' papers, etc.) 【评功】appraise
sb.'s merits ～摆好 speak of sb. in glowing terms 【评价】
appraise ～历史人物 evaluate historical figures 高度～
highly appraise 【评奖】decide on awards through discussion 【评理】decide which side is right/reason things out;
have it out 【评论】comment on; discuss/comment; commentary; review ～家 critic; reviewer ～员 commentator
【评判】pass judgment on; judge ～胜负 judge between
contestants ～优劣 judge which is superior ～员 judge;
adjudicator 【评薪】discuss and determine a person's wage-
grade 【评选】choose through public appraisal 【评议】ap-
praise sth. through discussion 【评语】comment; remark

坪 píng level ground 草～ lawn 停机～ aircraft park;
apron

苹 píng 【苹果】apple ～脯 preserved apple ～干 dried
apple slices ～酱 apple jam ～酒 cider; applejack

凭 píng ①lean on; lean against ～栏 lean on a railing
②rely on; depend on ～险抵抗 make use of a stra-

tegic vantage point to fight back ③evidence; proof 口说无～ verbal statements are no guarantee ④go by; base on; take as the basis ～票入场 admission by ticket only ～票付款 payable to bearer ⑤no matter (what, how, etc.)【凭单】a certificate (for drawing money, goods, etc.); voucher【凭借】depend on ～自己的力量 rely on one's own strength ～想象力 draw on one's imagination【凭据】evidence; proof【凭空】out of the void; without foundation; groundless【凭信】believe【凭照】permit; licence

屏

视～

píng ①screen 画～ painted screen ②a set of scrolls ③shield sb. or sth.【屏风】screen【屏幕】screen 电视～ telescreen【屏障】protective screen; natural defence

瓶

píng bottle; jar; flask 花～ flower vase【瓶胆】glass liner (of a thermos flask)【瓶装】bottled

萍

píng duckweed【萍水相逢】meet by chance like patches of drifting duckweed

PO

泊

pō lake 血～ pool of blood

坡

pō ①slope 陡～ a steep slope 平～ a gentle slope ②sloping; slanting 把板子～着放 put the board on a slant【坡地】hillside fields; sloping fields【坡度】slope

泼

pō ①sprinkle; splash; spill ～水 splash water ②rude and unreasonable; shrewish 撒～ act hysterically and refuse to see reason【泼妇】shrew【泼辣】rude and unreasonable; shrewish/pungent; forceful/bold and vigorous 工作～ be bold and vigorous in one's work【泼冷水】throw cold water on; dampen the enthusiasm of

颇

pō ①inclined to one side; oblique 偏～ biased; partial ②quite; rather 影响～大 exert a considerable influence ～为费解 rather difficult to understand

婆 pó ①old woman 媒～ woman matchmaker ②husband's mother; mother-in-law 【婆家】husband's family

叵 pǒ impossible 【叵测】unfathomable; unpredictable 居心～ with hidden intent

筶 pǒ 【筶箩】shallow basket

迫 pò ①compel; force; press ～于形势 under the pressure of events 为饥寒所～ be driven (to do sth.) by cold and hunger ②urgent; pressing 从容不～ calm and unhurried ③go towards 【迫不得已】have no alternative (but to); be forced to 【迫不及待】unable to hold oneself back 【迫害】persecute 政治～ political persecution 遭受～ suffer persecution 【迫切】urgent; pressing; imperative ～的需要 a crying need ～的心情 eager desire

破 pò ①broken; damaged; torn; worn-out ～衣服 ragged clothes ～房子 a dilapidated house ②break; split; cleave; cut ～浪前进 plough through the waves ③get rid of; destroy; break with ～纪录 break a record ④defeat; capture (a city, etc.) 城～之日 the day the city fell ⑤ expose the truth of; lay bare 看～ see through ⑥paltry; lousy ～笔 lousy pen 【破案】solve a case 【破冰船】ice-breaker 【破产】go bankrupt; become insolvent/come to naught 银行～ bank failure 阴谋～了 the plot has fallen through 【破除】get rid of; eradicate ～迷信 do away with superstitions or blind faith ～情面 not spare anybody's feelings 【破釜沉舟】break the cauldrons and sink the boats; burn one's boats 【破格】make an exception ～提升 break a rule to promote sb. ～接待 break proto-col to honour sb. 【破坏】destroy; wreck/do great damage to/violate (an agreement, regulation, etc.) ～名誉 damage sb.'s reputation ～桥梁 destroy a bridge ～生产 sabotage production ～团结 disrupt unity ～分子 saboteur ～活动 sabotage ～力 destructive power ～性 destructiveness 【破获】 unearth; uncover; crack (a criminal case, etc.) 【破旧】 old and shabby; worn-out; dilapidated 【破口大骂】 shout abuse 【破烂】 tattered; ragged/junk; scrap ～货 worthless stuff; rubbish 【破例】 break a rule; make an exception 【破裂】 burst; split; rupture; crack 谈判～ the negotiations broke down 【破落】 decline (in wealth and position); be reduced to poverty ～地主 an impoverished landlord ～户 a family that has gone down in the world 【破谜儿】 solve a riddle/ask a riddle 【破灭】 fall through; evaporate 幻想～ be disillusioned 希望～ one's hopes were shattered 【破碎】 tattered; broken / smash sth. to pieces; crush ～机 crusher; breaker 【破损】 damaged; worn; torn 【破涕为笑】 smile through tears 【破晓】 dawn; daybreak 【破绽】 a burst seam/flaw 看出～ spot sb.'s weak point 他的论据～百出 his argument is full of flaws 【破折号】 dash

魄 pò ①soul ②vigour; spirit 【魄力】 daring and resolution 工作有～ be bold and resolute in one's work

POU

剖 pōu ①cut open; rip open ～开鱼肚 cut open the belly of a fish ②analyse; examine 【剖面】 section 【剖析】 dissect

抔 póu hold sth. with cupped hand 一～土 a handful of earth—a grave

掊 pǒu 【掊击】 attack (in speech or writing); blast; lash out at

PU

仆 pū fall forward; fall prostrate

扑 pū ①throw oneself on; pounce on ～到怀里 throw oneself into sb.'s arms 猫向老鼠～去 the cat made a spring at the mouse ②rush at; attack ～蝴蝶 catch butterflies ③flap; flutter 鹰～着翅膀 the eagle flapped its wings ④bend over 【扑鼻】assail the nostrils 香气～ a sweet smell greeted us 【扑打】swat/beat; pat 【扑粉】face powder / talcum powder / apply powder 【扑克】playing cards/poker 打～ play cards 【扑空】fail to get or achieve what one wants; come away empty-handed 【扑面】blow on one's face 【扑灭】stamp out; extinguish / exterminate ～火灾 put out a fire ～蚊蝇 wipe out mosquitoes and flies 【扑腾】flop; throb; palpitate 【扑通】thump; splash

铺 pū ①spread; extend; unfold ～桌布 spread a tablecloth ②pave; lay ～路面 surface a road ～平道路 pave the way 【铺床】make the bed 【铺垫】bedding/foreshadowing 【铺盖】bedding; bedclothes ～卷儿 bedroll; luggage roll 【铺设】lay (a railroad track, etc.); build 【铺展】spread out 【铺张】extravagant

仆 pú servant 【仆从】footman; retainer; henchman ～国 vassal country

匍 pú 【匍匐】crawl; creep / lie prostrate ～前进 crawl forward ～植物 creeper

菩 pú 【菩萨】Bodhisattva/Buddha ～心肠 kindhearted and merciful

脯 pú chest; breast 【脯子】breast meat (of chicken, duck, etc.)

葡 pú 【葡萄】grape 一串～ a bunch of grapes ～干 raisin ～架 grape trellis ～酒 (grape) wine ～糖 glucose; grape sugar ～藤 grapevine ～园 vineyard

蒲 pú cattail 【蒲包】cattail bag; rush bag 【蒲绒】cattail wool 【蒲扇】cattail leaf fan 【蒲席】rush mat

朴 pǔ plain 【朴实】simple; plain/sincere and honest; guileless ～的工作作风 a down-to-earth style of work 【朴素】simple; plain 衣着～ simply dressed

圃 pǔ garden 菜～ vegetable plot 苗～ seed plot; (seedling) nursery

普 pǔ general; universal ～天下 all over the world 【普遍】general; widespread; common 有～意义 be of universal significance ～规律 universal law ～性 universality ～真理 universal truth 【普查】general survey 人口～ census 【普及】popularize; disseminate; spread / universal; popular ～本 popular edition ～教育 universal education ～文化科学知识 spread cultural and scientific knowledge among the people 【普通】ordinary; common; average ～一兵 an ordinary soldier ～人 the average person 【普选】general election 【普照】illuminate all things

谱 pǔ ①table; chart; register 食～ cookbook ②manual; guide 棋～ chess manual ③music score; music 歌～ music of a song ④compose (music) 【谱系】pedigree

蹼 pǔ web (of the feet of ducks, frogs, etc.) 【蹼趾】webbed toe 【蹼足】webfoot; palmate foot

铺 pù ①shop; store ②plank bed 【铺板】bed board 【铺面】shop front 【铺位】bunk; berth

瀑 pù 【瀑布】waterfall; falls; cataract

曝 pù expose to the sun 【曝光】exposure ～表 exposure meter 【曝露】exposed to the open air

Q

Qi

七 qī seven【七零八落】scattered here and there; in disorder【七拼八凑】piece together; knock together; rig up【七上八下】be agitated; be perturbed【七月】July/ the seventh moon

沏 qī infuse ～茶 infuse tea; make tea

妻 qī wife【妻离子散】breaking up or scattering of one's family

凄 qī ①chilly; cold ②bleak and desolate ～清 lonely and sad ③sad【凄惨】wretched; miserable; tragic【凄厉】sad and shrill (cries, etc.)【凄凉】dreary; desolate

栖 qī ①(of birds) perch ②dwell; stay【栖身】stay; sojourn 无处～ have no place to stay

戚 qī ①relative 皇亲国～ relatives of an emperor ② sorrow; woe 休～相关 share joys and sorrows

期 qī ①a period of time; phase; stage 假～ vacation 学～ school term ②scheduled time 到～ fall due ③ make an appointment 不～而遇 meet by chance【期待】 expect; await; look forward to【期刊】periodical ～阅 览室 periodical reading room【期考】terminal examination【期满】expire; run out; come to an end 合同 ～ on the expiration of the contract 服役～ complete one's term of service【期票】promissory note【期望】 hope 决不辜负人民的～ never disappoint the people's expectations【期限】allotted time; time limit 规定～ set a deadline 延长～ extend the time limit 在规定的～内

within the allotted time 付款～是哪一天 what is the prompt

欺 qī ①deceive ～人之谈 deceitful words ②bully; take advantage of ～人太甚 that's going too far 【欺负】 bully; treat sb. high-handedly 【欺凌】 bully and humiliate 【欺瞒】 hoodwink; dupe 【欺骗】 deceive; cheat; befuddle ～性 fraudulence; duplicity 【欺压】 bully and oppress 【欺诈】 cheat; swindle

漆 qī ①paint; lacquer ～盘 lacquer tray ～树 lacquer tree ②coat with lacquer; paint ～门 paint the door 【漆布】 varnished cloth 【漆工】 lacquering; painting/ lacquerer; painter 【漆黑】 pitch-dark; pitch-black

蹊 qī 【蹊跷】 odd; queer; fishy

齐 qí ①neat; even; uniform 剪得～ be evenly trimmed 长短不～ not of uniform length ②on a level with 雪深～膝 the snow was knee-deep ③together; simultaneously 一～动手 all pitched in 万炮～发 all the batteries fired at once ④all ready; all present 客人来～了 the guests are all present ⑤alike; similar 【齐备】 be all ready 【齐步走】 quick march 【齐唱】 (singing in) unison 【齐集】 assemble; gather; collect 【齐名】 be equally famous 【齐全】 complete; all in readiness 尺码～ have a complete range of sizes 装备～ be fully equipped 货物～ have a satisfactory variety of goods 【齐声】 in chorus; in unison ～回答 answer in chorus 【齐头并进】 advance side by side; do two or more things at once 【齐心】 be of one mind ～协力 work as one; make concerted efforts 【齐整】 neat; uniform 【齐奏】 playing (instruments) in unison; unison

祈 qí ①pray ～年 pray for a good harvest ②entreat 敬～指导 we respectfully request your guidance 【祈

祷】pray; say one's prayers 【祈求】earnestly hope; pray for 【祈使句】imperative sentence 【祈望】hope; wish

其 qí ①his (her; its; their) ～父 his father ②he (she, it, they) 促～早日实现 help bring it about at an early date ③that; such 正当～时 just at that time 不乏～人 there is no lack of such people 【其次】next; secondly; then/secondary 内容是主要的，形式还在～ content comes first, form second 【其实】actually; in fact; as a matter of fact 【其他】other; else 【其余】the others; the rest; the remainder ～就不必说了 the rest needs no telling 【其中】among (which, them, etc.); in (which, it)

奇 qí ①strange; queer; rare 一事 a strange affair ～花 exotic flowers ②surprise; wonder; astonish 【奇耻大辱】galling shame and humiliation 【奇功】outstanding service 【奇怪】strange; surprising; odd 【奇观】marvellous spectacle; wonder 【奇迹】miracle 医学上的～ a marvel of medical science 【奇景】wonderful view; extraordinary sight 【奇妙】marvellous; wonderful; intriguing 【奇巧】ingenious; exquisite 【奇谈】strange tale; absurd argument 【奇特】peculiar; queer; singular 【奇闻】sth. unheard-of 【奇袭】surprise attack; raid 【奇异】queer; bizarre/curious 【奇遇】happy encounter; fortuitous meeting / adventure 【奇装异服】exotic costume

歧 qí ①fork; branch ②divergent; different 【歧路】branch road; forked road 【歧视】discriminate against 【歧途】wrong road 误入～ go astray 【歧义】different meanings; various interpretations 有～ be equivocal

脐 qí navel; umbilicus 【脐带】umbilical cord

畦 qí rectangular pieces of land in a field, separated by ridges 菜～ a vegetable bed

崎 qí 【崎岖】rugged ～不平 rugged and rough ～的山路 a rugged mountain path

骑 qí ride ～马 ride a horse ～车回家 go home by bicycle 【骑兵】cavalryman; cavalry ～部队 mounted troops 【骑墙】sit on the fence ～派 fence-sitter 【骑士】knight; cavalier 【骑术】horsemanship

棋 qí chess 下盘～ play a game of chess 【棋迷】chess fan 【棋盘】chessboard 【棋谱】chess manual 【棋子】piece (in a board game); chessman

旗 qí flag; banner; standard 【旗杆】flagpole; flag post 【旗鼓相当】be well-matched 【旗舰】flagship 【旗开得胜】win victory in the first battle 【旗袍】cheongsam 【旗手】standard-bearer 【旗语】(signal by) semaphore

乞 qǐ beg (for alms, etc.); supplicate ～食 beg for food 【乞丐】beggar 【乞怜】beg for pity 【乞灵】resort to; seek help from 【乞降】beg to surrender

岂 qǐ 【岂敢】you flatter me; I don't deserve such praise or honour 【岂能】how could; how is it possible 【岂有此理】preposterous; outrageous

企 qǐ ①stand on tiptoe ②anxiously expect sth.; look forward to 【企鹅】penguin 【企求】desire to gain; seek for 【企图】attempt; try; seek 【企望】hope for; look foward to 【企业】enterprise; business 工矿～ factories, mines and other enterprises ～管理 business management ～家 entrepreneur; enterpriser

启 qǐ ①open 幕～ the curtain rises ②start; initiate ～行 start on a journey ③enlighten; awaken 【启程】set out 【启齿】open one's mouth; start to talk about sth. 【启动】start (a machine, etc) ; switch on 【启发】arouse; inspire; enlighten 【启封】unseal; remove the seal / open an envelop or wrapper 【启航】set sail; weigh anchor

【启蒙】impart rudimentary knowledge to beginners; initiate ～老师 the teacher who introduces one to a certain field of study ～课本 children's primer ～运动 the Enlightenment 【启示】enlightenment; inspiration; revelation 【启事】notice; announcement 【启运】start shipment (of goods)

起 qǐ ①rise; get up; stand up 早睡早～ early to bed and early to rise ②remove; extract; pull ～钉子 draw out a nail ③appear; raise ～水泡 get blisters ④rise; grow ～风 the wind is rising ～疑心 become suspicious ～作用 take effect ⑤draft; work out ～稿子 make a draft ⑥build; set up ～墙 build a wall ～伙 set up a mess ⑦begin 从今天～ starting from today ⑧case; instance/batch; group 分两～出发 set out in two groups 【起草】draft; draw up ～文件 draft a document ～人 draftsman ～委员会 drafting committee 【起程】leave; set out; start on a journey 【起初】originally; at first; at the outset 【起床】get up; get out of bed ～号 reveille 【起点】starting point 【起动】start (a machine, etc.) 【起飞】(of aircraft) take off 【起伏】rise and fall; undulate 【起航】set sail 【起哄】gather together to create a disturbance/jeer; boo and hoot 【起火】fire breaking out / cook meals 【起家】build up; make one's fortune, name, etc. 【起劲】vigorously; energetically 【起立】stand up; rise to one's feet 【起码】minimum; rudimentary; elementary/ at least 【起锚】weigh anchor; set sail 【起名儿】(give a) name 【起跑】start of a race ～线 starting line (for a race); scratch line (for a relay race) 【起讫】the beginning and the end 【起色】improvement; pickup 【起身】get up; get out of bed/leave; set out; get off 【起事】start armed struggle; rise in rebellion 【起誓】take an oath; swear

【起诉】bring a suit against sb.; sue; prosecute ～人 suit-or; prosecutor ～书 indictment 【起头】start; originate/beginning 万事～难 everything is hard in the beginning 【起先】at first 【起义】uprising; revolt ～军 insurrection-ary army 【起因】cause; origin 【起源】origin / originate; stem from 【起运】start shipment 【起重机】hoist; crane; derrick 【起子】bottle opener/baking powder/screwdriver

绮　qǐ damask 【绮丽】beautiful; gorgeous

气　qì ①gas 沼～ marsh gas ②air 开窗透透～ open the window to let in some fresh air ③breath 歇口～ catch one's breath ④smell; odour 香～ sweet smell 臭～ bad odour ⑤weather 秋高～爽 fine autumn weath-er ⑥airs; manner 官～ bureaucratic airs 书生～ bookish ⑦spirit; morale 打～ boost the morale; cheer on ⑧make angry; enrage 我故意～他 I got him angry on purpose ⑨be enraged ～得直哆嗦 tremble with rage ⑩bully; insult 受～ be bullied 【气冲冲】furious; beside oneself with rage 【气喘】asthma 【气窗】transom (window); fanlight 【气度】tolerance; bearing 【气氛】atmosphere 【气愤】indignant; furious 【气概】lofty quality; mettle; spirit 【气管】wind-pipe; trachea ～炎 tracheitis 【气候】climate/situation ～图 climatic chart ～学 climatology 【气急败坏】flustered and exasperated 【气节】integrity; moral courage 【气力】effort; energy; strength 【气量】tolerance ～大 large-mind-ed ～小 narrow-minded 【气流】air current; airflow/breath 【气门】(air) valve of a tyre ～心 valve inside 【气恼】take offence; be ruffled 【气馁】be discouraged; lose heart 【气派】manner; style; air 【气泡】air bubble 【气魄】boldness of vision; breadth of spirit; daring 【气枪】air gun 【气球】balloon 【气色】complexion; colour ～好

have a good colour ～不好 look pale; be off colour 【气势】 momentum; imposing manner ～汹汹 fierce; truculent; overbearing 【气体】 gas 【气筒】 inflator; bicycle pump 【气味】 smell; odour; flavour / smack; taste ～相投 be two of a kind 【气温】 air temperature 【气息】 breath / flavour; smell 有强烈的～生活 have the rich flavour of life ～奄奄 at one's last gasp 【气象】 meteorological phenomena / meteorology / atmosphere; scene ～观测 meteorological observation ～台 meteorological observatory ～图 meteorological map ～学 meteorology ～预报 weather forecast ～员 weatherman 【气象万千】 spectacular; majestic 【气呼呼】 panting; gasping for breath 【气压】 atmospheric pressure ～表 barometer 【气焰】 arrogance; bluster ～嚣张 be swollen with arrogance 【气质】 temperament; disposition / qualities; makings

讫 qì ①settled; completed 付～ paid 收～ received in full 验～ checked ②end

迄 qì up to; till ～今 up to now; to this day ②so far; all along ～无音信 have received no information so far

汽 qì vapour; steam 【汽车】 automobile; motor vehicle; car ～队 motor transport corps ～工业 auto industry ～库 garage ～修配厂 motor repair shop ～制造厂 automobile factory 【汽船】 steamship; steamer 【汽锤】 steam hammer 【汽灯】 gas lamp 【汽笛】 steam whistle; siren; hooter 【汽酒】 light sparkling wine 【汽水】 aerated water; soft drink; soda water 【汽艇】 motorboat 【汽油】 petrol; gasoline; gas

弃 qì throw away; discard; abandon ～之可惜 hesitate to discard sth.; be unwilling to throw away ～城 abandon the city 【弃旧图新】 turn over a new leaf 【弃权】 abstain from voting / waive the right (to play); forfeit【弃世】pass away; die【弃婴】abandon a baby/foundling【弃置】throw aside ～不用 be discarded

泣 qì ①weep; sob ～诉 accuse while weeping; accuse amid tears ～不成声 choke with sobs ②tears ～下如雨 weep copious tears

契 qì ①engrave; carve ②contract; deed 地～ land deed ③agree 默～ tacit agreement【契合】agree with; tally with【契机】moment/turning point; juncture【契约】deed

砌 qì ①build by laying bricks or stones ～墙 build a wall (with bricks, stones, etc.) ②step

器 qì ①implement; utensil; ware 玉～ jade article ②organ ③capacity; talent ～识 capability and judgment【器材】equipment; material【器官】organ; apparatus 发音～ organs of speech【器具】utensil; implement; appliance【器量】tolerance【器皿】household utensils; containers【器械】apparatus; appliance; instrument /weapon 医疗～ medical appliances 体育～ sports apparatus ～体操 gymnastics on or with apparatus【器乐】instrumental music ～曲 composition for an instrument【器重】think highly of; regard highly

QIA

掐 qiā ①pinch; nip ～花 nip off a flower 把烟卷～了 stub out the cigarette ②clutch ～脖子 seize sb. by the throat ～死 choke to death; throttle【掐断】nip off; cut off ～电线 disconnect the wire ～水源 cut off the water supply【掐头去尾】break off both ends

卡 qiǎ ①wedge; get stuck 鱼刺～在嗓子里 a fish bone sticks in one's throat ②clip; fastener 发～ hairpin【卡口灯泡】bayonet-socket bulb【卡口灯头】bayonet socket【卡子】clip; fastener/checkpost

洽 qià ①be in harmony; agree 意见不～ have different opinions ②consult; arrange with

恰 qià ①appropriate; proper ②just; exactly ～到好处 just right 【恰当】suitable; fitting 用词～ use proper words ～的措施 appropriate measures 你的话有点不～ your remarks were a bit out of place 【恰巧】by chance; fortunately; as chance would have it

QIAN

千 qiān ①thousand ～～万万 thousands upon thousands ②a great amount of ～百条建议 lots and lots of suggestions ～层饼 multi-layer steamed bread 【千变万化】ever changing 【千方百计】in a thousand and one ways; by every possible means 【千古】through-the ages; for all time ～奇闻 a fantastic story 【千里迢迢】thousands of li away; from afar 【千篇一律】stereotyped; following the same pattern 【千丝万缕】countless ties; a thousand and one links 【千头万绪】thousands of strands and loose ends; a multitude of things 【千万】ten million; millions upon millions 【千辛万苦】innumerable trials and tribulations; untold hardships 【千言万语】thousands and thousands of words

扦 qiān a short slender pointed piece of metal, bamboo, etc. 蜡～ candlestick 竹～ bamboo spike

迁 qiān ①move ～往他处 move to another place ② change 【迁就】accommodate oneself to; yield to 【迁居】change one's dwelling place; move (house) 【迁延】delay; defer; procrastinate ～时日 cause a long delay 【迁移】migrate

钎 qiān drill rod; drill steel; borer 【钎子】hammer drill; rock drill

牵 qiān ①lead along (by holding the hand, the halter, etc.); pull ~牛 lead an ox 手~手 hand in hand ②involve 【牵扯】involve; implicate; drag in 【牵掣】hold up; impede/pin down; check; contain 互相~ hold each other up 【牵动】affect; influence ~全局 affect the situation as a whole 【牵挂】worry; care 没有~ free from care 【牵累】tie down/implicate 【牵连】involve (in trouble); tie up with 【牵强】forced (interpretation, etc.); farfetched ~附会 draw a forced analogy; make a farfetched comparison 【牵涉】involve; drag in 【牵线】pull strings; pull wires/act as go-between ~人 wire-puller; go-between 【牵引】tow; draw ~车 tractor 【牵制】tie up; check; contain ~敌人 pin down the enemy

悭 qiān 【悭吝】stingy; miserly

铅 qiān lead 【铅笔】pencil ~刀 pen-knife ~盒 pencil-case ~画 pencil drawing ~芯 lead (in a pencil) 【铅球】shot 推~ shot put ~运动员 shot-putter 【铅印】letterpress printing; stereotype 【铅字】type; letter

谦 qiān modest 【谦恭】modest and courteous 【谦让】modestly decline 不要~了 don't decline out of modesty 【谦虚】modest; self-effacing/make modest remarks

签 qiān ①sign ②make brief comments on a document ③bamboo slips used for divination or drawing lots 抽~ draw lots ④label; sticker 航空邮~ air mail sticker ⑤a slender pointed piece of bamboo or wood 牙~ tooth pick 【签到】sign in ~簿 attendance book ~处 sign-in desk 【签订】conclude and sign (a treaty, etc.) ~合同 sign a contract 【签发】sign and issue (a document, certificate, etc.) 【签名】sign one's name; autograph 亲笔~的照片 an autographed picture ~簿 visitors' book

【签署】sign ～意见 write comments and sign one's name (on a document) 【签证】visa; visé 入(出)境～ entry (exit) visa 过境～ transit visa 【签字】sign; affix one's signature ～仪式 signing ceremony

前 qián ①front 楼～ in front of the buiding ②forward; ahead 向～看 look forward ③ago; before 日～ a few days ago 晚饭～ before supper ④preceding ——阶段 the preceding stage 战～ prewar ⑤former; formerly ～校长 former principal of a school ⑥first ～三排 the first three rows 【前辈】senior (person); elder 革命～ revolutionaries of the older generation 【前臂】forearm 【前边】in front; ahead / above; preceding 【前程】future; prospect ～远大 have brilliant prospects 【前导】lead the way; march in front; precede/guide 【前额】forehead 【前方】ahead / the front 注视～ look ahead 开赴～ be dispatched to the front 支援～ support the front 【前锋】vanguard/forward 【前赴后继】advance wave upon wave 【前后】around (a certain time); about / from beginning to end; altogether / in front and behind 十点～ around 10 o'clock ～来过四次 have been here four times altogether ～左右 on all sides; all around 【前进】advance; go forward; forge ahead 继续～ continue to make progress 大踏步～ make big strides forward 【前景】foreground/prospect; vista; perspective 【前排】front row 【前仆后继】no sooner has one fallen than another steps into the breach 【前期】earlier stage; early days 【前前后后】the whole story; the ins and outs (of a matter) 【前驱】forerunner; precursor; pioneer 【前人】forefathers; predecessors 【前任】predecessor ～书记 former secretary ～总统 ex-president 【前哨】outpost; advance guard ～战 skirmish 【前所未有】hitherto unknown; unprecedented

【前台】proscenium/(on) the stage【前提】premise/prerequisite; presupposition 必要的～ essential prerequisite【前天】.the day before yesterday ～晚上 the night before last【前厅】antechamber; vestibule【前途】future; prospect ～无量 have boundless prospects 很有～ have a great future【前往】go to; leave for; proceed to【前卫】vanguard【前夕】eve 解放～ on the eve of liberation【前线】front; frontline 上～ go to the front【前言】preface; foreword【前沿】forward position【前因后果】cause and effect; the entire process【前兆】omen; forewarning【前者】the former【前置词】preposition【前缀】prefix【前奏】prelude

荨 qián【荨麻】nettle【荨麻疹】nettle rash; urticaria

钳 qián ①pincers; pliers; tongs; forceps 手～ hand vice ②grip (with pincers); clamp ③restrain ～口不言 keep one's mouth shut【钳工】benchwork/fitter【钳制】clamp down on; suppress ～舆论 muzzle public opinion

虔 qián sincere【虔诚】pious; devout【虔敬】reverent

钱 qián ①copper coin; cash ②money 挣～ make money ③fund; sum ④qian, a unit of weight (= 5 grams)【钱包】wallet; purse【钱币】coin【钱财】wealth; money

掮 qián【掮客】broker 政治～ political broker

乾 qián male【乾坤】heaven and earth; the universe

潜 qián ①latent; hidden ～能 latent energy ②stealthily; secretly; on the sly【潜藏】hide; go into hiding【潜伏】hide; conceal; lie low ～特务 hidden enemy agent ～的危机 a latent crisis ～期 incubation period【潜力】latent capacity; potential 有很大～ have great potentialities

充分发挥～ bring the potential into full play 挖掘～ tap potentials 【潜入】 slip into; steal in / dive; submerge 【潜水】 go under water; dive ～员 diver; frogman ～衣 diving suit 【潜逃】 abscond 【潜艇】 submarine 【潜心】 with great concentration 【潜行】 move under water/slink 【潜移默化】 imperceptibly influence 【潜泳】 underwater swimming 【潜在】 latent; potential

黔 qián black 【黔驴之技】 tricks not to be feared; cheap tricks

浅 qiǎn ①shallow ～水 shallow water ②simple; easy 课文 ～ the lesson is easy ③superficial 认识 ～ have a superficial understanding ④not intimate; not close 交情 ～ not on familiar terms ⑤(of colour) light ～蓝 light blue ⑥ not long in time 【浅薄】 shallow; meagre 【浅海】 shallow sea 【浅见】 humble opinion 【浅近】 simple; plain; easy to understand 【浅陋】 meagre; mean 【浅说】 elementary introduction 【浅滩】 shoal; shallows 【浅易】 simple and easy ～读物 easy readings

遣 qiǎn ①send; dispatch 调兵～将 dispatch officers and men; deploy forces ②dispel; expel 消～ diversion; pastime 【遣词造句】 choice of words and building of sentences; wording and phrasing 【遣返】 repatriate ～战俘 repatriate prisoners of war 【遣散】 disband; dismiss; send away 【遣送】 send back ～回国 repatriate ～出境 deport

谴 qiǎn 【谴责】 condemn; denounce; censure ～帝国主义 condemn imperialism

缱 qiǎn 【缱绻】 deeply attached to each other ～之情 sentimental attachment

欠 qiàn ①owe; be behind with ～债 owe a debt ～租 be behind with the rent ～情 owe sb. a debt of gratitude ②not enough; lacking; wanting ～佳 not good enough ③ raise slightly 【欠款】arrears; balance due; debt 【欠缺】be deficient in; be short of/shortcoming 【欠身】raise oneself slightly; half rise from one's seat ～坐起 raise oneself to a half-sitting position 【欠妥】not proper 措词～ not properly worded 【欠息】debit interest 【欠帐】bills due

纤　qiàn a rope for towing a boat; tow line 拉～ track (a boat) 【纤夫】boat tracker

倩　qiàn ①pretty; handsome ②ask sb. to do sth.

堑　qiàn moat; chasm 天～ natural chasm 【堑壕】trench; entrenchment ～战 trench warfare

嵌　qiàn inlay; embed; set ～花的地面 a mosaic pavement

歉　qiàn ①apology 抱～ be sorry ②crop failure 以丰补～ make up for a crop failure with a bumper harvest 【歉年】lean year 【歉收】crop failure; poor harvest 【歉意】apology; regret 表示～ offer an apology; express one's regret 谨致～ please accept my apologies

QIANG

枪　qiāng ①rifle; gun; firearm ～架 rifle rack ②spear 红缨～ a red-tasselled spear 【枪把】the small of the stock; pistol grip 【枪毙】execute by shooting 【枪刺】bayonet 【枪弹】cartridge/bullet 【枪法】marksmanship 【枪杆子】the barrel of a gun; gun; arms 【枪管】barrel (of a gun) 【枪口】muzzle 【枪林弹雨】a hail of bullets 【枪杀】shoot dead 【枪伤】bullet wound 【枪声】shot; crack 【枪栓】rifle bolt 【枪膛】bore (of a gun) 【枪托】buttstock 【枪械】firearms 【枪眼】embrasure; loophole/bullet hole

戗　qiāng ①in an opposite direction ～风行船 sail against the wind ②clash; get to loggerheads

戕 qiāng kill 自～ kill oneself; commit suicide

腔 qiāng ①cavity 胸～ thoracic cavity ②tune; pitch 高～ high pitched tune ③accent 学生～ schoolboy talk ④speech 不开～ keep mum 【腔调】tune / accent

锵 qiāng clang; gong

镪 qiāng 【镪水】strong acid 硝～ nitric acid

强 qiáng ①strong; powerful 能力～ capable ～敌 formidable enemy ②by force ～取 take by force ③better ④slightly more than; plus 【强暴】violent; brutal/ferocious adversary 不畏～ defy brute force 【强大】big and powerful; formidable 力量越来越～ the forces are getting stronger and stronger 【强盗】robber; bandit 【强调】stress; emphasize; underline 【强度】intensity; strength 【强渡】force a river 【强风】strong breeze 【强攻】take by storm 【强固】strong; solid 【强国】powerful nation; power 现代化～ modern, powerful country 【强悍】intrepid; valiant 【强横】tyrannical 【强化】strengthen; intensify; consolidate 【强加】impose; force ～于人 force one's views on others 【强奸】rape; violate ～民意 defile public opinion 【强烈】strong; intense; violent ～的对比 a striking contrast ～谴责 vigorously denounce 【强权】power; might ～政治 power politics 【强盛】powerful and prosperous 【强行】force ～闯入 force one's way in ～通过议案 force through a bill 【强硬】strong; tough; unyielding ～抗议 strong protest ～路线 hard line ～态度 an uncompromising stand ～派 hardliner 【强占】forcibly occupy; seize 【强制】force; compel; coerce ～劳动 forced labour ～手段 coercive measure ～执行 enforce ～机关 institutions of coercion 【强壮】strong; sturdy; robust

墙 qiáng wall 【墙报】wall newspaper 【墙根】the foot of a wall 【墙角】a corner formed by two walls

蔷 qiáng 【蔷薇】rose ~科 the rose family

樯 qiáng mast 帆~如林 a forest of masts

抢 qiáng ①rob; loot ②snatch; grab 把信~过去 snatch away the letter ③vie for; scramble for ~球 scramble for the ball ④scrape 【抢夺】snatch; wrest; seize 【抢购】rush to purchase 【抢劫】rob; loot; plunder 【抢救】rescue; save; salvage 【抢时间】race against time 【抢收】rush in the harvest 【抢先】anticipate; forestall 【抢险】rush to deal with an emergency ~队 emergency squad 【抢修】do rush repairs 【抢占】race to control; seize 【抢种】rush-planting ~晚稻 rush-plant the late rice

强 qiǎng make an effort; strive ~作镇静 try hard to keep one's composure 【强词夺理】resort to sophistry; reason fallaciously 【强迫】force; compel; coerce ~命令 resort to coercion and commandism 【强求】insist on; impose 不能~一律 no uniformity should be imposed

褓 qiǎng 【襁褓】swaddling clothes ~中 be in one's infancy

呛 qiàng irritate (respiratory organs) 辣椒味~鼻子 the smell of red pepper irritates the nose

QIAO

悄 qiāo 【悄悄】quietly; on the quiet ~离开 leave quietly 他~跟我全说了 he told me everything on the quiet

跷 qiāo ①lift up (a leg); hold up (a finger) ~着腿坐着 sit with one's legs crossed ②on tiptoe ③stilts

【跷蹊】 fishy; dubious; queer

敲 qiāo ①knock; beat; strike ～门 knock at the door ②overcharge; fleece sb. 给～去五块钱 be stung for five *yuan* 【敲打】 beat; rap; tap 【敲诈】 extort; blackmail

锹 qiāo spade 挖一～深 dig a spade's depth 一～煤 a shovelful of coal

橇 qiāo sledge; sled; sleigh

乔 qiáo ①tall ②disguise 【乔林】 high forest 【乔木】 arbor; tree 【乔装】 disguise

侨 qiáo ①live abroad ②a person living abroad 【侨胞】 countrymen residing abroad 【侨汇】 overseas remittance 【侨居】 live abroad 【侨民】 a national of a particular country residing abroad 【侨务】 affairs concerning nationals living abroad

荞 qiáo 【荞麦】 buckwheat

桥 qiáo bridge 【桥洞】 bridge opening 【桥墩】 pier 【桥梁】 bridge 起～作用 serve as a link 【桥牌】 bridge

翘 qiáo ①raise (one's head) ②become warped 木板～了 the board has warped

憔 qiáo 【憔悴】 wan and sallow; thin and pallid

瞧 qiáo look; see 东～西看 look about 等着～ wait and see ～着办吧 do as you see fit 【瞧不起】 look down upon; hold in contempt 【瞧得起】 think much of sb.

巧 qiǎo ①skilful; ingenious; clever 手～ clever with one's hands; dexterous ②cunning; artful ～言 cunning words; deceitful talk ③opportunely; coincidentally; as it happens 来得～ arrive at a most opportune moment 【巧干】 work ingeniously; do sth. in a clever way 【巧合】

coincidence 【巧计】clever device; artful scheme 【巧克力】 chocolate 【巧立名目】invent all sorts of names 【巧妙】 ingenious; clever【巧取豪夺】secure (sb.'s belongings, right, etc.) by force or trickery 【巧遇】chance encounter

悄 qiǎo ①quiet; silent ②sad; worried 【悄然】sorrowfully; sadly / quietly; softly ～泪下 shed sad tears

壳 qiào shell; hard surface

俏 qiào ①pretty; smart 打扮得真～ be smartly dressed ②sell well ～货 goods in great demand 【俏丽】handsome; pretty 【俏皮】good-looking; smart / lively and delightful; witty ～话 witticism / sarcastic remark

诮 qiào censure; blame

窍 qiào ①aperture ②a key to sth. 【窍门】key; knack 找～ try to find the key to a problem

峭 qiào ①high and steep; precipitous ②severe; stern 【峭壁】cliff; precipice

翘 qiào stick up; hold up; bend upwards 【翘辫子】 kick the bucket 【翘尾巴】be cocky; get stuck-up

撬 qiào prize; pry ～开箱子 prize open a box 【撬杠】 crowbar

鞘 qiào sheath; scabbard

QIE

切 qiē cut; slice ～菜 cut up vegetables ～肉 slice meat 【切除】excision; resection 【切磋】learn from each other by exchanging views; compare notes 【切断】 cut off ～后路 cut off sb.'s retreat ～电源 cut off the electricity supply 【切面】tangent plane / section / cut noodles; machine-made noodles 【切片】 cut into slices

茄 qié 【茄子】 eggplant; aubergine

且 qiě just; for the time being ～等一下 just wait a little while 这事～放一下 let the matter rest for the time being 【且慢】 wait a moment; not go or do so soon

切 qiè ①correspond to; be close to 译文不～ the translation does not correspond to the original ②eager; anxious 回国心～ be anxious to return to one's country ③be sure to ～勿迟延 be sure not to delay 【切齿】 gnash one's teeth (in hatred) 【切合】 suit; fit in with ～实际 be geared to actual circumstances ～需要 fit in with the needs of sb. 【切记】 must always remember 【切忌】 must guard against; avoid by all means 【切身】 of immediate concern to oneself / personal ～利益 one's immediate or vital interests ～体会 personal understanding 【切实】 feasible; practical / conscientiously; earnestly ～改正错误 correct one's mistakes in real earnest 【切题】 keep to the point; be relevant to the subject 【切中】 hit (the mark)

妾 qiè concubine

怯 qiè timid; cowardly; nervous 【怯场】 have stage fright 【怯弱】 timid and weak-willed

窃 qiè ①steal; pilfer 行～ practise theft ～案 burglary ②secretly; furtively ～笑 laugh secretly ～～私议 exchange whispered comments 【窃国】 usurp state power ～大盗 arch usurper of state power 【窃据】 usurp ～要职 usurp a high post 【窃取】 steal; grab ～情报 steal (secret) information ～劳动果实 grab the fruits of other people's labour 【窃听】 eavesdrop; wiretap; bug ～器 tapping device 【窃贼】 thief; burglar

挈 qiè ①take along ～眷 take one's family along ②lift; raise; take up

惬 qiè be satisfied 【惬意】be pleased

锲 qiè carve; engrave 【锲而不舍】keep on carving unflaggingly/work with perseverance

QIN

亲 qīn ①parent 双～ parents ②blood relation; next of kin ～兄弟 blood brother ③relative 近～ close relative 远～ distant relative ④marriage; match 说～ act as a matchmaker ⑤close; intimate; dear ～如一家 as dear to each other as members of one family ⑥kiss ～孩子的脸 kiss the child on the cheek 【亲爱】dear; beloved ～的祖国 one's beloved country 【亲笔】(in) one's own handwriting ～签名 one's own signature; autograph ～信 a personal, hand-written message; an autograph letter 【亲口】(say sth.) personally 这是他～告诉我的 he told me this himself 【亲密】close; intimate ～战友 a close comrade-in-arms ～无间 be on very intimate terms with each other 【亲戚】relative 【亲切】cordial; kind ～的关怀 loving care ～的教导 kind guidance ～的谈话 a cordial conversation 【亲热】affectionate; intimate 【亲人】one's parents, spouse, children, etc.; one's family members 【亲善】goodwill (between countries) 【亲生】one's own (children, parents) 【亲事】marriage 【亲手】with one's own hands; personally; oneself 【亲属】kinsfolk; relatives 【亲王】prince 【亲信】trusted follower 【亲眼】with one's own eyes; personally 【亲友】relatives and friends; kith and kin 【亲自】personally; in person ～动手 do the job oneself 【亲嘴】kiss

侵 qīn invade; intrude into 【侵犯】 encroach on; violate ～人权 infringe upon human rights ～领土 violate a country's territorial integrity 公共财产不可～ public property shall be inviolable 【侵害】 encroach on 【侵略】 aggression; invasion ～别国 commit aggression against another country ～国 aggressor (nation) ～军 invading army ～行为 act of aggression ～战争 war of aggression ～者 aggressor; invader 【侵扰】 invade and harass ～边境 make border raids 【侵入】 invade; intrude into; make incursions into 【侵蚀】 corrode; erode 【侵吞】 misappropriate/swallow up; annex ～公款 embezzle public funds ～别国领土 annex another country's territory 【侵占】 seize ～公有土地 seize public land

钦 qīn ①admire; respect ②by the emperor himself 【钦差】 imperial envoy 【钦佩】 admire; esteem

芹 qín 【芹菜】 celery

琴 qín a general name for certain musical instruments 钢～ piano 口～ harmonica 【琴拨】 plectrum 【琴凳】 music stool 【琴键】 key 【琴弦】 string

禽 qín birds 家～ (domestic) fowls; poultry 【禽兽】 birds and beasts ～行为 bestial acts

勤 qín ①diligent; industrious ～学 study diligently ②frequently; regularly 夏雨雨水～ rain is frequent in summer ③attendance 考～ check on work attendance 【勤奋】 diligent; assiduous 学习～ be diligent in one's studies 【勤工俭学】 work-study programme 【勤俭】 hardworking and thrifty ～建国 build up the country through thrift and hard work ～持家 be industrious and thrifty in managing a household 【勤恳】 diligent and conscientious 【勤务】 duty; service ～员 odd-jobman

擒 qín capture; catch; seize 生～ capture alive ～贼先～王 to catch bandits, first catch the ringleader

噙 qín hold in the mouth or the eyes ～着眼泪 eyes brimming with tears

寝 qǐn ①sleep ②bedroom 就～ retire to rest; go to bed ③coffin chamber 陵～ mausoleum 【寝室】 bedroom; dormitory

沁 qìn ooze; seep; exude ～出汗珠 ooze sweat 【沁人心脾】 mentally refreshing

QING

青 qīng ①blue or green ～天 blue sky ～椒 green pepper ②black ～布 black cloth ③green grass; young crops 看～ keep watch on the ripening crops ④young ～工 young workers 【青菜】 green vegetables; greens/Chinese cabbage 【青草】 green grass 【青春】 youth; youthfulness ～的活力 youthful vigour ～期 puberty 【青翠】 verdant; fresh and green 【青豆】 green soya bean 【青果】 Chinese olive 【青梅】 green plum 【青霉素】 penicillin 【青苗】 young crops 【青年】 youth; young people ～时代 one's youth ～学生 young students ～工作 youth work ～运动 youth movement 【青山】 green hill 【青少年】 teen-agers; youngsters 【青史】 annals of history 【青饲料】 greenfeed 【青松】 pine 【青苔】 moss 【青铜】 bronze 【青蛙】 frog 【青贮】 ensiling ～饲料 ensilage; silage

轻 qīng ①light ～武器 light arms ②small in number, degree, etc. 年纪很～ be very young 病很～ the illness is not serious ③not important 责任～ carry a light responsibility ④gently; softly ～拿～放 handle gently ⑤rashly ～信 readily believe ⑥belittle; make light of 【轻便】 light; portable ～铁道 light railway ～桥 portable bridge 【轻薄】given to philandering; frivolous 【轻而易举】easy to do 这决不是～的事 it's certainly no easy job 【轻浮】flighty; light 举止～ behave frivolously 【轻工业】light industry 【轻活】light work; soft job 【轻机枪】light machine gun 【轻举妄动】act rashly 不可～ make no move without careful thought 【轻快】brisk; spry / lighthearted ～的曲调 lively tune ～的步子 brisk pace 【轻描淡写】touch on lightly; mention casually 【轻蔑】scornful; contemptuous ～的眼光 a disdainful look 【轻巧】light and handy / dexterous; deft 【轻伤】minor wound ～员 ambulant patient 【轻声】in a soft voice; softly ～低语 speak softly; whisper 【轻视】despise; look down on; underestimate 【轻率】rash; hasty; indiscreet ～的态度 reckless attitude ～从事 act rashly 【轻松】light; relaxed ～的工作 soft job 【轻佻】frivolous; skittish; giddy 【轻微】light; slight; trifling; to a small extent 【轻信】be credulous; readily place trust in ～口供 readily believe confessions 【轻型】light-duty; light ～卡车 light truck ～飞机 light aircraft 【轻易】easily / lightly; rashly 【轻音乐】light music 【轻盈】slim and graceful; lithe; lissom 【轻油】light oil 【轻重】weight/degree of seriousness; relative importance / propriety 两个箱子～不一样 the two boxes do not weight the same 此事无足～ it's a matter of no consequence 他说话不知～ he doesn't know the proper way to talk 【轻装】travel light ～就道 travel light ～前进 march with light packs 【轻罪】minor crime

氢 qīng hydrogen 【氢弹】hydrogen bomb ～头 H-warhead 【氢气】hydrogen ～球 hydrogen balloon

倾 qīng ①incline; lean; bend 向前～ lean forward ②deviation; tendency ③collapse 大厦将～ a great mansion on the point of collapse ④overturn and pour out; empty【倾倒】topple over / greatly admire 为之～ be infatuated with sb.【倾覆】overturn; topple; capsize【倾家荡产】lose a family fortune【倾慕】have a strong admiration for; adore【倾盆大雨】heavy downpour; torrential rain【倾诉】pour out (one's heart, troubles, etc.)【倾谈】have a good, heart-to-heart talk【倾听】lend an attentive ear to ～群众意见 listen attentively to the views of the masses【倾向】tendency; trend/be inclined to; prefer 我～于第一种方案 I prefer the first plan ～性 tendentiousness【倾销】dump (goods)【倾斜】tilt; incline; slope; slant ～度 gradient ～角 angle of inclination【倾心】admire; fall in love with/cordial 一见～ fall in love at first sight ～交谈 have a heart-to-heart talk【倾轧】engage in internal strife; jostle against each other

清 qīng ①unmixed; clear ～水 clear water ②distinct; clarified 说不～ hard to explain 数不～ countless ③quiet ④completely ⑤settle; clean up 帐～了吗 has the account been cleared up ⑥count【清白】pure; clean; stainless 历史～ have a clean personal record【清册】detailed list【清茶】green tea/tea served without refreshments【清查】check / uncover; comb out; ferret out【清偿】pay off (debts, etc.); clear off【清澈】limpid【清晨】early morning【清除】eliminate; get rid of ～垃圾 clear away the rubbish ～出党 clear sb. out of the Party【清楚】clear; distinct/be clear about; understand 字迹～ written in a clear hand 发音～ a clear pronunciation 头脑～ a clear head【清脆】clear and melodious【清单】detailed list【清淡】light; weak ～的绿茶 weak green tea ～的食物 light food 生意～ business is slack【清点】check; sort and count【清高】aloof (from politics and material pursuits)【清稿】fair copy【清官】honest and upright official【清规戒律】restrictions and fetters【清洁】clean 注意～卫生 pay attention to sanitation and hygiene ～队 cleaning squad ～工人 sanitation worker; street cleaner【清净】peace and quiet【清理】put in order; clear ～房间 clean up the room ～债务 clear up debts ～档案 sort out documents【清凉】·cool and refreshing ～饮料 cold drink; cooler ～油 cooling ointment【清爽】fresh and cool【清算】clear (accounts); square / expose and criticize【清晰】distinct; clear 她发音～ her pronunciation is clear ～可见 be clearly discernible ～度 clarity; articulation【清洗】rinse; wash; clean/purge; comb out【清闲】at leisure; idle【清醒】clear-headed/regain consciousness ～头脑 a cool head ～的估计 a sober estimate ～过来 come to one's senses【清秀】delicate and pretty 面貌～ of fine, delicate features【清样】final proof【清真】Islamic; Muslim ～教 Islam ～寺 mosque

蜻 qīng【蜻蜓】dragonfly

情 qíng ①feeling; affection 温～ tender sentiments ② love; passion 谈～说爱 be courting; talk love ③favour; kindness 求～ ask for a favour ④situation; circumstances 病～ patient's condition【情报】intelligence; information 搜集～ collect intelligence ～机关 intelligence agency【情不自禁】cannot refrain from; cannot help (doing sth.)【情操】sentiment【情调】emotional appeal【情分】mutual affection 朋友～ friendship 兄弟～ fraternity【情夫】lover【情妇】mistress【情感】emotion; feeling【情歌】love song【情话】lovers' prattle【情节】plot ～紧凑 a tightknit plot【情景】scene; sight【情况】situation; condition 在这种～下 under these circumstances 根据具体～ in accordance with specific conditions 在许

多～下 in many cases ～怎样 how do affairs stand 【情理】 reason; sense 合乎～ be reasonable 不近～ unreasonable 【情侣】 sweethearts; lovers 【情面】 feelings; sensibilities 留～ spare sb.'s feelings 不顾～ have no consideration for sb.'s feelings 【情势】 situation; trend of events 【情书】 love letter 【情态】 spirit; mood ～动词 modal verb 【情投意合】 find each other congenial 【情绪】 morale; feeling/depression; the sulks 【情义】 ties of friendship, comradeship, etc. 【情谊】 friendly feelings 战斗～ militant bonds of friendship 兄弟～ brotherly affection 【情意】 affection; goodwill 【情由】 the hows and whys 不问～ without asking about the circumstances or causes 【情有可原】 excusable; pardonable 【情欲】 sexual passion; lust 【情愿】 be willing to/would rather; prefer

晴 qíng fine; clear ～空 clear sky 【晴和】 warm and fine 【晴朗】 fine; sunny (day) 【晴天霹雳】 a bolt from the blue 【晴雨表】 barometer

擎 qíng prop up; hold up; lift up

顷 qǐng ①qǐng, a unit of area (＝6.6667 hectares) ② just ～接来信 I have just received your letter 【顷刻】 in a moment; instantly

请 qǐng ①request; ask ～他进来 ask him in ②invite; engage ～医生 send for a doctor ③please ～坐 please be seated ～不要笑 please don't laugh 【请便】 do as you wish; please yourself 【请假】 ask for leave 请病假回家 go home on sick leave ～条 written request for leave 【请教】 ask for advice; consult 向群众～ learn from the masses 【请客】 stand treat; invite sb. to dinner; entertain guests 这回我～ this is my treat 【请求】 ask; request 【请示】 ask for instructions 【请帖】 invitation 【请问】 excuse

me; please / we should like to ask; it may be asked ~
现在是什么时间 pray tell me the time【请勿】please don't
本室书籍~携出室外 please don't take the books out of
this room ~吸烟 no smoking ~践踏草地 keep off the
lawn【请愿】present a petition ～书 petition【请战】
ask for a battle assignment ~书 written request for a
battle assignment【请罪】apologize; admit one's error
and ask for punishment

庆 qìng ①celebrate; congratulate ～丰收 celebrate a
bumper harvest ②occasion for celebration【庆幸】
rejoice 值得~的事 a matter for rejoicing【庆祝】cele-
brate ～大会 celebration meeting

亲 qìng【亲家】parents of one's daughter-in-law or
son-in-law / relatives by marriage

罄 qìng use up; exhaust 告~ be all used up; run out
【罄竹难书】(of crimes, etc.) too numerous to record

QIONG

穷 qióng ①poor; poverty-stricken ②limit; end 无~
endless; inexhaustible ③thoroughly ～究 make a thorough inquiry ～追 go in hot pursuit【穷苦】impover-
ished【穷困】destitute; in straitened circumstances【穷人】
poor people【穷日子】days of poverty【穷奢极欲】(indulge in) luxury and extravagance; (live a life of) wanton extravagance【穷途末路】dead end【穷乡僻壤】a
remote, backward place【穷凶极恶】extremely vicious;
utterly evil; atrocious; diabolical

穹 qióng ①vault; dome ②the sky【穹苍】the sky; the
heavens

琼 qióng fine jade【琼脂】agar-agar; agar

QIU

丘 qiū ①mound; hillock 沙～ a sand dune ②grave 【丘陵】hills ～地带 hilly land 【丘疹】papule

秋 qiū ①autumn ～风 autumn wind ②harvest time 麦～ time for the wheat harvest ③year 千～万代 for thousands of years ④a period of time 多事之～ an eventful period 【秋波】bright eyes of a beautiful woman 送～ make eyes; ogle 【秋季】autumn ～作物 autumn crops 【秋凉】cool autumn days 【秋千】swing 打～ have a swing

蚯 qiū 【蚯蚓】earthworm

囚 qiū ①imprison 被～ be thrown into prison ②prisoner 死～ a convict sentenced to death 【囚车】prison van 【囚犯】convict 【囚禁】imprison; put in jail 【囚牢】prison; jail 【囚室】prison cell

求 qiú ①beg; request; entreat; beseech 有～于人 have to look to others for help ②seek; try ～进步 strive for further progress 一得一致 try to achieve a consensus ③demand 【求爱】pay court to 【求和】sue for peace 【求婚】make an offer of marriage; propose 【求见】request an interview 【求教】ask for advice 登门～ call on sb. for counsel 【求救】cry for help 发出～的信号 send an SOS 【求乞】beg 【求亲】seek a marriage alliance 【求情】plead; intercede 【求全】demand perfection / try to round sth. off 【求饶】beg for mercy 【求人】ask for help 【求胜】strive for victory ～心切 be anxious to gain victory 【求学】attend school/pursue one's studies 【求援】request reinforcements 【求知】seek knowledge

泅 qiū swim 【泅渡】swim across 武装～ swim across fully armed

酋 qiú ①chief of a tribe ②chieftain 匪～ bandit chief 【酋长】 chief of a tribe / sheik(h); emir

球 qiú ①sphere; globe ②ball 传～ pass the ball ③the globe; the earth 全～战略 global strategy 【球场】 court; field 【球胆】 bladder (of a ball) 【球队】 (ball game) team 【球门】 goal 【球赛】 (ball game) fan 【球拍】 (tennis, etc.) racket/(pingpong) bat 【球赛】 ball game; match 【球坛】 ball-playing circles 【球网】 net (for ball games) 【球鞋】 gym shoes; tennis shoes; sneakers 【球形】 globular; round 【球艺】 ball game skills

QU

区 qū ①area; district; region 山～ mountainous district 住宅～ residential quarters ②an administrative division 自治～ autonomous region ③classify; subdivide 【区别】 distinguish; differentiate / difference ～对待 deal with each case on its merits ～好坏 distinguish between good and bad 在意义上没有～ there is no difference in meaning 【区区】 trivial; trifling 【区域】 region; area

曲 qū ①bent; crooked ②bend (of a river, etc.) ③wrong; unjustifiable 【曲别针】 paper clip 【曲尺】 carpenter's square 【曲棍球】 field hockey/hockey ball 【曲解】 (deliberately) misinterpret; twist 你～了他的意思 you've misrepresented his meaning 【曲线】 curve 【曲折】 tortuous; winding / complications 【曲直】 right and wrong

驱 qū ①drive (a horse, car, etc.) ～车前往 drive (in a vehicle) to a place ②expel; disperse 【驱除】 drive out; get rid of 【驱散】 disperse; dispel; break up 【驱使】 order about / prompt; urge; spur on 为好奇心所～ be prompted by curiosity 【驱逐】 drive out; expel; banish ～出境 deport ～机 pursuit plane ～舰 destroyer

屈 qū ①bend; bow; crook ~臂 crook one's arm ②subdue; submit 不~不挠 unyielding ③wrong; injustice 受~ be wronged 叫~ complain about an injustice ④ in the wrong 理~ have a weak case 【屈服】surrender; yield; knuckle under ~于压力 yield to pressure 【屈辱】humiliation; mortification 【屈膝】bend one's knees

祛 qū dispel; remove ~暑 drive away summer heat 【祛除】dispel; get rid of; drive out ~疑虑 dispel one's misgivings ~邪魔 exorcize evil spirits

蛆 qū maggot

躯 qū the human body 血肉之~ mortal flesh and blood 【躯干】trunk; torso 【躯体】body

趋 qū ①hasten; hurry along ~前 hasten forward ②tend to become ~于稳定 tend towards stability ~于一致 reach unanimity 【趋势】trend; tendency 有恶化的~ be tending to deteriorate 【趋向】tend to; incline to/trend; direction ~好转 tend to improve ~动词 directional verb 【趋炎附势】curry favour with the powerful

渠 qú canal; channel 【渠道】irrigation ditch/medium of communication 外交~ diplomatic channels

曲 qū ①song; tune; melody 高歌一~ lustily sing a song 小~ ditty ②music (of a song) 【曲调】tune (of a song); melody 【曲艺】folk art forms including ballad singing, story telling, comic dialogues, clapper talks, etc.

取 qǔ ①take; get; fetch 去~行李 go to fetch one's luggage ②aim at; seek ~乐 seek pleasure ~信于人 win confidence ③adopt; assume 给孩子~名儿 choose a name for a child; give a name to a child 【取保】get sb. to go bail for one ~释放 be bailed out 【取材】draw materials 【取代】replace; substitute for; supersede; supplant 【取道】

by way of; via 【取得】gain; acquire ～经验 gain experience ～同意 obtain the consent ～一致意见 reach complete identity of views ～群众支持 enlist popular support ～成功 achieve success 【取缔】outlaw; suppress ～投机倒把 ban speculation and profiteering 【取给】draw (supplies, etc.) 【取决】be decided by; depend on 【取暖】warm oneself (by a fire, etc.) 【取巧】resort to trickery to serve oneself 【取舍】accept or reject; make one's choice 【取胜】win victory; score a success 【取消】cancel; call off; abolish ～会议 cancel a meeting ～决定 rescind a decision ～禁令 lift a ban ～主义 liquidationism 【取笑】ridicule; make fun of 【取样】sampling ～检查 take a sample to check 【取悦】try to please

娶 qǔ marry (a woman); take to wife 【娶亲】(of a man) get married

齲 qǔ 【齲齿】dental caries / decayed tooth

去 qù ①go; leave 他～多久了 how long has he been away ②remove; get rid of ～皮 remove the peel or skin; peel ③of last year ～冬 last winter 【去路】outlet; way 【去年】last year 【去世】die; pass away 【去伪存真】eliminate the false and retain the true 【去污粉】cleanser 【去向】the direction in which sb. or sth. has gone 不知～ be nowhere to be found 【去职】no longer hold the post

趣 qù ①interest; delight 有～ delightful; amusing ② interesting ～事 an interesting episode ③bent; purport 志～ aspirations and interests 【趣剧】farce 【趣味】interest; delight / taste; liking; preference 迎合低级 ～cater to vulgar tastes

覷 qù ①look; gaze 偷偷地～了他一眼 steal a glance at him ②narrow (one's eyes); squint

QUAN

圈 quān ①circle; ring 画~ draw a circle ②group 他不是~里人 he doesn't belong to the inner circle ③enclose; encircle 用篱笆把菜园~起来 enclose the vegetable garden with a fence ④mark with a circle 【圈套】 snare; trap 落入~ fall into a trap 【圈椅】 round-backed armchair

权 quán ①right 选举~ the right to vote ②power; authority 当~ be in power ③advantageous position 主动~ initiative ④tentatively; for the time being ~充 act temporarily as ⑤expediency 【权贵】 influential officials; bigwigs 【权衡】 weigh; balance ~利弊 weigh the advantages and disadvantages 【权力】 power; authority 【权利】 right 劳动的~ the right to work 受教育的~ the right to education 政治~ political rights 【权势】 power and influence 【权术】 political trickery; shifts in politics 玩弄~ play politics 【权威】 authority/a person of authority ~人士 authoritative person or sources 【权限】 limits of authority; jurisdiction; competence 【权宜】 expedient ~之计 an expedient measure; makeshift (device) 【权益】 rights and interests

全 quán ①complete 手稿已不~ the manuscript is no longer complete ②whole; entire; full; total ~中国 the whole of China ~称 full name ③entirely; completely ~错了 all wrong ~怪我 it's entirely my fault ④make perfect or complete; keep intact 【全部】 whole; complete; total; all 【全才】 a versatile person 【全场】 the whole audience; all those present / full-court; all-court 【全程】 whole journey; whole course 【全国】 the whole nation; countrywide; throughout the country ~人民 the people of the whole country ～冠军 national champion 【全会】plenary meeting 三中～ the Third Plenary Session 【全集】complete works 【全景】full view; whole scene 【全局】overall situation ～观点 adopt an overall point of view ～利益 general interests ～性问题 a matter of overall importance 【全军】the whole army 【全力】all-out; sparing no effort ～支持 support with all one's strength 竭尽～ exert all one's strength ～以赴 go all out; spare no effort 【全貌】full view 【全面】overall; all-round ～规划 overall planning ～总结 comprehensive summing-up ～崩溃 total collapse ～进攻 an all-out attack ～战争 a full-scale war ～地看问题 look at problems all-sidedly 【全民】the whole people; all the people ～皆兵 an entire nation in arms ～总动员 general mobilization of the nation ～所有制 ownership by the whole people 【全能】all-round ～运动员 all-rounder ～冠军 all-round champion 【全年】annual ～收入 annual income ～雨量 yearly rainfall 【全盘】comprehensive; wholesale ～考虑 give overall consideration to ～否定 total repudiation 【全球】the whole world ～战略 global strategy 【全权】full powers; plenary powers ～证书 full powers ～代表 plenipotentiary 【全日制】full-time ～教育 full-time schooling ～学校 full-time school 【全身】the whole body; all over (the body) ～不适 general malaise ～检查 a general physical checkup ～像 full-length picture 【全神贯注】be absorbed in; be preoccupied with 【全盛】flourishing; in full bloom ～时期 prime; heyday 【全速】full speed 【全体】all; entire ～工作人员 the whole staff 【全文】full text ～如下 the full text follows ～发表 publish in full 【全线】all fronts; the whole line ～出击 launch an attack on all fronts 【全心

全意] wholeheartedly; heart and soul 【全休】complete rest

泉 quán spring 温～ hot spring 【泉水】spring water 【泉源】springhead/source (of wisdom, strength, etc.)

拳 quán ①fist 挥～ shake one's fist ②boxing; pugilism 【拳打脚踢】cuff and kick; beat up 【拳师】boxing coach; pugilist 【拳术】Chinese boxing

痊 quán recover from an illness 【痊愈】be fully recovered 望早日～ I wish you a speedy recovery

蜷 quán curl up; huddle up 【蜷伏】lie with the knees drawn up 【蜷曲】coil; twist 【蜷缩】roll up; curl up

犬 quǎn dog 警～ police dog 丧家之～ a stray cur 【犬齿】canine tooth 【犬牙交错】jigsaw-like

劝 quàn ①advise; urge; try to persuade 规～ exhort ～他戒烟 advise him to give up smoking ②encourage ～学 encourage learning 【劝导】induce; talk sb. round 【劝架】try to reconcile parties to a quarrel 【劝解】help sb. to get over his worries, etc. / mediate; make peace between 【劝戒】admonish; expostulate 【劝慰】console; soothe 【劝阻】dissuade sb. from; advise sb. not to ～无效 try in vain to talk sb. out of doing sth.

券 quàn certificate; ticket 入场～ admission ticket 公债～ government bond

QUE

缺 quē ①be short of; lack ～人 be short of hands ～肥 lack manure 原料较～ the material is rather scarce ～一不可 not a single one can be omitted ②incomplete; imperfect 完美无～ flawless; perfect ③be absent ④vacancy; opening 补～ fill a vacancy 【缺德】mean; wicked; villainous 做～事 do sth. mean 【缺点】shortcoming; defect; weakness 【缺额】vacancy 【缺乏】lack; be wanting in

～经验 lack experience ～资源 be deficient in resources ～证据 want of proof 【缺货】 be in short supply; be out of stock 【缺课】 be absent from school 因病～ miss some classes on account of illness 【缺口】 breach; gap 【缺门】 gap (in a branch of learning, etc.) 【缺勤】 absence from duty ～率 absence rate 【缺少】 lack; be short of ～零件 lack spare parts 不可～的条件 indispensable conditions 【缺席】 absent (from a meeting, etc.) 因事～ be absent through being otherwise engaged 【缺陷】 drawback; flaw 生理～ physical defect

瘸 qué be lame; limp 一步一～ walk with a limp 【瘸子】 a lame person; cripple

却 què ①step back 退～ go back; retreat ②drive back; repulse ～敌 repulse the enemy ③decline; refuse ④but; yet; while 【却步】 step back (in fear or disgust); hang back 望而～ shrink back at the sight (of sth. dangerous or disgusting)

雀 què sparrow 【雀斑】 freckle 【雀跃】 jump for joy

确 què ①true; reliable; authentic ～证 ironclad proof ②firmly 【确保】 ensure; guarantee ～质量 guarantee quality 【确定】 define; fix; determine/definite 一日期 fix the date ～方案 decide on a plan 一任务 set the tasks ～的答复 a definite reply 【确立】 establish ～共产主义世界观 form a communist world outlook 【确切】 definite; exact ～的日期 an exact date ～的定义 a precise definition 【确认】 affirm; confirm; acknowledge 【确实】 true; reliable / really; indeed 【确信】 firmly believe; be convinced; be sure 【确诊】 make a definite diagnosis; diagnose 【确凿】 conclusive; authentic ～的证据 absolute proof ～的事实 irrefutable facts

鹊 què　magpie

QUN

裙 qún　skirt 绸～ silk skirt 【裙带】connected through one's female relatives 通过～关系 through petticoat influence

群 qún ①crowd; group 成～ in crowds; in flocks ～起而攻之 rally together to attack sb. or sth. ②group; herd; flock 一～孩子 a group of children 一～人 a crowd of people 一～牛 a herd of cattle 一～羊 a flock of sheep 一～蜜蜂 a swarm of bees 【群策群力】pool the wisdom and efforts of everyone 【群岛】archipelago 【群情】public sentiment; feelings of the masses ～振奋 everyone is exhilarated ～激昂 popular feeling ran high 【群众】the masses ～大会 mass rally ～观点 the mass viewpoint ～工作 mass work ～关系 one's relations with the masses ～路线 the mass line ～团体 mass organization ～性 of a mass character ～运动 mass movement

R

RAN

然 rán ①right; correct 不以为～ object to; not approve ②so; like that 不尽～ not exactly so 【然而】yet; but; however 【然后】then; after that; afterwards

燃 rán　burn; ignite; light ～起篝火 light a bonfire ～起革命的烈火 spark off the flames of revolution 【燃放】set off (fireworks, etc.) 【燃料】fuel 【燃烧】burn;

kindle / inflammation ～弹 incendiary bomb

染 rǎn ①dye ～布 dye a piece of cloth ②catch (a disease); acquire (a bad habit, etc.); soil; contaminate 【染料】dyestuff; dye 【染色】dyeing; colouring ～剂 colouring agent ～体 chromosome 【染指】encroach on

RANG

嚷 rāng 【嚷嚷】shout; yell; make an uproar / make widely known

瓤 ráng pulp; flesh; pith 西瓜～ the flesh of a watermelon

壤 rǎng ①soil ②earth 有霄～之别 there is a world of difference ③area 接～ have a common border

攘 rǎng ①reject; resist ～外 resist foreign aggression ②seize; grab ②push up one's sleeves

嚷 rǎng shout; yell; make an uproar 别～了 stop yelling

让 ràng ①give way; give ground; yield; give up 寸步不～ refuse to yield an inch 请一～ please step aside ②invite; offer 把客人～进里屋 invite guests into the inner room ③let; allow; make ～我想一想 let me think it over ④let sb. have sth. at a fair price 【让步】make a concession; give in 【让路】give way; give sb. the right of way 给重点工程～ make way for the main project 【让球】concede points 【让位】abdicate / yield to; change into 【让座】offer one's seat to sb.

RAO

饶 ráo ①rich; plentiful ～有风趣 full of wit and humour ②have mercy on; let sb. off 求～ beg for mercy

③give sth. extra 给你~一个 let you have one more 【饶命】spare sb.'s life 【饶恕】forgive; pardon

扰 rǎo harass; trouble 纷~ tumult 【扰乱】disturb; create confusion ~治安 disturb public order ~市场 disrupt the market ~军心 undermine the morale of an army ~视线 interfere with one's view

绕 rào ①wind; coil ~线 wind thread ②circle; revolve ~场一周 march around the arena ③make a detour; go round ~过暗礁 bypass hidden reefs 【绕道】make a detour; go by a roundabout route 【绕口令】tongue twister 【绕圈子】circle; go round and round / take a circuitous route 【绕弯儿】go for a stroll 【绕弯子】beat about the bush 【绕嘴】be difficult to articulate

RE

惹 rě ①invite; ask for ~麻烦 ask for trouble ~是非 provoke a dispute ②offend; tease 我~不起他 I cannot afford to offend him 我没~他 I did nothing to provoke him ③attract; cause ~人注意 attract attention ~人讨厌 make a nuisance of oneself 【惹祸】court disaster 【惹气】get angry 【惹事】stir up trouble

热 rè ①heat 传~ conduct heat ②hot ~水 hot water ③heat up; warm 把汤~ heat up the soup ④fever; temperature 发~ have a fever ⑤ardent; warmhearted 采取不冷不~的态度 take a lukewarm attitude ⑥craze; fad 乒乓~ ping-pong craze ⑦envious; eager 眼~ feel envious at the sight of sth. 【热爱】ardently love; have deep affection for ~工作 love one's work ~人民 have deep love for the people 【热补】vulcanize (tyre, etc.) 【热诚】warm and sincere ~欢迎 cordially welcome ~地希望 sincerely hope 【热带】the torrid zone; the tropics ~鱼

tropical fish ～植物 tropical plants ～作物 tropical crops
【热度】degree of heat; heat / fever; temperature 【热量】
quantity of heat 【热烈】warm; enthusiastic; ardent ～祝
贺 warm congratulations ～欢送 give sb. a warm send-
off 进行～的讨论 have a lively discussion 【热门】in
great demand; popular ～货 goods which sell well 赶～
follow a craze 【热闹】lively; bustling with noise, excitement and activity/liven up 看～ watch the fun 晚
会很～ it was a very lively evening party 【热能】heat
energy 【热气】steam; heat ～腾腾 steaming hot/seething
with activity 【热切】fervent; earnest 【热情】enthusiasm;
zeal/warm ～接待 warmly receive ～支持 fervently support 对旅客～ be warm towards the passengers 【热水袋】
hot-water bottle 【热水瓶】thermos; vacuum bottle 【热天】
hot days 【热望】ardently wish 【热心】ardent; warmhearted ～科学 eager to promote science 【热血】warm blood/
righteous ardour ～沸腾 burning with righteous indignation 【热饮】hot drinks 【热战】hot war 【热中】crave/
be keen on ～于名利 hanker after fame and gain

REN

人 rén ①human being; man; person; people 外国～
foreigner ②adult 长大成～ become a grown-up ③a
person engaged in a particular activity 工～ worker
④(other) people 助～为乐 take pleasure in helping people ⑤personality; character 为～公正 upright in character ⑥each; all ～手一册 everyone has a copy ～所共知
be known to all ⑦manpower; hand 缺～ be shorthanded
【人才】a person of ability; a talented person; talent
【人称】person 第一～ the first person 不定～ indefinite
person ～代词 personal pronoun 【人次】person-time 【人

道】humanity; human sympathy / human 不～ inhuman ～主义 humanitarianism【人浮于事】be overstaffed【人格】personality; character / human dignity ～化 personification【人工】man-made; artificial/manual work; work done by hand / manpower; man-day ～呼吸 artificial respiration ～降水 artificial precipitation ～流产 induced abortion【人家】household / family【人间】man's world【人口】population/number of people in a family ～密度 density of population ～普查 census【人类】mankind; humanity ～学 anthropology【人力】manpower; labour power ～资源 human resources【人马】forces; troops【人们】people; men; the public【人面兽心】a beast in human shape【人民】the people ～币 Renminbi ～代表大会 people's congress ～公社 people's commune ～性 affinity to the people ～战争 people's war ～政府 the People's Government【人命】human life ～案子 a case of homicide or manslaughter【人品】moral quality; character/looks; bearing【人情】human feelings/favour/present 不近～ not amenable to reason 做个～ do sb. a favour 送～ send gifts ～味 human touch ～世故 worldly wisdom; the ways of the world ～之常 natural and normal【人权】human rights【人群】crowd; multitude【人人】everyone【人身】living body of a human being; person ～安全 personal safety ～攻击 personal attack ～事故 personal injury caused by an accident ～自由 personal freedom【人参】ginseng【人生】life ～观 outlook on life ～哲学 philosophy of life【人声】voice ～嘈杂 a confusion of voices【人士】personage; public figure【人世】this world 不在～ be no longer living【人事】human affairs/personnel matters/ways of the world ～调动 transfer of personnel ～更迭 change of personnel ～处

personnel division ～制度 personnel system 【人手】manpower; hand 【人为】artificial; man-made 【人物】figure; personage/character 典型～ typical character ～塑造 characterization ～画 figure painting 【人像】portrait; image; figure 【人心】popular feeling; the will of the people 得～ enjoy popular support 不得～ go against the will of the people 【人行道】pavement; sidewalk 【人行横道】pedestrian crossing 【人性】human nature; humanity/normal human feelings; reason ～论 the theory of human nature 【人选】person selected 【人烟】signs of human habitation ～稀少 be sparsely populated 【人影】the shadow of a human figure/figure 【人员】personnel; staff 【人造】man-made; artificial ～宝石 imitation jewel ～冰 artificial ice ～革 leatherette ～棉 staple rayon ～丝 rayon ～卫星 man-made satellite ～纤维 man-made fibre 【人证】testimony ·of a witness

仁 rén ①benevolence; humanity ～政 policy of benevolence ②sensitive ③kernel 核桃～ walnut kernel 花生～ shelled peanuts 【仁爱】kindheartedness 【仁慈】merciful; kind 【仁义道德】virtue and morality

忍 rén ①bear; tolerate; put up with ～不住 unable to bear ～饥挨饿 endure the torments of hunger ～着眼泪 hold back one's tears ②be hardhearted enough to 于心不～ not have the heart to 【忍耐】exercise patience; restrain oneself 【忍气吞声】swallow an insult; submit to humiliation 【忍让】exercise forbearance 【忍受】endure; stand ～艰难困苦 endure hardships 【忍痛】reluctantly ～牺牲 reluctantly give up 【忍心】have the heart to

刃 rén ①the edge of a knife, sword, etc.; blade 刀～ knife blade ②sword; knife 利～ sharp sword ③kill with a sword or knife 手～ stab sb. to death 【刃具】

cutting tool

认 rèn ①recognize; know; make out ～出某人 identify a person ②adopt ～师傅 apprentice oneself to sb. ～闺女 adopt sb. as a daughter ③admit; recognize; own 公～ be generally acknowledged 【认错】admit a fault; make an apology 【认定】firmly believe; maintain; hold/ set one's mind on ～目标 set one's mind on the goal 【认购】offer to buy; subscribe ～公债 subscribe for bonds 【认可】approve 【认领】claim 【认清】see clearly; recognize; get a clear understanding of 【认生】(of a child) be shy with strangers 【认识】know; understand; recognize/ understanding; knowledge; cognition ～世界 understand the world ～错误 see one's mistake ～过程 process of cognition ～论 epistemology 【认输】admit defeat; give up 【认为】think; consider; hold; deem 你～怎样 what do you think of it 【认帐】acknowledge a debt / admit what one has said or done 【认真】conscientious; earnest; serious / take seriously; take to heart 【认字】know or learn how to read 【认罪】admit one's guilt; plead guilty

任 rèn ①appoint 新～校长 the newly appointed school-master ②assume a post; take up a job ～教多年 be a teacher for many years ③official post; office 上～ assume office 离～ leave office ④let; allow ～其自流 let things run their course ⑤no matter (how, what, etc.) 【任何】any; whichever; whatever 【任免】appoint and remove ～事项 appointments and removals 【任命】appoint ～为市长 appoint sb. mayor 【任期】term of office 【任情】to one's heart's content; as much as one likes 【任务】task; job 接受～ receive an assignment 完成～ fulfil one's mission 【任性】self-willed 【任意】wantonly; arbitrarily; wilfully 【任职】hold a post; be in office

妊 rèn be pregnant 【妊妇】pregnant woman 【妊娠】gestation; pregnancy ～期 gestational period

纫 rèn ①sew; stitch ②thread (a needle)

韧 rèn pliable but strong; tenacious; tough 【韧带】ligament 【韧性】toughness; tenacity

RENG

扔 rēng ①throw; toss; cast ～球 throw a ball ～炸弹 drop bombs ②throw away; cast aside 【扔下】abandon; put aside; leave behind

仍 réng ①remain ②still; yet ～有效力 be still effective ～未痊愈 have not yet recovered 这件事～是个谜 the affair rests riddle 【仍旧】remain the same/still; yet 他～是老样子 he still looked the same 有些问题～没有解决 some problems remain to be solved

RI

日 rì ①sun ～出 sunrise ～落 sunset ②daytime; day ～～夜夜 day and night ③day 今～ today ④daily; with each passing day 产量～增 output is going up every day ⑤time 春～ springtime 【日班】day shift 【日报】daily (paper) 【日常】day-to-day ～工作 routine duties ～生活 daily life ～用语 words and expressions for everyday use 【日场】day show; daytime performance 【日程】programme; schedule 【日光】sunlight; sunbeam ～灯 daylight lamp ～浴 sunbath ～疗法 heliotherapy 【日后】in the future; in days to come 【日积月累】accumulate over a long period 【日记】diary 记～ keep a diary 工作～ work diary ～本 diary 【日间】during the day 【日见】with each passing day; day by day 【日久】

in (the) course of time 【日历】calendar 【日内】in a few days; in a couple of days 【日期】date 【日食】solar eclipse 【日新月异】change with each passing day 【日用】daily expenses / of everyday use ～必需品 daily necessities ～工业品 manufactured goods for daily use ～品 articles of everyday use 【日语】Japanese 【日子·】day; date/time/life 定～ fix a day 走了有些～了 be away for some time 勤俭过～ lead an industrious and frugal life

RONG

荣 róng ①grow luxuriantly; flourish ②honour; glory ～归 return in glory 引以为～ take it as an honour 【荣获】have the honour to get or win ～冠军 win the championship ～奖章 be awarded a medal 【荣幸】be honoured 【荣誉】honour; credit; glory 赢得～ win honour ～感 sense of honour ～军人 disabled soldier

茸 róng ①fine and soft; downy 绿草～～ a carpet of green grass ②young pilose antler

绒 róng ①fine hair; down 鸭～ eiderdown ②cloth with a soft nap or pile 丝～ velvet ③fine floss for embroidery 【绒布】flannelette; cotton flannel 【绒花】velvet flowers, birds, etc. 【绒裤】sweat pants 【绒毛】fine hair; down; villus/nap; pile 【绒线】floss for embroidery / knitting wool ～衫 woollen sweater 【绒衣】sweat shirt

容 róng ①hold; contain 能～一千人 can hold a thousand people ②tolerate ③permit; allow 不～耽搁 allow of no delay 不～歪曲 brook no distortion 不～怀疑 admit of no doubt ④facial expression 怒～ an angry look ⑤appearance; looks 市～ the look of a city 【容光焕发】one's face glowing with health 【容积】volume 【容量】capacity 【容貌】appearance; looks 【容纳】hold; have a capacity of; accommodate 【容器】container; vessel 【容人】tolerant towards others; magnanimous 【容忍】tolerate; put up with; condone 【容易】easy/easily; likely; apt ～引起误会 be liable to cause misunderstanding

溶 róng dissolve 盐～于水 salt dissolves in water 【溶剂】solvent 【溶解】dissolve 【溶液】solution

熔 róng melt; fuse; smelt 【熔点】melting point 【熔化】melt 【熔解】fuse; fusion 【熔炉】furnace/crucible

融 róng ①melt; thaw ②blend; fuse; be in harmony 【融合】mix together; fuse; merge 【融化】melt; thaw 冰已～ the ice has already melted 【融会贯通】achieve mastery through a comprehensive study of the subject 【融洽】harmonious; on friendly terms

冗 rǒng ①redundant ～词 superfluous words ②full of trivial details 【冗长】tediously long; lengthy

ROU

柔 róu ①soft; supple; flexible ～枝 supple twigs ②gentle; yielding; mild ～中有刚 firm but gentle 【柔和】soft; gentle; mild ～的光线 soft light ～的声音 a mild voice 颜色～ a soft colour 【柔嫩】tender; delicate 【柔情】tender feelings; tenderness 【柔韧】pliable and tough 【柔软】soft; lithe ～体操 callisthenics 【柔弱】weak

揉 róu rub; knead ～眼睛 rub one's eyes ～面 knead dough ～成一团 crumple sth. into a ball

糅 róu mix; mingle 【糅合】mix; form a mixture (usu. of things which don't blend well)

蹂 róu 【蹂躏】trample on; ravage; make havoc of; devastate 遭到～ suffer devastation, oppression, etc.

肉 ròu ①meat; flesh 瘦～ lean meat 肥～ fat meat ②pulp; flesh (of fruit) 桂圆～ longan pulp 【肉饼】

meat pie 【肉搏】 fight hand-to-hand ～战 bayonet fighting 【肉店】 butcher's (shop) 【肉丁】 diced meat 【肉冻】 meat jelly; aspic 【肉末】 minced meat 【肉排】 steak 【肉皮】 pork skin 【肉片】 sliced meat 【肉色】 yellowish. pink 【肉丝】 shredded meat 【肉松】 dried meat floss 【肉汤】 broth 【肉体】 the human body; flesh 【肉丸】 meatball 【肉馅】 meat stuffing 【肉刑】 corporal punishment 【肉眼】 naked eye 【肉欲】 carnal desire 【肉汁】 gravy; (meat) juice

RU

如 rú ①in compliance with; according to ②like; as; as if ～临大敌 as if faced with a formidable enemy ～你所说 as you've said ③be as good as 我不～他 I can't compare with him ④for instance; such as; as ⑤if 【如常】 as usual 【如此】 so; such; in this way; like that ～而已 that's what it all adds up to 【如果】 if; in case; in the event of 【如何】 how; what 【如火如荼】 like a raging fire 【如获至宝】 as if one had found a treasure 【如今】 nowadays; now 【如梦初醒】 as if awakening from a dream 【如期】 as scheduled; on schedule 【如上】 as above ～所述 as stated above 【如实】 strictly according to the facts ～反映情况 reflect things as they really are 【如释重负】 as if relieved of a heavy load 【如数】 exactly the number or amount ～偿还 pay back in full ～到齐 all present and correct 【如同】 like 【如下】 as follows 全文 ～ the full text follows 发表～声明 make the following statement 【如意】 as one wishes ～算盘 wishful thinking 【如愿以偿】 achieve what one wishes 【如坐针毡】 be on pins and needles; be on tenterhooks

儒 rú ①Confucianism ②scholar; learned man 腐～ pedantic scholar 【儒家】 the Confucianists

孺 rú child 妇～ women and children

蠕 rú wriggle; squirm 【蠕虫】worm; helminth 【蠕动】wriggle; squirm

乳 rǔ ①breast ②milk ③any milk-like liquid 豆～ bean milk ④give birth to ⑤newborn (animal); sucking ～猪 sucking pig 【乳白】milky white; cream colour ～灯泡 opal bulb 【乳儿】suckling 【乳房】breast; mamma 【乳母】wet nurse 【乳牛】dairy cattle; milch cow ～场 dairy farm 【乳糖】milk sugar 【乳汁】milk 【乳脂】butterfat ～糖 toffee; taffy 【乳制品】dairy products

辱 rǔ ①disgrace; dishonour ②bring disgrace to; insult; humiliate 【辱骂】abuse; call sb. names

入 rù ①enter; entrance; admission 列～议程 put on the agenda ②join; be admitted into ～团 join the Chinese Communist Youth League ③income ～不敷出 income falling short of expenditure ④conform to; agree with ～情～理 fair and reasonable 【入党】join or be admitted to the Party 【入股】buy a share 【入骨】to the marrow 恨之～ bitterly hate 【入伙】join a gang / join a mess 【入境】enter a country ～登记 entrance registration ～签证 entry visa 【入门】learn the rudiments of a subject/elementary course 【入迷】be fascinated; be enchanted 【入侵】invade; intrude 【入手】begin with; proceed from 从调查研究～ start with investigation 【入睡】fall asleep 【入伍】join up 【入席】take one's seat at a banquet, ceremony, etc. 【入学】start school/enter a school 从～到毕业 from entrance to graduation ～考试 entrance examination ～年龄 school age 【入狱】be sent to jail

褥 rù cotton-padded mattress 被～bedding; bedclothes 【褥单】bed sheet 【褥套】bedding sack/mattress cover

RUAN

软 ruǎn ①soft; flexible; supple; pliable ～椅 soft chair ②mild; gentle ～语 soft words ③weak; feeble 腿发～ one's legs feel like jelly ④poor in quality, ability, etc. 工夫～ inadequate skill ⑤easily moved or influenced 心～ tenderhearted 【软缎】soft silk fabric in satin weave 【软腭】soft palate 【软膏】ointment; paste 【软化】soften/win over by soft tactics 使硬水～ soften hard water 态度～ become compliant 【软禁】place sb. under house arrest 【软磨】use soft tactics 【软木】cork 【软弱】weak; feeble; flabby ～无能 weak and incompetent ～可欺 be weak and easy to bully 【软食】soft diet 【软糖】soft sweets; jelly drops 【软梯】rope ladder 【软席】soft seat or berth 【软硬兼施】use both hard and soft tactics

RUI

蕊 ruǐ stamen or pistil 雄～ stamen 雌～ pistil

锐 ruì ①sharp; keen; acute ②vigour; fighting spirit 【锐利】sharp; keen ～的匕首 a sharp dagger 目光～ sharp-eyed 【锐敏】sensitive 【锐气】dash; drive

瑞 ruì auspicious; lucky 【瑞雪】auspicious snow ～兆丰年 a timely snow promises a good harvest

RUN

闰 rùn intercalary 【闰年】intercalary year 【闰月】intercalary month

润 rùn ①moist; smooth; sleek ②lubricate ～～嗓子 moisten one's throat ③polish ～饰 embellish; touch up ④profit 分～ share in the benefit 【润滑】lubricate

～油 lubricating oil【润色】polish (a piece of writing)

RUO

若 ruò ①like; seem; as if ～有所失 look distracted ～有所思 seem lost in thought; look pensive ～隐～现 appear indistinctly ②if【若非】if not; were it not for【若干】a certain number or amount ～年 a number of years ～次 several times ～地区 certain areas【若无其事】as if nothing had happened; calmly; casually

弱 ruò ①weak; feeble 由～变强 go from weakness to strength ②inferior【弱点】weakness; weak point

S

SA

撒 sā ①cast; let go; let out ～网 cast a net ～手 let go (one's hold) ②throw off all restraint; let oneself go ～酒疯 be roaring drunk【撒谎】tell a lie【撒娇】act like a spoiled child【撒尿】piss; pee【撒气】(of a ball, tyre, etc.) leak / vent one's anger or ill temper 别拿我～don't take it out on me【撒野】act wildly

洒 sǎ sprinkle; spray; spill ～泪 shed tears 把汤～了 spill the soup【洒扫】sprinkle water and sweep the floor【洒水车】watering car; sprinkler【洒脱】free and easy

撒 sǎ ①scatter; sprinkle; spread ～农药 dust crops with an insecticide ～种 sow seeds ②spill; drop ～了一地的盐 spill the salt all over the floor

飒 sà【飒然】soughing【飒飒】sough; rustle【飒爽】of martial bearing; valiant

SAI

塞 sāi ①fill in; squeeze in; stuff 再～点东西 squeeze a few more things in 管子～住了 the pipe is clogged up ②stopper; plug; spigot 软木～ cork

腮 sāi cheek【腮腺】parotid gland ～炎 parotitis

塞 sài a place of strategic importance 边～ frontier fortress

赛 sài ①match; game; competition; contest 田径～ track and field events ②be comparable to; surpass【赛车】cycle racing; motorcycle race; automobile race / racing bicycle【赛过】overtake; surpass; exceed【赛璐珞】celluloid【赛马】horse race【赛跑】race【赛艇】rowing/shell

SAN

三 sān ①three ②several; many ～思 think again and again; think twice (about doing sth.)【三部曲】trilogy【三岔路口】a fork in the road【三角】triangle/trigonometry ～板 set square ～架 tripod ～裤 panties; briefs【三轮车】tricycle; pedicab【三轮摩托车】motor tricycle【三轮汽车】three-wheeled automobile【三三两两】in twos and threes【三心二意】shilly-shally/half-hearted【三言两语】in a few words【三月】March/the third moon

伞 sǎn umbrella【伞兵】paratrooper; parachuter ～部队 paratroops

散 sǎn ①come loose; fall apart 背包～了 the blanket roll has come loose ②medicinal powder【散兵】skirmisher【散兵游勇】stragglers and disbanded soldiers【散光】astigmatism ～眼镜 astigmatic glasses【散居】live scattered【散漫】undisciplined; careless and sloppy/unorganized; scattered 【散文】 prose ～诗 prose poem 【散装】 bulk

散 sàn ①break up; disperse 乌云～了 dark clouds dispersed ②distribute; disseminate ～传单 give out handbills ③dispel; let out ～～烟 let the smoke out 【散布】 spread; scatter; diffuse ～流言蜚语 spread slanderous rumours 【散步】 take a walk 【散场】 empty after the show 【散发】 send out; diffuse; emit / distribute; issue 【散会】 be over; break up 宣布～declare the meeting over 【散伙】 dissolve; disband 【散开】 spread out; disperse; scatter 【散失】 scatter and disappear; be lost; be missing 【散心】 drive away one's cares; relieve boredom

SANG

丧 sāng funeral; mourning 【丧服】 mourning apparel 【丧礼】 obsequies 【丧事】 funeral arrangements 【丧葬】 burial ～费 funeral expenses 【丧钟】 funeral bell; knell

桑 sāng mulberry 【桑葚】 mulberry 【桑园】 mulberry field

嗓 sǎng ①throat; larynx ②voice 【嗓子】 throat; larynx/voice ～疼 have a sore throat ～好 have a good voice

丧 sàng lose 【丧胆】 be terror-stricken 【丧魂落魄】 be driven to distraction 【丧家之犬】 stray cur 【丧尽天良】 conscienceless; heartless 【丧命】 meet one's death 【丧气】 lose heart ～话 demoralizing words 【丧失】 lose; forfeit ～信心 lose confidence ～时机 miss the opportunity ～立场 depart from the correct stand 【丧心病狂】 frenzied; perverse

SAO

搔 sāo scratch ～痒 scratch where it itches ～首 scratch one's head

骚 sāo disturb; upset 【骚动】 disturbance; commotion; ferment / be in a tumult 【骚乱】 riot 【骚扰】 harass

缫 sāo reel 【缫丝】 silk reeling; filature ～厂 reeling mill ～机 reeling machine

臊 sāo the smell of urine; foul smell

扫 sǎo ①sweep; clear away ～雪 sweep away the snow ～清道路 clear the path ②pass quickly along or over ～了一眼 sweep one's eyes over sth. ～过夜空 sweep across the night sky ③put all together ～数归还 the whole amount returned 【扫除】 cleaning; cleanup / clear away; wipe out ～障碍 remove the obstacles 【扫荡】 mop up/ mopping-up operations 【扫地】 sweep the floor / be dragged in the dust 名誉～ be thoroughly discredited 威信～ be shorn of one's prestige 【扫雷】 mine sweeping ～舰 mine-sweeper 【扫盲】 wipe out illiteracy ～班 literacy class 【扫射】 strafe 【扫尾】 wind up ～工作 rounding-off work 【扫兴】 have one's spirits dampened

嫂 sǎo ①elder brother's wife; sister-in-law ②sister

扫 sào 【扫帚】 broom 【扫帚星】 comet

臊 sào shy; bashful ～得脸通红 blush scarlet

SE

色 sè ①colour 原～ primary colour ②look; countenance; expression 满面喜～ beaming with joy ③kind; description 各～人等 all kinds of people ④scene; scenery 山～ a landscape of mountains ⑤quality ⑥woman's looks 姿～ good looks 【色彩】 colour; hue; tint; shade

地方~ local colour 文学~ literary flavour 感情~ emotional colouring 【色盲】 colour blindness 【色情】 sexy ~文学 pornography 【色泽】 colour and lustre

涩 sè ①puckery; astringent 这柿子~不~ are these persimmons puckery ②unsmooth; hard-going

塞 sè 【塞责】 not do one's job conscientiously 敷衍~ perform one's duty in a perfunctory manner

SEN

森 sēn ①full of trees ②dark; gloomy 【森林】 forest 【森严】 stern; strict; forbiding 戒备~ heavily guarded 等级~ form a strict hierarchy

SENG

僧 sēng (Buddhist) monk 【僧侣】 monks and priests; clergy

SHA

杀 shā ①kill; slaughter ~人 commit murder ②fight; go into battle ~敌 fight the enemy ③weaken; reduce 风势稍~ the wind abated 【杀虫剂】 insecticide; pesticide 【杀风景】 spoil the fun 【杀菌】 disinfect; sterilize ~剂 germicide; bactericide 【杀戮】 massacre; slaughter 【杀气】 murderous look / vent one's ill feeling

沙 shā ①sand ②granulated; powdered 豆~ bean paste ③(of voice) hoarse; husky 【沙场】 battlefield 【沙船】 large junk 【沙袋】 sandbag 【沙丁鱼】 sardine 【沙发】 sofa; settee 【沙锅】 earthenware pot; casserole 【沙皇】 tsar 【沙坑】 jumping pit 【沙拉】 salad 【沙砾】 grit 【沙漠】 desert 【沙丘】 (sand) dune 【沙沙】 rustle 【沙滩】 sandy beach 【沙眼】 trachoma 【沙鱼】 shark 【沙洲】 shoal; sandbank

【沙子】sand; grit / small grains; pellets

纱 shā ①yarn ～厂 cotton mill ②gauze; sheer 铁～ wire gauze 【纱布】gauze 【纱窗】screen window 【纱灯】gauze lantern 【纱锭】spindle 【纱巾】gauze kerchief 【纱线】yarn 【纱罩】gauze or screen covering (over food)

刹 shā put on the brakes; stop; check ～住车子 brake a car ～住歪风 check an unhealthy tendency 【刹车】put on the brakes / turn off a machine / brake

砂 shā sand; grit 【砂布】emery cloth 【砂浆】mortar 【砂砾】gravel; grit 【砂糖】granulated sugar 【砂田】sandy land 【砂土】sandy soil; sand 【砂纸】sand paper

煞 shā ①stop; halt; check ～住脚 stop short ②tighten 把车上的东西～紧 firmly fasten a load on a vehicle; lash down 【煞尾】finish off; round off/final stage; end

傻 shǎ ①stupid; muddleheaded ～笑 laugh foolishly 装～ act dumb; pretend not to know 吓～ be stunned 别发～ don't be naive ②think or act mechanically 【傻瓜】fool; blockhead; simpleton 【傻呵呵】simpleminded; not very clever 【傻劲儿】foolishness / sheer enthusiasm

厦 shà a tall building; mansion 高楼大～ tall buildings and great mansions

煞 shà ①evil spirit; goblin ②very 【煞白】deathly pale; pallid 【煞费苦心】cudgel one's brains; take great pains

霎 shà a very short time; moment; instant 【霎时间】in a twinkling; in a split second; in a jiffy

SHAI

筛 shāi ①sieve; sifter; screen ②sift; riddle ～面 sift flour ～煤 screen coal ～砂子 riddle gravel

晒 shài ①(of the sun) shine upon 日～雨淋 be exposed to the sun and rain ②dry in the sun; bask ～

粮食 dry grain in the sun ～被子 air a quilt ～黑 be tanned 【晒台】 flat roof (for drying clothes, etc.) 【晒图】 make a blueprint ～员 blueprinter ～纸 blueprint paper

SHAN

山 shān hill; mountain 【山坳】 col 【山崩】 landslide 【山地】 hilly area; hilly country / fields on a hill 【山顶】 top of a mountain; hilltop 【山洞】 cave; cavern 【山峰】 mountain peak 【山冈】 low hill; hillock 【山歌】 folk song 【山沟】 gully; ravine 【山谷】 mountain valley 【山洪】 mountain torrents 【山货】 mountain products / household utensils made of wood, bamboo, clay, etc. 【山涧】 mountain stream 【山脚】 the foot of a hill 【山口】 mountain pass 【山林】 mountain forest 【山麓】 the foot of a mountain 【山脉】 mountain chain 【山盟海誓】 (make) a solemn pledge of love 【山明水秀】 green hills and clear waters — picturesque scenery 【山坡】 hillside 【山区】 mountain area 【山水】 water from a mountain / mountains and rivers; scenery with hills and waters ～画 landscape painting 【山头】 hilltop / mountain stronghold; faction 拉～ form a faction 【山崖】 cliff 【山羊】 goat / buck 【山腰】 half way up the mountain 【山药】 Chinese yam 【山楂】 (Chinese) hawthorn / haw ～糕 haw jelly 【山寨】 mountain fastness 【山珍海味】 dainties of every kind

删 shān delete; leave out ～去细节 cut out the details 【删除】 delete; strike out 【删改】 delete and change; revise (draft, etc.) 【删节】 abridge; abbreviate ～本 abridged edition; abbreviated version ～号 ellipsis; suspension points

衫 shān unlined upper garment 衬～ shirt 汗～ undershirt

姗 shān 【姗姗来迟】 be slow in coming; be late

珊 shān 【珊瑚】 coral ～虫 coral polyp; coral insect ～岛 coral island ～礁 coral reef

舢 shān 【舢板】 sampan

扇 shān ①fan ～扇子 fan oneself ②incite; instigate; fan up; stir up ～阴风 fan up an evil wind 【扇动】 fan; flap / incite; stir up ～翅膀 flap the wings ～派性 whip up factionalism ～群众闹事 stir up trouble among the masses 【扇风机】 ventilating fan 【扇惑】 incite ～人心 agitate people by demagogy

膻 shān the smell of mutton

闪 shān ①dodge; get out of the way 往边上一～ dodge swiftly to one side ②twist; sprain ～了腰 sprain one's back ③lightning 打～ flashes of lightning 【闪】 sparkle; shine 一～而过 streak past 脑子里一～过一个念头 an idea flashed through one's mind 【闪电】 lightning ～战 lightning war; blitz 【闪躲】 evade 【闪光】 flash of light/gleam; glisten; glitter ～灯 flash lamp; photoflash 【闪开】 get out of the way; jump aside; dodge 【闪闪】 sparkle; glisten; glitter 【闪烁】 twinkle; glimmer/evasive; vague ～其词 speak evasively; hedge 【闪现】 flash before one 【闪耀】 shine; radiate 他两眼～着刚毅的光芒 his eyes flashed with resolution

讪 shàn ①mock; ridicule ②awkward; shamefaced ～～地走开 walk away looking embarrassed 【讪笑】 deride

扇 shàn ①fan 电～ electric fan ②leaf 门～ door leaf 【扇骨】 the ribs of a fan 【扇面】 the covering of a fan 【扇形】 fan-shaped/sector

善 shàn ①good 改恶从～ give up evil and return to good ②satisfactory; good ～策 the best policy ③make a success of; perfect ④kind; friendly 友～ be friendly ⑤be good at; be expert in 不～经管 not good at management ～战 be skilful in battle ⑥properly ～为说辞 put in a good word for sb. ⑦be apt to ～变 be apt to change ～忘 be forgetful 【善后】 deal with problems arising from an accident, etc. 【善良】 good and honest; kindhearted ～愿望 the best of intentions 心地～ kindhearted 【善人】 philanthropist; charitable person 【善始善终】 start well and end well; see sth. through 【善心】 mercy; benevolence 【善意】 goodwill; good intentions 出于～ with the best intentions ～的批评 well-meaning criticism 【善于】 be good at; be adept in ～学习 be good at learning ～斗争 know how to struggle 【善终】 die a natural death; die in one's bed

缮 shàn ①repair; mend 房屋修～ house repairing ②copy; write out ～清 make a fair copy

擅 shàn ①arrogate to oneself; do sth. on one's own authority ～权 usurp power ～作主张 make a decision without authorization ②be expert in 不～辞令 lack facility in polite or tactful speech 【擅长】 be good at; be skilled in 【擅离职守】 be absent from one's post without leave 【擅自】 do sth. without authorization ～行动 act presumptuously

膳 shàn meals; board 【膳费】 board expenses 【膳食】 meals; food 【膳宿】 board and lodging

赡 shàn 【赡养】 support; provide for ～父母 support one's parents ～费 alimony

鳝 shàn eel; finless eel

SHANG

伤 shāng ①wound; injury 刀～ a knife wound 满身是～ be covered with cuts and bruises ②injure; hurt 摔～ fall and hurt oneself ～感情 hurt sb.'s feelings ③be distressed 哀～ sad; sorrowful ④get sick; develop an aversion to sth. 吃糖吃～了 get sick of eating sweets ⑤be detrimental to; hinder ～身体 be harmful to one's health 【伤疤】 scar 【伤兵】 wounded soldier 【伤病员】 the sick and wounded; noneffectives 【伤风】 catch cold; have a cold 【伤风败俗】 offend public decency; corrupt public morals 【伤感】 sick at heart; sentimental 【伤害】 injure; harm; hurt ～益鸟 harm beneficial birds ～自尊心 injure one's pride 【伤寒】 typhoid fever 【伤耗】 damage 【伤痕】 scar; bruise 【伤口】 wound; cut 洗～ bathe a wound 【伤脑筋】 troublesome; bothersome ～的问题 a knotty problem; headache 【伤神】 overtax one's nerves 【伤势】 the condition of an injury ～很重 be seriously wounded 【伤亡】 injuries and deaths; casualties 【伤心】 sad; grieved

商 shāng ①discuss; consult 有要事相～ I have important matters to discuss with you ②commerce; business 经～ engage in trade ③merchant; trader; dealer 私～ businessman 【商标】 trade mark ～注册 trade mark registration 【商场】 market; bazaar 【商船】 merchant ship 【商店】 shop; store 【商定】 decide through consultation; agree 【商贩】 small retailer; pedlar 【商港】 commercial port 【商会】 chamber of commerce 【商界】 business circles 【商量】 consult 【商品】 commodity; goods; merchandise ～交换 exchange of commodities ～经济 commodity economy ～粮 commodity grain ～流通 commodity circulation ～生产 commodity production 【商榷】 discuss;

deliberate 值得～ be open to question 【商人】 businessman; merchant; trader 【商谈】 exchange views; confer 派代表前来～ appoint representatives to come here for the negotiations 【商讨】 deliberate over 进行有益的～ hold useful discussions 【商务】 commercial affairs; business affairs ～参赞 commercial counsellor ～处 commercial counsellor's office 【商业】 commerce; trade; business ～部门 commercial departments ～区 business district

墙 shāng moisture in the soil 【墙情】 soil moisture content

晌 shǎng part of the day 前半～ morning 晚半～ dusk 【晌午】 midday; noon ～饭 midday meal; lunch

赏 shǎng ①grant a reward; award ②reward; award ③admire; enjoy; appreciate ～月 enjoy looking at the moon 【赏赐】 bestow a reward; award 【赏罚】 rewards and punishments ～严明 be strict and fair in meting out rewards and punishments 【赏格】 the size of a reward 【赏金】 money reward 【赏识】 recognize the worth of

上 shàng ①upper; up; upward ～铺 upper berth 往～看 look up ②higher; superior; better 向～反应情况 report the situation to the higher organization ③first (part); preceding; previous ～集 the first part; Part One; Volume One ～半夜 the first half of the night ④the emperor ～谕 imperial decree ⑤go up; get on ～山 go up a hill; go uphill ～公共汽车 get on a bus ～飞机 board a plane ～船 go on board ～岸 go ashore ～楼 go upstairs ⑥go to; leave for 你～哪儿去 where are you going ⑦supply; serve ～水 fill sth. with water ⑧set; fix 刀具 fix a cutting tool ⑨apply; paint; smear ～药膏 apply ointment ⑩be engaged (in work, study, etc.) at a fixed time ～大学 be in college ⑪up to; as many as ～百

up to a hundred ～万 as many as ten thousand 【上班】 go to work; be on duty 下午不～ no work this afternoon 八点钟～ start work at 8 上中班 be on the middle shift ～时间 work hours; office hours 【上臂】 the upper arm 【上操】 go out to drill 【上策】 the best plan 【上层】 upper strata; upper levels ～分子 upper-class elements ～建筑 superstructure ～人士 upper circles ～社会 upper-class society 【上场】 appear on the stage; enter/enter the court or field; join in a contest 【上床】 go to bed 【上当】 be taken in; be fooled 【上等】 first-class; first-rate 【上帝】 God 【上吊】 hang oneself 【上工】 go to work 【上古】 ancient times ～史 ancient history 【上级】 higher level; higher authorities ～党委 a Party committee of the higher level ～领导 a leading body at a higher level 报告～ report to one's superior 【上交】 turn over to the higher authorities; hand in 【上街】 go into the street 【上届】 previous term or session; last ～毕业生 last year's graduates 【上进】 go forward; make progress 不求～ not strive to make progress ～心 the desire to do better 【上课】 attend class; go to class/conduct a class; give a lesson 学校八点开始～ classes begin at 8 明天不～ there will be no school tomorrow 【上来】 come up 【上列】 the above-listed; the above ～各项 the items listed above 【上流】 upper reaches (of a river)/belonging to the upper circles; upper-class ～社会 high society; polite society 【上路】 set out on a journey; start off 【上马】 mount a horse/start (a project, etc.) 【上面】 above; over; on top of; on the surface of/above-mentioned/aspect; respect 【上年纪】 be getting on in years 【上铺】 upper berth 【上任】 assume office 【上身】 the upper part of the body/upper outer garment; shirt; blouse; jacket 【上升】 rise; go up; ascend 气温～

the temperature is going up 生产～ production is rising 【上市】go on the market 【上述】above-mentioned ～目标 the aforementioned objectives 【上税】pay taxes 【上司】 superior; boss 【上诉】appeal (to a higher court) 【上算】 paying; worthwhile 【上台】appear on the stage/come to power 【上文】preceding part of the text 见～ see above 【上午】forenoon; morning 【上下】high and low; old and young/from top to bottom/go up and down/relative superiority or inferiority/about; or so ～打量 look sb. up and down 【上学】go to school; attend school 上过几年学 have been to school for a few years 这孩子～了没有 is the child at school 【上演】put on the stage; perform 【上衣】upper outer garment; jacket 【上瘾】be addicted (to sth.); get into the habit (of doing sth.) 【上映】show (a film); screen 【上游】upper reaches (of a river)/advanced position 力争～ aim high; strive for the best 【上涨】rise; go up 【上肢】upper limbs

尚 shàng ①still; yet ～待进一步讨论 pending further discussion 为时～早 it is still too early 此事～未 解决 the matter remains to be settled ②esteem; value ～ 武 set great store by martial qualities

SHAO

烧 shāo ①burn ～掉废纸 burn up the waste paper ～了一个洞 burn a hole in sth. ②cook; bake; heat ～饭 prepare a meal ～水 heat up some water ～砖 bake bricks ③stew; fry; roast ～茄子 stewed eggplant ～鸡 roast chicken ④(run a) fever 病人～得厉害 the patient has a high temperature ～退了 the fever is down 【烧 饼】sesame seed cake 【烧火】make a fire; light a fire 【烧酒】white spirit 【烧伤】burn 【烧香】burn joss sticks

捎 shāo take along sth. to or for sb.; bring to sb. ～来点花生 bring sb. some peanuts ～个口信 take a message to sb. 【捎带】incidentally; in passing

梢 shāo tip; the thin end of a twig, etc. 鞭～ whiplash 树～ the top of a tree

稍 shāo a little; a bit ～加修改 make slight changes ～长 be a bit too long ～等一会儿 just a moment 【稍微】slightly; a trifle 【稍息】(stand) at ease

勺 sháo spoon; ladle; dipper; scoop

芍 sháo 【芍药】Chinese herbaceous peony

韶 sháo splendid 【韶光】beautiful springtime/glorious youth

少 shǎo ①few; little; less ～而精 fewer but better 以～胜多 defeat the many with the few ②be short; lack 缺医～药 be short of doctors and medicine ③lose; be missing ～一个字 there's a word missing ④a little while 请～候 wait a moment, please ⑤stop; quit ～废话 stop talking rubbish 【少不得】cannot do without 参考书～不得 reference books are indispensable ～要麻烦您 we may have to trouble you about it 【少量】a little; a few 【少数】small number; few ～人 a few people 他们是～ they are in the minority ～民族 minority nationality

少 shào ①young ②son of a rich family; young master 【少妇】young married woman 【少年】early youth ～犯罪 juvenile delinquency ～宫 Children's Palace ～运动员 juvenile athlete 【少女】young girl 【少先队】Young Pioneers ～员 Young Pioneer

捎 shào drive (a cart) backwards; back (a cart)

哨 shào ①(sentry) post 观察～ observation post 放～ stand guard ②whistle 吹～ blow a whistle 【哨兵】 sentry; guard 【哨所】 sentry post; post

涑 shào (of rain) slant in 东边～雨 the rain is driving in from the east

SHE

奢 shē ①luxurious 穷～极欲 (indulge in) luxury and extravagance ②excessive; inordinate ～望 extravagant hopes; wild wishes 【奢侈】 extravagant; wasteful 生活～ live in luxury ～品 luxuries 【奢华】 sumptuous

赊 shē buy or sell on credit 【赊购】 buy on credit 【赊欠】 give or get credit

舌 shé tongue 【舌尖】 the tip of the tongue 【舌头】 tongue/an enemy soldier captured for the purpose of extracting information 【舌战】 have a verbal battle with

折 shé break; snap 扁担～了 the shoulder pole broke 【折本】 lose money in business ～生意 a bad bargain

蛇 shé snake; serpent 【蛇形】 snakelike; S-shaped

舍 shě give up; abandon ～身救人 give one's life to rescue sb. 【舍不得】 hate to part with or use; grudge ～乱花一分钱 hate to waste a single cent 【舍得】 be willing to part with; not grudge

设 shè set up; establish; found ～新机构 set up a new organization 【设备】 equipment; installation; facilities 【设法】 think of a way; try; do what one can 【设防】 set up defences; fortify; garrison ～地带 fortified zone 【设计】 design; plan ～厂房 make designs for a factory building ～版面 lay out a printed page ～能力 designed capacity ～师 designer ～图 design drawing ～院 designing institute 【设立】establish; set up 【设身处地】put oneself in sb. else's position 【设想】imagine; conceive/ tentative plan; tentative idea/have consideration for 为群众~ take the interests of the masses into consideration 为青少年~ give thought to the needs of the younger generation 【设宴】give a banquet; fête (the distinguished guests, etc.) 【设置】set up; put up; install 课程~ courses offered in a college or school; curriculum

社 shè ①organized body; agency; society 出版~ publishing house ②people's commune ~办企业 commune-run enterprise 【社会】society ~财富 public wealth ~地位 social position ~工作 work, in addition to one's regular job, done for the collective; duty outside one's regular work ~关系 social relations / one's social connections ~学 sociology 【社会主义】socialism ~革命 socialist revolution ~建设 socialist construction 【社交】social contact 【社论】editorial 【社团】mass organizations 【社员】a member of a society, etc.

舍 shè house; shed; hut 校~ school buildings ②my ~弟 my younger brother ~间 my house

涉 shè ①wade; ford 远~重洋 travel all the way from across the oceans ②go through; experience ~险 go through dangers 【涉及】involve; relate to; touch upon 【涉外】concerning foreign affairs 【涉嫌】be a suspect

射 shè ①shoot; fire ~箭 shoot an arrow ~进一球 score a goal ②discharge in a jet 喷~ spout; spurt ③send out (light, heat, etc.) ~出强光 project powerful beams of light ④allude to sth. or sb. 影~ insinuate 【射程】range (of fire) 【射击】shoot; fire/shooting ~场 shooting range ~孔 embrasure 【射手】shooter; marksman 【射线】ray

赦 shè remit (a punishment); pardon 【赦罪】 absolve sb. from guilt

摄 shè ①absorb; assimilate ②take a photograph of; shoot ③conserve (one's health) 【摄取】 absorb; take in / shoot ～营养 absorb nourishment ～镜头 shoot a scene 【摄象机】 pickup camera 电视～ television camera 【摄影】 take a photograph / shoot a film ～留念 have a souvenir photograph taken ～机 camera ～记者 camera-man ～棚 film studio ～师 photographer 【摄制】 produce ～组 production unit

慑 shè fear; be awed 【慑服】 submit in fear; succumb/cow sb. into submission

麝 shè ①musk deer ②musk 【麝牛】 musk-ox 【麝鼠】 muskrat

SHEN

申 shēn state; express; explain 重～前令 reiterate the previous order 【申辩】 defend oneself; argue one's case 【申斥】 rebuke 【申明】 declare; avow ～立场 state one's position 【申请】 apply for ～入(出)境签证 apply for an entry (exit) visa ～人 applicant ～书 (written) application 【申述】 state; explain in detail ～来意 explain the purpose of one's visit ～观点 expound one's views 【申诉】 appeal 【申讨】 condemn; denounce 【申冤】 redress an injustice

伸 shēn stretch; extend ～懒腰 stretch oneself ～大拇指 hold up one's thumb 【伸手】 stretch out one's hand/ask for help, etc. ～拿碗 reach for the bowl 【伸缩】 stretch out and draw back; expand and contract; lengthen and shorten/flexible; elastic; adjustable 没有～余地 leave one no latitude 【伸展】 spread; extend 【伸张】 uphold ～正气 promote healthy tendencies

身 shēn ①body 转～ turn round ～负重伤 be seriously injured ②life 以～殉职 die a martyr at one's post ③oneself; personally ④one's moral character and conduct 修～ cultivate one's mind ⑤body 车～ the body of a car 【身边】 at one's side/with one ～没带钱 have no money on one 【身材】 stature; figure 【身段】 (woman's) figure/ (dancer's) posture 【身分】 status; capacity; identity/ dignity 不合～ incompatible with one's status ～不明 unidentified 暴露～ reveal one's identity 有失～ be beneath one's dignity ～证 identity card 【身高】 height (of a person) 【身教】 teach others by one's own example ～胜于言教 example is better than precept 【身强力壮】 strong; tough; sturdy 【身世】 one's life experience 【身手】 skill; talent 大显～ exhibit one's skill 【身受】 experience (personally) 感同～ I shall count it as a personal favour 【身体】 body/health 注意～ look after one's health

呻 shēn 【呻吟】 groan; moan 无病～ moan and groan without being ill

绅 shēn gentry 【绅士】 gentleman; gentry

参 shēn ginseng

深 shēn ①deep ～井 a deep well 水～ the depth of the water ②difficult; profound 这本书太～了 the book is too difficult ③thoroughgoing; penetrating; profound 功夫～ have put in a great deal of effort ④close; intimate 交情～ be on intimate terms ⑤dark ～蓝 dark blue 颜色～ the colour is deep ⑥late ～秋 late autumn 夜～了 it was late at night ⑦very; greatly; deeply ～恐 be very much afraid ～知 know very well ～感 feel deeply ～信 firmly believe ～受感动 be deeply moved 【深奥】

abstruse; profound; recondite 【深沉】 dark; deep / dull (sound, voice, etc.) 暮色～ the dusk is deepening ～的音调 deep notes; dull sound 【深处】 depths; recesses 在密林～ in the depths of the forest 在思想～ in one's heart of hearts 【深度】 degree of depth; depth/profundity 【深厚】 profound/solid ～的感情 deep feelings ～的友谊 profound friendship ～的基础 a solid foundation 【深化】 deepen 矛盾～ intensification of a contradiction 【深刻】 deep; deepgoing ～的印象 a deep impression ～的教育 a profound lesson 【深浅】 depth (of a river) /shade (of colour) 【深切】 heartfelt; deep ～怀念 dearly cherish the memory of ～哀悼 heartfelt condolences 【深情】 deep feeling; deep love ～厚谊 profound sentiments of friendship 【深入】 penetrate into/deepgoing ～实际 go deep into the realities of life ～基层 go down to the grass-roots units ～群众 go into the midst of the common people ～生活 plunge into the thick of life ～人心 strike root in the hearts of the people ～的思想工作 thoroughgoing ideological work ～浅出 explain the profound in simple terms 【深思】 ponder deeply over 值得～ be worth pondering ～熟虑 careful consideration 【深夜】 late at night 【深渊】 abyss 【深造】 pursue advanced studies 【深重】 very grave

什 shén 【什么】 what/when 他说～ what did he say 那是～颜色 what colour is it 他～时候走 when will he leave

神 shén ①god; deity; divinity ②supernatural; magical ～效 miraculous effect ③spirit; mind 凝～ focus one's attention 走～ be absentminded ④expression; look 眼～ expression in the eyes 【神采】 expression 【神化】 deify 【神话】 mythology; myth; fairy tale 【神魂】 state of mind; mind ～不定 be deeply perturbed ～颠倒 be infatuated

【神经】nerve ～病 neuropathy/mental disorder ～紧张 be nervous ～过敏 neuroticism/neurotic; oversensitive ～衰弱 neurasthenia 【神秘】mysterious; mystical ～主义 mysticism 【神妙】wonderful; marvellous 【神明】gods; deities 【神女】goddess 【神奇】mystical; miraculous ～的效果 magical effect 【神气】expression; air; manner/spirited; vigorous/putting on airs; cocky ～十足 very arrogant ～活现 as proud as a peacock 【神色】expression; look ～不对 look queer ～慌张 look flustered ～自若 be perfectly calm and collected 【神圣】sacred; holy ～职责 sacred duty ～权利 sacred right 【神速】with amazing speed 收效～ yield marvellously quick results 兵贵～ speed is precious in war 【神态】bearing; mien ～悠闲 look perfectly relaxed 【神通】remarkable ability ～广大 be infinitely resourceful 大显～ display one's prowess 【神童】child prodigy 【神往】be carried away; be rapt 【神威】martial prowess 【神仙】celestial being; immortal 【神学】theology 【神志】senses ～清醒 be in one's right mind ～昏迷 lose consciousness

审 shěn ①careful ～视 look closely at ②examine; go over ～稿 go over a manuscript or draft ③interrogate ～案 try a case 【审查】examine; investigate ～经费 check up on the funds 【审订】examine and revise ～教材 revise teaching materials 【审核】examine and verify ～预算 examine and approve a budget 【审理】try (a case); hear 【审美】appreciation of the beautiful ～观 aesthetic standards ～能力 aesthetic judgment 【审判】bring to trial ～程序 judicial procedure ～机关 judicial organ ～权 jurisdiction ～员 judge ～长 presiding judge 【审批】examine and approve 【审慎】cautious; careful; circumspect 【审问】question 【审讯】interrogate; try 【审议】consideration; deliberation; discussion 【审阅】check and approve

婶 shěn wife of father's younger brother; aunt

肾 shèn kidney 【肾炎】nephritis 【肾盂】renal pelvis

甚 shèn ①very; extremely ～为痛快 find it most satisfying ②more than 【甚至】even; (go) so far as to

渗 shèn ooze; seep 血～出来了 blood oozed out 【渗沟】sewer 【渗坑】seepage pit 【渗入】permeate ～地下 seep into the ground 【渗透】permeate; seep/infiltrate

慎 shèn careful; cautious 一着不～，满盘皆输 one careless move loses the whole game 【慎重】prudent; discreet 采取～的态度 adopt a prudent policy 经过～考虑 after careful consideration

SHENG

升 shēng ①rise; hoist; go up; ascend 太阳～起 the sun is rising ②promote 被提～ be promoted ③litre 一～啤酒 a litre of beer 【升班】go up (one grade in school) 【升级】go up (one grade, etc.) /escalation (of a war) 【升降机】elevator; lift 【升旗】raise a flag 【升学】go to a school of a higher grade; enter a higher school ～率 proportion of students entering schools of a higher grade

生 shēng ①give birth to (a child); bear ②grow ～根 take root ③life 一～ all one's life ④livelihood 谋～ make a living ⑤living ～物 living things ⑥get; have ～冻疮 get chilblains ⑦light (a fire, stove, etc.) ⑧unripe; green ～的苹果 a green apple ⑨raw; uncooked ～肉 raw meat ⑩unprocessed; unrefined; crude ～皮 rawhide ⑪unfamiliar; strange ～词 new word ⑫pupil; student 【生病】fall ill 【生产】produce; manufacture ～成本 cost of production ～定额 production quota ～队 production team ～力 productive forces ～率 productivity ～责任制 system of responsibility for (agricultural) production ～指标 production quota 【生存】 subsist; exist; live ～竞争 struggle for existence 【生动】 lively; vivid ～活泼 lively; vivid and vigorous 【生活】 life / live 日常～ daily life 政治～ political life 组织～ Party or League activities ～困难 be badly off ～必需品 daily necessities ～补助 extra allowance for living expenses ～方式 way of life; life style ～福利 welfare benefits ～来源 source of income ～水平 living standard ～条件 living conditions ～资料 means of livelihood ～作风 behaviour; conduct 【生火】 make a fire 【生机】 lease of life/life; vitality 充满～ be full of life 【生计】 livelihood 另谋～ try to find some other means of livelihood 【生姜】 ginger 【生理】 physiology ～作用 physiological action 【生力军】 fresh troops/fresh activists 【生路】 way out 杀出一条～ fight one's way out 【生命】 life ～力 life-force ～线 lifeline 【生僻】 uncommon; rare 【生平】 all one's life ～事迹 one's life story 作者～简介 a biographical note on the author 【生气】 take offence; get angry / life; vitality ～勃勃 vigorous; full of vitality 【生前】 before one's death 【生日】 birthday 【生色】 add colour to; add lustre to 【生事】 make trouble 【生手】 sb. new to a job 【生疏】 not familiar/out of practice; rusty/not as close as before 【生水】 unboiled water 【生丝】 raw silk 【生死】 life and death ～存亡的斗争 a life-and-death struggle ～攸关的问题 a matter of life and death 【生态】 ecology ～平衡 ecological balance 【生铁】 pig iron 【生物】 living things; living beings; organisms ～化学 biochemistry ～学 biology 【生效】 go into effect; become effective 【生涯】 career; profession 舞台～ a stage career【生意】business; trade 做～ do business 做成一笔～ make a deal ～经 the knack of doing business【生硬】stiff; rigid; harsh 态度～ be stiff in manner【生油】unboiled oil/peanut oil【生育】give birth to; bear ～子女 bear children 不能～ be sterile【生长】grow / grow up; be brought up【生殖】reproduction ～器 genitals

声 shēng ①sound; voice 脚步～ the sound of footsteps ②make a sound 不～不响 not utter a word【声辩】argue; justify【声波】sound wave【声称】profess; claim; assert【声带】vocal cords/sound track【声调】tone; note【声浪】voice; clamour【声明】state; declare; announce / statement; declaration【声色】voice and countenance 不动～ maintain one's composure ～俱厉 stern in voice and countenance【声势】impetus; momentum 虚张～ make a show of strength ～浩大 great in strength and impetus【声嘶力竭】shout oneself hoarse【声讨】denounce; condemn ～会 denunciation meeting【声望】popularity【声音】sound; voice【声誉】reputation; fame; prestige 亨有很高的～ enjoy great prestige【声援】express support for【声乐】vocal music【声张】make public; disclose

牲 shēng ①domestic animal ②animal sacrifice【牲畜】livestock【牲口】draught animals ～棚 stock barn

甥 shēng sister's son; nephew【甥女】sister's daughter; niece

绳 shéng ①rope; cord; string 麻～ hemp rope 钢丝～ wire rope ②restrict; restrain 要～之以法 must be dealt with according to law【绳梯】rope ladder

省 shěng ①economize; save ～时间 save time 能～的就～ economize wherever possible ②omit; leave out ～一道工序 eliminate one step from the process ③province ～长 governor of a province【省吃俭用】live frugally

【省得】so as to avoid 【省会】provincial capital 【省力】save effort; save labour 【省略】leave out 这些段落可以 ～ these paragraphs can be omitted 主语～了 the subject (of the sentence) is understood ～号 ellipsis (dots) ～句 elliptical sentence 【省钱】save money; be economical 【省事】save trouble; simplify matters 【省委】provincial Party committee 【省心】save worry

圣 shèng ①sage; saint ②holy; sacred 【圣诞】the birthday of Jesus Christ ～老人 Santa Claus ～树 Christmas tree ～节 Christmas Day 【圣地】sacred place; shrine 【圣经】the Bible 【圣人】sage 【圣旨】imperial edict

胜 shèng ①victory; success 得～ win (victory) ②surpass; be superior to; get the better of 聊～于无 better than nothing ③superb; wonderful; lovely ④be equal to; can bear 【胜地】famous scenic spot 【胜负】victory or defeat; success or failure 战争的～ the outcome of a war ～未定 victory hangs in the balance 【胜利】victory; triumph; win/successfully ～果实 fruits of victory ～会师 triumphantly join forces ～者 victor; winner 【胜任】competent; qualified ～工作 prove equal to the task 【胜仗】victorious battle; victory 打～ win a battle

盛 shèng ①flourishing; prosperous 鲜花～开 the flowers are in full bloom ②vigorous; energetic 火势很～ the fire is raging ③magnificent; grand ～举 a grand event ④abundant; plentiful ～意 great kindness ⑤popular; common ～传 be widely known ⑥greatly; deeply ～夸 praise highly 【盛产】abound in; teem with ～石油 be rich in oil 【盛大】grand; magnificent ～欢迎 a rousing welcome 【盛典】grand ceremony 【盛会】distinguished gathering; grand meeting 【盛极一时】be in fashion for a time 【盛况】spectacular event ～空前 an exceptionally grand occasion 【盛名】 great reputation 【盛气凌人】 domineering; arrogant ～的样子 imperious bearing 【盛情】 great kindness; boundless hospitality ～难却 it would be ungracious not to accept your invitation 【盛行】 midsummer 【盛行】 be current; be rife ～一时 be in vogue for a time; prevail for a time 【盛誉】 great fame; high reputation 【盛赞】 highly praise 【盛装】 splendid attire; rich dress

剩 shèng surplus; remnant ～货 surplus goods ～菜～饭 leftovers 【剩下】 be left (over); remain ～多少 how much is left (over) 【剩余】 surplus; remainder ～价值 surplus value ～物资 surplus materials

SHI

尸 shī corpse; dead body; remains 兽～ carcass 【尸骨】 skeleton

失 shī ①lose ～而复得 lost and found again ②miss; let slip 坐～良机 lose a good chance ③fail to achieve one's end 大～所望 be greatly disappointed ④defect; mistake 唯恐有～ fear that there may be some mishap ⑤break (a promise); go back on (one's word) 【失败】 be defeated; lose (a war, etc.) / fail ～是成功之母 failure is the mother of success ～情绪 defeatist sentiments ～主义 defeatism 【失策】 unwise; inexpedient 【失常】 not normal; odd 举止～ act oddly 精神～ be distraught 【失宠】 fall into disfavour 【失传】 be lost ～的艺术 a lost art 【失措】 lose one's head 【失当】 improper; inappropriate 处理～ be not properly handled 【失地】 lost territory 【失掉】 lose/miss ～联系 lose contact with ～权力 be stripped of power ～机会 miss a chance 【失火】 catch fire; be on fire 【失礼】 impoliteness; discourtesy 【失利】 suffer a defeat 军事上～ military reverses 【失恋】 be disappointed in a love affair 【失灵】 not work; be out of order 【失眠】 (suffer from) insomnia; have a sleepless night 【失明】 go blind 【失窃】 have things stolen 【失去】 lose ～知觉 lose consciousness ～信心 lose confidence ～时效 cease to be in force 【失散】 be separated from; be scattered 【失色】 turn pale / be eclipsed 【失神】 inattentive; absent-minded/ out of sorts 【失实】 inconsistent with the facts 【失势】 lose power and influence 【失事】 (have an) accident 【失手】 accidentally drop 【失算】 miscalculate; misjudge 【失调】 imbalance; dislocation / lack of proper care (after an illness, childbirth, etc.) 供求～ imbalance of supply and demand 经济～ economic dislocation 【失望】 lose hope/ be disappointed 【失物】 lost article ～招领处 Lost Property Office 【失误】 fault; muff 接球～ muff a ball 【失陷】 fall into enemy hands 【失效】 lose efficacy; cease to be effective / (of a treaty, etc.) be no longer in force 【失笑】 cannot help laughing 【失信】 break one's promise 【失修】 (of houses, etc.) be in bad repair 【失学】 be deprived of education; be unable to go to school 【失血】 lose blood ～过多 excessive loss of blood 【失言】 make an indiscreet remark 【失业】 be out of work; be unemployed ～率 rate of unemployment ～者 the unemployed; the jobless 【失意】 be frustrated; be disappointed 【失约】 fail to keep an appointment 【失职】 neglect one's duty 【失主】 owner of lost property 【失踪】 be missing 【失足】 lose one's footing; slip/take a wrong step in life

师 shī ①teacher; master 尊～ respect the teacher ② model; example ③ of one's master or teacher ～母 the wife of one's teacher or master ④division 步兵～ infantry division ⑤troops; army 正义之～ an army fighting for a just cause 【师部】 division headquarters

【师范】teacher-training; pedagogical/normal school ～学院 teachers college【师傅】master worker【师长】teacher/division commander【师资】teachers

虱 shī louse

诗 shī poetry; verse; poem【诗歌】poems and songs; poetry ～朗诵 recitation of poems【诗话】notes on poets and poetry【诗集】collection of poems【诗句】verse; line【诗剧】drama in verse【诗人】poet【诗兴】poetic inspiration; poetic mood【诗意】poetic quality or flavour

狮 shī lion【狮子狗】pug-dog【狮子头】large meatball

施 shī ①execute; carry out 无所～其技 no chance (for sb.) to play his tricks ②bestow; grant ～恩 bestow favour ③exert; impose ～压力 exert pressure ④use; apply ～肥 apply fertilizer【施放】discharge; fire ～烟幕 lay a smokescreen【施工】construction ～单位 unit in charge of construction ～人员 builder; constructor【施行】put in force; execute; apply/perform ～急救 administer first aid【施展】put to good use; give free play to ～本领 put one's ability to good use【施政】administration

湿 shī wet; damp; humid 别～了衣裳 don't get your clothes wet【湿度】humidity ～表 humidometer【湿淋淋】dripping wet; drenched【湿气】moisture; dampness【湿润】moist ～的土壤 damp soil 空气～ humid air

嘘 shī sh; hush

十 shí ①ten ～倍 ten times; tenfold ②topmost ～成 100 per cent【十二月】December/the twelfth moon【十分】very; fully ～难过 feel very sorry ～宝贵 most valuable ～有害 extremely harmful ～注意 pay close attention to 【十全十美】 be perfect in every way 【十一月】 November/the eleventh moon 【十月】 October/the tenth moon 【十之八九】 in eight or nine cases out of ten; most likely 【十字镐】 pick; pickaxe; mattock 【十字架】 cross 【十字路口】 crossroads 【十足】 out-and-out; sheer; downright 干劲~ full of energy

什 shí assorted; varied; miscellaneous 【什锦】 assorted; mixed ~饼干 assorted biscuits ~奶糖 assorted toffees

石 shí ①stone; rock ~板 slabstone; flag ②stone inscription 【石碑】 stone tablet; stele 【石笔】 slate pencil 【石壁】 cliff; precipice 【石雕】 stone carving / carved stone 【石方】 cubic metre of stone/stonework 【石膏】 gypsum; plaster stone ~夹板 plaster splint ~像 plaster statue 【石灰】 lime 【石匠】 stonemason 【石窟】 rock cave; grotto 【石榴】 pomegranate 【石棉】 asbestos 【石墨】 graphite 【石器】 stone artifact/stone vessel ~时代 the Stone Age 【石英】 quartz ~玻璃 quartz glass 【石油】 petroleum; oil ~工业 oil industry ~产品 petroleum products ~气 petroleum gas 【石子·】 cobble; pebble

识 shí ①know ②knowledge 【识别】 distinguish; discern; spot ~力 discernment ~干部 judge cadres 【识破】 see through; penetrate 【识字】 learn to read; become literate ~班 literacy class ~课本 reading primer

时 shí ①time; times; days 当~ at that time; in those days ②fixed time 按~上班 get to work on time ③hour 报~ give the time signal 上午八~ at 8 a.m. ④season ~菜 delicacies of the season ⑤current; present ⑥opportunity; chance 失~ miss the chance ⑦occasionally; from time to time ~有出现 occur now and then ⑧tense 过去~ the past tense 【时差】 time difference 【时常】 often; frequently 【时代】 times; age; era; epoch ~潮

流 the trend of the times ～需要 the needs of the times 青年～ youth 【时而】 from time to time; sometimes 【时光】 time/times; years; days 【时候】 (the duration of) time/ (a point in) time; moment 你花了多少～ how much time did you spend 现在是什么～ what time is it 【时机】 opportunity 等待～ wait for an opportunity; bide one's time 一到 when the opportunity arises ～不成熟 the time is not yet ripe 【时间】 time ～与空间 time and space ～紧 time is pressing ～到了 time's up 办公～ office hours ～性 timeliness 【时局】 the current political situation 【时刻】 time; hour; moment/constantly; always 关键～ a critical moment ～为人民利益着想 always keep the people's interests in mind ～表 timetable; schedule 【时令】 season ～不正 unseasonable weather 【时髦】 fashionable; stylish; in vogue 【时期】 period 【时尚】 fashion; fad 【时时】 often; constantly 【时势】 the current situation 【时事】 current events ～报告 report on current events ～述评 current events survey ～学习 study of current affairs 【时速】 speed per hour 【时态】 tense 【时势】 the trend of the times 【时鲜】 in season ～果品 fresh fruits 【时疫】 epidemic 【时运】 luck; fortune 【时针】 hands of a clock or watch/hour hand 【时装】 fashionable dress

实 shí ①solid ②true; real; honest ③reality; fact ④fruit; seed 结～ bear fruit 【实报实销】 be reimbursed for what one spends 【实词】 notional word 【实地】 on the spot ～考察 on-the-spot investigation 【实干】 do solid work ～家 man of action 【实话】 truth 说～ to tell the truth ～实说 not mince words 【实惠】 material benefit/substantial; solid 从中得到～ really benefit from it 【实际】 reality; practice / practical / real; actual 客观～ objective reality 从～出发 proceed from actual conditions ～上

in fact; in reality; actually ～经验 practical experience ～例子 a concrete instance ～情况 the actual situation ～收入 real income 【实价】 actual price 【实践】 practice/ put into practice 具体～ concrete practice ～诺言 keep one's word 【实况】 what is actually happening ～录音 on-the-spot recording ～转播 live broadcast; live telecast 【实力】 actual strength; strength ～相当 be well matched in strength ～地位 position of strength 【实例】 (living) example 【实情】 the true state of affairs; truth 【实权】 real power 【实施】 put into effect; implement; carry out 【实事求是】 seek truth from facts ～的工作作风 a practical and realistic style of work ～的批评 criticism based on facts 【实数】 the actual amount or number / real number 【实物】 material object / in kind ～交易 barter 【实习】 practice; fieldwork; field trip 进行教学～ do practice teaching ～生 trainee ～医生 intern 【实现】 realize; achieve ～改革 bring about a reform ～现代化 accomplish the modernization of 【实效】 actual effect; substantial results 注重～ emphasize practical results 【实行】 put into practice; implement ～土改 carry out agrarian reform ～专政 exercise dictatorship over 【实学】 real learning; sound scholarship 【实验】 experiment; test 做～ do an experiment; make a test ～室 laboratory ～员 laboratory technician 【实业】 industry and commerce; industry ～家 industrialist 【实用】 practical; pragmatic; functional ～美术 applied fine arts ～主义 pragmatism 【实在】 true; real; honest / indeed; really; honestly / in fact ～太好了 very good indeed 我～不知道 I really don't know 【实则】 actually; in fact; in reality 【实战】 actual combat 【实质】 substance; essence 问题的～ the crux of the matter ～上 in substance; in essence; essentially 【实足】 full;

solid ～一百斤 be a full 100 *jin* ～年龄 exact age

拾 shí pick up; collect ～麦穗 glean (stray ears of) wheat 【拾掇】 put in order/repair; fix

食 shí ①eat ②meal; food 主～ staple food ③feed 猪～ pig feed ④edible ～油 edible oil ⑤eclipse 月～ lunar eclipse 【食道】 esophagus 【食粮】 grain; food 【食品】 foodstuff; food; provisions ～部 food department ～厂 food products factory ～工业 food industry ～公司 food company ～加工 food processing ～商店 provisions shop 【食谱】 recipes; cookbook 【食堂】 dining room; mess hall; canteen 【食糖】 sugar 【食物】 food; eatables; edibles 【食言】 break one's promise 【食欲】 appetite ～不振 have a poor appetite 促进～ stimulate the appetite

蚀 shí ①lose 亏～ lose (money) in business ②erode; corrode 【蚀本】 lose one's capital ～生意 a business running at a loss; a losing proposition 【蚀刻】 etching

史 shǐ history 【史册】 history; annals 载入～ go down in history 【史料】 historical data 【史前】 prehistoric (age, times) 【史诗】 epic 【史实】 historical facts 【史书】 history; historical records 【史无前例】 without precedent in history; unprecedented 【史学】 the science of history; historical science ～家 historian

矢 shǐ ①arrow ②vow; swear ～志不移 vow to adhere to one's chosen course 【矢口否认】 flatly deny

使 shǐ ①send; tell sb. to do sth. ②use; employ; apply ～化肥 use chemical fertilizer ③make; cause; enable ④envoy; messenger 特～ special envoy 信～ courier; messenger ⑤if; supposing 【使出】 use; exert ～全副本领 use all one's resources 【使得】 can be used; usable / workable; feasible / make; cause 【使馆】 diplomatic mission; embassy ～工作人员 embassy personnel 【使节】 (diplomatic) envoy

【使劲】exert all one's strength ～干活 work hard ～划桨 strain at the oars 【使领馆】embassies and consulates 【使用】make use of; use; employ; apply ～种种手段 resort to every possible means ～方便 be easy to operate ～价值 use value ～率 rate of utilization ～权 right of use ～寿命 service life (of machines) ～说明书 operation instructions 【使者】emissary; envoy

始 shǐ ①beginning; start 不知～于何时 not know exactly when this came into being ②only then; not ... until 【始末】beginning and end—the whole story 【始业】the beginning of the school year 秋季～ the school year begins in autumn 【始终】from beginning to end; from start to finish; all along; throughout ～不渝 unswerving; steadfast ～如一 constant; consistent

驶 shǐ ①sail; drive ～入港口 sail into the harbour ②speed 疾～而过 speed by; fly past

屎 shǐ ①excrement; faeces 鸡～ chicken droppings 牛～ cow dung ②secretion (of the eye, ear, etc.) 耳～ earwax

士 shì ①bachelor ②scholar ③(commendable) person 勇～ brave fighter 【士兵】rank-and-file soldiers 【士气】morale 鼓舞～ boost morale 【士绅】gentry

氏 shì ①family name; surname ②née 李王～ Mrs. Li, née Wang 【氏族】clan ～社会 clan society ～制度 clan system

市 shì ①market 上～ be on the market ②city; municipality ～中心 city centre; downtown 【市场】marketplace; market; bazaar ～繁荣 the market is brisk ～价格 market price 【市集】fair 【市侩】sordid merchant 【市面】market conditions; business ～萧条 business is slack 【市民】residents of a city; townspeople 【市区】city proper; urban district 【市委】municipal Party committee 【市长】

mayor 【市镇】 towns 【市政】 municipal administration

示 shì show; notify; instruct 出~证件 produce one's papers 请~ ask for instructions 【示范】 set an example; demonstrate 起~作用 play an exemplary role ~表演 put on a demonstration 【示警】 give a warning; warn 【示弱】 give the impression of weakness; take sth. lying down 【示威】 demonstrate/display one's strength ~游行 demonstration; parade; march 【示意】 signal; hint ~他出去 motion to him to go out 以目~ give a hint with the eyes ~图 sketch map 【示众】 publicly expose

世 shì ①lifetime; life 今~ this present life ②generation ~交 friendship spanning many generations ③age; era ④world 举~闻名 well known all over the world 【世传】 be handed down through generations 【世代】 generation 【世故】 the ways of the world/worldly-wise 【世纪】 century 【世家】 old and well-known family 【世界】 world ~大战 world war ~观 world outlook ~冠军 world champion ~纪录 world record ~语 Esperanto ~主义 cosmopolitanism 【世面】 society; world; life 见过~ have seen the world; have experienced life 【世人】 common people 【世事】 affairs of human life 【世俗】 common customs/secular; worldly 【世态】 the ways of the world ~炎凉 inconstancy of human relationships 【世袭】 hereditary

仕 shì be an official; fill an office 【仕途】 official career

式 shì ①type; style 新~ new type ②pattern; form ③ceremony; ritual 开幕~ opening ceremony ④formula 分子~ molecular formula ⑤mood; mode 陈述~ indicative mood 【式样】 style; type; model ~美观 graceful-looking

试 shì try; test ~穿 try on (a garment, shoes, etc.) ~产 trial production ②examination; test 口~ oral examination 【试场】 examination hall 【试点】 make experiments; launch a pilot project / experimental unit 【试飞】 test flight ～驾驶员 test pilot 【试管】 test tube 【试剂】 reagent 【试金石】 touchstone 【试卷】 examination paper; test paper 【试探】 sound out; feel out; probe; explore 【试题】 test questions 【试图】 attempt; try 【试问】 may we ask 【试验】 trial; experiment; test ～场 proving ground ～田 experimental field 【试样】 (test) sample 【试映】 preview 【试用】 try out/on probation ～本 trial edition ～品 trial products ～期 probation period ～人员 probationer 【试纸】 test paper 【试制】 trial-produce

势 shì ①power; force; influence 仗～欺人 bully people on the strength of one's powerful connections ②momentum; tendency 来～甚猛 come with tremendous force. ③the outward appearance of a natural object 山～ the lie of a mountain ④situation; state of affairs; circumstances ～所必然 inevitably; as a matter of course ⑤sign; gesture 【势必】 certainly will; be bound to 【势不可当】 irresistible 【势不两立】 mutually exclusive; irreconcilable 【势均力敌】 match each other in strength 一场～的比赛 a close contest 【势力】 force; power; influence ～范围 sphere of influence 【势利】 snobbish ～小人 snob 【势头】 impetus; momentum; tendency 【势在必行】 be imperative (under the circumstances)

事 shì ①matter; affair; thing; business 国家大～ affairs of state ②trouble; accident 出～ have an accident 惹～ make trouble ③job; work 找～ look for a job ④be engaged in 无所～～ doing nothing 【事半功倍】 get twice the result with half the effort 【事倍功半】 get half the result with twice the effort 【事变】 incident/emergency; exigency/events 【事出有因】 there is good reason for it【事端】disturbance; incident 挑起～ provoke incidents 制造～ create disturbances【事故】accident; mishap 责任～ accident arising from sb.'s negligence【事后】after the event; afterwards【事迹】deed; achievement【事假】leave of absence【事件】incident; event【事理】reason; logic【事例】example; instance【事前】before the event; in advance; beforehand ～毫无准备 with no preparation at all ～请示 ask for instructions beforehand【事情】affair; matter; thing; business ～的真相 the facts of the case ～是这样的 it happened like this【事实】fact 与～不符 not tally with the facts ～俱在 the facts are all there ～如此 this is how things stand【事事】everything【事态】state of affairs; situation ～严重 the situation is serious【事务】work; routine / general affairs ～员 office clerk【事物】thing; object【事先】in advance; prior ～做准备 get ready beforehand ～打招呼 notify sb. in advance【事业】cause; undertaking / enterprise; facilities ～单位 institution ～费 operating expenses ～心 devotion to one's work; dedication【事与愿违】things go contrary to one's wishes【事主】the victim of a crime

侍 shì wait upon; attend upon; serve ～立 stand at sb.'s side in attendance【侍从】attendants; retinue【侍候】look after; attend【侍女】maid【侍者】waiter

视 shì ①look at ②regard ～如仇敌 look upon sb. as one's enemy ③watch【视察】inspect【视而不见】look but see not; turn a blind eye to【视角】angle of view【视界】visual field【视觉】visual sense; vision; sense of sight【视力】vision; sight【视听】seeing and hearing; what is seen and heard 混淆～ throw dust in people's eyes; confuse the public【视线】line of vision【视野】field of vision

饰 shì ①decorations; ornaments 服～ clothes and ornaments ②adorn; dress up; polish 文过～非 cover up one's mistakes ②play the role of; act the part of【饰词】 excuse; pretext【饰物】 jewelry / ornaments; decorations

室 shì room【室内】 indoor; interior 〜运动 indoor sport 〜游泳池 indoor swimming pool 〜装饰 interior decoration【室外】 outside 〜活动 outdoor activities

恃 shì rely on; depend on【恃才傲物】 be conceited and contemptuous【恃强凌弱】 use one's strength to bully the weak

拭 shì wipe away; wipe【拭目以待】 wait and see

柿 shì persimmon【柿饼】 dried persimmon【柿子椒】 sweetbell redpepper

是 shì ①correct; right 你说得～ what you said is right ②yes; right ③be 我～一个学生 I am a student【是的】 yes; right; that's it【是非】 right and wrong/quarrel; dispute 〜问题 a matter of right and wrong 搬弄〜 tell tales; sow discord 〜曲直 truth and falsehood; merits and demerits【是否】 whether or not; whether; if 〜符合实际 whether or not it corresponds to reality

适 shì ①fit; suitable; proper 〜于儿童读的书籍 books suitable for children 〜销对路 readily marketable ②right; opportune 〜量 just the right amount ③comfortable; well 感到不～ not feel well ④go; follow; pursue 无所～从 not know what course to pursue【适当】 suitable; proper 〜的安排 proper arrangemen、〜调整 appropriate readjustment【适得其反】 run counter to one's desire【适度】 appropriate measure【适合】 suit; fit 〜当地情况 be suited to local conditions 〜口味 suit one's taste【适可而止】 stop before going too far【适时】 at the right mo-

ment; timely ～播种 begin sowing in good time 【适宜】
suitable; fit; appropriate 【适意】 agreeable; enjoyable; comfortable 【适应】 suit; adapt; fit ～需要 suit the needs
of ～环境 adapt oneself to circumstances ～性 adaptability ～症 indication 【适用】 suit; be applicable 对我们这
个地区很～ be suitable for our area 【适中】 moderate/
well situated 大小～ moderate size

逝 shì ①pass 时光易～ time passes quickly ②die; pass
away 病～ die of illness 【逝世】 pass away; die

释 shì ①explain; elucidate ～义 explain the meaning
(of a word, etc.) ②clear up; dispel ～疑 remove
doubts ③let go; be relieved of ④set free 【释放】 release
(prisoners, energy, etc.)

嗜 shì have a liking for; be addicted to ～酒 be addicted to drink 【嗜好】 hobby/addiction; habit

誓 shì ①swear; vow; pledge ～将革命进行到底 vow to
carry the revolution through to the end ②oath 发～
take an oath; swear 【誓不罢休】 swear not to stop 【誓不
两立】 swear not to coexist with one's enemy; be irreconcilable 【誓词】 oath; pledge 【誓师】 a rally to pledge resolution before going to war/take a mass pledge ～大会 a
meeting to pledge mass effort 【誓约】 pledge; solemn promise

噬 shì bite 吞～ swallow up 反～ make a false coun-
tercharge

螫 shì sting 【螫针】 sting; stinger

SHOU

收 shōu ①receive ～报 receiving telegrams 我们不～
小帐 we don't accept gratuities 请～下作为纪念
please accept this as a souvenir ②put away; take in ～工具

put the tools away ③collect ～废品 collect scrap ④money received; receipts; income 税～ tax revenue ⑤harvest; gather in ～庄稼 harvest crops 秋～ autumn harvest⑥ close 伤～口了 the wound has healed 【收兵】 withdraw troops; call off a battle 【收藏】 collect; store up ～古画 collect old paintings ～家 collector (of books, antiques, etc.) 【收场】 wind up; end up; stop / end; ending 这件事不好～ it's hard to wind this matter up 草草～ wind up a matter hastily or perfunctorily 圆满的～ a happy ending 【收成】 harvest; crop ～不好 poor harvest 【收存】 receive and keep 【收到】 receive; get; achieve; obtain 【收发】 receive and dispatch/dispatcher ～室 office for incoming and outgoing mail 【收费】 collect fees; charge 【收复】 recover 【收割】 reap; harvest ～小麦 gather in the wheat ～机 harvester; reaper 【收工】 stop work for the day; knock off; pack up 【收购】 purchase; buy ～站 purchasing station 【收回】 take back; call in; regain; recall/ withdraw ～文件 recall the documents ～贷款 recall loans ～投资 recoup capital outlay ～建议 withdraw a proposal ～成命 countermand an order 【收获】 gather in the crops; harvest/results; gains 一次有～的访问 a rewarding visit 【收集】 collect; gather ～废铁 collect scrap iron 【收件人】 addressee; consignee 【收缴】 take over; capture 【收紧】 tighten up 【收据】 receipt 【收口】 (of a wound) close up; heal /(in knitting) binding off 【收款人】 payee 【收敛】 weaken or disappear/restrain oneself 【收留】 take sb. in; have sb. in one's care 【收罗】 collect; gather; enlist ～人才 recruit qualified personnel 【收买】 purchase; buy in/buy over; bribe ～旧书 buy used books ～人心 buy popular support 【收容】 take in; accept; house ～伤员 take in wounded soldiers ～难民 house refugees ～所 collecting post 【收入】 income; revenue; receipts; earnings; proceeds/ take in; include 集体～ collective income 财政～ state revenue 【收生】 midwifery 【收拾】 put in order; tidy; clear away/get things ready; pack ～屋子 tidy up the room ～床铺 make the bed ～碗筷 clear the table ～残局 clear up a messy situation 【收束】 bring together; collect 【收缩】 contract; shrink/concentrate one's forces; draw back 【收条】 receipt 【收听】 listen in ～新闻广播 listen to the news broadcast 【收尾】 wind up / ending (of an article, etc.) 【收文】 incoming dispatches ～簿 register of incoming dispatches 【收效】 yield results; bear fruit ～显著 bring notable results ～甚微 produce very little effect 【收信人】 the recipient of a letter; addressee 【收养】 ～孤儿 adopt an orphan 【收益】 income; profit; earnings; gains 【收音】 (of radio) reception / (of an auditorium, etc.) have good acoustics ～机 radio; wireless 【收支】 income and expenses ～平衡 revenue and expenditure are balanced

手 shǒu ①hand ～织的毛衣 a hand-knitted woollen sweater ②have in one's hand; hold 人～一册 everyone has a copy ③handy; convenient ④personally 【手背】 the back of the hand 【手臂】 arm 【手边】 on hand; at hand 【手表】 wrist watch 【手册】 handbook; manual 【手抄本】 hand-written copy 【手车】 handcart; wheelbarrow 【手电筒】 electric torch; flashlight 【手段】 means; medium; measure; method / trick; artifice 强制～ coercive method 艺术～ artistic medium 支付～ means of payment 采用种种～ use every artifice 【手法】 skill; technique/trick; gimmick 【手风琴】 accordion 【手扶拖拉机】 walking tractor 【手稿】 manuscript 【手工】 handwork / by hand; manual 做～ do handwork ～费 payment for a piece of handwork ～操作 done by hand【手工业】handicraft ～者 handicraftsman【手工艺】handicraft art～工人 craftsman; artisan ～品 handicrafts【手脚】movement of hands or feet; motion ～利落 nimble; agile ～不干净 sticky-fingered【手巾】towel【手锯】handsaw【手绢】handkerchief【手铐】handcuffs【手快】deft of hand【手雷】antitank grenade【手榴弹】hand grenade; grenade【手忙脚乱】in a frantic rush; in a muddle【手枪】pistol ～套 holster【手巧】skilful with one's hands; deft; dexterous【手勤】diligent; industrious【手球】handball【手软】be softhearted【手刹车】hand brake【手势】gesture; sign; signal 打～make a gesture; gesticulate ～语 sign language【手术】(surgical) operaton 动～perform or undergo an operation ～刀 scalpel ～室 operating room ～台 operating table【手套】gloves; mittens / baseball gloves; mitts【手提】portable ～包 handbag; bag ～箱 suitcase【手头】right beside one; on hand; at hand ～工作多 have a lot of work on hand ～紧 be short of money ～宽 be quite well off at the moment【手推车】handcart【手腕】artifice; finesse; stratagem 耍～ play tricks 政治～ political stratagem 外交～ diplomacy【手腕子】wrist【手无寸铁】bare-handed; unarmed【手舞足蹈】dance for joy【手写体】handwritten form; script【手心】the palm of the hand / control【手续】procedures; formalities 办～ go through formalities 行政～ administrative formalities 法律～ legal formalities ～费 service charge; commission【手艺】craftsmanship; workmanship/handicraft; trade 学～ learn the trade ～人 craftsman ～高 be highly skilled【手淫】masturbation【手印】an impression of the hand / thumb print; fingerprint【手掌】palm【手杖】stick【手指甲】finger nail【手纸】toilet paper【手指】finger【手镯】bracelet【手足】

brothers ～之情 brotherly affection 【手足无措】at a loss what to do

守 shǒu ①guard; defend ～城 defend a city ～球门 keep goal ～住阵地 hold the position ②keep watch ～着伤员 look after the wounded ③observe; abide by ～纪律 observe discipline ～规矩 behave well ～信用 keep one's promise 【守备】perform garrison duty; garrison ～部队 garrison force 【守财奴】miser 【守法】abide by the law; be law-abiding 【守寡】remain a widow; live in widowhood 【守候】wait for; expect / keep watch 【守护】guard; defend 【守旧】stick to old ways; be conservative ～派 old liners 【守军】defending troops; defenders 【守口如瓶】keep one's mouth shut 【守门】be on duty at the door or gate/keep goal ～员 goalkeeper 【守势】defensive 采取～ be on the defensive 【守卫】guard; defend 【守夜】keep watch at night 【守则】rules; regulations

首 shǒu ①head 昂～ hold one's head high ②first ～批 the first batch ③leader; head; chief 祸～ chief culprit ④bring charges against sb. 出～ inform against sb. 【首倡】initiate; start 【首车】first bus 【首创】originate; pioneer ～精神 creative initiative 【首次】for the first time; first ～航行 maiden voyage ～公演 opening performance 【首当其冲】be the first to be affected (by a disaster, etc.) 【首都】capital (of a country) 【首恶】chief criminal 【首领】chieftain; leader; head 【首脑】head (of government, etc.) ～会议 conference of heads of state; summit conference ～人物 leading figure 【首屈一指】come first on the list 【首饰】ornaments; jewelry ～盒 jewel case 【首尾】the beginning and the end / from beginning to end 【首位】(put in) the first place 【首席】seat of honour/ chief ～代表 chief representative 【首先】first/in the first place; first of all; above all 【首相】 prime minister 【首要】 of the first importance; first; chief ～任务 the most important task ～分子 major culprit, ringleader 【首长】 leading cadre; senior officer

寿 shòu ① longevity ②life; age 长～ long life ③birthday 祝～ congratulate sb. on his birthday ④for burial ～材 coffin 【寿礼】 birthday present 【寿命】 life-span; life 平均～ average life-span 【寿衣】 graveclothes

受 shòu ①receive; accept ～教育 receive an education ～礼 accept gifts ②suffer; be subjected to ～损失 suffer losses ～压迫 suffer oppression ③stand; endure; bear ～不了 cannot bear 【受潮】 be affected with damp 【受挫】 be foiled; be baffled 【受罚】 be punished 【受害】 suffer injury; fall victim; be affected ～不浅 suffer a lot ～者 victim 【受贿】 take bribes 【受奖】 be rewarded 【受惊】 be frightened 【受苦】 suffer (hardships) 【受累】 be put to much trouble; be inconvenienced 让您～了 sorry to have given you so much trouble 【受凉】 catch cold 【受命】 receive instructions 【受难】 be in distress 【受骗】 be deceived; be fooled 【受气】 suffer wrong 【受权】 be authorized ～发表如下声明 be authorized to issue the following statement ～宣布 announce upon authorization 【受热】 be heated / be affected by the heat 【受辱】 be insulted; be disgraced 【受伤】 be injured; be wounded 头部受重伤 sustain a severe head injury 【受审】 be tried 【受暑】 suffer from heatstroke 【受托】 be commissioned; be entrusted (with a task) 【受刑】 be tortured; be put to torture 【受训】 receive training 【受益】 profit by; benefit from; be benefited 【受用】 benefit from; profit by; enjoy 【受援】 receive aid ～国 recipient country 【受孕】 become pregnant; be impregnated; conceive 【受灾】 be hit by a natural adversity ～地区 disaster area【受罪】endure hardships, tortures, rough conditions, etc.; have a hard time

兽 shòu ①beast; animal ②beastly; bestial 人面～心 a beast in human shape【兽行】brutal act; brutality【兽性】brutish nature【兽医】veterinary surgeon; veterinarian; vet ～学 veterinary medicine; veterinary science ～站 veterinary station【兽欲】bestial desire

授 shòu ①award; vest; confer; give 授勋 present (sb. with) a flag ～以全权 vest sb. with full authority ②teach; instruct 函～ teach by correspondence【授奖】give a prize ～仪式 prize-giving ceremony【授精】insemination【授课】give lessons; give instruction【授命】give orders ～组阁 authorize sb. to form a cabinet【授权】empower; authorize ～新华社发表声明 authorize Xinhua News Agency to make a statement【授勋】confer orders or medals【授意】incite sb. to do sth.; inspire【授予】confer; award

售 shòu ①sell ～完 be sold out ②make (one's plan, trick, etc.) work; carry out (intrigues) 以～其奸 achieve one's treacherous purpose【售货】sell goods ～机 vending machine ～员 shop assistant; salesclerk【售价】selling price【售票处】ticket office【售票员】ticket seller

瘦 shòu ①thin; emaciated 脸～ be thin in the face ②lean ～肉 lean meat ③tight 腰身～了点 be a bit tight at the waist ④not fertile; poor【瘦长】long and thin; tall and thin【瘦弱】thin and weak; emaciated【瘦小】thin and small 身材～ slight of figure【瘦子】a lean person

SHU

书 shū ①write ②script 楷～ regular script ③ book ④letter 家～ a letter to or from home ⑤document【书包】

satchel; schoolbag 【书报】 books and newspapers 【书本】 book ～知识 book learning 【书橱】 bookcase 【书呆子】 pedant bookworm 【书挡】 bookend 【书店】 bookshop; bookseller's 【书法】 penmanship; calligraphy ～家 calligrapher 【书房】 study 【书后】 postscript 【书籍】 books; works; literature 【书记】 secretary/clerk ～处 secretariat 【书简】 letters 【书局】 publishing house; press 【书刊】 books and periodicals 【书面】 written; in written form ～材料 written material ～通知 written notice ～答复 answer in writing ～声明 written statement ～语 literary language 【书名】 title (of a book) ～页 title page 【书目】 booklist; title catalogue 参考～ a list of reference books; bibliography 【书皮】 (book) cover; jacket ～纸 paper for covering books 【书评】 book review 【书签】 bookmark 【书生】 intellectual; scholar ～之见 a pedantic view ～气 bookishness 【书摊】 bookstall 【书套】 slipcase 【书亭】 book-kiosk 【书写】 write ～标语 write slogans ～规则 rules for writing ～纸 writing paper 【书信】 letter ～体 epistolary style 【书页】 page 【书桌】 (writing) desk

抒 shū express; give expression to; convey 【抒发】 express; voice; give expression to 【抒情】 express one's emotion ～散文 lyric prose ～诗 lyric poetry; lyrics

枢 shū pivot; hub; centre 【枢纽】 axis; key position ～作用 a pivotal role 交通～ a hub of communications

叔 shū father's younger brother; uncle 【叔母】 wife of father's younger brother; aunt

殊 shū ①different ②outstanding; special; remarkable ③ very much; extremely 【殊不知】 little imagine; hardly realize 【殊死】 desperate; life-and-death (struggle) 【殊途同归】 reach the same goal by different routes

倏 shū swiftly 【倏忽】 in the twinkling of an eye ～不见 quickly disappear

淑 shū kind and gentle; fair ～女 a fair maiden

梳 shū ①comb 木～ wooden comb ②comb one's hair, etc. 【梳洗】 wash and dress ～用具 toilet articles 【梳妆】 dress and make up ～打扮 deck oneself out; dress smartly; be dressed up ～台 dressing table

舒 shū ①stretch; unfold ②easy; leisurely 【舒畅】 happy; entirely free from worry 心情～ have ease of mind 【舒服】 comfortable/be well 她今天不大～ she isn't well today 【舒适】 cosy; snug ～的生活 a comfortable life 【舒展】 unfold; extend; smooth out / limber up; stretch

疏 shū ①dredge (a river, etc.) ②thin; sparse; scattered ～星 scattered stars ③(of family or social relations) distant ④not familiar with 人地生～ be unfamiliar with the place and the people ⑤neglect ～于防范 neglect to take precautions ⑥scanty 志大才～ have great ambition but little talent ⑦disperse; scatter 【疏导】 dredge 【疏忽】 carelessness; negligence; oversight 【疏浚】 dredge (the waterways, a harbour, etc.) 【疏漏】 careless mission; slip; oversight 【疏落】 sparse; scattered 【疏散】 sparse; scattered; dispersed/evacuate ～人口 disperse the population 【疏失】 careless mistake; remissness 【疏松】 loose 【疏通】 mediate between two parties 【疏远】 drift apart

输 shū ①transport; convey ②lose; be beaten; be defeated 【输出】 export 【输电】 transmit electricity ～网 power transmission network ～线路 transmission line 【输理】 be in the wrong 【输入】 import 【输送】 carry; transport; convey ～新鲜血液 infuse new blood ～带 conveyer belt ～机 conveyer 【输血】 blood transfusion/give aid and support【输油管】petroleum pipeline

蔬 shū【蔬菜】vegetables; greens; greenstuff ～栽培 vegetable growing; vegetable farming

赎 shú ① redeem; ransom ②atone for (a crime)【赎当】redeem sth. pawned【赎价】ransom price【赎金】ransom money【赎买】redeem; buy out ～政策 policy of redemption【赎罪】atone for one's crime

塾 shú private school ～师 tutor of a private school

熟 shú ①ripe 桃子～了 the peaches are ripe ②cooked; done ～肉 cooked meat 饭～了 the rice is done ③processed ～皮 tanned leather ④familiar ⑤skilled; experienced ～手 practised hand ⑥deeply ～睡 be in a deep sleep【熟荤】cooked food; prepared food【熟记】learn by heart; memorize【熟客】frequent visitor【熟练】skilled; practised; proficient ～工人 skilled worker【熟路】familiar route; beaten track【熟能生巧】skill comes from practice【熟人】acquaintance; friend【熟视无睹】turn a blind eye to; ignore【熟识】be well acquainted with; know well【熟睡】sleep soundly; be fast asleep【熟思】ponder deeply; deliberate【熟悉】be familiar with; have an intimate knowledge of ～内情 know the ins and outs of the matter; be in the know ～情况 be familiar with the situation【熟习】be skilful at; have the knack of; be practised in ～业务 be well versed in one's field of work【熟语】idiom【熟知】know intimately【熟字】words already learned

属 shǔ ①category 金～ metals ②genus 亚～ subgenus ③under; subordinate to 所～单位 subordinate units ④belong to ～第三世界 belong to the Third World【属地】possession; dependency【属国】vassal state; dependent state【属性】property【属于】belong to; be part of.

暑 shǔ heat; hot weather 【暑假】summer vacation 【暑期】summer vacation time ～训练班 summer course 【暑气】(summer) heat 【暑天】hot summer days; dog days

署 shǔ ①a government office; office ②handle by proxy; act as deputy ～理部务 handle the ministry's affairs during the minister's absence 【署名】sign; put one's signature to ～人 the undersigned ～文章 a signed article

数 shǔ ①count 从一～到十 count from 1 to 10 ②enumerate; list 历～其罪 enumerate the crimes sb. has committed 【数一数二】count as one of the very best

鼠 shǔ mouse; rat 【鼠窜】scamper off like a rat 【鼠疫】the plague

薯 shǔ potato; yam 白～ sweet potato

曙 shǔ daybreak; dawn 【曙光】first light of morning; dawn 【曙色】light of early dawn

术 shù ①art; skill; technique 医～ doctor's skill ②method; tactics 【术语】technical terms; terminology

戍 shù defend; garrison (the frontiers)

束 shù ①bind; tie 腰～皮带 wear a belt round one's waist ②bundle; bunch; sheaf 一～鲜花 a bunch of flowers 一～稻草 a sheaf of straw ③control; restrain 无拘无～ without any restraint 【束缚】tie; bind up; fetter ～手脚 bind sb. hand and foot ～生产力 fetter the productive forces 【束手】have one's hands tied; be helpless ～就擒 allow oneself to be seized without putting up a fight ～待毙 helplessly wait for death ～无策 feel quite helpless 【束之高阁】lay aside and neglect; shelve

述 shù state; relate; narrate 略～经过 relate briefly how it happened 【述评】review; commentary

树 shù ①tree 苹果～ apple tree ②plant; cultivate ③set up; establish; uphold ～正气 foster healthy tendencies ～雄心 aim high 【树杈】crotch (of a tree) 【树丛】grove; thicket 【树敌】make an enemy of sb.; set others against oneself ～过多 antagonize too many people 【树墩】stump 【树干】trunk 【树冠】crown 【树胶】gum 【树立】set up; establish ～榜样 set an example 【树苗】set sb. up as a pacemaker 【树林】woods; grove 【树标兵】sapling 【树木】trees 【树皮】bark 【树梢】treetop 【树枝】branch 【树脂】resin

竖 shù ①vertical; upright; perpendicular ～线 vertical line ②set upright; erect; stand ～旗杆 erect a flagstaff 【竖井】(vertical) shaft 【竖立】erect; set upright; stand 【竖起】hold up; erect ～大旗 hoist a huge banner ～耳朵听 prick up one's ears 【竖琴】harp

恕 shù ①forgive; pardon; excuse ～罪 pardon an offence; forgive a sin ②beg your pardon ～不奉陪 excuse me (for not keeping you company)

庶 shù multitudinous; numerous 富～ rich and populous

数 shù ①number; figure ～以万计 number tens of thousands 心中有～ know what's what ②number 单～ singular number ③several; a few ～百人 several hundred people 【数词】numeral 序～ ordinal number 基～ cardinal number 【数额】number; amount 【数据】data 科学～ scientific data ～处理 data processing ～库 data base 【数量】quantity; amount ～和质量 quantity and quality ～上的差别 quantitative difference 【数学】mathematics ～家 mathematician 【数字】numeral; figure; digit / quantity

漱 shù gargle; rinse 【漱口】rinse the mouth; gargle ～杯 a glass or mug for mouth-rinsing or teeth-cleaning; tooth glass ～剂 gargle

SHUA

刷 shuā ①brush 牙～ toothbrush ②brush; scrub ～鞋 brush shoes ～锅 clean a pot ③daub; paste up ～墙 whitewash a wall ～标语 paste up posters ④rustle 【刷新】renovate; refurbish/break ～纪录 break a record

耍 shuǎ ①play ②play with; flourish ～刀 flourish a sword ～猴儿 put on a monkey show ③play (tricks) ～两面派 be double-faced 【耍笔杆】wield a pen 【耍花招】play tricks 他在～了 he is up to his tricks 【耍滑】act in a slick way 【耍赖】act shamelessly 【耍流氓】take liberties with women; act indecently 【耍弄】make fun of; make a fool of; deceive 【耍脾气】get into a huff 【耍威风】make a show of authority 【耍无赖】be perverse

刷 shuà 【刷白】white; pale 脸变得～ turn pale

SHUAI

衰 shuāi decline; wane 体力渐～ get weaker physically 【衰败】decline; wane; be at a low ebb 【衰竭】exhaustion 心力～ heart failure 【衰老】old and feeble; decrepit; senile 【衰落】decline; be on the wane; go downhill 【衰弱】weak; feeble 【衰颓】weak and degenerate 【衰退】fail; decline 视力～ failing eyesight 记忆力～ be losing one's memory 经济～ economic recession 【衰亡】become feeble and die; decline and fall

摔 shuāi ①fall; tumble; lose one's balance ②hurtle down; plunge 飞机～下来了 the plane plunged to the ground ③cause to fall and break; break 我把玻璃杯～了 I broke a glass ④cast; throw; fling 把帽子一～ throw one's cap 【摔打】beat; knock / rough it; temper oneself 【摔

跟头】tumble; trip and fall / trip up; make a blunder 【摔交】tumble/come a cropper/wrestling ～运动员 wrestler

甩 shuǎi ①move backward and forward; swing ～胳膊 swing one's arms ～鞭子 crack a whip ②throw; fling; toss ～手榴弹 throw hand grenades ③leave sb. behind; throw off ～掉尾巴 throw off a pursuer ～掉包袱 cast off a burden 【甩手】 swing one's arms/refuse to do

帅 shuài ①commander in chief ②beautiful; graceful; smart 字写得～ write a beautiful hand

率 shuài ①lead; command ～师 command troops ②rash; hasty 草～ careless; cursory ③frank; straightforward ④generally; usually 【率领】lead; head; command ～代表团 lead a delegation 由他～ be under his command 【率先】be the first to do sth. 【率直】straightforward; unreserved

SHUAN

闩 shuān ①bolt; latch 门～ door bolt ②fasten with a bolt or latch 把门～好 bolt the door

拴 shuān tie; fasten ～马 tether a horse 把船～住 make the boat fast

栓 shuān ·①bolt; plug 消火～ fireplug 枪～ rifle bolt ②stopper; cork

涮 shuàn ①rinse ～衣服 rinse the clothes 把瓶子～一下 give this bottle a rinse ②instant-boil ～羊肉 instant-boiled mutton

SHUANG

双 shuāng ①two; twin; both; dual ②pair 一～鞋 a pair of shoes ③even ④double; twofold ～份 double the amount 【双胞胎】twins 【双边】bilateral ～会谈 bilateral talks ～贸易 bilateral trade; two-way trade ～条约 bilateral treaty 【双层】 double-deck; having two layers; of two thicknesses ～床 double-decker (bed, bunk) ～玻璃窗 double window 【双重】 double; dual; twofold ～任务 double task ～标准 double standard ～领导 dual leadership 【双唇音】 bilabial (sound) 【双打】 doubles 【双方】 both sides; the two parties ～同意 by mutual consent 【双幅】 double width 【双杠】 parallel bars 【双关】 having a double meaning 一语 a phrase with a double meaning ～语 pun 【双轨】 double track ～铁路 double-track railway 【双号】 even numbers (of tickets, seats, etc.) 【双簧管】 oboe 【双季稻】 double-harvest rice 【双料】 of reinforced material; extra quality 【双面】 two-sided; reversible ～刀片 a double-edged razor blade 【双亲】 (both) parents; father and mother 【双全】 complete in both respects; possessing both 智勇～ possessing both wisdom and courage 文武～ be adept with both the pen and the sword 【双人床】 double bed 【双人舞】 dance for two people 【双日】 even-numbered days (of the month) 【双生】 twin ～姐妹 twin sisters 【双手】 both hands 【双数】 even numbers 【双月刊】 bimonthly 【双职工】 working couple 【双周刊】 biweekly

霜 shuāng ①frost ②frostlike powder 糖～ icing ③white; hoar ～鬓 hoary temples 【霜冻】 frost 【霜害】 frostbite; frost injury 【霜花】 frostwork 【霜叶】 red leaves

孀 shuāng widow 【孀居】 be a widow; live in widowhood

爽 shuǎng ①bright; clear; crisp ②frank; straightforward; openhearted 豪～ forthright ③feel well 身体不～ not feel well ④deviate 毫厘不～ not deviating a hair's breadth 【爽口】 tasty and refreshing 【爽快】 refreshed; comfortable/ frank; outright / with alacrity; readily 为人～ be frank and straightforward 办事～ work readily and briskly

【爽朗】bright and clear / hearty; candid; frank and open ～的笑声 hearty laughter ～的性格 a frank and open personality 【爽利】efficient and able 【爽身粉】talcum powder

SHUI

谁 shuí ①who 他是～ who is he 这是～的意见 whose idea is it ②someone; anyone ～都不甘落后 nobody wanted to lag behind

水 shuǐ ①water ②a general term for rivers, lakes, seas, etc. 【水坝】dam 【水泵】water pump 【水表】water meter 【水兵】seaman; sailor 【水彩】watercolour ～画 watercolour (painting) ～颜料 watercolours 【水草】water and grass/waterweeds; water plants 【水产】aquatic product ～品 aquatic product 【水车】waterwheel/watercart; water wagon 【水池】pond; pool 【水道】water course/waterway 【水稻】paddy (rice); rice 【水电】water and electricity ～供应 water and electricity supply ～费 charges for water and electricity ～站 hydropower station 【水分】moisture content 吸收～ absorb moisture 【水沟】ditch; drain; gutter 【水管】waterpipe 【水果】fruit ～罐头 tinned fruit ～软糖 fruit jelly ～糖 fruit drops 【水壶】kettle/canteen/watering can 【水花】spray 【水火】fire and water — two things diametrically opposed to each other/extreme misery ～不相容 be incompatible as fire and water 救民于～ save the people from untold miseries ～无情 floods and fires have no mercy for anybody 【水饺】boiled dumplings 【水晶】(rock) crystal 【水井】well 【水坑】puddle; pool 【水库】reservoir 【水雷】mine 【水力】waterpower; hydraulic power ～发电站 hydroelectric station ～资源 waterpower resources 【水利】water conservancy/irrigation works ～工程 water conservancy project ～灌溉网 irrigation network 【水流】 rivers; streams; waters / current; flow 【水龙】 (fire) hose 【水龙头】 (water) tap 【水陆】 land and water ～运输 transportation by land and water 【水路】 waterway; water route 【水落石出】 come to light 辩个～ argue a matter out 把这事弄个～ get to the bottom of this matter 【水门】 water valve 【水母】 jellyfish; medusa 【水泥】 cement ～标号 cement grade ～厂 cement plant 【水鸟】 aquatic bird; water bird 【水牛】 (water) buffalo 【水暖工】 plumber 【水泡】 bubble / blister 【水疱】 blister 【水瓢】 (gourd) water ladle 【水平】 horizontal / standard; level 认识～ level of one's understanding 【水球】 water polo 【水渠】 ditch; canal 【水上飞机】 seaplane; hydroplane 【水上运动】 aquatic sports 【水手】 seaman; sailor ～长 boatswain 【水塔】 water tower 【水獭】 otter 【水塘】 pond; pool 【水田】 paddy field 【水桶】 pail; bucket 【水土】 water and soil/natural environment and climate ～流失 soil erosion ～不服 not acclimatized 【水汪汪】 bright and intelligent 【水位】 water level 地下～ groundwater level 【水文】 hydrology ～工作者 hydrologist ～站 hydrometric station ～资料 hydrological data 【水系】 river system 【水仙】 narcissus 【水线】 waterline 【水乡】 a region of rivers and lakes 【水箱】 water tank 【水泻】 watery diarrhoea 【水星】 Mercury 【水性】 ability in swimming 【水压】 water pressure ～机 hydraulic press 【水银】 mercury; quicksilver ～灯 mercury-vapour lamp 【水印】 watercolour block printing/watermark 【水域】 waters; water area 【水源】 the source of a river/source of water 【水运】 water transport 【水灾】 flood; inundation 【水藻】 algae 【水闸】 sluice; water gate 【水蒸汽】 steam; water vapour 【水珠】 drop of water 【水柱】 water column 【水准】 level; standard 【水族】 aquatic animals

税 shuì tax; duty 【税额】the amount of tax to be paid 【税款】tax payment 【税率】tax rate 【税收】tax revenue ~政策 tax policy 【税务局】tax bureau 【税务员】tax collector 【税则】tax regulations 【税制】taxation

睡 shuì sleep 他~着了 he's asleep 【睡觉】sleep 睡午觉 take a nap after lunch 睡懒觉 get up late; sleep late 【睡帽】nightcap 【睡梦】sleep; slumber 【睡眠】sleep ~不足 not have enough sleep ~疗法 physiological sleep therapy 【睡醒】wake up 【睡衣】night clothes 【睡意】sleepiness; drowsiness 有~ be drowsy

SHUN

顺 shùn ①in the same direcion as; with ~流而下 go downstream ②along ~着这条道走 follow this road ③obey; yield to ④suitable; agreeable 不~他的意 not fall in with his wishes ⑤in sequence 号码是一~的 these are serial numbers 【顺便】conveniently; in passing 这一点现在~提一下 I mention this point now in passing ~说一句 by the way 【顺畅】smooth; unhindered 【顺次】in order; in succession 【顺从】be obedient to; submit to; yield to 【顺风】have a tail wind / favourable wind 【顺口】read smoothly/say offhandedly ~答应 agree without thinking 【顺口溜】doggerel; jingle 【顺利】smoothly; successfully 会议进行得很~ the meeting went off without a hitch 【顺路】on the way/direct route 这么走不~ this is not the most direct route 【顺手】smoothly; without difficulty/conveniently/convenient and easy to use 【顺序】sequence; order/in proper order; in turn 【顺延】postpone 【顺眼】pleasing to the eye 看着不~ be offensive to the eye 【顺应】comply with ~历史发展的潮流 conform to the historical trend of the times

瞬 shùn wink【瞬息】twinkling ～间 in the twinkling of an eye ～万变 fast changing

SHUO

说 shuō ①speak; talk; say 请～慢一点儿 please speak more slowly 你～得对 what you say is true 俗话～ as the saying goes ②explain 我一～他就明白了 I told him how and he caught on at once ③theory; teachings; doctrine 著书立～ write books to expound a theory ④ scold ～了他一顿 give him a scolding【说不得】unspeakable; unmentionable/scandalous【说不定】perhaps; maybe【说不来】cannot get along (with sb.)【说不上】cannot say / not worth mentioning【说穿】reveal; disclose【说大话】brag; boast; talk big【说到底】in the final analysis; at bottom【说到做到】do what one says【说得过去】justifiable; passable【说得来】can get along; be on good terms【说定】settle; agree on【说法】way of saying a thing; wording / statement; version 换一个～ say it in another way 这种～是正确的 this argument is sound【说服】persuade; convince; talk sb. over【说好】come to an agreement or understanding【说合】bring two (or more) parties together / talk over【说话】speak; talk; say / chat; gossip 学～ learn to speak 爱～ like to talk 人家要～的 people will talk 我们～是算数的 we mean what we say 我找他～去 I'd like to have a chat with him【说谎】tell a lie【说教】deliver a sermon; preach【说来话长】it's a long story【说理】argue; reason things out【说媒】act as matchmaker【说明】explain; illustrate; show / explanation ～理由 give reasons ～真相 give the facts ～实际问题 elucidate practical problems ～书 (a booklet of) directions; (technical) manual; synopsis (of a play or film) ～文 expository writing; exposition 图片下有～ there is a caption under the picture 【说情】plead for mercy for sb.; intercede for sb. 【说书】story-telling

烁 shuò bright; shining 闪～ twinkle; glimmer 【烁烁】glitter; sparkle

朔 shuò ①new moon ②the first day of the lunar month ③north ～风 north wind 【朔望】syzygy

硕 shuò large 【硕大】gigantic 【硕果】rich fruits; great achievements ～仅存 rare survival 【硕士】Master ～学位 Master's degree

数 shuò frequently; repeatedly 【数见不鲜】common occurrence; nothing new

SI

司 sī ①take charge of; attend to; manage 各～其事 each attends to his own duties ②department (under a ministry) 【司法】administration of justice; judicature ～部门 judicial departments ～机关 judicial organs ～鉴定 expert testimony ～权 judicial powers 【司号员】bugler; trumpeter 【司机】driver 火车～ engine driver 【司空见惯】a common sight; a common occurrence 【司令】commander; commanding officer ～部 headquarters; command 【司炉】stoker; fireman 【司务长】mess officer/company quarter-master 【司药】pharmacist; druggist; chemist 【司仪】master of ceremonies

丝 sī ①silk ②a threadlike thing 蜘蛛～ cobweb 铜～ copper wire ③a tiny bit; trace 一～不差 not a bit of difference 【丝绸】silk cloth; silk 【丝带】silk ribbon; silk braid 【丝糕】steamed corn cake 【丝瓜】towel gourd ～络 loofah; vegetable sponge 【丝毫】a bit; a particle 【丝绵】silk floss; silk wadding 【丝绒】velvet; velour 【丝

线] silk thread (for sewing); silk yarn 【丝织品】silk fabrics/silk knit goods 【丝状】filiform

私 sī ①personal; private ~信 personal letter ②selfish 无~ unselfish; selfless ③secret ~话 confidential talk ④illicit; illegal ~设公堂 set up an illegal court 【私奔】elopement 【私弊】corrupt practices 【私产】private property 【私娼】unlicensed prostitute 【私仇】personal enmity 【私德】personal morals 【私法】private law 【私房】private savings/confidential ~钱 private savings of a family member 叙~话 exchange confidences 【私愤】personal spite 【私货】smuggled goods; contraband goods 【私利】selfish interests 图~ pursue private ends 不谋~ seek no personal gain 【私囊】private purse 饱~ line one's pockets 【私念】selfish ideas 【私情】personal relationships 【私人】private; personal/one's own man ~访问 private visit 任用~ fill a post with one's own man; practise nepotism ~代表 personal representative ~秘书 private secretary ~企业 private enterprise 【私商】businessman; merchant; trader 【私生活】private life 【私生子】illegitimate child; bastard 【私逃】abscond 【私通】have secret communication with (the enemy)/illicit intercourse; adultery 【私下】in private; in secret ~商议 discuss a matter in private 【私相授受】make an illicit transfer 【私心】selfish motives; selfishness ~杂念 selfish ideas and personal considerations 【私刑】illegal punishment (meted out by a kangaroo court) 【私蓄】private savings 【私营】privately owned; privately operated ~工商业 privately owned industrial and commercial enterprises ~企业 private enterprise 【私有】privately owned; private ~财产 private property ~观念 private ownership mentality ~制 private ownership (of means of production) 【私语】whisper/confidence 【私欲】 selfish desire 【私章】 personal seal; signet

思 sī ①think; consider; deliberate 前～后想 think over again and again ②think of; long for ～亲 think of one's parents with affection ③thought; thinking 文～ train of thought in writing 【思潮】 trend of thought; ideological trend / thoughts ～起伏 disquieting thoughts surging in one's mind 【思考】 think deeply; ponder over; reflect on ～问题 ponder a problem 【思量】 consider; turn sth. over in one's mind 【思路】 train of thought; think-ing 打断～ interrupt one's train of thought 【思虑】 con-sider carefully; contemplate; deliberate 【思慕】 think of sb. with respect; admire 【思念】 long for; miss 【思索】 think deeply; ponder 反复～这个问题 turn the problem over and over in one's mind 【思想】 thought; idea ～见面 have a frank exchange of ideas 有～准备 be mentally prepared ～内容好 have good ideological content ～跟不上 lag behind in one's understanding ～包袱 sth. weigh-ing on one's mind ～斗争 ideological struggle ～方法 way of thinking ～改造 ideological remoulding ～家 thinker ～觉悟 political consciousness ～意识 ideology

斯 sī ①this ～时 at this moment ②then; thus 【斯文】 refined; gentle

撕 sī tear; rip ～下一页 tear a page ～下假面具 unmask 【撕毁】 tear to shreds ～协定 tear up an agreement

嘶 sī ①neigh 人喊马～ men shouting and horses neighing ③hoarse 声～力竭 hoarse and exhausted

死 sī ①die ～人 the dead 打～ beat to death ②to the death ～战 fight to the death ③extremely 累～ be tired to death 渴～ be dying for a drink 咸～ terribly salty ④implacable; deadly ～对头 sworn enemy ⑤fixed; rigid ～规矩 a rigid rule ～教条 lifeless dogma ⑥impassable; closed 把漏洞堵～ plug the holes 【死板】 rigid; inflexible; stiff 办事～ work in a mechanical way 【死党】 diehard followers 【死得其所】 die a worthy death 【死敌】 deadly enemy; implacable foe 【死读书】 study mechanically; be a bookworm 【死光】 death ray 【死鬼】 devil 【死寂】 deathly stillness 【死角】 dead angle 【死结】 fast knot 【死里逃生】 have a narrow escape 【死力】 (with) all one's strength 出～ exert one's utmost effort 【死路】 blind alley / the road to ruin 【死面】 unleavened dough 【死命】 doom; death / desperately ～挣扎 struggle desperately 【死气沉沉】 lifeless; spiritless; stagnant 【死去活来】 half alive 被打得～ be beaten half dead 哭得～ weep one's heart out 【死尸】 corpse; dead body 【死水】 stagnant water 【死亡】 death; doom ～率 death rate; mortality 【死心】 drop the idea forever; give up the idea 【死心塌地】 be dead set; be hell-bent 【死心眼儿】 stubborn/a person with a one-track mind 【死信】 dead letter 【死刑】 death penalty; capital punishment 【死讯】 news of sb.'s death 【死硬】 stiff; inflexible/very obstinate; die-hard ～派 diehards 【死有余辜】 even death would be too good for him 【死于非命】 die an unnatural death 【死者】 the dead; the deceased 【死罪】 capital crime

四 sì four 【四边】 (on) four sides ～形 quadrilateral 【四处】 all around; everywhere ～逃窜 flee in all directions ～奔走 go hither and thither ～寻找 search high and low 【四方】 all sides; all quarters / square; cubic 【四季】 the four seasons 【四邻】 one's near neighbours 【四面】 (on) four sides; (on) all sides ～出击 hit out in all directions 【四散】 scatter in all directions 【四月】 April/the fourth moon 【四肢】 the four limbs; arms and legs 【四周】 all around

寺

sì temple 清真～ mosque【寺院】temple; monastery

似

sì ①similar; like 内容相～ be similar in content ②seem; appear ～曾相识 seem to have met before【似乎】it seems; as if; seemingly【似是而非】apparently right but actually wrong ～的说法 a specious argument

伺

sì watch; await【伺机】watch for one's chance ～而动 wait for the opportune moment to go into action

饲

sì raise; rear【饲草】forage grass【饲料】forage; fodder; feed 猪～ pig feed ～加工厂 feed-processing plant ～作物 forage crop【饲养】raise ～家禽 rear poultry ～牲畜 raise livestock ～场 feed lot ～员 stockman

肆

sì wanton; unbridled【肆虐】indulge in wanton massacre or persecution; wreak havoc【肆无忌惮】brazen; unscrupulous【肆意】recklessly; wilfully

SONG

松

sōng ①pine ②loose; slack 土质很～ the soil is loose 绳子～了 the rope is slack ③loosen; relax; slacken ～开手 relax one's hold ～一口气 have a breathing spell ④not hard up 现在手头～些 be better off ⑤light and flaky; soft ⑥dried meat floss; dried minced meat【松弛】limp; flabby; slack/lax 肌肉～ flaccid muscles 纪律～ lax discipline【松花】preserved egg【松节油】turpentine【松劲】relax one's efforts; slacken (off) ～情绪 slack mood【松软】soft; spongy; loose【松散】loose/inattentive 文章结构～ the article is loosely organized【松手】loosen one's grip; let go【松鼠】squirrel【松土】loosen the soil【松香】rosin【松懈】relax; slacken; slack ～斗志 relax one's will to fight 工作～ be slack in one's work【松针】pine needle【松子】pine nut

怂 sǒng 【丛恿】instigate; incite; egg sb. on; abet

耸 sǒng ①towering; lofty ②alarm; shock 【耸动】shrug (one's shoulders)/create a sensation 【耸立】tower aloft 【耸人听闻】deliberately exaggerate so as to create a sensation ～的谣言 a sensational rumour

讼 sòng ①bring a case to court ②dispute; argue 【讼棍】legal pettifogger; shyster 【讼事】lawsuit; litigation

送 sòng ①deliver; carry ～信 deliver a letter ②give (as a present) ～他一本书 give him a book ③see sb. off or out ～她回家 escort her home 到车站～人 see sb. off at the station 把客人～到门口 walk a guest to the gate ～孩子上学 take a child to school ～他到机场 accompany him to the airport 【送殡】attend a funeral 【送风机】blower 【送话器】microphone 【送还】give back; return 【送货】deliver goods 【送交】deliver; hand over 【送客】see a visitor out 【送礼】give sb. a present; present a gift to sb. 【送命】lose one's life; get killed 【送人情】do favours at no great cost to oneself/make a gift of sth. 【送死】court death 【送行】wish sb. bon voyage/give a send-off party 【送葬】take part in a funeral procession

诵 sòng ①read aloud; chant ②recite

颂 sòng ①praise; extol; eulogize; laud ②song; ode; paean; eulogy 【颂词】panegyric 【颂扬】sing sb.'s praises

SOU

搜 sōu search ～身 search the person 【搜捕】track down and arrest 【搜查】ransack; rummage ～证 search warrant 【搜刮】extort; plunder 【搜集】collect ～情报 gather information ～史料 collect historical data 【搜罗】

gather; recruit (qualified persons) 【搜】hunt for; scout around ～失踪船只 search for missing boats ～枯肠 rack one's brains (for fresh ideas, etc.) 【搜寻】search for; look for; seek 【搜腰包】search sb.'s pockets

馊 sōu sour; spoiled ～主意 rotten idea; lousy idea 牛奶～了 the milk has turned sour

SU

苏 sū ①revive; come to 死而复～ come back to life 【苏打】soda ～饼干 soda biscuit 【苏醒】revive; regain consciousness; come to

酥 sū ①crisp; short ～糖 crunchy candy ②shortbread 杏仁～ almond shortbread 【酥脆】crisp 【酥麻】limp and numb 【酥软】limp; weak; soft 【酥油】butter

俗 sú ①custom; convention 移风易～ break with old customs ②popular; common ③vulgar ～不可耐 unbearably vulgar ④secular; lay 【俗话】common saying ～说 as the saying goes 【俗名】popular name; local name 【俗气】vulgar; in poor taste 【俗套】convention 不落～ conform to no conventional pattern 【俗语】folk adage

凤 sù ①early in the morning ②long-standing; old ～志 long-cherished ambition

诉 sù ①tell; relate; inform ②complain; accuse 倾～ pour out (one's feelings, troubles, etc.) ③appeal to ～诸武力 resort to force; appeal to arms 【诉苦】vent one's grievances 【诉讼】lawsuit; litigation 提出～ take legal proceedings against sb. 撤消～ drop a lawsuit ～代理人 legal representative ～法 procedural law ～条例 rules of procedure 【诉状】plaint; indictment

肃 sù ①respectful ②solemn 【肃反】elimination of counterrevolutionaries 【肃静】solemn silence 【肃立】stand (as a mark of respect) ～默哀 stand in silent mourning 【肃穆】solemn and respectful 【肃清】eliminate; clean up

素 sù ①white ～服 white clothing ②plain; simple; quiet ～色 plain colour ③vegetable 吃～ be a vegetarian ④native ～性 one's disposition ⑤basic element 色～ pigment ⑥usually; always 我和他～不相识 I don't know him at all 【素材】(source) material 【素菜】vegetable dish 【素常】usually; habitually; ordinarily 【素描】sketch / literary sketch 【素食】vegetarian diet / be a vegetarian ～者 vegetarian 【素席】vegetarian feast 【素雅】simple but elegant 【素养】accomplishment; attainment 【素油】vegetable oil 【素质】quality

速 sù ①fast; rapid; quick; speedy 收效甚～ produce quick results ②speed; velocity 音～ velocity of sound 【速成】speeded-up educational program ～班 accelerated course; crash course ～教学法 quick method of teaching 【速度】speed; velocity/rate; pace; tempo 加快～ increase speed 生产～ the tempo of production 工业化的～ the pace of industrialization ～滑冰 speed skating 【速记】shorthand ～员 stenographer 【速决】quick decision ～战 war of quick decision 【速射】rapid fire ～炮 quick-firing gun 【速效】quick results 【速写】sketch/literary sketch

宿 sù ①lodge for the night; stay overnight ②longstanding; old ～志 long-cherished ambition ③veteran ～将 veteran general 【宿命论】fatalism 【宿舍】hostel; living quarters; dormitory 学生～ students' hostel 职工～ living quarters for staff and workers 【宿营】take up quarters 【宿怨】old grudge 【宿愿】long-cherished wish

溯 sù ①go against the stream ～流而上 go upstream ②trace back; recall 回～往事 recall past events 【溯源】trace to the source

塑 sù model; mould ～像 mould a statue 泥～ clay sculpture 【塑料】 plastics ～薄膜 plastic film

簌 sù 【簌簌】①rustle ②(tears) streaming down

SUAN

酸 suān ①acid 醋～ acetic acid ②sour ～果 tart fruit ～梨 sour pear ③tingle; ache 腰～背痛 have a pain in the back 【酸菜】 Chinese sauerkraut 【酸梅】 smoked plum; dark plum ～汤 sweet-sour plum juice 【酸牛奶】 sour milk 【酸软】 aching and limp 【酸痛】 ache 浑身～ ache all over 【酸味】 tart flavour; acidity 【酸性】 acidity

蒜 suàn garlic 一瓣～ a braid of garlic 【蒜瓣儿】 garlic clove 【蒜黄】 blanched garlic leaves 【蒜苗】 garlic bolt 【蒜泥】 mashed garlic 【蒜头】 the head of garlic

算 suàn ①calculate; reckon; compute; figure 能写会～ good at writing and reckoning ②include; count 把我也～上 count me in ③plan; calculate 失～ miscalculate 暗～ plot against sb. ④at long last; in the end 问题～解决了 the problem is finally solved 【算计】 calculate; reckon/scheme; plot 暗中～别人 secretly scheme against others 【算命】 fortune-telling ～先生 fortune-teller 【算盘】 abacus ～子 beads (of an abacus) 【算术】 arithmetic 做～ do sums 【算数】 count; hold; stand 个别情况不～ isolated instances do not count 【算学】 mathematics / arithmetic 【算帐】 do accounts; balance the books / square accounts with sb ; get even with sb.

SUI

尿 suī urine

虽 suī though; although; even if ～死犹荣 honoured though dead

绥 suī ①peaceful ②pacify 【绥靖】 appease ～政策 policy of appeasement

随 suī ①follow ～我来 come along with me ②comply with; adapt to ～顺 yield and comply ③let (sb. do as he likes) ～你的便 do as you please ④along with (some other action) 【随笔】 informal essay; jottings 【随便】 casual; random; informal/careless; slipshod ～说了几句 make some casual remarks 说话～ not be careful about the way one talks ⑤any ～什么时候来都行 come any time you like 【随波逐流】 drift with the tide 【随从】 accompany (one's superior); attend / retinue; suite 【随带】 going along with/have sth. taken along with one 【随地】 anywhere 【随风转舵】 trim one's sails 【随和】 amiable; obliging 【随机应变】 act according to circumstances 【随即】 immediately; presently 【随口】 speak thoughtlessly or casually ～答应 agree without thinking 【随身】 (carry) on one's person; (take) with one ～行李 personal luggage 【随声附和】 echo what others say 【随时】 at any time; at all times/whenever necessary; as the occasion demands 【随手】 conveniently ～关门 shut the door after you 【随同】 be in company with 【随心所欲】 have one's own way; do as one pleases 【随行人员】 suite; party 【随意】 at will; as one pleases 【随员】 suite; retinue 【随着】 along with; in the wake of; in pace with ～时间的推移 as time goes on

髓 suī ①marrow ②pith

岁 suī ①year ～首(末) the beginning (end) of the year ～入(出) annual income (expenditure) ② year (of age) 两～女孩儿 a two-year-old girl 【岁月】 years 艰苦

斗争的～ years of arduous struggle ～不居 time and tide wait for no man

祟 suì evil spirit; ghost 作～ act like an evil spirit; haunt and plague

遂 suì ①satisfy; fulfil ～愿 have one's wish fulfilled ②succeed 所谋不～ fail in an attempt 【遂心】 after one's own heart; to one's liking

碎 suì ①break to pieces; smash 玻璃杯打～了 the glass is smashed to pieces ②broken; fragmentary ～瓷片 broken bits of china ～布 oddments of cloth ③garrulous; gabby 嘴太～ talk too much; be a regular chatterbox 【碎步】 quick short steps 【碎石】 crushed stones; broken stones ～机 stone crusher ～路 broken stone road

隧 suì 【隧道】 tunnel

燧 suì ①flint ②beacon fire 【燧石】 flint ～玻璃 flint glass

穗 suì ①the ear of grain; spike 麦～ the ear of wheat ②tassel; fringe

SUN

孙 sūn ①grandson ②generations below that of the grand-child 曾～ great-grandson 【孙女】 granddaughter

笋 sǔn bamboo shoot 【笋干】 dried bamboo shoots 【笋瓜】 winter squash 【笋鸡】 young chicken; broiler

损 sǔn ①decrease; lose 增～ increase and decrease ② harm; damage ～公肥私 seek private gain at public expense 【损害】 harm; damage; injure ～庄稼 damage crops ～健康 impair one's health ～视力 be bad for one's eyes 【损耗】 loss; wear and tear/wastage; spoilage ～费 cost of wear and tear ～率 proportion of goods damaged

【损坏】damage; injure【损人利己】harm others to benefit oneself【损失】lose/damage 遭受重大～ sustain heavy losses

SUO

唆 suō instigate; abet【唆使】instigate ～者 instigator; abettor

梭 suō shuttle【梭鱼】(redeye) mullet【梭子】shuttle/clip 打了一～子弹 fire a whole clip of ammunition

缩 suō ①contract; shrink 热胀冷～ expand with heat and contract with cold ②draw back; withdraw; recoil【缩短】shorten; curtail ～距离 reduce the distance ～战线 contract the front【缩减】reduce; cut ～开支 reduce spending ～行政人员 retrench administrative staff【缩小】reduce; lessen; narrow; shrink ～范围 narrow the range【缩写】abbreviation/abridge ～本 abridged edition

所 suō place 住～ dwelling place【所长】one's strong point; one's forte【所得】income; earnings; gains ～税 income tax【所谓】what is called/so-called【所向披靡】carry all before one【所向无前】be invincible【所以】so; therefore; as a result【所有】own; possess / possessions ～格 possessive case ～权 proprietary rights; ownership; title ～制 (system of) ownership【所在】place; location ～地 location; seat; site【所致】be caused by

索 suō ①large rope 船～ ship's rigging ②demand; ask; exact ～价 ask a price; charge ～债 demand payment of a debt ～赔 claim damages【索道】cableway; ropeway 高架～ telpher【索取】ask for; demand【索引】index 卡片～ card index 书名～ title index

琐 suō trivial; petty【琐事】trifles; trivial matters 家庭～ household affairs【琐碎】trifling【琐闻】bits of news

锁 suǒ ①lock 挂～ padlock ②lock up ～门 lock a door
～在保险箱里 be locked up in a safe ③lockstitch
～眼 do a lockstitch on a buttonhole ～边 lockstitch a
border 【锁匠】 locksmith 【锁链】 chain/shackles; fetters

T

TA

它 tā it 【它们】 they

他 tā ①he ～俩 the two of them ～家在农村 his home
is in the countryside ②other; another; some other
调往～处 be transferred to another place 留作～用 reserve for other uses 【他们】 they ～俩 the two of them
～的学校规模很大 theirs is a big school 【他人】 another
person; other people; others 【他日】 some other time; some
day; later on 【他杀】 homicide 【他乡】 an alien land

她 tā she 【她们】 they

塌 tā ①collapse; fall down; cave in 墙～了 the wall
has fallen 天不会～下来 the sky won't fall down ②
sink; droop ～鼻梁 a flat nose ③calm down ～下心去
settle down to (work, etc.) 【塌方】 cave in; collapse/land-
slide; landslip 【塌实】 steady and sure; dependable/free
from anxiety; having peace of mind 工作～ be steadfast
in one's work 觉得～ have one's mind set at rest; feel
secure about sth. 【塌陷】 subside; sink; cave in

塔 tǎ ①pagoda ②tower 水～ water tower 【塔吊】 tower
crane

榻 tà couch 竹~ bamboo couch 藤~ rattan couch 同~ sleep in the same bed; share a bed

踏 tà step on; tread; stamp ~上人生的道路 tread the path of life 把火~灭 tread out a fire 【踏板】treadle (of a sewing machine, etc.); footboard; footrest/footstool 卡车的~ the step of a truck 【踏步】mark time

TAI

胎 tāi ①foetus; embryo ~发 foetal hair 怀~ become or be pregnant ②birth 头~ first baby ③padding; stuffing; wadding 棉花~ the cotton padding of a quilt, etc. ④tyre 内~ inner tube (of a tyre) 【胎衣】afterbirth

台 tái ①platform; stage; terrace 讲~ rostrum 下不了 ~ unable to get off the spot ②stand; support 灯~ lampstand ③table; desk 写字~ (writing) desk ④broadcasting station 电视~ television broadcasting station ⑤ a special telephone service 长途~ trunk call service; long distance 【台本】a playscript with stage directions 【台布】tablecloth 【台秤】platform scale 【台词】actor's lines 【台灯】desk lamp; reading lamp 【台风】typhoon 【台阶】a flight of steps; steps leading up to a house, etc. 跑下~ run down the steps 给他个~下吧 give him an out 【台历】desk calendar 【台球】billiards/billiard ball 【台柱子】leading light; pillar; mainstay

抬 tái ①lift; raise ~桌子 lift (up) the table ②carry ~担架 carry a stretcher 【抬杠】argue for the sake of arguing; bicker; wrangle 【抬价】force up commodity prices 【抬举】praise or promote sb. to show favour 【抬头】raise one's head/gain ground; look up; rise

苔 tái liver mosses 【苔藓植物】bryophyte 【苔原】tundra

太 tài highest; greatest; remotest ～空 outer space ② excessively; too; over ～晚 too late ③extremely ～感谢你了 thanks a lot ④very 不～好 not very good【太古】 remote antiquity【太后】empress dowager; queen mother【太监】(court) eunuch【太平】peace and tranquility ～龙头 fire plug ～门 exit ～梯 fire escape ～间 mortuary【太太】Mrs.; madame; lady【太阳】the sun/ sunshine; sunlight 晒～ bask in the sun ～灯 sunlamp ～电池 solar cell ～光 the sun's rays; sunlight; sunbeam ～镜 sunglasses ～历 solar calendar ～炉 solar furnace ～帽 sun helmet; topee ～能 solar energy ～年 solar year ～穴 the temples ～系 the solar system ～灶 solar cooker【太阴】the moon/lunar【太子】crown prince

汰 tài discard; eliminate

态 tài ①form; appearance; condition 形～ shape; morphology ②state 气～ gaseous state ③voice 主动语～ the active voice【态度】manner; bearing/attitude; approach 劳动～ attitude towards labour

泰 tài ①safe; peaceful 国～民安 the country is prosperous and the people live in peace ②extreme; most【泰然】calm; composed ～自若 be self-possessed

TAN

坍 tān collapse; fall; tumble 墙～了 the wall collapsed【坍方】cave in; collapse/landslide; landslip

贪 tān ①corrupt; venal ～官 corrupt official ②have an insatiable desire for ～财 be greedy for money ～大求全 go in for grandiose projects ③covet; hanker after【贪婪】avaricious; greedy; rapacious ～的目光 greedy eyes【贪便宜】anxious to get things on the cheap【贪图】seek;

hanker after; covet ～安逸 seek ease and comfort ～小利 covet small advantages ～享乐 seek pleasure 【贪污】 corruption; graft ～盗窃 graft and embezzlement ～腐化 corruption and degeneration ～分子 grafter; embezzler 【贪心】 greed; avarice; rapacity / greedy; insatiable; voracious 【贪小失大】 covet a little and lose a lot 【贪赃】 take bribes; practise graft ～枉法 take bribes and bend the law 【贪嘴】 greedy (for food); gluttonous

滩 tān ①beach; sands 海～ seabeach 沙～ sand bank ②shoal 险～ dangerous shoals

摊 tān ①spread out 把豆子～开 spread the beans out ②take a share in ③vendor's stand; booth: stall 水果～ fruit stand ④一～泥 a mud puddle ～血 a pool of blood ⑤fry batter in a thin layer ～煎饼 make pancakes ～鸡蛋 make an omelet 【摊贩】 street pedlar 【摊牌】 lay one's cards on the table; show one's hand; have a showdown 【摊派】 apportion (expenses, etc.) 【摊子】 vendor's stand; stall/the structure of an organization; setup

瘫 tān paralysis 吓～ be paralysed with fright 【瘫痪】 paralysis; palsy / be paralysed; break down; be at a standstill 【瘫软】 weak and limp 【瘫子】 paralytic

坛 tán ①altar 日～ the Altar to the Sun ②a raised plot of land for planting flowers, etc. 花～ (raised) flower bed ③forum 讲～ speaker's platform ④circles; world 文～ literary circles ⑤earthen jar 酒～ wine jug

昙 tán covered with clouds 【昙花】 broad-leaved epiphyllum ～一现 last briefly

谈 tán ①talk; chat; discuss ～得来 get along well ② what is said or talked about 奇～ strange talk; fantastic tale 【谈不到】 out of the question 【谈到】 speak of; talk about; refer to 【谈锋】 eloquence ～甚健 talk volubly 【谈话】 conversation; talk 书面～ written statement 【谈家常】 engage in small talk; chitchat 【谈论】 discuss; talk about 【谈判】 negotiations; talks 举行～ hold talks 开始～ enter into negotiations with ～中断 the talks broke down ～桌 conference tabie 【谈天】 chat; make conversation 【谈吐】 style of conversation 【谈笑风生】 talk cheerfully and humorously 【谈心】 heart-to-heart talk

弹 tán ①shoot; send forth ～石子 shoot pebbles with a catapult ②spring; leap 球～回来 the ball rebounded ③flick; flip ～烟灰 flick the ash off a cigarette ～灰尘 flick the dust off ④fluff; tease ～棉花 fluff cotton (with a bow) ⑤play (a stringed musical instrument); pluck ～钢琴 play the piano ～琵琶 pluck the *pipa* ⑥elastic 忄生 elasticity ⑦accuse 【弹劾】 impeach (a public official) 【弹簧】 spring ～秤 spring balance ～床 spring bed ～门 swing door ～圈 spring coil ～锁 spring lock 【弹力】 elastic force; elasticity; resilience; spring ～袜 stretch socks 【弹球】 (play) marbles 【弹射】 launch (as with a catapult); catapult; shoot off; eject ～器 ejector 【弹跳】 bounce; spring 【弹压】 quell

痰 tán phlegm; sputum 【痰盂】 spittoon; cuspidor

潭 tán ①deep pool; pond ②pit; depression

檀 tán wingceltis 【檀板】 hardwood clappers 【檀香】 sandalwood ～扇 sandalwood fan ～皂 sandal soap

忐 tǎn 【忐忑】 perturbed; mentally disturbed ～不安 uneasy; fidgety

坦 tǎn ①level; smooth ②calm; composed ③open 【坦白】 honest; frank; candid / confess; make a confession; own up (to) ～对你说 to be frank with you ～交代

make a clean breast of (one's crimes) ～从宽 leniency to those who confess their crimes【坦荡】magnanimous; bighearted【坦克】tank ～兵 tank forces ～手 tankman【坦然】calm; unperturbed; having no misgivings ～自若 completely at ease【坦率】candid; frank; straightforward 为人～ be frank and open ～地交换意见 have a frank exchange of views【坦途】level road; highway

祖 tǎn ①leave (the upper part of the body) uncovered; be stripped to the waist or have one's shirt unbuttoned ②shield; shelter 偏～ be partial to【祖护】give unprincipled protection to; shield

毯 tǎn blanket; rug; carpet 毛～ woollen blanket

叹 tàn ①sigh 长～ heave a deep sigh ②exclaim in admiration; acclaim ～为奇迹 admire and praise sth. as a wonderful achievement【叹词】interjection; exclamation【叹服】gasp in admiration【叹气】sigh

炭 tàn charcoal 烧～ make charcoal【炭笔】charcoal pencil【炭画】charcoal (drawing)【炭火】charcoal fire【炭盆】charcoal brazier【炭窑】charcoal kiln

探 tàn ①try to find out; explore; sound ～路 explore the way ②scout; spy; detective 敌～ enemy scout ③visit ～亲访友 visit one's relatives and friends ④stretch forward ～进头来 pop one's head in 不要～身窗外 don't lean out of the window【探测】survey; sound; probe ～水深 take soundings ～器 sounder【探访】seek by inquiry or search/pay a visit to; visit【探监】visit a prisoner【探究】make a thorough inquiry; probe into ～原因 look into the causes【探口气】find out sb.'s opinions or feelings; sound sb. out【探矿】prospect【探明】ascertain; verify【探亲】go home to visit one's family or go to visit one's relatives ～假 home leave 【探求】seek; pursue; search after 【探索】explore; probe ～秘密 probe the secrets of sth. ～事物的本质 probe into the essence of things ～真理 seek truth 星际～ space exploration 【探讨】inquire into; probe into 【探听】try to find out; make inquiries ～下落 inquire about the whereabouts of sb. or sth. ～消息 fish for information 【探望】look about/ visit 【探问】make cautious inquiries about / inquire after 【探悉】ascertain; learn; find out 【探险】explore; make explorations ～队 exploration party ～家 explorer 【探照灯】searchlight ～光 searchlight beam 【探针】probe

碳 tàn carbon 【碳水化合物】carbohydrate 【碳酸】carbonic acid ～钠 soda ～气 carbon dioxide

TANG

汤 tāng ①hot water ②soup; broth 清～ clear soup 姜～ginger tea 【汤匙】soupspoon 【汤面】noodles in soup 【汤勺】soup ladle 【汤碗】soup bowl 【汤药】a decoction of medicinal ingredients

蹚 tāng ①wade; ford ～水过河 wade (across) a stream ②turn the soil and dig up weeds (with a hoe, etc.)

堂 táng ①the main room of a house ②a hall for a specific purpose 讲～ lecture room 课～ classroom ③court of law 过～ be tried ④relationship between cousins, etc. of the same paternal grandfather or great-grandfather; of the same clan ～兄弟 cousins on the paternal side; cousins 【堂皇】grand; stately; magnificent 【堂堂】dignified; impressive/imposing; awe-inspiring ～正正 open and aboveboard 【堂屋】central room

塘 táng ①dyke; embankment 河～ river embankment ②pool; pond 鱼～ fish pond ③hot-water bathing pool 澡～ bathhouse 【塘泥】pool sludge

搪 táng ①ward off; keep out ～风 keep out the wind ②spread (clay, paint, etc.) over; daub ～炉子 line a stove with clay 【搪瓷】enamel ～茶缸 enamel mug 【搪塞】stall sb. off; do sth. perfunctorily

膛 táng ①thorax; chest ②an enclosed space inside sth.; chamber 炉～ stove chamber

糖 táng ①sugar 冰～ crystal sugar ②sugared; in syrup ～蒜 garlic in syrup ③sweets; candy 【糖厂】sugar refinery 【糖醋】sugar and vinegar; sweet and sour ～鱼 fish in sweet and sour sauce 【糖果】sweets; candy; sweetmeats ～店 sweet shop; candy store; confectionery 【糖葫芦】sugarcoated haws on a stick 【糖浆】syrup 【糖精】saccharin; gluside 【糖萝卜】beet / preserved carrot 【糖蜜】molasses 【糖水】syrup ～桔子 tangerines in syrup 【糖衣】sugarcoating ～炮弹 sugarcoated bullet

倘 tǎng if; supposing; in case ～有不测 in case of accidents

淌 tǎng drip; shed; trickle ～汗 be dripping with sweat ～眼泪 shed tears ～口水 slaver; slobber 伤口～血 blood trickled from the wound

躺 tǎng lie; recline ～下歇歇 lie down and rest a while 【躺倒】lie down ～不干 stay in bed—refuse to shoulder responsibilities any longer 【躺椅】deck chair; sling chair

烫 tàng ①scald; burn 让开水～了 be scalded by boiling water ②heat up in hot water; warm ～脚 bathe one's feet in hot water ③very hot 汤真～ this soup is boiling hot ④iron; press ～衣服 iron clothes ⑤perm 冷～ cold wave 【烫发】give or have a permanent wave; perm 【烫金】gilding; bronzing 布面～ cloth gilt

TAO

叨 tāo be favoured with; get the benefit of 【叨光】much obliged to you 【叨教】many thanks for your advice

涛 tāo great waves; billows

掏 tāo ①draw out; pull out; fish out ～手枪 draw a pistol ～炉灰 clear the ashes from a stove ～耳朵 pick one's ears ②dig (a hole, etc.); hollow out ③steal from sb.'s pocket 【掏腰包】pay out of one's own pocket; foot a bill/pick sb.'s pocket

滔 tāo inundate; flood 【滔滔】torrential; surging/keeping up a constant flow of words 【滔天】(of billows, etc.) dash to the skies/heinous; monstrous (crimes)

韬 tāo ①sheath or bow case ②hide; conceal ③the art of war 【韬晦】conceal one's true features or intentions; lie low 【韬略】military strategy

逃 táo ①run away; escape; flee ～出监狱 escape from the prison ②evade; dodge; shirk; escape ～税 evade a tax 【逃避】escape; evade; shirk ～现实 try to escape reality ～斗争 evade struggle ～责任 shirk responsibility ～困难 dodge a difficulty 【逃兵】deserter 【逃窜】run away; flee in disorder 【逃遁】flee; escape; evade 【逃犯】escaped criminal or convict 【逃荒】flee from famine 【逃命】fly for one's life 【逃难】flee from a calamity; be a refugee 【逃匿】escape and hide; go into hiding 【逃跑】flee; take flight 【逃散】become separated in flight 【逃脱】make good one's escape ～责任 succeed in evading responsibility ～不了惩罚 never escape punishment 【逃亡】become a fugitive; flee from home; go into exile ～地主 runaway landlord 【逃学】play truant; cut class

桃 táo ①peach 【桃脯】 preserved peach 【桃红】 pink 【桃花】 peach blossom 【桃仁】 peach kernel/walnut meat

陶 táo ①pottery; earthenware ～俑 pottery figurine ②make pottery ③cultivate; mould; educate 熏～ exert a gradual influence on ④contented; happy 【陶瓷】 pottery and porcelain; ceramics ～工 potter ～业 ceramic industry 【陶器】 pottery; earthenware 【陶土】 pottery clay 【陶冶】 make pottery and smelt metal / mould (a person's temperament) 【陶醉】 be intoxicated (with success etc.); revel in 自我～ be intoxicated with self-satisfaction

淘 táo ①wash in a pan or basket ～米 wash rice ②clean out; dredge ～井 dredge a well 【淘金】 panning 【淘箩】 a basket for washing rice in 【淘气】 naughty; mischievous ～鬼 a regular little mischief 【淘汰】 eliminate through selection or competition / die out; fall into disuse; be obsolete ～赛 elimination series

讨 tǎo ①send armed forces to suppress ～平叛乱 put down a rebellion ②denounce; condemn ③demand; ask for; beg for ～帐 demand the payment of a debt; dun ④marry (a woman) ～老婆 take a wife ⑤incur; invite ～没趣儿 court a rebuff; ask for a snub ～喜欢 likable; cute 【讨伐】 send a punitive expedition against 【讨饭】 beg for food; be a beggar 【讨好】 fawn on; toady to / be rewarded with a fruitful result 【讨还】 get sth. back ～血债 make sb. pay his blood debt 【讨价】 ask a price ～还价 bargain; haggle 【讨教】 ask for advice 【讨论】 discuss; talk over 参加～ join in the discussion ～会 discussion; symposium 【讨便宜】 seek undue advantage; look for a bargain 【讨乞】 beg alms 【讨巧】 act artfully to get what one wants; choose the easy way out 【讨饶】 beg for mercy; ask for forgiveness 【讨嫌】 disagreeable; annoying 【讨厌】 disgusting; repugnant/hard to handle; troublesome; nasty/detest; loathe; be disgusted with ～的天气 abominable weather ～的病 a nasty illness 工人～他 the workers dislike him

套 tào ①sheath; case; cover; sleeve 枕～ pillowcase 椅～ slipcover for a chair ②cover with; slip over; encase in ～上一件毛衣 slip on a sweater ③that which covers (other garments, etc.) ～袖 oversleeve ～鞋 overshoes ④overlap; interlink 一环～一环 one ring linked with another — a closely linked succession ⑤traces; harness (for a draught animal) 拉～ pull a plough or cart ⑥harness (an animal); hitch up (an animal to a cart) ⑦knot; loop; noose 活～slipknot ⑧put a ring, etc. round; tie ～上救生圈 put on a life ring ⑨model on; copy ～公式 apply a formula ⑩convention; formula 老一～ the same old stuff ⑪coax a secret out of sb.; pump sb. about sth. ⑫try to win (sb.'s friendship) ～近乎 cotton up to ⑬set; suit 两～衣服 two suits of clothes 一～房间 a flat 【套包】 collar (for a horse) 【套车】 harness an animal to a cart 【套购】 fraudulently purchase (state-controlled commodities); illegally buy up 【套间】 a small room opening off another; inner room/apartment; flat 【套裤】 trouser legs worn over one's trousers; leggings 【套色】 colour process ～版 colourplate ～木刻 coloured woodcut 【套用】 apply mechanically; use indiscriminately 【套语】 polite formula 【套种】 interplanting

TE

特 tè ①special; particular; unusual; exceptional ～使 special envoy ②for a special purpose; specially ～为此事而来 come specially for this purpose ③secret agent;

spy 敌～ enemy agent 【特别】 special; particular/especially; particularly ～会议 special meeting; special session ～开支 special expenses ～快车 express 【特产】 special (local) product; speciality 【特长】 strong point; speciality 他有什么～ what is he skilled in 【特出】 extraordinary ～成绩 outstanding achievements ～作用 a prominent role 【特大】 especially big; the most ～喜讯 excellent news ～丰收 an exceptional bumper harvest ～洪水 a catastrophic flood ～号服装 outsize garments 【特等】 special class; top grade ～舱 stateroom 【特地】 for a special purpose; specially 【特点】 distinguishing feature; peculiarity; trait 生理～ physiological characteristics 【特定】 specially designated/specific; specified 在～的条件下 under given conditions 【特工】 secret service ～人员 special agent 【特混舰队】 (naval) task force 【特级】 special grade; superfine ～教师 teacher of a special classification ～战斗英雄 special-class combat hero 【特急】 extra urgent (telegram) 【特辑】 special issue of a periodical / a special collection of short films 【特技】 stunt; trick/special effects ～飞行 stunt flying ～镜头 trick shot ～摄影 trick photography 【特价】 special offer ～出售 sell at a bargain price 【特刊】 special (number) 【特快】 express 【特派】 specially appointed ～记者 special correspondent 【特遣部队】 task force 【特权】 privilege; prerogative 外交～ diplomatic privileges ～阶层 privileged stratum ～思想 the idea that prerogatives and privileges go with position 【特色】 distinguishing feature 艺术～ artistic characteristics 有民族～ with distinctive national features 【特赦】 special pardon/special amnesty ～令 decree of special pardon or amnesty 【特殊】 particular; peculiar ～情况 an exceptional case; special circumstances ～性 particularity; peculiarity

～规律 specific law【特殊化】become privileged 不搞～ seek no personal privileges 反对～ oppose privileges【特为】for a special purpose; specially【特务】special task (battalion, etc.)/special agent; spy ～活动 espionage ～机关 secret service; espionage agency ～组织 secret service; spy organization【特效】specially good effect; special efficacy ～药 specific drug; effective cure【特写】feature article or story; feature/close-up ～镜头 close-up (shot)【特性】specific property【特许】special permission ～证书 special permit; letters patent【特邀】specially invite ～代表 specially invited representative【特有】peculiar; characteristic【特约】engage by special arrangement ～稿 special contribution (to a publication) ～记者 special correspondent【特征】feature; trait 面部～ facial characteristics【特指】refer in particular to【特种】special type; particular kind ～工艺 special arts and crafts ～战争 special warfare

TENG

疼 téng ①ache; pain; sore 头～ have a headache 浑身～ be aching all over ②love dearly; be fond of ～小孙子 dote on one's little grandson

誊 téng transcribe; copy out【誊清】make a fair copy of ～稿 fair copy

腾 téng ①gallop; jump; prance ～身而过 jump over sth. ②rise; soar 升～ ascend ③make room; clear out; vacate ～房子 vacate one's room【腾空】soar; rise to the sky【腾腾】steaming; seething 热气～ steaming hot 烟雾～ hazy with smoke

藤 téng ①cane; rattan ～椅 cane chair ～盔 rattan helmet ③vine 葡萄～ grape vine【藤牌】cane shield

TI

体 tī 【体己】intimate; confidential/private savings ～话 things one says only to one's intimates

剔 tī ①pick ～骨头 pick a bone ～牙 pick one's teeth ②pick out and throw away; reject 【剔除】get rid of

梯 tī ①ladder; steps; stairs ②terraced 【梯队】echelon 【梯级】stair; step 【梯田】terraced fields; terrace 【梯形】ladder-shaped/trapezoid; trapezium 【梯子】stepladder

踢 tī ①kick 把门～开 kick the door open 把凳子～翻 kick over a stool 这马～人 this horse kicks ②play (football); kick ～进一球 score a goal 【踢皮球】play children's football/pass the buck 【踢踏舞】step dance

提 tí ①carry ～着篮子 carry a basket ②lift; raise; promote 一只手就能～起来 can lift it with one hand ～价 raise the price ③shift to an earlier time; move up a date ④bring up; raise ～问题 ask a question ～意见 make a criticism ～抗议 lodge a protest ～条件 put forward conditions ～要求 make demands ～方案 suggest plans ⑤draw out; extract ～款 draw money ⑥mention; refer to 别再～那件事了 don't bring that up again 【提案】motion; proposal 【提拔】promote 【提包】handbag; bag; valise 【提倡】advocate; promote; encourage; recommend ～计划生育 advocate family planning 值得～deserve recommendation 【提成】deduct a percentage (from a sum of money, etc.) 【提出】advance; pose; raise ～建议 put forward a proposal ～新的理论 advance a new theory ～警告 give a warning ～了新的课题 put new questions before sb. 【提词】prompt/prompter 【提法】formulation; wording 【提纲】outline ～挈领 concentrate on the main points; bring out the essentials 【提高】raise; increase;

improve ～水位 raise the water level ～警惕 enhance one's vigilance ～觉悟 heighten one's awareness ～认识 deepen one's understanding ～战斗力 increase the combat effectiveness ～工作效率 raise working efficiency ～产品质量 improve the quality of products 【提供】provide; supply; furnish; offer ～原料 supply sth. with raw materials ～援助 give aid; provide assistance ～贷款 offer a loan 【提货】pick up goods; take delivery of goods ～单 bill of lading 【提交】submit (a problem, draft resolution, etc.) to; refer to 【提炼】extract and purify; abstract; refine (cane sugar, etc.) ～金属 extract metal 【提名】nominate (sb. for representative, etc.) 【提起】mention; speak of/raise; arouse; brace up ～精神 raise one's spirits; brace oneself up ～人们的注意 call people's attention 【提前】shift to an earlier date; move up (a date); advance/in advance; ahead of time; beforehand ～通知我们 notify us in advance ～召开大会 convene the congress before the due date 【提琴】the violin family 小～ violin 中～ viola 大～ cello 低音～ contrabass 【提请】submit sth. to ～大会批准 submit to the congress for approval 【提取】draw; collect/extract; abstract 到车站～行李 pick up one's luggage at the railway station ～石油 extract oil 【提神】refresh oneself 【提审】bring (a prisoner) before the court; bring (sb. in custody) to trial; fetch (a detainee) for interrogation 【提升】promote / elevate ～机 elevator 【提示】point out; prompt 【提问】put questions to; quiz 回答老师的～ answer the teacher's questions 【提箱】suitcase 【提心吊胆】have one's heart in one's mouth 【提醒】remind; warn; call attention to 【提要】abstract; epitome; synopsis 本书内容～ capsule summary (of the book) 【提议】propose; suggest; move/proposal; motion 我～休会 I move the meeting be adjourned 【提早】be earlier than planned or expected

啼 tí ①cry; wail; weep aloud ②crow; caw 鸡～ cocks crow 【啼笑皆非】not know whether to laugh or cry

题 tí ①topic; subject; title; problem 讨论～ topic for discussion 考～ examination questions ②inscribe ～诗 inscribe a poem 【题材】subject matter; theme ～范围 range of subjects 【题词】write a few words of encouragement, appreciation or commemoration/inscription; dedication/foreword 【题解】explanatory notes on the title or background of a book/key to exercises or problems

蹄 tí hoof 马～ horse's hoofs 炖猪～ stewed pig's trotters 【蹄筋】tendons (of beef, mutton or pork)

体 tǐ ①body; part of the body 肢～ limbs ②(state of a) substance 固～ solid ③style; form 旧～诗 old-style poems ④personally do or experience sth. 身～力行 earnestly practise what one advocates ⑤system 国～ state system ⑥aspect (of a verb) 【体裁】types or forms of literature 【体操】gymnastics ～表演 gymnastic exhibition ～服 gym outfit ～器械 gymnastic apparatus 【体察】experience and observe 【体罚】physical punishment 【体格】physique; build ～检查 health checkup 【体会】know or learn from experience; realize 深有～ have an intimate knowledge of sth. 【体积】volume (of a container, etc.); bulk ～大 bulky 【体力】physical strength 增强～ build up one's strength 消耗～ be a drain on one's strength; consume one's strength ～劳动 manual labour 【体谅】show understanding and sympathy for; make allowances for 【体面】dignity; face / honourable; creditable 有失～ be a loss of face 维持～ keep up appearances 不～的行为 disgraceful conduct 【体态】posture; carriage ～轻盈

a graceful carriage 【体贴】 give every care to ～病人 show a patient every consideration ～入微 look after with meticulous care 【体统】 decorum; propriety; decency 不成～ most improper 有失～ be disgraceful 【体味】 appreciate; savour 【体温】 (body) temperature 【体无完肤】 have cuts and bruises all over the body / be thoroughly refuted 【体系】 system 【体现】 embody incarnate; reflect; give expression to 【体形】 bodily form; build 【体型】 type of build or figure 【体验】 learn through practice or one's personal experience ～生活 observe and learn from real life 【体育】 physical culture; physical training; sports ～场 stadium ～道德 sportsmanship ～锻炼 physical training ～馆 gymnasium; gym ～活动 sports activities ～课 physical education (PE) ～疗法 physical exercise therapy ～用品 sports goods 【体制】 system of organization 国家～ state system 【体质】 physique; constitution 【体重】 (body) weight ～增加 put on weight

屉 tì ①a food steamer with several trays; steamer tray ②桌 three-drawer desk 三～桌

剃 tì shave ～胡子 have a shave ～头 have one's head shaved; have a haircut 【剃刀】 razor

涕 tì ①tears 痛哭流～ shed bitter tears 感激～零 be moved to tears of gratitude ②snivel 【涕泣】 weep

惕 tì cautious; watchful 警～ be on the alert; watch out

替 tì ①take the place of; replace; substitute for 谁～他 who'll take his place ②for; on behalf of ～别人买火车票 buy a train ticket for someone ～顾客着想 think about the interests of the customers 【替代】 substitute for; replace; supersede 【替工】 work as a temporary substitute/ temporary substitute 找一个～ find a substitute 【替换】

substitute for; displace; take the place of 带上一套~的
衣服 take a change of clothes with you 【替身】 substitute; replacement; stand-in/scapegoat

嚏 tì sneeze 【嚏喷】 sneeze

TIAN

天 tiān ①sky; heaven ②overhead ~桥 overline bridge
③day 忙了一~ have had a busy day ④a period of
time in a day 五更~ around four in the morning ⑤sea-
son 春~ spring ⑥weather 下雨~ wet weather ⑦nature
~灾 natural calamity ⑧God; Heaven ~知道 God knows
【天窗】 skylight 【天地】 heaven and earth; world; universe / field of activity; scope of operation 【天鹅】 swan
~绒 velvet 【天翻地覆】 earthshaking 一的变化 tremendous changes 【天分】 natural gift; talent 【天赋】 inborn;
innate / endowments 【天宫】 heavenly palace 【天国】 the
Kingdom of Heaven; paradise 【天花】 smallpox 【天花板】
ceiling 【天昏地暗】 dark all round / in a state of chaos
and darkness 【天经地义】 unalterable principle — right
and proper; perfectly justified 【天井】 small yard; courtyard / skylight 【天空】 the sky; the heavens 【天蓝】 sky
blue; azure 【天理】 heavenly principles / justice 【天良】
conscience 【天亮】 daybreak; dawn 【天罗地网】 nets above
and snares below; tight encirclement 布下~ spread a
dragnet 【天幕】 the canopy of the heavens / backdrop
(of a stage) 【天平】 balance; scales 【天气】 weather ~
要变 the weather is changing ~转晴 it's clearing up ~
图 weather map ~预报 weather forecast 【天堑】 natural
moat 【天然】 natural ~财富 natural resources ~景色
natural scenery ~障碍物 natural barrier ~气 natural

gas【天壤】heaven and earth ～之别 as far apart as heaven and earth; a world of difference【天日】the sky and the sun; light 重见～ once more see the light of day — be delivered from oppression or persecution【天色】colour of the sky; weather ～已晚 it is getting dark 看～要晴 it seems to be clearing up【天生】born; inborn; inherent; innate【天时】weather; climate ～不正 abnormal weather【天使】angel【天堂】paradise; heaven【天体】celestial body【天天】every day; daily; day in, day out【天王星】Uranus【天文】astronomy ～观测 astronomical observation ～馆 planetarium ～数字 astronomical figure; enormous figure ～台 (astronomical) observatory【天下】land under heaven — the world or China【天险】natural barrier【天线】aerial; antenna【天性】nature【天涯】the end of the world【天真】innocent; naïve【天职】bounden duty; vocation【天主教】Catholicism ～徒 Catholic【天资】natural gift; talent【天子】the emperor

添

tiān add; increase ～煤 put in more coal; stoke ～衣服 put on more clothes 给你们～麻烦了 sorry to have troubled you【添补】replenish; get more【添枝加叶】embellish a story【添置】add to one's possessions; acquire ～家具 buy more furniture

田

tiān field; farmland 型～ plough a field 油～ oilfield 煤～ coalfield【田地】field; cropland【田埂】ridge【田鸡】frog【田间】field; farm ～管理 field management ～劳动 field labour【田径】track and field ～队 track and field team ～赛 track and field meet ～赛项目 track and field events ～运动 track and field sports; athletics ～运动员 athlete【田螺】river snail【田赛】field events【田鼠】(field) vole【田野】field; open country【田园】fields and gardens; countryside ～生活 idyllic life

～风光 rural scenery ～诗 idyll; pastoral poetry ～诗人 pastoral poet 【田庄】country estate

恬 tián ①quiet; tranquil; calm ②not care at all; remain unperturbed 【恬不知耻】have no sense of shame

甜 tián ①sweet; honeyed ②sound 睡得～ have a sweet sleep; sleep soundly 【甜菜】beet/beetroot ～糖 beet sugar 【甜瓜】muskmelon 【甜美】sweet; luscious/pleasant; refreshing 味道～ taste sweet ～的桃儿 luscious peaches 【甜蜜】sweet; happy ～的回忆 happy memories 【甜面酱】a sweet sauce made of fermented flour 【甜食】sweet food; sweetmeats 爱吃～ have a sweet tooth 【甜头】sweet taste; pleasant flavour / good; benefit (as an inducement) 尝到 ～ draw benefit from it 【甜味】sweet taste 【甜言蜜语】sweet words and honeyed phrases; fine-sounding words

填 tián ①fill; stuff 往坑里～土 fill a pit with earth ②write; fill in ～表 fill in a form 【填补】fill (a vacancy, gap, etc.) ～空白 fill in the gaps 【填充】fill up; stuff / fill in the blanks (in a test paper) 【填空】fill a vacant position; fill a vacancy 【填平】fill and level up ～弹坑 fill up craters ～补齐 fill up the gaps

TIAO

挑 tiāo ①choose; select; pick ～最好的作种子 select the best for seeds ～毛病 pick faults; find fault ②carry; shoulder ～一担菜 carry two baskets of vegetables on a shoulder pole 【挑拣】pick and choose 【挑剔】nit-pick; be hypercritical; be fastidious 【挑选】choose; select; pick out ～接班人 choose successors 【挑子】carrying pole with its load; load carried on a shoulder pole

条 tiáo ①twig 柳～儿 willow twigs ② a long narrow piece; strip; slip 布～ a strip of cloth ③item; article

逐～ item by item; point by point ④order 有～不紊 in perfect order; orderly ⑥一～肥皂 a bar of soap 一～香烟 a carton of cigarettes 一～裤子 a pair of trousers 【条案】 a long narrow table 【条播】 drilling 【条幅】 scroll 【条件】 condition; term; factor / requirement; prerequisite 利用有利的～ make use of the favourable factors 在目前～下 under present circumstances 提出～ list the prerequisites; put forward the requirements 【条款】 clause; article; provision 【条理】 proper arrangement or presentation; orderliness; method 他工作有～ he works with system 【条例】 regulations; rules; ordinances 组织～ organic rules 【条目】 clauses and subclauses/entry (in a dictionary) 【条条框框】 rules and regulations; conventions 【条文】 article; clause 【条纹】 stripe; streak 【条约】 treaty; pact 【条子】 strip / a brief informal note

迢 tiáo far; remote 【迢迢】 far away; remote 千里～ from a thousand li away; from afar

调 tiáo ①mix; adjust ～色 mix colours ～弦 tune a stringed instrument ②suit well; fit in perfectly ③mediate ④tease; provoke 【调羹】 spoon 【调和】 be in harmonious proportion/mediate; reconcile/compromise; make concessions 这两种颜色很～ these two colours blend well 进行不～的斗争 wage uncompromising struggles 没有～的余地 there is no room for compromise 【调剂】 make up a prescription/adjust; regulate ～劳动力 redistribute labour power ～生活 enliven one's life 【调节】 adjust; regulate (the room temperature, etc.) 市场～作用 role of regulation through the market ～器 regulator; conditioner 【调解】 mediate; make peace 【调理】 nurse one's health; recuperate/take care of; look after 【调料】 condiment; seasoning 【调皮】 naughty;

mischievous / unruly; tricky 【调情】 flirt 【调唆】 incite;
instigate 【调停】 mediate; intervene 居间 ~ mediate between two parties 对争端进行 ~ mediate a dispute 【调
味】 flavour; season ~品 flavouring; seasoning; condiment 【调戏】 take liberties with (a woman); assail (a
woman) with obscenities 【调笑】 make fun of; poke fun
at; tease 【调谐】 harmonious 【调养】 take good care of
oneself (after an illness); be nursed back to health 【调整】
adjust; regulate; revise 工资 ~ adjustment of wages (usu.
upwards) ~价格 readjust prices ~国民经济 adjust the
national economy

笤 tiáo 【笤帚】 whisk broom

挑 tiáo ①push sth. up with a pole or stick; raise ~
帘子 raise the curtain ②poke; pick ~刺 pick out a
splinter ~水泡 prick a blister with a needle ③instigate
【挑拨】 instigate; incite; sow discord ~是非 foment discord ~离间 sow dissension; incite one against the other
【挑动】 provoke; stir up; incite ~内战 provoke civil war
【挑逗】 provoke; tease; tantalize 【挑花】 cross-stitch work
【挑唆】 abet 【挑衅】 provoke 故意 ~ deliberate provocation ~性问题 provocative questions 【挑战】 throw down
the gauntlet; give a challenge/challenge sb. to a contest
接受~ take up the gauntlet; accept a challenge

眺 tiào look into the distance from a high place 远~
look far into the distance

跳 tiào ①jump; leap; spring; bounce 高兴得~起来
jump for joy ~下自行车 jump off a bicycle ~过
一条沟 leap over a ditch ②move up and down; beat 心
~正常 one's heartbeat is normal ③skip (over); make
omissions ~过了三页 skip over three pages ~一针 drop

a stitch 【跳班】 (of pupils) skip a grade 【跳板】 gangplank / springboard; diving board 【跳动】 beat; pulsate 【跳高】 high jump 【跳高运动员】 high jumper 【跳脚】 stamp one's foot 气得～ stamp with rage 【跳栏】 hurdle race; the hurdles 【跳马】 vaulting horse/horse-vaulting 【跳棋】 Chinese checkers; Chinese draughts 【跳伞】 parachute; bale out/parachute jumping 【跳绳】 rope skipping 【跳水】 dive 【跳台】 diving tower 【跳舞】 dance 【跳远】 long jump; broad jump 【跳蚤】 flea

TIE

贴 tiē ①paste; stick; glue ～邮票 stick on a stamp ②keep close to 紧～在妈妈身边 nestle closely to one's mother ③subsidies; allowance 房～ housing allowance 【贴边】 hem (of a garment) 【贴补】 subsidize ～家用 help out with the family expenses 【贴切】 (of words) apt; suitable; appropriate 措词～ aptly worded; well-put 【贴身】 next to the skin ～衣服 underclothes 【贴心】 intimate; close ～话 words spoken in confidence

铁 tiě ①iron ～工厂 ironworks ②arms; weapon 手无寸～ bare-handed ③hard or strong as iron ～拳 iron fist ④indisputable; unalterable ～的事实 ironclad evidence ～的纪律 iron discipline ⑤resolve; determine ～了心 be unshakable in one's determination 【铁板】 iron plate ～一块 a monolithic bloc 【铁饼】 discus/discus throw 【铁道】 railway; railroad ～兵 railway corps 【铁饭碗】 iron rice bowl — a secure job 【铁工】 ironwork/ironworker; blacksmith 【铁镐】 iron hoop 【铁管】 iron pipe 【铁轨】 rail 【铁环】 iron hoop 滚～ trundle a hoop 【铁甲】 armour ～车 armoured car 【铁匠】 blacksmith ～铺 smithy; blacksmith's shop 【铁矿】 iron ore / iron mine ～石 iron ore 【铁链】 iron chain; shackles 【铁路】 railway; railroad ～线 railway line 【铁门】 iron gate 【铁皮】 iron sheet 白～ tinplate 黑～ black sheet 【铁骑】 cavalry 【铁器】 ironware ～时代 the Iron Age 【铁锹】 spade; shovel 【铁青】 ashen; livid 【铁纱】 wire gauze; wire cloth 【铁石心肠】 be ironhearted 【铁水】 molten iron 【铁丝】 iron wire ～网 wire netting; wire entanglement 【铁索】 cable; iron chain ～桥 chain bridge 【铁腕】 iron hand ～人物 an ironhanded person; strong man 【铁锈】 rust 【铁证】 ironclad proof

帖 tiè a book containing models of handwriting or painting for learners to copy 字～ calligraphy models

TING

厅 tīng ①hall 餐～ dining hall; restaurant 会议～ conference hall ②office 办公～ general office ③ a government department at the provincial level 教育～ the Education Department

听 tīng ①listen; hear ～广播 listen to the radio 请～我讲完 please hear me out ②heed; obey ～党的话 do as the Party says ③allow; let ～任摆布 allow oneself to be ordered about ④tin; can 【听便】 as one pleases; please yourself 【听从】 obey; heed; comply with ～吩咐 be at sb.'s beck and call ～劝告 accept sb.'s advice 【听而不闻】 hear but pay no attention 【听候】 wait for (a decision, settlement, etc.) ～分配 wait for one's assignment (to work) 【听话】 be obedient 【听见】 hear 【听讲】 listen to a talk; attend a lecture 【听觉】 sense of hearing 【听课】 visit a class/attend a lecture 【听力】 hearing / aural comprehension (in language teaching) 【听命】 take orders from; be at sb.'s command 【听其自然】 let things take their own course 【听起来】 sound ～不错 it sounds all right 【听取】 listen to ～群众的意见 heed the opinions of the masses ～汇报 hear reports (from below); debrief 【听筒】 (telephone) receiver / headphone; earphone / stethoscope 【听写】 dictation 教师让学生～ the teacher gave the pupils dictation 【听信】 wait for information / believe (what one hears) 【听众】 audience; listeners 【听装】 tinned

廷 tíng the court of a feudal ruler; the seat of a monarchical government 清～ the Qing government

亭 tíng pavilion; kiosk 书～ bookstall 【亭亭】 erect; upright ～玉立 slim and graceful; tall and erect

庭 tíng ①front courtyard; front yard ②law court 【庭园】 flower garden; grounds 【庭院】 courtyard

停 tíng ①stop; cease; halt; pause 雨～了 the rain has stopped 他不～地写着 he kept on writing ②stop over; stay ③(of cars) be parked; (of ships) lie at anchor 【停办】 close down 【停泊】 anchor; berth ～处 anchorage; roadstead 【停产】 stop production 【停车】 stop; pull up/ park/(of a machine) stall; stop working ～场 car park 【停当】 ready; settled 【停电】 power cut 【停顿】 stop; halt / pause (in speaking) 陷于～状态 be at a standstill 【停放】 park; place 【停工】 stop work; shut down 【停火】 cease fire ～协议 cease-fire agreement 【停机坪】 aircraft parking area 【停刊】 stop publication (of a newspaper, magazine, etc.) 【停课】 suspend classes 学校～了 classes were suspended 【停留】 stay for a time; stop; remain 过夜 make an overnight stop 短暂～ have a brief stopover 【停水】 cut off the water supply 【停妥】 be well arranged; be in order 【停息】 stop; cease 【停歇】 stop doing business; close down/stop; cease/stop for a rest; rest 【停学】 stop going to school/suspend sb. from school 【停业】

stop doing business; close down 修理内部，暂时～ closed temporarily for repairs 【停战】armistice; truce 【停职】suspend sb. from his duties ～反省 be temporarily relieved of one's post for self-examination 【停止】stop; cease; halt ～工作 stop working ～营业 business suspended ～广播 stop broadcasting ～罢工 call off a strike 谈话～了 the talking quenched 暴风雨～了 the storm quieted down 【停滞】stagnate; be at a standstill; bog down

挺 tǐng ①straight; erect; stiff ～立 stand erect; stand firm ②stick out; straighten up (physically) ～胸 throw out one's chest ～起腰杆 straighten one's back ③endure; stand; hold out 你～得住吗 can you stand it ④rather; quite ～好 very good 【挺拔】tall and straight/forceful 【挺进】(of troops) boldly drive on; press onward; push forward 【挺举】clean and jerk 【挺身】straighten one's back ～反抗 stand up and fight ～而出 step forward bravely; come out boldly 【挺秀】tall and graceful

铤 tǐng (run) quickly 【铤而走险】risk danger in desperation; make a reckless move

艇 tǐng a light boat 汽～ steamboat 炮～ gunboat 登陆～ landing craft

TONG

通 tōng ①open; through 路～了 the road is now open 电话打～了 the call has been put through ② poke; jab ～炉子 poke the fire ③lead to; go to 直～北京 go straight to Beijing ④connect; communicate 两个房间是～的 the two rooms are connected ⑤notify; tell 一个电话给 sb. a ring ⑥understand; know ～三种语言 know three languages ⑦authority; expert 中国～ an old China hand ⑧logical; coherent 文理不～ ungrammatical and incoherent (writing) ⑧general; common ～称 a general term ⑩all; whole ～身 the whole body【通报】circulate a notice (of commendation, etc.)/circular (on the situation, etc.) / bulletin; journal【通病】common failing【通常】general; usual; normal 在～惰况下 under normal conditions【通车】(of a railway or highway) be open to traffic/have transport service【通称】be generally called/ a general term【通达】understand【通道】thoroughfare; passage【通敌】collude with the enemy; have illicit relations with the enemy【通电】electrify; energize/circular telegram 【通牒】diplomatic note【通风】ventilate ～机 ventilator 【通告】give public notice; announce / public notice; announcement【通过】pass through; get past; traverse/adopt; pass / by means of; through 船～海峡 the ship passed the channel ～决议 adopt a resolution ～协商 through consultation【通航】be open to navigation or air traffic【通红】very red; red through and through【通话】converse / communicate by telephone【通婚】be related by marriage; intermarry【通货】currency; current money ～膨胀 inflation ～收缩 deflation【通缉】order the arrest of a criminal at large 下～令 issue a wanted circular【通奸】commit adultery【通栏标题】banner【通联】communications and liaison【通令】circular order ～嘉奖 issue an order of commendation【通路】thoroughfare【通盘】overall; all-round; comprehensive ～计划 overall planning【通情达理】showing good sense; reasonable【通融】make an exception in sb.'s favour / accommodate sb. with a short-term loan【通商】 (of nations) have trade relations ～条约 a trade treaty ～口岸 trading port【通史】comprehensive history; general history【通顺】clear and coherent; smooth 文理～ coherent writing【通俗】popular; common ～易懂 easy to understand ～读物 books for popular consumption; popular literature ～化 popularization 【通条】 poker/cleaning rod 【通同】 collude; gang up ～作弊 act fraudulently in collusion with sb. 【通宵】 all night; throughout the night ～值班 on duty all night 【通晓】 thoroughly understand; be proficient in ～中国历史 be well versed in Chinese history 【通心粉】 macaroni 【通信】 communicate by letter; correspond ～处 mailing address ～鸽 Homing pigeon ～犬 messenger dog ～员 messenger 【通行】 pass through/current; general ～证 pass; permit 【通讯】 communication / correspondence ～报导 news report ～方法 means of communication ～录 address book ～社 news agency ～设备 communication apparatus ～卫星 communications satellite 【通用】 in common use; current; general/interchangeable 全国～教材 national textbooks ～语种 commonly used languages ～月票 a monthly ticket for all urban and suburban lines 【通邮】 accessible by postal communication 【通知】 notify; inform/notice; circular 请～他 please notify him ～书 notice

同 tóng ①same; alike; similar ～类 the same kind ②be the same as ③together; in common ～甘苦, 共患难 share weal and woe ④with ～群众商量 consult with the masses 我～你一起去 I'll go with you 【同班】 in the same class ～同学 classmate 【同伴】 companion 【同胞】 born of the same parents/fellow countryman ～兄弟 full brothers 【同辈】 of the same generation 【同病相怜】 misery loves company 【同窗】 study in the same school/schoolmate 【同等】 on an equal basis ～重要 of equal importance ～对待 put on an equal footing ～学力 (have) the same educational level (as graduates or a certain grade of students) 【同房】 of the same branch of a family/sleep together; have sexual intercourse 【同感】 the same feeling 【同工同酬】 equal pay for equal work 【同归于尽】 perish together 【同行】 of the same trade or occupation / a person of the same trade or occupation 【同化】 assimilate (ethnic groups) ～政策 the policy of national assimilation ～作用 assimilation 【同伙】 work in partnership; collude (in doing evil) / partner; confederate 【同居】 live together/cohabit 【同流合污】 wallow in the mire with sb. 【同路】 go the same way ～人 fellow traveller 【同盟】 alliance; league 结成～ form an alliance ～国 ally ～军 allied forces ～条约 treaty of alliance 【同名】 of the same name 【同谋】 conspire (with sb.) / confederate 【同情】 sympathize with; show sympathy for ～心 sympathy; fellow feeling 【同时】 at the same time; meanwhile; in the meantime / moreover; besides ～发生 happen at the same time; coincide ～存在 exist simultaneously 【同事】 work in the same place; work together/ colleague; fellow worker 【同岁】 of the same age 【同位语】 appositive 【同乡】 a person from the same village, town or province; a fellow villager, townsman or provincial 【同心】 concentric / with one heart ～同德 be of one heart and one mind ～协力 make concerted efforts 【同行】 travel together 【同性】 of the same sex / of the same nature or character ～恋爱 homosexuality 【同姓】 of the same surname 他与我～ he is my namesake 【同学】 be in the same school: be a schoolmate of sb./fellow student; schoolmate/a form of address used in speaking to a student 【同样】 same; equal ～情况下 under similar circumstances 【同业】 the same trade or business/a person of the same trade or business ～公会 trade council 【同一】 same; identical 【同义词】 synonym 【同意】 agree;

approve 我～你的意见 I'm of your mind【同音词】homonym; homophone【同志】comrade【同宗】of the same clan

桐 tóng a general term for paulownia, phoenix tree and tung tree【桐油】tung oil ～树 tung tree

铜 tóng copper ～丝 copper wire ～像 bronze statue ～扣子 brass button【铜版】copperplate ～画 copperplate etching ～印刷 copperplate printing ～纸 art (printing) paper【铜管乐队】brass band【铜管乐器】brass wind【铜匠】coppersmith【铜模】matrix; (copper) mould【铜器】bronze, brass or copper ware【铜钱】copper cash【铜墙铁壁】bastion of iron — impregnable fortress

童 tóng ①child ②virgin ～男 virgin boy ～女 maiden; virgin ③bare; bald ～山 bare hills【童工】child labourer/child labour【童话】children's stories; fairy tales【童年】childhood【童声】child's voice ～合唱 children's chorus【童心】childlike innocence; childishness【童谣】children's folk rhymes【童贞】virginity【童子】boy; lad

瞳 tóng pupil (of the eye)【瞳孔】pupil 放大～ have one's pupils dilated

统 tǒng ①interconnected system 传～ tradition ②gather into one; unite 由他～管 be under his overall leadership【统舱】steerage【统筹】plan as a whole ～全局 take the whole situation into account and plan accordingly ～规划 overall planning ～兼顾 unified planning with due consideration for all concerned【统共】altogether; in all【统购统销】state monopoly for purchase and marketing【统计】statistics / add up; count 据不完全～ according to incomplete statistics ～出席人数 count up the number of people present (at a meeting, etc.) ～资料 statistical data【统帅】commander (in chief) / command

~部 supreme command 【统率】command 【统统】all; completely; entirely 【统辖】have under one's command; exercise control over; govern 【统一】unify; unite; integrate/unified; unitary ~思想 seek unity of thinking ~行动 act in unison ~领导 unified leadership ~计划 unified planning ~分配 centralized distribution ~的意见 consensus of opinion ~体 entity; unity ~性 unity ~战线 united front 【统治】rule 占~地位 occupy a dominant position ~阶级 ruling class ~者 ruler 【统制】control

捅 tǒng ① poke; stab ~炉子 give the fire a poke ~马蜂窝 stir up a hornets' nest ②disclose; give away 把秘密~出去 let out a secret ~娄子 make a mess of sth.; get into trouble

桶 tǒng tub; pail; bucket; keg; barrel 水~ water bucket 汽油~ petrol drum 一~牛奶 a pail of milk

筒 tǒng ①a section of thick bamboo 竹~ bamboo tube ②a tube-shaped object or part 枪~ barrel of a gun 烟~ chimney 袜~ the leg of a stocking 袖~ sleeve

痛 tòng ①ache; pain 头~ (have a) headache ②sadness 悲~ deep sorrow; grief ③extremely; deeply ~骂 severely scold; scathingly denounce 【痛处】tender spot 【痛感】keenly feel 【痛恨】hate bitterly 【痛觉】sense of pain 【痛哭】cry bitterly; wail 一场~ have a good cry ~流涕 weep bitterly ~失声 be choked with tears 【痛苦】pain; suffering; anguish 精神上的~ mental agony 【痛快】very happy; delighted; joyful/to one's heart's content; to one's great satisfaction/simple and direct; forthright; straightforward 喝个~ drink one's fill 玩个~ have a wonderful time 说话很~ speak simply and directly 他~地答应了 he readily agreed 【痛切】with intense sorrow; most sorrowfully 【痛恶】bitterly detest; abhor 【痛惜】deeply regret; deplore 【痛心】 pained; distressed; grieved

TOU

偷 tōu ①steal; pilfer; make off with 钱包被～ have one's purse stolen ②stealthily; secretly; on the sly ～看 steal a glance; peek; peep ③find (time) 【偷安】 seek temporary ease 【偷工减料】 do shoddy work and use inferior material 【偷懒】 loaf on the job; be lazy 【偷情】 carry on a clandestine love affair 【偷生】 drag out an ignoble existence 【偷税】 evade taxes 【偷偷】 stealthily; secretly; covertly ～地溜走 sneak away ～告诉他 tell him on the quiet 【偷偷摸摸】 furtively; surreptitiously 【偷袭】 sneak attack; surprise attack 【偷闲】 snatch a moment of leisure

头 tóu ①head 从～到脚 from head to foot ②hair 梳～ comb the hair 平～ crew cut ③top; end 山～ hilltop ④beginning or end 从～讲起 tell the story from the very beginning 提个～儿 give sb. a lead ⑤remnant; end 铅笔～ pencil stub 烟～ cigarette end ⑥chief; head ⑦side; aspect 事情不能只顾一一～ we mustn't pay attention to only one aspect of the matter ⑧first 【头版】 front page (of a newspaper) 【头等】 first-class; first-rate ～大事 a major event ～舱 first-class cabin ～品 first-rate goods 【头顶】 the top of the head 【头发】 hair ～夹子 hairpin 【头号】 number one; size one/first-rate ～字 size one type ～大米 top-grade rice 【头昏】 dizzy; giddy 【头角】 brilliance; talent 初露～ begin to show ability or talent 【头巾】 scarf; kerchief 【头里】 in front; ahead/in advance; beforehand 【头面人物】 prominent figure; bigwig 【头目】 head of a gang; ringleader; chieftain 【头脑】 brains; mind 有～ have plenty of brains 不用～ not use one's head 有政治～ be politically-minded 【头皮】 scalp / scurf 【头

生] firstborn 【头套】 actor's headgear 【头疼】 (have a) headache 【头衔】 title 【头像】 head (portrait or sculpture) 【头绪】 main threads (of a complicated affair) ～太多 have too many things to attend to 理出～ get things into shape 【头油】 hair oil 【头子】 chieftain; chief; boss

投 tóu ①throw; fling; hurl ～手榴弹 throw a hand grenade ②put in; drop 把信～进信箱 drop a letter into the letter-box ③throw oneself into (a river, well, etc. to commit suicide) ④send; deliver ⑤fit in with; agree with ～其所好 cater to sb.'s likes 【投案】 give oneself up to the police 【投奔】 go to (a friend or a place) for shelter 【投标】 submit a tender; enter a bid 【投产】 put into production 【投诚】 surrender 【投敌】 go over to the enemy 【投递】 deliver (letters) ～员 postman; letter carrier 【投合】 agree; get along/cater to 脾气～ be quite congenial 【投机】 agreeable/speculate; engage in speculation/ be opportunistic ～分子 opportunist; political speculator ～商 speculator; profiteer 【投考】 sign up for an examination 【投靠】 go and seek refuge with sb. 【投篮】 shoot (a basket) 【投票】 vote; cast a vote ～赞成 vote for ～反对 vote against ～表决 decide by ballot ～箱 ballot box 【投入】 throw into; put into ～生产 put into production 【投宿】 seek temporary lodging; put up for the night 【投降】 surrender; capitulate ～派 capitulators; capitulationist clique 【投资】 invest/money invested 国家～ state investment 智力～ intellectual investment

透 tòu ①penetrate; pass through ②fully; thoroughly 熟～ be quite ripe 湿～ be wet through 【透彻】 penetrating; thorough 有～的了解 have a thorough understanding 【透镜】 lens 【透亮】 bright; transparent / perfectly clear 【透露】 divulge; leak; reveal ～风声 disclose information

【透明】transparent ～度 transparency ～纸 cellophane (paper)【透气】ventilate; let air in / breathe freely【透视】perspective / fluoroscopy ～图 perspective drawing

TU

凸 tū protruding; raised ～面 convex【凸版】relief printing plate ～印刷 letterpress【凸透镜】convex lens

秃 tū ①bald; bare ～山 bare hills ②blunt; without a point 铅笔～了 the pencil is blunt ③incomplete; unsatisfactory【秃顶】bald【秃子】baldhead

突 tū ①dash forward; charge ～入敌阵 charge into enemy positions ②sudden; abrupt ～变 sudden change【突出】protruding; sticking out/prominent/stress ～的岩石 projecting rocks ～的成就 outstanding achievements ～重点 stress the main points ～自己 push oneself forward【突飞猛进】advance by leaps and bounds; make giant strides【突击】assault / do a crash job / shock ～队 shock brigade ～任务 rush job; shock work ～手 shock worker ～战术 shock tactics【突破】make a breakthrough/ surmount; break ～防线 break through a defence line ～难关 break the back of a tough job ～定额 overfulfil a quota ～点 breakthrough point ～口 breach; gap【突起】break out; suddenly appear / rise high; tower 战事～ hostilities broke out 奇峰～ peaks tower magnificently【突然】suddenly; abruptly; unexpectedly ～停止 suddenly stop ～哭起来 burst into tears【突围】break out of an encirclement【突袭】surprise attack

图 tú ①picture; drawing; chart; map 制～ make a drawing or chart 插～ illustration; plate ②scheme; plan; attempt ③pursue; seek ～私利 pursue private ends ～一时痛快 seek momentary satisfaction ④intention; intent

【图案】pattern; design 装饰～ decorative pattern 几何～ geometrical pattern 【图表】chart; diagram; graph 【图钉】drawing pin; thumbtack 【图画】drawing; picture; painting ～纸 drawing paper 【图记】seal; stamp 【图解】diagram; graph; figure / graphic solution ～法 graphic method 【图景】view; prospect 【图例】legend (of a map, etc.); key 【图谋】scheme; conspire ～不轨 hatch a sinister plot 【图片】picture; photograph ～展览 picture exhibition ～说明 caption 【图谱】a collection of illustrative plates; atlas 【图书】books ～资料 books and reference materials ～馆 library ～馆管理员 librarian ～目录 catalogue of books; library catalogue 【图像】picture; image 【图形】graph; figure 【图样】pattern; design; drawing; draft (for a machine, etc.) 【图章】seal; stamp 【图纸】blueprint; drawing (of a building, etc.)

涂 tú ①spread on; apply; smear ～漆 apply a coat of paint; paint ②scribble; scrawl ③blot out ～掉几个字 cross out a few words 【涂层】coat; coating 【涂改】alter ～无效 invalid if altered 【涂料】coating; paint 【涂抹】daub; smear/scribble 【涂脂抹粉】apply powder and paint; prettify 为自己～ try to whitewash oneself

途 tú way; road; route 沿～ along the way ～中 on the way 【途经】by way of; via 【途径】way; channel

徒 tú ①on foot ～涉 wade through; ford ②empty; bare ～手 bare-handed; unarmed ③merely; only ～具形式 be a mere formality ④in vain; to no avail ～费唇舌 waste one's breath ⑤apprentice; pupil 门～ pupil; disciple ⑥follower; believer 佛教～ Buddhist ⑦person; fellow 无耻之～ a shameless person ⑧(prison) sentence; imprisonment 【徒步】on foot ～旅行 travel on foot 【徒弟】apprentice; disciple 【徒工】apprentice 【徒劳】futile

effort; fruitless labour ～往返 make a futile journey
～无功 make a futile effort; work to no avail 【徒然】
in vain; for nothing; to no avail 【徒刑】 imprisonment;
(prison) sentence

屠 tú ①slaughter ②massacre 【屠刀】 butcher's knife 【屠
夫】 butcher/a ruthless ruler 【屠杀】 massacre; butcher

土 tǔ ①soil; earth ～路 dirt road ②land; ground 领一
territory; domain ③local; native ～产 local product
④homemade ～办法 indigenous methods ⑤unrefined; unenlightened 【土崩瓦解】 crumble; fall apart 【土布】 hand-
woven cloth; homespun cloth 【土地】 land; soil/territory
～法 land law ～证 land deed 【土方】 cubic metre of
earth/earthwork/folk recipe 【土匪】 bandit; brigand 【土改】
land reform 【土豪】 local tyrant 【土话】 local, colloquial
expressions; local dialect 【土皇帝】 local despot; local
tyrant 【土货】 local product; native produce 【土牢】 dun-
geon 【土木】 building; construction ～工程 civil engineering ～工程师 civil engineer 【土坯】 sun-dried mud brick;
adobe 【土气】 rustic; uncouth; countrified 【土壤】 soil ～
改良 soil improvement ～结构 soil structure ～学 soil
science ～学家 pedologist 【土人】 natives 【土色】 ashen;
pale 面如～ turn deadly pale 【土星】 Saturn 【土音】 local
accent 【土著】 original inhabitants

吐 tǔ ①spit ～核儿 spit out the pips, stone or pits
～痰 spit; expectorate ～舌头 put out one's tongue
②say; tell; pour out ～实 tell the truth ～怨气 vent one's
grievances 【吐露】 reveal; tell ～真情 unbosom oneself
【吐弃】 spurn; cast aside; reject

吐 tù ①vomit; throw up 恶心要～ feel sick; feel like
vomiting ②give up unwillingly; disgorge (ill-gotten gains) 【吐沫】 saliva; spittle 【吐血】 spitting blood

兔 tù hare; rabbit 【兔死狐悲】 the fox mourns the death of the hare — like grieves for like

TUAN

湍 tuān ①(of a current) rapid; torrential ②rapids; rushing waters 【湍急】 rapid; torrential; swift 水流 ～ the current is swift

团 tuán ①round; circular ～扇 round fan ②sth. shaped like a ball 汤～ boiled rice dumpling ③roll (sth. into a ball) ～药丸 roll pills ④unite; conglomerate ⑤group; society; organization 剧～ drama troupe 代表～ delegation ⑥regiment ⑦the League 入～ join the League ～籍 League membership 【团粉】 cooking starch 【团结】 unite; rally ～就是力量 unity is strength 【团聚】 reunite 全家～ family reunion 【团体】 organization; group; team 群众～ mass organization ～操 group callisthenics ～冠军 team title ～票 group ticket ～赛 team competition 【团团】 round and round; all round ～围住 surround completely; encircle 【团员】 member of a delegation/a member of the Communist Youth League of China; League member 【团圆】 reunion ～饭 family reunion dinner 【团长】 regimental commander/head of a delegation, troupe, etc. 【团子】 dumpling 饭～ rice ball

TUI

推 tuī ①push; shove ～车 push a cart 把门～开 shove the door open ～铅球 put the shot ②turn (a mill or grindstone); grind ③cut; pare ～头 have a haircut or cut sb.'s hair (with clippers) ④push forward; promote; advance ⑤infer; deduce 类～ analogize ⑥push away; shirk; shift ⑦put off; postpone 不能老是往后～

can't put it off day after day ⑧elect; choose 【推测】 infer; conjecture; guess 根据～ by inference 不过是～ mere guesswork 【推陈出新】 weed through the old to bring forth the new 【推迟】 put off; postpone; defer 【推崇】 hold in esteem 【推辞】 decline (an appointment, invitation, etc.) 【推倒】 push over; overturn / repudiate; cancel; reverse 【推动】 promote; give impetus to ～工作 push the work forward ～社会向前发展 propel the society forward ～力 motive force 【推断】 infer; deduce 作出正确的～ draw a correct inference 【推翻】 overthrow; overturn; topple/cancel; reverse ～协议 repudiate an agreement ～原定计划 cancel the original plan 【推广】 popularize; spread; extend ～先进经验 spread advanced experience 【推荐】 recommend ～文学作品 recommend literary works 【推进】 push on; carry forward; advance; give impetus to/ move forward; push; drive ～力 driving power ～器 propeller 【推究】 examine; study 【推举】 elect; choose/ press 【推理】 inference; reasoning 【推力】 thrust 【推论】 inference, deduction; corollary; weigh; deliberate ～词句 weigh one's words; seek the right word 经过反复～ after repeated deliberation 经得起～ can stand close scrutiny 【推求】 inquire into; ascertain 【推却】 refuse decline 【推让】 decline (a position, favour, etc. out of modesty) 【推三阻四】 decline with all sorts of excuses 【推算】 calculate; reckon 【推土机】 bulldozer 【推推搡搡】 push and shove 【推托】 offer as an excuse 【推想】 imagine; guess 【推销】 market; peddle ～商品 promote the sale of goods ～员 salesman 【推卸】 shirk (responsibility) 【推行】 carry out; pursue; practise ～新的政策 pursue a new policy ～经济责任制 introduce the system of economic responsibility 【推选】 elect; choose 【推移】 (of time) elapse; pass / develop; evolve 随着时间的～ as time goes on【推重】have a high regard for【推子】hair-clippers

颓 tuí ①ruined; dilapidated ～垣断壁 crumbling walls and dilapidated houses ②declining; decadent 衰～ on the decline ③dejected【颓废】dispirited ～情绪 decadent sentiments ～派 the decadents【颓丧】listless【颓势】declining tendency 挽回～ turn the tide in one's favour

腿 tuǐ ①leg 大～ thigh 小～ shank ～勤 tireless in running around ②a leglike support 桌子～ legs of a table【腿肚子】calf (of the leg)【腿腕子】ankle

退 tuì ①move back; retreat ～了几步 step back a few paces ～一步说 even if that is so; even so ②cause to move back; remove ～敌 repulse the enemy ～子弹 unload a gun ③withdraw from; quit ～党 withdraw from a political party ④decline; recede; ebb 潮水～了 the tide has receded ⑤fade ⑥return; give back; refund ～礼 return the gift ～货 return merchandise ～钱 refund ⑦cancel; break off【退避】withdraw and keep off; keep out of the way【退兵】retreat; withdrawal/force the enemy to retreat【退步】lag behind; retrogress/room for manoeuvre 留～ leave some leeway【退潮】ebb tide【退出】withdraw from; secede; quit ～战斗 withdraw from action ～会场 walk out of a meeting ～组织 withdraw from an organization ～比赛 withdraw from a competition; scratch【退化】degeneration/degenerate; deteriorate; retrograde【退还】return ～公物 return public property【退换】replace a purchase【退回】return; give back/go back 原稿已经～ the manuscript has been sent back【退婚】break off an engagement【退伙】withdraw from a mess【退路】route of retreat/leeway【退票】return a ticket; get a refund for a ticket【退坡】fall off; backslide

【退却】withdraw/shrink back; flinch 【退让】make a concession; yield; give in 决不～一步 never yield an inch 【退色】fade 这种布～吗 will this cloth fade 【退烧】bring down a fever/come down 他已经～了 his fever is gone ～药 antipyretic 【退缩】shrink back 【退位】abdicate 【退伍】be demobilized; leave the army ～军人 demobilized soldier; veteran 【退席】leave a banquet or a meeting/walk out (in protest, etc.) 【退休】retire ～工人 retired worker ～金 retirement pay; pension ～年龄 retirement age 【退学】leave school; discontinue one's schooling 因病～ leave school owing to bad health 勒令～ order to quit school 【退役】retire or be released from military service (on completing the term of reserve) ～军官 retired officer ～军人 ex-serviceman 【退隐】go into retirement 【退赃】give up ill-gotten gains 【退职】resign or be discharged from office; quit working

蜕 tuì ①slough off; exuviate; moult ②exuviae 蛇～ snake slough 【蜕变】change qualitatively; transform; transmute/decay 【蜕化】slough off; exuviate/degenerate

裉 tuì ①take off (clothes); shed (feathers) ②(of colour) fade

TUN

吞 tūn ①swallow; gulp down ～药丸 swallow the pills 一口～掉 devour in one gulp ②take possession of; annex 独～ take exclusive possession of 【吞并】annex; gobble up 【吞没】embezzle/swallow up; engulf ～巨款 misappropriate a huge sum 被波浪～ be engulfed in the waves 【吞声】gulp down one's sobs 【吞噬】swallow; gobble up; engulf 【吞吐】swallow and spit — take in and send out in large quantities ～量 handling capacity (of a harbour) 【吞吞吐吐】 hesitate in speech

屯 tún ①collect; store up ~粮 store up grain ～聚 assemble; collect ②station (troops); quarter

囤 tún store up; hoard ～货 store goods 【囤积】 hoard for speculation; corner (the market) ～小麦 corner the wheat market ～居奇 hoarding and cornering

豚 tún ①suckling pig ②pig 【豚鼠】 guinea pig; cavy

臀 tún buttocks 【臀部】 buttocks 在～打一针 give or have an injection in the buttock

氽 tǔn ①float; drift ②deep-fry 油～花生米 fried peanuts

褪 tùn slip out of sth. ～下一只袖子 slip one's arm out of one's sleeve

TUO

托 tuō ①hold in the palm; support with the hand or palm ～着盘子 hold a tray on one's palm ②sth. serving as a support 枪～ the stock of a rifle, etc. ③serve as a foil; set off ④ask; entrust ～人订票 ask sb. to book a ticket for one ～人照看孩子 leave a child in sb.'s care ⑤plead; give as a pretext ～病 plead illness ⑥rely upon; owe to 【托词】 find a pretext; make an excuse/pretext; excuse; subterfuge ～谢绝 decline on some pretext 【托儿所】 nursery; child-care centre; crèche 【托付】 entrust; commit sth. to sb.'s care 【托拉斯】 trust 【托盘】 (serving) tray 【托名】 do sth. in sb. else's name 【托人情】 gain one's end through pull; seek the good offices of sb. 【托运】 consign for shipment; check 你的行李～了吗 have you checked your baggage 【托子】 base; support

拖 tuō ①pull; drag; haul ~出箱子 drag a trunk out ~地板 mop the floor ~人下水 get sb. into hot water ~住敌人 pin down the enemy ②delay; drag on; procrastinate 【拖把】 mop 【拖车】 trailer 【拖带】 traction; pulling; towing 【拖拉】 dilatory; slow; sluggish 办事~ be dilatory in doing things ~作风 dilatory style of work 【拖拉机】 tractor ~厂 tractor plant ~手 tractor driver ~站 tractor station 【拖累】 encumber; be a burden on/implicate; involve 受家务~ be tied down by household chores 【拖轮】 tugboat; tug; towboat 【拖泥带水】 messy; sloppy; slovenly 【拖欠】 be behind in payment; be in arrears; default 【拖网】 trawlnet; trawl; dragnet ~渔船 trawler 【拖鞋】 slippers 【拖延】 delay; put off; procrastinate ~时间 play for time; stall (for time)

脱 tuō ①(of hair, skin) shed; come off 头发~光了 lose all one's hair ②take off; cast off ~鞋 take off one's shoes ③escape from; get out of ~险 escape danger ④miss (out) 这儿~一行 a line is missing here 【脱班】 be late for work/(of a bus, train, etc.) be behind schedule 【脱产】 be released from production or one's regular work (to take on other duties or for study) ~干部 a cadre not engaged in production 【脱党】 quit a political party; give up party membership 【脱缰之马】 a runaway horse — uncontrollable; running wild 【脱节】 come apart; be disjointed; be out of line with 理论与实践不能~ theory must not be divorced from practice 【脱口而出】 say sth. unwittingly; blurt out; let slip 【脱离】 separate oneself from; break away from ~群众 be divorced from the masses ~队伍 drop out of the ranks ~实际 lose contact with reality ~关系 break off relations; cut ties ~危险 be out of danger 【脱粒】 threshing/

shelling ～机 thresher 【脱漏】 be left out; be omitted; be missing ～一针 drop a stitch (in knitting) 【脱落】 drop; fall off; come off 【脱毛】 lose hair or feathers; moult; shed 【脱帽】 raise one's hat (in respect) ～致敬 take off one's hat in salutation 【脱期】 fail to come out on time 【脱手】 slip out of the hand/get off one's hands; dispose of; sell 不好～ be difficult to dispose of 【脱水】 loss of body fluids/dehydration ～蔬菜 dehydrated vegetables 【脱胎】 emerge from the womb of; be born out of ～换骨 be reborn; cast off one's old self 【脱险】 escape danger; be out of danger 【脱销】 out of stock 书～了 the book is sold out 【脱脂】 de-fat; degrease ～棉 absorbent cotton ～奶粉 de-fatted milk powder; nonfat dried milk

驮 tuó carry on the back 【驮畜】 pack animal 【驮筐】 pannier 【驮马】 pack horse

陀 tuó 【陀螺】 top 抽～ whip a top ～仪 gyroscope; gyro

驼 tuó ①camel ②hunchbacked 【驼背】 hunchback 【驼绒】 camel's hair/camel hair cloth 【驼色】 light tan

鸵 tuó 【鸵鸟】 ostrich ～政策 ostrich policy; ostrichism

妥 tuǒ ①appropriate; proper 欠～ not proper; not quite satisfactory 请～为保存 please look after it carefully ②ready; settled; finished 款已备～ the money is ready 事已办～ the matter has been settled 【妥当】 appropriate; proper 【妥善】 proper; well arranged ～安排 make appropriate arrangements 需要～处理 need careful and skilful handling 【妥协】 come to terms; compromise

椭 tuǒ 【椭圆】 ellipse

拓 tuò open up; develop 【拓荒】 open up virgin soil; reclaim wasteland ～者 pioneer; pathbreaker

唾 tuò ①saliva; spittle ②spit 【唾骂】 spit on and curse; revile 【唾沫】 saliva; spittle 【唾弃】 cast aside; spurn 【唾手可得】 extremely easy to obtain 【唾液】 saliva

W

WA

洼 wā ①hollow ②low-lying area 水～ a waterlogged depression 【洼地】 depression; low-lying land

挖 wā dig; excavate ～井 dig a well ～隧道 excavate a tunnel ～塘泥 scoop up sludge from a pond ～根 uproot 【挖补】 mend by replacing a damaged part 【挖沟】 ditch; trench 【挖掘】 excavate; unearth ～古物 excavate ancient relics ～地下宝藏 unearth buried treasure ～潜力 tap the latent power 【挖苦】 speak sarcastically or ironically ～话 ironical remarks; verbal thrusts 【挖泥船】 dredger; dredge 【挖墙脚】 undermine the foundation; cut the ground from under sb.'s feet

蛙 wā frog 【蛙人】 frogman 【蛙式打夯机】 frog rammer 【蛙泳】 breaststroke

娃 wá ①baby; child ②newborn animal 鸡～ chick 猪～ piglet

瓦 wǎ ①tile ②made of baked clay ～器 earthenware 【瓦房】 tile-roofed house 【瓦工】 bricklaying, tiling or plastering/bricklayer; tiler; plasterer 【瓦解】 disintegrate 敌军全线～ the whole enemy front crumbled 【瓦砾】 rubble debris 【瓦斯】 gas ～爆炸 gas explosion

瓦 wà cover (a roof) with tiles; tile 【瓦刀】(brick-layer's) cleaver

袜 wà socks; stockings; hose 【袜带】suspenders; garters 【袜套】socks; ankle socks 【袜筒】the leg of a stocking

WAI

歪 wāi ①askew; aslant; inclined; slanting ～戴帽子 have one's hat on crooked ～着头 with one's head tilted to one side ②devious; underhand 【歪风】evil wind; unhealthy trend 打击～ combat evil trends 【歪曲】dis-tort; misrepresent; twist ～事实 distort the facts

外 wài ①outer; outward; outside ～屋 outer room 窗～ outside the window ②other ～省 other provinces ③foreign; external ～商 foreign merchants ④(relatives) of one's mother, sisters or daughters ～孙 daughter's son; grandson ⑤not of the same organization, class, etc.; not closely related 见～ regard sb. as an outsider 电话不～借 this telephone is not for public use ⑥in addition; beyond 此～ besides; into the bargain ⑦unofficial (biography) 【外币】foreign currency 【外边】outside; out/exterior 到～散步 go out for a walk 上～去谈 let's go outside to talk ～工作 work somewhere away from home 【外表】out-ward appearance; exterior; surface 【外宾】foreign guest 【外部】outside; external / exterior 【外层空间】outer space 【外敷】apply (ointment, etc.) ～药 medicine for exter-nal application 【外国】foreign country ～朋友 foreign friends 到～学习 go abroad to study ～人 foreigner ～语 foreign language 【外行】layman; nonprofessional / lay; unprofessional ～话 lay language 【外号】nickname 【外患】foreign aggression 【外汇】foreign exchange ～兑换率 rate of exchange ～官价 official exchange rate ～管理 exchange control ～行情 exchange quotations ～交易 foreign exchange transaction 【外货】 foreign goods 【外籍】 foreign nationality ～工作人员 foreign personnel 【外加】 more; additional; extra 【外间】 outer room/the external world; outside circles 【外交】 diplomacy; foreign affairs 大使级 ～关系 diplomatic relations at ambassadorial level ～部 the Ministry of Foreign Affairs ～部长 Foreign Minister ～官 diplomat ～信使 diplomatic courier ～政策 foreign policy 【外界】 the external world/outside 【外景】 outdoor scene; exterior 拍摄～ film the exterior; shoot a scene on location 【外科】 surgical department ～病房 surgical ward ～手术 surgical operation ～学 surgery ～医生 surgeon 【外壳】 shell; case 热水瓶～ the outer casing of a thermos flask 【外快】 extra income 【外来】 outside; external; foreign ～干涉 outside interference ～人 a person from another place; nonnative ～语 word of foreign origin; foreign word; loanword 【外力】 outside force/external force 【外流】 outflow; drain 黄金～ gold bullion outflow 【外贸】 foreign trade; external trade ～部 the Ministry of Foreign Trade 【外貌】 appearance; exterior; looks 【外面】 outward appearance; exterior; surface/outside; out 搬到～去 take sth. out 今天在～吃饭 eat out today 【外婆】 (maternal) grandmother 【外侨】 foreign national; alien 【外勤】 work done outside the office or in the field/field personnel 【外人】 stranger; outsider/foreigner; alien 【外伤】 an injury or wound; trauma 【外甥】 sister's son; nephew 【外甥女】 sister's daughter; niece 【外事】 foreign affairs 【外孙】 daughter's son; grandson 【外孙女】 daughter's daughter; granddaughter 【外胎】 tyre (cover) 【外逃】 flee to some other place/flee the country 【外套】 overcoat/loose coat; outer garment 【外头】 outside; out 【外围】 periphery ～

防线 outer defence line ~组织 peripheral organization 【外文】 foreign language 【外侮】 foreign aggression 【外线】 exterior lines / outside (telephone) connections 【外乡】 another part of the country; some other place ~口音 a nonlocal accent 【外向】 extroversion 【外销】 for sale abroad or in another part of the country ~产品 products for export; articles for sale in other areas 【外形】 appearance; external form 【外衣】 coat; jacket; outer clothing; outer garment / semblance; appearance; garb 【外因】 external cause 【外用】 external use; external application ~药水 lotion 只能~ for external use only 【外语】 foreign language ~教学 foreign language teaching ~学院 institute of foreign languages 【外域】 foreign lands 【外援】 foreign aid; outside help 【外在】 extrinsic; external 【外债】 external debt; foreign debt 【外资】 foreign capital 【外族】 people not of the same clan/foreigner; alien/other nationalities 【外祖父】 (maternal) grandfather 【外祖母】 (maternal) grandmother

WAN

弯 wān ①curved; tortuous; crooked 一~新月 a crescent moon ②bend; flex ~弓 bend a bow ~着腰插秧 bend over to transplant rice ③curve; bend 拐~ turn a corner 【弯路】 crooked road; tortuous path / roundabout way 少走~ avoid detours 工作走了~ take a roundabout course in one's work 【弯曲】 winding; meandering; zigzag; curved ~的小道 a winding path 【弯子】 turn

剜 wān cut out; gouge out; scoop out

湾 wān ①a bend in a stream 河~ river bend ②gulf; bay ③cast anchor; moor

蜿 wān 【蜿蜒】 ①(of snakes, etc.) wriggle ②wind; zigzag; meander

豌 wān 【豌豆】 pea ～黄 pea flour cake

丸 wán ①ball; pellet 泥～ mud ball ②pill; bolus 每服两～ take two pills each time 【丸药】 pill of Chinese medicine 【丸子】 a round mass of food; ball / pill

纨 wán fine silk fabrics 【纨袴子弟】 profligate son of the rich; fop; dandy; playboy 【纨扇】 round silk fan

完 wán ①intact; whole ～好 in good condition; intact ②run out; use up 听～别人的话 hear sb. out 信纸用～了 the writing pad is used up ③finish; complete; be over; be through 会开～了 the meeting is over ④pay (taxes) 【完备】 complete; perfect 指出不～之处 point out the imperfections 【完毕】 finish; complete; end 一切准备～ everything is ready 【完成】 complete; bring to success ～任务 accomplish a task ～计划 fulfil the plan ～生产指标 fulfil the production quota 【完蛋】 be done for; be finished 【完稿】 complete the manuscript 【完工】 complete a project, etc.; finish doing sth.; get through 【完婚】 (of a man) get married; marry 【完结】 end; be over; finish 事情并没有～ this is not the end of the matter 【完满】 satisfactory; successful ～的解决办法 a satisfactory solution 【完美】 perfect; consummate ～无疵 flawless ～无缺 leave nothing to be desired 【完全】 complete; whole / fully; entirely ～错了 be completely wrong ～不同 be totally different ～相反 be the exact opposite ～正确 perfectly right; absolutely correct ～同意 fully agree with 【完人】 perfect man 【完事】 finish; get through; come to an end 你～了没有 have you finished (the job) 【完整】 complete; integrated; intact ～的工业体系 a comprehensive industrial system

玩 wán ①play; have fun; amuse oneself ～牌 play cards 真好～ that's great fun 说着～儿的 say it for fun; be only joking ②employ; resort to ～手段 play tricks ③treat lightly ～法 trifle with the law ④enjoy; appreciate ～月 enjoy looking at the moon ～邮票 make a hobby of collecting stamps ⑤object for appreciation 【玩忽】 trifle with; neglect (of duty) 【玩火】 play with fire ～自焚 whoever plays with fire will perish by fire 【玩具】 toy; plaything ～汽车 toy car ～店 toyshop 【玩弄】 dally with (women) / play with; juggle with / resort to; employ ～词句 juggle with words; go in for rhetoric ～花招 employ some tricks 【玩偶】 doll; toy figurine 【玩命】 play with one's life; risk one's life needlessly 【玩赏】 enjoy; take pleasure in ～风景 admire the scenery 【玩世不恭】 be cynical 【玩味】 ponder; ruminate 值得～ be worth pondering 【玩物】 plaything; toy ～丧志 riding a hobby saps one's will to make progress 【玩笑】 joke; jest 开～ play a joke on; make jests

顽 wán ①stupid; dense ～石 hard rock; insensate stone ②stubborn; obstinate ～敌 stubborn enemy 【顽固】 obstinate; stubborn; headstrong/die-hard ～不化 incorrigibly obstinate ～分子 diehard; die-hard element ～派 the diehards 【顽抗】 stubbornly resist 【顽皮】 naughty; mischievous 【顽强】 indomitable; staunch 进行～的斗争 carry on a tenacious struggle against sth. 【顽童】 naughty child; urchin 【顽症】 persistent ailment

宛 wǎn winding; tortuous 【宛然】 as if 【宛如】 just like 【宛延】 meander

挽 wǎn ①draw; pull 手～着手 arm in arm ②roll up ～起袖子 roll up one's sleeves ③lament sb.'s death

①coil up 【挽歌】dirge; elegy 【挽回】retrieve; redeem ～败局 retrieve a defeat ～面子 save face ～劣势 improve one's position ～损失 retrieve a loss ～影响 redeem one's reputation 无可～ irredeemable; irretrievable 【挽救】save; remedy; rescue ～病人的生命 save the patient's life 有效的～办法 an effective remedy 【挽联】elegiac couplet 【挽留】urge sb. to stay 【挽马】draught horse

惋

wǎn sigh 【惋惜】feel sorry for sb. or about sth.; sympathize with

晚

wǎn ①evening; night 今～ this evening; tonight ②far on in time; late 睡得～ go to bed late ～做总比不做好 better late than never 【晚安】good night 【晚班】night shift 【晚报】evening paper 【晚辈】the younger generation; one's juniors 【晚场】evening show; evening performance 【晚车】night train 【晚稻】late rice 【晚点】(of a train, ship, etc.) late; behind schedule 火车～了 the train is late 【晚饭】supper; dinner 【晚会】soiree; social evening; evening party 【晚婚】marry at a mature age 提倡～ favour late marriage 【晚节】integrity in one's later years 【晚景】evening scene / one's circumstances in old age 【晚年】old age; one's remaining years 【晚期】later period ～作品 sb.'s later works 【晚秋】late autumn ～作物 late-autumn crops 【晚上】(in the) evening; (at) night 【晚熟】late-maturing ～品种 late variety 【晚霞】sunset glow; sunset clouds

婉

wǎn ①gentle; gracious; tactful ～商 consult with sb. tactfully ～顺 complaisant; obliging ②beautiful; graceful; elegant ～丽 lovely 【婉辞】gentle words; euphemism/graciously decline; politely refuse 【婉言】tactful expressions ～相劝 gently persuade ～谢绝 graciously decline; politely refuse 【婉转】mild and indirect; tactful/

sweet and agreeable 措词~ put it tactfully 歌喉~ a sweet voice; sweet singing

辁 wǎn ①pull; draw ~车 pull a cart or carriage ② lament sb.'s death【辁歌】dirge【辁联】elegiac couplet

绻 wǎn coil up 把头发~起来 coil one's hair ~个扣儿 tie a knot

碗 wǎn bowl 摆~筷 put out bowls and chopsticks for a meal; lay the table

万 wàn ①ten thousand ② a very great number ~里长空 vast clear skies ③absolutely; by all means ~不得已 out of absolute necessity; as a last resort【万般】all the different kinds/utterly; extremely ~无奈 have no alternative (but to)【万端】multifarious 变化~ kaleidoscopic changes【万恶】extremely evil; absolutely vicious ~的旧社会 the vicious old society ~之源 the root of all evil【万分】very much; extremely【万古】through the ages; eternally; forever ~长存 last forever; be everlasting ~长青 remain fresh forever【万花筒】kaleidoscope【万籁俱寂】all is quiet; silence reigns supreme【万难】extremely difficult; utterly impossible/all difficulties ~ 照办 impossible to do as requested ~同意 can by no means agree【万能】omnipotent; all-powerful/universal ~胶 all-purpose adhesive【万年】ten thousand years; all ages; eternity ~历 perpetual calendar【万千】multifarious; myriad 变化~ eternally changing【万全】perfectly sound; surefire ~之计 a surefire plan【万世】all ages; generation after generation【万事】all things; everything ~大吉 everything is just fine ~亨通 everything goes well ~通 know-all【万万】absolutely; wholly/hundred million【万无一失】no risk at all【万象】every phenomenon on earth; all manifestations of nature【万

幸】 very lucky 【万一】 just in case; if by any chance

腕

wàn　wrist

蔓

wàn　a tendrilled vine

WANG

汪

wāng　(of liquid) collect; accumulate 【汪洋】 (of a body of water) vast; boundless (ocean)

亡

wáng　①flee; run away 出～ flee; live in exile ② lose; be gone ③die; perish 阵～ fall in battle ④deceased ～妻 deceased wife ⑤conquer; subjugate 【亡故】 die; pass away; decease 【亡国】 subjugate a nation; let a state perish/a conquered nation ～奴 a slave without a country; a conquered people 【亡命】 flee; seek refuge; go into exile/desperate ～之徒 desperado

王

wáng　king; monarch 【王朝】 imperial court; royal court/dynasty 【王储】 crown prince 【王道】 kingly way; benevolent government 【王法】 the law of the land; the law 【王宫】 (imperial) palace 【王冠】 imperial crown; royal crown 【王国】 kingdom/realm; domain 独立～ independent kingdom; private preserve 【王后】 queen (consort) 【王浆】 royal jelly 【王牌】 trump card ～军 elite troops; crack units 【王室】 royal family / imperial court; royal court 【王位】 throne 【王子】 king's son; prince

网

wǎng　①net 鱼～ fishnet ②network 铁路～ railway network ③catch with a net ～着了一条鱼 net a fish 【网兜】 string bag 【网篮】 a basket with netting on top 【网罗】 a net for catching fish or birds; trap / enlist the services of ～人材 enlist able men 【网球】 tennis/tennis ball ～场 tennis court ～拍 tennis racket 【网眼】 mesh

枉 wǎng ①crooked 矫～ straighten sth. crooked; right a wrong ②twist; pervert ～法 pervert the law ③treat unjustly; wrong ～死 be wronged and driven to death 【枉费】 waste; try in vain; be of no avail ～唇舌 be a mere waste of breath ～心机 rack one's brains in vain; scheme without avail 【枉然】 in vain; to no purpose

往 wǎng ①go 来来～ coming and going ②in the direction of; toward ～东走 go in an eastward direction ③past; previous ～事 the past 【往常】 habitually in the past ～不这样 be not like that before 【往返】 go there and back; journey to and fro 【往复】 move back and forth; reciprocate 【往还】 contact; dealings; intercourse 【往来】 come and go/contact; dealings 贸易～ trade contacts 友好～ friendly intercourse ～密切 be in close contact ～帐 current account 【往年】 (in) former years 【往日】 (in) former days 【往事】 past events; the past 回忆～ recollections of the past 【往往】 often; frequently

惘 wǎng feel frustrated; feel disappointed 【惘然】 frustrated; disappointed ～若失 feel lost

妄 wàng ①absurd; preposterous ②presumptuous; rash ～加评论 make improper comments 【妄动】 (take) rash action 【妄念】 wild fancy; improper thought 【妄求】 inappropriate request 【妄图】 try in vain; vainly attempt 【妄想】 vain hope 【妄自菲薄】 unduly humble oneself

忘 wàng ①forget; dismiss from one's mind 把这事全～了 forget all about it ②overlook; neglect 别～了锁门 don't omit locking the door 别～了给我打电话 don't forget to phone me ～了开钟 neglect to wind the clock 【忘本】 forget one's class origin; forget one's past suffering 【忘恩负义】 devoid of gratitude; ungrateful 【忘乎所以】 forget oneself; be carried away 【忘我】 oblivious of oneself; selfless ～地工作 work selflessly

旺 wàng prosperous; flourishing 购销两～ both purchasing and marketing are brisk 人畜两～ both men and livestock are flourishing 【旺季】 peak period; busy season 【旺盛】 vigorous; exuberant 士气～ have high morale ～的生命力 exuberant vitality

往 wǎng to; toward ～左拐 turn to the left ～前看 look forward 【往后】 from now on; later on

望 wàng ①gaze into the distance; look over ～了他一眼 shoot a glance at him ②call on; visit 拜～ call to pay one's respects ③hope; expect ～速归 hoping you'll return as soon as possible ～回信 awaiting your reply ④reputation; prestige 【望尘莫及】 too far behind to catch up; too inferior to bear comparison 【望而生畏】 be terrified by the sight of 【望风】 be on the lookout; keep watch ～而逃 flee at the mere sight of the oncoming force 【望远镜】 telescope; opera glasses

WEI

危 wēi ①danger; peril ②endanger; imperil ～及生命 endanger one's life ③dying 病～ be critically ill; be dying 【危害】 harm; endanger ～革命 endanger the revolution ～治安 jeopardize public security ～公共利益 harm the public interest ～性 harmfulness; perniciousness 【危机】 crisis ～重重 bogged down in crises ～四伏 beset with crises; crisis-ridden 【危急】 critical; in imminent danger; in a desperate situation ～关头 critical time 情况～ the situation is desperate 伤势～ the wound may be fatal 【危局】 a dangerous situation 【危难】 danger and disaster; calamity 【危亡】 in peril; at stake 【危险】 dangerous; perilous 冒生命～ at the risk of one's life 有生

命～ be in jeopardy of one's life 脱离～ out of danger
～品 dangerous articles ～人物 a dangerous person

威 wēi ①impressive strength; might; power 军～ the
might of an army ②by force【威逼】threaten by force;
coerce; intimidate ～利诱 alternate intimidation and bri-
bery【威风】power and prestige/imposing; impressive ～凛
凛 majestic-looking; awe-inspiring ～扫地 with every
shred of one's prestige swept away — completely dis-
credited【威名】prestige; renown【威权】authority; power
【威慑】terrorize with military force; deter ～力量 deter-
rent (force)【威士忌】whisky【威势】power and influ-
ence【威望】prestige【威武】might; force; power / powerful; mighty ～不能屈 not to be subdued by force ～雄
壮 full of power and grandeur【威胁】threaten; menace
～世界和平 imperil world peace【威信】prestige; popular
trust【威严】dignified; stately; majestic/prestige; dignity

逶 wēi【逶迤】winding; meandering

萎 wēi decline 火～了 the fire is going out

偎 wēi snuggle up to; lean close to【偎抱】hug; cud-
dle【偎依】lean close to

煨 wēi ①cook over a slow fire; stew; simmer ～牛肉
stewed beef ②roast in fresh cinders

微 wēi ①minute; tiny微甚 相差甚 the difference is slight
～雨 drizzle ～风 gentle breeze ②profound; abstruse
精～ subtle ③decline 衰～ on the decline【微薄】meagre;
little; scanty 收入～ have a meagre income【微不足
道】not worth mentioning; insignificant【微观】micro-
cosmic ～世界 microcosmos【微乎其微】very little; next
to nothing【微贱】humble; lowly【微妙】delicate; sub-

tle 关系～ subtle relations 谈判进入～阶段 the negotiations have entered a delicate stage 【微末】 trifling;
insignificant 【微弱】 faint; feeble; weak 呼吸～ faint
breath 脉搏～ feeble pulse ～的多数 a slender majority
【微生物】 microorganism; microbe ～学 microbiology 【微
微】 slight; faint 一～笑 smile faintly 【微细】 very small
【微小】 small; little 【微笑】 smile 【微型】 miniature; mini-
～汽车 minicar; mini ～照相机 miniature camera

巍 wēi towering; lofty 【巍峨】 towering; lofty

为 wéi ①do; act 敢作敢～ act with daring ②act as;
serve as 以此～凭 this will serve as a proof ③become 一分～二 one divides into two ④be; mean ⑤by ～
人民所爱戴 be loved and respected by the people 【为非
作歹】 do evil; commit crimes 【为富不仁】 be rich and
cruel 【为难】 feel embarrassed; feel awkward/make things
difficult for 【为期】 (to be completed) by a definite date
～一个月 last a month 【为人】 behave; conduct oneself
～正直 be upright 【为生】 make a living 【为时过早】 premature; too early; too soon 【为首】 with sb. as the leader; headed by 【为数】 amount to; number ～不少 come
up to a large number ～不多 have only a small number
【为所欲为】 do as one pleases; do whatever one likes 【为
伍】 associate with 【为限】 be within the limit of; not exceed 【为止】 up to; till 迄今～ up to now; so far

违 wéi ①disobey; violate ～令 disobey orders ～警
violation of police regulations ②be separated 久～了
I haven't seen you for ages 【违碍】 taboo; prohibition
【违背】 violate; go against ～原则 violate a principle
～自己的诺言 go back on one's word ～事实 be contrary to the facts 【违法】 break the law; be illegal

~乱纪 violate the law and discipline ~行为 illegal activities 【违反】transgress ~劳动纪律 violate labour discipline ~决议的精神 be contrary to the spirit of the resolution 【违犯】violate; infringe; act contrary to ~纪律 breach of discipline 【违禁】violate a ban ~品 contraband (goods) 【违抗】disobey (orders, etc.); defy (one's superiors, etc.) 【违心】against one's will ~之论 obviously insincere talk 【违约】break a contract/break one's promise 【违章】break rules and regulations ~行驶 drive against traffic regulations

围 wéi ①enclose; surround ~炉而坐 sit around a fire ②all round; around 四~都是山 there are mountains all round 【围城】encircle a city/besieged city 【围攻】besiege; lay siege to/jointly attack sb. 遭~ come under attack from all sides 【围歼】surround and annihilate 【围剿】encircle and suppress 【围巾】muffler; scarf 【围困】hem in; pin down 【围拢】crowd around 【围棋】weiqi; go 【围墙】enclosure; enclosing wall 【围裙】apron 【围绕】round; around/centre on; revolve round

桅 wéi mast 【桅灯】mast head light; range light/barn lantern

惟 wéi ①only; alone ~你是问 you'll be held personally responsible ②but 【惟恐】for fear that; lest ~落后 for fear that one should lag behind ~天下不乱 desire to see the world plunged into chaos; desire to stir up trouble 【惟利是图】be bent solely on profit; be intent on nothing but profit ~的思想 profit-before-everything mentality 【惟一】only; sole ~合法的政府 the sole legitimate government ~出路 the only way out

唯 wéi only; alone 【唯物辩证法】materialist dialectics 【唯物论】materialism 【唯物史观】materialist conception of history; historical materialism【唯物主义】materialism【唯心论】idealism【唯心史观】idealist conception of history; historical idealism【唯心主义】idealism

维 wéi ①tie up; hold together ~系 maintain ②safeguard; preserve; maintain; defend; uphold ③thinking; thought【维持】keep; maintain, preserve ~秩序 keep order ~现状 maintain the *status quo*; let things go on as they are ~生活 support oneself or one's family【维护】safeguard; defend ~团结 uphold unity ~人民的利益 safeguard the people's interests ~国家主权 defend state sovereignty【维妙维肖】remarkably true to life; absolutely lifelike【维尼纶】vinylon【维生素】vitamin【维新】reform; modernization【维修】keep in (good) repair ~房屋 maintain houses and buildings ~汽车 service a car 设备~ maintenance of equipment ~费 maintenance cost; upkeep ~工 maintenance worker

伪 wěi ①false; fake; bogus ~证 false witness ~钞 forged bank note ~科学 pseudoscience ②puppet; collaborationist ~政权 puppet regime【伪币】counterfeit money; forged bank note/money issued by a puppet government【伪军】puppet army or soldier【伪君子】hypocrite【伪善】hypocritical ~的言词 hypocritical words ~者 hypocrite【伪造】forge; falsify ~签名 forge a signature ~证件 forge a certificate ~帐目 falsify accounts ~历史 fabricate history【伪装】pretend; feign/guise; mask/camouflage ~进步 pretend to be progressive ~中立 feign neutrality ~工事 camouflage works

伟 wěi big; great ~力 mighty force【伟大】great; mighty ~的胜利 a signal victory【伟绩】great feats; great exploits; brilliant achievements【伟人】a great man【伟业】great cause

苇 wěi reed 【苇箔】reed matting 【苇塘】reed pond 【苇席】reed mat

纬 wěi ①weft; woof ②latitude 北～四十度 forty degrees north latitude

尾 wěi ①tail 牛～ ox-tail ②end 排～ (a person) standing at the end of a line ③remaining part; remnant 扫～工程 the final phase of a project 【尾巴】tail 飞机～ the tail of a plane 甩掉～ throw off one's tail 【尾声】coda/epilogue/end 会谈已接近～ the talks are drawing to an end 【尾数】odd amount in addition to the round number 【尾随】tail behind; tag along after 【尾追】hot on the trail of

委 wěi ①entrust; appoint ～以重任 entrust sb. with an important task ②throw away; cast aside ～弃 discard ③shift ～过于人 put the blame on sb. else ④indirect; roundabout 【委顿】tired; exhausted; weary 【委靡】listless; dispirited ～不振 in low spirits; dejected and apathetic 【委派】appoint; delegate; designate 【委屈】feel wronged; nurse a grievance / put sb. to great inconvenience 你只好～一点 you'll have to put up with it 对不起,～你了 sorry to have made you go through all this 【委任】appoint ～状 certificate of appointment 【委托】entrust; trust 这事就～你了 I leave this matter in your hands ～商店 commission shop; commission house 【委婉】mild and roundabout; tactful ～的语气 a mild tone ～语 euphemism 【委员】committee member ～会 committee; commission; council

娓 wěi 【娓娓】(talk) tirelessly ～动听 speak with absorbing interest ～而谈 talk volubly

萎 wěi wither; wilt; fade 【萎缩】wither; shrivel / (of a market; economy, etc.) shrink; sag

唯 wěi yea 【唯唯诺诺】 be a yes-man; be obsequious

猥 wěi ①numerous; multifarious ②base; obscene; salacious; indecent 【猥贱】 lowly; humble 【猥亵】 obscene; salacious / act indecently towards (a woman)

卫 wěi ①defend; guard; protect 【卫兵】 guard; bodyguard 【卫队】 squad of bodyguards ~长 captain of the guard 【卫生】 hygiene; health; sanitation 讲~ pay attention to hygiene ~带 sanitary towel ~队 medical unit ~间 toilet ~局 public health bureau ~科 health section ~裤 sweat pants ~球 camphor ball; mothball ~设备 sanitary equipment ~室 clinic ~衣 sweat shirt ~员 health worker ~纸 toilet paper 【卫戍】 garrison ~部队 garrison force 【卫星】 satellite; moon/artificial satellite; man-made satellite ~城 satellite town ~国 satellite state; satellite country

为 wěi ①for ②for the sake of; in order to 【为此】 to this end; for this reason; in this connection 【为何】 why; for what reason 【为虎作伥】 help a villain do evil 【为民请命】 plead for the people 【为什么】 why

未 wěi ①have not; did not 尚~恢复健康 not yet recovered ②not ~知可否 not know whether sth. can be done 【未必】 may not 他~知道 he doesn't necessarily know 【未便】 not be in a position to; find it hard to ~擅自处理 cannot do it without authorization ~立即答复 find it difficult to give an immediate reply 【未卜先知】 foresee; have foresight 【未尝】 have not; did not 那也~不可 that should be all right ~没有可取之处 not without its merits 【未成年】 not yet of age; under age 【未定】 uncertain; undecided; undefined 行期~ the date of departure is not yet fixed ~稿 draft ~界 undefined

boundary 【未婚】 unmarried; single ～夫 *fiancé* ～妻
fiancée 【未决】 unsettled; outstanding 胜负～ the outcome
is not yet decided ～犯 culprit 【未可】 cannot ～乐观
nothing to be optimistic about 前途～限量 have a brilliant future ～厚非 give no cause for much criticism
【未来】 coming; approaching; next / future 在～的斗争中
in the struggle to come 【未老先衰】 prematurely senile;
old before one's time 【未了】 unfinished; outstanding ～
事宜 unfinished business ～的手续 formalities still to be
complied with 【未免】 rather; a bit too; truly 这～太
过份 this is really going too far 【未能】 cannot ～实现
fail to materialize ～取得预期的结果 fail to achieve the
expected result 【未遂】 not accomplished 政变～ the coup
d'état aborted 自杀～ an attempted suicide ～罪 attempted
crime 【未完】 unfinished ～待续 to be continued 【未详】
unknown 作者～ the author is unknown 病因～ what
brought on the illness is not clear 【未央】 not ended 夜
～ the night is yet young 【未雨绸缪】 provide for a rainy
day; take precautions 【未知数】 unknown (number); uncertain

位 wèi ①place; location 座～ seat ②position 名～ fame
and position ③throne 即～ come to the throne ④
place; figure; digit 个～ unit's place 十～ ten's place
【位次】 precedence; seating arrangement 【位于】 be located; be situated; lie 【位置】 seat; place / position

味 wèi ①taste; flavour 甜～ a sweet taste ②smell;
odour 香～ a sweet smell 臭～ a foul smell ③inter-
est 语言无～ insipid language ④distinguish the flavour
of 玩～ ponder; ruminate 【味道】 taste; flavour 【味精】
monosodium glutamate; gourmet powder 【味觉】 sense of
taste

畏 wèi ①fear 不～强敌 stand in no fear of a formidable enemy ②respect 后生可～ youth are to be regarded with respect 【畏避】 recoil from; flinch from 【畏惧】 fear; dread 【畏难】 be afraid of difficulty ～情绪 fear of difficulty 【畏怯】 cowardly; timid; chickenhearted 【畏缩】 recoil; shrink; flinch ～不前 hesitate to press forward; hang back 【畏罪】 dread punishment for one's crime ～潜逃 abscond to avoid punishment ～自杀 commit suicide to escape punishment

胃 wèi stomach 【胃病】 stomach trouble 【胃口】 appetite / liking ～好 have a good appetite 没有～ have no appetite 对～ to one's liking 【胃溃疡】 gastric ulcer

谓 wèi ①say 或～ someone says ②call; name 所～ so-called ③meaning; sense 无～的话 senseless talk; twaddle 【谓语】 predicate

尉 wèi 【尉官】 a junior officer

喂 wèi ①hello; hey ②feed ～猪 feed pigs 【喂奶】 breastfeed; suckle; nurse 【喂养】 raise; feed ～家禽 keep fowls

蔚 wèi ①luxuriant; grand ②colourful 【蔚蓝】 azure; sky blue 【蔚然成风】 become common practice; become the order of the day

慰 wèi ①console; comfort ～勉 comfort and encourage ②be relieved 【慰劳】 bring gifts to, or send one's best wishes to, in recognition of services rendered 【慰问】 extend one's regards to; convey greetings; salute ～袋 gift bag ～团 a group sent to convey greetings and appreciation ～信 a letter expressing one's appreciation or sympathy ～演出 a special performance as an expression of gratitude or appreciation

WEN

温 wēn ①warm ～水 lukewarm water ②temperature (of the body) ③warm up ～酒 warm up the wine ④ review; revise ～课 review one's lessons 【温床】hotbed/ breeding ground 【温存】attentive / gentle; kind 【温带】 temperate zone 【温度】temperature ～计 thermograph ～ 表 thermometer 【温和】temperate; moderate / gentle; mild 气候 a temperate climate 性情 a gentle disposition 语气 a mild tone ～派 moderates 【温厚】gentle and kind; good-natured 【温暖】warm 天气～ warm weather 感到～ feel the warmth of sth. 【温情】tender feeling/ too softhearted ～脉脉 full of tender feeling ～主义 excessive tenderheartedness 【温泉】hot spring 【温柔】gentle and soft 【温室】greenhouse 【温顺】docile; meek

瘟 wēn acute communicable diseases 【瘟神】god of plague 【瘟疫】pestilence

文 wén ①character; script; writing ②language 英～ the English language ③literary composition; writing ～如其人 the writing mirrors the writer ④literary language 半～半白 half literary and half vernacular ⑤culture ～物 cultural relic ⑥formal ritual 虚～ a mere formality ⑦civilian; civil ～职 civilian post ⑧gentle; refined ⑨certain natural phenomena 天～ astronomy 水～ hydrology ⑩cover up; paint over ～过饰非 conceal faults and gloss over wrongs 【文本】text; version 【文笔】style of writing ～流利 write in an easy and fluent style 【文才】literary talent 【文采】rich and bright colours/literary grace 【文辞】diction; language ～优美 exquisite diction 【文牍】official documents and correspondence ～主义 red tape 【文法】grammar 【文风】style of writing 【文稿】

manuscript; draft 【文告】statement; message 【文工团】art troupe; cultural troupe 【文官】civil official 【文豪】literary giant; great writer 【文化】civilization; culture/education; schooling; culture; literacy 学～ acquire literacy; learn to read and write; acquire an elementary education ～宫 cultural palace ～馆 cultural centre ～界 cultural circles ～课 literacy class ～人 cultural worker ～事业 cultural undertakings ～水平 cultural level ～用品 stationery 【文火】slow fire 【文集】collected works 【文件】documents; papers; instruments ～袋 documents pouch; dispatch case ～柜 filing cabinet 【文教】culture and education ～界 cultural and educational circles ～事业 culture and education 【文静】gentle and quiet 【文具】writing materials; stationery ～店 stationer's; stationery shop 【文科】liberal arts ～学校 liberal arts school ～院校 colleges of arts 【文库】library 【文盲】an illiterate person 【文明】civilization; culture/civilized 物质～ material civilization; material development ～古国 a country with an ancient civilization 【文凭】diploma 【文人】man of letters; scholar 【文史】literature and history ～馆 Research Institute of Culture and History ～资料 historical accounts of past events 【文书】document; official dispatch/copy clerk 【文思】the train of thought in writing ～敏捷 have a ready pen 【文坛】the literary circles; the world of letters 【文体】type of writing; literary form; style/recreation and sports ～活动 recreational and sports activities 【文物】historical relic 【文献】document; literature ～记录片 documentary (film) 【文选】selected works 【文学】literature ～家 writer; man of letters ～流派 schools of literature ～批评 literary criticism ～作品 literary works ～语言 standard speech; literary language

【文雅】elegant; refined; cultured 【文言】classical Chinese ～文 writings in classical Chinese; classical style of writing 【文艺】literature and art ～创作 literary and artistic creation ～工作 work in the literary and artistic fields ～工作者 literary and art workers ～会演 theatrical festival ～节目 theatrical items ～界 the world of literature and art ～理论 theory of literature and art ～批评 literary or art criticism ～思潮 trend of thought in literature and art ～团体 theatre troupe ～作品 literary and artistic works 【文娱】cultural recreation; entertainment ～活动 recreational activities 【文责】author's responsibility ～自负 the author takes sole responsibility for his views 【文摘】abstract; digest 【文章】essay; article/ literary works; writings 【文职】civilian post ～人员 nonmilitary personnel 【文质彬彬】gentle; suave 【文绉绉】genteel 【文字】characters; script; writing/written language ～宣传 written propaganda ～游戏 play with words ～清通 lucid writing ～学 philology

纹 wén lines; veins; grain 【纹理】veins; grain 【纹丝不动】absolutely still

闻 wén ①hear ～讯 hear the news 听而不～ listen but not hear ②news; story 要～ important news ③ famous ～人 well-known figure ④reputation 秽～ ill repute ⑤smell 你～～这是什么味儿 smell this and see what it is 【闻风而动】go into action without delay 【闻名】famous; renowned/be familiar with sb's name ～全国 well-known throughout the country

蚊 wén mosquito 【蚊香】mosquito-repellent incense 【蚊帐】mosquito net 【蚊子】mosquito

刎 wěn cut one's throat

吻 wěn ①lips ②kiss ③an animal's mouth 【吻合】be identical; coincide; tally 意见～ have identical views

紊 wěn disorderly; confused 【紊乱】disorder; chaos; confusion 秩序～ in a state of chaos

稳 wěn ①steady; firm 站～ stand firm 坐～ sit tight 企图～住阵脚 try to maintain one's position ②sure; certain 这事你拿得～吗 are you quite sure of it 【稳步】with steady steps ～发展 steady growth ～前进 advance steadily 生产～上升 production is going up steadily 【稳当】reliable; secure; safe ～的办法 a reliable method 【稳定】stable; steady/stabilize 物价～ prices remain stable 情绪～ be in a calm, unruffled mood ～的多数 a stable majority ～物价 stabilize commodity prices ～情绪 set sb.'s mind at rest; reassure sb. 【稳固】firm; stable ～的基础 a solid foundation ～的政权 a stable government 【稳健】firm; steady 迈着～的步子 walk with firm steps 办事～ go about things steadily ～派 moderates 【稳妥】safe; reliable ～的计划 a safe plan 【稳重】steady; staid; sedate

问 wèn ①ask; inquire ～路 ask the way 不懂就～ if you don't know; just ask ②inquire after 他信里～起你 he asks after you in his letter ③interrogate; examine ④hold responsible 出了事唯你是～ you'll be held responsible if anything goes wrong 【问安】pay one's respects; wish sb. good health 【问案】hear a case 【问答】questions and answers ～练习 question-and-answer drills 【问好】send one's regards to; say hello to 请代我向你父亲～ remember me to your father 他向您～ he wished to be remembered to you 【问号】question mark/unknown factor; unsolved problem 【问候】send one's respects to; extend greetings to 【问世】be published; come out 【问题】question; problem; issue/trouble; mishap 我提个～

may I ask a question ～的关键 the heart of the matter 一路上没出～ the trip went off without mishap 【问心无愧】 have a clear conscience 【问心有愧】 have a guilty conscience 【问讯】 inquire; ask ～处 inquiry office; information desk 【问罪】 denounce; condemn

WENG

翁　wēng ①old man 渔～ an old fisherman ②father ③father-in-law ～姑 a woman's parents-in-law

嗡　wēng drone; buzz; hum

瓮　wēng urn; earthen jar 水～ water jar 【瓮声瓮气】 in a low, muffled voice

WO

涡　wō whirlpool; eddy (of. water) 【涡轮】 turbine

莴　wō 【莴苣】 lettuce 【莴笋】 asparagus lettuce

窝　wō ①nest 鸟～ bird's nest ②lair; den 贼～ thieves' den ③pit 心～ the pit of the stomach ④place 挪～儿 move sth. to some other place ⑤shelter; harbour (stolen goods) ⑥hold in; check ～火 be simmering with rage ⑦bend 别把画片～了 be careful not to bend the picture ⑧litter; brood 一～小鸡 a brood of chickens 【窝藏】 harbour ～罪犯 give shelter to a criminal 【窝工】 holdup in the work through poor organization 【窝头】 steamed bread of corn, sorghum, etc. 【窝主】 a person who harbours criminals, loot or contraband goods

 蜗　wō 【蜗牛】 snail

我 wǒ ①I ②we ～方 our side ～军 our army ③self 自～牺牲 'self-sacrifice 【我们】we 【我行我素】persist in one's old ways (no matter what others say)

沃 wò ①fertile; rich ～土 fertile soil ～野千里 a vast expanse of fertile land ②irrigate (farmland)

卧 wò ①lie 仰～ lie on one's back ②for sleeping in 【卧病】be confined to bed; be laid up 【卧车】sleeping car; sleeper/automobile; car; limousine; sedan 【卧床】lie in bed 【卧倒】drop to the ground; take a prone position 【卧铺】sleeping berth; sleeper 【卧射】prone fire 【卧式】horizontal 【卧室】bedroom 【卧榻】bed

握 wò hold; grasp 【握别】shake hands at parting; part 【握力】the power of gripping; grip ～器 spring-grip dumb-bells 【握拳】make a fist 【握手】shake hands

斡 wò 【斡旋】mediate/good offices

龌 wò 【龌龊】dirty; filthy 卑鄙～ sordid; foul

WU

乌 wū ①crow ②black; dark ～云 black clouds 【乌龟】tortoise/cuckold ～壳 tortoiseshell 【乌合之众】a motley crowd; rabble; mob 【乌黑】pitch-black; jet-black 【乌七八糟】in a horrible mess; in great disorder/obscene; dirty; filthy 【乌纱帽】black gauze cap / official post 丢～ be dismissed from office 【乌托邦】Utopia 【乌鸦】crow 【乌烟瘴气】foul atmosphere 搞得～ foul up 【乌有】nothing; naught 化为～ come to nothing 【乌贼】inkfish

污 wū ①dirt; filth 血～ blood stains ②dirty; filthy; foul ～泥 mud; mire; sludge ③corrupt (officials) ④defile; smear 【污点】spot; blemish; smirch 洗去～ wash off stains 【污迹】 smudge 【污蔑】 slander/sully 【污染】 pollute; contaminate 【污辱】 humiliate; insult/defile; tarnish 【污水】 foul water; sewage; slops ～处理 sewage treatment ～管道 sewer line ～灌溉 sewage irrigation

巫 wū shaman witch 【巫婆】 witch; sorceress 【巫师】 wizard; sorcerer 【巫术】 witchcraft; sorcery

鸣 wū toot; hoot; zoom 【鸣呼】 alas; alack / die ～哀哉 dead and gone/all is lost 【鸣咽】 sob; whimper

诬 wū accuse falsely 【诬告】 bring a false charge against ～案件 trumped-up case 【诬赖】 calumniate; malign 【诬蔑】 falsely incriminate ～好人 incriminate innocent people 【诬蔑】 slander; vilify 【诬陷】 frame sb.

屋 wū ①house ②room 【屋顶】 roof; housetop ～花园 roof garden 【屋脊】 ridge (of a roof) 【屋檐】 eaves

钨 wū tungsten; wolfram 【钨钢】 tungsten steel 【钨砂】 tungsten ore 【钨丝】 tungsten filament

无 wú ①nothing; nil 从～到有 grow out of nothing ②not have; without ～一定计划 without a definite plan ③not ～碍大局 not affect the situation as a whole ④regardless of; no matter whether, what, etc. 【无比】 incomparable; unparalleled; matchless 【无边无际】 boundless; limitless; vast 【无补】 of no help; of no avail 【无不】 all without exception; invariably 【无产阶级】 the proletariat ～化 acquire proletarian qualities ～专政 proletarian dictatorship 【无偿】 free; gratuitous ～援助 aid given gratis 【无耻】 impudent ～谰言 shameless slander ～之尤 brazen in the extreme ～之徒 a shameless person 【无从】 have no way (of doing sth.) ～答复 be in no position to answer (such questions) ～说起 not know where to begin 【无党派人士】 nonparty personage 【无敌】 invincible ～于天下 unmatched anywhere in the world 【无的

放矢】shoot at random 【无动于衷】aloof and indifferent; unmoved 【无恶不作】stop at no evil 【无法】unable; incapable ～应付 unable to cope with ～形容 beyond description 【无妨】there's no harm; may as well 【无非】nothing but; no more than 【无辜】innocent/an innocent person 【无故】without cause ～缺席 be absent without reason 【无怪】no wonder; not to be wondered at 【无关】have nothing to do with ～大局 it does not matter very much ～紧要 of no importance 【无轨电车】trolleybus 【无花果】fig 【无机】inorganic ～肥料 inorganic fertilizer ～化学 inorganic chemistry 【无稽】unfounded; absurd ～之谈 fantastic talk 【无计可施】at one's wits' end 【无济于事】of no avail; to no effect 【无精打采】listless; in low spirits; out of sorts 【无拘束】unrestrained; unconstrained 【无可厚非】give no cause for much criticism 【无可讳言】there is no hiding the fact ～的事实 indisputable fact 【无可救药】incorrigible 【无可奈何】have no way out; have no alternative 【无可争辩】indisputable 【无可置疑】indubitable 【无愧】have a clear conscience 问心～ feel no qualms upon self-examination 【无赖】rascally; scoundrelly / rascal 【无理】unreasonable; unjustifiable ～指责 unwarranted accusations ～取闹 wilfully make trouble 【无力】lack strength; feel weak/unable; incapable 【无量】measureless; immeasurable 【无聊】bored/senseless; silly; stupid 【无论】no matter what, how, etc.; regardless of 【无论如何】in any case 【无名】nameless; unknown / indefinable; indescribable ～英雄 an unknown hero ～指 the third finger 【无奈】cannot help but; have no alternative 【无能】incompetent; incapable 【无能为力】powerless; helpless 【无期徒刑】life imprisonment 【无情】merciless; ruthless

【无穷】infinite; endless 【无权】have no right 【无人】unmanned/depopulated (zone) /self-service (bookstall, etc.) 【无声】noiseless; silent ～手枪 pistol with a silencer 【无时无刻】all the time; incessantly 【无事生非】make trouble out of nothing 【无视】ignore; disregard; defy 【无数】innumerable; countless / not know for certain 【无双】unparalleled; matchless 【无私】selfless ～的援助 disinterested assistance 【无所不为】stop at nothing; do all manner of evil 【无所事事】have nothing to do 【无所谓】cannot be designated as / be indifferent; not matter 采取～的态度 adopt an indifferent attitude 【无条件】unconditional; without preconditions 【无暇】have no time; be too busy 【无限】infinite; limitless; immeasurable ～热爱 have boundless love for ～忠诚 absolute devotion to ～的创造力 unlimited creative power ～公司 unlimited company 【无限制】unrestricted; unlimited 【无线电】radio ～传真 radiofacsimile ～发射机 radio transmitter ～收音机 radio receiver 【无效】of no avail; invalid; null and void 医治～ fail to respond to medical treatment 宣布合同～ declare a contract invalid 【无懈可击】unassailable; invulnerable 【无心】not be in the mood for / unwittingly; inadvertently 他说这话是～的 he didn't say it intentionally 【无形】invisible (shackles, fronts, etc.) 【无形中】imperceptibly; virtually 【无疑】beyond doubt; undoubtedly 【无异】not different from; the same as 【无用】useless; of no use 【无原则】unprincipled (dispute, etc.) 【无缘无故】without cause or reason; for no reason at all 【无政府主义】anarchism 【无知】ignorant 出于～ out of ignorance 【无止境】have no limits; know no end【无足轻重】insignificant 【无罪】innocent; not guilty ～释放 set a person free with a verdict of "not guilty"

芜 wú ①overgrown with weeds 荒～ lie waste ②grassland ③mixed and disorderly ～杂 miscellaneous

梧 wú 【梧桐】Chinese parasol (tree)

蜈 wú 【蜈蚣】centipede

五 wǔ five ～十 fifty ～倍 fivefold; puintuple ～分之一 one fifth ～十年代 the fifties 【五彩】the five colours (blue, yellow, red, white and black) /multicoloured ～缤纷 colourful; blazing with colour 【五斗柜】chest of drawers 【五分制】the five-grade marking system 【五更】the five watches of the night / the fifth watch of the night; just before dawn 【五谷】the five cereals (rice, two kinds of millet, wheat and beans) / food crops ～丰登 an abundant harvest of all food crops 【五官】the five sense organs (ears, eyes, lips, nose and tongue) / facial features ～端正 have regular features 【五光十色】multicoloured; bright with many colours / of great variety; of all kinds 【五湖四海】all corners of the land 【五花八门】multifarious; of a rich variety 【五角星】five-pointed star 【五金】the five metals (gold, silver, copper, iron and tin) /metals; hardware ～厂 hardware factory ～店 hardware store 【五味】the five flavours (sweet, sour, bitter, pungent and salty) / all sorts of flavours 【五线谱】staff; stave 【五香】the five spices (prickly ash, star aniseed, cinnamon, clove and fennel) / spices ～豆 spiced beans 【五星红旗】the Five-Starred Red Flag 【五颜六色】of various colours; multicoloured; colourful 【五月】May/ the fifth moon 【五脏】the five internal organs (heart, liver, spleen, lungs and kidneys) 【五指】the five fingers (thumb, index finger, middle finger, third finger and little finger)

午 wǔ noon; midday 【午饭】 midday meal; lunch 【午后】 afternoon 【午前】 forenoon; before noon; morning 【午睡】 afternoon nap; noontime snooze / take a nap after lunch 【午休】 noon break 【午夜】 midnight

妖 wǔ 【妩媚】 lovely; charming

忤 wǔ ①disobedient (to parents, etc.) ②uncongenial 与人无~ bear no ill will against anybody

武 wǔ ①military ~官 military officer ②valiant; fierce 【武斗】 resort to violence 【武断】 arbitrary decision 【武工】 skill in acrobatics 【武力】 force / military force; armed strength ~镇压 armed suppression 诉诸~ resort to force 【武器】 weapon; arms 放下~ lay down one's arms 拿起~ take up arms ~装备 weaponry 【武士】 palace guards in ancient times / man of prowess; warrior 【武装】 arms; military equipment; battle outfit / armed forces / equip with arms; arm ~部队 armed forces ~冲突 armed clash ~带 Sam Browne belt ~斗争 armed struggle ~干涉 armed intervention ~力量 armed power; armed forces ~起义 armed uprising ~人员 armed personnel

侮 wǔ insult; bully 不可~ not to be bullied 【侮慢】 slight; treat disrespectfully 【侮辱】 humiliate

捂 wǔ seal; cover; muffle ~鼻子 cover one's nose with one's hand ~耳朵 stop one's ears ~盖子 keep the lid on; cover up the truth

舞 wǔ ①dance 集体~ group dance ②flourish; wield; brandish; wave 【舞伴】 dancing partner 【舞弊】 malpractices 【舞场】 dance hall; ballroom 【舞蹈】 dance ~动作 dance movement ~家 dancer 【舞会】 dance; ball 举行~ hold a dance 【舞剧】 dance drama; ballet 【舞女

dancing girl; taxi dancer 【舞曲】dance (music) 【舞台】stage; arena ～布景 (stage) scenery ～工作人员 stagehand ～记录片 stage documentary ～监督 stage director ～设计 stage design ～效果 stage effect ～艺术 stagecraft

勿 wù no; not 请～吸烟 no smoking ～谓言之不预也 do not say that you have not been forewarned

务 wù ①affair; business 公～ official business 任～ task; job ②be engaged in; devote one's efforts to ～农 be a farmer 【务必】must 你～去看他 be sure to go and see him 【务使】make sure; ensure

坞 wù a depressed place 船～ dock 花～ sunken flower-er-bed

物 wù ①thing; matter 废～ waste matter 以～易～ barter ②content; substance 言之无～ talk or writing devoid of substance 【物产】products; produce 【物归原主】return sth. to its rightful owner 【物价】(commodity) prices ～稳定 prices remain stable 【物理】innate laws of things / physics ～变化 physical change ～疗法 physiotherapy ～学 physics ～学家 physicist 【物力】material resources 【物品】article 【物色】look for; seek out; choose 【物体】body; substance; object 【物证】material evidence 【物质】matter; substance; material ～财富 material wealth ～储备 reserve supply ～刺激 material incentive ～鼓励 material reward 【物种】species 【物资】goods and materials ～交流 interflow of commodities

误 wù ①mistake; error 笔～ a slip of the pen ②miss ～了火车 miss a train ③harm 人子弟 harm the younger generation ④by mistake; by accident ～伤 accidentally injure 【误差】error 【误点】late; overdue; behind schedule 【误工】delay one's work / loss of working time 【误会】mistake; misconstrue 你～了我的意思 you've mistaken my meaning 消除～ dispel misunderstanding 【误解】 misread; misunderstand 【误入歧途】 go astray; be misled 【误杀】 manslaughter 【误事】 cause delay in work or business; hold things up / bungle matters

悟 wù realize; awaken ～出其中的道理 realize why it should be so 【悟性】 comprehension

恶 wù loathe; dislike; hate 好～ likes and dislikes 可～ loathsome; hateful

晤 wù meet; interview; see 【晤谈】 meet and talk; have a talk

雾 wù ①fog 浓～ dense fog 薄～ mist ②fine spray 喷～器 sprayer

X

XI

夕 xī ①sunset ②evening; night 【夕烟】 evening mist 【夕阳】 the setting sun 【夕照】 evening glow

汐 xī tide during the night; nighttide

西 xī ①west ～屋 west room ～风 west wind 往～去 head west ②Occidental; Western 【西餐】 Western-style food 【西方】 the west/the West; the Occident ～国家 the Western countries 【西服】 Western-style clothes 【西瓜】 watermelon ～子 watermelon seed 【西红柿】 tomato 【西葫芦】 pumpkin 【西式】 Western style ～点心 Western-style pastry 【西洋景】 peep show / hanky-panky; trickery 拆穿～ expose sb.'s tricks 【西药】 Western medicine 【西医】 Western medicine / a doctor trained in Western medicine

【西乐】Western music 【西装】Western-style clothes

吸 xī ①inhale; breathe in; draw ～新鲜空气 inhale fresh air ②absorb; suck up ～水 absorb water ③attract; draw to oneself 【吸尘器】dust catcher 【吸毒】drug taking ～者 drug addict 【吸力】suction; attraction 【吸墨纸】blotting paper 【吸取】absorb; draw; assimilate ～精华 absorb the quintessence ～教训 draw a lesson 【吸食】suck; take in 【吸收】absorb; suck up; draw/recruit; enrol; admit ～养分 assimilate nutriment ～水分 suck up moisture ～知识 imbibe knowledge ～作用 absorption 【吸吮】suck; absorb 【吸铁石】magnet; lodestone 【吸血鬼】bloodsucker; vampire 【吸烟】smoke ～室 smoking room 【吸引】attract; draw; fascinate ～注意力 attract attention

希 xī ①hope ～准时到会 please get to the meeting on time ②scarce 【希罕】rare; uncommon/value as a rarity; cherish 【希冀】hope for; wish for 【希奇】rare; strange; curious 【希图】harbour the intention of; attempt to ～蒙混过关 try to wangle ～牟取暴利 go after quick profits 【希望】hope; wish; expect 把～变成现实 turn hopes into reality 大有成功的～ promise high hopes of success

昔 xī former times; the past 今胜于～ the present is superior to the past 【昔日】in former days

析 xī ①divide; separate ②analyse; dissect ～义 analyse the meaning (of a word, etc.) ～疑 resolve a doubt

牺 xī sacrifice 【牺牲】sacrifice oneself; die a martyr's death/give up; do sth. at the expense of ～个人利益 sacrifice one's personal interests ～品 victim; prey

息 xī ①breath 一～尚存 so long as there is breath left in one ②news 信～ message ③cease; stop ～怒 cease to be angry ④rest ⑤interest 年～ annual interest 【息票】interest coupon 【息息相关】be closely linked; be closely bound up

惜 xī ①cherish; value highly; care for tenderly ～寸阴 value every bit of time ②spare; grudge; stint 不～工本 spare no expense ③have pity on sb.; feel sorry for sb. 【惜别】be reluctant to part; hate to see sb. go

悉 xī ①all; entirely ～力 go all out ②know; learn 熟～ know very well 惊～ be shocked to learn 【悉心】devote all one's attention; take the utmost care

稀 xī ①rare; scarce; uncommon 物以～为贵 when a thing is scarce, it is precious ②sparse; scattered ③watery; thin ～粥 thin gruel 吃～的 have some liquid food 【稀薄】thin; rare 空气～ the air is thin 【稀饭】rice or millet gruel; porridge 【稀客】rare visitor 【稀烂】completely mashed; pulpy / smashed to pieces 【稀少】few; rare; scarce 人口～ a sparse population 【稀释】dilute 【稀疏】few and scattered; thin; sparse 【稀松】poor; sloppy / unimportant; trivial 【稀有】rare; unusual ～金属 rare metal

犀 xī rhinoceros 【犀角】rhinoceros horn 【犀利】sharp; incisive; trenchant ～的目光 sharp eyes

溪 xī small stream; brook; rivulet 【溪涧】mountain stream

锡 xī tin 【锡箔】tinfoil paper 【锡匠】tinsmith 【锡矿】tin ore 【锡纸】silver paper; tinfoil

熄 xī extinguish; put out ～灯 put out the light 【熄灯号】lights-out; taps 【熄灭】go out; die out

熙 xī ①bright; sunny ②prosperous ③merry 【熙攘攘】bustling with activity; with people bustling about

蜥 xī 【蜥蜴】lizard

膝 xī knee 【膝盖】knee ～骨 kneecap; patella 【膝关节】knee joint

嬉 xī play; sport【嬉皮笑脸】grinning cheekily; smiling and grimacing【嬉笑】be laughing and playing

熹 xī dawn; brightness【熹微】dim; pale 晨光～ the dim light of dawn

蟋 xī 【蟋蟀】cricket

习 xí ①practise; exercise 复～ review (one's lessons) ②get accustomed to; be used to 不～水性 be not good at swimming ③habit; custom; usual practice 积～ old habit【习惯】be accustomed to; be used to; be inured to/ habit 旧～ outmoded customs ～法 common law; customary law ～势力 force of habit【习见】(of things) commonly seen【习气】bad habit; bad practice【习俗】custom; convention【习题】exercises (in school work)【习性】habits and characteristics【习以为常】be accustomed to sth.【习用】habitually use【习语】idiom【习字】practise penmanship ～帖 copybook; calligraphy model【习作】do exercises in composition / an exercise in composition

席 xí ①mat 草～ straw mat ②seat; place 入～ take one's seat ③feast; banquet【席次】the order of seats; seating arrangement【席地】(sit) on the ground【席卷】roll up like a mat; take away everything / sweep across; engulf【席棚】mat shed / mat hoarding【席位】seat

袭 xí ①make a surprise attack on; raid 夜～ night raid ②follow the pattern of 因～ carry on (an old tradition, etc.)【袭击】surprise; raid 受台风的～ be hit by a typhoon【袭扰】harassing attack

媳 xí daughter-in-law【媳妇】son's wife; daughter-in-law/the wife of a relative of the younger generation

檄 xí 【檄文】an official call to arms / an official denunciation of the enemy

洗 xǐ ①wash; bathe ～碟子 wash dishes ～头 wash one's hair ～伤口 bathe a wound ②baptize 受～ be baptized ③redress; right ～冤 right a wrong ④kill and loot ⑤develop (a film) ⑥shuffle (cards, etc.) 【洗尘】 give a dinner of welcome (to a visitor from afar) 【洗涤】 wash; cleanse ～剂 detergent 【洗涤剂】 shampoo 【洗劫】 loot; sack 【洗礼】 baptism / severe test 炮火的～ the baptism of fire 【洗脸盆】 washbasin; washbowl 【洗染店】 laundering and dyeing shop 【洗手】 (of a thief, bandit, etc.) stop doing evil and reform oneself / wash one's hands of sth. 【洗刷】 wash and brush; scrub / wash off; clear oneself of (opprobrium, stigma, guilt, etc.) 【洗心革面】 turn over a new leaf 【洗雪】 wipe out (a disgrace); redress (a wrong) 【洗眼杯】 eyecup 【洗衣】 wash clothes; do one's washing ～板 washboard ～店 laundry ～粉 washing powder ～机 washing machine; washer 【洗澡】 bathe

玺 xǐ imperial or royal seal

徙 xǐ move (from one place to another) 【徙居】 move house

铣 xǐ mill 【铣床】 miller 【铣刀】 milling cutter 【铣工】 milling (work) /miller

喜 xǐ ①happy; delighted; pleased ～不自胜 be delighted beyond measure ～降瑞雪 there was a welcome fall of seasonable snow ②happy event (esp. wedding); occasion for celebration 大～的日子 a day of great happiness ③ pregnancy 有～ be expecting ④like ～读书 be fond of reading 【喜爱】 like; love; be fond of; be keen on 【喜报】 a bulletin of glad tidings 【喜出望外】 be overjoyed; be pleasantly surprised 【喜欢】 like; love; be fond of; be keen on/happy; elated; filled with joy 他～这样做 it pleased him to do so 【喜酒】 wine drunk at a wedding feast / wedding feast 【喜剧】 comedy 【喜气洋洋】 full of joy; jubilant 【喜庆】 joyous; jubilant / happy event 【喜鹊】 magpie 【喜人】 satisfactory 形势~ the situation is gratifying 【喜色】 joyful look 面有~ wear a happy expression 【喜事】 happy event; joyous occasion / wedding 【喜闻乐见】 love (to see and hear) 【喜新厌旧】 love the new and loathe the old — be fickle in affection 【喜形于色】 be visibly pleased; light up with pleasure 【喜讯】 happy news; good news; glad tidings 【喜洋洋】 beaming with joy; radiant 【喜雨】 seasonable rain 【喜悦】 joyous

戏 xì ①play; sport 嬉~ have fun ②make fun of; joke ~言 say something for fun ③drama; play; show 马~ circus show 去看~ go to the theatre 【戏班】 theatrical troupe 【戏词】 actor's lines 【戏法】 conjuring; juggling; tricks; magic 变~ juggle; conjure 【戏剧】 drama; play; theatre ~家 dramatist ~界 theatrical circles ~评论 dramatic criticism 【戏迷】 theatre fan 【戏目】 theatrical programme 【戏弄】 make fun of; play tricks on; tease; kid 【戏曲】 traditional opera 【戏台】 stage 【戏谑】 banter; crack jokes 【戏院】 theatre 【戏装】 theatrical costume

系 xì ①system; series 太阳~ the solar system 语~ (language) family 派~ faction ②department (in a college); faculty 哲学~ the department of philosophy ③tie; fasten ~马 tether a horse ④feel anxious; be concerned 【系词】 copula / copulative verb; linking verb 【系列】 series; set 一~的问题 a series of problems 一~政策 a whole set of policies 【系念】 be anxious about; feel concerned about 【系数】 coefficient 【系统】 system/systematic 作~的研究 make a systematic study ~地说明 explain in a systematic way ~化 systematize

细 xì ①thin; slender ～铁丝 thin wire ②in small particles; fine ～沙 fine sand ③thin and soft ～嗓子 a threadly voice ④fine; exquisite; delicate ～瓷 fine porcelain ⑤meticulous; detailed ～看 examine carefully ～问 ask about details ⑥minute; trifling 分工很～ have an elaborate division of labour 【细胞】cell 【细布】fine cloth 【细长】long and thin; tall and slender 【细节】details; particulars 【细菌】germ; bacterium ～武器 germ weapon ～学 bacteriology ～学家 bacteriologist ～战 germ warfare 【细粮】flour and rice 【细毛】fine, soft fur ～羊 fine-wool sheep 【细密】thin and closely woven; close; meticulous 质地～ of close texture 针脚～ in fine close stitches ～的分析 a detailed analysis 【细目】detailed catalogue / detail 【细嫩】delicate; tender 【细腻】fine and smooth/exquisite ～的描写 a minute description ～的表演 an exquisite performance 【细巧】exquisite; dainty; delicate 【细弱】thin and delicate; slim and fragile 【细纱】spun yarn ～机 spinning frame 【细声细气】in a soft voice; soft-spoken 【细水长流】economize to avoid running short / go about sth. little by little without a letup 【细微】fine; subtle ～的变化 slight changes ～差别 a fine distinction 【细小】very small; tiny; fine; trivial 【细心】careful; attentive 【细雨】drizzle; fine rain 【细则】detailed rules and regulations

隙 xì ①crack; chink; crevice 墙～ a crack in the wall ②gap; interval ③opportunity 无～可乘 no loophole to take advantage of

XIA

虾 xiā shrimp ～群 a shoal of shrimps 【虾酱】shrimp paste 【虾米】dried, shelled shrimps 【虾皮】dried small shrimps 【虾仁】 shrimp meat 【虾油】 shrimp sauce 【虾子】 shrimp roe ～酱油 shrimp-roe soy sauce

瞎 xiā ①blind ～了一只眼 blind in one eye ②foolishly; to no purpose ～诽 speak groundlessly ～花钱 spend money foolishly ～干 go it blind ～猜 make a wild guess 【瞎话】 untruth; lie 说～ tell a lie; lie 【瞎闹】 act senselessly; mess about/fool around; be mischievous 【瞎说】 talk irresponsibly; talk rubbish 【瞎指挥】 issue confused orders; give arbitrary and impracticable directions 【瞎子】 a blind person

匣 xiá 【匣子】 a small box; casket

狎 xiá 【狎昵】 be improperly familiar with

侠 xiá 【侠客】 a person adept in martial arts and given to chivalrous conduct (in olden times) 【侠义】 having a strong sense of justice and ready to help the weak; chivalrous

峡 xiá gorge 海～ strait 【峡谷】 gorge; canyon 【峡湾】 fiord

狭 xiá narrow 【狭隘】 narrow ～的看法 a narrow view 心胸～ be narrow-minded 【狭义】 narrow sense 【狭窄】 narrow; cramped / limited

遐 xiá far; distant / lasting; long ～龄 advanced age 【遐想】 reverie; daydream

瑕 xiá ①flaw in a piece of jade ②flaw; defect; shortcoming 【瑕疵】 blemish

暇 xiá free time; leisure 无～兼顾 be too busy to attend to other things

辖 xiá ①linchpin ②have jurisdiction over; administer; govern 【辖区】 area under one's jurisdiction

霞 xiá rosy clouds; morning or evening glow 【霞光】 rays of morning or evening sunlight

下 xià ①below; down; under 树～ under the tree 山 ～ at the foot of the hill ②lower; inferior 等 lower grade; inferior ③next; latter ～一步怎么做 what's our next move ④downward; down 物价～跌 prices dropped ⑤descend; get off ～山 descend the mountain ～床 get out of bed ～楼 descend the stairs; go or come downstairs ⑥(of rain, snow, etc.) fall ⑦issue; deliver; send ～命令 issue orders ⑧go to ～车间 go to the workshop ⑨exit; leave 从左边门儿～ exit from the left door ⑩put in; cast ～作料 put in the condiments ～面 条 cook noodles ⑪take away; dismantle ⑫form (an opinion, idea, etc.) ～结论 draw a conclusion ～决心 make a resolution; be determined ～定义 give a definition; define ⑬apply; use ～力气 put forth strength ⑭give birth to; lay ～蛋 lay eggs 【下巴】 the lower jaw / chin 【下班】 come or go off work; knock off 【下半场】 second half (of a game) 【下半旗】 fly a flag at half-mast 【下半夜】 the latter half of the night 【下笔】 put pen to paper; begin to write or paint 【下策】 a bad plan; an unwise decision 【下层】 lower levels / lower strata 【下场】 go off stage; exit/leave the playing field/end; fate 【下沉】 sink; subside; submerge 【下船】 go ashore; disembark 【下垂】 hang down; droop 【下达】 make known to lower levels 任务已 经～ the task has been assigned 【下地】 go to the fields/ leave a sickbed 【下毒手】 strike a vicious blow 【下颚】 the lower jaw; mandible 【下放】 transfer to a lower level 【下风】 leeward / disadvantageous position 占～ be at a disadvantage 【下岗】 come or go off sentry duty 【下工 夫】 put in time and energy; concentrate one's efforts

【下跪】 kneel down 【下海】 go to sea 【下级】 lower level/ subordinate ～干部 junior cadre ～机关 government office at a lower level 【下贱】 low; base; mean; degrading 【下降】 descend; drop; fall; decline 飞机开始～ the plane began to descend 生产成本～ production costs come down 出生率～ a decline in the birth rate 【下课】 get out of class; finish class ～后再去 go there after class 现在～ the class is over 【下来】 come down 【下列】 listed below; following 【下令】 give orders 【下流】 lower reaches (of a river) / mean; dirty; coarse ～的玩笑 obscene jests ～话 foul language; obscenities 【下落】 whereabouts / drop; fall 【下马】 get down from a horse/discontinue (a project, etc.) 【下面】 below; under / next; following / lower level ～该谁了 who's next 听～的意见 listen to the views of one's subordinates 【下坡路】 downhill path 走～ go downhill; be on the decline 【下棋】 play chess 【下去】 go down; descend 【下身】 the lower part of the body/private parts/trousers 【下手】 put one's hand to; start; set about; set to / right-hand seat / assistant; helper 打～ act as assistant 【下属】 subordinate 【下水】 (of a ship) enter the water; be launched/fall into evil ways ～典礼 launching ceremony 【下水道】 sewer 【下台】 step down from the stage or platform / fall out of power; leave office 【下文】 what follows in the passage, paragraph, article, etc./later development; outcome ～再作阐述 be explained in the ensuing chapters or paragraphs 【下午】 afternoon 【下乡】 go to the countryside 【下旬】 the last ten-day period of a month 【下游】 lower reaches (of a river)/backward position 【下肢】 legs

吓 xià frighten; scare; intimidate ～我一跳 give me a start

夏 xià summer 【夏布】 grass cloth; grass linen 【夏历】 the lunar calendar 【夏令】 summer; summertime/summer weather ～商品 commodities for summer use ～营 summer camp 【夏收】 summer harvest

仙 xiān celestial being; immortal 【仙丹】 elixir of life 【仙鹤】 red-crowned crane 【仙境】 fairyland; wonderland 【仙女】 female celestial 【仙人掌】 cactus

先 xiān ①earlier; before; first; in advance ～人后己 put others before oneself 我～说几句 let me say a few words first 您～请 after you ②elder generation; ancestor ③deceased; late ～父 my late father 【先导】 guide; forerunner; precursor 【先发制人】 gain the initiative by striking first; forestall the enemy 【先锋】 van 打～ fight in the van; be a pioneer ～队 vanguard 【先后】 early or late; priority; order / successively; one after another 【先进】 advanced ～单位 advanced unit ～分子 advanced element 【先决】 prerequisite 【先例】 precedent 开～ set a precedent 有～可援 have a precedent to go by 【先烈】 martyr 【先前】 before; previously 【先遣】 sent in advance ～队 advance party 【先驱】 pioneer; forerunner 【先入为主】 first impressions are strongest; be prejudiced 【先声】 first signs; herald 【先生】 teacher/mister (Mr.); gentleman; sir 【先天】 congenital; inborn / innate ～不足 be congenitally deficient; suffer from an inherent shortage 【先行】 go ahead of the rest; start off before the others / beforehand ～通知 notify in advance ～者 forerunner 【先兆】 omen; portent; sign 【先哲】 sage

纤 xiān fine; minute 【纤巧】 dainty; delicate 【纤弱】 slim and fragile 【纤维】 fibre; staple ～板 fibreboard ～素 cellulose【纤细】very thin; slender; tenuous

掀 xiān lift (a cover, etc.) ～门帘 lift the door curtain ～盖子 take the lid off【掀动】lift; start; set in motion【掀起】lift; raise / surge / set off (a movement)

锨 xiān shovel

鲜 xiān ①fresh ～奶 fresh milk ②bright-coloured; bright ③delicious; tasty ④delicacy 时～ delicacies of the season ⑥aquatic foods 海～ seafood【鲜红】bright red; scarlet【鲜花】(fresh) flowers【鲜美】delicious; tasty【鲜明】bright / clear-cut; distinct; distinctive ～的对照 sharp contrast 主题～ have a distinct theme【鲜嫩】fresh and tender【鲜血】blood【鲜艳】bright-coloured; gaily-coloured

闲 xiān ①not busy; idle ～不住 refuse to stay idle 星期日我就～了 I'll be disengaged on Sunday ②not in use; unoccupied; lying idle ～房 unoccupied room or house ③spare time; leisure 不得～ have no time to spare【闲逛】saunter; stroll; loaf【闲话】digression/complaint; gossip【闲聊】chat【闲气】anger about trifles【闲钱】spare cash【闲人】an unoccupied person; idler/persons not concerned ～免进 no admittance except on business【闲散】free and at leisure; at a loose end / unused; idle ～资金 idle capital ～土地 scattered plots of unutilized land【闲事】a matter that does not concern one / unimportant matter 别管～ none of your business 老爱管～ be always meddling【闲适】leisurely and comfortable【闲书】light reading【闲谈】engage in chitchat【闲暇】leisure【闲心】leisurely mood【闲杂】without fixed duties ～人员 miscellaneous personnel【闲置】leave unused; set aside

贤 xiān ①virtuous; worthy; able ②an able and virtuous person 让～ relinquish one's post in favour of sb.

better qualified 【贤达】prominent personage 【贤惠】virtuous 【贤良】able and virtuous 【贤明】sagacious

弦 xián ①bowstring; string ②the string of a musical instrument 【弦外之音】overtones; implication 【弦乐队】string orchestra 【弦乐器】stringed instrument

咸 xián salted; salty ~鱼 salt fish ~蛋 salted egg ~菜 salted vegetables; pickles ~肉 salt meat; bacon

娴 xián ①refined ②adept; skilled ~于辞令 be gifted with a silver tongue 【娴静】gentle and refined 【娴熟】adept; skilled ~的技巧 consummate skill

舷 xián the side of a ship; board 左~ port 右~ starboard 【舷窗】porthole 【舷梯】gangway ladder / ramp

衔 xián ①hold in the mouth ~着烟斗 have a pipe between one's teeth ②harbour; bear ~冤 nurse a bitter sense of wrong ③rank; title 【衔接】link up; join

嫌 xián ①suspicion 避~ avoid suspicion ②enmity; ill will ③dislike; mind; complain of ~麻烦 not want to take the trouble 【嫌弃】dislike and avoid; cold-shoulder 【嫌恶】detest; loathe 【嫌疑】suspicion ~犯 suspect ~分子 suspected person 【嫌怨】grudge; resentment

险 xián ①a place difficult of access; narrow pass ②danger; peril; risk 遇~ meet with danger ③vicious; venomous 阴~ sinister ④by a hair's breadth; by inches; nearly ~遭不幸 come within an ace of death 【险恶】dangerous; perilous; ominous / malicious; treacherous 处境~ be in a perilous position 病情~ be dangerously ill ~的用心 vicious intentions; evil motives 【险境】dangerous situation 【险滩】rapids 【险些】narrowly (escape from sth. untoward); nearly 【险要】strategically located and difficult of access 【险症】dangerous illness 【险阻】(of roads) dangerous and difficult

显 xiǎn ①apparent; obvious 效果不～ the effect is not noticeable ②show; display; manifest 不～脏 not show the dirt 【显达】 illustrious and influential 【显得】 look; seem; appear 他～有点紧张 he seems a bit nervous 屋子～宽敞多了 the room looks much more spacious 【显而易见】 obviously; evidently; clearly 【显赫】 illustrious; celebrated 声势～ have a powerful influence ～的名声 great renown 【显露】 become visible; appear; manifest itself 【显明】 manifest; distinct; marked ～的道理 an obvious truth ～的特点 marked characteristic 【显然】 obvious; evident; clear 【显身手】 display one's talent or skill 【显示】 show; display; demonstrate; manifest ～力量 display one's strength 【显微镜】 microscope 【显象管】 kinescope 【显形】 show one's (true) colours; betray oneself 【显眼】 showy 【显要】 powerful and influential/influential figure; important personage 【显影】 develop ～机 developing machine ～剂 developer ～纸 developing-out paper 【显著】 notable; striking 收效～ yield notable results ～的进步 marked progress ～的成就 remarkable success ～的特征 outstanding characteristics

县 xiàn county 【县城】 county town 【县委】 county Party committee 【县长】 county magistrate

现 xiàn ①present; current ～阶段 the present stage ～况 the existing situation ②(do sth.) in time of need ～写一首诗 improvise a poem ③(of money) on hand ～钱 ready money; cash ④cash; ready money 付～ pay cash ⑤show; appear ～出一丝笑容 a faint smile appeared on sb.'s face 【现场】 scene (of an incident) / site; spot 保护～ keep the scene intact 工作～ worksite 试验～ testing ground ～会议 on-the-spot meeting 【现成】 ready-made ～衣服 ready-made clothes ～饭 food ready for the table; unearned gain ～话 an onlooker's unsolicited comments; a kibitzer's comments 【现代】 modern times/modern; contemporary ～派 modernist school ～史 contemporary history 【现代化】 modernize ～企业 modernized enterprise ～设备 sophisticated equipment 实现四个～ achieve the four modernizations (of agriculture, industry, national defence, and science and technology) 【现金】 ready money; cash / cash reserve in a bank ～付款 cash payment ～交易 cash transaction ～帐book cash book ～支出 out-of-pocket expenses 【现任】 at present hold the office of/currently in office; incumbent 【现实】 reality; actuality/real; actual 脱离～ be divorced from reality 面对～ face the facts ～生活 real life ～意义 practical or immediate significance ～态度 a realistic attitude ～主义 realism 【现世】 this life / lose face; be disgraced 【现象】 appearance (of things); phenomenon 社会～ social phenomenon 不良～ unhealthy phenomena 【现行】 in effect; in force; in operation / active ～法令 decrees in effect ～规章制度 rules and regulations in force ～政策 present policies ～反革命分子 active counterrevolutionary ～犯 criminal caught in, before or immediately after the act 【现形】 betray oneself 【现役】 active service; active duty ～军官 officer on the active list ～军人 serviceman 【现有】 existing ～材料 materials now available; available information 【现在】 now; at present; today 【现状】 present situation; *status quo*

限 xiàn limit; bounds 以年底为～ set the end of the year as the deadline ②set a limit; restrict 每人～购四张票 each customer is limited to four tickets 人数不～ there is no restriction on the number of people 【限定】 prescribe a limit to; limit; restrict 【限度】 limit; limitation 超过～ go beyond the limit 【限额】 norm; limit; quota 【限量】 limit the quantity of; set bounds to 【限期】 within a definite time / time limit; deadline ～报到 report for duty by the prescribed time ～撤退 withdraw within a stated time ～已满 the time limit has been reached 【限于】 be confined to; be limited to 不～青年 be not confined to the young people ～篇幅 as space is limited 【限制】 restrict; limit; confine 年龄～ age limit

线 xiàn ①thread; string; wire ～团 a reel of thread ② made of cotton thread ～衣 ～裤 cotten knitwear ③ line; route 直～ straight line 供应～ supply route 海岸～ coastline ④brink; verge 在死亡～上 on the verge of death ⑤一～希望 a ray of hope 一一光明 a gleam of light 一一生机 a slim chance of life 【线路】 circuit/line; route 【线绳】 cotton rope 【线索】 clue; thread 破案的～ clues for solving a case 故事的～ threads of a story 【线毯】 cotton (thread) blanket 【线条】 line 【线装】 thread binding ～书 thread-bound Chinese book

宪 xiàn ①statute ②constitution 制～ draw up a constitution 【宪兵】 military police ～队 military police corps 【宪法】 constitution ～草案 draft constitution 【宪章】 charter 【宪政】 constitutionalism

陷 xiàn ①get stuck; be bogged down in ～进泥里 get stuck in the mud ～于孤立 find oneself isolated ② sink; cave in 地基下～ the foundations have sunk 【陷害】 frame (up) ～好人 frame up an innocent person 政治～ political frame-up 【陷阱】 pitfall; pit; trap 【陷落】 subside; sink in; cave in/(of territory) fall into enemy hands 【陷入】 sink into; be caught in / be immersed in; be deep in ～被动 fall into a passive position ～重围 find oneself tightly encircled ～困境 land in a predicament; be cornered ～僵局 come to a deadlock ～沉思 be lost in thought

馅 xiàn filling; stuffing 肉～ meat filling 饺子～ stuffing for dumplings 【馅儿饼】 meat pie

羡 xiàn admire 人人称～ be the admiration of everyone 【羡慕】 admire; envy

献 xiàn ①offer; present; dedicate; donate ～花圈 lay a wreath ～血 donate blood for sb. ～出生命 give one's life for ②show; put on; display ～殷勤 show sb. excessive attentions; pay one's addresses 【献宝】 present a treasure/offer a valuable piece of advice/show off what one treasures 【献策】 offer advice; make suggestions 【献词】 congratulatory message 【献计】 offer advice; make suggestions 【献技】 show one's skill 【献礼】 present a gift 【献媚】 try to ingratiate oneself with; make up to 【献旗】 present a banner 【献身】 dedicate oneself to; give one's life for

腺 xiàn gland 汗～ sweat gland

XIANG

乡 xiāng ①country; village; rural area ②native place; home village or town 回～ return to one's native place ③township 【乡亲】 a person from the same village or town / local people; villagers; folks 【乡绅】 country gentleman; squire 【乡思】 homesickness; nostalgia 【乡土】 native soil; home village / of one's native land; local ～风味 local flavour ～观念 provincialism 【乡下】 village; countryside ～人 country folk

相 xiāng each other; one another; mutually ～安 live in peace with each other 素不～识 not know each

other ～距太远 too far apart 【相比】compare 二者不能
～ there's no comparison between the two (of them) 【相
差】differ 两者～无几 there's hardly any difference
between the two 【相称】match; suit 颜色～ the colours
match well 【相持】be locked in a stalemate 双方～不下
neither side was ready to yield 【相处】get along 不好
difficult to get along with ～得好 get on well with each
other 【相传】tradition has it that...; according to leg-
end/hand down or pass on from one to another 【相当】
match; be equal to/suitable; fit/quite; fairly 得失～
the gains balance the losses 年龄～ be well-matched in age ～
好 fairly good ～成功 be quite a success 【相等】be equal
数量～ be equal in amount 【相抵】offset; balance; coun-
terbalance 收支～ the expenses balance the receipts 【相
对】opposite/relative ～而坐 sit face to face ～稳定 relatively stable 地说 comparatively speaking ～真理
relative truth ～值 relative value ～主义 relativism 【相
反】opposite; contrary ～方向 opposite direction 与愿望
～ contrary to one's expectations ～相成 oppose each
other and yet also complement each other 【相仿】similar;
more or less the same 内容～ be similar in content 年
纪～ be about the same age 【相逢】meet (by chance);
come across 【相符】conform to; tally with; correspond
to 【相辅相成】supplement each other 【相干】be concerned with 这事与你不～ this has nothing to do with you
【相隔】be separated by; be apart; be at a distance of ～
万里 be a long way away from each other ～多年 after
an interval of many years 【相关】be interrelated 【相好】
be on intimate terms/intimate friend/have an affair with/
lover or mistress 【相互】mutual; reciprocal; each other
～影响 influence each other; interact ～关系 mutual re-

lation; interrelation 〜作用 interaction; interplay 【相继】
one after another 〜发言 speak in succession 【相间】
alternate with 黑白〜 in black and white check 【相交】
intersect / make friends with 〜有年 have been friends
for years 【相近】 close; near / be similar to 比分〜 the
score was very close 【相距】 apart; away from 【相连】 be
linked together; be joined 【相劝】 persuade; offer advice
【相商】 consult 【相识】 be acquainted with each other/ac-
quaintance 素不〜 have never met 老〜 an old acquaintance 【相思】 yearning between lovers 单〜 unrequited
love 〜病 lovesickness 【相似】 resemble; be similar; be
alike 面貌〜 look alike 【相提并论】 mention in the same
breath; place on a par 【相通】 communicate with each
other; be interlinked 两间〜的屋子 two communicating
rooms 【相同】 identical; the same; alike 观点〜 have the
same views on sth. 毫无〜之处 have nothing in common
【相投】 agree with each other 兴趣〜 find each other
congenial 【相象】 resemble; be similar; be alike 【相信】
believe in; be convinced of 〜真理 believe in truth 〜
群众 have faith in the masses 【相形见绌】 prove definitely inferior 【相依】 be interdependent 〜为命 depend on
each other for survival 【相宜】 suitable; fitting 【相应】
corresponding; relevant 采取〜措施 take appropriate measures 通过〜决议 pass relevant resolutions 【相映】 set
each other off 〜成趣 form a delightful contrast

香 xiāng ①sweet-smelling; aromatic; scented 〜花 fragrant flowers ②savoury; appetizing 这饭真〜 this
rice is really appetizing ③with good appetite 吃得〜 eat
with relish; enjoy the food ④perfume; spice 檀〜 sandalwood ⑤incense; joss stick 盘〜 incense coil 【香槟酒】
champagne 【香菜】 coriander 【香草】 sweetgrass 【香肠】

sausage 【香粉】 face powder 【香菇】 *Xianggu* mushroom 【香瓜】 muskmelon 【香蕉】 banana 【香精】 essence 【香客】 pilgrim 【香料】 perfume / spice ～厂 perfumery 【香炉】 incense burner 【香喷喷】 sweet-smelling/savoury; appetizing 【香水】 perfume; scent 【香甜】 fragrant and sweet/ (sleep) soundly 【香味】 sweet smell; fragrance; scent; perfume 【香烟】 cigarette / incense smoke ～盒 cigarette case ～头 cigarette butt 【香油】 sesame oil 【香皂】 perfumed soap; toilet soap 【香脂】 face cream/balm; balsam

厢 xiāng ①wing; wing-room ②railway carriage or compartment; (theatre) box ③side 一～情愿 one-sided wish

箱 xiāng chest; box; case; trunk 大木～ wooden trunk 货～ packing box 书～ a box for books

襄 xiāng assist; help 【襄理】 assistant manager 【襄助】 assist

镶 xiāng ①inlay; set; mount ～宝石 set gems 给窗子 ～玻璃 glaze a window ②rim; edge; border 给裙子 ～花边 edge a skirt with lace 【镶牙】 put in a false tooth

详 xiáng ①detailed; minute ～谈 speak in detail ②details; particulars ～见附录 for details, see the appendix ③know clearly 不～ be unknown 【详细】 detailed ～的记载 a detailed record ～的调查 a thorough investigation ～的研究 an exhaustive study 【详情】 detailed information ～后报 details to follow ～请向办事处 please apply to the office for particulars 【详图】 detail (drawing) 【详细】 detailed; minute ～了解情况 acquire detailed knowledge of the situation ～占有资料 collect all the available material 请近～点 please explain in greater detail ～地描述 give a minute description

降 xiáng surrender; capitulate 【降伏】 subdue; vanquish; tame 【降服】 yield; surrender; break in (a wild horse)

祥 xiáng auspicious; propitious; lucky 【祥瑞】auspicious sign

翔 xiáng circle in the air 翱～ soar; hover 【翔实】full and accurate

享 xiǎng enjoy 共～胜利的欢乐 share the joy of victory 【享福】enjoy a happy life 【享乐】indulge in creature comforts ～思想 preoccupation with pleasure-seeking ～主义 hedonism 【享年】die at the age of 【享受】enjoy/enjoyment; treat ～公费医疗 enjoy public health services 贪图～ seek ease and comfort 【享用】enjoy (the use of) 【享有】enjoy (rights, prestige, etc.)

响 xiǎng ①sound; noise 一声炮～ the report of a cannon ②make a sound; ring 电话铃～了 the telephone rang ③noisy; loud 【响彻】resound through (the skies, etc.) ～山谷 reverberate in the valley 【响动】sound of sth. astir 【响亮】resonant; sonorous ～的回答 a loud and clear reply ～的声音 a resounding voice 【响应】respond; answer ～党的号召 respond to the Party's call

饷 xiǎng ①entertain (with food and drink) ②pay (for soldiers, policemen, etc.) 月～ monthly pay

想 xiǎng ①think 想～问题 think over a problem ～办法 think of a way ②suppose; reckon; consider 我～他今天不会来 I don't think he'll be coming today ③want to; would like to 我～试试 I'd like to have a try ④remember with longing; miss 我们都很～你 we all missed you 【想必】presumably; most likely 【想不到】unexpected ～变化这么大 I never expected it would have changed so much 【想不开】take things too hard; take a matter to heart 【想当然】assume sth. as a matter of course; take for granted 【想到】think of; call to mind 【想得开】not take to heart 【想法】idea; opinion

按我的～ in my opinion; to my mind 把你的～说出来 speak your mind out 【想方设法】do everything possible; try every means 【想见】infer; gather 【想来】it may be assumed that; presumably 【想念】long to see again; miss 【想起】remember; recall; think of; call to mind 【想入非非】indulge in fantasy; allow one's fancy to run wild 【想通】straighten out one's thinking; become convinced 【想望】desire; long for 【想象】imagine; fancy; visualize/imagination 难以～ hard to imagine ～不到的困难 unimaginable difficulties ～力 imaginative power

向 xiàng ①direction 风～ wind direction ②face; turn towards 这间房子～东 this room faces east ③take sb.'s part; be partial to ～理不～人 side with whoever is right ④to; from ～上级汇报工作 report to one's superior on one's work ～纵深发展 develop in depth 【向导】guide 【向来】always; all along ～如此 it has always been so 我～不抽烟 I have never smoked 【向前】forward; onward; ahead 奋勇～ forge ahead 采取～看的态度 adopt a forward-looking attitude 【向日葵】sunflower 【向上】upward; up 【向往】yearn for ～幸福的新生活 look forward to a happy new life ～共产主义 cherish the ideal of communism 【向下】downward; down 【向阳】exposed to the sun; sunny / with a sunny (usu. southern) exposure 这间屋～ the room has a southern exposure 【向着】turn towards; face / take sb.'s part; side with

巷 xiàng lane; alley 【巷战】street fighting

项 xiàng ①nape (of the neck) ②sum (of money) 进～ income 欠～ liabilities ③term 【项链】necklace 【项目】item 基本建设～ capital construction project 训练～ training courses 田径～ track and field events

相 xiāng ①looks; appearance 长~ a person's appearance 可怜~ a pitiful appearance ②bearing; posture ③look at and appraise ~马 look at a horse to judge its worth ④ photograph 照个~ take a photo 【相册】photo album 【相机】watch for an opportunity/camera ~行事 act as the occasion demands ~而动 bide one's time 【相角】photo corner 【相貌】facial features; looks; appearance ~端正 have regular features 【相片】photograph; photo 【相声】comic dialogue; cross talk 说~ perform a comic dialogue 【相纸】photographic paper

象 xiàng ①elephant ②appearance; shape; image ③resemble 这兄弟俩长得很~ the two brothers are very much alike 这孩子~他父亲 the child takes after its father ④look as if; seem ~要下雨了 it looks like rain ⑤such as; like 【象棋】(Chinese) chess 【象牙】elephant's tusk; ivory ~雕刻 ivory carving ~制品 ivories ~之塔 ivory tower 【象样】up to the mark; presentable; decent; sound ~的桌子 a decent table ~的理由 a sound reason 【象征】symbolize; signify; stand for / symbol; token 友谊的~ emblem of friendship ~性 symbolic

像 xiàng ①likeness (of sb.); portrait; picture 铜~ bronze statue ②image 【像章】badge

橡 xiàng ①oak ②rubber tree 【橡胶】rubber ~厂 rubber plant ~轮胎 rubber tyre 【橡皮】rubber/eraser ~船 rubber boat ~膏 adhesive plaster ~筋 rubber band ~泥 plasticine ~手套 rubber gloves ~艇 rubber dinghy ~图章 rubber-stamp

XIAO

削 xiāo ①pare (with a knife) ~苹果 peel an apple ~铅笔 sharpen a pencil ②cut; chop ~球 cut; chop

哮

xiāo ①heavy breathing; wheeze ②roar; howl 【哮喘】 asthma

消

xiāo ①disappear; vanish 云～雾散 the clouds dispersed and the fog lifted ②eliminate; dispel; remove ～愁解闷 dispel depression or melancholy ③while away (the time) ～夏 pass the summer in a leisurely way 【消沉】 downhearted; low-spirited; dejected; depressed 意志～ demoralized; despondent 【消除】 eliminate; dispel ～分歧 iron out differences ～顾虑 dispel misgivings ～隐患 remove a hidden danger ～误会 clear up a misunderstanding 【消毒】 disinfect; sterilize ～剂 disinfectant ～牛奶 sterilized milk 【消防】 fire control ～车 fire engine ～队 fire brigade ～人员 fire fighter ～设备 fire-fighting equipment ～水龙 fire hose ～站 fire station 【消费】 consume ～城市 consumer-city ～合作社 consumers' cooperative ～品 consumer goods ～者 consumer ～资料 means of subsistence 【消耗】 use up; deplete; expend ～精力 consume one's energy ～战 war of attrition 【消化】 digest 好～ digestible; easy to digest 帮助学生～所学的东西 help the students digest what they have learnt ～不良 indigestion; dyspepsia ～系统 digestive system 【消火栓】 fire hydrant 【消极】 negative/passive; inactive ～因素 negative factor ～影响 negative influence ～抵抗 passive resistance 态度～ remain inactive 情绪～ be dispirited ～怠工 be slack in work 【消灭】 die out; pass away / eliminate; abolish 自行～ perish of itself ～剥削制度 eliminate the system of exploitation ～敌人一个师 wipe out an enemy division 【消磨】 wear down; fritter away / idle away ～岁月 while away the time ～时间 kill time; pass the time 【消气】 cool down; be mollified 【消遣】 divert oneself; while away the time/

pastime; diversion 【消融】 melt 【消散】 scatter and disappear; dissipate 雾～了 the mist has lifted 【消失】 disappear; vanish; die away ～在人群中 be lost in a crowd 【消逝】 fade away; elapse 随着时间的～ with the lapse of time 【消瘦】 become thin; emaciate 【消亡】 wither away; die out 【消息】 news; information / tidings

宵 xiāo night 通～ throughout the night 【宵禁】 curfew 实行～ impose a curfew 解除～ lift a curfew

逍 xiāo 【逍遥】 free and unfettered ～自在 be leisurely and carefree ～法外 go scot-free; be at large

萧 xiāo desolate; dreary 【萧瑟】 rustle in the air/bleak; desolate 秋风～ the autumn wind is soughing 【萧条】 bleak/depression 经济～ economic depression; slump

硝 xiāo ①nitre; saltpetre ②tawing 【硝镪水】 nitric acid 【硝酸】 nitric acid 【硝烟】 smoke of gunpowder

销 xiāo ①melt (metal) ②cancel; annul 注～ write off ～案 close a case ③sell; market 畅～ sell well 滞～ sell poorly ④expend; spend 开～ expenditure 【销毁】 destroy by melting or burning ～罪证 destroy incriminating evidence 【销魂】 feel transported 【销假】 report back after leave of absence 【销路】 sale; market ～好 have a good sale 没有～ find no sale 【销声匿迹】 keep silent and lie low; disappear from the scene 【销售】 sell; market ～价格 selling price ～量 sales volume ～总额 total sales

潇 xiāo (of water) deep and clear 【潇洒】 natural and unrestrained 【潇潇】 whistling and pattering/drizzly

箫 xiāo a vertical bamboo flute

霄 xiāo ①clouds 高入云～ towering into the clouds ②sky; heaven 【霄壤】 heaven and earth 有～之别 be as far apart as heaven and earth

嚣 xiāo clamour; hubbub; din 【嚣张】 arrogant; aggressive ～一时 run rampant for a time

淆 xiáo confuse; mix 混～ mix up; obscure ～惑 bewilder 【淆乱】 confuse; befuddle

小 xiǎo ①small; little; petty ～姑娘 a little girl ～问题 a minor question ～声说话 speak in a low voice ②for a short time ～坐 sit for a while ～住 stay for a few days ③young ～儿子 the youngest son ～鸡 chick; chicken 【小班】 the bottom class in a kindergarten 【小半】 less than half 【小报】 tabloid 【小辈】 younger member of a family; junior 【小本经营】 business with a small capital/do business in a small way 【小便】 urinate; pass water/urine ～处 urinal 【小辫儿】 short braid; pigtail 【小辫子】 vulnerable point; handle 抓住～不放 get a handle on sb. to make things hard for him 【小标题】 subheading; subhead 【小册子】 booklet; pamphlet 【小产】 miscarriage; abortion 【小肠】 small intestine 【小车】 handcart; pushcart / sedan (car) 【小吃】 snack; refreshments / cold dish; made dish ～部 snack counter ～店 snack bar; lunchroom 【小丑】 clown; buffoon 【小葱】 shallot; spring onion 【小聪明】 petty trick 【小刀】 small sword / pocket knife 【小道消息】 hearsay; grapevine 【小调】 ditty / minor 【小动作】 petty action; little trick 【小豆】 red bean 【小队】 team; squad 【小恩小惠】 petty favours 【小儿】 children ～科 (department of) paediatrics 【小贩】 pedlar; vendor 【小费】 tip 【小工】 unskilled labourer 【小鬼】 imp; goblin/little devil 【小孩】 child 【小伙子】 lad; young fellow 【小集团】 clique 【小将】 young general/ young militant; young pathbreaker 【小轿车】 sedan (car); limousine 【小节】 small matter; trifle 生活～ matters concerning personal life 不拘～ not bother about small matters; not be punctilious 【小结】 preliminary summary; brief sum-up ～前阶段的工作 summarize briefly the work done in the previous stage 【小姐】 Miss/ young lady 【小看】 look down upon; belittle 【小康】 comparatively well-off ～之家 a comfortable family 【小考】 mid-term examination; quiz 【小老婆】 concubine 【小麦】 wheat 【小卖部】 a small shop attached to a school, factory, theatre, etc./buffet; snack counter 【小米】 millet ～粥 millet gruel 【小名】 pet name for a child; childhood name 【小拇指】 little finger 【小脑】 cerebellum 【小农】 small farmer ～经济 small-scale peasant economy 【小朋友】 children / little boy or girl; child 【小便宜】 small gain 贪～ go after petty advantages 【小品】 a short, simple creation; sketch 历史～ short historical essay ～文 (familiar) essay 【小气】 stingy; niggardly; mean/narrow-minded; petty 【小巧玲珑】 small and exquisite 【小曲】 ditty; popular tune 【小圈子】 small circle of people 搞～ form a small coterie ～主义 "small circle" mentality 【小人】 a person of low position / a base person; vile character ～得志 villains holding sway 【小人书】 picture-story book 【小人物】 an unimportant person; a nobody 【小商品】 small commodities ～经济 small commodity economy ～生产者 small commodity producer 【小生产】 small production ～者 small producer 【小时】 hour 【小时候】 in one's childhood; when one was young 【小市民】 urban petty bourgeois 【小事】 trifle; petty thing 【小手小脚】 stingy; mean / lacking boldness; timid; niggling 【小数】 decimal ～点 decimal point 【小说】 novel; fiction ～家 novelist; writer of fiction 【小算盘】 selfish calculations ～打得精 be very calculating 【小提琴】 violin ～手 violinist 【小题大作】 make a fuss over a trifling matter

【小偷】petty thief ～小摸 pilfering 【小腿】shank 【小写】 small letter 【小心】take care; be careful; be cautious ～火烛 guard against fire ～轻放 handle with care ～油 漆 mind the wet paint 【小型】small-sized; small-scale; miniature ～企业 small enterprise ～拖拉机 baby tractor ～照相机 miniature camera 【小熊猫】lesser panda 【小学】primary school ～生 pupil; schoolchild; schoolboy or schoolgirl 【小样】galley proof 【小业主】small proprietor 【小夜曲】serenade 【小意思】small token of kindly feelings; mere trifle 【小灶】special mess 【小帐】tip; gratuity 【小照】small-sized photograph 【小传】brief biography 【小资产阶级】petty bourgeoisie 【小字】small character 【小组】group ～讨论 group discussion

晓 xiǎo ①dawn; daybreak 拂～ foredawn ②know ③let sb. know; tell ～以利害 warn sb. of the consequences 【晓得】know 【晓示】tell explicitly; notify

孝 xiào ①filial piety ②mourning 带～ in mourning 【孝服】mourning (dress) 【孝敬】give presents (to one's elders or superiors) 【孝顺】show filial obedience 【孝子】dutiful son / son in mourning

肖 xiào resemble; be like 【肖像】portrait; portraiture ～画 portrait-painting

效 xiào ①effect 见～ produce an effect; prove effective ②imitate ③devote (one's energy or life) to; render (a service) 【效法】follow the example of; model oneself on; learn from 【效果】effect; result/sound effects ～不大 not be very effective 取得良好的～ achieve good results 【效劳】work in the service of; work for 乐于～ be glad to offer one's services 【效力】render a service to; serve (one's country, etc.) /effect 这药很有～ the medicine is efficacious 【效率】efficiency ～高 efficient

~低 inefficient 提高~ raise efficiency【效命】go all out to serve sb. regardless of the consequences【效能】efficacy; usefulness【效益】beneficial result; benefit 提高经济~ achieve better economic results【效忠】pledge loyalty to; devote oneself heart and soul to

校 xiào ①school ~办工厂 school-run workshop ②field officer【校车】school bus【校风】school spirit【校官】field officer【校规】school regulations【校徽】school badge【校刊】school magazine; college journal【校历】school calendar【校庆】anniversary of the founding of a school or college【校舍】schoolhouse; school building【校外】outside school; after school ~辅导员 after-school activities counsellor ~活动站 after-school activities club【校务】administrative affairs of a school or college【校医】school doctor【校友】alumnus or alumna【校园】campus; school yard【校长】headmaster; principal / president【校址】the location of a school or college

笑 xiào ①smile; laugh; grin ②ridicule 别~他 don't laugh at him【笑柄】laughingstock; butt; joke 成为~become a standing joke【笑哈哈】laughingly; with a laugh【笑话】joke; jest / laugh at 说~crack a joke 闹~make a fool of oneself 等着看~wait to have a good laugh at sb.【笑剧】farce【笑里藏刀】with murderous intent behind one's smiles【笑脸】smiling face ~相迎 greet sb. with a smile 陪~meet rudeness with a flattering smile【笑容】smiling expression; smile【笑谈】object of ridicule【笑窝】dimple【笑嘻嘻】grinning; smiling broadly【笑颜】smiling face【笑逐颜开】beam with smiles; be wreathed in smiles

嘯 xiào ①whistle ②howl; roar 虎~the roar of a tiger【嘯聚】band together; gang up ~山林 go to the greenwood

XIE

些 xiē some; few 前～日子 a few days ago; sometime ago 买～东西 do some shopping 好～人 a lot of people 这～ these 【些微】slightly; a little; a bit

歇 xiē ①have a rest ～口气 stop for a breather; take a breather ②stop (work, etc.) 【歇班】be off duty 【歇工】stop work; knock off 【歇晌】take a midday nap or rest 【歇手】stop doing sth. 【歇斯底里】hysteria 【歇息】have a rest/go to bed 【歇业】close a business

蝎 xiē scorpion 【蝎虎】gecko; house lizard

协 xié ①joint; common ～办 do sth. jointly ②assist 【协定】agreement; accord/reach an agreement on sth. 【协会】association; society 【协力】unite efforts; join in a common effort 【协商】consult; talk things over 民主～ democratic consultation ～会议 consultative conference 【协调】coordinate; concert; harmonize ～委员会 coordination committee 【协同】work in coordination with; cooperate-with ～作战 fight in coordination ～动作 coordinated action 【协议】agree on/agreement 达成～ reach an agreement 【协助】assist; help; give assistance; provide help 【协奏曲】concerto 【协作】cooperation; coordination; combined efforts

邪 xié evil; heretical; irregular 不信～ not believe in heresy 【邪道】evil ways; vice 走～ lead a depraved life 【邪恶】wicked; vicious 【邪门歪道】crooked ways; dishonest practices 【邪魔】evil spirit; demon 【邪念】evil thought; wicked idea 【邪气】perverse trend; evil influence; unhealthy trend 【邪说】heresy; heretical ideas

胁 xié ①the upper part of the side of the human body ②coerce; force 裹~ force to take part 【胁从】be an accomplice under duress ~分子 reluctant follower

挟 xié ①hold sth. under the arm ②coerce; force sb. to submit to one's will ③harbour (resentment, etc.) 【挟持】seize sb. on both sides by the arms/hold sb. under duress 【挟制】force sb. to do one's bidding

谐 xié ①in harmony; in accord ②humorous 【谐和】concordant 【谐谑】banter 【谐音】homophonic/partials

偕 xié together with; in the company of ~行 travel together 【偕老】husband and wife grow old together 【偕同】in the company of

斜 xié oblique; slanting; inclined; tilted 线~了 the line is slanting ~躺在沙发上 recline on a sofa 把桌子~过来 turn the table sideways 【斜坡】slope 【斜视】strabismus/cast a sidelong glance 目不~ not look sideways 【斜体字】italics 【斜纹】twill (weave) ~布 twill; drill 【斜线】oblique line ~号 slant 【斜眼】strabismus/wall-eye or cross-eye 【斜阳】setting sun

携 xié ①carry; take along ~眷 bring one's wife and children along ~款潜逃 abscond with funds ②take sb. by the hand; join (hands) 【携带】carry; take along ~方便 be easy to carry about 随身~的物品 things carried on one's person 旅客每人可~行李二十公斤 each passenger can take up to twenty kilograms of luggage 【携手】hand in hand ~并进 go forward hand in hand

鞋 xié shoes 【鞋带】shoelace; shoestring 【鞋底】sole 【鞋垫】shoe-pad; insole 【鞋跟】heel 【鞋匠】shoe-maker; cobbler 【鞋扣】shoe buckle 【鞋里】shoe lining 【鞋面】instep; vamp 【鞋刷】shoe brush 【鞋楦】shoe tree 【鞋样】shoe pattern; outline of sole 【鞋油】shoe polish

写 xiě ①write ~得一手好字 write a good hand ②compose ~诗 compose a poem ~日记 make an entry in one's diary ~科学论文 write scientific papers ③describe; depict ~景 describe the scenery 【写稿】 write for a magazine, etc. 为儿童刊物~ contribute to children's magazines 【写生】 paint from life; draw, paint or sketch from nature 人物~ portrait from life ~画 sketch 【写实】 write or paint realistically 【写照】 portrayal; portraiture 【写真】 portray a person; draw a portrait/portrait/describe sth. as it is 【写字台】 (writing) desk 【写作】 writing 从事~ take up writing as one's career ~班子 writing group ~技巧 writing technique

血 xiě blood ~的教训 a lesson paid for in blood 流了一点~ there was a little bleeding 【血晕】 bruise

泻 xiè ①flow swiftly; rush down; pour out ②have loose bowels 【泻盐】 salts 【泻药】 laxative

泄 xiè ①let out; release ~洪 release floodwater ②leak (news, secrets, etc.) ③vent ~私愤 give vent to personal spite 【泄漏】 leak; divulge; give away ~秘密 let out a secret 消息~了 the news has leaked out 【泄露】 let out; reveal 【泄气】 lose heart / disappointing

卸 xiè ①unload; discharge; lay down ~船 unload a ship ~担子 lay down a burden ~牲口 unhitch a draught animal ②remove; strip ~零件 remove parts from a machine 把门~下来 lift a door off its hinges ③get rid of; shirk (the responsibility) 【卸车】 unload goods, etc. from a vehicle 【卸货】 discharge cargo; unload 【卸任】 be relieved of one's office 【卸装】 remove stage makeup and costume

屑 xiè ①bits; scraps; crumbs 纸~ scraps of paper 煤~ (coal) slack 面包~ crumbs (of bread) ②trifling

械 xiè ①tool; instrument 机～ machine ②weapon 军～ arms; ordnance 【械斗】 fight with weapons between groups of people

谢 xiè ①thank 多～ thanks a lot ②decline 敬～不敏 beg to be excused ③(of flowers, leaves) wither 【谢忱】 gratitude; thankfulness 谨致～ allow us to express our thanks for 【谢词】 thank-you speech 【谢绝】 refuse; decline 婉言～ politely refuse ～参观 not open to visitors 【谢幕】 answer a curtain call 【谢天谢地】 thank goodness; thank heaven 【谢帖】 a thank-you note 【谢谢】 thanks; thank you 【谢意】 gratitude; thankfulness 预致～ thank you in anticipation 谨致薄礼，聊表～ please accept this gift and my gratitude 【谢罪】 offer an apology

亵 xiè ①treat with irreverence; be disrespectful ②obscene; indecent 【亵渎】 blaspheme; profane; pollute

榭 xiè a pavilion or house on a terrace 水～ waterside pavilion 歌台舞～ halls for the performance of songs and dances

懈 xiè slack; lax 松～ slacken; relax; let up 作不～的努力 make unremitting efforts 【懈怠】 sluggish

邂 xiè 【邂逅】 meet (a relative, friend, etc.) unexpectedly; run into sb.; meet by chance

蟹 xiè crab 【蟹粉】 crab meat 【蟹黄】 the ovary and digestive glands of a crab

XIN

心 xīn ①the heart ②heart; mind; feeling; intention 羞耻之～ sense of shame 伤人的～ hurt sb.'s feelings ③centre; core 手～ the hollow of the palm 白菜～ the heart of a Chinese cabbage 【心爱】 love; treasure ～的人 loved one ～的东西 treasured possession 【心安理得】

feel at ease and justified 【心病】 worry; anxiety / sore point; secret trouble ～在不焉 absent-minded; inattentive 【心肠】 heart; intention / state of mind; mood 【心潮】 surging thoughts and emotions ～澎湃 feel an upsurge of emotion ～翻滚 one's mind being in a tumult 【心得】 what one has learned from work, study, etc. 【心地】 a person's mind, character, moral nature, etc. ～坦白 candid; open ～单纯 simpleminded ～善良 good-hatured; kindhearted 【心烦】 be vexed; be perturbed ～意乱 be terribly upset 【心浮】 flighty and impatient; unstable 【心服】 be genuinely convinced; acknowledge (one's defeat, mistake, etc.) sincerely 【心腹】 trusted subordinate; reliable agent / confidential 说～话 confide in sb.; exchange confidences ～事 a secret in the depth of one's heart ～之患 disease in one's vital organs — serious hidden trouble or danger 【心甘情愿】 be most willing to; be perfectly happy to 【心肝】 conscience / darling; deary 没～ heartless 【心狠】 cruel; merciless ～手辣 cruel and evil; wicked and merciless 【心花怒放】 burst with joy; be elated 【心怀】 harbour; entertain; cherish / intention; purpose/state of mind; mood ～叵测 harbour dark designs ～不满 feel discontented ～鬼胎 entertain dark schemes 【心慌】 be flustered; be nervous/(of the heart) palpitate ～意乱 be alarmed and nervous 【心灰意懒】 be disheartened; be downhearted 【心机】 thinking; scheming 枉费～ rack ons's brains in vain; make futile efforts 费尽～ take great pains; cudgel one's brains 【心迹】 the true state of one's mind 表明～ lay bare one's true feelings 【心急】 impatient; short-tempered 【心计】 calculation; planning 工于～ adept at scheming 做事很有～ do things intelligently 【心焦】 anxious; worried 【心惊胆战】 tremble with fear; be filled with apprehension 【心境】state of mind; mental state ～不好 be in a bad mood ～愉快 be in a happy mood 【心静】calm 【心坎】the bottom of one's heart 【心口】the pit of the stomach 【心口如一】say what one thinks 【心旷神怡】carefree and joyous 【心理】psychology; mentality 这是一般人的～ this is how ordinary people feel about it ～病态 morbid state of mind ～分析 psychoanalysis ～疗法 psychotherapy ～学 psychology ～学家 psychologist 【心力】mental and physical efforts ～交瘁 be mentally and physically exhausted 【心里】in the heart; at heart; in (the) mind ～不痛快 feel bad about sth. 记在～ keep in mind ～有事 have sth. on one's mind 活在我们～ live in our hearts 【心里话】one's innermost thoughts and feelings 【心灵】clever; intelligent; quick-witted/heart; soul; spirit ～深处 deep in one's heart 【心领神会】understand tacitly; readily take a hint 【心满意足】be perfectly content 【心明眼亮】see and think clearly 【心目】mind; mental view 在某些人的～中 in some people's eyes 在我的～中 to my mind 【心平气和】even-tempered and good-humoured; calm 【心窍】capacity for clear thinking 权迷～ be obsessed by a lust for power 【心情】state of mind ～愉快 be in a cheerful frame of mind; be in a good mood ～激动 be excited ～舒畅 have ease of mind 【心软】be tenderhearted 【心神】mind ～不定 have no peace of mind 【心声】heartfelt wishes; thinking 表达人民的～ voice the aspirations of the people 言为～ what the heart thinks the tongue says 【心事】a load on one's mind; worry ～重重 be weighed down with care 了结一桩～ take a load off one's mind 有～ have something on one's mind 【心想】thought; idea/thinking/mood 坏～ a wicked idea 想

~ ponder; contemplate 用~ think hard 白费~ rack one's brains in vain 没~看戏 not be in the mood to see a play 【心酸】 be grieved; feel sad 【心算】 mental arithmetic 【心疼】 love dearly / feel sorry; be distressed 【心跳】 palpitation 【心头】 mind; heart 记在~ keep in mind ~恨 rankling hatred 【心窝】 the pit of the stomach 【心细】 careful; scrupulous 【心弦】 heartstrings 动人~ tug at one's heartstrings 【心心相印】 have mutual affinity; be kindred spirits 【心绪】 state of mind ~不宁 in a flutter ~烦乱 emotionally upset 【心血】 painstaking effort 费尽~ expend all one's energies ~来潮 be seized by a whim 【心眼儿】 heart; mind/intention/cleverness 没安好~ have bad intentions ~好 kindhearted ~多 full of unnecessary misgivings; oversensitive 有~ be alert and thoughtful 【心意】 regard; kindly feelings/ intention; purpose 【心硬】 hardhearted 【心有余悸】 have a lingering fear 【心愿】 cherished desire; aspiration; wish; dream 【心悦诚服】 feel a heartfelt admiration; be completely convinced 【心脏】 the heart ~病 heart disease ~地带 heartland 【心照】 understand without being told ~不宣 have a tacit understanding 【心直口快】 frank and outspoken 【心中有数】 have a pretty good idea of; know fairly well; know what's what 做到~ get to know how things stand 【心醉】 be charmed; be enchanted

辛 xīn ①hot (in taste, flavour, etc.); pungent ②hard; laborious 艰~ hardships ③suffering 【辛苦】 hard; toilsome / work hard; go through hardships 你得一~一趟 了 you'll have to take the trouble of going there 【辛辣】 pungent; hot ~的味道 a sharp flavour ~的讽刺 bitter irony 【辛劳】 pains; toil 不辞~ spare no pains 【辛勤】 industrious; hardworking ~劳动 work hard; labour assiduously【辛酸】sad; bitter; miserable ～泪 hot and bitter tears ～的往事 sad memories 饱尝～ taste to the full the bitterness of life【辛辛苦苦】take a lot of trouble

欣
xīn glad; happy ～悉 be glad to learn ～逢佳节 on the happy occasion of the festival【欣然】joyfully ～接受 accept with pleasure ～同意 gladly consent; readily agree【欣赏】appreciate; admire 音乐～ music appreciation ～风景 enjoy the scenery【欣慰】be gratified【欣喜】happy ～若狂 be wild with joy; go into raptures【欣欣向荣】thriving; flourishing; prosperous

锌
xīn zinc【锌版】zinc plate ～印刷术 zincography

新
xīn ①new; fresh ～社会 the new society ～技术 up-to-date technique 最～消息 the latest news ②newly; freshly; recently ～建的工厂 a newly built factory 他是～来的 he's a new arrival【新陈代谢】metabolism/ the new superseding the old【新仇旧恨】old scores and new【新村】new residential quarter 工人～ new workers' housing estate【新房】bridal chamber【新婚】newly-married ～夫妇 newly-married couple; newlyweds【新纪元】new era; new epoch【新近】recently; lately【新居】new home; new residence【新郎】bridegroom【新名词】new term【新年】New Year ～好 Happy New Year ～献词 New Year message【新娘】bride【新篇章】new page【新奇】strange; novel; new ～的想法 a novel idea【新人】people of a new type / new personality; new talent / newlywed, esp. the bride【新生】newborn; newly born/new life; rebirth; regeneration/new student ～力量 newly emerging force; new force ～事物 newly emerging things; new things【新诗】free verse written in the vernacular【新式】latest type; new-style ～农具 new types

of farm implements.～武器 modern weapons 【新手】 new hand; raw recruit 【新闻】 news ～处 office of information ～稿 press release ～工作者 journalist ～公报 press *communiqué* ～广播 newscast ～记者 newsman; reporter; journalist ～简报 news summary ～界 press circles; the press ～片 newsreel; news film ～司 department of information ～纸 newsprint 【新鲜】 fresh/new; novel ～空气 fresh air ～经验 new experience 【新兴】 new and developing; rising; burgeoning ～工业城市 a developing industrial city ～势力 the rising forces 【新型】 new type; new pattern 【新颖】 new and original; novel 题材～ original in choice of subject 式样～ in a novel style 【新月】 crescent/new moon 【新装】 new clothes

薪 xīn ①firewood; fuel ②salary; pay; wages 发～ pay out the salary 【薪炭林】 fuel forest

馨 xīn strong and pervasive fragrance 【馨香】 fragrance / smell of burning incense

寻 xīn 【寻死】 (try to) commit suicide ～觅活 repeatedly attempt suicide 【寻思】 think sth. over; consider

芯 xīn core 【芯子】 ①fuse; wick 蜡烛～ candle wick

信 xīn ①true ②confidence; faith 取～于民 win the people's trust ～得过 trustworthy ③believe ～不～由你 believe it or not ～以为真 accept sth. as true 他没有～错人 his trust was not misplaced ④profess faith in; believe in ～佛 profess Buddhism ⑤at will; at random; without plan ⑥sign; evidence 印～ official seal ⑦letter; mail 证明～ certification ⑧message; word; information 还没有～儿 no news yet 【信步】 take a leisurely walk; stroll; walk aimlessly 【信贷】 credit ～资金 credit funds 【信风】 trade (wind) ～带 trade-wind zone 【信封】

envelope 【信奉】believe in ～基督教 be a Christian 【信服】completely accept; be convinced 令人～的论据 convincing argument 【信鸽】carrier pigeon; homer 【信管】fuse 【信号】signal ～兵 signaiman ～弹 signal flare ～灯 signal lamp ～枪 flare pistol 【信汇】mail transfer 【信笺】letter paper; writing paper 【信件】letters; mail 【信教】profess a religion; be religious 【信口开河】talk irresponsibly 【信赖】trust; count on; have faith in 【信任】have confidence in 【信守】stand by ～诺言 keep a promise 【信条】creed; precept; tenet 【信筒】pillar-box 【信徒】believer; disciple; adherent 【信托】trust; entrust ～公司 trust company ～基金 trust fund ～商店 commission shop 【信息】information; news; message 【信心】confidence; faith 【信仰】faith; belief; conviction 政治～ political conviction 【信用】trustworthiness; credit 讲～ keep one's word 失去～ lose one's credit 【信誉】prestige; credit; reputation 享有很高的～ enjoy high prestige 【信纸】letter paper

衅 xìn quarrel; dispute 寻～ pick a quarrel with sb. 桃～ provoke

XING

兴 xīng ①prosper; rise; prevail; become popular ～衰 rise and decline; ups and downs ②start; begin ～工 start construction ～兵 send an army ③encourage; promote ～利除弊 promote what is beneficial and abolish what is harmful 【兴办】initiate; set up 【兴奋】be excited / excitation ～剂 excitant; stimulant ～性 excitability 【兴风作浪】stir up trouble; fan the flames of disorder 【兴建】build; construct 【兴隆】prosperous; thriving; flourishing; brisk 生意～ business is brisk 【兴起】rise; spring up; be on the upgrade 【兴盛】prosperous; in the ascendant 国家～ prosperity of the nation 【兴亡】 rise and fall (of a nation) 【兴修】 start construction; build

星 xīng ①star ～空 starlit sky ②heavenly body 彗～ comet 卫～ satellite ③bit; particle 一～半点 a tiny bit 火～儿 spark 【星辰】 stars 【星号】 asterisk 【星火】 spark/shooting star; meteor ～燎原 a single spark can start a prairie fire 急如～ most urgent 【星际】 interplanetary; interstellar ～飞行 space flight 【星罗棋布】 spread all over the place 【星期】 week/Sunday 今天～几 what day (of the week) is it today 本～ this week 上～ last week 下～ next week ～休息 Sunday is our day off ～日 Sunday ～一 Monday ～二 Tuesday ～三 Wednesday ～四 Thursday ～五 Friday ～六 Saturday 【星球】 heavenly body 【星团】 cluster 【星系】 galaxy 【星云】 nebula 【星座】 constellation

惺 xīng 【惺忪】 not yet fully open on waking up 睡眼～ sleepy eyes 【惺惺】 clearheaded; awake/wise

猩 xīng orangutan 【猩红】 scarlet; bloodred 【猩红热】 scarlet fever 【猩猩】 orangutan 大～ gorilla

腥 xīng ①raw meat or fish ②having the smell of fish, seafood, etc.; fishy 【腥臭】 stinking smell (as of rotten fish); stench 【腥膻】 smelling of fish or mutton

刑 xíng ①punishment ～满释放 be released after serving a sentence ②torture 用～ put sb. to torture; administer corporal punishment 受～ suffer corporal punishment 【刑场】 execution ground 【刑罚】 penalty; punishment 【刑法】 penal code; criminal law 【刑具】 instruments of torture 【刑律】 criminal law 触犯～ violate the criminal law 【刑期】 prison term 【刑事】 criminal; penal ～案件 criminal case ～处分 criminal sanction ～法庭 criminal court ～犯 criminal (offender) ～犯罪 crimi-

nal offence; crime ～诉讼 criminal suit ～责任 responsibility for a crime【刑讯】inquisition by torture

行　xíng ①go 日～百里 cover a hundred *li* a day ②
travel 非洲之～ a trip to Africa ③temporary ～灶
makeshift cooking stove ④be current; prevail; circulate
风～一时 be popular for a time ⑤do; perform; carry out;
engage in 简便易～ simple and easy to do ⑥behaviour;
conduct 言～ words and deeds ⑦capable; competent ⑧
all right; O.K.【行不通】won't do; get nowhere 计划～ this
plan won't work【行车】drive a vehicle ～速率 driving
speed ～执照 driver's license【行程】route or distance
of travel【行船】sail a boat; navigate【行刺】assassinate
【行动】move about / act / action ～不便 have difficulty
getting about ～缓慢 move slowly ～起来 go into action 按计划～ proceed according to plan 军事～ military operations ～纲领 programme of action【行方便】
make things convenient for sb.【行贿】(offer a) bribe;
resort to bribery【行劫】commit robbery; rob【行进】
march forward; advance【行经】go by; pass by【行径】
act; action; move【行军】(of troops) march ～床 camp bed;
camp cot ～锅 field cauldron ～壶 canteen ～灶 field kit-
chen【行乐】indulge in pleasures; make merry【行礼】salute
【行李】luggage; baggage ～车 luggage van; baggage car
～寄存处 checkroom ～架 luggage rack ～卷儿 bedroll ～
票 luggage check【行旅】traveller; wayfarer【行期】date
of departure【行乞】beg one's bread【行人】pedestrian
【行善】do good works【行驶】(of a vehicle, ship, etc.)
go; ply; travel 向南～ be going south【行事】act; handle
matters / behaviour; conduct【行为】action; behaviour;
conduct 正义的～ righteous action 不法～ illegal act【行
销】be on sale; sell【行星】planet【行刑】carry out a

death sentence; execute 【行凶】 commit physical assault or murder; do violence 【行医】 practise medicine (usu. on one's own) 【行营】 field headquarters 【行政】 administration ～部门 administrative unit; executive branch ～处分 disciplinary sanction ～命令 administrative decree 【行之有效】 effective (in practice); effectual 【行装】 outfit for a journey; luggage 整理～ pack (for a journey) 【行踪】 track ～不定 be of uncertain whereabouts 【行走】 walk

形 xíng ①form; shape 不成～ shapeless; formless ② body; entity 有～ tangible 无～ intangible ③appear; look 喜～于色 look very pleased ④compare 相～之下 by contrast 【形成】 take shape; form ～鲜明的对比 form a sharp contrast ～风气 become a common practice 一僵局 come to a deadlock 【形而上学】 metaphysics 【形迹】 a person's movements and expression/formality ～可疑 suspicious-looking 不拘～ without formality 【形容】 appearance; countenance/describe ～憔悴 looking wan 难以～ difficult to describe 【形容词】 adjective 【形式】 form; shape 艺术～ artistic form ～逻辑 formal logic ～上 in form; formal 【形势】 terrain; topographical features/situation; circumstances ～险要 strategically important terrain ～逼人 the situation is pressing 【形似】 be similar in form or appearance 【形态】 form; shape; pattern/formation ～学 morphology 【形体】 shape (of a person's body); physique; body / form and structure 【形象】 image; figure ～思维 thinking in (terms of) images 【形形色色】 of every hue; of all shades 【形状】 form; appearance; shape

型 xíng ①mould 砂～ sand mould ②type; pattern 新～ new model 血～ blood group 【型号】 model; type

省 xǐng ①examine oneself critically ②visit ～亲 pay a visit to one's parents or elders (living at another place) ③become conscious; be aware 不～人事 lose consciousness 【省视】 call upon/examine carefully; inspect

醒 xǐng ①regain consciousness; sober up 他～过来了 he's come to ②wake up; be awake 如梦初～ like awakening from a dream 他还～着 he is still awake ③be clear in mind 头脑清～ keep a cool head ④be striking to the eye 【醒目】 catch the eye; attract attention ～的标语 eye-catching slogans ～的标题 bold headline 【醒悟】 come to see the truth, one's error, etc.

擤 xǐng blow (one's nose) ～鼻涕 blow one's nose

兴 xìng mood or desire to do sth.; interest 游～ the mood for sight-seeing 酒～ excitement due to drinking 【兴高采烈】 in high spirits; in great delight; jubilant 【兴趣】 interest 【兴头】 enthusiasm 【兴味】 interest ～索然 uninterested; bored stiff ～盎然 with keen interest 【兴致】 mood to enjoy ～勃勃 full of zest

杏 xìng apricot 杏红 apricot pink 【杏黄】 apricot yellow 【杏仁】 apricot kernel; almond

性 xìng ①nature; character; disposition 本～ inherent character ②property; quality 药～ medicinal properties ③sex ～行为 the sex act ④gender 【性别】 sexual distinction; sex 【性病】 venereal disease 【性格】 nature; disposition 【性急】 impatient; short-tempered 【性交】 sexual intercourse 【性命】 life ～交关 (a matter of) life and death; of vital importance 【性能】 function (of a machine, etc.); property ～试验 performance test 【性情】 temperament; temper ～温柔 have a gentle disposition ～暴躁 be short-tempered 【性欲】 sexual desire 【性质】 quality; nature 中国革命的～ the character of the Chinese revolution 【性状】 properties 【性子】 temper 使～ get into a temper

幸 xìng ① (have) good fortune 有～ be lucky ～甚 very fortunate indeed ②rejoice 庆～ congratulate oneself; rejoice ③luckily ～未成灾 fortunately it didn't cause a disaster 【幸福】happiness; well-being/happy 为人民谋～ work for the well-being of the people 祝你～ I wish you happiness ～的回忆 happy memories ～的晚年 a happy life in one's remaining years 【幸亏】fortunately; luckily 【幸免】escape by sheer luck; have a narrow escape ～于难 escape death by sheer luck 【幸事】good fortune; blessing 【幸运】good luck/fortunate; lucky ～儿 fortune's favourite; lucky fellow 【幸灾乐祸】take pleasure in others' misfortune

姓 xìng surname; family name 【姓名】surname and personal name; full name

悻 xìng 【悻悻】angry; resentful ～而去 go away angry

凶 xiōng ①inauspicious; ominous ～兆 ill omen ②crop failure ～年 a bad year ③fierce; ferocious 样子真～ look really fierce ④terrible; fearful 病势很～ terribly ill ⑤act of violence; murder 行～ commit physical assault or murder 【凶暴】fierce and brutal 【凶残】savage and cruel 【凶多吉少】bode ill rather than well 【凶恶】ferocious; fiendish 【凶犯】murderer 【凶猛】violent; ferocious 来势～ with a terrifying force 【凶器】lethal weapon 【凶杀】homicide; murder 【凶神】demon; fiend ～恶煞 devils 【凶手】murderer; assassin; assailant 【凶险】in a very dangerous state; critical 【凶宅】haunted house

兄 xiōng elder brother 胞～ elder brother of the same parents 【兄弟】brothers/fraternal/younger brother

洶 xiōng 【洶洶】the sound of roaring waves/violent/agitated 气势～ blustering and truculent 【洶涌】tempestuous 波涛～ turbulent waves ～澎湃 surging

胸 xiōng ①chest; bosom; thorax 挺～ throw out one's chest ②mind; heart ～怀祖国 have the whole country in mind 【胸襟】(breadth of) mind ～开阔 broadminded 【胸腔】thoracic cavity 【胸围】chest measurement; bust 【胸像】(sculptured) bust 【胸有成竹】have a well-thought-out plan, strategem, etc.

雄 xiōng ①male ～猫 male cat ～鸡 cock ②grand; imposing ③powerful; mighty ～兵 a powerful army 【雄辩】convincing argument; eloquence 【雄才大略】great talent and bold vision; rare gifts and bold strategy 【雄厚】rich; solid 资金～ abundant funds 【雄浑】vigorous and firm; forceful 【雄健】robust; vigorous; powerful 【雄赳赳】valiantly; gallantly 【雄图】great ambition; grandiose plan 【雄伟】grand; imposing; magnificent 【雄心】great ambition 树～，立壮志 foster lofty ideals, set high goals; set up high aims and lofty aspirations 【雄壮】full of power and grandeur; magnificent 【雄姿】majestic appearance; heroic posture

熊 xiōng bear 【熊猫】panda 【熊熊】flaming; ablaze ～烈火 raging flames 【熊掌】bear's paw

休 xiū stop; cease 争论不～ argue ceaselessly 【休会】adjourn 【休假】have a holiday or vacation; be on leave ～一周 have a week's holiday 回国～ go home on furlough 【休克】shock 【休戚】joys and sorrows ～与共 share weal and woe ～相关 be bound by a common cause 【休息】take a rest ～一会儿 rest for a while 幕间～ intermission; interval 课间～ break (between classes) ～一天 have a day off ～室 lounge 【休想】don't imagine (that it's possible) 【休学】suspend one's schooling without losing one's status as a student 【休养】recuperate; convalesce 【休业】suspend business; be closed down 今天～ closed today 【休战】truce; cease-fire; armistice 【休整】(of troops) rest and reorganization

修 xiū ①embellish 装～铺面 paint and decorate the front of a shop ②repair; overhaul ～收音机 repair a radio ～鞋 mend shoes ③study; cultivate 自～ study by oneself ④build; construct ～铁路 build a railway ～渠 dig irrigation ditches ⑤trim; prune ～指甲 trim one's fingernails ⑥long; tall and slender ～竹 tall bamboos ⑦revisionism 反～ combat revisionism 【修补】mend; patch up; repair; revamp 【修辞】rhetoric ～学 rhetoric 【修道】cultivate oneself according to a religious doctrine ～院 monastery; convent 【修订】revise ～条约 revise a treaty ～教学计划 revise a teaching plan ～本 revised edition 【修复】repair; restore ～铁路 repair a railway ～老建筑物 renovate old buildings 【修改】revise; modify; alter ～计划 revise a plan ～宪法 amend a constitution 【修剪】prune; trim; clip ～果枝 prune fruit trees 【修建】build; construct; erect ～机场 build an airport ～桥梁 construct a bridge 【修旧利废】repair and utilize old or discarded things 【修理】mend; fix ～机器 repair a machine 正在～ be under repair ～店 fix-it shop; repair shop ～行业 repairing trades 【修配】make repairs and supply replacements ～车间 repair and spare parts workshop 【修饰】decorate; adorn; embellish/make up and dress up / polish (a piece of writing) / qualify; modify ～语 modifier 【修养】accomplishment; training; mastery/self-cultivation 有艺术~ be artistically accomplished 【修业】study at school ~年限 length of schooling ~证书 certificate showing courses attended 【修正】revise; amend; correct ~错误 correct one's mistakes ~草案 a revised draft ~案 amendment 【修正主义】revisionism 【修筑】build ~工事 construct defences; build fortifications

羞 xiū ①shy; bashful; coy ~红了脸 blush ~于言谈 be coy of speech ②shame; disgrace 遮 ~ hide one's shame ③feel ashamed ~与为伍 consider it beneath one to associate with sb. 【羞惭】be ashamed 满面~ be shamefaced 【羞耻】shame ~之心 sense of shame 【羞愧】abashed ~难言 be ashamed beyond words 【羞怯】timid; sheepish 【羞人】feel embarrassed 【羞辱】dishonour; humiliation / humiliate; put sb. to shame

朽 xiǔ ①rotten; decayed ②senile 老~ old and useless 【朽木】rotten wood or tree / a hopeless case

秀 xiù ①put forth flowers or ears ~穗 put forth ears ②elegant; beautiful 眉清目~ having well-chiselled features; handsome 山清水~ beautiful hills and waters ③excellent 【秀丽】pretty 【秀美】graceful; elegant 【秀气】delicate; fine / refined; urbane

袖 xiù ①sleeve ②tuck inside the sleeve 【袖口】cuff (of a sleeve) 【袖手旁观】look on with folded arms; look on unconcerned 【袖章】armband 【袖珍】pocket-size; pocket ~字典 pocket dictionary ~照相机 vest-pocket camera ~潜艇 midget submarine ~本 pocket edition

绣 xiù embroider 【绣花】embroider; do embroidery ~被面 embroidered quilt cover ~丝线 floss silk ~鞋 embroidered shoes ~针 embroidery needle

臭 xiù odour; smell 纯空气是无色无~的 pure air is colourless and odourless

锈 xiù ①rust ②become rusty 锁～住了 the lock is rusty and won't open

嗅 xiù smell; scent; sniff 【嗅觉】smell; scent ～很灵 have a keen sense of smell

XU

吁 xū sigh 长～短叹 sighs and groans 气喘～～ pant; puff hard

须 xū ①must; have to ～作出很大努力 have to make a great effort ②beard; mustache 留～ grow a beard 【须知】one should know that; it must be understood that/points for attention; notice 游览～ tourist guide; information for tourists 旅客～ notice to travellers, etc.

虚 xū ①void; emptiness 太～ the great void; the universe ②empty; void; unoccupied 座无～席 there was no empty seat ③diffident; timid 心里有点～ feel rather diffident ④in vain 不～此行 have not made the trip in vain ⑤false; nominal ～名 false or undeserved reputation ⑥weak; in poor health 身体～ be weak physically 【虚报】make a false report ～帐目 cook accounts 【虚词】function word; form word 【虚度】spend time in vain; waste ～光阴 fritter away one's time ～青春 trifle through one's youth 【虚浮】impractical 作风～ have a superficial style of work 【虚构】fabricate ～的情节 a made-up story ～的人物 a fictitious character 纯属～ a sheer fabrication 【虚幻】unreal; illusory 【虚假】false; sham ～繁荣 false prosperity ～的可能性 spurious possibility 【虚惊】false alarm 受了一场～ be the victim of a false alarm 【虚拟】invented; fictitious / suppositional ～语气 the subjunctive mood 【虚情假意】false display of affection; hypocritical show of friendship 【虚荣】van-

ity 不慕～ not affected by vanity; not vain ～心 vanity
【虚弱】in poor health; weak; debilitated/feeble 病后身体
～ be weak after an illness 兵力～ weak in military
strength 【虚妄】unfounded; invented 【虚伪】sham; false;
hypocritical 【虚无】nihility; nothingness ～主义 nihil-
ism ～主义者 nihilist 【虚线】dotted line or line of
dashes / imaginary line 【虚心】open-minded; modest

需 xū ①need; want 急～巨款 badly require a big sum
of money 孩子～人照料 the child wants sb. to look
after it ②necessaries; needs 军～ military supplies 【需求】
requirement; demand 【需要】need; require; demand/needs
这所房子～修理 the house wants repairing 从群众的
～出发 make the needs of the masses our starting point

嘘 xū ①breathe out slowly ②utter a sigh ③hiss; boo
【嘘寒问暖】be solicitous about sb.'s health

徐 xú slowly; gently 【徐步】walk slowly 【徐徐】gen-
tly 红旗～升起 the red flag slowly went up the pole

许 xǔ ①praise 赞～ commend ②allow; permit 不～拖
延 permit of no delay 【许多】many; much; a great
deal of; a lot of ～人 many people 有～工作要做 have
a lot of work to do 【许久】for a long time; for ages
【许可】permit; allow ～证 licence; permit 【许诺】prom-
ise 【许配】betroth a girl 【许愿】make a vow (to a god) /
promise sb. a reward

栩 xǔ 【栩栩】vivid; lively ～如生 lifelike; to the life
旭 xǔ brilliance of the rising sun 【旭日】the rising
sun ～东升 the sun rising in the eastern sky
序 xù ①order; sequence ②preface; foreword 【序列】
alignment; array 战斗～ battle array 【序幕】prologue;
prelude 【序曲】overture 【序数】ordinal (numbers)

恤 xù pity; sympathize ②give relief; compensate 【恤金】pension

叙 xù ②talk; chat ～家常 chitchat ②narrate; relate③ assess; appraise ～功 assess service and give credit for it 【叙旧】talk about the old days 【叙事】narrate ～诗 narrative poem ～文 narrative 【叙述】recount; tell; relate

畜 xù raise (domestic animals) 【畜产】livestock products 【畜牧】raise livestock or poultry ～场 animal farm ～业 animal husbandry

酗 xù 【酗酒】excessive drinking ～滋事 get drunk and create a disturbance

绪 xù thread 【绪言】introduction

续 xù ①continuous; successive ②continue; extend; join 待～ to be continued ③add; supply more 炉子该～煤了 the fire needs more coal 【续订】renew one's subscription 【续集】continuation (of a book); sequel 【续假】extend leave ～一星期 have one's leave extended for another week 【续借】renew (a library book)

絮 xù ①(cotton) wadding ②wad with cotton ～被子 wad a quilt with cotton 【絮叨】garrulous 【絮棉】cotton for wadding

婿 xù ①son-in-law ②husband 妹～ younger sister's husband

蓄 xù ①store up ～水 store water ②grow ～须 grow a beard ～发 wear one's hair long ③entertain (ideas); harbour 【蓄电池】storage battery; accumulator 【蓄积】store up; save up ～粮食 store up grain 【蓄谋】premeditate 【蓄意】premeditated; deliberate ～挑衅 premeditated provocation ～破坏 deliberately sabotage

XUAN

轩 xuān ①high; lofty ②a small room or veranda with windows 【轩然大波】a great disturbance

宣 xuān declare; announce ～示 make known publicly 【宣布】declare; proclaim ～会议开始 call a meeting to order ～无效 declare sth. invalid ～一件事 make an announcement 【宣称】assert; profess 【宣传】conduct propaganda; propagate; give publicity to ～共产主义思想 disseminate communist ideas ～党的方针政策 publicize the Party's general and specific policies ～车 propaganda car ～队 propaganda team ～工具 means of propaganda or publicity; mass media ～工作者 propagandist ～画 picture poster ～品 publicity material ～员 propagandist 【宣读】read out (in public) 【宣告】proclaim ～成立 proclaim the founding of ～破产 declare bankruptcy 【宣讲】explain and publicise 【宣教】propaganda and education 【宣判】pronounce judgment 【宣誓】swear an oath; make a pledge 庄严～ make a solemn vow 入党～ take the oath on being admitted to the Party ～就职 be sworn in 【宣泄】lead off (liquids); drain/get sth. off one's chest; unbosom oneself 【宣言】declaration; manifesto 【宣扬】publicise; advocate; advertise ～好人好事 give publicity to good people and their good deeds 【宣战】declare war

喧 xuān noisy 【喧哗】confused noise; uproar 请勿～ quiet, please 【喧闹】bustle; racket 【喧嚷】clamour; din; hubbub 【喧扰】noise and disturbance; tumult

玄 xuān ①black; dark ～狐 a black fox ②profound; abstruse ③unreliable; incredible 【玄妙】mysterious; abstruse 【玄虚】deceitful trick; mystery 故弄～ purposely turn simple things into mysteries

旋 xuán ①revolve; circle ②return; come back ～里 return home 【旋律】melody 【旋绕】curl up; wind around 【旋涡】whirlpool; vortex; eddy 【旋转】revolve; gyrate; rotate; spin

悬 xuán ①hang; suspend ～梯 hanging ladder ②outstanding; unresolved ～而未决的问题 an outstanding question ③far apart ～隔 be separated by a great distance 【悬案】unsettled law case / outstanding issue; unsettled question 【悬挂】hang ～在空中的气球 a balloon suspended in mid air 【悬赏】offer a reward (for) 【悬殊】great disparity 力量～ a great disparity in strength 贫富～ a wide gap between the rich and the poor 【悬想】imagine; fancy 【悬崖】steep cliff; precipice ～绝壁 sheer precipice and overhanging rocks ～勒马 rein in at the brink of the precipice—wake up to and escape disaster at the last moment

选 xuǎn ①select; choose; pick 比赛前～场地 choose sides before a contest ②elect ～她当队长 elect her leader of a team 入～ be chosen; be elected ③selections; anthology 民歌～ selections of folk songs 【选拔】select; choose ～运动员 select athletes ～赛 (selective) trials 【选材】select (suitable) material 【选读】selected readings (in literature, etc.) 【选购】pick out and buy; choose 【选集】selected works; selections 【选举】elect ～程序 electoral procedure ～法 electoral law ～结果 election results ～权 the right to vote; franchise 【选民】voter; elector ～榜 list of eligible voters ～登记 registration of voters ～证 elector's certificate 【选票】vote; ballot 【选区】electoral district 【选曲】selected songs 【选手】(selected) contestant; player 【选修】take as an elective course ～英语 take English as an elective course ～课 elective course 【选择】select; choose; opt 【选种】seed selection

炫 xuàn ①dazzle ②display 自～其能 show off one's ability 【炫耀】make a display of ～力量 flaunt one's strength ～武力 make a show of force ～学问 parade one's learning

绚 xuàn gorgeous 【绚烂】splendid ～的朝霞 gorgeous morning clouds 【绚丽】magnificent ～多彩 bright and colourful

眩 xuàn ①dizzy; giddy 头晕目～ feel dizzy ②dazzled; bewildered ～于名利 dazzled by the prospect of fame and wealth

旋 xuàn ①whirl ～风 whirlwind ②turn sth. on a lathe; lathe 【旋床】lathe

渲 xuàn 【渲染】apply colours to a drawing / play up; exaggerate ～战争恐怖 play up the horrors of war

楦 xuàn ①shoe last ②hat block ③shape with a last or block ～鞋 last a shoe

XUE

削 xuē pare; cut 剥～ exploit 【削壁】precipice; cliff 【削价】cut prices 【削减】reduce; slash; whittle down ～开支 cut down expenditures 【削弱】weaken ～敌人的力量 cripple the enemy

靴 xuē boots 马～ riding boots 雨～ rubber boots

穴 xué ①cave; den; hole ～居 live in caves 虎～ tiger's lair ②grave ③acupoint

学 xué ①study; learn ～文化 learn to read and write ～外语 learn a foreign language ～先进 emulate the advanced ②imitate ～鸡叫 mimic the crowing of a cock ③learning; knowledge ④school; college 小～ primary school 【学报】 (learned) journal 【学潮】 student strike 【学费】 tuition (fee) 【学分】 credit ~制 the credit system 【学风】 style of study 【学府】 seat of learning; institution of higher learning 【学好】 learn from good examples; emulate good 【学会】 learn; master / learned society; institute 【学籍】 one's status as a student 【学科】 course; subject 【学力】 knowledge; academic attainments 具有同等~ have the same educational level (as school graduates) 【学历】 record of formal schooling 【学龄】 school age (children) 【学名】 scientific name / formal name 【学年】 school year ~考试 year-end examination 【学派】 school (of thought) 【学期】 (school) term; semester 【学生】 student; pupil / disciple; follower 医科~ a medical student ~运动 student movement ~时代 school days ~会 student association ~证 student's identity card 【学时】 class hour 【学识】 learning; knowledge 【学士】 scholar / bachelor 【学术】 learning; science ~报告 learned report ~交流 academic exchanges ~界 academic circles ~论文 scientific paper; thesis ~讨论会 academic discussion ~团体 learned society ~研究 academic research 【学说】 theory; doctrine 【学徒】 apprentice; trainee ~工 apprentice 【学位】 (academic) degree 【学问】 learning; scholarship 做~ do research 【学习】 study; learn ~别人的长处 emulate other's strong points ~班 study class ~成绩 school record ~年限 period of schooling 【学衔】 academic rank 【学校】 school; educational institution 【学业】 one's studies; school work 【学院】 college; academy; institute 美术~ school of art 音乐~ conservatory of music 【学者】 scholar; learned man 【学制】 educational system / length of schooling ~改革 reform in the school system 缩短~ shorten the period of schooling

雪 xuě ①snow ②wipe out (a humiliation) ～耻 avenge an insult 【雪白】snow-white 【雪崩】snowslide 【雪堆】snow drift 【雪糕】ice cream 【雪花】snowflake 【雪花膏】vanishing cream 【雪茄】cigar 【雪里红】potherb mustard 【雪亮】bright as snow; shiny 【雪橇】sled; sledge

血 xuě ①blood 流～ shed blood 出～ bleed ②related by blood ～亲 blood relation 【血案】murder case 【血管】blood vessel 【血迹】bloodstain 【血浆】(blood) plasma 【血库】blood bank 【血泪】tears of blood ～帐 debts of blood and tears ～史 history written in blood and tears 【血泊】pool of blood 【血气】sap; vigour/courage and uprightness ～方刚 full of sap 【血清】(blood) serum 【血球】blood cell 【血肉】flesh and blood ～之躯 the human body ～相连 as close as flesh and blood 【血色】redness of the skin; colour 脸上没有～ look pale 【血统】blood lineage 有中国～ be of Chinese extraction 中国～的外国人 foreign nationals of Chinese descent 【血腥】bloody ～味 smell of blood ～统治 sanguinary rule ～的镇压 bloody suppression 【血压】blood pressure 【血液】blood 新鲜～ fresh blood 【血缘】ties of blood; blood relationship 【血债】a debt of blood 【血战】bloody battle ～到底 fight to the bitter end

谑 xuè crack a joke 戏～ banter; tease ～而不虐 tease without embarrassing

XUN

勋 xūn merit; achievement; contribution 【勋劳】meritorious service 【勋章】medal; decoration

熏 xūn ①smoke; fumigate ～蚊子 smoke out mosquitoes ②treat (meat, etc.) with smoke; smoke ～鱼 smoked fish 【熏染】exert a gradual, corrupting influence on 【熏

陶】nurture; edify 起～作用 exert an edifying influence on

旬 xún ①a period of ten days 上(中,下)～ the first (second, last) ten days of a month ②a period of ten years in a person's age 八～老母 80-year-old mother

驯 xún ①tame and docile ～象 a tame elephant ② tame; domesticate 善于～虎 good at taming tigers ～马 break in a horse 【驯服】docile; tame; tractable / break; domesticate 【驯化】domestication; taming 【驯鹿】reindeer 【驯养】raise and train (animals)

寻 xún ①search; seek ～物 look for sth. lost ～欢 作乐 seek pleasure 【寻常】ordinary; usual; common 【寻根究底】get to the bottom of things 【寻求】explore; go in quest of ～真理 seek truth 【寻衅】pick a quarrel

巡 xún patrol; make one's rounds ～夜 go on night patrol 【巡查】make one's rounds 【巡回】go the rounds; tour; make a circuit of ～放映队 mobile film projection unit ～医疗队 mobile medical team 【巡逻】(go on) patrol ～队 patrol party ～艇 patrol boat 【巡视】make an inspection tour 【巡洋舰】cruiser

询 xún ask; inquire 查～make inquiries 【询问】ask about ～病状 inquire about sb.'s illness

循 xún follow; abide by ～例 follow a precedent 【循环】circulate; cycle ～赛 round robin ～系统 the circulatory system 【循序】in proper order or sequence ～渐进 follow in order and advance step by step 【循循善诱】be good at giving systematic guidance; teach with skill and patience

讯 xùn message; dispatch 据新华社～ according to a Xinhua dispatch 【讯问】interrogate; inquire; question

训 xùn lecture; teach; train ～人 give sb. a dressing down 受～ undergo training 【训斥】reprimand; rebuke【训词】admonition; instructions【训话】(give) an admonitory talk to subordinates【训诫】admonish; advise/ rebuke; reprimand【训练】train; drill 班 training class

汛 xùn flood; high water 防～ flood control【汛期】flood season

迅 xùn fast; swift【迅猛】swift and violent【迅速】rapid; speedy 动作～ swift in action ～取得成效 produce speedy results ～作出决定 come to a prompt decision

逊 xùn ①abdicate ②modest 出言不～ speak insolently【逊色】be inferior 毫无～ be by no means inferior

殉 xùn sacrifice one's life for【殉国】die for one's country【殉葬】be buried alive with the dead ～品 sacrificial object【殉职】die at one's post

Y

YA

丫 yā fork【丫杈】fork (of a tree)【丫头】girl / slave girl

压 yā ①press; push down; weigh down ～扁 press flat ～碎 crush (to pieces) ②control; keep under; quell ～低嗓门 speak under one's breath ～住怒火 control one's anger ③suppress; daunt; intimidate 不受捧, 不怕 ～ withstand both flattery and pressure ④shelve 这份文件～了不少时间 this document was pigeonholed for quite some time【压倒】overwhelm; overpower ～一切的任务 an overriding task ～多数 an overwhelming majority【压服】force sb. to submit【压价】demand a lower price ～出售 undersell【压力】pressure / overwhelming force 施加～ bring pressure to bear on sb.【压路机】(road) roller【压迫】oppress; repress ～阶级 oppressor class ～者 oppressor【压缩】compress; condense; cut down ～开支 reduce expenses; retrench ～机 compressor ～空气 compressed air【压抑】constrain; inhibit; depress; hold back/oppressive; stifling 心情～ feel constrained 胸口感到～ feel tight in the chest【压榨】press; squeeze / oppress and exploit; bleed ～甘蔗 press sugar cane ～机 squeezer【压制】suppress; stifle; inhibit ～批评 suppress criticism ～不同意见 stifle differing opinions

呀 yā ①ah; oh ②creak 门～的一声开了 the door opened with a creak

押 yā ①mortgage; pawn; pledge ②detain; take into custody 在～犯 criminal in custody ③escort ～行李 escort luggage【押当】pawn sth./a small pawnshop【押金】cash pledge; deposit【押送】send under escort; escort

鸦 yā crow【鸦片】opium【鸦雀无声】silence reigns

鸭 yā duck 公～ drake 小～ duckling【鸭蛋】duck's egg【鸭绒】duck's down ～被 eiderdown quilt【鸭舌帽】peaked cap【鸭胗儿】duck's gizzard

牙 yá ①tooth ②ivory【牙齿】tooth【牙床】gum/ivory-inlaid bed【牙雕】ivory carving【牙粉】tooth powder【牙膏】toothpaste【牙关】mandibular joint 咬紧～ clench one's teeth【牙科】(department of) dentistry ～医生 dentist ～诊疗所 dental clinic【牙轮】gear【牙签】toothpick【牙刷】toothbrush【牙痛】toothache【牙龈】gum

芽 yá bud; sprout; shoot【芽豆】sprouted broad bean

涯 yá margin; limit

崖 yá　precipice; cliff

哑 yǎ　①mute; dumb ②hoarse; husky 嗓子喊～了 shout oneself hoarse【哑巴】a dumb person【哑剧】dumb show; pantomime【哑口无言】be left without an argument【哑铃】dumbbell【哑谜】puzzling remark; enigma; riddle

雅 yǎ　①standard; proper; correct ②refined; elegant 古～ of classic elegance【雅观】refined (in manner, etc.); in good taste 很不～ most unseemly; rather unsightly【雅兴】aesthetic mood【雅致】refined; tasteful【雅座】private room (in a restaurant, etc.)

轧 yà　①roll; run over ～平路面 roll a road surface 被车～伤 get run over and injured by a car ②oust; push out 倾～ engage in internal strife【轧花】cotton ginning ～厂 cotton ginning mill ～机 cotton gin

亚 yà　inferior; second【亚军】second place (in a sports contest); runner-up 获～ win second place【亚麻】flax ～布 linen (cloth) ～子 linseed【亚洲】Asia

YAN

咽 yān　pharynx【咽喉】throat / strategic passage; key link

烟 yān　①smoke ②tobacco ③cigarette 抽支～ have a cigarette ④opium【烟草】tobacco【烟囱】chimney; funnel【烟斗】(tobacco) pipe【烟盒】cigarette case【烟灰】tobacco or cigarette ash ～缸 ashtray【烟火】fireworks 放～ let off fireworks【烟具】smoking set【烟煤】soft coal【烟幕】smoke screen ～弹 smoke shell【烟丝】pipe tobacco【烟头】cigarette end【烟土】crude opium【烟雾】smoke; mist; vapour; smog ～弥漫 full of smoke【烟消云散】vanish like mist and smoke; completely vanish

【烟叶】tobacco leaf 【烟瘾】a craving for tobacco ～大 be a heavy smoker 【烟子】soot 【烟嘴儿】cigarette holder

胭 yān 【胭脂】rouge ～红 carmine

淹 yān flood; submerge 【淹没】flood; inundate 【淹死】drown

阉 yān castrate or spay ～鸡 capon ～猪 hog 【阉割】castrate or spay/deprive a theory, etc. of its essence; emasculate

湮 yān ①fall into oblivion ②clog up; stop 【湮灭】bury in oblivion; annihilate 【湮没】be neglected

腌 yān preserve in salt; pickle; cure ～菜 pickled vegetables; pickles ～鱼 salted fish ～肉 bacon

嫣 yān handsome; beautiful 【嫣红】bright red 【嫣然】beautiful; sweet ～一笑 give a winsome smile

延 yán ①prolong; extend; protract 蔓～ spread ②postpone; delay 拖～ procrastinate ③engage ～医 send for a doctor 【延长】lengthen ～管道 extend a pipeline 会议～了两天 the conference was prolonged for two more days 【延缓】delay; put off ～工作进度 retard the progress of work 【延年益寿】(of tonics, etc.) prolong life; promise longevity 【延期】postpone; defer ～付款 defer payment 因雨～ put off on account of rain 【延烧】(of fire) spread 【延伸】stretch; elongate 【延误】incur loss through delay ～时机 miss an opportunity because of a delay ～时日 lose time 【延续】continue; go on; last

言 yán ①speech; word 无～以对 have nothing to say in reply ②say; talk; speak ～明 state explicitly; clearly stipulate ③character; word 【言不由衷】speak insincerely 【言传】explain in words 只可意会, 不可～ only to be sensed, not explained ～身教 teach by personal example as well as verbal instruction 【言辞】one's words ~恳切 be sincere in what one says 【言归于好】 make it up with sb. 【言归正传】 to return to the subject 【言过其实】 overstate 【言简意赅】 concise and comprehensive; compendious 【言教】 give verbal directions 【言论】opinion on public affairs; speech ~自由 freedom of speech 【言谈】 the way one speaks or what he says ~举止 speech and deportment 【言外之意】 implication; what is actually meant 【言行】 words and deeds ~不一 one's deeds do not match one's words ~的 be as good as one's word 【言语】 spoken language; speech

严 yán ①tight 关~ shut sth. tight 嘴~ be tight-mouthed ②strict; severe; rigorous ~加批驳 sternly refute 【严办】 deal with severely 【严惩】 punish severely ~入侵之敌 deal the invaders a crushing blow 【严词】 in strong terms; in stern words ~谴责 sternly condemn ~拒绝 sternly refuse 【严冬】 severe winter 【严防】 take strict precautions against 【严格】 rigid; stringent ~训练，要求 go in for rigorous training and set strict demands; train hard and strictly ~说来 strictly speaking 【严寒】 severe cold 【严谨】 strict/compact ~的科学态度 a rigorous scientific approach 文章结构~ the essay is well-knit 【严禁】 strictly prohibit ~体罚 strictly forbid corporal punishment 【严峻】 stern ~的考验 a severe test ~的局势 a grim situation 【严酷】 harsh; grim ~的现实 harsh reality ~的教训 a bitter lesson ~的斗争 a grim struggle 【严厉】 stern; severe ~制裁 apply stern sanctions 【严密】 tight ~封锁 impose a tight blockade ~监视 keep close watch over 组织~ be well-organized 【严明】 strict and impartial 赏罚~ give rewards and punishments impartially 纪律~ be highly disciplined 【严肃】 serious; solemn ~地

指出 point out in all earnestness ~的态度 a serious attitude 【严刑】 cruel torture ~拷打 cruelly beat up ~峻法 severe law 【严正】 serious and principled; stern ~立场 solemn and just stand ~警告 serve a stern warning 【严重】 serious; grave ~后果 serious consequences ~关头 critical juncture 病情~ be seriously ill 事态~ the situation is grave ~警告 serious warning

沿 yán ①along ~着海岸航行 sail along the coast ② follow (a tradition, pattern, etc.) ③edge; border 炕~儿 the edge of a *kang* 【沿岸】 along the bank or coast 【沿革】 evolution 【沿海】 along the coast; coastal ~城市 coastal city ~岛屿 offshore islands ~地区 coastal areas ~国家 coastal state 【沿路】 along the road; on the way 【沿途】 throughout a journey 【沿袭】 carry on as before; follow (convention, etc.) 【沿线】 along the (railway, etc.) line 【沿用】 continue to use (an old method, name, etc.)

炎 yán ①scorching; burning hot ~夏 hot summer ② inflammation 嗓子发~ suffer from an inflammation of the throat 【炎热】 blazing 冒着~ braving the sweltering heat 【炎暑】 sweltering summer days; dog days

岩 yán ①rock ②cliff; crag 【岩层】 rock stratum 【岩洞】 grotto 【岩浆】 magma 【岩石】 rock

研 yán ①grind; pestle ~成粉末 grind into fine powder ②study 钻~ study intensively 【研钵】 mortar 【研杵】 pestle; pounder 【研究】 study; research / consider; discuss; deliberate; discuss 这些问题正在~ these matters are under review ~工作者 research worker ~生 graduate student ~所 research institute ~员 research fellow ~院 research institute 【研磨】 grind; pestle/abrade; polish 【研讨】 deliberate; discuss 【研制】 prepare; manufacture ~新式武器 develop new weapons

盐 yán salt【盐场】saltern【盐池】salt pond【盐碱化】salinization (of soil)【盐井】salt well【盐矿】salt mine【盐卤】bittern【盐瓶】saltcellar【盐水】salt solution; brine【盐酸】hydrochloric acid【盐业】salt industry

阎 yán【阎王】Yama; King of Hell / an extremely cruel and violent person ～殿 the Palace of Hell ～帐 usurious loan

筵 yán feast; banquet 喜～ a wedding feast【筵席】seats arranged at a banquet / feast

颜 yán ①face; countenance ②prestige; face 无～见人 not have the face to appear in public ③colour 五～六色 of all colours; colourful【颜料】pigment; colour; dyestuff【颜色】colour / countenance; facial expression

檐 yán ①eaves ②ledge; brim 帽～儿 the visor of a cap; the brim of a hat

奄 yǎn ①cover; overspread ②suddenly【奄奄】feeble breathing ～一息 at one's last gasp

掩 yǎn ①cover; hide ～口而笑 hide one's smile ②shut; close ～卷 close a book ③by surprise ～杀 launch a surprise attack; pounce on (the enemy)【掩盖】cover; conceal【掩护】screen; shield; cover ～进攻 screen an advance ～战友 shield one's comrade-in-arms【掩人耳目】deceive the public【掩饰】cover up; conceal ～错误 gloss over one's mistakes ～真实的意图 conceal one's true intentions【掩体】bunker【掩映】set off (one another)

眼 yǎn ①eye 亲～看见 see with one's own eyes ②look; glance 瞥了他一～ shoot a glance at him ③small hole; aperture 打个～ bore a hole ④key point 节骨儿 critical juncture【眼光】eye / sight; insight; vision 锐利的～ sharp eyes ～远大 farsighted ～短浅 shortsighted 政治～ political foresight 历史～ historical perspective 【眼红】 covet; be envious / furious 【眼花】 have dim eyesight ～缭乱 be dazzled 【眼尖】 have sharp eyes 【眼角】 the corner of the eye; canthus 【眼睫毛】 eyelash 【眼界】 field of view; outlook 扩大～ widen one's field of vision 【眼镜】 glasses; spectacles 戴～ wear glasses 【眼睛】 eye 【眼科】 (department of) ophthalmology ～医生 oculist; eye-doctor 【眼眶】 eye socket; orbit / rim of the eye 【眼泪】 tears ～汪汪 eyes brimming with tears 【眼力】 eyesight; vision/judgment ～好（差）have good (poor) eyesight 看人有～ be good at sizing people up 【眼里】 within one's vision; in one's eyes 【眼帘】 映入～ come into view; meet the eye 【眼明手快】 quick of eye and deft of hand 【眼皮】 eyelid 【眼前】 before one's eyes / at the moment; at present ～利益 immediate interests 只顾～ think only of the present 【眼球】 eyeball 【眼圈】 eye socket; orbit/rim of the eye 【眼色】 hint given with the eyes; meaningful glance; wink 使～ tip sb. the wink; wink at sb. 看～行事 take one's cue from sb. 【眼神】 expression in one's eyes / eyesight ～不济 have poor eyesight 【眼生】 look unfamiliar 【眼熟】 look familiar 【眼药】 eye ointment or eyedrops 【眼中钉】 thorn in one's flesh

演 yǎn ①develop; evolve 愈～愈烈 grow in intensity ②elaborate 推～ deduce ③drill; practise ～算 perform mathematical calculations ④perform; play; act; put on 电影 show a film ～五场 give five performances 【演变】 develop; evolve 【演唱】 sing (in a performance) 【演出】 perform; show; put on a show 登台～ appear on the stage ～结束后 after the final curtain ～些什么节目 what's on the programme ～本 acting version; script ～单位 producer ～节目 items on the programme; programme 【演化】 evolution 【演技】 acting 【演讲】 give a lecture 【演示】 demonstrate 【演说】 deliver a speech; make an address/speech 【演算】 perform mathematical calculations 【演习】 manoeuvre; exercise; drill; practice 【演戏】 put on a play; act in a play/playact; pretend 别再～了 stop playacting 【演义】 historical romance 【演绎】 deduction ～法 the deductive method 【演员】 actor or actress; performer ～表 cast 【演奏】 play a musical instrument

厌 yàn ①be disgusted with ～弃 detest and reject ② be tired of 看～了 have seen more than enough of sth. 吃～了 be sick of eating sth. 【厌烦】 be fed up with 【厌倦】 be weary of 【厌世】 be world-weary; be pessimistic 【厌恶】 detest; abominate; be disgusted with 【厌战】 be weary of war ～情绪 war-weariness

沿 yàn water's edge; bank 河～ riverside 沟～儿 edge of a ditch

砚 yàn inkstone; inkslab

咽 yàn swallow 细嚼慢～ chew carefully and swallow slowly 【咽气】 breathe one's last; die

宴 yàn ①entertain at a banquet ～客 entertain guests at a banquet ②feast 【宴会】 banquet; dinner party ～厅 banquet hall 【宴请】 entertain (to dinner); fête

晏 yàn ①late ～起 get up late ②ease and comfort

艳 yàn ①gorgeous; colourful; gaudy 百花争～ flowers blossom in a riot of colour ②amorous ～诗 love poem in a flowery style 【艳丽】 bright-coloured and beautiful ～夺目 of dazzling beauty 词藻～ flowery diction 打扮得非常～ be gorgeously dressed

唁 yàn extend condolences 【唁电】 telegram of condolence; message of condolence

验 yàn ①examine; check; test ～护照 check a passport ②prove effective; produce the expected result 屡试屡～ prove successful in every test 【验方】proved recipe 【验光】optometry 【验尸】autopsy 【验收】check and accept; check upon delivery ～单 receipt 【验算】checking computations 【验血】blood test 【验证】test and verify

谚 yàn proverbs; saying 农～ peasants' proverb 【谚语】saying; adage; saw

焰 yàn flame; blaze 烈～ raging flames 【焰火】fireworks

雁 yàn wild goose

燕 yàn swallow 家～ house swallow 【燕麦】oats 【燕尾服】swallowtail; tails 【燕窝】edible bird's nest

赝 yàn counterfeit; spurious; fake 【赝本】spurious edition or copy 【赝品】sham

YANG

央 yāng ①entreat ②centre ③end; finish 夜未～ the night is not yet spent 【央告】beg; ask earnestly; plead

殃 yāng ①calamity; misfortune 遭～ meet with disaster ②bring disaster to

秧 yāng ①seedling 黄瓜～ cucumber sprout ②rice seedling 插～ transplant rice seedlings ③vine 白薯～ sweet potato vine ④young; fry 【秧歌】yangko (dance)

羊 yáng sheep 山～ goat 母～ ewe 公～ ram 【羊羔】lamb 【羊倌】shepherd 【羊圈】sheep pen 【羊毛】sheep's wool; fleece ～衫 woollen sweater; cardigan ～袜 woollen stockings 【羊皮】sheepskin 【羊肉】mutton

阳 yáng ①the sun ～历 solar calendar ②in relief ～文 characters cut in relief ③belonging to this world

～间 this world ④positive ～离子 positive ion 【阳电】
positive electricity 【阳奉阴违】 comply in public but
oppose in private; feign compliance 【阳沟】 open drain;
ditch 【阳光】 sunlight; sunshine ～充足 full of sunlight;
sunny 【阳极】 positive pole 【阳伞】 parasol; sunshade 【阳
台】 balcony 【阳性】 positive / masculine gender

扬 yáng ①raise ～起灰尘 raise a dust ②throw up and
scatter; winnow (the chaff from the grain) ③spread;
make known 宣～ propagate; publicize 【扬眉吐气】 feel
proud and elated 【扬名】 make a name for oneself ～天下
become world-famous 【扬弃】 develop what is useful or
healthy and discard what is not/sublate 【扬琴】 dulcimer
【扬声器】 loudspeaker 【扬言】 threaten (that one is going
to take action) ～要进行报复 threaten to retaliate

杨 yáng poplar 【杨柳】 poplar and willow/willow 【杨
梅】 red bayberry

佯 yáng pretend; feign; sham ～死 feign death ～攻
feign attack; make a feint

洋 yáng ①vast; multitudinous ②ocean ③foreign ～房
Western-style house ④modern ～办法 modern methods
【洋白菜】 cabbage 【洋菜】 agar 【洋葱】 onion 【洋服】
Western-style clothes 【洋行】 foreign firm (in preliber-
ation China) 【洋灰】 cement 【洋火】 matches 【洋泾浜】
pidgin (English) 【洋奴】 slave of a foreign master; flun-
key of imperialism ～思想 slavish mentality towards
all things foreign ～哲学 blind worship of everything
foreign 【洋气】 foreign flavour; Western style/outlandish
ways 【洋人】 foreigner 【洋为中用】 make foreign things
serve China 【洋溢】 be permeated with; brim with 热情～
的讲话 a speech brimming with warm feeling ～着热烈
气氛 be permeated with a warm atmosphere

仰 yǎng ①face upward ~着睡 sleep on one's back ②admire; respect 瞻~ look at with reverence 【仰慕】 admire; look up to 【仰望】 look up at / respectfully seek guidance or help from 【仰卧】 lie on one's back 【仰泳】 backstroke 【仰仗】 rely on; look to sb. for support

养 yǎng ①provide for ~家 support a family ②raise ~鸭 raise ducks ~鸟 keep pet birds ~花 grow flowers ③give birth to ④foster; adoptive ~父 foster father ~子 adopted son ⑤form; acquire ~成良好的习惯 cultivate good habits ⑥rest; convalesce ~身体 recuperate ~伤 heal one's wounds ⑦keep in good repair ~路 maintain a road 【养兵】 maintain an army 【养病】 take rest and nourishment to regain one's health 在家~ recuperate at home 【养分】 nutrient 【养活】 support; feed (a family) 【养精蓄锐】 conserve strength and store up energy 【养老】 provide for the aged / live out one's life in retirement ~金 old-age pension 【养料】 nutriment 吸收~ draw nourishment 【养神】 rest to attain mental tranquility 闭目~ sit in repose with one's eyes closed 【养生】 preserve one's health ~之道 the way to keep in good health 【养育】 bring up; rear ~子女 bring up children 【养殖】 breed (aquatics) ~海带 cultivate kelp 【养尊处优】 enjoy high position and live in ease and comfort; live in clover

氧 yǎng oxygen 【氧化】 oxidize ~剂 oxidizer ~物 oxide ~作用 oxidation 【氧气】 oxygen ~瓶 oxygen cylinder

痒 yǎng itch; tickle 浑身发~ itch all over 搔到~处 scratch where it itches — hit the nail on the head

快 yàng 【怏怏】 disgruntled; sullen ~不乐 unhappy about sth.; morose

恙 yàng ailment; illness 无～ in good health 偶染微～ feel slightly indisposed

样 yàng ①appearance; shape ②sample; model; pattern 鞋～ outline of a shoe ③kind; type 三～菜 three kinds of vegetables; three dishes 【样板】 sample plate/templet/model; prototype 【样本】 sample book 【样品】 sample; specimen 【样式】 type; style; form 【样样】 every kind; all 【样张】 specimen page

漾 yàng ①ripple 荡～ undulate ②brim over; overflow

YAO

夭 yāo 【夭折】 die young / come to a premature end

吆 yāo 【吆喝】 cry out; call / cry one's wares / loudly urge on (an animal)

约 yāo weigh 给我～二斤肉 weigh me out two *jin* of meat ～多重 see how much it weighs

妖 yāo ①goblin; demon; evil spirit ②evil and fraudulent ～术 sorcery; witchcraft ③bewitching; coquettish 打扮得～里～气 be seductively dressed 【妖风】 evil wind; noxious trend 【妖怪】 monster; bogy 【妖精】 demon/alluring woman 【妖媚】 seductively charming 【妖魔鬼怪】 demons and ghosts; monsters of every description 【妖孽】 person or event associated with evil or misfortune/evildoer 【妖娆】 enchanting; fascinating 【妖言】 heresy; fallacy 【妖艳】 pretty and coquettish

要 yāo ①demand; ask ②force; coerce 【要求】 ask; require; claim ～入党 ask to join the Party ～发言 ask to be heard 严格～自己 be strict with oneself 达到质量～ fulfil quality requirements ～赔偿 claim compensation 【要挟】coerce; put pressure on; threaten

腰 yāo ①waist; small of the back 弯～ bend down ～酸腿疼 aching back and legs 扭了～ sprain one's back muscles ②waist (of a garment) 【腰带】waistband; belt; girdle 【腰杆子】back / backing; support ～硬 have strong backing 【腰鼓】waist drum 【腰身】waistline; waist; girth 【腰痛】lumbago 【腰子】kidney

邀 yāo ①invite; request 应～出席 be present by invitation ②intercept ～击 intercept (the enemy); waylay 【邀集】invite to meet together; call together 【邀请】invite ～他参加会议 ask him to a meeting 发出～ send an invitation ～赛 invitational tournament

肴 yáo meat and fish dishes 【肴馔】sumptuous courses at a meal

窑 yáo ①kiln 砖～ brickkiln ②(coal) pit 小煤～ small coal pit 【窑洞】cave dwelling

谣 yáo ①rhyme 民～ ballad ②rumour 造～ start a rumour 【谣传】rumour; hearsay / it is rumoured that 【谣言】groundless allegation 散布～ spread rumours

遥 yáo distant; remote; far 【遥测】telemetering 【遥控】remote control; telecontrol ～飞机 telecontrolled airplane ～无人驾驶飞机 drone (aircraft) 【遥望】look into the distance 【遥相呼应】echo each other at a distance 【遥遥】far away; a long way off ～领先 be far ahead ～相对 stand far apart, facing each other 【遥远】faraway ～的将来 the distant future 路途～ a long way to go

摇 yáo shake; rock; turn (a windlass, etc.) ～铃 ring a bell ～扇子 wave a fan ～船 row a boat ～手 (头) shake one's hand (head) ～尾巴 wag the tail 【摇摆】sway; swing 船身～ the ship rocked 左右～ vacillate now to the left, now to the right ～舞 rock and roll

【摇动】wave; shake; sway; rock 【摇撼】give a violent shake to 【摇篮】cradle ~曲 lullaby; cradlesong 【摇旗呐喊】bang the drum for sb. 【摇钱树】a ready source of money 【摇身一变】suddenly change one's identity, etc. 【摇摇欲坠】tottering; crumbling; on the verge of collapse 【摇曳】sway ~的灯光 flickering light 【摇椅】rocking chair

傜 yáo 【傜役】corvée

杳 yáo distant and out of sight ~无踪迹 disappear without a trace; vanish ~无音信 have never been heard of since

咬 yáo ①bite; snap at ~不动 too tough to chew ~一口 take a bite ~紧牙关 grit one's teeth ②(of a dog) bark ③pronounce ~字清楚 clear articulation ④be nitpicking (on words) 【咬耳朵】whisper (in sb.'s ear) 【咬文嚼字】pay excessive attention to wording 【咬牙】grit one's teeth/grind one's teeth (in sleep) ~切齿 gnash one's teeth (in hatred) 【咬住】bite into; grip with one's teeth/grip; take firm hold of ~敌人 be close on the heels of the enemy ~敌机 get on the tail of the enemy plane

窈 yáo 【窈窕】(of a woman) gentle and graceful

舀 yáo ladle out; spoon up; scoop up ~汤 ladle out soup 【舀子】dipper; ladle; scoop

药 yào ①medicine; drug; remedy 服~ take medicine ②certain chemicals 火~ gunpowder ③kill with poison ~老鼠 poison rats 【药材】medicinal materials; crude drugs 【药草】medicinal herbs 【药厂】pharmaceutical factory 【药方】prescription 【药房】drugstore; chemist's shop / hospital pharmacy; dispensary 【药费】charges for medicine 【药粉】(medicinal) powder 【药膏】ointment;

salve 【药剂】 medicament ～师 pharmacist ～学 pharmacy 【药酒】 medicinal liquor 【药力】 efficacy of a drug ～发作 the drug is taking effect 【药片】 tablet 【药品】 medicines and chemical reagents 【药瓶】 medicine bottle 【药铺】 herbal medicine shop 【药水】 liquid medicine / lotion 【药丸】 pill; bolus 【药味】 herbal medicines in a prescription / flavour of a drug 【药物】 medicines; medicaments 【药箱】 medical kit 【药性】 property of a medicine 【药皂】 medicated soap 【药渣】 dregs of a decoction

要 yào ①important; essential ～事 an important matter ②want; ask for; wish; desire 谁没有票，问她～ anyone without a ticket can ask her for one ③ask sb. to do sth. ～我写封信 ask me to write a letter ④want to; wish to ～见司令员 wish to see the commander 我还有几句话～说 I'd like to say a few more words ⑤ must; should; it is necessary ～相信群众 we must have faith in the masses ⑥shall; will; be going to ～下雨了 it's going to rain ⑦need; take 这活儿～不了这么多人 you don't need so many people for this job ⑧if; suppose; in case 他～来不了呢 suppose he can't come 【要隘】 strategic pass 【要不】 otherwise; or else; or 【要不得】 no good; intolerable 【要不是】 if it were not for; but for 【要冲】 communications centre 【要道】 thoroughfare 【要地】 important place; strategic point 【要点】 main points; essentials; gist / key strongpoint 抓住～ grasp the main points 讲话的～ the gist of a speech 战略～ strategic point 【要犯】 important criminal 【要害】 vital part; crucial point ～部位 vital part ～部门 key department 击中～ hit home 【要好】 be on good terms / eager to improve oneself 【要价】 ask a price; charge ～过高 demand an exorbitant price; ask too much 【要紧】important; essential / be critical; be serious; matter 【要领】main points; essentials; gist / essentials 掌握～ grasp the essentials 【要么】or; either ... or ... 【要面子】be keen on face-saving 【要强】be eager to excel 【要人】very important person 【要塞】fort; fortress 【要是】if; suppose; in case 【要素】essential factor 【要闻】important news 【要职】important post 身居～ hold an important post 【要旨】gist; main idea

钥

yào 【钥匙】key

鹞

yào ①harrier ②sparrow hawk

耀

yào ①shine; illuminate ～眼 dazzling ②boast of; laud 夸～ boast about ③honour; credit 【耀武扬威】make a show of one's strength

YE

耶

yē 【耶稣】Jesus ～基督 Jesus Christ ～教 Protestantism

掖

yē tuck in; thrust in between 把被角～好 tuck in the corner of the quilt 腰里～着枪 with a pistol in one's belt

椰

yē coconut palm; coconut tree; coco 【椰干】copra 【椰蓉】shredded coconut stuffing 【椰油】coconut oil 【椰枣】date palm / date 【椰子】coconut palm / coconut ～肉 coconut meat ～糖 coconut candy ～汁 coconut milk

噎

yē choke 留神别～着 be careful not to choke

爷

yé ① father ② grandfather 【爷爷】grandfather / grandpa

揶 yé 【揶揄】 ridicule; deride

也 yě ①also; too; as well; either 你不去，我～不去 if you're not going, I'm not going either 【也好】 it may not be a bad idea; may as well 说明一下～ better give an explanation 【也许】 perhaps; probably; maybe ～是这样的 it may possibly be so

冶 yě ①smelt (metal) ②seductively dressed or made up 【冶金】 metallurgy ～工业 metallurgical industry 【冶炼】 smelt ～厂 smeltery ～炉 smelting furnace

野 yě ①open country; the open ②limit; boundary 分～ line of demarcation ③not in power; out of office 下～ be forced to relinquish power ④wild; uncultivated; undomesticated ～花 wild flower ～鸭 wild duck ⑤rude; rough 动作太～ rough play ⑥unrestrained; abandoned; unruly 【野菜】 edible wild herbs 【野餐】 picnic 【野草】 weeds ～丛生 be overgrown with weeds 【野地】 wilderness 【野果】 wild fruit 【野火】 prairie fire 【野鸡】 (ring-necked) pheasant 【野蛮】 uncivilized; savage / barbarous; cruel; brutal 【野猫】 wildcat / stray cat 【野牛】 wild ox 【野炮】 field gun 【野禽】 wild fowl 【野人】 savage 【野生】 wild; uncultivated; feral ～动物 wild animal ～植物 wild plant 【野史】 unofficial history 【野兽】 wild beast; wild animal 【野兔】 hare 【野外】 open country; field 在～工作 do fieldwork ～生活 outdoor life 【野味】 game (as food) 【野心】 wild ambition; careerism ～不死 cling to one's ambitious designs ～勃勃 be overweeningly ambitious ～家 careerist 【野性】 wild nature; unruliness 【野营】 camp; bivouac 出外～ go camping ～训练 camp and field training 【野战】 field operations ～工事 fieldwork ～军 field army ～医院 field hospital 【野猪】 wild boar

业 yè ①line of business; trade; industry 矿～ mining industry ②occupation; profession; employment; job 失～ be out of a job ③course of study 结～ complete a course of study; graduate ④cause 创～ start an enterprise ⑤estate 家～ family property ⑥engage in ～农 engage in farming ⑦already ～已核实 have already been verified ～已批准 have been approved【业绩】outstanding achievement【业务】vocational work; professional work; business 钻研～ diligently study one's profession ～范围 scope of business ～水平 vocational level ～学习 vocational study ～知识 professional knowledge【业余】sparetime; after-hours; amateur ～教育 sparetime education ～学校 sparetime school【业主】owner; proprietor

叶 yè ①leaf; foliage 落～ fallen leaves ②part of a historical period 二十世纪中～ the middle of the twentieth century【叶绿素】chlorophyll【叶脉】vein

页 yè page; leaf 打开新的一～ open up a new chapter【页边】margin【页码】page number

曳 yè drag; haul; tug; tow【曳光弹】tracer【曳力】drag force

夜 yè night; evening【夜班】night shift【夜长梦多】a long delay means many hitches【夜场】evening show【夜车】night train 开～ work deep into the night【夜大学】evening university【夜工】night work 打～ work at night【夜光表】luminous watch【夜壶】chamber pot【夜间】at night ～施工 carry on construction work at night ～演习 night exercise【夜景】night scene【夜阑人静】in the dead of night【夜幕】curtain of night ～降临 night has fallen【夜色】the dim light of night 趁着～ by starlight or moonlight【夜袭】night attack【夜宵】refreshments taken late at night; midnight snack

【夜校】night school; evening school 【夜行军】night march 【夜以继日】day and night; round the clock 【夜莺】nightingale 【夜战】night fighting 【夜总会】nightclub

液 yè liquid; fluid; juice ~ body fluid 【液化】liquefaction ~器 liquefier ~石油气 liquefied petroleum gas 【液态】liquid state ~空气 liquid air 【液体】liquid ~燃料 liquid fuel 【液压】hydraulic pressure

掖 yè ①support sb. by the arm ②help; assist; promote

谒 yè call on (a superior); pay one's respects to 【谒见】have an audience with

腋 yè ①axilla; armpit ②axil 【腋毛】armpit hair 【腋窝】armpit

YI

一 yī ①one ②alone; only one ③same ④whole; all; throughout ~冬 the whole winter ⑤each; per; every time ~小时六十公里 at 60 kilometres per hour 【一般】same as; just like/general; ordinary; common ~号召 general calls ~工作人员 ordinary personnel 【一般化】vague generalization 【一半】one half; half; in part ~以上 more than half 【一辈子】all one's life 【一边】one side/at the same time; simultaneously ~喝茶, ~聊天 chat over a cup of tea 【一并】along with all the others 【一场空】all in vain; futile 【一筹莫展】can find no way out 【一触即发】be on the verge of breaking out 【一次】once 【一旦】in a single day; in a very short time / once; in case 【一刀两断】sever at one blow — make a clean break 【一道】together; side by side; alongside 【一等】first-class; top-grade ~品 first-rate product 【一点儿】a bit; a little ~不累 not feel the least bit tired ~都不知

道 have not the faintest idea ～用处也没有 utterly useless 还有～希望 there is still a gleam of hope 【一定】fixed; specified; definite; regular/certainly; surely; necessarily/given; particular; certain ～的生产指标 fixed production quotas ～来啊 be sure to come 在～条件下 under given conditions 【一度】 once; for a time 【一帆风顺】 plain sailing 【一方面】 one side/on the one hand ..., on the other hand ...; for one thing ..., for another ... 【一概】 one and all; without exception; totally 【一干二净】 thoroughly; completely 【一共】 altogether; in all; all told 【一贯】 consistent; persistent; all along 【一回事】 one and the same (thing)/one thing 【一会儿】 a little while/in a moment; presently 我～就来 I won't be a minute 【一技之长】 professional skill; speciality 【一见钟情】 fall in love at first sight 【一举】 with one action; at one stroke ～成名 become famous overnight 【一两得】 kill two birds with one stone 【一句话】 in a word; in short 【一口】 a mouthful; a bite/with certainty; flatly ～答应 readily agree ～回绝 flatly refuse 【一口气】 one breath/in one breath; without a break ～干完 finish the work at one go 【一块儿】 at the same place/together 【一览】 general survey; bird's-eye view ～表 table; schedule ～无余 take in everything at a glance 【一揽子】 wholesale; package ～计划 package plan ～交易 package deal 【一劳永逸】 get sth. done once and for all ～的解决办法 a permanent solution 【一力】 do all one can ～成全 do one's best to help 【一连】 in a row; in succession; running 【一连串】 a succession of; a series of; a string of; a chain of ～的事件 a succession of events ～问题 a series of questions 【一溜烟】 (run away) swiftly 【一路】 all the way / of the same kind ～平安 have a good trip ～货 one of a kind ～纵队 single column 咱们是～吗 are we going the same way 【一律】 same; alike; uniform/all; without exception 【一面】 one side; one aspect / at the same time; simultaneously ～教，～学 learn while teaching 【一瞥】 a quick glance/a glimpse; a brief survey 【一齐】 at the same time; in unison 【一起】 in the same place/together; in company 【一窍不通】 know nothing about (a subject) 【一切】 all; every; everything 【一如既往】 just as in the past; as before; as always 【一色】 of the same colour/of the same type; uniform 【一身】 all over the body/a suit ～新衣服 a new suit of clothes 【一生】 all one's life; throughout one's life 【一声不响】 not utter a sound 【一时】 a period of time / for a short while; temporary; momentary 【一事无成】 accomplish nothing; get nowhere 【一视同仁】 treat equally without discrimination 【一手】 proficiency; skill/single-handed; all alone 露～ show off one's skill 业务上有～ be proficient in one's own line ～包办 keep everything in one's own hands 【一瞬】 an instant; a flash; the twinkling of an eye 一即逝 vanish in a flash 【一丝不苟】 not be the least bit negligent 【一丝不挂】 not have a stitch on 【一丝一毫】 a tiny bit; an iota; a trace 【一塌糊涂】 in a complete mess; in an awful state 【一天】 a day/one day (in the past) / the whole day; all (the) day 【一条心】 be of one mind; be at one 【一同】 together; at the same time and place 【一团和气】 keep on good terms with everyone at the expense of principle 【一团漆黑】 pitch-dark — utterly hopeless 【一团糟】 a complete mess; chaos 【一味】 blindly; stubbornly ～迁就 make endless concessions 【一文不名】 penniless 【一窝蜂】 like a swarm of bees 【一无所长】 have no special skill 【一无所有】 not have a thing to one's name 【一无所知】 know nothing about 【一系列】 a series of ～问题 a whole series of questions ～的事件 a whole train of events 【一线】 a ray of; a gleam of ～希望 a gleam of hope ～光明 a ray of light 【一问】 earlier on; lately/consistently; all along 【一些】 a number of; certain; some; a few; a little 【一心】 wholeheartedly; heart and soul/of one mind; at one ～一德 be of one heart and one mind 【一言不发】 not say a word 【一言难尽】 it is hard to explain in a few words; it's a long story 【一言为定】 that's settled then 【一样】 the same; equally; alike; as . . . as . . . 【一一】 one by one; one after another 【一应】 everything ～俱全 everything needed is there 【一元化】 centralized; unified 【一月】 January 【一再】 time and again; repeatedly 【一早】 early in the morning 【一针见血】 hit the nail on the head 【一阵】 a burst; a fit; a peal ～掌声 a burst of applause ～咳嗽 a fit of coughing ～阵笑声 peals of laughter ～大风 a blast of wind ～枪声 a burst of gunfire 【一阵子】 a period of time; a spell 【一知半解】 have scanty knowledge 【一直】 straight / continuously; always; all along; all the way 【一致】 showing no difference; consistent 观点～ hold identical views 步调～ march in step 提案～通过 the resolution was adopted unanimously 言行～ match words with deeds 【一专多能】 expert in one thing and good at many

衣 yī ①clothing; clothes; garment 穿(脱)衣 put on (take off) one's clothes 和～而睡 sleep in one's clothes ～不蔽体 be dressed in rags ②coating; covering 糖～ sugar coating 【衣胞】 (human) afterbirth 【衣服】 clothing; clothes 【衣钩】 clothes hook 【衣柜】 wardrobe 【衣架】 coat hanger/clothes tree 【衣料】 material for clothing; dress material 【衣帽间】 cloakroom 【衣物】 clothing and other articles of daily use【衣箱】suitcase; trunk【衣着】clothing, headgear and footwear

伊 yī he or she【伊始】beginning 就职～ upon assuming office【伊斯兰教】Islam; Islamism ～国家 Islamic country ～徒 Moslem

医 yī ①doctor (of medicine) ②medical science; medical service; medicine 行～ practise medicine ③cure; treat 把他的病～好 cure him of his illness【医科】medical courses in general; medicine ～大学 medical university【医疗】medical treatment ～队 medical team ～机构 medical establishment ～卫生工作 medical and health work ～站 medical station; health centre【医生】doctor; medical man 内科～ physician 外科～ surgeon【医士】practitioner with secondary medical school education【医术】medical skill; art of healing【医务】medical matters ～工作者 medical worker ～人员 medical personnel ～所 clinic【医学】medical science; medicine ～科学院 academy of medical sciences ～文献 medical literature【医药】medicine ～常识 general medical knowledge ～费 medical expenses【医院】hospital【医治】cure; treat; heal

依 yī ①depend on ～存 depend on sb. or sth. for existence ②comply with; listen to; yield to ③according to ～我看 in my view; as I see it【依此类推】and so on and so forth【依次】in proper order; successively ～入座 take one's seats in proper order【依从】comply with; yield to【依附】attach oneself to【依据】according to; on the basis of/foundation ～上述意见 in accordance with the above views 提供科学～ provide scientific basis for sth.【依靠】rely on; depend on/support; backing ～政策和科学 rely on (correct) policies and on science 寻找～ seek support 生活有～ have one's livelihood assured 【依赖】rely on ～别人 be dependent on others ～思想 the dependent mentality ～性 dependence 【依恋】be reluctant to leave 【依然】still; as before ～有效 still hold good ～如故 remain as before 【依顺】be obedient 【依依】reluctant to part ～不舍 cannot bear to part 【依仗】rely on ～权势 count on one's powerful connections 【依照】in the light of ～指示办事 act in accordance with the directives ～情况而定 decide as circumstances require

揖 yī (make a)bow with hands clasped

仪 yí ①appearance 威～ dignified bearing ②rite ③gift 贺～ present for wedding, birthday, etc. ④apparatus; instrument 【仪表】appearance; bearing/meter ～堂堂 noble and dignified ～大方 poised and graceful ～厂 instrument and meter plant 【仪器】instrument; apparatus ～制造工业 instrument-making industry 【仪容】looks; appearance 【仪式】ceremony; rite; function 【仪态】bearing; deportment 【仪仗】flags, weapons, etc. carried by a guard of honour ～队 honour guard

夷 yí ①smooth; safe 化险为～ turn danger into safety ②raze ～为平地 level to the ground; raze

宜 yí ①suitable; appropriate; fitting 老幼咸～ suitable for both young and old ～于饮用的水 water good to drink ②should; ought to 不～操之过急 you should not act in haste 【宜人】pleasant; delightful 气候～ pleasant weather 景物～ attractive scenery

怡 yí happy; joyful; cheerful 【怡然】contented ～自得 happy and pleased with oneself

饴 yí maltose 【饴糖】maltose; malt sugar

贻 yí ①make a gift of sth.; present ②leave behind ～患 sow seeds of disaster 【贻害】 leave a legacy of trouble ～无穷 entail untold troubles 【贻误】 bungle ～工作 affect the work adversely ～战机 forfeit a chance for combat ～青年 mislead young people

姨 yí ①one's mother's sister; aunt ②one's wife's sister; sister-in-law 【姨表】 maternal cousin ～兄弟 (姐妹) male (female) maternal cousins 【姨夫】 the husband of one's maternal aunt; uncle 【姨母】 maternal aunt; aunt

胰 yí pancreas 【胰岛】 pancreas islet ～素 insulin

移 yí ①move; remove; shift ～走 move away ②change; alter 【移风易俗】 change prevailing habits and customs 【移行】 divide (a word) with a hyphen at the end of a line 【移交】 turn over; transfer/hand over one's job to a successor 【移居】 move one's residence; migrate 【移植】 transplant

遗 yí ①lose ②omit 补～ addendum ③leave behind (at one's death); bequeath; hand down ～风 customs handed down from past generations ～骨 remains (of the dead) 【遗产】 legacy; inheritance; heritage 历史～ a legacy of history 文化～ cultural heritage ～承受人 legatee 【遗传】 heredity; inheritance ～病 hereditary disease 【遗憾】 regret; pity 表示～ express regret 不感到～ have no regrets 【遗恨】 eternal regret 【遗迹】 vestige; traces 【遗留】 leave over; hand down 【遗漏】 omit; leave out 【遗弃】 abandon; cast off; forsake (one's wife, children, etc.) 【遗失】 lose ～借书证 lose one's library card ～声明 lost property notice 【遗事】 incidents of past ages/deeds of those now dead 【遗孀】 widow; relict 【遗体】 remains (of the dead) 【遗忘】 forget 【遗物】 things left behind by the deceased 【遗像】 a portrait of the deceased 【遗言】 words of the deceased 【遗愿】 last wish; behest 【遗址】 ruins; relics 【遗志】 unfulfilled wish 【遗嘱】 will; dying words 【遗著】 posthumous work (of an author)

颐 yí ①cheek 支～ cheek in palm ②keep fit; take care of oneself

疑 yí ①doubt; disbelieve; suspect 坚信不～ firmly believe ②doubtful; uncertain ～点 questionable point 存～ leave the question open 【疑案】 doubtful case; open question; mystery 【疑惑】 feel uncertain; not be convinced ～不解 feel puzzled; have doubts 【疑虑】 misgivings; doubt 消除～ clear one's mind of doubt 【疑难】 difficult; knotty ～问题 a knotty problem ～病症 difficult and complicated cases (of illness) 【疑团】 doubts and suspicions ～顿释 the suspicions were cleared up at once 【疑问】 query; question; doubt 毫无～ without question ～句 interrogative sentence 【疑心】 suspicion 起～ become suspicious 【疑义】 doubt 毫无～ no doubt

乙 yǐ ①second; ～等 the second grade; grade B 【乙醚】 ether 【乙炔】 ethyne 【乙种粒子】 beta particle

已 yǐ ①stop; cease; end 争论不～ argue endlessly ②already 问题～解决 the problem has already been solved ～成定局 be a foregone conclusion 【已故】 deceased; late 【已经】 already 【已然】 be already so; have already become a fact 【已前】 before; previously; in the past 【已知数】 known number

以 yǐ ①use; take ～攻为守 use attack as a means of defence ～丰补歉 store up in fat years to make up for lean ones ②according to ～到达先后为序 in order of arrival ③because of 不～人废言 not reject a saying because the speaker is what or who he is ④in order to;

so as to ～示区别 so as to distinguish this from other cases ～应急需 in order to answer an urgent need 【以便】so that; in order to; so as to 【以德报怨】return good for evil 【以毒攻毒】combat poison with poison 【以讹传讹】incorrectly relay an erroneous message 【以寡敌众】pit the few against the many 【以后】after; afterwards; later; hereafter 【以及】as well as; along with; and 【以来】since 长期～ for a long time past 三年～ in the past three years 【以免】in order to avoid; so as not to; lest 【以内】within; less than 【以前】before; formerly; previously 在我回来～不要走开 stay here till I return 【以求】in order to; in an attempt to 【以上】more than; over; above/the above; the foregoing 五十人～ more than fifty people 十岁～的孩子 children of ten and over 【以身作则】set an example with one's own conduct 【以退为进】retreat in order to advance 【以外】beyond; outside; other than; except 【以往】before; formerly; in the past 【以为】think; believe; consider 我还～是她呢 I thought it was her 【以下】below; under/the following 零度～ sub-zero 三岁～儿童 children under three ～是代表名单 the following is a list of the delegates 【以怨报德】return evil for good 【以至】down to; up to/to such an extent as to . . .; so . . . that . . . 【以致】so that; with the result that; consequently; as a result 【以资】as a means of ～证明 in testimony thereof ～鼓励 as an encouragement

蚁 yǐ ant 兵～ soldier ant 工～ worker ant 【蚁巢】ant nest 【蚁丘】ant hill

倚 yǐ ①lean on or against; rest on or against ～重 rely heavily on sb.'s service ～栏 lean on the parapet ②rely on; count on ～势欺人 take advantage of one's position to bully people ③biased; partial

椅 yǐ chair

义 yì ①justice; righteousness ②equitable; just ～战 just war ～行 righteous deed ③ significance 词～ the meaning of a word ④adopted; adoptive ～母 adoptive mother ⑤artificial (limb, etc.); false (hair, tooth, etc.) 【义不容辞】 be duty-bound; have an unshirkable duty 【义愤】 moral indignation 激于～ be roused to righteous indignation ～填膺 be filled with indignation 【义卖】 charity bazaar 【义旗】 banner of righteousness 【义气】 personal loyalty 讲～ be loyal (to one's friends) 【义师】 righteous army 【义士】 righteous man 【义务】 duty; obligation/volunteer; voluntary 尽～ do voluntary service ～兵 compulsory serviceman ～教育 compulsory education ～劳动 voluntary labour 【义演】 benefit performance 【义勇军】 (army of) volunteers ～进行曲 March of the Volunteers 【义正词严】 speak with the force of justice; speak sternly out of a sense of justice

亿 yì a hundred million 【亿万】 hundreds of millions; millions upon millions ～富翁 billionaire

忆 yì recall; recollect ～苦思甜 recall past suffering and think over the source of present happiness

艺 yì ①skill 球～ skill in a ball game ②art ～苑 the realm of art and literature 【艺名】 stage name 【艺人】 actor or artist / artisan; handicraftsman 【艺术】 art / skill; craft ～标准 artistic criterion ～风格 artistic style ～技巧 artistry ～家 artist ～界 art circles ～品 work of art ～团 art ensemble ～形式 forms of art ～性 artistic quality ～指导 art director

刈 yì mow; cut down 【刈草机】 mowing machine; mower

议 yì ①opinion; view 提～ propose; move ②discuss; exchange views on; talk over ～而不决 discuss sth. without reaching a decision 【议案】proposal; motion 【议程】agenda 列入～ place on the agenda 【议定书】protocol 【议和】negotiate peace 【议会】parliament; legislative assembly 召开(解散)～ convene (dissolve) parliament 【议价】negotiate a price/negotiated price 【议论】comment; talk; discuss 【议题】subject under discussion 【议员】member of a legislative assembly 【议长】speaker; president

亦 yì also; too 【亦步亦趋】imitate sb.'s every move 【亦即】that is; i.e.; namely

屹 yì towering like a mountain peak 【屹立】stand erect 【屹然】towering; majestic

异 yì ①different ～词 dissenting words; disagreement ②strange; unusual ～兆 strange omen ～香 extraordinary fragrance ③surprise 深以为～ it strikes one as very strange ④other; another ～日 some other day ～地 a strange land 【异常】unusual; abnormal/extremely ～现象 abnormal phenomena 神色～ not be one's usual self ～危险 extremely dangerous ～丰富 exceedingly rich ～需要 particularly necessary 【异端】heterodoxy; heresy ～邪说 unorthodox opinions 【异国】foreign land ～情调 an exotic atmosphere 【异己】dissident; alien 排除～ get rid of dissidents 【异教】paganism ～徒 pagan 【异口同声】with one voice; in unison 【异体字】a variant form of a Chinese character 【异乡】foreign land; strange land 【异想天开】indulge in the wildest fantasy 【异心】infidelity; disloyalty 【异性】the opposite sex/different in nature 【异样】difference/unusual; peculiar ～服装 peculiar dress ～的眼光 curious eyes 【异议】objection; dissent 提出～ raise an objection 【异族】different race or nation

译 yì translate; interpret ～成英语 translate into English ～成密码 enciphering 【译本】 translation 【译电】 encode; encipher/decode; decipher ～员 decoder 【译码】 decode; decipher 【译名】 translated term or name 【译述】 translate freely 【译文】 translated text 【译意风】 simultaneous interpretation installation 【译音】 transliteration 【译员】 interpreter 【译者】 translator 【译制】 dub ～片 dubbed film

抑 yì restrain; repress; curb 【抑郁】 depressed; despondent; gloomy ～不平 feel disgruntled ～症 depression 【抑制】 restrain; control; check/inhibition ～愤怒 restrain one's anger ～感情 control one's emotion

呓 yì 【呓语】 talk in one's sleep/crazy talk; ravings 狂人～ ravings of a madman

邑 yì ①city 通都大～ big city; metropolis ②county

役 yì ①labour; service 劳～ corvée ②use as a servant 奴～ enslave ③servant ④battle; campaign 【役畜】 draught animal 【役使】 work (an animal); use

诣 yì ①call on (sb. one respects); visit ②(academic or technical) attainments

易 yì ①easy 不～解决 not easy to solve ～患感冒 catch cold easily ②amiable 平～近人 amiable and easy of access ③change ～手 change hands ④exchange ～货协定 an agreement on the exchange of commodities

疫 yì epidemic disease; pestilence 【疫苗】 vaccine 【疫情】 epidemic situation

益 yì ①benefit; profit; advantage 受～ receive benefit ②beneficial ③increase ④all the more; increasingly 多多～善 the more the better 【益虫】 beneficial insect 【益鸟】 beneficial bird 【益友】 friend and mentor

谊 yì friendship 深情厚～ profound friendship

逸 yì ①ease; leisure 有劳有～ alternate work with rest ②escape【逸乐】comfort and pleasure【逸事】anecdote

翌 yì next ～日 next day ～年 next year

溢 yì ①overflow; spill 河水四～ the river overflowed ②excessive ～美 undeserved praise; compliment

意 yì ①meaning; idea 词不达～ the words fail to convey the meaning ②wish; desire 好～ a good intention ③anticipate; expect 不～ unexpectedly ④suggestion; hint; trace 颇有秋～ make one feel that autumn has set in【意见】idea; view; opinion/objection; differing 交换～ exchange ideas 听取群众的～ listen to the views of the masses ～一致 have identical views ～分歧 have a difference of opinion 我对这种办法很有～ I strongly object to this method 大家对你～很大 people have a lot of complaints about you ～簿 visitors' book; customers' book ～箱 suggestion box【意境】artistic conception【意料】anticipate; expect 这是～中的事 that's to be expected【意气】will and spirit/temperament/personal feelings ～相投 be congenial with each other ～用事 be swayed by personal feelings ～之争 a dispute caused by personal feelings【意气风发】high-spirited and vigorous; daring and energetic【意趣】interest and charm 【意识】consciousness/be aware of; be conscious of ～流 stream of consciousness ～形态 ideology【意思】meaning; idea/wish; desire/suggestion; hint; trace/interest; fun 你这是什么～ what do you mean by that 照自己的～办 act up to one's opinions 天有点要下雨的～ it looks like rain 打乒乓球很有～ ping-pong is a lot of fun【意图】intention; intent

领会上级～ understand the intentions of the higher organization 【意外】 unexpected; unforeseen / accident; mishap 感到～ be surprised 以免发生～ so as to avoid accidents 【意味】 significance; implication/interest ～深长的一笑 a meaning smile 带有文学～ with a literary flavour ～着 signify; mean; imply 【意想】 imagine; expect ～不到的效果 unexpected results 【意向】 intention; purpose 【意象】 image; imagery 【意兴】 interest; enthusiasm ～素然 have not the least interest 【意义】 meaning; sense; significance 在某种～上 in a sense 这样做没有～ there's no point in doing that 这个词有三个～ this word has three distinct meanings 【意译】 free translation 【意愿】 wish; desire; aspiration 【意在言外】 the meaning is implied 【意志】 will ～坚强 strong-willed ～消沉 demoralized 锻炼～ temper one's willpower 【意中人】 person of one's heart

裔 yì ①descendants; posterity 华～美国人 an American of Chinese descent ②borderland; distant land

肆 yì study in school or at college 【肄业】 study in school or at college 大学～二年 be in college for two years

毅 yì firm; resolute 【毅力】 willpower; will; stamina 【毅然】 resolutely; firmly; determinedly

臆 yì ①chest ②subjectively 【臆测】 conjecture; surmise; guess 【臆说】 assumption; supposition 【臆造】 fabricate (a story, reason, etc.); concoct

翼 yì the wing of a bird, aeroplane, etc. 从两～夹攻敌人 attack the enemy on both flanks

YĪN

因 yīn ①follow; carry on 陈陈相～ follow a set routine ②in accordance with; in the light of 疗效～人

而异 the curative effect varies from person to person ③cause: reason 外～ external cause 事出有～ there is good reason for it ④because; for ～病请假 ask for sick leave ～公牺牲 die while on duty ～故改期 be postponed for some reason 【因材施教】 teach students in accordance with their aptitude 【因此】 therefore; for this reason; consequently 【因地制宜】 suit measures to local conditions 【因而】 thus; as a result; with the result that 【因果】 cause and effect ～关系 causality ～律 law of causation 【因势利导】 adroitly guide action according to circumstances 【因素】 factor; element 【因为】 because; for; on account of 【因袭】 follow (old customs, methods, rules, etc.) 【因小失大】 try to save a little only to lose a lot 【因循】 continue in the same old rut / procrastinate

阴 yīn ①the moon ～历 lunar calendar ②overcast 天～了 the sky is overcast ③shade 树～ the shade of a tree ④in intaglio ～文 characters cut in intaglio ⑤hidden; secret ～谋 sinister plot ⑥of the nether world ～间 the nether world ⑦negative ～离子 negative ion; anion ⑧private parts (esp. of the female) 【阴暗】 dark ～的角落 a dark corner ～的脸色 a glum face ～的心理 mentality marked by antipathy and gloom ～面 the dark side of things 【阴部】 private parts; pudenda 【阴沉】 cloudy; overcast; gloomy; sombre 【阴电】 negative electricity 【阴风】 evil wind 【阴沟】 sewer 【阴魂】 soul; spirit ～不散 the spirit refuses to leave 【阴极】 negative pole; cathode 【阴凉】 shady and cool ～地儿 cool place; shade 【阴霾】 haze 【阴谋】 plot; scheme ～破坏 plot sabotage ～手段 conspiratorial means ～集团 conspiratorial clique ～家 schemer; conspirator 【阴森】 gloomy; ghastly 【阴私】 shameful secret 【阴天】

cloudy day 【阴险】 sinister; insidious; treacherous 【阴性】 negative/feminine gender 【阴影】 shadow 【阴郁】 dismal; depressed 心情~ feel gloomy 【阴云】 dark clouds

音 yīn ①sound 噪~ noise ②news; tidings 佳~ welcome news ③tone 【音标】 phonetic symbol 【音波】 sound wave 【音叉】 tuning fork 【音调】 tone 【音符】 note 【音高】 pitch 【音阶】 scale 【音节】 syllable 【音量】 volume (of sound) 【音律】 temperament 【音容】 the likeness of the deceased ~宛在 as if the person were in the flesh 【音色】 tone colour; timbre 【音诗】 tone poem 【音素】 phoneme 【音速】 speed of sound 【音位】 phoneme 【音响】 sound; acoustics ~效果 sound effects 【音信】 mail; message; news 互通~ communicate with each other 【音译】 transliteration 【音域】 range; compass 【音乐】 music ~会 concert ~家 musician ~片 musical (film) ~厅 concert hall ~学院 conservatory of music 【音韵学】 phonology

茵 yīn mattress 绿草如~ a carpet of green grass

洇 yīn (of ink) spread and sink in 这种纸写字容易~ ink blots on this paper

姻 yīn marriage 联~ connect by marriage 【姻亲】 relation by marriage 【姻缘】 the happy fate which brings lovers together 美满~ a happy marriage; conjugal felicity

荫 yīn shade 【荫蔽】 be shaded or hidden by foliage / cover; conceal ~集结 concentrate under cover

殷 yīn ①abundant; rich ②eager; ardent 期望甚~ cherish high hopes ③hospitable 【殷切】 eager ~的期望 ardent expectations 【殷勤】 eagerly attentive 受到~接待 be accorded solicitous hospitality 【殷实】 substantial (firm, etc.); well-off (families)

吟 yín chant; recite ～诗 recite or compose poetry ～咏 recite (poetry) with a cadence

淫 yín ①excessive ～雨 excessive rains ②loose; wanton ③lewd ～乱 (sexually) promiscuous ④obscene ～书 pornographic book ～画 obscene picture 【淫荡】loose in morals; lascivious; licentious 【淫秽】salacious; bawdy 【淫威】abuse of power; despotic power

银 yín ①silver ②silver-coloured ～发 silver hair ～色 silvery 【银杯】silver cup 【银币】silver coin 【银耳】tremella 【银根】money ～紧(松) money is tight (easy) 【银行】bank ～存款 bank deposit ～存折 bankbook; passbook ～家 banker ～信贷 bank credit 【银河】the Milky Way ～系 the Galaxy 【银婚】silver wedding 【银匠】silversmith 【银楼】silverware shop 【银幕】screen 【银牌】silver medal 【银器】silverware 【银圆】silver dollar

引 yín ①lead; guide ～路 lead the way ②lure; attract ～入圈套 lure into a trap ～火 kindle a fire ③cause; make ～得大家笑起来 set everybody laughing ④quote; cite ～某人的话 quote sb. ～以为荣 cite sth. as an honour 【引爆】ignite; detonate ～装置 igniter 【引出】draw forth; lead to ～正确的结论 draw correct conclusions 【引导】guide; lead 【引渡】extradite 【引号】quotation marks 【引火柴】kindling 【引见】introduce; present 【引进】recommend/introduce from elsewhere ～技术装备 import technology and equipment 【引经据典】quote the classics 【引力】gravitation 【引起】give rise to; touch off; cause ～严重后果 lead to grave consequences ～连锁反应 set off a chain reaction ～公愤 arouse public indignation ～怀疑 arouse suspicion ～注意 bring to sb.'s attention ～讨论 evoke a discussion 【引人入胜】fascinating; enchanting; bewitching 【引人注目】noticeable ～的特点 conspicuous features ～的变化 spectacular changes【引入】lead into; draw into ～歧途 lead sb. astray【引申】extend (the meaning of a word, etc.) ～义 extended meaning【引水】pilot a ship into harbour / draw or channel water ～灌田 channel water into the fields ～工程 diversion works ～员 pilot【引退】retire from office; resign【引文】quoted passage; quotation【引信】detonator; fuse【引言】foreword; introduction【引以为戒】learn a lesson; take warning【引用】quote; cite【引诱】lure; seduce

饮 yǐn drink ～茶 drink tea【饮料】drink; beverage【饮食】food and drink; diet ～店 eating house ～卫生 dietetic hygiene ～业 catering trade【饮用水】drinking water

隐 yǐn ①hidden ～伏 lie concealed ②secret ～痛 secret anguish ～忧 secret worry【隐蔽】conceal; take cover ～活动 covert activities【隐藏】hide; conceal; remain under cover【隐患】hidden trouble; hidden danger 消除～ remove a hidden peril【隐讳】avoid mentioning; cover up【隐晦】obscure; veiled 写得很～ be couched in ambiguous terms【隐疾】unmentionable disease【隐居】live in seclusion; be a hermit【隐瞒】hide; hold back ～错误 conceal one's mistakes ～事实 withhold the truth; hide the facts【隐情】facts one wishes to hide【隐忍】bear patiently; forbear (from speaking)【隐射】insinuate; hint【隐士】hermit【隐私】one's secrets【隐退】retire from political life【隐姓埋名】conceal one's identity; live incognito【隐隐】indistinct; faint ～雷声 a distant roll of thunder ～作痛 feel a dull pain【隐语】enigmatic language【隐喻】metaphor【隐约】indistinct; faint ～可见 faintly visible ～其词 speak in equivocal terms; use ambiguous language【隐衷】feeling or troubles one wishes to keep to oneself

瘾 yǐn ①addiction; habitual craving 吸毒上～ be addicted to drugs 发烟～ have an urge to smoke 过～ satisfy a craving ②strong interest (in a sport or pastime) 有球～ have a passion for ball games

印 yǐn ①seal; stamp; chop 盖～ affix one's seal ②print; mark 脚～ footprint ③print ～书 print books 付～ put (an article, etc.) into print 一在脑子里 be engraved on one's mind ④tally; conform 【印版】(printing) plate 【印发】 print and distribute 【印盒】 seal box 【印花】 printing / revenue stamp ～布 prints; printed calico ～厂 printworks ～机 printing machine ～棉布 cotton print ～丝绸 printed silk ～税 stamp tax 【印泥】 red ink paste used for seals 【印染】 printing and dyeing (of textiles) ～厂 printing and dyeing mill 【印数】 printing; impression 【印刷】 printing ～厂 printing house; press ～错误 misprint ～工人 printer ～机 printing machine; press ～品 printed matter ～体 block letter; print hand ～纸 printing paper 【印台】 ink pad; stamp pad 【印相纸】 photographic paper 【印象】 impression ～好 have a good impression 留下深刻的～ leave a deep impression on 一派 impressionist school; impressionist ～主义 impressionism 【印信】 official seal 【印行】 publish 【印油】 stamp-pad ink 【印章】 seal; signet; stamp 【印证】 confirm; verify 有待～ yet to be confirmed

饮 yǐn give (animals) water to drink; water ～马 water a horse

荫 yǐn shady; damp and chilly 【荫庇】 protection by one's elders or ancestors 【荫凉】 shady and cool

YING

应 yīng ①answer; respond ～声开门 answer the door ②agree (to do sth.); promise; accept ～允 assent; consent ③should; ought to; must ～予考虑 merit consideration ～予纠正 it should be corrected 【应得】(well) deserved; due 【应届毕业生】graduating students or pupils; this year's graduates 【应有】due; proper; deserved 发挥它～的作用 play its proper role ～尽有 have everything that one expects to find

英 yīng hero; outstanding person 【英镑】pound sterling 【英才】person of outstanding ability 【英尺】foot 【英寸】inch 【英国】Britain; England ～人 the British 【英俊】eminently talented; brilliant / handsome and spirited; smart 【英里】mile 【英两】ounce 【英灵】spirit of the brave departed; martyr 【英名】illustrious name 【英明】wise ～论断 brilliant thesis ～远见 sagacity and farsightedness 【英亩】acre 【英气】heroic spirit 【英武】of soldierly bearing 【英雄】hero 女～ heroine ～本色 the true quality of a hero ～气概 heroic spirit; mettle ～主义 heroism 【英勇】valiant; brave; gallant ～奋斗 fight heroically ～善战 brave and skilful in battle ～就义 die a heroic death 【英语】English (language) 【英姿】heroic bearing

莺 yīng warbler; oriole

婴 yīng 【婴儿】baby; infant ～车 perambulator; baby carriage

罂 yīng 【罂粟】opium poppy ～花 poppy flower

缨 yīng ①tassel 红～枪 red-tasselled spear ②sth. shaped like a tassel 萝卜～子 radish leaves ③ribbon

樱 yīng ①cherry ②oriental cherry 【樱花】oriental cherry 日本~ Japanese flowering cherry 【樱桃】cherry

鹦 yīng 【鹦鹉】parrot ~学舌 repeat the words of others like a parrot; parrot

鹰 yīng hawk; eagle 【鹰钩鼻子】aquiline nose 【鹰犬】falcons and hounds — lackeys; hired thugs

迎 yíng ①go to meet; greet; welcome; receive ②move towards; meet face to face 【迎风】facing the wind / down the wind; with the wind ~飘扬 flutter in the wind 【迎合】cater to ~对方心理 go along with the other side ~低级趣味 pander to low tastes 【迎候】await the arrival of 【迎击】meet (an approaching enemy) head-on 【迎接】meet; welcome; greet ~贵宾 meet a distinguished guest 【迎面】head-on; in one's face 【迎刃而解】(of a problem) be readily solved 【迎头】head-on; directly ~痛击 deal head-on blows ~赶上 try hard to catch up 【迎新】see the New Year in / welcome new arrivals ~晚会 an evening party to welcome newcomers

盈 yíng ①be full of ②have a surplus of 【盈亏】profit and loss 【盈利】profit; gain 【盈余】surplus; profit

荧 yíng ①glimmering ②dazzled; perplexed 【荧光】fluorescence ~灯 fluorescent lamp ~屏 fluorescent screen

莹 yíng ①jade-like stone ②lustrous and transparent

营 yíng ①seek ~利 seek profits ②operate; run 国~ state-run ③camp; barracks 扎~ pitch a camp ④battalion ~部 battalion headquarters 【营地】campsite; camping ground 【营房】barracks 【营火】campfire ~会 campfire party 【营救】succour; rescue 【营私】seek private gain ~舞弊 engage in malpractices for selfish ends; practise graft【营养】nutrition 富于～ nourishing ～不良 malnutrition ～价值 nutritive value ～品 nutriment ～素 nutrient ～学 nutriology【营业】do business 暂停～ business temporarily suspended 照常～ business as usual ～额 turnover ～时间 business hours ～收入 business income ～税 business tax ～员 shop employees【营造】construct; build【营长】battalion commander【营帐】tent

萤 yíng firefly; glowworm【萤石】fluorite; fluorspar

萦 yíng entangle; encompass【萦怀】occupy one's mind【萦回】hover; linger

蝇 yíng fly【蝇拍】flyswatter; flyflap【蝇头】small as the head of a fly; tiny ～小利 petty profits

赢 yíng ①win; beat 这场比赛谁～了 who won the game ②gain (profit)【赢得】win; gain ～独立 attain independence【赢利】profit; gain【赢余】surplus; profit

颖 yíng ①glume; grain husk ②clever【颖慧】bright; intelligent

影 yíng ①shadow; reflection; image 倒～ inverted image ②photograph; picture 合～ group photo ③film; movie ～迷 film fan【影集】photo album【影片】film; movie【影评】film review【影射】allude to; hint obliquely at ～攻击 attack by innuendo【影响】effect; impact/affect; influence 产生显著～ make a notable impact 受气候～ be influenced by the weather ～质量 impair the quality ～威信 lower one's prestige ～工程进度 hold up the project ～积极性 chill the enthusiasm ～工作 interfere with one's work【影印】photo offset process ～版 process plate ～本 photo-offset copy【影院】cinema

应 yìng ①answer; respond 呼～ echo ②comply with; grant 为～广大读者需要 to meet the needs of the broad reading public ③suit; respond to ～景 do sth. for the occasion ④deal with; cope with 从容～敌 meet the enemy calmly【应变】meet an emergency ～措施 emergency measure【应承】agree (to do sth.); promise【应酬】have social intercourse with; treat with courtesy 不善～ socially inept ～几句 exchange a few polite words【应对】reply; answer 善于～ good at repartee【应付】deal with; cope with; handle / do sth. perfunctorily; do sth. after a fashion / make do【应急】meet an urgent need; meet a contingency ～计划 contingency plan【应考】take an examination【应时】seasonable; in season ～瓜果 fruits of the season【应验】come true; be confirmed【应邀】at sb.'s invitation; on invitaton【应用】apply; use 理论～于实践 apply theory to practice ～化学 applied chemistry ～科学 applied science ～文 practical writing【应战】meet an enemy attack /accept a challenge ～书 letter accepting a challenge【应诊】see patients【应征】be recruited (into the army) /respond to a call for contributions

映 yìng reflect; mirror; shine ～在湖面上 be mirrored on the lake【映衬】set off【映射】shine upon; cast light upon【映象】image【映照】shine upon

硬 yìng ①hard; stiff; tough ～领 stiff collar ②strong; firm 话说得很～ express oneself in strong terms ③ manage to do sth. with difficulty ～撑着干 force oneself to work hard ④good (quality); able (person)【硬币】coin; specie【硬功夫】masterly skill【硬骨头】hard bone — a dauntless, unyielding person【硬煤】hard coal【硬木】hardwood【硬拼】fight recklessly【硬水】hard water【硬说】stubbornly insist; assert; allege【硬挺】endure with all one's will【硬通货】hard currency【硬席】hard seats (on a train) ～卧铺 hard sleeper【硬性】rigid; stiff; inflexible 【硬仗】 tough battle/formidable task

YONG

佣 yōng ①hire (a labourer) ②servant 女~ woman servant; maid

拥 yōng ①hold in one's arms 把孩子紧紧~在怀里 hug the child tightly ②gather around 一群人~着他走出来 he came out, surrounded by a group of people ③crowd; throng; swarm ~向门口 surge towards the gate ④support 军爱民，民~军 the army cherishes the people and the people support the army ⑤have; possess ~兵十万 have an army of 100,000 【拥抱】 embrace; hug 【拥戴】 support (sb. as leader) 【拥护】 support; uphold; endorse ~这个决定 endorse this decision 【拥挤】 crowd; push and squeeze 【拥塞】 jam; congest 【拥有】 possess

庸 yōng ①commonplace; mediocre ②inferior; second-rate 【庸碌】 mediocre and unambitious 【庸人】 mediocre person ~自扰 worry about troubles of one's own imagining 【庸俗】 vulgar; philistine; low ~作风 the vulgar ways ~化 vulgarize; debase 【庸医】 quack; charlatan

雍 yōng harmony 【雍容】 natural, graceful and poised ~华贵 elegant and poised

壅 yōng stop up; obstruct 【壅塞】 clogged up; jammed; congested 水道~ the waterway is blocked up

臃 yōng 【臃肿】 too fat to move/overstaffed 穿得太~ be cumbersomely dressed

永 yōng perpetually; forever; always ~葆革命青春 always keep one's revolutionary spirit young ~不变心 remain loyal till one's dying day 【永别】 part forever 【永恒】 eternal; perpetual ~的真理 eternal truth ~运动 perpetual motion 【永久】 permanent; everlasting; for good (and all) 【永诀】 be separated by death 【永生】 eternal life/immortal 【永世】 forever 【永远】 always; forever

甬 yǒng 【甬道】 paved path leading to a main hall or a tomb/corridor

泳 yǒng swim 仰～ backstroke 蛙～ breaststroke

咏 yǒng chant; intone 吟～ recite (a poem) 【咏叹】 intone; chant; sing ～调 aria

俑 yǒng tomb figure; figurine 陶～ pottery figurine 武士～ warrior figure

勇 yǒng brave; valiant ～冠三军 distinguish oneself by peerless valour in battle 【勇敢】 brave ～善战 courageous and skilful in battle 【勇猛】 bold and powerful ～前进 march boldly forward 【勇气】 courage; nerve 【勇士】 a brave and strong man; warrior 【勇往直前】 advance bravely 【勇于】 have the courage to ～负责 be brave in shouldering responsibilities ～创新 be bold in making innovations

涌 yǒng ①gush; well; pour; surge 泪如泉～ tears well up in one's eyes ②rise; surge; emerge 巨浪～向石滩 huge waves surged over the rocks 往事～上心头 memories of the past welled up in one's mind 【涌现】 emerge in large numbers; spring up; come to the fore

踊 yǒng leap up; jump up 【踊跃】 leap; jump / eagerly; enthusiastically

用 yòng ①use; employ; apply ～手摸 touch with one's hand ②expenses; outlay 家～ family expenses ③usefulness; use 没～ useless; worthless 有点～ be of some use ④(no) need 不～开灯 there's no need to turn on the light ⑤eat; drink 请～茶 won't you have some tea, please 【用兵】 resort to arms 善于～ well versed in the art of war 【用不了】have more than is needed/less than 【用不着】have no use for / there is no need to 【用处】use; good 各有各的～ each has its own use 【用得着】find sth. useful; need / there is need to; it is necessary to 【用度】expenditure; outlay 【用法】use; usage ～说明 directions (for use) 【用费】expense; cost 【用功】diligent; studious ～读书 study diligently 【用户】consumer; user 电话～ telephone subscriber 【用具】utensil; apparatus; appliance 【用力】put forth one's strength 【用品】articles for use 生活～ daily necessities 办公～ things for office use 【用人】make use of personnel 善于～ know how to choose the right person for the right job ～不当 not choose the right person for the job 【用人】servant 女～ maidservant 【用途】use 【用心】diligently; attentively / motive; intention ～学习 concentrate on one's studies ～听讲 listen attentively to a lecture 【用以】in order to; so as to 【用意】intention; purpose 【用语】wording/term ～不当 inappropriate choice of words 商业～ commercial phraseology

佣 yòng commission 【佣金】commission; brokerage; middleman's fee

YOU

优 yōu excellent; fine 质～价廉 fine in quality and low in price 【优待】give favoured treatment ～外宾 give special consideration to foreign guests ～券 complimentary ticket 【优等】first-rate; excellent ～品 high-class product ～生 top student 【优点】merit; advantage; virtue 【优厚】munificent; liberal; favourable 待遇～ excellent pay and conditions 【优惠】preferential; favourable 【优良】fine; good 成绩～ get good marks 【优美】graceful; fine; exquisite 【优胜】winning; superior ～奖 winning prize ～者 winner; champion 【优势】superiority; preponderance ～兵力 superior force 占～ occupy a dominant position 【优先】have priority; take precedence ～权 priority; preference 【优秀】excellent; splendid ～作品 (literary or artistic) works of excellence ～电影 highly rated films ～的共产党员 an exemplary Communist 【优异】outstanding; exceedingly good 考试成绩～ do exceedingly well in an examination 作出了～的成绩 perform brilliant exploits 【优裕】affluent; abundant 生活～ be well-off 【优越】superior; advantageous ～条件 favourable conditions ～感 sense of superiority ～性 advantage 【优质】high quality ～钢 high-quality steel

忧 yōu ① worry ～国～民 be concerned about one's country and one's people ②sorrow; anxiety 无～无虑 carefree 【忧愁】sad; depressed 【忧患】suffering; misery; hardship 【忧惧】worried and apprehensive 【忧虑】anxious; concerned 【忧闷】feeling low 【忧伤】weighed down with sorrow; laden with grief 【忧心】heavyhearted; care-laden ～如焚 burning with anxiety 【忧郁】melancholy

幽 yōu ①deep and remote; dim ～谷 a deep and secluded valley ～林 a secluded wood ②secret; hidden ～居 live in seclusion ③tranquil ～深 deep and quiet ④of the nether world ～魂 ghost ⑤imprison ～禁 put under house arrest 【幽暗】dim; gloomy 【幽愤】hidden resentment 【幽会】a lovers' rendezvous; tryst 【幽寂】secluded and lonely 【幽静】quiet and secluded 【幽灵】spectre; spirit 【幽默】humorous ～感 sense of humour

悠 yōu ①long-drawn-out; remote in time or space ② leisurely ②swing (across) 【悠荡】swing (to and fro); sway (back and forth) 【悠久】long; age-old 历史～ have a long history ～的文化 a civilization of long standing

~的传统 an age-old tradition【悠闲】leisurely and care-free【悠扬】(of music, etc.) rising and falling; melodious

尤 yóu ①outstanding 择~ pick out the best ②fault 效~ knowingly follow the example of a wrongdoer【尤其】especially; particularly

由 yóu ①cause; reason. ②because of; due to 咎~自取 have only oneself to blame ③through ~此入内 this way in ④follow; obey ~他去吧 let him do as he pleases ⑤by ~群众推荐 be recommended by the masses 须~支部大会通过 be subject to acceptance by a general meeting of the Party branch ⑥from ~浅入深 proceed from the easy to the difficult ~下而上 from bottom to top【由不得】not be up to sb. to decide; be beyond the control of 这件事~我 it's not up to me【由此】from this ~看来 judging from this; in view of this ~产生的一切后果 all consequences arising therefrom ~可见 thus it can be seen; this shows; that proves【由来】origin 分歧的~ origin of differences ~已久 long-standing; time-honoured【由于】thanks to; as a result of; due to; in virtue of ~健康关系 on health grounds ~同志们的共同努力 owing to the concerted efforts of the comrades【由衷】sincere; heartfelt ~之言 sincere words

邮 yóu ①post; mail ②postal ~路 postal route【邮包】(postal) parcel【邮车】postal car【邮船】(ocean) liner; packet ship【邮戳】postmark【邮袋】mailbag; post-bag; pouch【邮递】send by post / postal delivery ~员 postman【邮电】post and telecommunications ~部 Ministry of Posts and Telecommunications ~局 post and telecommunications office【邮费】postage ~免收 post-free【邮购】mail-order ~部 mail-order department【邮汇】remit by post【邮寄】(send by) post【邮件】postal matter;

post; mail 挂号～ registered post 航空～ air mail 小包
～ a postal packet 【邮局】post office 【邮票】postage
stamp 一套纪念～ a set of commemorative stamps【邮亭】
postal kiosk 【邮筒】postbox; mailbox 【邮政】postal service ～编码 postcode ～代办所 postal agency ～汇票
postal (money) order ～局 post office ～局长 postmaster
～信箱 post-office box 【邮资】postage ～已付 postage paid

犹 yóu ①just as; like; as if 虽死～生 live on in spirit
②still 记忆～新 be still fresh in one's memory 【犹
豫 yù】hesitate; be irresolute ～不决 remain undecided

油 yóu ①oil; fat; grease 猪～ lard ②apply tung oil or
paint ～门窗 paint the doors and windows ③be stained with oil or grease ④oily; glib 嘴挺～ have a glib
tongue 【油饼】deep-fried dough cake / oil cake 【油布】
oilcloth 【油彩】greasepaint 【油菜】rape ～籽 rapeseed 【油
层】oil reservoir 【油茶】tea-oil tree; oil-tea camellia / a
gruel of sweetened, fried flour 【油船】tanker 【油灯】oil
lamp 【油橄榄】olive 【油膏】ointment 【油管】oil pipe / oil
tube 【油罐】oil tank 【油光】glossy; shiny 【油壶】oilcan
【油滑】slippery; foxy 【油画】oil painting 画～ paint in
oils 【油灰】putty 【油迹】oil stains; grease spots 【油井】
oil well 【油库】oil depot 【油矿】oil deposit/oil field 【油
料作物】oil crops 【油门】throttle/accelerator 踩～ step on
the accelerator 【油墨】printing ink 【油母页岩】oil shale
【油泥】greasy filth; grease 表该擦～了 the watch needs
cleaning and oiling 【油腻】greasy; oily / greasy food 【油
漆】paint / cover with paint 一层～ a coat of paint ～
未干 wet paint ～工人 painter 【油腔滑调】glib; unctu-
ous 【油然】spontaneously; involuntarily 【油石】oilstone
【油水】grease/profit ～不大 not very profitable 捞到一
点～ make a profit 【油酥】short; crisp; flaky ～点心

short pastry 【油田】 oil field 开发～ exploit an oil field 【油条】 deep-fried twisted dough sticks 【油桐】 tung oil tree 【油桶】 oil drum 【油头滑脑】 slick; flippant 【油箱】 fuel tank 【油烟】 lampblack 【油印】 mimeograph ～一百份 mimeograph a hundred copies 【油渣】 dregs of fat 【油毡】 asphalt felt 【油脂】 oil; fat 【油纸】 oilpaper

铀
yóu uranium 浓缩～ enriched uranium

游
yóu ①swim ～了一会儿(水) have a swim ②wander; travel; tour ～山玩水 go on trips to different scenic spots ③roving; itinerant ～民 vagrant ④reach 上～ the upper reaches 【游伴】 travel companion 【游荡】 loaf about; loiter 【游动】 move about; go from place to place ～哨 a roving sentry 【游逛】 go sight-seeing; stroll about 【游击】 guerrilla warfare 打～ fight as a guerrilla ～队 guerrilla forces ～队员 guerrilla; partisan ～区 guerrilla area ～战 guerrilla war 【游记】 travel notes; travels 【游街】 parade sb. through the streets 【游客】 visitor (to a park, etc.); tourist; sightseer 【游览】 go sight-seeing; tour; visit ～车 tourist coach ～地 place for sight-seeing; excursion centre 【游廊】 covered corridor; veranda 【游离】 dissociate; drift away 【游历】 travel (for pleasure) 【游牧】 rove around as a nomad ～部落 nomadic tribe～生活 nomadic life 【游手好闲】 idle about; loaf 【游说】 go about selling an idea; go canvassing 【游丝】 gossamer/hairspring 【游艇】 yacht; pleasure-boat 【游玩】 amuse oneself; play/stroll about 【游戏】 recreation; game/play 做～ play games 【游行】 parade; march 节日～ gala parade 抗议～ protest march 举行～示威 hold a demonstration ～队伍 procession 【游移】 waver; wobble ～不定 keep on vacillating 【游艺】 entertainment; recreation ～室 recrea-

tion room【游泳】swim 去～ go swimming ～比赛 swimming contest ～池 swimming pool ～裤(帽) swimming trunks (cap) ～衣 swimsuit【游资】idle fund

友 yǒu ①friend 好～ close friend 战～ comrade-in-arms ②friendly ～军 friendly forces【友爱】friendly affection; fraternal love 团结～ fraternal unity 阶级～ class brotherhood【友邦】friendly nation【友好】(close) friend/friendly; amicable ～访问 friendly visit 在～的气氛中 in a friendly atmosphere ～代表团 goodwill mission ～人士 friendly personage; friend ～条约 treaty of friendship ～协会 friendship association【友情】friendly sentiments【友善】amicable【友谊】friendship 建立～ forge ties of friendship ～赛 friendship match

有 yǒu ①have; possess 我～一个弟弟 I have a younger brother ②there is; exist 屋里～人吗 is there anyone in the room【有碍】get in the way of; obstruct ～交通 hinder traffic【有备无患】preparedness averts peril【有待】remain; await ～解决 remain to be solved ～证明 have yet to be proved ～进一步讨论 pending further discussion【有点儿】some; a little / somewhat; rather; a bit ～反感 feel a bit resentful ～不好意思 be somewhat embarrassed 我只是～认识她 I barely know her【有功】have performed meritorious service 对革命～ have rendered service to the revolution【有关】have something to do with; relate to; concern ～的文件 the relevant documents ～部门 the department concerned ～当局 the authorities concerned ～方面 the parties concerned【有轨电车】tramcar; streetcar【有鬼】there's something fishy 这里面～ one smells a rat here 心里～ have a guilty conscience【有害】harmful; detrimental 对健康～ harmful to one's health ～的影响 pernicious effects【有机】organic

～的整体 an organic whole ～玻璃 plexiglass ～肥料 organic manure ～化学 organic chemistry ～体 organism 【有机可乘】there's an opportunity to take advantage of 【有计划】in a planned way; according to plan 【有赖】depend on; rest on 【有理】reasonable; justified; in the right 【有力】strong; powerful; forceful 进行～的斗争 conduct a vigorous struggle 给以～的支援 give effective support 提供～的证据 furnish convincing proof 【有利】advantageous; beneficial; favourable ～于改进作风 help improve the style ～可图 stand to gain; be profitable ～时机 opportune time ～条件 favourable condition 【有名】well-known; famous 【有名无实】merely nominal; titular 【有目共睹】be obvious to all 【有期徒刑】set term of imprisonment 【有钱】rich; wealthy ～的人 the rich 【有趣】interesting; fascinating; amusing 【有色】coloured ～金属 nonferrous metal ～人种 coloured race 【有生力量】effective strength 【有声片】sound film; talkie 【有声有色】vivid and dramatic 【有识之士】a man of insight 【有时】sometimes; at times; now and then 【有始有终】carry sth. through to the end 【有事】if sth. happens/occupied; busy ～同群众商量 consult with the masses when problems crop up 你今晚～吗 have you anything on this evening 我现在～ I'm busy now 【有数】know exactly how things stand 我们心里～ we know where we are 怎样做我～ I know what I'm doing 【有条不紊】in an orderly way; methodically 【有为】promising 【有限】limited; finite 为数～ limited in number; not many ～公司 limited company 【有线】wired ～广播 wired broadcasting 【有效】efficacious; effective; valid 采取～步骤 take effective steps 三日内～ be valid for three days ～期 term of validity; time of efficacy 【有些】some/rather ～不满 be somewhat dissatisfied ～失望 be rather disappointed 【有心】 have a mind to/intentionally; purposely 【有益】 profitable; beneficial; useful ～的贡献 valuable contributions ～于健康 good for 'one's health ～于人民 be of value to the people 【有意】 have a mind to; be inclined to/purposely ～帮忙 be disposed to help ～歪曲 deliberately distort ～习难 make things difficult for sb. on purpose 【有意识】 consciously 【有意思】 significant; meaningful / interesting; enjoyable 【有勇无谋】 be brave but not resourceful 【有余】 have a surplus 粮食自给～ have grain enough and to spare 绰绰～ more than enough 【有助于】 contribute to; be conducive to; conduce to

又 yòu ①again 读了～读 read again and again 一年～一年 year after year ②but 我想去，～怕没时间 I'd like to go, but I'm not sure if I can find the time ～便宜～好 cheap but good ③and 一～二分之一 one and a half ～红～专 both red and expert·

右 yòu ①the right (side) 靠～走 keep to the right 无出其～ second to none ②the Right 【右派】 the Right; the right wing/Rightist 【右倾】 Right deviation ～思想 Right-deviationist thinking ～机会主义 Right opportunism 【右手】 the right hand 【右首】 the right-hand side; the right 【右翼】 right wing; right flank /the Right

幼 yòu ①young; under age ～芽 young shoot ～畜 young animal ②children; the young 【幼虫】 larva 【幼儿】 child; infant ～教育 preschool education ～园 kindergarten; nursery school; infant school 【幼苗】 seedling 【幼年】 childhood; infancy 【幼小】 immature 【幼稚】 young/ childish; puerile; naive ～可笑 ridiculously childish ～的想法 naive ideas ～病 infantilism / infantile disorder 【幼子】 the youngest son

佑 yòu help; protect; bless

诱 yòu ①guide; lead ~发 induce; bring out; cause to happen ②seduce; entice ~敌深入 lure the enemy in deep 【诱饵】bait 【诱供】induce a person to make a confession 【诱拐】abduct 【诱惑】tempt; lure 【诱奸】seduce 【诱骗】inveigle; cajole; trap; trick 【诱杀】trap and kill

YU

迂 yū ①circuitous; winding; tortuous ②pedantic ~论 pedantic talk 【迂腐】pedantry ~的见解 pedantic ideas 【迂回】roundabout/outflank ~曲折 full of twists and turns ~前进 advance by a roundabout route ~战术 outflanking tactics【迂阔】high-sounding and impracticable

淤 yū ①become silted up ②silt 引~肥田 fertilize the soil with silt ③stasis (of blood) 【淤积】silt up; deposit 【淤泥】silt; sludge; ooze 【淤塞】silt up; be choked with silt 【淤血】extravasated blood

于 yú ①in; at 位~郊外 be situated in the suburbs 运动正处~高潮 the movement is at its high tide ②for 求助~人 ask people for help ③to 忠~祖国 be loyal to one's country ④from; of 出~自愿 of one's own free will 出~无知 out of ignorance 【于是】thereupon; hence; consequently; as a result

余 yú ①surplus; spare; remaining ~钱 spare money ②more than; odd; over 五十~年 fifty odd years ③beyond; after 工作之~ after working hours; after work 【余波】repercussions 【余存】balance; remainder 【余党】remaining confederates 【余地】leeway; room; latitude 回旋的~ room for manoeuvre 改进的~ room for improvement 留有~ leave some margin 没有怀疑的~ there is no place for doubt 【余毒】residual poison; pernicious influence 【余额】vacancies yet to be filled / remaining sum 【余悸】lingering fear 心有~ have a lingering fear 【余烬】ashes; embers 【余可类推】the rest may be inferred by analogy 【余粮】surplus grain ~户 grain-surplus household 【余年】one's remaining years 【余孽】leftover evil 封建~ dregs of feudalism 【余生】one's remaining years / survival (after a disaster) 【余剩】surplus; remainder 【余威】remaining prestige or influence 【余味】agreeable aftertaste ~无穷 leave a lasting and pleasant impression 【余暇】spare time; leisure time 【余下】remaining ~的同志 the other comrades 【余兴】lingering interest / entertainment after a meeting or a dinner party 【余音】lingering sound

鱼 yú fish 【鱼叉】fish spear 【鱼翅】shark's fin 【鱼虫】water flea 【鱼刺】fishbone 【鱼饵】(fish) bait 【鱼粉】fish meal 【鱼肝油】cod-liver oil 【鱼竿】fishing rod 【鱼钩】fishhook 【鱼雷】torpedo ~发射管 torpedo tube ~快艇 torpedo boat 【鱼鳞】(fish) scale ~坑 fish-scale pits 【鱼卵】(fish) roe 【鱼米之乡】a land of fish and rice — a land of plenty 【鱼苗】fry 【鱼目混珠】pass off fish eyes as pearls — pass off the sham as the genuine 【鱼群】shoal of fish 【鱼水】fish and water ~情深 be close as fish and water 【鱼松】dried fish floss 【鱼网】fishnet; fishing net 【鱼尾号】boldface square brackets 【鱼鲜】seafood 【鱼汛】fishing season 【鱼秧】fingerling 【鱼子】roe ~酱 caviare

诨 yú flatter 阿~ flatter and toady ~辞 flattering words; flattery

娱 yú ①give pleasure to; amuse 聊以自~ just to amuse oneself ②joy 耳目之~ pleasures of the senses

【娱乐】amusement; entertainment; recreation ～场所 public place of entertainment ～室 re creation room

隅 yú ①corner; nook 城～ the corner of a city wall ②outlying place; border 海～ seaboard

渔 yú fishing ～船 fishing boat ～村 fishing village 【渔产】aquatic products 【渔场】fishery 【渔港】fishing port 【渔具】fishing tackle 【渔利】reap unfair gains / easy gains; spoils 从～ cash in on other people's efforts 坐收～ profit from others' conflict 【渔轮】fishing vessel 【渔民】fisherman 【渔业】fishery ～区 fishing zone

渝 yú (of one's attitude or feeling) change 始终不～ unswerving; consistent

愉 yú pleased; happy 面有不～之色 wear an annoyed expression; look displeased 【愉快】joyful; cheerful ～的微笑 a happy smile ～的事 something pleasant; a joyful event 心情～ be in a cheerful frame of mind

逾 yú ①exceed; go beyond ～额 exceed the allowed amount ～常 unusual 【逾期】exceed the time limit; be overdue 【逾越】exceed ～权限 overstep one's authority 不可～的鸿沟 an impassable gulf

愚 yú ①stupid; foolish ～不可及 couldn't be more foolish ②make a fool of 为人所～ be duped by sb. ③I ～见 my humble opinion 【愚蠢】foolish; silly; stupid; clumsy 【愚钝】slow-witted 【愚昧】ignorant; benighted 【愚弄】deceive; hoodwink; dupe

瑜 yú ①fine jade; gem ②lustre of gems—virtues; good points 瑕不掩～ the defects do not obscure the virtues

榆 yú 【榆树】elm

舆 yú public 【舆论】public opinion 作～准备 prepare public opinion 国际～ world opinion ～工具

mass media ～界 the media; press circles

与 yǔ ①give; offer; grant ～人方便 give help to others; make things easy for others ②help; support ～人为善的批评 criticism aimed at helping those criticized ③to ～困难作斗争 strive to overcome difficulties ～人民为敌 be hostile to the people ④and 工业～农业 industry and agriculture【与日俱增】grow with each passing day【与众不同】out of the ordinary

予 yǔ give; grant; bestow 授～奖状 award sb. a citation of merit 免～处分 exempt sb. from punishment ～人口实 give people a handle

宇 yǔ ①eaves ②house 庙～ temple ③space; universe; world ～内 in the world【宇宙】universe; cosmos ～飞船 spaceship ～飞行 space flight ～飞员 spaceman ～观 world view ～航行 astronavigation; space navigation ～火箭 space rocket ～空间 cosmic space ～速度 cosmic velocity

屿 yǔ small island; islet 岛～ islands and islets; islands

羽 yǔ feather【羽毛】feather; plume ～丰满 become full-fledged ～未丰 unfledged; young and immature ～球 badminton / shuttlecock ～扇 feather fan【羽纱】camlet【羽翼】wing / assistant

雨 yǔ rain【雨布】waterproof cloth; waterproof【雨点】raindrop【雨后春笋】(spring up like) bamboo shoots after a spring rain【雨季】rainy season【雨具】rain gear (i.e. umbrella, raincoat, etc.)【雨量】rainfall ～计 rain gauge【雨露】rain and dew / favour; grace; bounty【雨帽】rain cap / hood【雨伞】umbrella【雨水】rainwater; rainfall; rain ～足 adequate rainfall ～调和 the rainfall is just right【雨鞋】rubber boots; rubbers

【雨衣】raincoat; waterproof

语 yǔ ①language; tongue; words 汉～ the Chinese language ②speak; say 低～ speak in a low voice; whisper ③set phrase; proverb ④sign; signal 旗～ flag-signal 【语病】faulty wording or formulation 【语词】words and phrases 【语调】intonation 【语法】grammar 【语汇】vocabulary 【语句】sentence 【语录】quotation 【语气】tone; manner of speaking / mood ～友好 a friendly tone 祈使～ imperative mood 【语态】voice 主动～ active voice 被动～ passive voice 【语体】type of writing; style 口语～ colloquialism 科学～ scientific style of writing ～文 prose written in the vernacular 【语文】Chinese / language and literature 【语系】language family 【语序】word order 【语言】language ～科学 linguistic science ～学 linguistics ～学家 linguist 【语义学】semantics 【语音】speech sounds / pronunciation ～课 phonetics class ～学 phonetics ～学家 phonetician 【语源学】etymology 【语重心长】sincere words and earnest wishes

与 yù participate in a conference 【与会】participate in a conference ～国 participating countries ～者 conferee 【与闻】be let into (a secret, etc.) ～其事 be in the know; have a participant's knowledge of matter

玉 yù jade 【玉雕】jade carving ～工人 jade carver 【玉米】maize; Indian corn; corn/ear of maize ～花 popcorn ～粒 kernel of corn ～面 maize flour; corn-meal ～芯 corncob; cob ～粥 maize gruel 【玉器】jade article; jadeware ～工厂 jade workshop 【玉蜀黍】maize

驭 yù drive (a carriage) 【驭手】soldier in charge of pack animals; driver of a military pack train

芋 yù ①taro ②tuber crops 洋～ potato 山～ sweet potato

育 yù ①give birth to 生儿～女 give birth to children ②rear; raise; bring up ～苗 grow seedlings ～种 breeding ～秧 raise rice seedlings ③educate

郁 yù ①strongly fragrant ②luxuriant ③gloomy; sad 【郁积】pent-up ～的愤怒 pent-up fury ～的不满 smouldering discontent 【郁闷】depressed; oppressive 【郁郁】lush/melancholy; gloomy

狱 yù ①prison; jail 入～ be imprisoned ②lawsuit; case 断～ hear and pass judgment on a case

浴 yù bath; bathe 【浴场】outdoor bathing place 海滨～ bathing beach 【浴池】common bathing pool/public bathhouse 【浴巾】bath towel 【浴盆】bathtub 【浴室】bathroom 【浴血】bathed in blood ～奋战 fight a bloody battle 【浴衣】bathrobe

预 yù in advance; beforehand ～付 pay in advance ～致谢意 thanks in anticipation ～祝成功 wish sb. success 【预报】forecast 【预备】prepare; get ready ～功课 prepare lessons 你们～好了吗 are you all ready ～党员 probationary Party member 【预卜】reserve force; reserves ～期 probationary period ～役 reserve duty 【预卜】augur; foretell ～吉凶 try to predict good or bad fortune 尚难～ be hard to foretell 【预测】calculate; forecast 【预产期】expected date of childbirth 【预处理】pretreatment 【预订】book; place an order for ～杂志 subscribe to a magazine ～火车票 book a train ticket 【预定】fix in advance; predetermine 在～时间 at the fixed time ～在明年完成 be scheduled for completion next year 【预断】prejudge 【预防】prevent; guard against ～火灾 take precautions against fire ～注射 preventive inoculation 【预感】premonition/have a premonition 不祥的～ an ominous presentiment 【预告】announce in advance; herald/advance notice 【预购】 purchase in advance 【预计】 calculate in advance; estimate 【预见】 foresee; predict/foresight; prevision ～不到的困难 unforeseen difficulties 英明的～ brilliant foresight ～性 farsightedness 【预科】 preparatory course (in a college) 【预料】 expect; anticipate 和我们的～相反 contrary to our expectations 【预谋】 plan beforehand ～杀人 premeditated murder 【预期】 expect 达到～的效果 achieve the desired results 结果和～的相反 the results are contrary to expectations 【预赛】 preliminary (contest); trial 【预示】 betoken; indicate; presage 【预算】 budget 【预习】 (of students) prepare lessons before class 【预先】 in advance ～通知 notify in advance ～声明 state explicitly beforehand ～警告 forewarn ～感谢 thank sb. in anticipation 【预言】 prophesy; foretell/prediction ～家 prophet 【预演】 preview (of a performance, etc.) 【预约】 make an appointment ～挂号 have an appointment with a doctor 【预展】 preview (of an exhibition) 【预兆】 omen; presage; sign; harbinger 【预制】 prefabricate ～构件 prefabricated components

欲 yù ①desire; longing; wish 食～ a desire for food 求知～ thirst for knowledge ②wish; want 畅所～言 speak one's mind freely ③about to; just going to 【欲罢不能】 cannot help carrying on 【欲望】 desire; wish; lust

域 yù land within certain boundaries; territory; region 异～ foreign lands 绝～ inaccessible remote areas

谕 yù instruct; tell 面～ tell sb. in person 上～ imperial edict

寓 yù ①reside; live ②residence; abode 公～ apartment house ③imply; contain 这个故事～有深意 this story contains a profound lesson 【寓所】 residence; abode 【寓言】 fable; allegory; parable 【寓意】 implied meaning; import ～深刻 be pregnant with meaning

裕 yù abundant; plentiful 富～ affluent; well-to-do 【裕如】effortlessly; with ease 应付～ handle with ease

遇 yù ①meet 不期而～ meet by chance ～雨 be caught in a rain ②treat; receive 优～ treat sb. with special consideration ③chance; opportunity 机～ favourable circumstances 【遇刺】be attacked by an assassin ～身死 be assassinated 【遇到】run into; encounter; meet; come across 【遇救】be rescued; be saved 【遇难】die in an accident/be murdered 【遇事】when anything crops up ～不慌 be unruffled whatever happens ～和群众商量 consult with the masses when matters arise 【遇险】meet with a mishap; be in danger; be in distress ～船只 ship in distress ～信号 distress signal

喻 yù ①explain; inform ～之以理 reason with sb. ② understand; know 家～户晓 known to every household ③analogy 比～ metaphor

御 yù ①drive (a carriage) ～者 carriage driver ②imperial ～花园 imperial garden ③resist; ward off ～敌 resist the enemy ～寒 keep out the cold ～侮 resist foreign aggression 【御用】for the use of an emperor/be in the pay of ～报刊 hired press; paid press ～文人 hired scribbler; hack writer

誉 yù ①reputation; fame ～满全球 of world renown; famed the world over ②praise; eulogize 毁～参半 be as much censured as praised

愈 yù ①heal; recover; become well 病～ recover from an illness ②the more..., the more...～多～好 the more the better ～辩～明 become clearer through debate 【愈合】heal 伤口～了 the wound healed 【愈加】all the more; even more; further

YUAN

冤 yuān ①wrong; injustice 不白之～ unrighted wrong ②hatred; enmity 【冤仇】rancour 【冤家】enemy; foe 【冤屈】wrong; treat unjustly/wrongful treatment 受～ suffer an injustice 【冤枉】wrong; treat unjustly / not worthwhile ～好人 wrong an innocent person 花～钱 waste money 走～路 go the long way 【冤狱】an unjust charge or verdict 反平～ reverse an unjust verdict

鸳 yuān 【鸳鸯】mandarin duck/an affectionate couple

渊 yuān deep pool 深～ abyss 【渊博】broad and profound; erudite 【渊薮】den; haunt 盗贼的～ a den of bandits and thieves 罪恶的～ a hotbed of crime; a sink of iniquity 【渊源】origin; source

元 yuán ①first; primary ～月 the first month of the year; January ②unit; component 【元旦】New Year's Day 【元件】element; component; cell 【元老】senior statesman; founding member (of a political organization, etc.) 【元年】the first year of an era or the reign of an emperor 【元气】vitality; vigour 大伤～ sap one's vitality 恢复～ regain one's strength 【元首】head of state 【元帅】marshal 【元素】element 【元凶】prime culprit 【元勋】a man of great merit; founding father 【元音】vowel

园 yuán ①an area of land for growing plants 果～ orchard ②a place for public recreation 动物～ zoo 【园地】garden plot / field; scope 【园丁】gardener 【园林】gardens; park 【园田】vegetable garden 【园艺】gardening

员 yuán ①a person engaged in some field of activity 炊事～ cook 售货～ shop assistant ②member 工会会～ member of a trade union 【员工】staff; personnel

原 yuán ①primary; original; former ~义 primary meaning ~计划 original plan ~班人马 the former staff ②raw ~矿石 raw ore ~粮 unprocessed food grains ③excuse; pardon 情有可~ pardonable ④open country 平~ plain 【原版】original edition (of a book, etc.) 【原本】 master copy/the original 【原材料】raw and processed materials 【原动力】motivity 【原封】intact ~不动 be left intact 【原稿】original manuscript 【原告】plaintiff; prosecutor 【原级】positive degree 【原籍】ancestral home 【原来】original; former ~的想法 original idea 【原理】principle; tenet 【原谅】excuse; forgive; pardon 【原料】raw material 【原煤】raw coal 【原棉】raw cotton 【原木】log 【原始】original; firsthand / primeval; primitive ~记录 original record ~资料 source material ~森林 virgin forest ~社会 primitive society 【原委】the whole story; all the details 【原文】original text 【原先】former; original ~的计划 original plan 他~是个海员 he used to be a sailor 【原形】original shape ~毕露 show one's true colours 【原野】open country; champaign 【原意】meaning; original intention 曲解~ distort the meaning 这不是我们的~ this is not what we meant 【原因】cause; reason 【原油】crude oil; crude 【原则】principle ~问题 a matter of principle ~分歧 differences in principle ~上同意 agree in principle ~立场 the principled stand 【原址】former address 【原主】original owner 物归~ return sth. to its (rightful) owner 【原著】original work; original 【原状】original state; previous condition 恢复~ restore to the former state 【原子】atom ~弹 atom bomb ~反应堆 atomic reactor ~核 atomic nucleus ~量 atomic weight ~能 atomic energy ~武器 atomic weapon 【原作】original work

圆 yuán ①round; circular; spherical ～孔 a round hole ②circle ③justify 自～其说 justify oneself ～谎 patch up a lie ④yuan, the monetary unit of China 【圆规】 compasses 【圆滑】 slick and sly 【圆括号】 parentheses; curves 【圆满】 satisfactory ～成功 complete success ～的答案 a satisfactory answer ～解决 be solved satisfactorily ～结束 be rounded off 【圆圈】 circle; ring 【圆润】 mellow and full 【圆熟】 skilful; proficient 【圆舞曲】 waltz 【圆心】 the centre of a circle 【圆形】 circular; round 【圆周】 circumference 【圆珠笔】 ball-pen 【圆柱】 cylinder 【圆锥】 circular cone; taper 【圆桌】 round table

援 yuán ①help; aid 求～ ask for help ②cite; quote ～例 cite a precedent 【援救】 rescue; save 【援军】 reinforcements; relief troops 【援外】 foreign aid ～物资 materials in aid of a foreign country 【援助】 help; support; aid 技术～ technical assistance

源 yuán source 河～ river source 财～ source of income 【源泉】 fountainhead 【源源】 in a steady stream

猿 yuán ape 【猿猴】 apes and monkeys 【猿人】 ape-man

缘 yuán ①reason 无～无故 for no reason at all ②edge; fringe; brink 外～ outer edge 沙漠南～ southern fringe of the desert 【缘故】 cause 【缘起】 genesis; origin

辕 yuán shafts of a cart or carriage 【辕马】 shaft-horse

远 yuǎn far; distant; remote ～～超过 far exceed ～隔重洋 be separated by vast oceans 【远大】 long-range; broad ～的计划 an ambitious plan ～的理想 lofty ideals 【远道】 a long way ～而来 come from afar 【远方】 distant place ～的来客 a guest from afar 【远古】 remote antiquity 【远见】 foresight; vision 【远郊】 outer suburbs【远景】distant view; prospect ～规划 a long-range plan【远亲】distant relative; remote kinsfolk【远视】long sight ～眼镜 spectacles for long sight【远行】go on a long journey【远洋】ocean / oceanic ～货轮 oceangoing freighter ～渔业 deep-sea fishing【远因】remote cause【远征】expedition ～军 expeditionary army【远足】hike

怨 yuàn ①resentment 结～ arouse sb.'s enmity ～色 a resentful look ②blame; complain 这件事～我 I am to blame for this【怨愤】discontent and indignation【怨恨】have a grudge against sb.; hate / resenfment; grudge; enmity; hatred【怨气】complaint 出～ air one's grievances; vent one's resentment 一肚子～ be full of complaints【怨声载道】cries of discontent rise all round【怨言】grumble 从未发过一句～ never utter a word of complaint

院 yuàn ①courtyard; yard 前～ front yard 居民大～ neighbourhood compound ②a designation for certain government offices and public places 科学～ the academy of sciences 电影～ cinema【院士】academician

愿 yuàn ①hope; wish; desire 平生之～ a lifelong wish ②be willing ③vow 还～ redeem a vow【愿望】wish; aspiration 从团结的～出发 start from the desire for unity【愿意】be willing; be ready / wish; like; want ～作出牺牲 be willing to make sacrifice

YUE

日 yuē ①say ②call; name 美其名～ give sth. the fine-sounding name of

约 yuē ①make an appointment (with sb.); arrange ②ask or invite in advance ～他来 ask him to come ③pact; agreement 立～ make a pact 践～ keep an appointment ④restrict; restrain; bind ⑤economical; frugal ⑥ simple; brief ～言之 in brief; in a word ①about; around ～五十人 about fifty people 【约定】agree on; appoint; arrange ～会晤地点 agree on a meeting place 在～的时间 at the appointed time 【约会】appointment; engagement; date 我今晚有～ I have an engagement this evening 【约计】count roughly; come roughly to 【约略】rough; approximate 【约期】fix a date; appoint a time 【约请】invite; ask 【约束】keep within bounds; restrain; bind ～力 binding force 【约数】approximate number/divisor

月 yuè ①the moon 新～ a new moon ②month ～底 the end of the month ～产量 monthly output 【月报】monthly magazine / monthly report 【月饼】moon cake 【月份】month 上～ last month 【月光】moonlight; moonbeam 【月经】menses; period ～带 sanitary belt 【月刊】monthly (magazine) 【月历】monthly calendar 【月票】monthly ticket 【月食】lunar eclipse 【月台】railway platform ～票 platform ticket 【月息】monthly interest 【月薪】monthly pay

乐 yuè music 奏～ play music 【乐池】orchestra (pit) 【乐队】orchestra; band ～指挥 conductor; bandmaster 【乐谱】music (score) ～架 music stand 【乐器】(musical) instrument 【乐曲】(musical) composition; music 【乐团】philharmonic society or orchestra 【乐音】musical sound; tone 【乐章】movement

岳 yuè ①high mountain ②wife's parents 【岳父】wife's father; father-in-law 【岳母】wife's mother; mother-in-law

钥 yuè key

悦 yuè ①happy; pleased; delighted 不～ displeased ②please; delight 取～于人 try to please sb. 【悦耳】pleasing to the ear; sweet-sounding ～的音乐 melodious music 歌声~ the singing is pleasant 【悦服】 heartily admire 【悦目】 pleasing to the eye; good-looking

阅 yuè ①read; go over ~卷 go over examination papers ②review; inspect 【阅兵】 review troops ~场 parade ground ~式 military review; parade 【阅读】 read 【阅览】 read ~室 reading room 【阅历】 see, hear or do for oneself/experience 有~ have seen much of the world ~浅 having little experience; inexperienced

跃 yuè leap; jump 一~而起 get up with a jump ~居世界首位 leap to first place in the world 【跃进】 make a leap; leap forward 【跃跃欲试】 be eager to have a try

越 yuè ①get over; jump over ~墙而逃 escape by climbing over the wall ②exceed; overstep ~出常规 exceed conventional rules ~出范围 exceed the limits ~出政策界限 go beyond the bounds of policy ③the more ..., the more... ~多~好 the more the better ~战~强 grow stronger with the fighting 【越轨】 exceed the bounds; transgress ~行为 transgression 【越过】 cross; negotiate ~障碍 surmount obstacles 【越界】 cross the border 【越境】 cross the boundary illegally 【越权】 exceed one's authority 【越狱】 escape from prison

YUN

晕 yūn ①dizzy; giddy 有点头~ feel a bit dizzy ②swoon; faint 【晕倒】 fall in a faint; pass out 【晕头转向】 confused and disoriented

云 yún ①say 人~亦~ repeat what others say ②cloud 【云层】 cloud layer 【云集】 gather; converge 【云梯】 scaling ladder 【云雾】 cloud and mist 【云霄】 the skies

匀 yún ①even 颜色涂得不~ the colour is not evenly spread ②even up; divide evenly ③spare 我们可以~

给你们一些 we can spare you some 【匀称】well-balanced; symmetrical 身材～ of proportional build 【匀净】uniform

耘 yún weed 春耕夏～ spring ploughing and summer weeding 【耘锄】hoe

允 yǔn ①permit; allow ～从 comply ②fair; just 公～ equitable 【允许】permit; allow; consent; undertake

陨 yǔn fall from the sky or outer space 【陨石】aerolite; stony meteorite ～雨 meteorite shower 【陨铁】meteoric iron 【陨星】meteorite

殒 yǔn perish; die 【殒命】meet one's death; perish

孕 yùn pregnant 【孕妇】pregnant woman 【孕期】pregnancy 【孕育】be pregnant with; breed

运 yùn ①carry; transport ～往河边 carry to the riverside ②use; wield; utilize ～笔 wield the pen ③fortune; fate 不走～ be out of luck 【运筹学】operational research 【运动】motion / sports; athletics; exercise / movement; campaign; drive 直线～ rectilinear motion 室内～ indoor sports 群众～ mass movement ～场 sports ground ～服 sportswear ～会 sports meet; games ～员 sportsman or sportswoman; athlete; player ～战 mobile war 【运费】transportation expenses; freight 【运河】canal 【运气】fortune; luck 【运输】transport; carriage; conveyance ～船 cargo ship ～队 transport corps ～工具 means of transport ～公司 transport company ～机 transport plane ～业 transport service 【运送】ship; convey 【运算】operation ～误差 arithmetic error 【运行】be in motion 在轨道上～ move in orbit ` 列车～时 while the train is in motion 【运用】utilize; wield; apply; put to use ～自如 handle very skilfully ～价值规律 utilize the law of value 【运转】revolve; turn round / work; operate 机器～正常 the machine is running well

晕 yùn ①dizzy; giddy; faint 头~目眩 have a dizzy spell ②halo 日~ solar halo 月~ lunar halo 【晕车】 carsickness 【晕船】 seasickness

酝 yùn 【酝酿】 brew; ferment / deliberate on 此事~已久 it has been brewing for a long time ~候选人名单 consider and talk over the list of candidates

愠 yùn angry; irritated 而有~色 look irritated 【愠怒】 be inwardly angry

韵 yùn ①musical sound ②rhyme ~文 literary composition in rhyme; verse ~书 rhyming dictionary ③charm ~味 lingering charm; lasting appeal

熨 yùn iron; press ~衣服 iron clothes 【熨斗】 flatiron; iron 电~ electric iron

蕴 yùn accumulate 【蕴藏】 hold in store; contain ~着极大的积极性 have a vast reservoir of enthusiasm ~量 reserves; deposits

Z

ZA

扎 zā tie; bind ~小辫儿 tie up one's plaits ~彩 hang up festoons

杂 zá ①sundry; mixed ~事 miscellaneous affairs ~而不乱 mixed but not confused ②mix; mingle 【杂拌儿】 assorted preserved fruits; mixed sweetmeats 【杂草】 weeds; rank grass 【杂费】 incidental expenses; incidentals/sundry fees 【杂烩】 mixed stew; hotchpotch/mixture; miscellany 【杂货】 sundry goods; groceries ~店 grocery

【杂记】jottings; notes / miscellanies (as a type of literature) 【杂技】acrobatics ～团 acrobatic troupe ～演员 acrobat 【杂交】hybridize; cross ～水稻 hybrid rice ～玉米 crossbred maize 【杂粮】food grains other than wheat and rice 【杂乱】mixed and disorderly; in a jumble; in a muddle ～无章 disorderly and unsystematic; disorganized 【杂念】distracting thoughts 【杂牌】a less known and inferior brand 【杂耍】variety show; vaudeville 【杂文】essay 【杂务】odd jobs 【杂音】noise / murmur 【杂志】magazine 【杂质】impurity 【杂种】crossbreed / bastard

砸 zá ①pound; tamp ～了脚 have one's foot squashed ②break; smash 把门～开 smash the door open

ZAI

灾 zāi ①calamity 天～ natural disaster ②personal misfortune; adversity 没病没～ good health and good luck 【灾荒】famine due to crop failures 【灾民】victims of a natural calamity 【灾难】suffering ～深重 disaster-ridden ～性的后果 disastrous consequences 避免一场大～ avert a catastrophe 带来巨大～ bring great suffering to sb. 【灾情】the condition of a disaster ～严重 the losses caused by the disaster were serious 【灾区】disaster area

栽 zāi ①plant; grow ～树 plant trees ～花 grow flowers ②stick in; insert; plant ～杆子 erect a pole ③force sth. on sb.; impose ～赃 plant stolen or banned goods on sb.; frame sb.; fabricate a charge against sb. ④fall 从自行车上～下来 tumble off a bicycle 【栽跟头】tumble / suffer a setback 【栽培】cultivate; grow / foster

宰 zǎi ①slaughter; butcher ～猪 butcher pigs ②govern; rule 主～ dominate; dictate 【宰割】invade, oppress and exploit 任人～ allow oneself to be trampled upon

【宰相】 prime minister (in feudal China); chancellor

载 zǎi ①year ②put down in writing; record ～入记录 place on record 据报～ according to press reports

再 zài ①another time; again; once more ～试一次 try again 一而～、～而三 again and again ～创纪录 set another record ②come back; return 青春不～ one's youth never returns 良机难～ opportunity knocks but once 【再版】 second edition/reprint; second impression 【再次】 once more; once again 【再见】 good-bye; see you again 【再接再励】 make persistent efforts 【再起】 recurrence; revival 【再三】 over and over again; time and again; repeatedly 【再生产】 reproduction 【再说】 what's more; besides 【再现】 reappear 在银幕上～ be reproduced on the screen

在 zài ① exist; be living 这问题还～ the problem still exists ②be 我父母～农村 my parents are in the countryside 你的钢笔～桌子上呢 your pen is on the table ③at; in ～会上发言 speak at a meeting ～我看来 in my opinion ～理论上 in theory ～这种情况下 under these circumstances ～这方面 in this respect ④rest with; depend on 主要～自己努力 depend mainly on one's own efforts 【在案】 be on record 记录～ be put on record 【在场】 be on the spot; be present 【在行】 be expert at sth. 【在乎】 care about; mind 满不～ not care a bit 【在家】 be at home 【在理】 reasonable; right 【在世】 be living 他～的时候 in his lifetime 他妈要是还～ if his mother were alive 【在逃】 has escaped; be at large 【在望】 be visible, be in sight 胜利～ victory is in sight 【在握】 be under one's control 大权～ with power in one's hands 胜利～ victory is within grasp 【在先】 formerly; in the past; before 【在押】 be in prison ～犯 criminal in custody;

prisoner 【在野】be out of office ～党 a party not in office 【在于】lie in; rest with / be determined by; depend on 【在职】be on the job ～干部 cadres at their posts 【在座】be present (at a meeting, banquet, etc.)

载 zài carry; hold ～客 carry passengers ～货 carry cargo 【载运】convey (by vehicles, ships, etc.); transport 【载重】load; carrying capacity ～汽车 truck; lorry

ZAN

簪 zān ①hairpin ②wear in one's hair ～花 wear flowers in one's hair 【簪子】hair clasp

咱 zán 【咱们】we ～军民是一家 we, the army and the people, are all one family ～商量一下 let's talk it over

攒 zǎn accumulate; hoard; save ～钱 save up money 好不容易～几个钱 scrape up a little sum

暂 zàn ①of short duration ②for the time being; for the moment ～别 temporary separation ～代 act for sb. ～住 stay temporarily (at a place) ～不答复 put off replying 【暂定】tentative; provisional ～办法 provisional measures ～两年 be tentatively fixed at two years 【暂缓】postpone; defer ～决定 put off making a decision 【暂时】temporary ～现象 transient phenomenon ～停刊 temporarily suspend publication 【暂停】suspend/time-out ～付款 suspend payment 【暂行】provisional ～条例 provisional regulations ～规定 temporary provisions

赞 zàn ①support; favour ～助 assistance; help ②praise; commend ～不绝口 be profuse in praise 【赞成】approve of; favour; agree with; endorse 我完全～ I'm all for it ～意见 assenting views ～票 affirmative vote 【赞歌】paean 【赞美】eulogize; extol ～诗 hymn 【赞赏】appreciate; admire 【赞叹】gasp in admiration; highly praise 【赞许】speak favourably of 得到～ win the approval of 值得～ be commendable; be worthy of praise

ZANG

赃 zāng ①stolen goods; spoils 分～ share the booty ② bribes 贪～ practise graft 【赃官】corrupt official 【赃款】money stolen, embezzled or received in bribes; illicit money

脏 zāng dirty; filthy ～衣服 soiled clothes; dirty linen ～水 filthy water; slops; sewage ～东西 muck; garbage ～字 obscene word; swearword

脏 zāng internal organs of the body (usu. referring to the heart, liver, spleen, lungs, kidneys, etc.); viscera

葬 zàng bury; inter 【葬礼】funeral (rites) 【葬身】be buried ～鱼腹 be drowned 【葬送】ruin

藏 zàng storing place; depository 宝～ precious (mineral) deposits

ZAO

遭 zāo suffer ～难 meet with misfortune ～殃 suffer disaster ～灾 be hit by a natural calamity 险～不测 have a near escape 【遭到】suffer; come across; encounter ～失败 meet with defeat ～拒绝 be turned down ～困难 encounter difficulties ～破坏 be damaged 【遭受】be subjected to ～挫折 suffer setbacks ～损失 sustain losses ～水灾 be hit by floods 【遭遇】meet with; run up against/ (bitter) experience; (hard) lot 与敌人～ encounter the enemy 我们有共同的～ we have shared the same experiences ～战 an encounter action

糟 zāo ①(distillers') grains ②be pickled with grains or in wine ～鱼 pickled fish ③rotten; poor 木板～

了 the board is rotten 身体很～ be in very poor health ④in a terrible state; in a mess 把事情搞～了 make a mess of sth.【糟糕】how terrible; what bad luck; too bad【糟粕】waste matter; dross; dregs【糟蹋】ruin; spoil/ insult; ravage ～粮食 waste grain ～妇女 violate a woman 【糟心】vexed; annoyed; dejected

凿 záo ①chisel ②cut a hole; chisel ～井 dig a well ～个窟窿 bore a hole ～冰 make a hole in the ice 把船～沉 scuttle the ship

早 zǎo ①(early) morning ②long ago; for a long time ～知道了 know that long ago ～在二十世纪初 as early as the beginning of the twentieth century ③early; beforehand ～点儿来 come early ～作准备 get prepared in advance ④good morning【早班】morning shift【早餐】 breakfast【早操】morning exercises【早产】premature delivery【早场】morning show【早春】early spring【早稻】early (season) rice【早点】(light) breakfast【早婚】 marrying too early【早年】one's early years【早期】early stage ～作品 sb.'s early works【早日】early; soon 请～答复 your early reply is requested 祝你～恢复健康 I hope you'll get well soon【早熟】precocity/early-ripe ～的孩子 a precocious child ～品种 early variety ～作物 early-maturing crop【早退】leave early【早晚】morning and evening/sooner or later ～服务部 before-and-after-hours shop 【早先】previously【早已】long ago

枣 zǎo jujube; (Chinese) date; tsao【枣红】purplish red; claret【枣泥】jujube paste【枣树】jujube tree

蚤 zǎo flea 沙～ beach flea 水～ water flea

澡 zǎo bath【澡盆】bathtub【澡堂】public baths; bath-house

藻 zǎo ①algae ②aquatic plants ③literary embellishment 辞～ ornate diction

灶 zǎo ①kitchen range; cooking stove ②kitchen; mess; canteen 学生～ students' dining room 【灶台】 the top of a kitchen range

皂 zǎo ①black ②soap 香～ toilet soap 药～ medicated soap

造 zǎo ①make; build; create ～纸 make paper ～房子 build a house ～舆论 create public opinion ～表 draw up a form or list ～册 compile a register ②invent; cook up; concoct ～假帐 cook accounts ③train; educate 深～ pursue advanced studies 【造成】 create; cause; give rise to ～革命声势 build up revolutionary momentum ～既成事实 bring about a *fait accompli* ～巨大损失 cause enormous losses ～假象 put up a facade 【造船】 shipbuilding ～厂 shipyard 【造反】 rebel; revolt 【造福】 benefit ～人类 bring benefit to mankind 为后代～ benefit future generations 【造价】 cost 【造就】 train; bring up (a new generation, etc.)/achievements; attainments 【造句】 sentence-making 【造林】 afforestation 【造型】 modelling; mould-making/model; mould ～艺术 plastic arts 【造谣】 cook up a story; start a rumour ～生事 stir up trouble by rumourmongering 【造诣】 attainments ～很高 of great attainments 【造作】 affected; artificial

噪 zǎo ①chirp ②a confusion of voices 鼓～ make an uproar 名～一时 be a celebrity for a time 【噪音】 noise ～污染 noise pollution

燥 zǎo dry ～热 hot and dry

躁 zǎo rash; impetuous 性子～ quick-tempered ～动 move restlessly ～急 restless; uneasy

ZE

则 zé ①standard; norm; criterion ②rule; regulation

责 zé ①duty ②demand; require 严以～己 be strict with oneself ③question closely ④reproach; rebuke; blame 自～ reprove oneself ⑤punish【责备】blame; reprove; take sb. to task ～的眼光 a look of reproach 受到良心的～ feel a prick of conscience【责成】instruct (sb. to fulfil a task); charge (sb. with a task); enjoin (sb. to do sth.)【责罚】punish【责令】order; instruct; charge【责骂】scold; rebuke; dress down【责难】censure; blame【责任】duty; responsibility 负起～来 shoulder your responsibility 追究～ ascertain where the responsibility lies ～事故 accident due to negligence ～心 sense of duty ～制 system of (job) responsibility【责问】call sb. to account【责无旁贷】be duty-bound

泽 zé ①pool; pond ②damp; moist ③lustre (of metals, pearls, etc.) 光～ gloss; sheen 色～ colour and lustre

择 zé select; choose; pick 交～ choose friends 二者任～其一 choose either of the two

啧 zé ①compete for a chance to speak; dispute ②click of the tongue ～～称羡 click the tongue in admiration ～～叹赏 be profuse in one's praise

ZEI

贼 zéi ①thief ～喊捉 a thief crying "Stop thief" ② traitor; enemy ③crooked; wicked; evil; furtive ～头～脑 stealthy ～眼 shifty eyes【贼船】pirate ship 上～ board the pirate ship—join a reactionary faction

ZEN

怎 zěn why; how 【怎么】what; why; how ～办 what's to be done 你～啦 what's the matter with you 你～没去看电影 why didn't you go to the film 这个词～拼 how do you spell the word 该～办就～办 do what must be done ～得了 where will it all end 【怎么样】what; how 骑车去～ what about going by bike

ZENG

曾 zēng relationship between great-grandchildren and great-grandparents 【曾孙】great-grandson 【曾孙女】great-granddaughter 【曾祖】(paternal) great-grandfather 【曾祖母】(paternal) great-grandmother

憎 zēng hate; detest; abhor 面目可～ repulsive in appearance 【憎恶】loathe; abominate

增 zēng increase; gain; add 产量猛～ output increased sharply ～兵 throw in more troops 【增补】augment; supplement ～本 enlarged edition 【增产】increase production 【增订】revise and enlarge (a book) ～本 revised and enlarged edition 【增多】grow in number or quantity; increase 【增光】add lustre to; add to the prestige of; do credit to 为国～ do credit to one's country 【增加】increase; raise; add ～收入 increase income ～工资 get a raise in pay ～困难 add to the difficulties ～体重 put on weight ～抵抗力 build up one's resistance to disease 产量～一倍 output is double 【增进】enhance; further ～友谊 promote friendship ～健康 improve one's health ～食欲 whet one's appetite 【增刊】supplement; supplementary issue 【增强】strengthen; enhance ～战斗力 increase combat effectiveness ～信心 heighten one's confidence 【增删】additions and

deletions【增添】add; increase ～设备 get additional equip-
ment【增援】reinforce ～部队 reinforcements【增长】
increase; rise; grow 控制 人口～ control population growth
～才干 enhance one's abilities ～知识 broaden one's knowledge ～率 growth rate【增值】rise in value; increment

赠 zèng give as a present ～书 present sb. with a book
某某敬～ with the compliments of so-and-so【赠品】
gift; giveaway【赠送】present as a gift ～花篮 present a
basket of flowers ～仪式 presentation ceremony【赠阅】
given free by the publisher ～本 complimentary copy

ZHA

扎 zhā ①prick; run or stick (a needle, etc.) into 手
指上～了一根刺 prick one's finger on a thorn ～一
刀 stab with a knife ②plunge into; get into ～进水里
dive into the water ～进书堆里 bury oneself in books
【扎根】take root (among the masses, etc.)【扎实】sturdy;
strong/solid; sound 工作很～ do a solid job【扎针】give or
have an acupuncture treatment

渣 zhā ①dregs; sediment 豆腐～ soya-bean residue 猪
油～ cracklings ②broken bits 面包～ (bread) crumbs

揸 zhā ①pick up sth. with the fingers ②spread one's
fingers

扎 zhá pitch (a tent, etc.)【扎营】pitch a tent or camp;
encamp

札 zhá letter【札记】reading notes

轧 zhá roll (steel)【轧钢】steel rolling ～厂 steel rolling mill ～机 rolling mill【轧制】rolling

闸 zhá ①floodgate; sluice gate ②dam up water ③brake
踩～ step on the brake 捏～ apply the hand brake

④switch 扳~ operate a switch; switch on or off【闸门】sluice gate / throttle valve

炸 zhá deep-fry ~豆腐 deep-fried bean curd ~糕 fried cake【炸酱】fried bean sauce ~面 noodles served with fried bean sauce

铡 zhá ①hand hay cutter; fodder chopper ②cut up with a hay cutter【铡草机】hay cutter; chaffcutter【铡刀】hand hay catter; fodder chopper

眨 zhǎ blink; wink 眼睛一~ blink (one's eyes) 他向我~了~眼 he winked at me【眨眼】very short time; twinkle 一~的工夫 in the twinkling of an eye

乍 zhà ①first; for the first time ~一听 at first hearing ~一看 at first glance ②suddenly; abruptly 天气~冷~热 the temperature changes abruptly

诈 zhà ①cheat; swindle ~人钱财 get money by fraud ②pretend; feign ~降 pretend to surrender ~死 fake death; play dead ~败 feign defeat ③bluff sb. into giving information 他是拿话~我 he was trying to draw me out【诈唬】bluff; bluster【诈骗】defraud ~犯 swindler

炸 zhà ①explode; burst 暖瓶~了 the thermos flask has burst ②blow up ~桥 blow up a bridge ~毁 demolish ~平 bomb flat ~沉 bomb and sink【炸弹】bomb ~坑 bomb-crater【炸药】explosive (charges); dynamite ~包 pack of dynamite; explosive package

栅 zhà railings; paling; bars; boom 木~ palisade 铁~ metal rails; iron bars 炉~ grate

蚱 zhà 【蚱蜢】grasshopper

榨 zhà press; extract ~甘蔗 press sugar cane ~油 extract oil【榨菜】hot pickled mustard tuber【榨取】squeeze; extort【榨油机】oil press

ZHAI

斋 zhāi ①vegetarian diet (adopted for religious reasons) ②give alms (to a monk) ③room or building 书~ study 【斋戒】abstain from meat, wine, etc.; fast

摘 zhāi ①pick; pluck; take off—棉花 pick cotton—花 pluck flowers—眼镜(帽子) take off one's glasses (hat or cap) ~灯泡 remove the bulb ②select; make extracts from ~译 translation of selected passages 【摘抄】take passages; extract / extracts 【摘除】excise (an abdominal tumour, etc.) 【摘记】take notes/excerpts 【摘录】make extracts/extracts 【摘要】make a summary/summary; abstract ~发表 publish excerpts of sth. 【摘引】quote 【摘由】key extracts (of a document)

宅 zhái residence; house 【宅门】gate of an old-style big house / family living in such a house

择 zhái select; choose; pick ~菜 trim vegetables for cooking

窄 zhǎi ①narrow ~轨铁路 narrow-gauge railway ② petty 心眼儿~ oversensitive

债 zhài debt 欠~ be in debt 还~ pay one's debt 借~ borrow money 【债款】loan 【债权】creditor's rights ~国 creditor nation ~人 creditor 【债券】bond; debenture 【债务】debt; liabilities ~国 debtor nation ~人 debtor

寨 zhài ①stockade ②stockaded village ③camp ④mountain stronghold 【寨子】stockaded village

ZHAN

占 zhān practise divination ~课 divine by tossing coins ~梦 divine by interpreting dreams ~星 divine by astrology

沾 zhān ①be stained with ～水 get wet ～泥 be stained with mud ②touch 烟酒不～ touch neither tobacco nor alcohol 【沾光】benefit from association with sb. or sth. 【沾染】be contaminated by ～细菌 be infected with germs ～坏习气 be tainted with bad habits 【沾沾自喜】feel complacent; be pleased with oneself

毡 zhān felt ～帽 felt hat ～房 yurt 【毡子】felt rug; felt blanket

粘 zhān glue; stick; paste 把信封～上 seal (up) an envelope 【粘连】adhesion

谵 zhān rave; be delirious 【谵妄】delirium 【谵语】delirious speech

瞻 zhān look up or forward 【瞻前顾后】look ahead and behind — be overcautious and indecisive 【瞻望】look forward; look far ahead ～未来 look to the future 【瞻仰】look at with reverence ～烈士陵园 pay a visit to the martyrs' mausoleum

斩 zhǎn ①chop; cut 快刀～乱麻 cut the Gordian knot ②behead; decapitate ～尽杀绝 kill all 【斩钉截铁】resolute and decisive; categorical

展 zhǎn ①open up; spread out; unfold; unfurl ～翅 spread the wings; get ready for flight 风～红旗 the red flags are fluttering in the wind ②put to good use; give free play to 大～宏图 carry out a great plan ③postpone; prolong ～限 extend a time limit ④exhibition 预～ preview 【展开】spread out; unfold; open up / launch; develop; carry out ～攻势 unfold an offensive ～思想斗争 wage an ideological struggle ～讨论 set off a discussion 【展览】put on display; exhibit; show ～馆 exhibition hall ～会 exhibition ～品 exhibit ～室 showroom 【展期】extend a time limit; postpone / duration of an exhibition 会议～ the meeting has been postponed ～两天结束 be extended for another two days【展示】reveal; show; lay bare【展望】look into the distance/look ahead/forecast; prospect ～未来 look forward to the future; look into the future 八十年代～ prospects for the 1980 s; 1980's in prospect【展现】emerge; develop

盏 zhǎn ①small cup ②一～灯 a lamp

崭 zhǎn 【崭新】brand-new; completely new

揎 zhǎn 【揎布】dishcloth; dish towel

辗 zhǎn 【辗转】pass through many hands or places/toss about (in bed) ～流传 spread from place to place ～反侧 toss and turn restlessly

占 zhàn ①occupy; seize; take 多吃多～ grab more than one's share ～不少时间 take up much time ②make up; account for ～多(少)数 constitute the majority (minority) ～统治地位 hold a dominant position【占据】occupy; hold【占领】capture; seize ～军 occupation army ～区 occupied area【占便宜】profit at other people's expense/advantageous; favourable【占先】take precedence; take the lead; get ahead of【占线】the line's busy【占有】own; possess; have/occupy; hold ～生产资料 own the means of production ～第一手资料 have firsthand data ～重要地位 occupy an important place

战 zhàn ①war; warfare; battle 夜～ night fighting ②fight ～而胜之 fight and defeat the enemy【战败】be defeated/defeat; vanquish; beat ～国 vanquished nation【战报】war *communiqué*; battlefield report【战备】war preparedness; combat readiness ～工作 preparations against war【战场】battleground; battlefront 开辟~ open another front 奔赴~ go to the front【战地】battlefield; combat zone ~记者 war correspondent ~指挥部 field headquarters【战抖】tremble; shiver; shudder【战斗】battle; combat; action/fighting 投入~ go into battle ~友谊 militant friendship ~岗位 fighting post ~部队 combat forces ~队 fighting force ~机 fighter ~力 combat effectiveness ~任务 fighting task ~性 militancy ~英雄 combat hero ~员 fighter【战犯】war criminal【战费】war expenses【战俘】prisoner of war ~营 prisoner-of-war camp【战歌】battle song【战功】meritorious military service【战鼓】war drum【战果】results of battle; combat success 取得辉煌~ achieve splendid results on the battlefield 扩大~ exploit the victory【战壕】trench【战后】postwar ~时期 postwar period【战火】flames of war【战祸】disaster of war【战机】opportunity for combat 丧失~ miss the opportunity to win a battle【战绩】military successes; combat gains【战舰】warship【战局】war situation【战况】situation on the battlefield【战利品】spoils of war; war booty【战列舰】battleship【战列巡洋舰】battle cruiser【战乱】chaos caused by war【战略】strategy ~家 strategist ~思想 strategic thinking ~要地 strategic area ~马 battle steed【战前】prewar ~时期 prewar period ~动员 mobilization before a battle【战区】war zone【战胜】triumph over; vanquish ~敌人 defeat the enemy ~困难 overcome difficulties ~自然灾害 conquer natural disasters ~国 victorious nation【战时】wartime ~编制 war footing ~内阁 wartime cabinet【战士】soldier; man/champion; warrior; fighter【战事】war; hostilities ~结束 conclusion of the war【战书】letter of challenge【战术】(military) tactics【战线】battle line; front ~太长

overextended battle line 【战役】 campaign; battle ～性的进攻 offensive campaign 【战友】 comrade-in-arms 【战战兢兢】 trembling with fear; with fear and trepidation/with caution; gingerly 【战争】 war ～状态 state of war

栈 zhàn ①warehouse ②inn ③shed; pen 【栈房】 warehouse; storehouse

站 zhàn ①stand ～起来 stand up; rise to one's feet ～在党的立场上 uphold the stand of the Party ②stop; halt 中途不～ make no stops along the way ③station; stop 终点～ terminal; terminus ④centre 服务～ service centre 拖拉机～ tractor station 【站队】 line up; stand in line 【站岗】 stand guard; be on sentry duty 【站台】 platform (in a railway station) ～票 platform ticket 【站稳】 come to a stop/stand firm; take a firm stand 【站长】 head of a station, etc. 火车站～ station-master

绽 zhàn split; burst 鞋开～了 the shoe has split open

湛 zhàn ①profound; deep 精～ consummate; exquisite ②crystal clear 【湛蓝】 azure

颤 zhàn · tremble; shiver; shudder

蘸 zhàn dip in ～墨水 dip in ink ～酱 dip in thick sauce

ZHANG

张 zhāng ①open; spread; stretch ～嘴 open one's mouth (to say sth.) ～开手 open one's hand ～开双臂 stretch out both arms ～帆 make sail ②set out; display 大～筵席 lay on a feast ③look 东～西望 gaze around 【张大】 magnify ～其词 exaggerate ～其事 publicize the matter widely 【张灯结彩】 be decorated with lanterns and coloured streamers 【张口结舌】 be agape and tongue-tied 【张罗】 take care of; get busy about / raise (funds); get together (money, etc.)/greet and entertain (guests); attend to (customers, etc.) 【张贴】 put up (a notice, poster, etc.) 【张望】 peep (through a crack, etc.)/look around 【张扬】 make widely known; make pubilc 四处～ publicize everywhere 别～出去 don't spread it around

章 zhāng ①chapter; section 共二十一～ have twenty chapters ②order 杂乱无～ disorderly and unsystematic ③ rules; regulations 党～ the Party Constitution ④seal; stamp 盖～ affix one's seal ⑤badge; medal 【章鱼】 octopus

彰 zhāng clear; evident; conspicuous 【彰明较著】 very obvious; easily seen

樟 zhāng camphor tree 【樟木】 camphorwood 【樟脑】 camphor ～丸 camphor ball; mothball ～油 camphor oil

长 zhǎng ①older; elder; senior 比我年～ older than me ②eldest; oldest 一女 eldest daughter ③chief; head 科～ section chief ④grow; develop 庄稼～得好 the crops are growing well ⑤come into being; begin to grow; form ～ 疮 have a boil 【长辈】 elder member of a family; elder; senior 【长大】 grow up; be brought up 【长官】 senior officer or official; commanding officer 【长机】 lead aircraft; leader 【长进】 progress 学习有～ make progress in one's studies 【长孙】 son's eldest son; eldest grandson 【长相】 looks; features; appearance ～好 be good-looking 【长者】 elder; senior/venerable elder 【长子】 eldest son

涨 zhǎng (of water, etc.) rise; go up 【涨潮】 rising tide 【涨风】 upward trend of prices 【涨价】 rise in price 【涨落】 (of water, prices, etc.) rise and fall; fluctuate

掌 zhǎng ①palm ②strike with the palm of the hand ～嘴 slap sb. on the face ③be in charge of; control

~兵权 wield military power ④pad 脚~ sole 鸭~ duck's foot 熊~ bear's paw ⑤shoe sole or heel ⑥horseshoe 【掌舵】 be at the helm; operate the rudder 【掌故】 anecdotes 【掌管】 be in charge of; administer 【掌柜】 shopkeeper; manager (of a shop) 【掌权】 be in power; wield power 【掌声】 clapping; applause 【掌握】 grasp; master; know well/ take into one's hands; control ~党的政策 have a good grasp of the Party's policies ~新情况 keep abreast of new developments ~一门外国语 have a good command of a foreign language ~局势 have the situation under control ~主动权 have the initiative in one's hands ~自己的命运 be master of one's own destiny ~会议 preside over a meeting ~分寸 exercise sound judgment; act or speak properly 【掌心】 the centre of the palm

丈 zhàng *zhang*, a unit of length (= 3¹/₃ metres) 【丈夫】 husband 【丈量】 measure (land) 【丈母娘】 wife's mother; mother-in-law 【丈人】 wife's father; father-in-law

仗 zhàng ①weaponry; weapons 【仗剑】 hold a sword ②depend on ~恃 rely on (an advantage) ④battle; war 打~ go to war 【仗势欺人】 take advantage of one's or sb. else's power to bully people 【仗义疏财】 be generous in aiding needy people

杖 zhàng cane; stick 拐~ walking stick 擀面~ rolling pin

帐 zhàng ①curtain; canopy ~幕 tent ②account 记~ keep accounts ③debt; credit 还~ repay a debt 【帐簿】 account book 【帐单】 bill; check 【帐户】 account 在银行开立(结束)~ open (close) an account with a bank 【帐款】 funds on account; credit 【帐目】 accounts 清理~ square accounts 公布~ publish the accounts ~不清 the accounts are not in order 【帐篷】 tent 搭(拆)~ pitch (strike) a tent 【帐子】 bed-curtain/mosquito net

胀 zhàng ①expand; distend ②swell 肿～ swollen 吃多了，肚子发～ feel bloated after overeating

涨 zhàng ①swell after absorbing water, being soaked, etc. ②be swelled by a rush of blood 气得～红了脸 redden with anger 头昏脑～ feel one's head swimming

障 zhàng ①hinder ②barrier; block 路～ roadblock 【障碍】 hinder / obstruction; impediment 扫清～ clear away obstacles 制造～ erect barriers ～赛跑 steeplechase ～物 obstacle; barrier 【障蔽】 block; shut out; obstruct

瘴 zhàng miasma 【瘴疠 疬】 communicable subtropical diseases

ZHAO

招 zhāo ①beckon ～手要我进去 beckon me in ②recruit; enlist; enrol ～工 recruit workers ③attract; incur; court ～苍蝇 attract flies ～灾 court disaster ④provoke; tease 别～他 don't tease him ⑤confess; own up 不打自～ confess without being pressed ⑥trick; device; move 【招标】 invite tenders 【招兵】 recruit soldiers ～买马 raise or enlarge an army; recruit followers 【招待】 receive (guests); serve (customers) ～客人 entertain guests 谢谢你们的热情～ thank you for your kind hospitality ～费 entertainment allowance or expenses ～会 reception ～券 complimentary ticket ～所 guest house; hostel 【招供】 confess 【招呼】 hail; greet; say hello to/notify; tell/ take care of (old people, etc.) 先给我打个～ let me know beforehand 【招架】 ward off blows ～不住 unable to hold one's own 【招考】 give public notice of entrance examination; admit (students, applicants, etc.) by examination 【招徕】 solicit ～顾客 solicit customers 【招揽】

solicit ～生意 canvass business orders; drum up trade 【招领】 announce the finding of lost property 失物 ～ Found 【招牌】 shop sign; signboard 【招聘】 invite applications for a job ～技术工人 advertise for skilled workers 【招惹】 provoke; incur; court/tease ～是非 bring trouble on oneself 【招认】 confess one's crime; plead guilty 【招生】 recruit students ～制度 enrolment system 【招收】 recruit; take in ～工人 recruit workers ～大学生 enrol new students in universities and colleges 【招手】 beckon; wave ～致意 wave one's greetings 【招贴】 poster; placard; bill ～画 pictorial poster 【招降】 summon sb. to surrender ～纳叛 recruit deserters and traitors 【招摇】 act ostentatiously ～过市 swagger through the streets — blatantly seek publicity 【招摇撞骗】 swindle and bluff 【招引】 attract; induce 【招展】 flutter; wave 【招致】 recruit (followers) /incur; lead to ～失败 cause defeat

昭　zhāo clear; obvious 【昭示】 declare publicly 【昭雪】 exonerate; rehabilitate 冤案得到～ the wrong has been righted 【昭彰】 clear; manifest; evident 罪恶～ have committed flagrant crimes 【昭著】 evident; obvious

着　zhāo ①a move in chess 走错一～ make a false move ②trick; device 没～儿了 be at the end of his tether

朝　zhāo ①early morning; morning ～阳 morning sun ②day 今～ today; the present 【朝晖】 morning sunlight 【朝气】 youthful spirit; vigour; vitality ～蓬勃 full of youthful spirit; full of vigour and vitality 【朝夕】 morning and evening / a very short time / day and night; daily 【朝霞】 rosy clouds of dawn; rosy dawn

着　zháo ①touch 说话不～边际 not speak to the point ②feel; be affected by (cold, etc.) ③burn 火～得旺 the fire is burning briskly ④fall asleep 他躺下就～ he fell asleep as soon as he lay down 【着慌】 get alarmed; become flustered 【着火】 catch fire; be on fire 【着急】 feel anxious 着什么急 there's nothing to worry about 等得～了 become impatient with waiting 【着凉】 catch cold 【着忙】 be in a hurry 【着迷】 be fascinated

爪 zhǎo claw; talon 【爪牙】 talons and fangs — lackeys; underlings

找 zhǎo ①look for; try to find; seek ～矿 look for mineral deposits ～到油田 discover an oil field ～工作 hunt for a job ～机会 seek an opportunity ～出路 seek a way out ～原因 seek the cause ～答案 try to find the answer ～对象 look for a partner in marriage ②want to see; call on; approach; ask for 有人～你 someone wants to see you 明天再来～你 I'll call on you again tomorrow ～我有什么事 what can I do for you ③give change 两不～ that's just right 【找补】 make up a deficiency 【找碴】 find fault 【找麻烦】 look for trouble/cause sb. trouble 自～ ask for trouble 【找头】 change

沼 zhǎo natural pond 【沼气】 marsh gas; firedamp; methane 【沼泽】 marsh; swamp; bog ～地 marshland

召 zhǎo convene 【召唤】 call; summon 时刻听从党的～ always heed the Party's call 【召回】 recall ～大使 recall an ambassador 【召集】 call together ～干部 call the cadres together ～会议 convene a conference ～人 convener 【召见】 call in (a subordinate) / summon (an envoy) to an interview 【召开】 convoke (a conference)

兆 zhào ①sign; omen; portent 不祥之～ an ill omen ②foretell ③million; mega- ～周 megacycle ④billion

照 zhào ①shine; illuminate; light (up) ～～路 light the way ②reflect; mirror ～镜子 look in the mirror ③take a picture; photograph; film; shoot 我想～一张相

I want to have a picture taken ④photograph; picture 剧～ stage photo; still ⑤license; permit 无～行车 drive without a license ⑥take care of; look after ⑦notify 知～ inform ⑧contrast 对～ check against ⑨understand 心～ have a tacit understanding ⑩in the direction of; towards ～这个方向走 go in this direction ⑪according to; in accordance with ～他们的说法 according to what they say【照搬】indiscriminately imitate; copy【照办】act accordingly; act in accordance with; comply with【照本宣科】repeat what the book says【照常】as usual ～营业 business as usual【照抄】copy word for word【照发】issue as before/approved for distribution【照顾】give consideration to; make allowance(s) for / look after; care for; attend to ～全局 take the whole into account ～实际需要 consider actual needs ～他的困难 take his difficulties into account 给予适当～ give appropriate preferential treatment ～伤员 look after the wounded【照管】look after; tend ～孩子 look after a child ～机器 tend a machine ～仓库 be in charge of a storehouse【照会】present a note to (a government)/note 提出～ deliver a note 交换～ exchange notes【照价】(pay) according to the set price【照旧】as before; as usual; as of old【照看】attend to; look after; keep an eye on ～病人 attend to a patient【照例】as a rule; as usual; usually【照料】take care of; attend to【照明】illumination; lighting ～弹 flare; star shell ～装置 lighting installation【照片】photograph; picture【照射】shine; light up; irradiate【照说】ordinarily; as a rule【照相】take a picture; photograph ～簿 photo album ～馆 photo studio ～机 camera ～纸 photographic paper【照样】after a pattern or model / in the same old way; all the same; as before 照这个样儿做 do it this way ～办理 act in the same way; follow suit 【照耀】 shine; illuminate 【照应】 coordinate; correlate / look after

罩 zhào ①cover; overspread; wrap ～好仪器 cover the instruments ②shade; hood; casing 玻璃～ glass cover 发动机～ hood 【罩袍】 overall; dust-robe 【罩衣】 dustcoat

肇 zhào ①start; commence; initiate ②cause (trouble, etc.) 【肇事】 create a disturbance ～者 troublemaker

ZHE

折 zhē ①roll over; turn over ～个跟斗 turn a somersault ②pour back and forth between two containers 【折腾】 turn from side to side; toss about / do sth. over and over again / get sb. down

蜇 zhē sting 马蜂～了我的手指 a wasp stung me on the finger

遮 zhē ①hide from view; cover; screen 用帘子把窗户 ～起来 cover the window with a curtain ②obstruct; impede ～道 block the way ③keep out ～风挡雨 keep out wind and rain 【遮蔽】 cover; screen/obstruct; block ～视线 obstruct the view 【遮丑】 hide one's shame; cover up one's defect 【遮挡】 shelter from; keep out 【遮盖】 overspread/hide; conceal; cover up 【遮羞】 hush up a scandal ～布 fig leaf 【遮眼法】 camouflage 【遮阳】 sunshade

折 zhé ①break; snap ～断树枝 break off branches ～断腿 fracture one's leg ②suffer the loss of; lose ③bend; twist 曲～ twists and turns ④turn back; change direction 边界～向西南 the boundary turns southwestward ⑤be convinced; be filled with admiration 心～ be deeply convinced ⑥convert into; amount to 把市斤～成公 斤 change *jin* into kilograms ⑦discount; rebate 打八～ give 20% discount ⑧fold ～信 fold the letter 【折尺】 folding rule 【折叠】fold ～报纸 fold up the newspaper ～床(椅) folding bed (chair) 【折服】subdue; bring into submission/be convinced; be filled with admiration 令人～compel admiration 【折合】convert into; amount to 一英镑～成人民币是多少 how much is a pound in terms of Renminbi 【折回】turn back (halfway) 【折价】convert into money; evaluate in terms of money 【折旧】depreciation 【折扣】discount; rebate 这价钱已经打了～this is the discounted price 【折磨】cause suffering; torment 受疾病的～ suffer severely from a lingering illness 受尽～ suffer a lot 【折扇】folding fan 【折射】refraction 【折算】convert 【折帐】pay a debt in kind 【折中】compromise ～方案 a compromise proposal ～主义 eclecticism

哲 zhé ①wise; sagacious ②wise man; sage 【哲理】philosophic theory 【哲学】philosophy ～家 philosopher

辙 zhé ①the track of a wheel; rut ②rhyme (of a song, poetic drama, etc.) 合～ in rhyme

者 zhě -er; -or 读～ reader 出版～ publisher 胜利～ victor 医务工作～ medical worker 前(后)～ the former (latter) 马克思主义～ Marxist

褶 zhě pleat; crease 把衬衫上的～儿熨平 iron the wrinkles out of the shirt 【褶皱】wrinkle/fold

这 zhè ①this ～地方 this place ～一回 this time ～就对了 that's better ②now 我～就走 I'm leaving right now 【这边】this side; here 【这次】this time; present ～会议 the present session ～运动 the current movement 【这会儿】now; at the moment; at present 【这里】here 【这么】so; such; this way; like this ～点儿 such a little bit ～些 so much; so many 【这些】these

蔗 zhè sugarcane 【蔗农】sugarcane grower 【蔗糖】sucrose/cane sugar

ZHEN

贞 zhēn ①loyal; faithful 坚～ staunch and faithful ②chastity or virginity ～洁 chaste and undefiled

针 zhēn ①needle 毛线～ knitting needle ②stitch 缝两～ sew a couple of stitches ③injection; shot 打～ give or have an injection ④acupuncture【针刺疗法】acupuncture treatment【针对】be directed against; be aimed at / in the light of; in accordance with ～这种倾向 to counter this tendency ～这种情况 in view of this situation【针锋相对】give tit for tat; be diametrically opposed to ～的斗争 tit-for-tat struggle【针箍】thimble【针剂】injection【针尖】the point of a needle; pinpoint【针脚】stitch【针灸】acupuncture and moxibustion【针头】syringe needle【针线】needlework ～包 sewing kit ～活 needlework; stitching; sewing【针眼】the eye of a needle/pinprick【针织】knitting ～厂 knitting mill ～机 knitting machine ～品 knit goods; knitwear

侦 zhēn detect; scout【侦查】investigate (a crime)【侦察】reconnoitre; scout ～敌情 gather intelligence about the enemy ～部队 reconnaissance troops ～机 reconnaissance plane; scout ～卫星 spy satellite ～员 scout【侦探】do detective work / spy ～小说 detective story

珍 zhēn ①treasure 奇～ rare treasures ②precious; valuable ～禽 rare birds ③value highly【珍爱】treasure; love dearly; be very fond of【珍宝】jewellery; treasure【珍本】rare edition; rare book【珍藏】collect (rare books, art treasures, etc.)【珍贵】valuable; precious【珍品】treasure【珍闻】news titbits; fillers 世界～ world briefs【珍惜】treasure; value; cherish ～时间 value one's time【珍馐】delicacies; dainties【珍重】highly value; set great store by/take good care of yourself【珍珠】pearl

膣

zhēn gizzard【膣肝儿】gizzard and liver (esp. chicken's or duck's)

真

zhēn ①true; genuine ～丝 real silk ②really; truly; indeed 我～不知道 I really don't know 他～信了 he actually believed it ③clearly; unmistakably【真才实学】real ability and learning; genuine talent【真诚】genuine; true ～的愿望 a sincere wish ～的友谊 true friendship ～合作 sincerely cooperate【真谛】true essence; true meaning【真迹】authentic work【真空】vacuum ～管 vacuum valve ～吸尘器 vacuum cleaner【真理】truth 坚持 ～ uphold the truth【真面目】true features 认清其～ see sb. in his true colours【真名实姓】real name【真凭实据】conclusive evidence; hard evidence【真切】vivid; clear; distinct 看得～ see clearly【真情】the real situation; the facts; truth/real sentiments ～的流露 a revelation of one's true feelings【真善美】the true, the good and the beautiful【真实】true; real; authentic ～记录 authentic records ～感 sense of reality ～性 truthfulness; authenticity【真率】unaffected; straightforward【真髓】essence【真相】the real facts 掩盖～ cover up the facts 弄清事情的～ clarify the truth of the matter 大白 whole truth has come out 这就是事情的～ this is the actual state of affairs【真心】wholehearted; heartfelt ～话 sincere words ～实意 genuinely and sincerely; truly and wholeheartedly【真正】genuine; true; real ～的朋友 a true friend ～负起责任来 shoulder the responsibilities in earnest【真知】genuine knowledge 实践出～ real knowledge comes from practice ～灼见 real knowledge and deep insight; penetrating judgment【真珠】pearl【真主】Allah

砧 zhēn hammering block; anvil 【砧板】 chopping block

斟 zhēn pour (tea or wine) 【斟酌】 consider; deliberate ～词句 weigh one's words ～办理 act as one sees fit

甄 zhēn discriminate ～选 select 【甄别】 screen / reexamine a case ～委员会 screening committee

箴 zhēn ①admonish; exhort ②a type of didactic literary composition 【箴言】 admonition; maxim

诊 zhěn examine (a patient) ～病 diagnose a disease 【诊断】 diagnose ～书 medical certificate 【诊疗】 make a diagnosis and give treatment ～器械 medical instruments ～室 consulting room ～所 clinic; dispensary

枕 zhěn ①pillow ②rest the head on ～着一本书睡觉 sleep with one's head resting on a book 【枕巾】 a towel used to cover a pillow 【枕木】 sleeper; tie 【枕套】 pillowcase 【枕心】 pillow (without the pillowcase)

疹 zhěn rash 荨麻～ nettle rash 【疹子】 measles

缜 zhěn 【缜密】 careful; meticulous ～的计划 a deliberate plan ～的分析 a minute analysis

阵 zhèn ①battle array 长蛇～ singleline battle formation ②position; front ①position; front 上～ go to the front ③a period of time 那一～子 in those days ④blast; spasm 一～雨 a spatter of rain 一～风 a gust of wind 一～寒潮 a cold spell 一～咳嗽 a fit of coughing 一～热烈的掌声 a burst of warm applause 【阵地】 position; front 进入～ get into position ～战 positional warfare 【阵脚】 front line/ situation 稳住～ secure one's position 乱了～ be thrown into confusion 【阵容】 battle array/lineup ～强大 have a strong lineup 演员～整齐 a well-balanced cast 【阵势】 battle formation; a disposition of combat forces /situation; condition 摆开～ deploy the ranks in battle array 【阵亡】be killed in action 【阵线】front; ranks 阶级 ～ class alignment 【阵营】camp 【阵雨】shower

振 zhèn shake; flap ～臂 raise one's arm ～翅 flap the wings ②rise with force and spirit; brace up 精神为之一～ feel one's spirits buoyed up 士气大～ the morale was greatly boosted 【振动】vibration 【振奋】rouse oneself; be inspired with enthusiasm/inspire; stimulate ～人心 inspire people ～士气 boost the morale (of the troops) 【振兴】promote ～教育事业 vitalize education ～工业 vigorously develop industry 【振作】exert oneself; display vigour ～精神 bestir oneself; cheer up

赈 zhèn relieve; aid 以工代～ provide work as a form of relief 【赈济】relieve; aid ～灾民 aid the victims of natural calamities 【赈款】relief fund

震 zhèn ①shake; vibrate 地～ earthquake ②greatly excited; deeply astonished ～骇 shocked; stunned 【震动】shake; shock; vibrate; quake ～全国 reverberate through the whole country 引起了广泛的～ produce wide repercussions 【震惊】amaze; astonish ～中外 shock the country and the whole world 【震怒】be enraged

镇 zhèn ①press down; keep down; ease ～痛 ease pain ②calm; tranquil; at ease ③guard ～守 garrison ④ garrison post ⑤town ⑥cool with cold water or ice 冰 ～啤酒 iced beer 【镇定】calm; cool 神色～ be calm and collected 保持～ keep cool; remain calm 【镇静】composed; unruffled 遇到紧急情况要～ keep calm in an emergency 努力～下来 compose oneself with an effort ～剂 sedative; tranquillizer 【镇压】suppress; repress / execute (a counterrevolutionary) ～叛乱 put down a rebellion 【镇纸】paperweight

ZHENG

正 zhēng 【正月】 the first month of the lunar year; the first moon ～初一 the lunar New Year's Day

争 zhēng ①contend; vie; strive ～名～利 scramble for fame and gain ～挑重担 rush to carry the heaviest load ～分夺秒 work against time ～着发言 try to have the floor before others ②argue; dispute 你们在～什么 what are you arguing about 【争霸】 struggle for hegemony; strive for supremacy 【争辩】 argue; debate; contend 无可～ indisputable; incontestable 【争吵】 quarrel; wrangle; squabble ～不休 bicker endlessly 【争持】 refuse to give in 【争斗】 fight; struggle; strife 【争端】 controversial issue; conflict 国际～ an international dispute 调解～ act as mediator in a conflict 【争夺】 fight for; contend for; enter into rivalry with sb. over sth. ～市场 scramble for markets ～势力范围 scramble for spheres of influence 【争光】 win honour for 为国～ bring credit to our country 【争论】 controversy; debate 激烈的～ a heated dispute ～双方 the two contending sides ～之点 the point at issue 自由～ free contention 【争鸣】 contend 【争气】 try to make a good showing; try to win credit for 【争取】 strive for; fight for ～群众 win over the masses ～入党 strive to qualify for Party membership ～时间 race against time ～主动 take the initiative 【争权夺利】 scramble for power and profit 【争先】 try to be the first to do sth. 【争先恐后】 vie with each other in doing sth. 【争议】 dispute; controversy 有～的地区 a disputed area 【争执】 disagree ～不下 each sticks to his own stand

怔 zhēng seized with terror; terrified; panic-stricken

征 zhēng ①go on a journey ～帆 a ship on a long journey ②go on an expedition ～马 battle steed ③levy (troops); call up 应～入伍 be drafted into the army ④levy (taxes); impose ～粮 collect grain taxes ⑤ask for ～稿 solicit contributions (to a journal, etc.) ⑥evidence; proof 有实物为～ there is solid evidence ⑦portent － 候 sign 【征兵】conscription; draft; call-up ～法 draft law ～制 conscription system 【征调】call up ～物资和人员 requisition supplies and draft personnel 【征伐】go on a punitive expedition 【征服】conquer; subjugate ～自然 conquer nature 【征购】requisition by purchase 粮食～ grain purchases by the state ～任务 state purchase quotas 【征集】collect/draft; call up ～签名 collect signatures ～物资 the acquisition of supplies ～新兵 recruitment 【征求】solicit; seek; ask for ～意见 solicit opinions; ask for criticisms ～订户 canvass for subscriptions 【征实】levies in kind; grain levies 【征收】levy; collect; impose 【征税】levy taxes; taxation 【征途】journey 踏上革命的～ embark on the road of revolution 【征文】solicit articles or essays 【征象】sign; symptom 【征询】seek the opinion of; consult 【征用】commandeer; requisition ～～城乡土地 take over for use urban and rural land 【征召】call up; conscript ～入伍 enlist in the army

挣 zhēng 【挣扎】struggle ～着坐起来 struggle to a sitting position 进行垂死的～ put up a last-ditch struggle

峥 zhēng 【峥嵘】lofty and steep; towering / outstanding; extraordinary ～岁月 eventful years

狰 zhēng 【狰狞】savage; hideous ～面目 ferocious features; a vile visage

症 zhēng 【症结】crux; crucial reason 这就是问题的～所在 therein lies the crux of the problem

睁 zhēng open (the eyes) ～一只眼，闭一只眼 turn a blind eye to sth. ～着眼睛说瞎话 tell a barefaced lie

蒸 zhēng ①evaporate ②steam ～饭 steam rice ～饺 steamed dumpling 【蒸发】evaporate 【蒸锅】steamer 【蒸馏】distillation ～器 distiller; retort ～水 distilled water 【蒸笼】food steamer 【蒸气】vapour 【蒸汽】steam ～锅炉 steam boiler ～机 steam engine ～机车 steam locomotive ～浴 steam bath 【蒸腾】(of steam) rising 热气 ～ steaming 【蒸蒸日上】flourishing; thriving

拯 zhěng 【拯救】save; rescue; deliver

整 zhěng ①whole; complete; full; entire ～砖 a whole brick ～夜 all night long 一～页 a full page 十二点～ twelve o'clock sharp ②in good order; neat; tidy 衣冠不～ not properly dressed ③put in order; rectify ～党 consolidate the Party organization ④repair; mend ～修 renovate ～旧如新 repair sth. old and make it as good as new ⑤make sb. suffer; punish; fix 挨～ be the target of criticism or attack 【整编】reorganize (troops) 【整队】dress the ranks; line up ～出发 get the ranks in good order and set out ～入场 file into the arena, auditorium, etc. 【整顿】rectify; reorganize ～纪律 strengthen discipline ～组织 overhaul and consolidate an organization ～现有企业 consolidate existing enterprises 【整风】rectification of incorrect styles of work ～运动 rectification movement 【整个】whole; entire ～社会 the whole of society ～说来 on the whole; by and large 【整洁】clean and tidy; neat; trim 【整理】put in order; arrange ～房间 tidy a room ～资料 sort out the data ～财政 regulate finances ～行装 pack one's things for a journey 【整齐】in good order; neat; tidy/even; regular 字写

得清楚～ clear and neat handwriting ～的牙齿 regular teeth 阵容～ have a well-balanced lineup 【整容】 tidy oneself up/face-lifting 【整数】 whole number/round number 【整套】 a whole set of ～设备 a complete set of equipment 【整体】 whole; entirety ～利益 overall interests ～观念 the concept of viewing the situation as a whole 【整天】 the whole day; all day (long) 【整形】 plastic ～手术 plastic operation ～外科 plastic surgery; plastics 【整修】 rebuild; recondition ～房屋 renovate a house 【整装】 get one's things ready (for a journey, etc.) ～待发 ready and waiting ～待命 be ready for orders

正 zhèng ①straight; upright 把柱子扶～ set the post upright ～北 due north ②situated in the middle; main ～门 main entrance ～厅 main hall ③(time) punctually; sharp 九点～ at nine o'clock sharp ④obverse; right ～面 the right side ⑤honest; upright 方～ righteous ⑥correct ～路 the right way ～论 a correct and sensible view ⑦pure; right ～黄 pure yellow ⑧principal; chief ～驾驶员 first pilot ⑨regular ～八边形 regular octagon ⑩positive ～电 positive electricity ～号 positive sign; plus sign ⑪rectify; set right ～音 correct one's pronunciation ⑫just ～如你所说的 just as you say 大小～合适 just the right size 【正比】 direct ratio 【正比例】 direct proportion 【正常】 normal; regular 在～情况下 under normal conditions 恢复～ return to normal 【正大】 upright; honest ～光明 open and aboveboard 【正当】 just when; just the time for 【正当】 proper; appropriate; legitimate 【正道】 the right way 走～ follow the correct path 【正点】 on schedule; on time; punctually ～运行 running on schedule 火车～到达 the train arrived on time 【正方】 square 【正规】 regular; standard ～部队 regular troops;

regulars ～化 regularize ～军 regular army ～学校 regular school ～战争 regular warfare 【正轨】the right path 纳入～ put on the right track 【正好】just in time; just right / happen to; chance to 【正经】decent; respectable; honest/serious ～人 a decent person ～事 serious affairs ～货 standard goods 【正面】front (of a house, etc.)/the right side/positive ～进攻 frontal attack 布的～ the right side of the cloth ～教育 positive education ～人物 positive character 【正派】upright; honest; decent ～人 a decent person 作风～ honest and upright in one's ways 【正气】healthy tendency ～上升 a healthy atmosphere prevails 【正巧】happen to/just in time 【正确】right; proper ～的立场 a correct stand ～估计形势 accurately appraise the situation 【正式】formal; official; regular ～党员 full Party member ～访问 official visit ～会谈 formal talks ～记录 official records ～声明 official statement 【正视】face squarely; look squarely at ～困难 face up to difficulties ～现实 look reality in the face ～缺点 acknowledge one's shortcomings 【正事】one's proper business 谈～ talk business 【正题】topic (of a talk or essay) 转入～ come to the subject 【正文】main body (of a book, etc.); text 【正误】correct (typographical) errors ～表 errata; corrigenda 【正业】regular occupation 不务～ not attend to one's proper duties 【正义】justice/just; righteous 主持～ uphold justice ～立场 a just stand ～感 sense of justice 【正直】honest

证 zhèng ①prove; demonstrate 求～ seek to prove ② proof; testimony 作～ give evidence 物～ material evidence ③certificate; card 许可～ permit 【证词】testimony 【证婚人】chief witness at a wedding ceremony 【证件】credentials; papers 【证据】evidence; proof 搜集～

collect evidence 提出～ offer testimony 【证明】prove; testify; bear out/certificate; identification 医生～ medical certificate 【证券】negotiable securities ～交易所 stock exchange 【证人】witness ～席 witness stand 【证实】confirm; verify 【证章】badge

诤 zhèng criticize sb.'s faults frankly; expostulate 【诤言】forthright admonition

郑 zhèng 【郑重】serious; earnest 态度～ be serious in one's attitude ～声明 solemnly declare

政 zhèng politics; political affairs ～事 government affairs 【政变】coup d'état; coup 发动～ stage a coup d'état 【政策】policy 【政党】political party 【政敌】political opponent 【政法】politics and law ～学院 institute of political science and law 【政府】government ～部门 government departments ～机构 government apparatus 【政纲】political programme 【政界】political circles 【政局】political situation 【政客】politician 【政令】government decree 【政论】political comment ～家 political commentator ～文 political essay 【政权】political power; regime ～机关 organs of state power 【政体】system of government 【政委】(political) commissar 【政务】government administration 【政治】politics; political affairs ～表现 political behaviour or record ～部 political department ～待遇 political treatment ～犯 political offender ～家 statesman ～觉悟 political consciousness ～局 the Political Bureau ～立场 political stand ～权利 political rights ～信仰 political conviction ～学 political science; government

挣 zhèng ①struggle to get free ～命 struggle to save one's life ～脱枷锁 throw off the shackles ②earn; make ～钱 make money ～饭吃 earn a living

症 zhèng disease; illness 不治之～ incurable disease 【症候】disease / symptom

ZHI

之 zhī ①someone; something 取而代～ replace someone 偶一为～ do something once in a while ②of 钟鼓 ～声 the sound of drums and bells 原因～— one of the reasons 【之后】later; after 【之前】before; prior to

支 zhī ①prop up; put up ～帐篷 put up a tent ②protrude; raise ～着耳朵听 prick up one's ears ③support; sustain; bear ～前 support the front ④send away 把他～开 put him off with excuses ⑤pay or draw (money) 预～一百元 get an advance of 100 *yuan* ⑥branch; offshoot ～店 branch store 【支部】branch 党～ Party branch ～大会 general membership meeting of the branch ～书记 branch secretary ～委员 member of the branch committee 【支撑】prop up; sustain; support 【支持】sustain; hold out; bear / support; back; stand by ～不住 cannot hold out any longer 得到广泛的～ enjoy wide support 给予坚决的～ give strong backing to 【支出】pay(money); expend; disburse/expenses; expenditure 【支队】detachment 【支付】pay (money); defray 【支架】support; stand; trestle 【支离】fragmented; broken; disorganized; incoherent ～破 碎 torn to pieces; broken up 【支流】tributary; affluent / minor aspects 【支脉】offshoot; branch range 【支配】arrange; allocate / dominate; govern; control ～劳动力 allocate the labour force ～时间 budget one's time 受 人～ be controlled by others 【支票】cheque 开～ write a cheque ～簿 chequebook 【支气管】bronchus ～炎 bronchitis 【支取】draw (money, one's deposit, etc.) 【支使】order about / send away; put sb. off 【支线】branch line;

feeder (line) 【支援】support; assist; help 【支柱】pillar

汁 zhī juice 橘~ orange juice 牛肉~ beef extract 椰子~ coconut milk

只 zhī single; one only ~字不提 not say a single word 【只身】alone ~在外 be away from home all by oneself

芝 zhī 【芝麻】sesame / sesame seed ~酱 sesame paste ~油 sesame oil

枝 zhī branch; twig 【枝节】branches and knots — minor matters / complication ~问题 a minor problem

知 zhī ①know; realize ~过必改 always correct an error when one becomes aware of it ②knowledge 求~欲 thirst for knowledge 【知道】know; realize 你的意思我~ I see your point 我们~有困难 we are aware that there will still be difficulties 【知己】intimate; understanding ~话 intimate words ~朋友 bosom friend 【知觉】consciousness 【知名】noted; famous ~人士 well-known personage; public figure 【知情】be in the know ~人 person in the know; insider 【知趣】be sensible; be tactful 【知识】knowledge / intellectual 技术~ technical know-how 书本~ book learning ~分子 intellectual ~青年 school leavers; school graduates 【知悉】learn; be informed of 【知足】be content with one's lot

肢 zhī limb 四~ the four limbs 【肢体】limbs / limbs and trunk

织 zhī ①weave ~席 weave a mat ②knit ~毛衣 knit a sweater 【织补】darning; invisible mending 【织布】weaving (cotton cloth) 【织物】fabric

指 zhī 【指甲】nail ~刀 nail clippers ~油 nail polish

脂 zhī ①fat; grease; tallow/rouge 【脂肪】fat 【脂粉】rouge and powder; cosmetics

掷 zhī throw; cast ～色子 throw dice; play dice

蜘 zhī 【蜘蛛】spider ～丝 the thread of a spider web ～网 spider web; cobweb

执 zhí ①hold; grasp 手～红旗 hold a red banner ②take charge of; direct; manage ～教 be a teacher ③stick to (one's views, etc.); persist ④catch; capture 被～ be captured 【执笔】write; do the actual writing 【执法】execute the law ～如山 enforce the law strictly 【执迷不悟】obstinately stick to a wrong course; be perverse 【执拗】stubborn; wilful 【执行】carry out; implement ～任务 perform a mission ～命令 execute an order ～政策 implement a policy ～机构 executive body ～机关 executive organ ～委员会 executive committee ～主席 presiding chairman 【执意】insist on; be determined to 【执照】license; permit 【执政】be in power; be in office ～党 the party in power 【执著】inflexible; rigid

直 zhí ①straight 街道很～ the streets are straight ②straighten ～起腰来 stand up straight ③vertical; perpendicular ～上云霄 soar straight up into the sky ④just; upright 正～ fair-minded ⑤frank; straightforward ～认不讳 admit frankly ～说 speak frankly ⑥directly 一～走 go straight ahead 【直达】through; nonstop ～车 through train or through bus ～车票 through ticket ～路线 through route 【直观】audio-visual ～教具 audio-visual aids ～教学 object teaching ～教学课 object lesson 【直角】right angle 【直接】immediate; direct 【直接原因】direct cause ～会晤 meet sb. in person ～交涉 negotiate directly with sb. ～宾语 direct object 【直截了当】straightforward; blunt; point-blank 【直径】diameter 【直觉】intuition 【直升飞机】helicopter; copter ～母舰 helicopter carrier

【直率】frank; candid 【直爽】straightforward; forthright
【直线】straight line / steep; sharp (rise or fall) 【直言】
speak bluntly; state outright ～不讳 not mince words
【直译】literal translation 【直至】till; until / up to

侄 zhí brother's son; nephew 【侄女】brother's daughter; niece

指 zhí 【指头】finger / toe

值 zhí ①value 而～ currency value ⓐbe worth 这～
多少钱 what is this worth 不～一提 not worth
mentioning ⓐtake one's turn at sth. 轮～ work in shifts
【值班】be on duty 今天谁～ who's on duty today ～员
person on duty 【值得】be worth; deserve ～买 be worth
buying ～注意 merit attention ～怀疑 be open to doubt
～考虑 warrant consideration ～一读 be worth reading
【值钱】costly; valuable 【值勤】(of policemen, etc.) be
on point duty 【值日】be on duty for the day 今天谁
～打扫教室 whose turn is it to clean the classroom today
～生 student on duty 【值星】(of army officers) be on
duty for the week

职 zhí ①duty; job 尽～ fulfil one's duty ②post; office
调～ be transferred to another post 【职称】the title
of a technical or professional post 【职工】staff and workers
【职能】function (of money, etc.) 【职权】powers or authority of office 行使～ exercise one's functions and
powers ～范围 terms of reference 【职位】position 【职
务】post; duties; job 【职业】occupation; profession; vo-
cation ～病 occupational disease ～团体 professional organization ～外交官 career diplomat ～学校 vocational
school ～运动员 professional athlete 【职员】office worker;
staff member 【职责】duty; obligation; responsibility

植 zhí plant; grow ～树 plant trees 【植树造林】afforestation 【植物】plant; flora ～保护 plant protection ～界 plant kingdom ～学 botany ～学家 botanist ～油 vegetable oil ～园 botanical garden

殖 zhí breed; multiply 生～ reproduce 【殖民】establish a colony; colonize ～地 colony ～国家 colonialist power ～战争 colonialist war ～主义 colonialism

止 zhǐ ①stop ～付 stop payment ～痒 stop the itching ～渴 quench one's thirst 打一针能～痛 the injection can relieve pain ②to; till 到目前为～ to date; till now ③only 不～一次 not just once 【止步】halt; stop; go no further 游人～ no visitors 【止境】end; limit 【止咳】relieve a cough ～糖浆 cough syrup 【止息】cease; stop 【止血】stop bleeding; stanch bleeding ～药 haemostatic

只 zhǐ only; merely ～剩一个 there is only one left 【只得】be obliged to; have to 【只顾】be absorbed in/merely; simply 【只管】by all means 你～干下去 go ahead by all means 【只好】have to ～作罢 be forced to give up ～另想办法 cannot but seek other means 【只是】merely; only; just / simply 这～个时间问题 it is merely a question of time 他～笑,不回答 he simply laughed without replying 【只要】so long as; provided 【只有】alone ～他知道内情 he alone knows the inside story

旨 zhǐ ①purport; purpose; aim ②decree 【旨趣】objective 【旨意】decree; order

址 zhǐ location; site 厂～ factory site 地～ address

纸 zhǐ paper 一张白～ a blank sheet of paper 一～空文 a mere scrap of paper 【纸板】paperboard ～盒 cardboard box 【纸币】paper money; note 【纸花】paper flower 【纸浆】(paper) pulp 【纸老虎】paper tiger 【纸牌】

playing cards 【纸绳】 paper string 【纸型】. paper mould

指 zhǐ ①finger ②point at; point to ③indicate; refer to ～出正确方向 point out the correct way ～出缺点 point out sb.'s shortcomings 他的话不是～你说的 his remarks were not directed at you ④depend on; count on 【指标】 target; quota; norm; index 生产～ production target 质量～ quality index 【指斥】 reprove; denounce 【指导】 guide; direct ～思想 guiding ideology ～员 political instructor 【指点】 give directions; show how (to do sth.) 【指定】 appoint; assign ～地点 the designated place 【指环】 (finger) ring 【指挥】 command; direct; conduct/commander; director/conductor ～连队 command a company ～交通 direct traffic ～乐队 conduct an orchestra ～棒 baton ～部 command post; headquarters ～刀 officer's sword ～官 commander ～系统 command system 【指教】 give advice or comments 请多～ kindly give us your advice 【指靠】 depend on (for one's livelihood); look to (for help); count on 【指控】 accuse; charge 【指令】 instruct; order; direct / instructions 【指名】 name ～攻击 assail sb. by name ～道姓 name names 【指明】 show clearly; demonstrate ～出路 point the way out 【指南】 guide; guidebook ～针 compass 【指派】 appoint; designate 【指使】 instigate; incite 受人～ act on sb.'s instigation 【指示】 indicate; point out/instruct/directive ～代词 demonstrative pronoun ～灯 indicator lamp 【指数】 index 【指望】 look to; count on/prospect; hope 他的病还有～吗 is there still hope of his recovery 【指纹】 loops and whorls on a finger/fingerprint 【指引】 point (the way); guide; show 【指印】 fingerprint; finger mark 【指责】 censure; criticize; find fault with 受舆论～ be subjected to the censure of public opinion 【指针】 indicator

趾

zhǐ ①toe ②foot 【趾高气扬】 strut about and give oneself airs 【趾甲】 toenail

至

zhì ①to; until 从左~右 from left to right 截~上月底为止 up to the end of last month ②most ~宝 most valuable treasure 【至诚】 complete sincerity/sincere; straightforward 出于~ in all sincerity ~的朋友 a sincere friend 【至迟】 at (the) latest 【至多】 at (the) most 【至高无上】 most lofty; paramount; supreme 【至交】 best friend 【至今】 up to now; to this day; so far 【至亲】 close relative 【至少】 at (the) least 【至于】 as for; as to

志

zhì ①will; ideal 胸怀大~ have lofty aspirations 立~当科学家 be determined to become a scientist ②keep in mind 永~不忘 forever bear in mind 【志气】 aspiration; ambition 【志趣】 inclination; bent 【志士】 person of ideals and integrity 爱国~ noble-minded patriot 【志同道合】 have a common goal 【志愿】 aspiration; wish; ideal/do sth. of one's own free will; volunteer ~兵 volunteer (soldier) ~军 volunteers ~书 application form

治

zhì ①rule; govern; administer; manage ~家 manage a household ②order; peace 天下大~ great order across the land ③treat (a disease); cure ~好创伤 heal a wound ④control; harness (a river) ~沙 sand-control ⑤study; research ~史 make a study of history 【治安】 public order; public security 【治本】 take radical measures 【治标】 take stopgap measures 【治病救人】 cure a sickness to save the patient 【治国】 run a country; manage state affairs 【治理】 administer (a country); govern / harness 【治疗】 treat; cure ~效果 therapeutic effect 在医院~ be hospitalized; be under treatment in hospital 【治学】 pursue one's studies; do scholarly research 【治罪】 punish sb. (for a crime)

质 zhì ①nature; character ②quality ～的飞跃 a qualitative leap ③simple; plain 言之 to put it bluntly ④question ～疑 call in question; query 【质变】qualitative change 【质地】texture; grain/character; disposition 【质量】quality ～好 of high quality ～不高 of low quality; inferior 【质料】material 【质朴】simple; unaffected; plain 【质问】interrogate; call to account; query 提出～ bring sb. to account 【质询】address inquiries to

制 zhì ①make; manufacture 机～ machine-made ②work out ③restrict; control ④ system 【制裁】sanction; punish 实行～ impose sanctions (upon) 受法律～ be punished according to law 【制成品】finished products; manufactures 【制导】control and guide (a missile, bomb, etc.) 【制定】lay down; draw up; draft ～政策 formulate a policy ～计划 work out a plan ～法律 make laws 【制动】brake 【制度】system; institution 【制伏】bring under control ～风沙 check wind and sand ～敌人 subdue the enemy 【制服】uniform ～呢 uniform cloth 【制图】charting; map-making/drafting ～仪器 drawing instrument ～员 cartographer; draftsman 【制药】pharmacy ～厂 pharmaceutical factory 【制约】restrict; condition 互相～ condition each other; interact 【制造】make; manufacture/engineer; create; fabricate 中国～ made in China ～商 manufacturer ～业 manufacturing industry ～纠纷 create trouble ～紧张局势 create tension ～分裂 foment splits ～假象 put up a false front ～障碍 raise obstacles ～舆论 mould public opinion 【制止】check; curb; prevent; stop ～通货膨胀 halt inflation ～派别活动 put an end to factional activities

峙 zhì stand erect; tower 对～ stand up against each other; confront each other ～立 stand towering

桎 zhì fetters 【桎梏】 fetters and handcuffs; shackles 打碎精神上的～ smash spiritual shackles

致 zhì ①send; deliver ～电 send a telegram ～贺 extend one's congratulations ②devote (one's efforts, etc.) 专心～志 be wholly absorbed in ③incur; result in; cause 招～失败 cause defeat ④fine; delicate 精～ exquisite 细～ meticulous 【致辞】 make a speech 向大会～ address the conference 新年～ New Year message 【致敬】 salute; pay one's respects to ～电 message of greeting 【致力】 dedicate oneself to; work for 【致命】 fatal; mortal ～的打击 a deadly blow ～伤 a vital wound ～的弱点 fatal weakness 【致使】 cause; result in 【致死】 causing death; lethal; deadly ～原因 cause of death ～剂量 lethal dose 【致谢】 express one's gratitude; extend thanks to 谨此～ we hereby express our thanks 【致意】 give one's regards; give one's best wishes 挥手～ wave a greeting

秩 zhì 【秩序】 order; sequence 工作～ sequence of work 维护社会～ maintain public order 紧张而有～的工作 intense but orderly work

挚 zhì sincere; earnest 真～的友谊 true friendship 【挚友】 intimate friend; bosom friend

掷 zhì throw; cast; fling ～电 send a telegram ～标枪 javelin throw ～铁饼 discus throw 【掷弹筒】 grenade discharger

窒 zhì stop up; obstruct ～塞 block ～闷 close; stuffy 【窒息】 stifle; suffocate

痔 zhì 【痔疮】 haemorrhoids; piles 【痔漏】 anal fistula

滞 zhì stagnant; sluggish 【滞留】 be detained; be held up 【滞销】 unsalable ～货 drug; slow-selling goods

痣 zhì nevus; mole 色～ pigmented mole 胎～ birthmark

智 zhì wisdom; resourcefulness; wit ～穷才尽 at the end of one's wits 【智慧】 wisdom 【智力】 intelligence; intellect ～测验 intelligence test 【智谋】 resourcefulness 【智囊】 brain truster ～团 brain trust 【智取】 take (a fort, town, etc.) by strategy 【智术】 trickery; stratagem 【智勇双全】 both brave and resourceful 【智育】 intellectual education

置 zhì ①place; put 搁～ put aside ②set up; establish; install ～酒款待 give a feast to entertain sb. ③buy; purchase ～家具 buy furniture 【置若罔闻】 turn a deaf ear to; pay no heed to 【置身】 place oneself; stay ～事外 stay aloof from the affair; keep out of the business 【置之不理】 ignore; pay no attention to 【置之度外】 give no thought to; have no regard for

稚 zhì young; childish 【稚气】 childishness 【稚子】 (innocent) child

ZHONG

中 zhōng ①centre; middle 居～ in the centre ②China ③in; among; amidst 跳入水～ jump into the water ④middle 月～ in the middle of a month ⑤medium; intermediate ～号 medium-sized ⑥mean 适～ moderate ⑦intermediary 作～ act as an intermediary ⑧in the process of 在修建～ being built; under construction ⑨fit for; good for 不～用 good for nothing 【中波】 medium wave 【中部】 central section; middle part 【中餐】 Chinese meal; Chinese food 【中草药】 Chinese herbal medicine 【中策】 the second best plan 【中层】 middle-level ～干部 middle-level cadres 【中常】 middling ～年景 average harvest 【中等】 medium; moderate; middling / secondary ～城市 medium-sized city ～教育 secondary school education ～专

科学校 technical secondary school 【中断】suspend; break off ~谈判 break off the negotiations 交通~ traffic was held up 【中队】squadron 【中国】China ~话 the Chinese language; Chinese ~画 traditional Chinese painting ~共产党 the Communist Party of China; the Chinese Communist Party ~人 Chinese ~字 Chinese characters 【中华】China ~民族 the Chinese nation ~人民共和国 the People's Republic of China 【中级】middle rank; intermediate ~人民法院 intermediate people's court 【中坚】nucleus; hard core; backbone ~分子 backbone elements 【中间】among; between / centre; middle ~突破 make a breakthrough at the centre ~剥削 middleman's exploitation ~道路 middle road 【中看】be pleasant to the eye 【中立】neutrality 守~ observe neutrality 保持~ remain neutral ~地带 neutral zone ~国 neutral state ~政策 policy of neutrality ~主义 neutralism 【中流】midstream ~砥柱 mainstay 【中落】(of family fortunes) decline; ebb 【中年】middle age ~人 a middle-aged person 【中农】middle peasant 【中篇小说】novelette 【中秋节】the Mid-autumn Festival (15th day of the 8th lunar month) 【中人】go-between 【中枢】centre ~神经系统 central nervous system 【中提琴】viola 【中听】pleasant to the ear 【中途】halfway; midway ~停留 stop halfway ~下汽车 get off the car midway 【中文】Chinese ~书刊 books and magazines in Chinese 【中午】noon; midday 【中心】centre; heart; core; hub ~城市 key city ~工作 central task ~环节 key link ~思想 central idea; gist ~问题 central issue 【中型】middle-sized ~词典 a medium-sized dictionary 【中性】neutral / neuter ~反应 neutral reaction ~名词 neuter noun 【中学】middle school ~生 middle school student 【中央】centre; middle/central authorities

～机构 central organs ～银行 central bank ～直属机关 departments under the Party Central Committee 【中药】 traditional Chinese medicine ～铺 Chinese pharmacy 【中医】 traditional Chinese medical science / doctor of traditional Chinese medicine 【中游】 middle reaches/the state of being middling 【中止】 discontinue; break off ～谈判 suspend negotiations 【中指】 middle finger 【中专】 special or technical secondary school; polytechnic school 【中转】 change trains ～站 transfer station 【中装】 traditional Chinese clothing 【中子】 neutron ～弹 neutron bomb

忠 zhōng loyal; devoted; honest 【忠臣】 official loyal to his sovereign 【忠诚】 loyal; faithful; staunch ～党的教育事业 be devoted to the Party's educational task 【忠告】 sincerely advise 【忠厚】 honest and tolerant 【忠实】 true; faithful ～于原文 true to the original ～信徒 faithful disciple 【忠心】 loyalty; devotion ～耿耿 most faithful and true 【忠言】 earnest advice ～逆耳 good advice jars on the ear 【忠于】 true to; faithful to ～祖国、～人民 be loyal to one's country and people ～职守 be loyal to one's duty

终 zhōng ①end; finish 年～ end of the year ～局 outcome ②death; end 临～ on one's deathbed ③eventually; in the end ～非良策 it's not a good plan after all ④whole; entire; all ～岁 the whole year ～日 all day long; all day 【终点】 terminal point; destination/finish 旅行的～ destination of a journey ～线 finishing line ～站 terminus 【终极】 ultimate ～目标 ultimate aim 【终结】 end; final stage 【终了】 end (of a period) 学期～ the end of the (school) term 【终身】 lifelong; all one's life ～伴侣 lifelong companion ～事业 one's lifework 【终于】 at (long) last; in the end; finally 【终止】 stop;

end/termination; annulment ～日期 closing date

盅 zhōng handleless cup 茶～ teacup 酒～ winecup

钟 zhōng ①bell 敲～ toll a bell ②clock 电～ electric clock ③time as measured in hours and minutes 六点～ six o'clock 十分～ ten minutes ④concentrate (one's affections, etc.)【钟爱】dote on (a child); cherish【钟摆】pendulum【钟表】clocks and watches; timepiece 店 watchmaker's shop【钟楼】bell tower; belfry / clock tower【钟情】be deeply in love

衷 zhōng inner feelings; heart【衷心】heartfelt 表示～的感激 express one's heartfelt gratitude ～拥护 give wholehearted support 表示～祝贺 extend cordial greetings

肿 zhǒng swelling 我的腿～了 my legs are swollen ～消了 the swelling has gone down【肿瘤】tumour

种 zhǒng ①species 本地～ endemic species ②race 黄～ the yellow race ③seed; strain; breed 麦～ wheat seeds ④kind; sort; type 各～仪器 all kinds of instruments【种畜】stud stock【种类】type ～繁多 a great variety【种马】stud ～场 stud farm【种牛】bull kept for covering【种种】all sorts of; a variety of 由于～原因 for a variety of reasons 用～手段 resort to every means【种子】seed ～处理 seed treatment ～田 seed-breeding field ～选手 seeded player; seed【种族】race ～主义 racism

中 zhòng ①hit; fit exactly 猜～ guess right 你说～了 you've hit it ②be hit by; be affected by; suffer 腿上～了一枪 be shot in the leg ～计 fall into a trap ～煤气 be gassed【中的】hit the mark【中毒】poisoning 食物～ food poisoning【中风】apoplexy【中奖】win a prize in a lottery; get the winning number in a bond【中肯】apropos; pertinent 回答～ the reply was to the

point 【中签】 be the lucky number (in drawing lots, etc.)
【中伤】 slander; malign; vilify 【中暑】 suffer heatstroke/
sunstroke 【中意】 be to one's liking

众 zhòng ①many; numerous ②crowd; multitude 【众多】
multitudinous 【众寡悬殊】 a great disparity in nu-
merical strength 【众口一词】 with one voice 【众叛亲离】
be opposed by the masses and deserted by one's followers; be utterly isolated 【众人】 everybody 【众矢之的】
target of public criticism 【众说纷纭】 opinions vary 【众
所周知】 as everyone knows 【众望】 people's expectations;
popular confidence 不孚～ fall short of people's expectations ～所归 enjoy popular confidence

仲 zhòng ①second 一～春 second month of spring ②mid-
dle; intermediate 【仲裁】 arbitrate (a dispute, etc.)
～法庭 arbitration tribunal ～人 arbitrator ～书 award

种 zhòng grow; plant; cultivate ～水稻 grow rice ～
庄稼 plant crops ～花 grow flowers ～地 cultivate
land; go in for farming 【种痘】 vaccination (against
smallpox) 【种田】 till the land; farm 【种植】 plant; grow

重 zhòng ①weight 这条鱼有三斤～ this fish weighs
three *jin* ②heavy; weighty 工作～ have a heavy
work load ～税 heavy taxation 分别轻～ distinguish the
trivial from the important ③considerable in amount or
value ～赏 a handsome reward ④deep; serious 情意～
deep affection 病～ be seriously ill 受～伤 be severely
injured ⑤attach importance to ～调查研究 lay stress on
investigation and study ～男轻女 regard men as superior
to women 【重办】 severely punish (a criminal) 【重兵】
massive forces 有～把守 be heavily guarded 【重创】 inflict
heavy losses on; maul (heavily) 【重大】 great; weighty
～成就 tremendous achievements ～胜利 a signal victory

~问题 vital problem; major issue ~损失 heavy losses 【重担】 heavy burden 把~子留给自己 take the difficult tasks for oneself 【重点】 focal point; stress; emphasis 突出~ make the key points stand out ~工程 major project ~高等院校 key institutes of higher learning ~企业 key enterprises ~进攻 attacks against key sectors 工作~ focal point of the work 【重读】 stress ~音节 stressed syllable 【重工业】 heavy industry 【重价】 high price 【重力】 gravity 【重利】 high interest/huge profit ~盘剥 practise usury 【重量】 weight 【重任】 heavy responsibility 身负~ be charged with important tasks 【重视】 attach importance to; pay attention to; think highly of; value ~这件事 take the matter seriously 【重型】 heavy-duty ~卡车 heavy truck 【重要】 important; significant ~关头 critical juncture ~任务 vital task ~原则 cardinal principle 【重音】 stress; accent 句子~ sentence stress 单词~ word stress ~符号 stress mark; accent 【重用】 put sb. in an important position 【重油】 heavy oil

ZHOU

州 zhōu ①an administrative division ②(autonomous) prefecture

舟 zhōu boat 轻~ a light boat 泛~ go boating

诌 zhōu fabricate (tales, etc.); make up 别胡~了 stop making up wild stories

周 zhōu ①circumference; periphery; circuit 绕场一~ make a circuit of the arena ②all; whole ~身 the whole body ③thoughtful; attentive 计划不~ not planned carefully enough 招待不~ not be attentive enough to guests ④week 上~ last week 【周报】 weekly (publication)

【周波】cycle 【周到】attentive and satisfactory; considerate 服务～ offer good service 想得很～ be very thoughtful 安排得很～ be carefully worked out 【周刊】weekly 【周密】careful; thorough ～的分析 a detailed analysis ～的计划 a well-conceived plan 【周末】weekend 【周年】anniversary 【周期】period; cycle ～表 periodic table ～性 periodicity; cyclicity 【周围】around; round; about ～环境 surroundings; environment 【周旋】mix with other people; socialize/deal with 【周游】travel round; journey round 【周折】twists and turns 几经～ after many setbacks 这事要费一番～ this business will cause us a good deal of bother 【周转】turnover / have enough to meet the need ～资金 working fund

洲 zhōu ①continent ②islet in a river; sand bar 【洲际】intercontinental ～导弹 intercontinental missile

粥 zhōu gruel (made of rice, millet, etc.); porridge; congee 小米～ millet gruel

妯 zhóu 【妯娌】wives of brothers; sisters-in-law

轴 zhóu ①axle; shaft 车～ car axle 地～ the earth's axis ②spool; rod 线～儿 spool (for thread) 【轴承】bearing 【轴线】spool thread; spool cotton 【轴心】axis

肘 zhǒu elbow 【肘子】upper part of a leg of pork/elbow

咒 zhòu ①incantation 念～ chant incantations ②damn 【咒骂】curse; swear; abuse; revile

胄 zhòu ①helmet 甲～ armour and helmet ②descendants; offspring

昼 zhòu daytime; daylight; day ～伏夜出 hide by day and come out at night 【昼夜】day and night ～看守 keep watch round the clock

皱 zhòu wrinkle; crease 别把地图弄～ don't crumple the map 【皱眉】knit one's brows; frown 【皱纹】wrinkles; lines ～纸 crepe paper 【皱褶】fold

骤 zhòu ①(of a horse) trot 驰～ gallop ②sudden; abrupt 狂风～起 a sudden gale struck 【骤然】suddenly

ZHU

朱 zhū ①vermilion; bright red ②cinnabar 【朱漆】red paint; red lacquer 【朱砂】cinnabar

诛 zhū ①put (a criminal) to death 伏～ be executed 【诛求无已】make endless exorbitant demands

侏 zhū dwarf 【侏儒】dwarf; midget; pygmy

珠 zhū ①pearl ②bead 露～ beads of dew 【珠宝】pearls and jewels; jewelry; ornaments made with pearls, jade, etc. ～店 a jeweller's (shop) ～商 jeweller 【珠算】calculation with an abacus; reckoning by the abacus

株 zhū ①trunk of a tree; stem of a plant ②(individual) plant 幼～ sapling 【株连】involve (others) in a criminal case; implicate

诸 zhū all; various 【诸侯】dukes or princes under an emperor 【诸如】such as ～此类 things like that; such (as these); and so on and so forth 【诸位】you 欢迎～提意见 you are welcome to put forward your views

猪 zhū pig; hog; swine 小～ pigling 母～ sow 公～ boar 【猪草】greenfeed for pigs 【猪场】pig farm 【猪肝】pork liver 【猪倌】swineherd 【猪圈】pigsty; pigpen; hogpen 【猪排】pork chop 【猪皮】pigskin 【猪肉】pork 【猪食】pig feed; swill 【猪油】lard 【猪鬃】(hog) bristles

蛛 zhū spider 【蛛丝马迹】thread of a spider and trail of a horse — clues; traces 【蛛网】spider web; cobweb

潴 zhū ①(of water) collect; accumulate; store ②puddle; pool 【潴留】 retention 尿～ retention of urine

竹 zhú bamboo ～篓 bamboo basket ～林 groves of bamboo 【竹板】 bamboo clappers 【竹竿】 bamboo (pole) 【竹排】 bamboo raft 【竹器】 articles made of bamboo 【竹笋】 bamboo shoots

烛 zhú ①candle ～心 candlewick ②illuminate 火光～天 leaping flames lit up the sky ③watt 二十五～灯泡 a 25-watt bulb 【烛光】 candlepower; candle 【烛花】 snuff 【烛台】 candlestick

逐 zhú ①pursue; chase ②drive out; expel ～出门外 drive out of the door ③one by one ～项 item by item ～日 day by day; every day ～月 month by month ～年 year after year ～条 point by point 【逐步】 progressively; step by step ～加以解决 settle sth. step by step 【逐渐】 gradually; by degrees 天～暗下来了 it's getting darker and darker 【逐字】 word for word; verbatim ～记录 verbatim record

主 zhǔ ①host ②owner; master 当家作～ be master in one's own house ③main; primary ～航道 principal channel 预防为～ put prevention first ④manage ～办 direct; sponsor ～事 be in charge of the business ⑤hold a definite view about sth. ～和 advocate peace 【主编】 chief editor / supervise the publication of (a newspaper, magazine, etc.); edit 【主宾席】 seat for the guest of honour 【主持】 take charge of; manage; direct/preside over; chair/uphold; stand for 一日常事务 take care of routine matters ～讨论 chair a discussion ～正义 uphold justice 【主词】 subject 【主次】 primary and secondary 【主从】 principal and subordinate 【主导】 dominant; guiding 起～作用 play a leading role ～思想 dominant ideas 【主动】

initiative 争取~ try to gain the initiative ~帮助人 help others of one's own accord 【主队】 host team 【主犯】 prime culprit; principal (criminal) 【主妇】 housewife; hostess 【主攻】 main attack ~部队 main attack force ~方向 main direction of attack 【主顾】 customer; client 【主观】 subjective ~努力 subjective efforts ~愿望 subjective desire; wishful thinking ~世界 subjective world ~能动性 subjective initiative ~唯心主义 subjective idealism ~主义 subjectivism 【主管】 be responsible for; be in charge of/person in charge ~部门 department responsible for the work ~机关 responsible institution 【主见】 one's own judgment 没有~ have no definite views of one's own 有~ know one's own mind 【主讲】 be the speaker; give a lecture 【主将】 chief commander 【主教】 bishop 大~ archbishop 红衣~ cardinal 【主句】 principal clause 【主角】 leading role; lead; protagonist 在该片中演~ play the lead in the film 女~ a leading lady 【主考】 be in charge of an examination/chief examiner (in a school, etc.) 【主课】 major course 【主力】 main force ~兵团 main formations ~队员 top players of a team ~舰 capital ship ~军 principal force 【主流】 main stream; main current/essential or main aspect; main trend ~和支流 principal and secondary aspects 【主谋】 head a conspiracy/ chief instigator 【主脑】 control centre/leader; chief 【主权】 sovereign rights; sovereignty ~国家 a sovereign state 【主人】 master/owner/host 女~ hostess 房子的~ owner of the house 【主人公】 leading character in a novel, etc.; hero or heroine; protagonist 【主人翁】 master 【主任】 director; head; chairman 【主食】 staple food 【主使】 instigate; incite; abet 【主题】 theme; subject; motif 诗的~ the subject of a poem 作品的~思想 the theme of a literary work ～歌 theme song 【主体】 main body; principal part/subject ～工程 principal part of a project 【主席】 chairman (of a meeting); president (of an organization or a state) 当～ be in the chair; preside over a meeting ～台 rostrum; platform ～团 presidium 【主修】 specialize (in a subject); major ～物理 major in physics ～科目 major subjects 【主演】 act the leading role (in a play or film) 【主要】 main; chief ～敌人 chief enemy ～矛盾 principal contradiction ～目的 major objective ～因素 primary factor ～农作物 staple crops 【主义】 doctrine; -ism 【主意】 idea; plan/decision; definite view 好～ a good idea 打定～ make a decision; make up one's mind 改变～ change one's mind 拿不定～ be in two minds (about sth.) 【主语】 subject 【主宰】 dominate; dictate ～自己的命运 decide one's own destiny 【主张】 advocate; stand for; maintain; hold/view; position; stand; proposition ～改革 favour reforms 这是我们一贯的～ that has been our consistent stand 【主旨】 purport; substance; gist 【主治医生】 physician-in-charge; doctor in charge of a case 【主子】 master; boss

挂 zhǔ lean on (a stick, etc.) ～着拐棍走 walk with a stick

属 zhǔ ①join; combine 前后相～ (of two parts) join together ②centre (one's attention, etc.) upon ～望 centre one's hope on ～意 fix one's mind on sb.

煮 zhǔ boil; cook ～鸡蛋 boil eggs ～饭 cook rice

嘱 zhǔ enjoin; advise; urge 【嘱咐】 tell; exhort ～他保守秘密 enjoin him to secrecy 【嘱托】 entrust

瞩 zhǔ gaze; look steadily 【瞩目】 fix one's eyes upon; focus one's attention upon 【瞩望】 look forward to

助 zhù help; assist; aid ～消化 aid digestion ～人为乐 find it a pleasure to help others 【助产士】 midwife 【助动词】 auxiliary verb 【助攻】 holding attack ～部队 holding element 【助教】 assistant (of a college faculty) 【助理】 assistant 部长～ assistant minister 【助手】 assistant; helper; aide 【助听器】 audiphone; deaf-aid 【助威】 boost the morale of; cheer for 【助兴】 liven things up; add to the fun 【助学金】 stipend 领～的学生 a grant-aided student 【助战】 assist in fighting/bolster sb.'s morale 【助长】 abet; foster; foment; encourage

住 zhù ①live; reside; stay ～旅馆 stay at a hotel ② stop; cease 雨～了 the rain has stopped 【住处】 residence; dwelling (place); lodging; domicile; quarters 找到～没有 have you found accommodation 我不知道他的～ I don't know where he lives 【住房】 housing; lodgings ～问题 the housing problem; accommodation 【住户】 household; resident 【住口】 shut up; stop talking 【住手】 stay one's hand; stop 【住宿】 stay; put up; get accommodation 在旅店～ put up at an inn 给客人安排～ find lodgings for the visitors 【住院】 be in hospital; be hospitalized ～部 inpatient department ～处 admission office ～费 hospitalization expenses ～医生 resident (physician) 【住宅】 residence; dwelling 【住址】 address

注 zhù ①pour 大雨如～ the rain poured down ②concentrate; fix 全神贯～ be engrossed in; be preoccupied with ③stakes' (in gambling) ④annotate; notes 【注册】 register ～组 registrar's office ～商标 registered trademark 【注定】 be doomed; be destined ～失败 be doomed to failure 命中～ predestined 【注脚】 footnote 【注解】 annotate; explain with notes / (explanatory) note; annotation 【注明】 give clear indication of ～出处 give sources 【注目】 gaze at; fix one's eyes on 引人～ spectacular 【注入】 pour into; empty into 【注射】 inject ～器 injector; syringe 【注视】 look attentively at; gaze at 【注释】 explanatory note; annotation ～读物 annotated readings 【注销】 cancel; write off ～借条 cancel an I.O.U. 帐已～ the account has been written off 【注意】 pay attention to; take note of ～工作方法 pay attention to methods of work ～力 attention ～事项 points for attention 【注音】 phonetic notation ～字母 the national phonetic alphabet 【注重】 pay attention to; attach importance to ～基本功的训练 lay stress on basic training

贮 zhù store; save; lay aside ～粮ði荒 store grain against a lean year 【贮备】 have in reserve 【贮藏】 store up ～白菜 lay in cabbages 【贮存】 keep in storage

驻 zhù ①halt; stay ～足 make a temporary stay ②be stationed ～英大使 ambassador to Britain ～京记者 resident correspondent in Beijing 【驻地】 place where troops, etc. are stationed 【驻守】 garrison; defend

炷 zhù ①wick (of an oil lamp) ②burn ～香 burn a joss stick

祝 zhù ①wish ～你健康 I wish you the best of health ～你旅途愉快 have a pleasant journey 【祝词】 congratulatory speech; congratulations 【祝福】 blessing; benediction 【祝贺】 congratulate ～演出成功 congratulate the artists on their successful performance 向你～ congratulations 【祝捷】 celebrate a victory ～大会 victory celebration (meeting) 【祝酒】 toast 向来宾们～ toast the guests 致～辞 propose a toast 答谢～ reply to a toast 【祝寿】 congratulate (an elderly person) on his or her birthday 【祝颂】 express good wishes 【祝愿】 wish 致以良好的～ with best wishes

柱 zhù post; upright; pillar; column 门～ doorposts 水～ water column 【柱石】pillar; mainstay

著 zhù ①marked; outstanding ② distinguished ② show; prove 颇～成效 prove rather effective ③write ～书 write books ④book; work 名～ a famous work 新～ sb.'s latest work 【著名】famous; well-known 【著者】author 【著作】work; writings / write ～权 copyright

蛀 zhù (of moths, etc.) eat; bore through 给虫子～了 be moth-eaten 【蛀齿】decayed tooth 【蛀虫】moth

筑 zhù build; construct ～路 construct a road ～提 build a dyke

铸 zhù casting; founding ～字 typecasting ～钟 cast a bell ～钱 coin money ～成大错 make a gross error

ZHUA

抓 zhuā ①grab; seize; clutch ～权 grab power ～机会 seize an opportunity ～起帽子 snatch up one's cap ②scratch ～痒 scratch an itch ③arrest; catch; press-gang (able-bodied men) ～特务 catch an enemy agent ④pay special attention to ～重点 stress the essentials ⑤take charge of; be responsible for 【抓差】draft sb. for a particular task 【抓工夫】find time (to do sth.) 【抓紧】firmly grasp ～时间 make the best use of one's time 【抓阄儿】draw lots 【抓住】seize hold of; grip/catch; capture

爪 zhuǎ claw; talon 鹰～ eagle's talons 【爪儿】paw (of a small animal) 猫～ cat's paws

ZHUAI

拽 zhuài pull; drag; haul 一把～住不放 catch hold of sb. or sth. and not let go

ZHUAN

专 zhuān ①focussed on one thing 心不～ not concentrate (on any one thing) ②special ～车 special train or car ～程 special trip ③expert 又红又～ be both red and expert ④monopolize (power) 【专案】(special) case ～材料 dossier ～组 special group for the examination of a case 【专长】speciality; special skill or knowledge 学有～ be expert in a special field of study 【专场】special performance 【专断】act arbitrarily 【专号】special issue (of a periodical) 【专横】imperious; peremptory 【专机】special plane / private plane 【专家】expert; specialist 【专刊】special issue or column / monograph 【专科学校】training school 【专款】special fund ～专用 earmark a fund for its specified purpose only 【专栏】special column ～作家 columnist 【专利】patent 【专卖】monopoly 【专门】special; specialized ～机构 special organ ～人材 people with professional skill ～术语 technical terms ～知识 specialized knowledge; expertise 【专名】proper noun 【专区】prefecture 【专任】full-time; regular ～教员 full-time teacher 【专题】special subject ～报告 report on a special topic ～讨论 seminar ～研究 monographic study ～著作 monograph 【专线】special railway line/special telephone line 【专心】concentrate one's attention ～致志 wholly absorbed 【专修】specialize in (mathematics, chemistry, etc.) ～科 special (training) course 【专业】special field of study; speciality; discipline / specialized trade or profession; special line ～队伍 professional contingent ～化 specialization ～课 specialized course ～人员 personnel in a specific field ～学校 vocational school ～知识 professional knowledge 【专一】single-minded; concentrated 爱情～ be constant in love【专用】for a special purpose ～电话 telephone for special use【专员】assistant director; commissioner 商务～ commercial attaché【专政】dictatorship ～对象 object of dictatorship ～工具 instrument of dictatorship ～机关 organ of dictatorship【专职】sole duty; specific duty/full-time【专制】autocracy/despotic ～帝王 despotic emperor ～君主 autocrat【专著】monograph; treatise

砖 zhuān brick ～房 brick house ～墙 brick wall【砖茶】brick tea【砖厂】brickyard【砖坯】unfired brick

转 zhuǎn ①turn; shift; change ～车 change trains or buses ～败为胜 turn defeat into victory ②pass on; transfer 这封信请你～给他 please pass the letter on to him【转变】change; transform ～立场 change one's stand【转播】relay (a radio or TV broadcast) ～台 relay station【转达】pass on; convey 请向他～我的问候 please give him my regards【转动】turn; move; turn round【转告】communicate; transmit【转换】change; transform ～方向 change direction ～话题 change the subject of conversation【转机】a turn for the better【转嫁】transfer; shift (off one's responsibility)【转交】pass on; transmit【转让】make over【转入】change over to; shift to; switch to ～地下 go underground ～正常 return to normal【转身】(of a person) turn round; face about【转手】sell what one has bought【转述】report; relate sth. as told by another【转送】pass on; transmit on/make a present of what one has been given【转弯】turn a corner; make a turn【转学】transfer to another school【转眼】in the twinkling of an eye【转业】be transferred to civilian work ～军人 armyman transferred to civilian work【转移】shift; transfer; divert/change; transform ～兵力 shift forces ～视线 divert sb.'s attention ～目标 distract people's attention from sth. or sb. ～社会风气 change prevalent social customs 【转义】transferred meaning 【转运】transport ～公司 transport company ～站 transfer post 【转载】reprint 【转帐】transfer accounts 【转折】a turn in the course of events/transition (of an essay) ～点 turning point 【转正】become a full member after completion of the probationary period/become a regular worker

传 zhuàn ①commentaries on classics ②biography ③a novel or story written in historical style 【传略】biographical sketch; profile

转 zhuàn ①turn; revolve; rotate 地球绕着太阳～ the earth revolves round the sun ②revolution 【转轮手枪】revolver 【转台】revolving stage 【转椅】swivel chair; revolving chair 【转悠】turn; move from side to side/stroll; saunter

赚 zhuàn make a profit; gain ～钱 make money ～钱生意 a profitable business; a paying proposition

撰 zhuàn write; compose 为报纸～稿 write articles for a newspaper

ZHUANG

妆 zhuāng ①apply makeup; make up ②woman's personal adornments ③trousseau 【妆饰】adorn; dress up

庄 zhuāng ①village ②a place of business 饭～ restaurant 【庄户】peasant household ～人家 peasant family 【庄家】banker (in a gambling game) 【庄稼】crops ～地 cropland ～活 farm work ～人 peasant; farmer 【庄严】solemn; dignified; stately ～声明 solemnly declare 态度～ dignified in manner 【庄园】manor 【庄重】serious; grave

桩
zhuāng ①stake; pile 打～ drive piles ②～～大事 an important matter 一～买卖 a business transaction

装
zhuāng ①dress up; play the part of; act; deck ②outfit; clothing 春～ a spring outfit ③stage makeup and costume 上～ dress and put on makeup ④pretend; feign; make believe ～病 pretend sickness ～死 feign death ～傻 pretend to be naive or stupid ～糊涂 feign ignorance ⑤pack; hold ～车 load a truck or cart ～箱 pack a box ⑥install; fit; assemble 给门～锁 fit a lock on the door 【装扮】attire; deck out / disguise 【装备】equip; fit out/ equipment; outfit ～新式武器 be equipped with modern weapons 军事～ military equipment 【装订】binding ～车间 bindery ～工人 bookbinder 【装疯卖傻】play the fool 【装潢】mount (a picture, etc.); decorate; dress/decoration; mounting; packaging 【装甲】plate armour/armoured ～兵 armoured force ～车 armoured car ～师 armoured division 【装聋作哑】pretend to be ignorant of sth. 【装门面】put up a front 【装模作样】be affected; put on an act 【装配】assemble; fit together ～机器 assemble a machine ～车间 fitting shop ～工 assembler ～线 assembly line 【装腔】be artificial ～作势 strike a pose 【装饰】decorate; adorn; deck ～品 ornament ～图案 decorative pattern 【装束】dress; attire 【装卸】load and unload (a truck, ship, etc. or goods)/assemble and disassemble ～工 loader; stevedore 【装修】fit up (a house, etc.) 【装样子】put on an act; do sth. for appearance sake 【装运】load and transport; ship 【装载】loading ～量 loading capacity 【装帧】binding and layout (of a book, magazine, etc.) 【装置】install; fit/installation; unit; device

壮
zhuàng ①strong; robust ～苗 strong sprout 身体～ have a strong physique ②magnificent; grand 雄～

full of grandeur ⑨strengthen; make better ～声势 to lend impetus and strength 【壮大】grow in strength 【壮胆】embolden; boost sb.'s courage 【壮丁】able-bodied man 【壮工】unskilled labourer 【壮举】magnificent feat 【壮丽】majestic; glorious ～的景色 magnificent scenery ～的史诗 glorious epic 【壮烈】heroic; brave ～牺牲 die a hero's death 【壮年】the more robust years of a person's life 【壮士】heroic man; hero 【壮实】sturdy 【壮志】lofty ideal

状 zhuàng ①form; shape 其～不一 of different forms ②state; condition 现～ present state of affairs ③describe 不可名～ indescribable ④written complaint 告～ lodge an accusation ⑤certificate (of commendation, etc.) 【状况】condition 健康～ state of health 经济～ financial or economic situation 【状态】state; state of affairs 心理～ state of mind 战争～ state of war 【状语】adverbial modifier; adverbial 【状元】Number One Scholar/ the very best (in any field) 【状子】plaint

撞 zhuàng ①bump against; strike; collide ～车 collision of vehicles ～墙 bump against a wall 被卡车 ～倒 be knocked down by a truck ②meet by chance; run into 在路上～到他了 bump into him on the road ③rush; dash; barge 【撞击】ram; dash against; strike 【撞见】meet or discover by chance; run across; catch sb. in the act 【撞骗】swindle 【撞锁】spring lock

ZHUĪ

追 zhuī ①chase after; pursue ～兵 pursuing troops ～上他 catch up with him 紧～不舍 be hot on sb.'s trail ②trace ～本溯源 trace to its source; get at the root of the matter ③seek; go after ～名逐利 seek fame and wealth ④recall ～念往事 reminisce about the past 【追

捕】pursue and capture 【追查】investigate; trace; find out ～谣言 trace a rumour to its source 【追悼】mourn over a person's death ～会 memorial meeting 【追赶】run after; pursue 【追回】recover (stolen property, etc.) 【追悔】regret ～莫及 too late to repent 【追击】pursue and attack; follow up 【追记】write down afterwards, or from memory / award posthumously 【追加】add to (the original amount) ～预算 supplement a budget 【追剿】pursue and wipe out 【追究】look into; investigate ～责任 investigate and affix the responsibility; find out who is to blame 【追求】seek; pursue / woo; court; chase; run after ～真理 seek truth ～数量 concentrate on quantity 【追溯】trace back to; date from 【追随】follow ～者 follower 【追问】make a detailed inquiry 【追寻】search; track down 【追忆】recollect; recall 【追逐】pursue; chase / seek; quest ～高额利润 seek exorbitant profits 【追踪】follow the trail of; track; trace

椎 zhuī vertebra 颈～ cervical vertebra 胸～ thoracic vertebra

锥 zhuī ①awl ②anything shaped like an awl ③bore; drill ～孔 make a hole with an awl ④cone

坠 zhuì ①fall; drop ～马 fall off a horse ②weigh down ③weight 扇～ pendant of a fan 【坠毁】(of a plane, etc.) fall and break; crash 【坠落】fall; drop

缀 zhuì ①sew; stitch ②put words together correctly; compose (an essay) ③embellish; decorate

惴 zhuì 【惴惴不安】be anxious and fearful; be alarmed and on tenterhooks

赘 zhuì superfluous; redundant 【赘述】say more than is needed; give unnecessary details 不必～ it is unnecessary to go into details

ZHUN

谆 zhūn 【谆谆】 earnestly and tirelessly ～教导 earnestly instruct ～告诫 repeatedly admonish

准 zhǔn ①allow; grant; permit ～假两周 grant sb. two weeks' leave ②standard; norm 以此为～ take this as the standard ③accurate; exact 投篮不～ inaccurate shooting (in basketball) 这表走得～ the watch keeps good time ④definitely; certainly 我明天一去 I'll certainly be there tomorrow ⑤quasi-; para- 军事组织 paramilitary organization 【准备】 prepare; get ready / intend; plan 作最坏的～ prepare for the worst 你～好了吗 are you ready ～下星期一开始试验 plan to start the experiment next Monday ～活动 warming-up exercise ～阶段 preparatory stage 【准确】 accurate; exact; precise 【准时】 punctual; on time; on schedule 请～出席 please be punctual 【准则】 norm; criterion

ZHUO

拙 zhuō ①clumsy; awkward; dull ～于言词 be inarticulate; ②my ～著 my writing ～见 my humble opinion 【拙劣】 inferior; clumsy ～表演 a bad show

卓 zhuō ①tall and erect ～立 stand upright ②eminent; outstanding 【卓见】 brilliant idea 【卓识】 sagacity 【卓有成效】 fruitful; highly effective 【卓越】 brilliant; remarkable 作出～的贡献 make outstanding contributions

捉 zhuō ①clutch; hold; grasp ～住 seize hold of sb. or sth. ②catch; capture 活～ capture sb. alive 【捉迷藏】 (play) hide-and-seek 【捉拿】 arrest; catch ～逃犯 arrest an escaped prisoner ～归案 bring sb. to justice 【捉弄】 tease; make fun of; embarrass

桌 zhuō table; desk 三～客人 three tables of guests (at a dinner party)【桌布】tablecloth【桌灯】desk lamp

灼 zhuó ①burn; scorch ～热 scorching hot ②bright; luminous【灼见】profound. view【灼灼】shining; brilliant 目光～ with keen, sparkling eyes

茁 zhuó【茁壮】healthy and strong; sturdy 小麦长得～ the wheat has grown sturdy

浊 zhuó ①turbid; muddy ～水 turbid water ②deep and thick ～声～气 in a raucous voice【浊音】voiced sound

酌 zhuó ①pour out (wine); drink 独～ drink alone ② a meal with wine 便～ informal dinner ③consider; think over ～办 do as one thinks fit 请～加修改 make any alterations as you may think fit【酌量】deliberate; use one's judgment【酌情】take into cosideration the circumstances; use one's discretion ～处理 settle a matter as one sees fit

着 zhuó ①wear (clothes) ②touch 附～ adhere to ③apply; use ～墨不多 sketchily painted or described ④ whereabouts 经费无～ no funds available【着笔】begin to write or paint【着陆】land; touch down【着落】whereabouts / assured source 遗失的行李已经有～了 the missing luggage has been found 这笔经费还没有～ we still don't know where to get the funds from【着色】put colour on; colour【着实】really; indeed / severely ～说了他一顿 lecture him severely【着手】put one's hand to; set about【着想】consider (the interests of sb. or sth.)【着眼】see from the angle of ～于人民 have the people in mind ～点 starting point【着重】stress; emphasize ～指出 emphatically point out

啄 zhuó peck 小鸡～米 the chicks are pecking at the rice【啄木鸟】woodpecker

琢 zhuó chisel; carve 【琢磨】 carve and polish (jade) / improve (literary works); polish; refine

擢 zhuó ①pull out; extract ②raise (in rank) 【擢升】 promote; advance (to a higher position or rank)

镯 zhuó bracelet 玉~ jade bracelet

ZI

吱 zī ①(of mice) squeak ②(of small birds) chirp; peep 【吱声】 utter sth.; make a sound

孜 zī 【孜孜】 diligent; industrious; hardworking ~以求 diligently strive after ~不倦 indefatigably

咨 zī 【咨询】 seek advice from; hold counsel with; consult ~机关 advisory body

姿 zī ①looks; appearance ~色 good looks ②gesture 舞~ a dancer's posture and movements 【姿势】 posture; gesture ~优美 have a graceful carriage 【姿态】 carriage / attitude; pose

资 zī ①money 川~ travelling expenses ②subsidize; support ~敌 give supplies to the enemy ③provide; supply 以~补救 to serve as a remedy ④natural ability 天~ natural endowments ⑤qualifications 年~ years of service; seniority 【资本】 capital / what is capitalized on ~家 capitalist ~主义 capitalism 【资财】 capital and goods; assets 【资产】 property / capital (fund) / assets ~负债表 balance sheet ~阶级 the capitalist class; the bourgeoisie 【资方】 capital ~代理人 agent of a capitalist 【资格】 qualifications / seniority 具备必要的~ be qualified 取消比赛~ be disqualified from the contest 摆老~ flaunt one's seniority 【资金】 fund 【资力】 financial strength ~雄厚 have a large capital 【资历】 qualifications and record of service 【资料】 means / data; material ～室 reference room 【资源】 resources ～丰富 abound in natural resources 开发～ tap natural resources 【资助】 subsidize

滋 zī ①grow; multiply ～事 create trouble ②more 为害～甚 cause greater havoc than ever 【滋补】 nourishing; nutritious; tonic 【滋蔓】 grow and spread; grow vigorously 【滋润】 moist / moisten 【滋生】 multiply; breed; propagate / create; provoke 蚊蝇～ breeding of flies and mosquitoes 【滋味】 taste; flavour 【滋养】 nourish/nutriment ～品 nourishing food 【滋长】 grow; develop

辐 zī 【辎重】 impedimenta; supplies and gear of an army; baggage

子 zǐ ①son; child 独生～ an only son ②person 男～ male person; man ③seed 瓜～ melon seed ④egg 鸡～ hen's egg ⑤young; tender; small ～鸡 chick ⑥something small and hard 棋～ chessman; piece 枪～ bullet ⑦copper (coin) 一个～儿也没有 penniless 【子弹】 bullet; cartridge ～带 cartridge belt ～箱 cartridge box 【子弟】 juniors; children 职工～ children of the workers and staff (of a factory, etc.) 【子宫】 uterus; womb 【子女】 sons and daughters; children 【子孙】 descendants

仔 zǐ young ～猪 piglet; pigling 【仔细】 careful; attentive/be careful; look out ～分析 analyse carefully

姊 zǐ elder sister 【姊妹】 elder and younger sisters; sisters ～篇 companion volume

紫 zǐ purple; violet 【紫菜】 laver 【紫丁香】 (early) lilac 【紫红】 purplish red 【紫罗兰】 violet; common stock 【紫药水】 gentian violet

字 zì ①word; character ～义 meaning of a word ②pronunciation (of a word or character) 咬～清楚 pronounce every word clearly ③style of handwriting;

printing type 黑体~ boldface ④scripts; writings 【字典】 dictionary 查~ consult a dictionary 【字句】 words and expressions; writing ~通顺 coherent and smooth writing 【字据】 written pledge 【字里行间】 between the lines 【字谜】 a riddle about a character or word 【字面】 literal ~上的意思 literal meaning 从~上看 taken literally 【字模】 (type) matrix 【字母】 letters of an alphabet; letter 英语~ the English alphabet 【字幕】 captions (of motion pictures, etc.); subtitles 中文~ Chinese subtitles 【字盘】 case 【字体】 script; typeface/style of calligraphy 【字条】 brief note 【字帖】 copybook (for calligraphy) 【字眼】 wording; diction 玩弄~ play with words 【字样】 model of written characters/printed or written words 【字斟句酌】 weigh every word 【字纸篓】 wastepaper basket

自 zì ①self; oneself; one's own ~不量力 overestimate one's strength or oneself ②certainly; of course ~当努力 will certainly do one's best ~不待言 it goes without saying ③from; since ~即日起生效 become effective (as) from this date; with effect from ~古以来 since ancient times ~幼 since childhood 【自爱】 self-respect 【自拔】 free oneself (from pain or evildoing) 不能~ unable to extricate oneself 【自白】 make clear one's meaning or position; vindicate oneself 【自卑】 feel oneself inferior ~感 sense of inferiority 【自备】 provide for oneself ~碗筷 bring one's own bowls and chopsticks 【自便】 at one's convenience 听其~ let him do as he pleases 请~ please do as you like 【自称】 claim to be; profess ~内行 call oneself an expert 【自吹自擂】 blow one's own trumpet 【自动】 voluntarily; of one's own accord/automatic ~参加 participate voluntarily ~交待

confess of one's own accord ～控制 automatic control ～铅笔 propelling pencil ～装配线 automatic assembly line 【自发】 spontaneous 【自费】 at one's own expense 【自负】 be responsible for one's own action, etc./think highly of oneself; be conceited 【自负盈亏】 (of an enterprise) assume sole responsibility for its profits or losses 【自供】 confess ～状 confession 【自豪】 be proud of sth. ～感 sense of pride 【自己】 oneself/closely related; own 生～的气 be angry with oneself ～动手 use one's own hands ～弟兄 one's own brothers ～人 people on one's own side; one of us 【自给】 self-sufficient ～自足 self-sufficiency; autarky 【自荐】 recommend oneself (for a job); offer one's services 【自救】 save oneself 生产～ provide for and help oneself by engaging in production 【自觉】 conscious; aware ～遵守纪律 conscientiously observe discipline 【自夸】 sing one's own praises 【自来水】 running water; tap water ～厂 waterworks 【自来水笔】 fountain pen 【自立】 support oneself; earn one's own living 【自力更生】 regeneration through one's own efforts; self-reliance 【自流】 (of water) flow by itself / (of a thing) take its natural course / (of a person) do as one pleases 【自留地】 family plot; private plot 【自满】 complacent 【自欺欺人】 deceive oneself as well as others 【自取灭亡】 take the road to one's doom 【自取其咎】 have only oneself to blame 【自然】 nature / naturally / of course ～规律 natural law ～环境 natural environment ～界 natural world ～经济 natural economy ～科学 natural science ～现象 natural phenomena ～主义 naturalism 【自然】 at ease; natural 态度相当～ be quite at ease 【自然而然】 naturally; spontaneously; of oneself 【自如】 freely; smoothly 操纵～ operate with facility 运用～ wield skilfully 【自若】 self-possessed; composed 神态～ appear calm and at ease 【自杀】commit suicide 【自上而下】from above to below; from top to bottom 【自始至终】from start to finish; from beginning to end 【自首】voluntarily surrender oneself; give oneself up/make a political recantation 【自私】selfish; self-centred 【自讨苦吃】ask for trouble 【自投罗网】bite the hook 【自卫】defend oneself/self-defence ～能力 the capacity to defend oneself ～反击 fight back in self-defence ～反击战 counterattack in self-defence ～军 self-defence corps ～行动 an act in self-defence ～战争 war of self-defence 【自我】self; oneself ～介绍 introduce oneself ～暴露 self-exposure ～辩解 self-justification ～表现 self-expression ～改造 self-remoulding ～检查 self-examination ～教育 self-education ～批评 self-criticism ～牺牲 self-sacrifice 【自习】study by oneself in scheduled time or free time ～时间 time for individual study 【自下而上】from bottom to top; from below 【自相残杀】kill each other; cause death to one another 【自相矛盾】contradict oneself; be self-contradictory 【自新】turn over a new leaf 【自信】self-confident ～由自在 by oneself / of oneself; of one's own accord ～解决 settle (a problem) by oneself ～其是 act as one thinks fit; go one's own way 【自行车】bicycle; bike 【自修】study by oneself; have self-study / study on one's own; study independently ～法语 teach oneself French 【自学】study on one's own 培养～能力 foster one's ability to study independently ～课本 teach-yourself books 【自寻死路】bring about one's own destruction 【自言自语】talk to oneself; think aloud 【自以为是】consider oneself (always) in the right; be opinionated 【自用】for private use; personal ～物品 personal effects 【自由】freedom; liberty / free;

unrestrained ～讨论 have a free exchange of views ～选择 be free to choose ～散漫 slack; lax in discipline ～化 liberalization ～竞争 free competition ～恋爱 freedom to choose one's spouse ～诗 free verse ～市场 free market ～体操 free exercise ～主义 liberalism 【自圆其说】 make one's statement consistent; justify oneself 【自愿】 voluntary; of one's own accord 出于～ on a voluntary basis 【自在】 free; unrestrained / comfortable; at ease 【自找】 ask for it ～麻烦 be looking for trouble 【自知之明】 self-knowledge 无～ lack of self-knowledge 【自治】 autonomy; self-government ～机关 organ of self-government ～区 autonomous region 【自制】 made by oneself / self-control; self-restraint 失去～ lose self-control 【自重】 be self-possessed / dead weight 【自主】 act on one's own; decide for oneself 【自传】 autobiography 【自转】 rotation 【自尊】 self-respect; self-esteem 伤了他的～心 injure his self-esteem; wound his pride ～感 sense of self-respect 【自作自受】 suffer from one's own actions; lie in the bed one has made 【自作聪明】 think oneself clever

恣 zì throw off restraint; do as one pleases 【恣意】 reckless; unbridled; wilful ～妄为 behave unscrupulously

渍 zì ①steep; soak; ret ～麻 ret flax, jute, etc. ②be soiled (with grease, etc.) ③stain; sludge 油～ oil sludge

ZONG

宗 zōng ①ancestor ②clan 同～ of the same clan ③sect; faction 正～ orthodox school ④principal aim; purpose 开～明义 make clear the purpose and main theme from the very beginning ⑤take as one's model ⑥model; great master 【宗法】 patriarchal clan system ～社会 patriarchal society 【宗教】 religion ～改革 religious reform ～

信仰 religious belief ~仪式 religious rites; ritual 【宗派】faction; sect ~斗争 factional strife ~活动 factional activities ~主义 sectarianism 【宗旨】aim; purpose 【宗族】patriarchal clan/clansman

综 zōng put together; sum up ~上所述 to sum up 【综合】synthesize/synthetical; multiple ~报导 composite dispatch ~报告 summing-up report ~大学 university ~规划 unified plan ~考察 comprehensive survey ~利用 comprehensive utilization ~平衡 overall balance ~研究 synthetical study 【综计】sum up; add up

棕 zōng ①palm ②palm fibre; coir ~绳 coir rope 【棕榈】palm ~油 palm oil 【棕色】brown

踪 zōng footprint; trace 【踪迹】track 不留~ not leave a trace 【踪影】sign 毫无~ leaving without a trace

鬃 zōng hair on the neck of a pig, horse, etc. 马~ horse's mane 猪~ pig's bristles ~刷 bristle brush

总 zōng ①assemble; put together ~起来说 to sum up ②general; overall 抓~ assume overall responsibility ~开关 master switch ~产量 total output ~趋势 general trend ~根源 root cause ~的说来 by and large ③chief; head ~工程师 chief engineer ~部 general headquarters ~书记 general secretary ~头目 chief boss ④always; invariably ~是站在第一线 always stand in the forefront ⑤anyway; after all; inevitably ~是要解决的 be settled sooner or later 【总得】must; have to; be bound to ~想个办法 have got to find a way out 【总动员】general mobilization 【总额】total 【总而言之】in short; in a word; in brief 【总方针】general policy; general principle 【总纲】general programme; general principles 【总工会】federation of trade unions 【总攻】general offensive 【总共】in all; altogether; in the aggregate 【总管】manager 【总归】

anyhow; eventually 事实～是事实 after all, facts are facts 【总和】sum; total 各部分的～ summation of individual parts 【总汇】come or flow together/confluence; concourse 【总机】switchboard; telephone exchange 【总计】grand total/amount to; add up to; total 【总结】sum up; summarize/ summary ～经验 sum up one's experience ～工作 summarize one's work 作～ make a summary ～报告 summary report ～会 summing-up meeting 【总揽】assume overall responsibility ～大权 assume a dominant role 【总理】premier; prime minister 国务院～ the Premier of the State Council 【总领事】consul general ～馆 consulate general 【总目】comprehensive table of contents 【总评】general comment 【总数】total 【总司令】commander in chief ～部 general headquarters 【总算】at long last; finally/considering everything; on the whole 【总体】overall; total ～规划 overall plan ～战 general war 【总统】president (of a republic) ～府 presidential palace; the residence and office of a president 【总务】general affairs/person in charge of general affairs ～科 general affairs section ～司 general service department 【总则】general rules; general principles 【总帐】general ledger 【总之】in a word; in short; in brief 【总支】general (Party or Youth League) branch 【总值】total value 生产～ total output value 国民生产～ gross national product 【总指挥】commander in chief/general director ～部 general headquarters

纵 zòng ①vertical; longitudinal; lengthwise ～剖面 vertical section ②release; set free ③let loose; let go ～酒 drink to excess ～欲 indulge in sensual pleasures 放～ indulge; let sb. have his way ～声大笑 have a hearty laugh ④jump up 【纵队】column; file 一路～ single file 二路～ column of twos 【纵火】set on fire;

commit arson ～犯 arsonist 【纵情】to one's content; as much as one likes; as 一直 sing heartily 【纵然】even if; even though 【纵容】connive; wink at ～孩子 indulge a child 在某人一下 with the connivance of sb. 受～ be winked at 【纵身】jump; leap 一一跳 jump up 上马 leap onto a horse 【纵深】depth 向～发展 develop in depth ～防御 defence in depth 【纵谈】talk freely

粽 zòng 【粽子】a pyramid-shaped dumpling made of glutinous rice wrapped in bamboo or reed leaves

ZOU

走 zǒu ①walk; go 一直往前～ go straight ahead ～远路 walk a long distance ～回头路 turn back ～弯路 make a detour ～错房间 get into the wrong room ～群众路线 follow the mass line ②run; move 钟不一了 the clock has stopped ③leave; go away 我们该～了 it's time for us to leave ④visit; call on ～亲戚 call on relatives ⑤through; from 咱们～这个门进去吧 let's go in through this door ⑥leak; escape ～气了 the gas is leaking ～风 let out a secret ⑦depart from the original 说话～题儿 speak beside the point 【走动】walk about; stretch one's legs/visit each other 出去～～吧 let's go out for a stroll 病人能～了 the invalid is able to get about now 【走读】attend a day school ～生 day student 【走访】interview/pay a visit to; go and see 【走狗】running dog; lackey 【走后门】get in by the back door; secure advantages through pull or influence 【走火】(of firearms) discharge accidentally/go too far in what one says 【走廊】corridor; passage 【走漏】leak out; divulge (a secret) 【走路】walk; go on foot 【走失】wander away; be lost; be missing 【走兽】beast; quadruped 【走私】smuggle ～

的货物 smuggled goods 【走投无路】 have no way out; be in an impasse 逼得～ be driven to the wall 【走味】 lose flavour 【走向】 run; trend; alignment / head for; be on the way to ～胜利 advance towards victory ～反面 change into one's opposite 【走样】 lose shape; go out of form 【走运】 be in luck; have good luck 不～ have bad luck 【走着瞧】 wait and see 【走卒】 pawn; cat's-paw

奏 zòu ①play (music); perform (on a musical instrument) ～国歌 play the national anthem ②achieve; produce ③present a memorial to an emperor 【奏捷】 win a battle 【奏凯】 win victory 【奏效】 prove effective; be successful 【奏乐】 play music; strike up a tune

揍 zòu ①beat; hit; strike ～他一顿 beat him up 挨～ get a thrashing

ZU

租 zū rent; hire; charter ～一条小船 hire a boat ② rent out; let out; lease 此屋招～ room to let ③rent 房～ house rent 收～ collect rent ④land tax 【租金】 rent; rental 【租用】 take on lease ～礼堂 hire a hall

足 zú ①foot; leg 赤～ barefoot ②full; as much as 路上～～走了两个钟头 the journey took fully two hours 【足够】 enough; ample; sufficient 有～的时间吗 is there enough time 【足迹】 footmark; footprint; track 【足见】 it serves to show; one can well perceive 【足金】 pure gold; solid gold 【足球】 soccer; football ～队 football team ～运动员 footballer 【足智多谋】 resourceful; wise and full of stratagems

卒 zú ①soldier 小～ private; a mere pawn ②servant 走～ underling; lackey ③finish; end ～业 finish a course of study ④die 生～年月 dates of birth and death

族 zú ①clan 合～ the whole clan ～人 clansman ～长 clan elder ②race; nationality ③a class or group of things with common features 语～ a family of languages

阻 zǔ hinder; obstruct 拦～ hold back 通行无～ go through without hindrance 【阻碍】block; impede ～交通 block the traffic 遇到～ meet with obstruction 【阻挡】stem; resist; obstruct 【阻隔】separate; cut off 【阻击】block; check ～战 blocking action 【阻拦】stop; obstruct; bar the way 【阻力】obstruction; resistance 【阻挠】thwart; stand in the way 【阻止】prevent; stop ～事态恶化 prevent the situation from deteriorating ～敌军前进 check the enemy's advance

诅 zǔ 【诅咒】curse; swear; wish sb. evil; imprecate

组 zǔ ①organize; form ～阁 set up a cabinet ②group ③set; series 一～邮票 a set of stamps 【组成】make up; compose 水的～ the composition of water ～部分 component (part) 【组稿】solicit contributions 【组合】consitute/association; combination 【组织】organize; form/organization ～劳力 organize a labour force ～座谈 organize a discussion ～演出 get up a performance 群众～ mass organizations ～关系 membership credentials ～生活 regular activities of an organization ～条例 organic rules ～委员 committee member in charge of organizational work

祖 zǔ ①grandfather ②ancestor ③founder (of a craft, religious sect, etc.); originator 【祖传】handed down from one's ancestors 【祖父】(paternal) grandfather 【祖国】one's country; motherland; fatherland 【祖籍】original family home 【祖母】(paternal) grandmother 【祖先】ancestry; ancestors; forbears; forefathers

ZUAN

钻 zuān ①drill; bore ～孔 drill a hole ②get into; go through ～进树林 go into a forest 【钻牛角尖】split hairs/get into a dead end 【钻探】drilling ～工 driller ～机 drilling machine 【钻研】study intensively; dig into ～业务 dig into one's job or a subject; work hard to perfect oneself professionally 【钻营】secure personal gain

钻 zuàn ①drill; auger ②diamond; jewel ～戒 diamond ring ③bore; drill ～个眼 bore a hole 【钻床】driller 【钻机】(drilling) rig 【钻井】well drilling ～队 drilling team ～工人 driller 【钻石】diamond/jewel (used in a watch) 【钻塔】boring tower 【钻头】bit (of a drill)

攥 zuàn grip; grasp ～着斧子 hold an axe ～紧拳头 clench one's fist ～住他的手 clasp him by the hand

ZUI

嘴 zuǐ mouth 闭～ keep one's mouth shut 【嘴笨】clumsy of speech 【嘴馋】fond of good food 【嘴唇】lip 咬着～ bite one's lips 【嘴尖】sharp-tongued 【嘴角】corners of the mouth 【嘴紧】tight-lipped; secretive 【嘴快】have a loose tongue 【嘴脸】look; features 【嘴碎】loquacious; garrulous 【嘴甜】ingratiating in speech; honey-mouthed 【嘴稳】able to keep a secret

最 zuì most; -est ～小 the smallest ～为积极 be the most active ～快 the fastest ～大的幸福 supreme happiness 【最初】initial; first ～阶段 the initial stage ～的印象 first impressions 【最低】lowest; minimum ～价格 lowest price 【最多】at most; maximum 【最高】highest; supreme; tallest; maximum 达到～峰 reach the climax 创历史～纪录 hit an all-time high ～权力 supreme power ～速度 maximum speed～统帅 supreme commander【最高级】highest; summit/the superlative degree ～会谈 summit talks ～会议 summit conference【最好】best; first-rate/it would be best ～的办法 the best way 你～今天把它搞完 you'd better finish it today【最后】final; last; ultimate ～胜利 final victory ～挣扎 last-ditch struggle ～一排 last row ～通牒 ultimatum【最近】recently; lately; of late/in the near future; soon 我～很忙 I've been very busy recently ～几天 in the last few days ～的消息 recent news ～要上演许多新电影 many new films will be released soon【最终】final; ultimate ～结果 the final outcome ～目的 the ultimate aim

罪 zuì ①crime; guilt ～上加～ be doubly guilty ～有应得 deserve the punishment ②fault; blame 归～于人 lay the blame on others ③suffering; hardship 受～ be in pain ④put the blame on ～己 bear the blame oneself【罪案】details of a criminal case; case【罪恶】crime; evil ～多端 be guilty of all kinds of evil【罪犯】criminal; offender【罪过】fault; offence; sin【罪魁】chief criminal【罪名】charge; accusation【罪孽】sin ～深重 sinful【罪人】guilty person; sinner【罪行】guilt; offence【罪责】responsibility for an offence【罪证】evidence of a crime; proof of one's guilt【罪状】facts about a crime; charges in an indictment

醉 zuì ①drunk; intoxicated; tipsy 烂～ be dead drunk ②steeped in liquor ～蟹 liquor-saturated crab【醉鬼】drunkard; inebriate【醉汉】drunken man【醉生梦死】lead a befuddled life【醉心】be bent on; be wrapped up in; be infatuated with【醉醺醺】sottish【醉意】signs or feeling of getting drunk 他已有几分～ he is a bit tipsy

ZUN

尊 zūn ①senior; of a senior generation ～长 elders and betters ②venerate; honour ～师爱生 respect the teacher and love the student ③your ～夫人 your wife ～府 your residence ～姓大名 may I know your name 【尊称】a respectful form of address; honorific title/address sb. respectfully 【尊崇】worship; revere 【尊贵】honourable; respectable 【尊敬】respect; esteem 【尊严】dignity 国家～ national dignity 法律的～ sanctity of the law 【尊重】respect; value ～群众的首创精神 value the initiative of the masses

遵 zūn abide by; obey; observe ～医嘱 follow the doctor's advice 【遵从】defer to; follow ～上级的指示 in compliance with the directives of the leadership ～老师的教导 follow the teacher's advice 【遵命】comply with your wish; obey your command 【遵守】observe; abide by ～纪律 observe discipline ～时间 be on time ～法律 abide by the law 【遵循】follow; adhere to 【遵照】conform to; comply with; obey ～政策办事 act in accordance with the policies

撙 zūn save 【撙节】retrench; practise economy ～开支 cut down expenses

ZUO

作 zuō workshop 洗衣～ laundry 【作坊】workshop 【作弄】tease; make a fool of; poke fun at

zuó 【作践】spoil; waste / run sb. down; disparage / humiliate; insult 【作料】condiments; seasoning

昨 zuó yesterday ～晚 yesterday evening; last night

琢 zuó 【琢磨】 turn sth. over in one's mind; ponder ～出个办法 figure out a way (to do sth.)

左 zuǒ ①the left side ～上方 the upper left 向～转 turn left ②the Left 在 "～" 的思想影响下 under the influence of the "Left" ideology ③different; contrary; 意见相～ hold different views 【左近】 in the vicinity; nearby 【左轮】 revolver 【左面】 the left side; the left-hand side 【左派】 the Left; the left wing/Leftist 【左倾】 left-leaning; progressive/"Left" deviation 【左手】 the left hand 【左首】 the left-hand side 【左翼】 left wing; left flank/the left wing; the Left 【左右】 the left and right sides/about/master; influence ～摇摆 vacillate now to the left and now to the right 八点钟～ around eight o'clock 一个月～ a month or so 十元～ about 10 *yuan* ～局势 be master of the situation 为人所～ be controlled by sb. ～手 right-hand man 【左右为难】 in a dilemma; in an awkward predicament

坐 zuò ①sit; take a seat 请～ please sit down ②travel by (a plane, etc.) ③have its back towards 房子～北朝南 the house faces south ④put (a pan, pot, kettle, etc.) on a fire 【坐等】 sit back and wait 【坐垫】 cushion 【坐牢】 be in jail; be imprisoned 【坐立不安】 be fidgety; be on tenterhooks 【坐落】 be situated; be located 【坐视】 sit by and watch ～不理 sit by idly and remain indifferent 【坐位】 seat 这个～有人吗 is this seat occupied 留几个～ reserve some seats 【坐以待毙】 await one's doom

作 zuò ①do; make ～功课 do one's homework ～报告 make a report ～结论 reach a conclusion ②write; compose ～诗 compose a poem ～画 paint a picture ③writings; work 新～ a new work ④pretend; affect 故怒容 pretend to be angry ⑤regard as 视～英雄 regard sb.

as a hero ⑥feel; have ～冷 feel a chill ⑦act as; be 【作案】 commit a crime or an offence 【作罢】 drop; relinquish; give up 事情只好～ the matter had to be dropped 【作保】 be sb.'s guarantor; go bail for sb. 【作弊】 practise fraud; cheat; indulge in corrupt practices 【作操】 do gymnastics; do exercises 【作对】 set oneself against; oppose 【作恶】 do evil 【作法】 way of doing things; practice 文章～ technique of writing; art of composition 他这种～是行不通的 his course of action will get him nowhere 【作废】 become invalid 宣布～ declare invalid 过期～ become invalid after a specified date 【作风】 style; way ～正派 be honest and upright 生活～ way of life 民主～ a democratic style of work 【作怪】 do mischief; make trouble 【作家】 writer ～协会 the Writers' Union 【作乐】 make merry; enjoy oneself 【作乱】 stage an armed rebellion 【作难】 feel awkward / make things difficult for sb. 【作呕】 feel sick 【作品】 works (of literature and art) 【作曲】 write music; compose ～家 composer 【作数】 count; be valid 【作祟】 (of ghosts, spirits, etc.) haunt/make mischief; cause trouble 【作为】 conduct; deed; action/ accomplish; do sth. worthwhile / regard as; look on as; take for ～借口 use sth. as an excuse ～靠山 look upon sb. as one's prop 【作文】 write a composition / composition 【作物】 crop 【作息】 work and rest 按时～ work and rest according to schedule ～时间表 daily schedule; timetable; work schedule 【作业】 school assignment / work; task; operation; production 做～ do one's assignment 家庭～ homework 改～ correct students' papers 野外～ field work ～班 work team ～计划 production plan 【作用】 act on; affect / action; function / effect 【作战】 fight; conduct operations; do battle ～部队 combat troops ～

部署 operational preparations ～地图 battle map ～方法 method of fighting ～方针 concept of operations【作者】author; writer【作证】testify; give evidence 在法庭上～ bear witness in a lawcourt【作主】decide 我作不了主 I am not in a position to decide

座 zuò ①seat; place 请入～ please be seated ②stand 花瓶～儿 vase stand ③constellation 大熊～ the Great Bear【座谈】have an informal discussion ～会 forum; symposium【座位】seat; place【座右铭】motto; maxim【座子】stand; pedestal; base / saddle (of a bicycle, etc.)

做 zuò ①make; produce; manufacture ～衣服 make clothes ②cook; prepare ～饭 prepare a meal ～菜 cook a dish ③do; act; engage in ～好事 do good ～生意 do business ④be; become ～演员 become an actor or actress ⑤write; compose ～一首诗 write a poem ⑥be used as 可以～教材 may be used as teaching material ⑦form or contract a relationship ～朋友 make friends with ～对头 set oneself against sb.【做伴】keep sb. company【做到】accomplish; achieve【做东】play the host; host sb.【做法】way of doing or making a thing; method of work; practice【做工】do manual work; work/charge for the making of sth./workmanship ～精美 of excellent workmanship【做官】be an official【做客】be a guest【做礼拜】go to church; be at church【做媒】be a matchmaker【做梦】have a dream; dream / have a pipe dream; daydream【做人】conduct oneself; behave / be an upright person 重新～ turn over a new leaf【做事】handle affairs; do a deed; act / work; have a job【做寿】celebrate the birthday【做文章】write an essay / make an issue of【做戏】act in a play / put on a show; playact【做贼心虚】have a guilty conscience【做作】affected; ar-

凿 zuò ①certain; authentic; irrefutable ②mortise 【凿凿】true; verified, ～有据 with irrefutable evidence 言之～ say sth. with certainty

附　录

化学元素表

1. 氢　hydrogen (H)
2. 氦　helium (He)
3. 锂　lithium (Li)
4. 铍　beryllium (Be)
5. 硼　boron (B)
6. 碳　carbon (C)
7. 氮　nitrogen (N)
8. 氧　oxygen (O)
9. 氟　fluorine (F)
10. 氖　neon (Ne)
11. 钠　sodium (Na)
12. 镁　magnesium (Mg)
13. 铝　aluminium (Al)
14. 硅　silicon (Si)
15. 磷　phosphorus (P)
16. 硫　sulphur (S)
17. 氯　chlorine (Cl)
18. 氩　argon (Ar)
19. 钾　potassium (K)
20. 钙　calcium (Ca)
21. 钪　scandium (Sc)
22. 钛　titanium (Ti)
23. 钒　vanadium (V)
24. 铬　chromium (Cr)
25. 锰　manganese (Mn)
26. 铁　iron (Fe)
27. 钴　cobalt (Co)
28. 镍　nickel (Ni)
29. 铜　copper (Cu)
30. 锌　zinc (Zn)
31. 镓　gallium (Ga)
32. 锗　germanium (Ge)
33. 砷　arsenic (As)
34. 硒　selenium (Se)
35. 溴　bromine (Br)
36. 氪　krypton (Kr)
37. 铷　rubidium (Rb)
38. 锶　strontium (Sr)
39. 钇　yttrium (Y)
40. 锆　zirconium (Zr)
41. 铌　niobium (Nb)
42. 钼　molybdenum (Mo)
43. 锝　technetium (Tc)
44. 钌　ruthenium (Ru)
45. 铑　rhodium (Rh)
46. 钯　palladium (Pd)
47. 银　silver (Ag)
48. 镉　cadmium (Cd)
49. 铟　indium (In)
50. 锡　tin (Sn)
51. 锑　antimony (Sb)
52. 碲　tellurium (Te)
53. 碘　iodine (I)
54. 氙　xenon (Xe)

55.	铯	cesium (Cs)	80.	汞 mercury (Hg)
56.	钡	barium (Ba)	81.	铊 thallium (Tl)
57.	镧	lanthanum (La)	82.	铅 lead (Pb)
58.	铈	cerium (Ce)	83.	铋 bismuth (Bi)
59.	镨	praseodymium (Pr)	84.	钋 polonium (Po)
60.	钕	neodymium (Nd)	85.	砹 astatine (At)
61.	钷	promethium (Pm)	86.	氡 radon (Rn)
62.	钐	samarium (Sm)	87.	钫 francium (Fr)
63.	铕	europium (Eu)	88.	镭 radium (Ra)
64.	钆	gadolinium (Gd)	89.	锕 actinium (Ac)
65.	铽	terbium (Tb)	90.	钍 thorium (Th)
66.	镝	dysprosium (Dy)	91.	镤 protactinium (Pa)
67.	钬	holmium (Ho)	92.	铀 uranium (U)
68.	铒	erbium (Er)	93.	镎 neptunium (Np)
69.	铥	thulium (Tm)	94.	钚 plutonium (Pu)
70.	镱	ytterbium (Yb)	95.	镅 americium (Am)
71.	镥	lutecium (Lu)	96.	锔 curium (Cm)
72.	铪	hafnium (Hf)	97.	锫 berkelium (Bk)
73.	钽	tantalum (Ta)	98.	锎 californium (Cf)
74.	钨	wolfram (W)	99.	锿 einsteinium (Es)
75.	铼	rhenium (Re)	100.	镄 fermium (Fm)
76.	锇	osmium (Os)	101.	钔 mendelevium (Md)
77.	铱	iridium (Ir)	102.	锘 nobelium (No)
78.	铂	platinum (Pt)	103.	铹 lawrencium (Lr)
79.	金	gold (Au)		

二十四节气

立春 the Beginning of Spring
雨水 Rain Water
惊蛰 the Waking of Insects
春分 the Spring Equinox
清明 Pure Brightness
谷雨 Grain Rain
立夏 the Beginning of Summer
小满 Grain Full
芒种 Grain in Ear
夏至 the Summer Solstice
小暑 Slight Heat
大暑 Great Heat

立秋 the Beginning of Autumn
处暑 the Limit of Heat
白露 White Dew
秋分 the Autumnal Equinox
寒露 Cold Dew
霜降 Frost's Descent
立冬 the Beginning of Winter
小雪 Slight Snow
大雪 Great Snow
冬至 the Winter Solstice
小寒 Slight Cold
大寒 Great Cold

我国主要节日

一月一日　元旦　New Year's Day

三月八日　国际劳动妇女节　International Working Women's Day

五月一日　国际劳动节　International Labour Day

五月四日　中国青年节　Chinese Youth Day

六月一日　国际儿童节　International Children's Day

七月一日　中国共产党成立纪念日　Anniversary of the Founding of the Communist Party of China

八月一日　中国人民解放军建军节　Army Day (Anniversary of the Founding of the Chinese Liberation Army)

十月一日　国庆节　National Day

主要传统节日

农历正月初一　春节　1st of the first month of the Chinese lunar calendar　Spring Festival

农历正月十五　元宵节；灯节　15th of the first month of the Chinese lunar calendar　Lantern Festival

农历五月初五　端午节　5th of the fifth month of the Chinese lunar calendar　Dragon-Boat Festival

农历八月十五　中秋节　15th of the eighth month of the Chinese lunar calendar　Mid-Autumn Festival; the Moon Festival

度量衡换算表

中国市制	公　　制		美　　制	
1尺 (chǐ)	1/3 米 (metre)		1.0936 英尺 (feet)	
1里 (lǐ)	1/2 公里 (kilometre)		0.3107 英里 (mile)	
1亩 (mu)	1/15公顷 (hectare)		0.1644 英亩 (acre)	
1两 (liang)	50克 (grammes)		1.7637 英两 (ounces)	
1斤 (jin)	1/2 公斤 (kilogramme)		1.1023 磅 (pounds)	
1担 (dan)	50公斤 (kilogrammes)		0.9842 英担 (hundred-weight) (cwt)	
1担 (dan)	1/20吨 (metric ton)		0.0492 英吨 (long ton)	
			0.0551 美吨 (short ton)	
1升 (sheng)	1 公升 (litre)		0.22 加仑 (British gallon)	
1斗 (dou)	10公升 (litres)		2.2 加仑 (British gallons)	

公　制	中国市制	英　美　制
1米　(metre)	3 尺　(chi)	3.2808 英尺　(feet)
1公里　(kilometre)	2 里　(li)	0.6214 英里　(mile)
1平方公里　(square km)	4 平方里 (sq. li)	0.3861平方英里 (sq. mile)
1平方米　(sq. metre)	9 平方尺 (sq. chi)	10.7636平方英尺 (sq. feet)
1公顷　(hectare)	15 亩　(mu)	2.471 英亩　(acres)
1公斤　(kilogramme)	2 斤　(jin)	2.2046 磅　(pounds)
1吨　(metric ton)	2,000斤　(jin)	0.9842 英吨　(long ton)
1立方米　(cubic metre)	27 立方尺 (cubic chi)	35.3166立方英尺 (cubic feet)
1公升　(litre)	1 升　(sheng)	0.22 加仑　(British gallon)
		0.264加仑(美)　(S.U. gallon)

英　美　制	公　　制	中国市制
1英尺 (foot)	0.3048 米 (metre)	0.9144 尺 (chi)
1码 (yard)	0.9144 米 (metre)	2.7432 尺 (chi)
1英里 (mile)	1.6093 公里 (kilometres)	3.2187 里 (li)
1平方英里 (sq. mile)	2.59平方公里 (sq. kilometres)	10.36平方里 (sq. li)
1英亩 (acre)	0.405 公顷 (hectare)	6.07 亩 (mu)
1磅 (pound)	0.4536 公斤 (kilogramme)	0.9072 斤 (jin)
1英吨 (long ton)	1.016 公斤 (kilogrammes)	2,032 斤 (jin)
1美吨 (short ton)	907 公斤 (kilogrammes)	1,814 斤 (jin)
1加仑 (British gallon)	4.546 升 (litre)	4.546 升 (sheng)

数字用法

零　0　nought; zero; O
十　10　ten
二百　200　two hundred
三千　3,000　three thousand
四万四千　44,000　forty-four thousand
五十万　500,000　five hundred thousand
六百万　6,000,000　six million
七千七百万　77,000,000　seventy-seven million
八亿　800,000,000　eight hundred million

• • •

五百四十三　543　five hundred and forty-three
一千五百　1,500　fifteen hundred; one thousand five hundred
四千四百零二　4,402　four thousand four hundred and two
五万六千七百八十九　56,789　fifty-six thousand, seven hundred and eighty-nine
二百一十三万四千六百五十四　2,134,654　two million, one hundred and thirty-four thousand six hundred and fifty-four
十亿八千万　1,080,000,000　one billion and eighty million
二百亿　20,000,000,000　twenty billion
三千亿　300,000,000,000　three hundred billion
四万亿　4,000,000,000,000　four million million

• • •

分数　fractions

二分之一　1/2　one-half; a half

三分之一，三分之二　1/3, 2/3　one-third, two-thirds

五分之一，五分之三　1/5, 3/5　one-fifth, three-fifths

十分之一　1/10　one-tenth; a tenth

五十分之一　1/50　one-fiftieth; a fiftieth

百分之一　1/100　one-hundredth; one per cent

千分之一　1/1,000　one-thousandth

万分之一　1/10,000　one ten-thousandth

一又二分之一　one and a half; a ... and a half

五又六分之五　five and five-sixths

• •

百分比　percentages

百分之百　100%　one hundred per cent

百分之零点五　0.5%　point five per cent

百分之零点二五　0.25%　point two five per cent

• •

小数　decimals

3.07　three point nought seven; three point O seven

5.002　five point nought nought two; five point O O two

35.12　thirty-five point one two

双倍，加倍　(to) double

是去年的二倍（即加倍）　to be double that of last year

比一九六五年增加一倍以上　to be more than double the
1965 figure

比一九四九年增加了十多倍　to be a dozen times that of
1949

是去年的五倍　to be five times that of last year; to increase fivefold compared with last year; to increase by
400 per cent over last year

象……一样多　as many as, as much as

是···的三倍　three times as many (much) as

去年的钢产量比一九六六年增加两倍多　(to make) over three times as much steel last year as in 1966

去年自行车的销售量比一九四九年增长了二百一十一倍　(to sell) 212 times as many bicycles last year as in 1949

比上一年增长百分之五十　to jump 50 per cent above the previous year

增加百分之百（即加倍，原数的二倍）　to increase by one hundred per cent; to double; to increase to twice as many (much) as

增加　to go up by; to shoot up by; to rise by (to); to be raised by

增加百分之一　to increase by one-hundredth

增加百分之十　to increase by one-tenth

增加百分之五十　to increase by one-half

增加百分之八十　an increase of eighty per cent; an eighty-per cent increase

•　　　•　　　•

下降，减少　to go down by; to fall by (to); to reduce by

下降（减少）百分之八十　a reduction (fall) of eighty per cent

下降百分之一　to decrease by one-hundredth; to reduce by one-hundredth

下降百分之十（或十分之一）　to decrease by ten per cent; to reduce by ten per cent; to reduce to nine-tenths; to be reduced to nine-tenths

下降百分之二十（或五分之一）　to decrease by one-fifth; to reduce by one-fifth; to reduce to four-fifths; to be reduced to four-fifths

下降百分之二十五（或四分之一）　to decrease by one quarter; to reduce by one quarter; to reduce to three-fourths;

to be reduced to three-fourths

下降百分之五十（一半）to decrease by one-half; to reduce
by one-half; to reduce to one-half; to be reduced to one-
half

封面设计:张灵芝

本书原为一百二十八开本,经订正后,另出
这种六十四开本,以满足部分读者的需要。

小小汉英词典

严 英 编

外语教学与研究出版社出版
(北京市西三环北路19号)

北京广播学院印刷厂排版
北京印刷三厂印刷
新华书店北京发行所发行

开本 787×1092 1/64 14印张 736千字
1982年9月第一版 1987年10月北京第三次印刷
印数 300,001—335,000 册

ISBN 7-5600-0211-0/H·60

书号:9215·160 定价:3.85元